CHAPTER 168

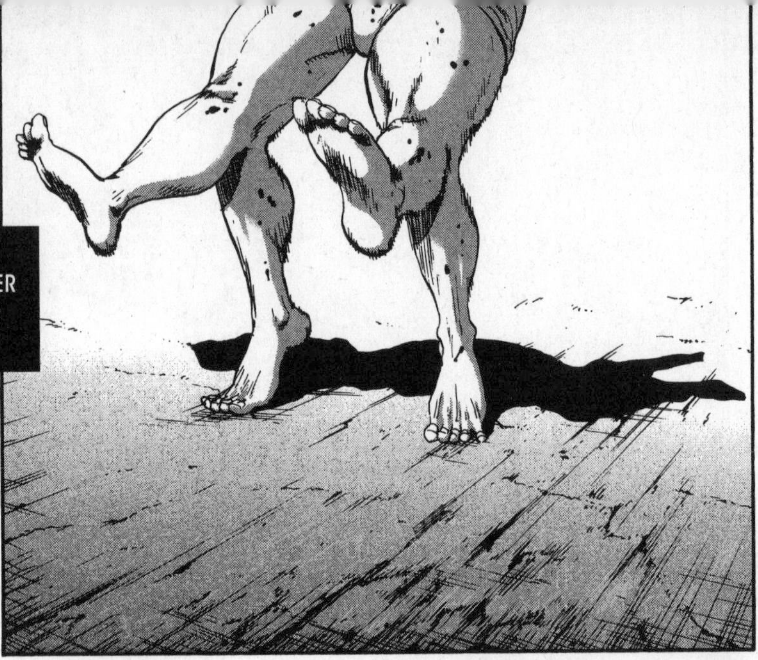

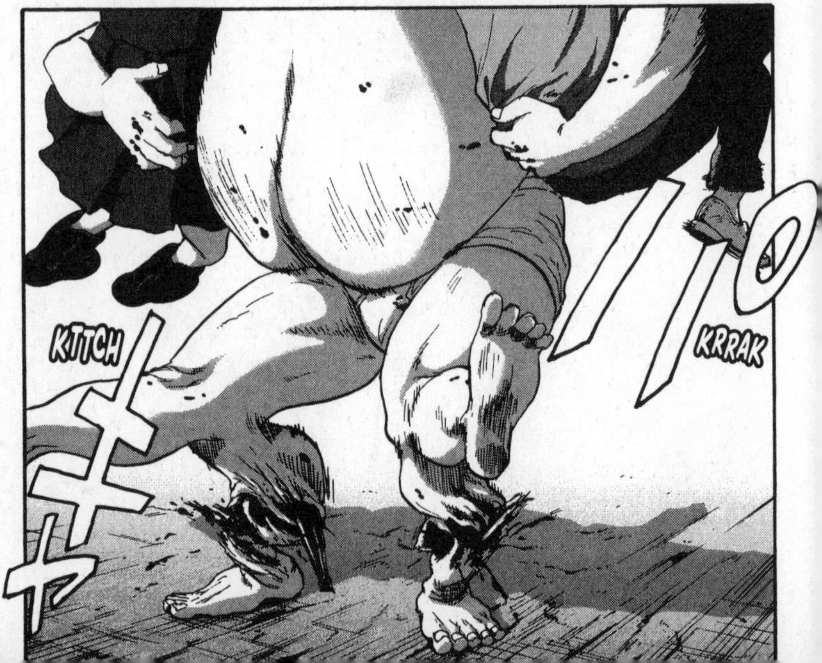
KRRAK
KITTCH

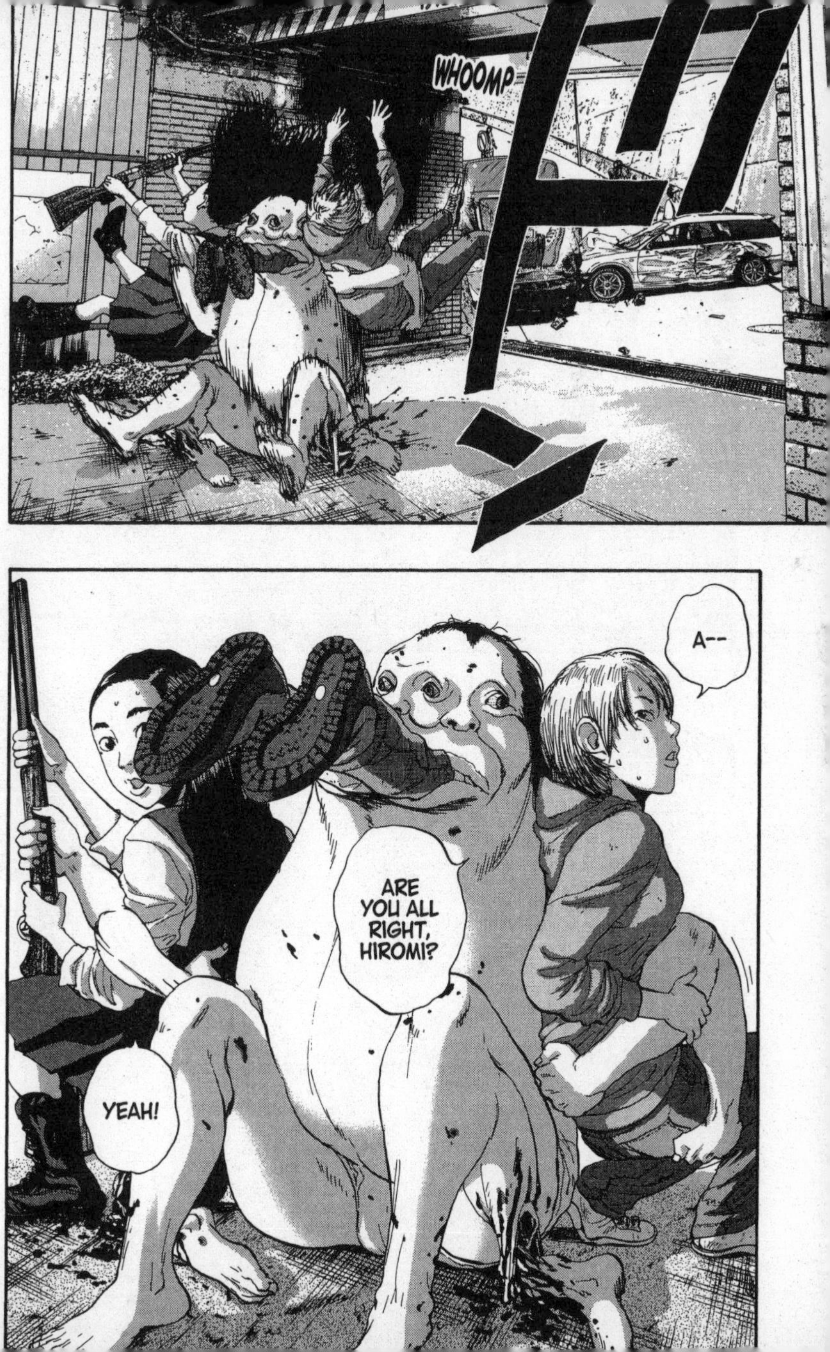
WHOOMP
A--
ARE YOU ALL RIGHT, HIROMI?
YEAH!

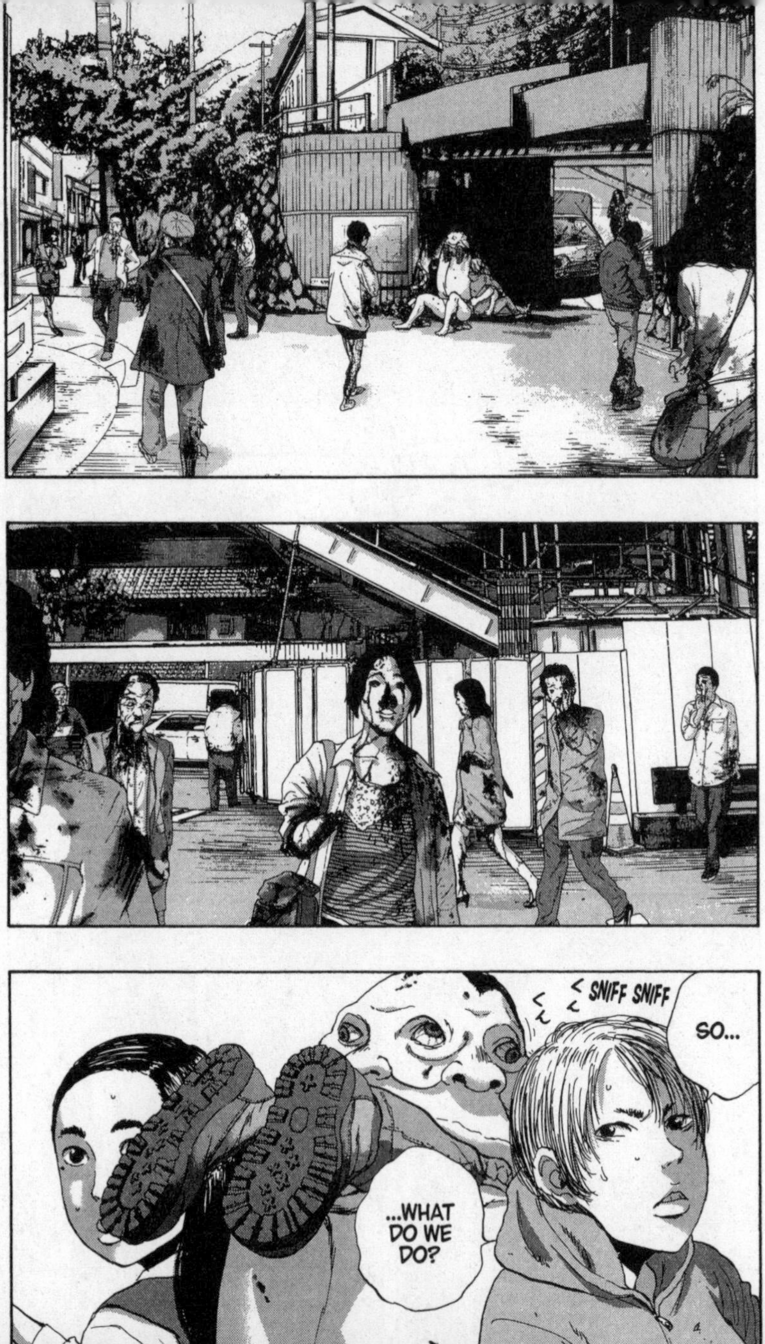
SNIFF SNIFF
SO...
...WHAT DO WE DO?

ぐぐっ
HRRGG
MISTER, YOU'RE HURT!
NNF
RNNF
GRARRF
NNHRRF

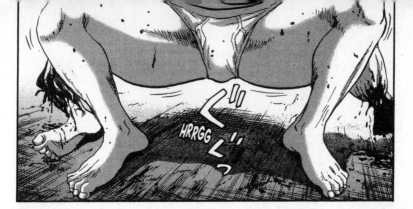

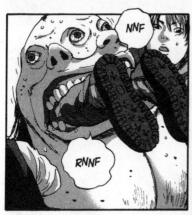

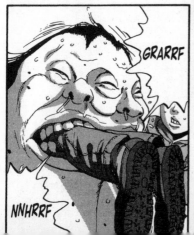

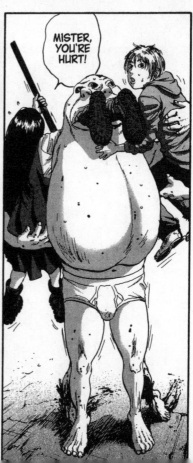

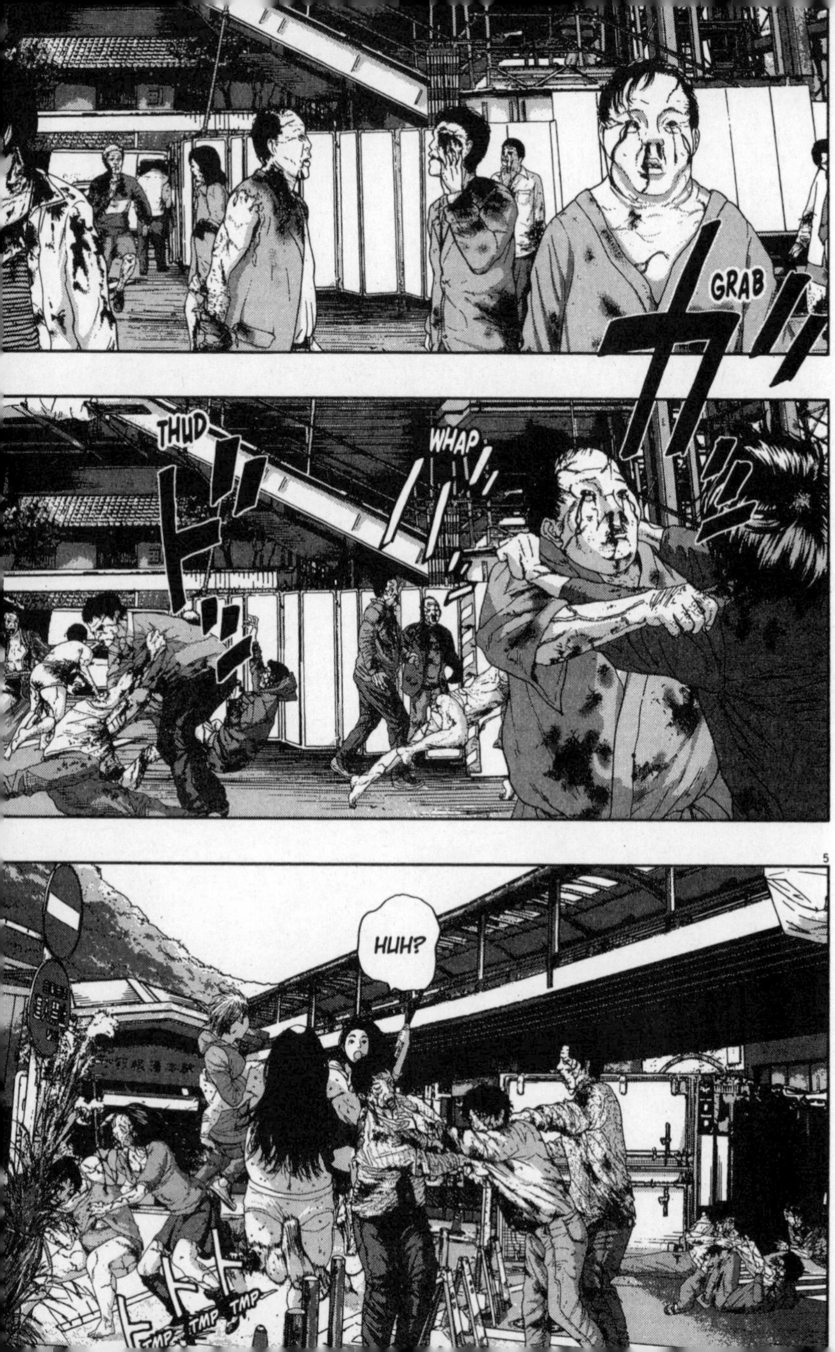
GRAB
WHAP
THUD
HUH?
TMP TMP TMP TMP

5

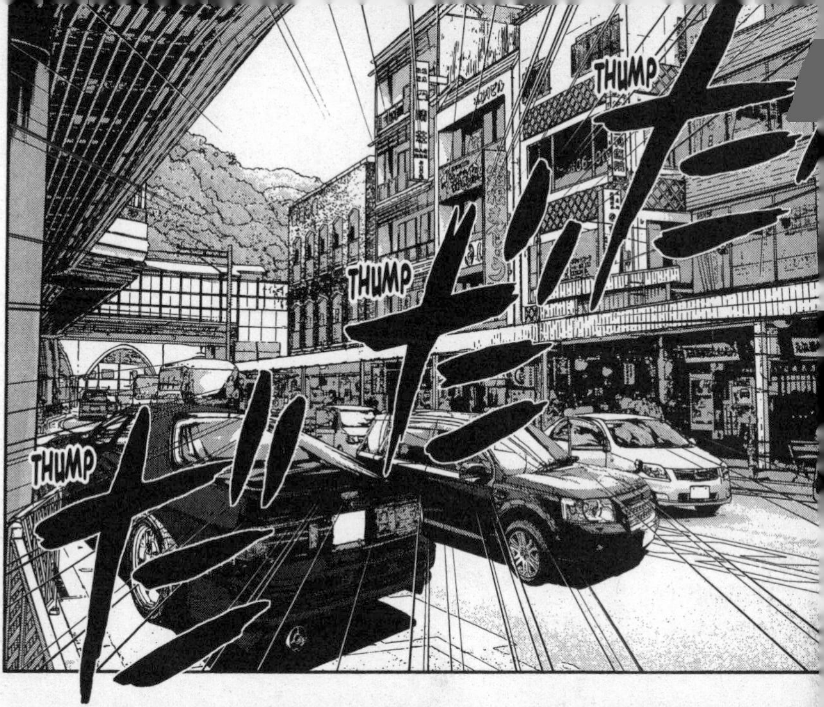
THUMP
THUMP
THUMP

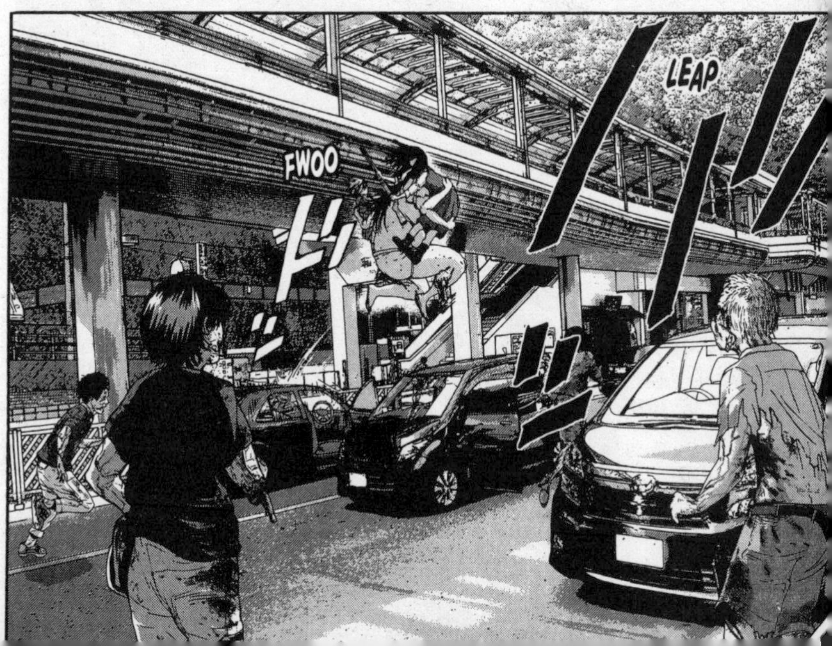
LEAP
FWOO

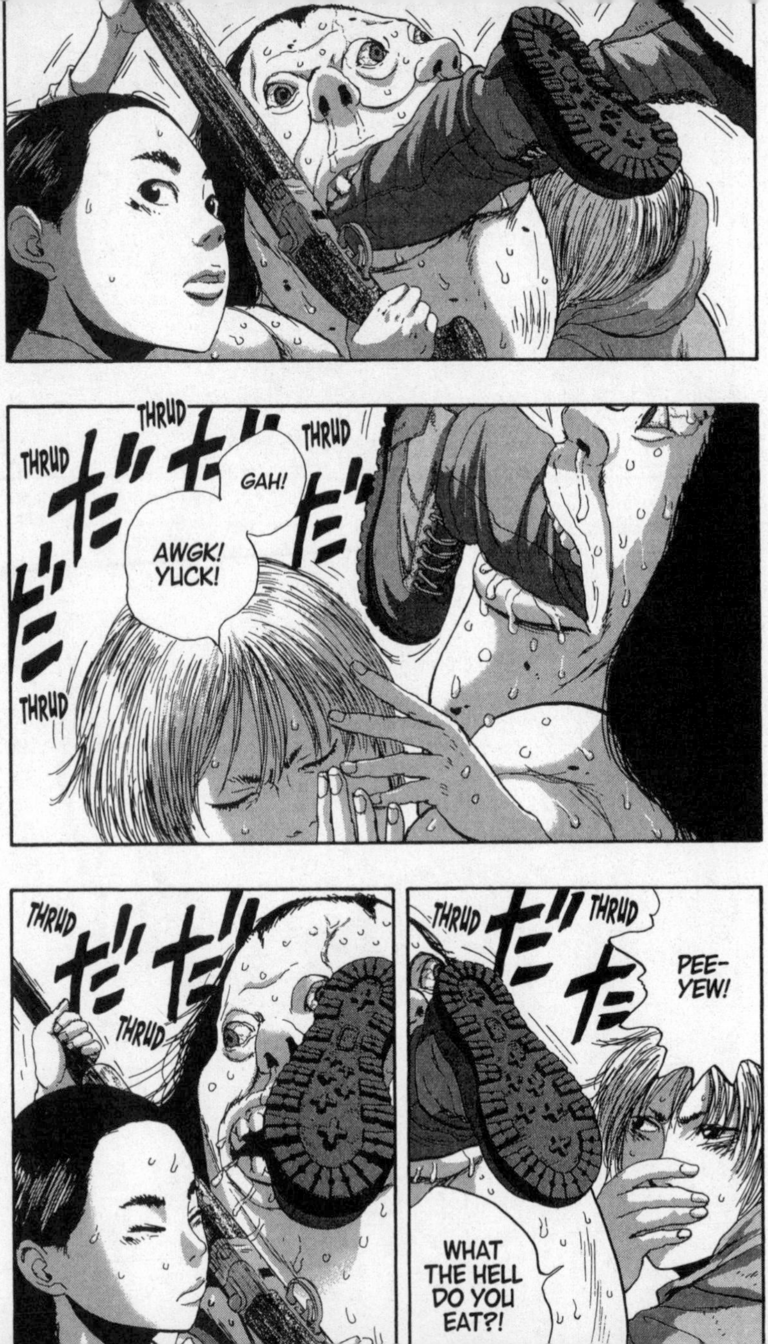
THRUD
GAH!
THRUD
THRUD
AWGK! YUCK!
THRUD
THRUD
THRUD
PEE-YEW!
WHAT THE HELL DO YOU EAT?!
THRUD
THRUD

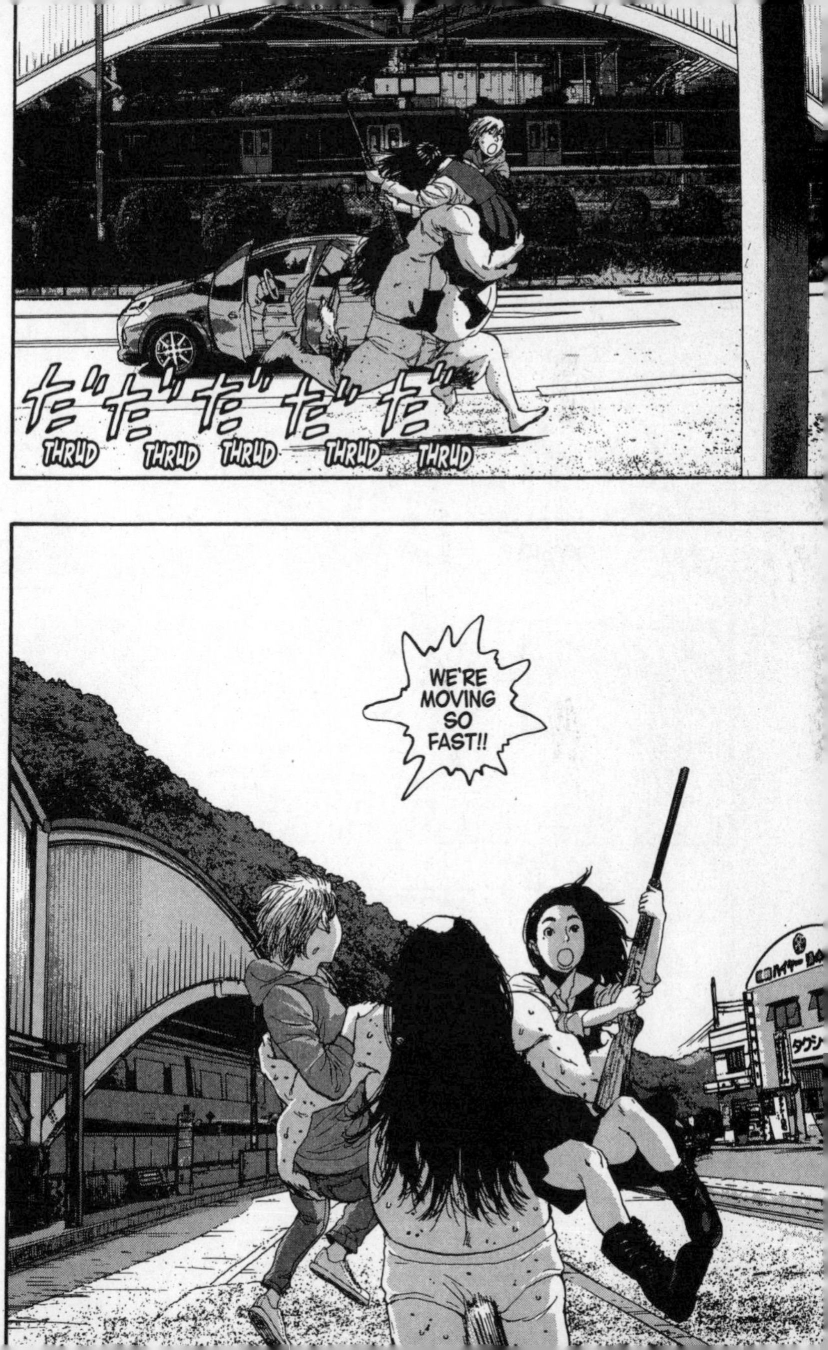
だだだだだ
THRUD THRUD THRUD THRUD THRUD
WE'RE MOVING SO FAST!!
タクシ

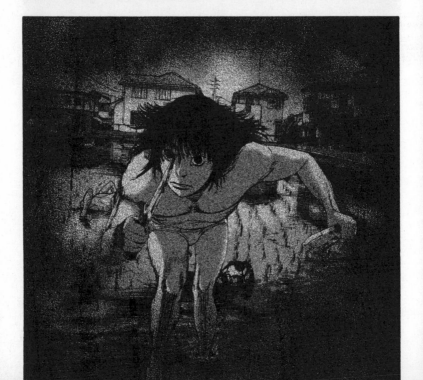

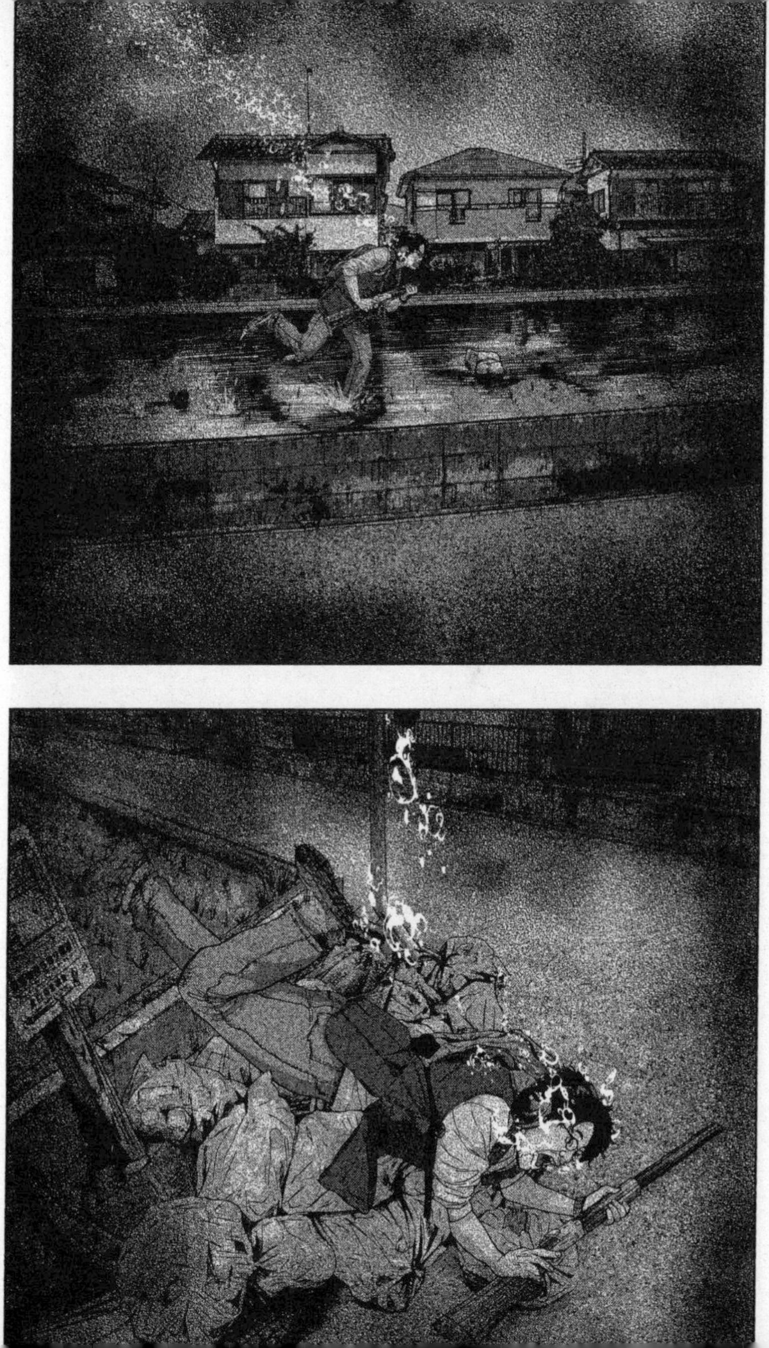

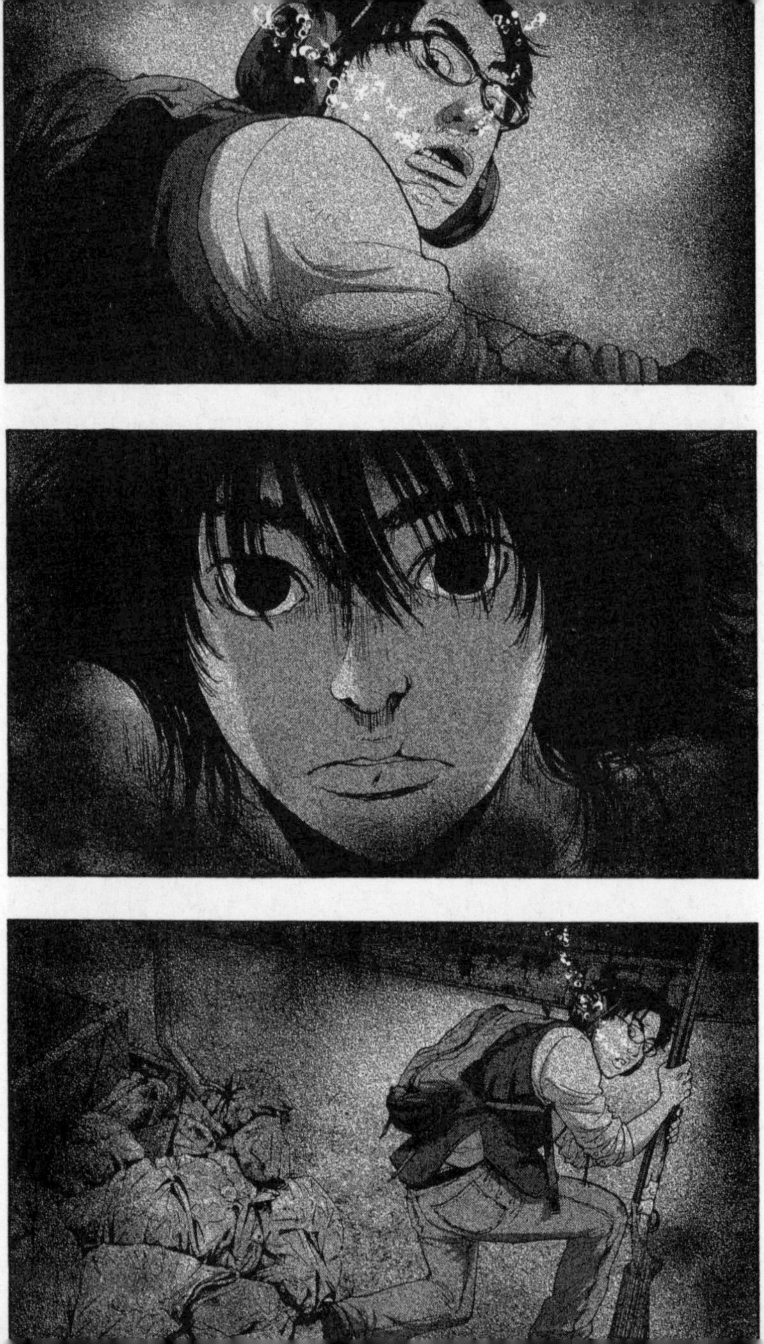

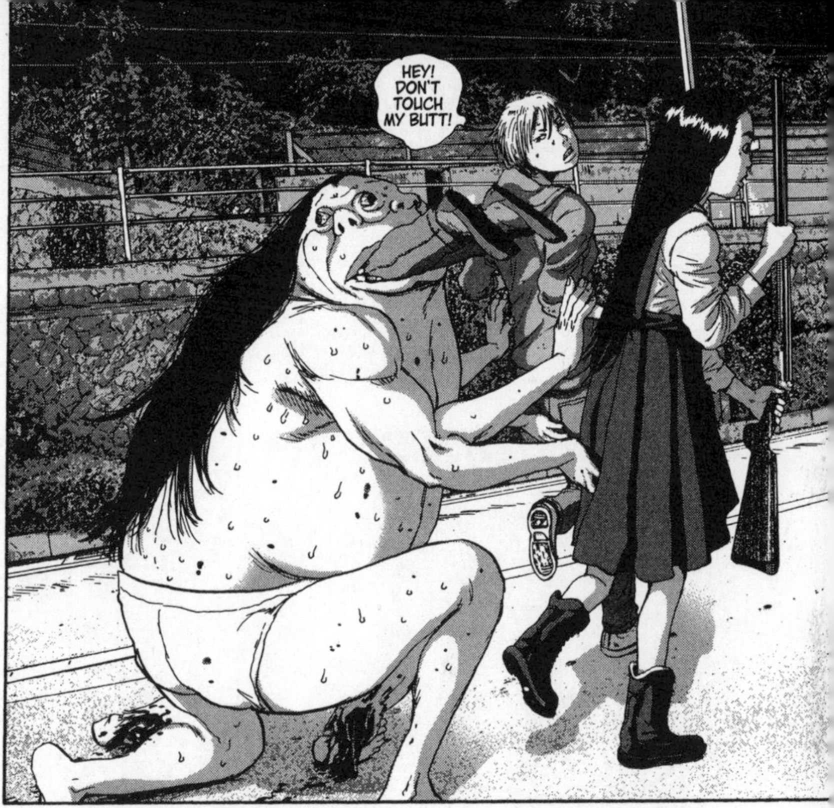
HEY! DON'T TOUCH MY BUTT!
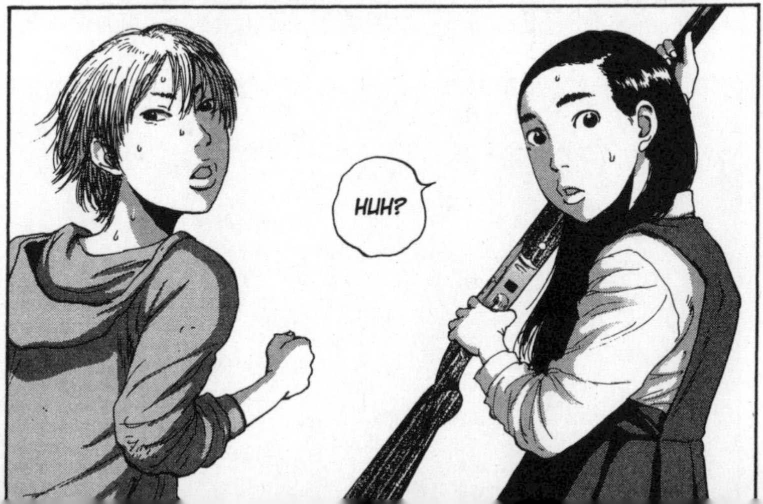
HUH?

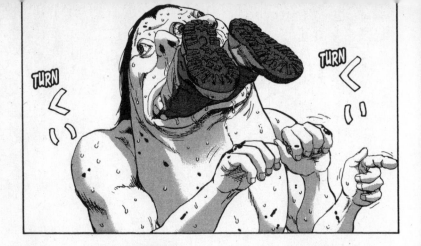

TURN

TURN

A CAR!!

HE'S SAYING TO FIND A CAR AND DRIVE AWAY!!

WHAT IS IT NOW?!

I'M RUN-NING!

RUN, MISS ODA!!

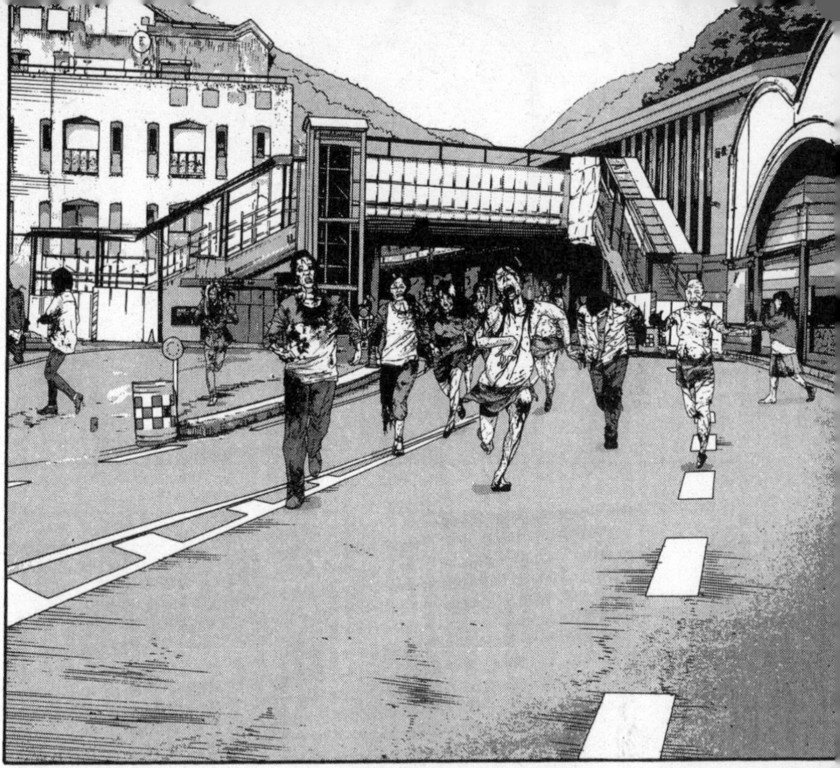

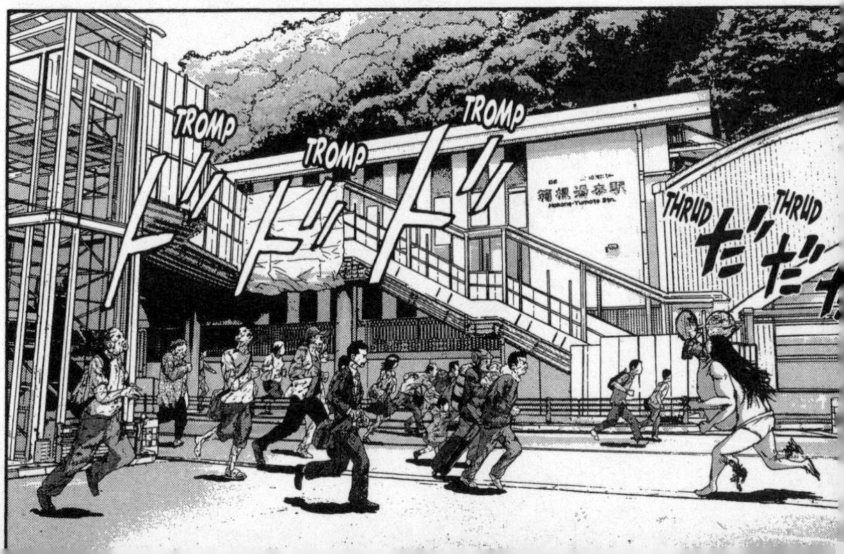
THRUD
THRUD
箱根湯本駅
TROMP
TROMP
TROMP
ドッドッドッ

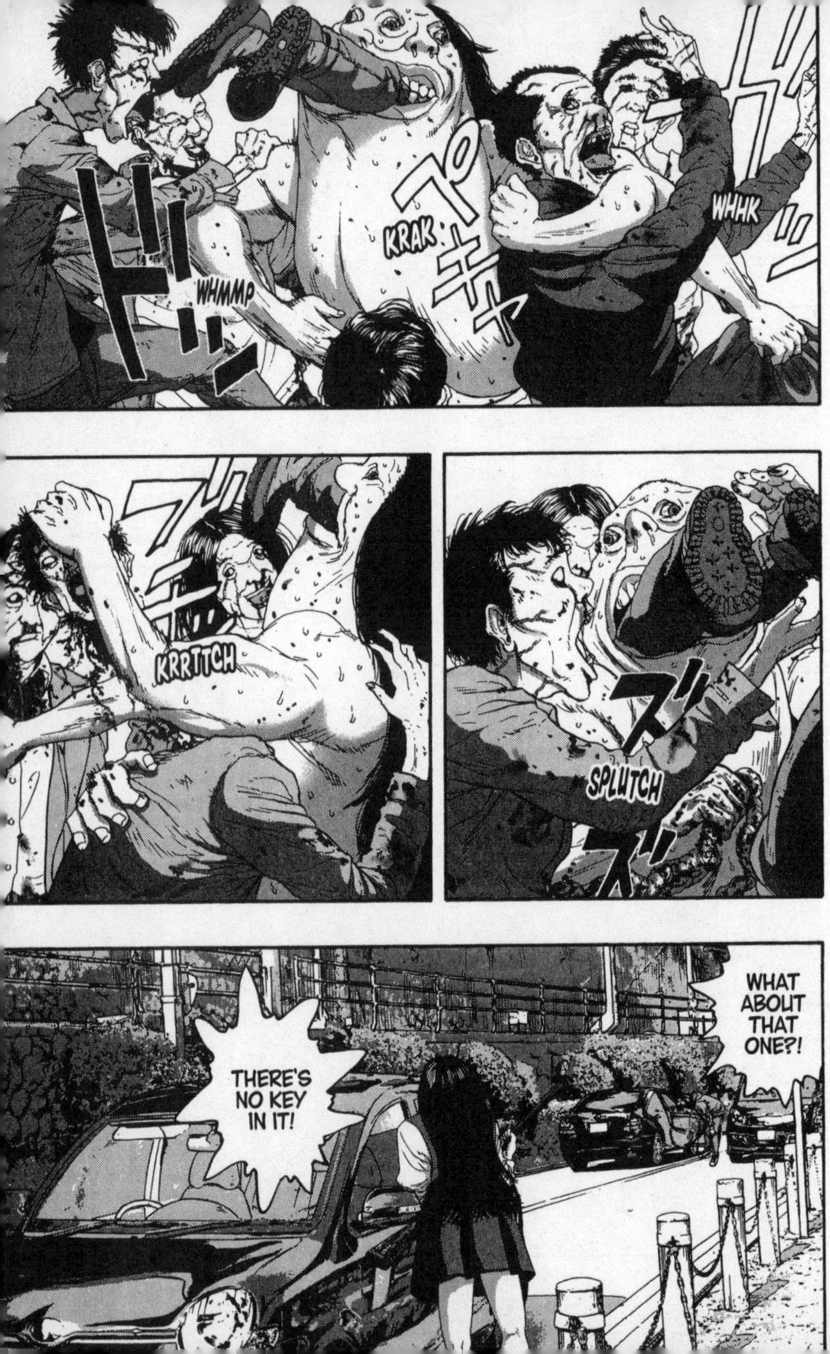
WHHK
KRAK
WHMMP
SPLUTCH
KRRTTCH
WHAT ABOUT THAT ONE?!
THERE'S NO KEY IN IT!

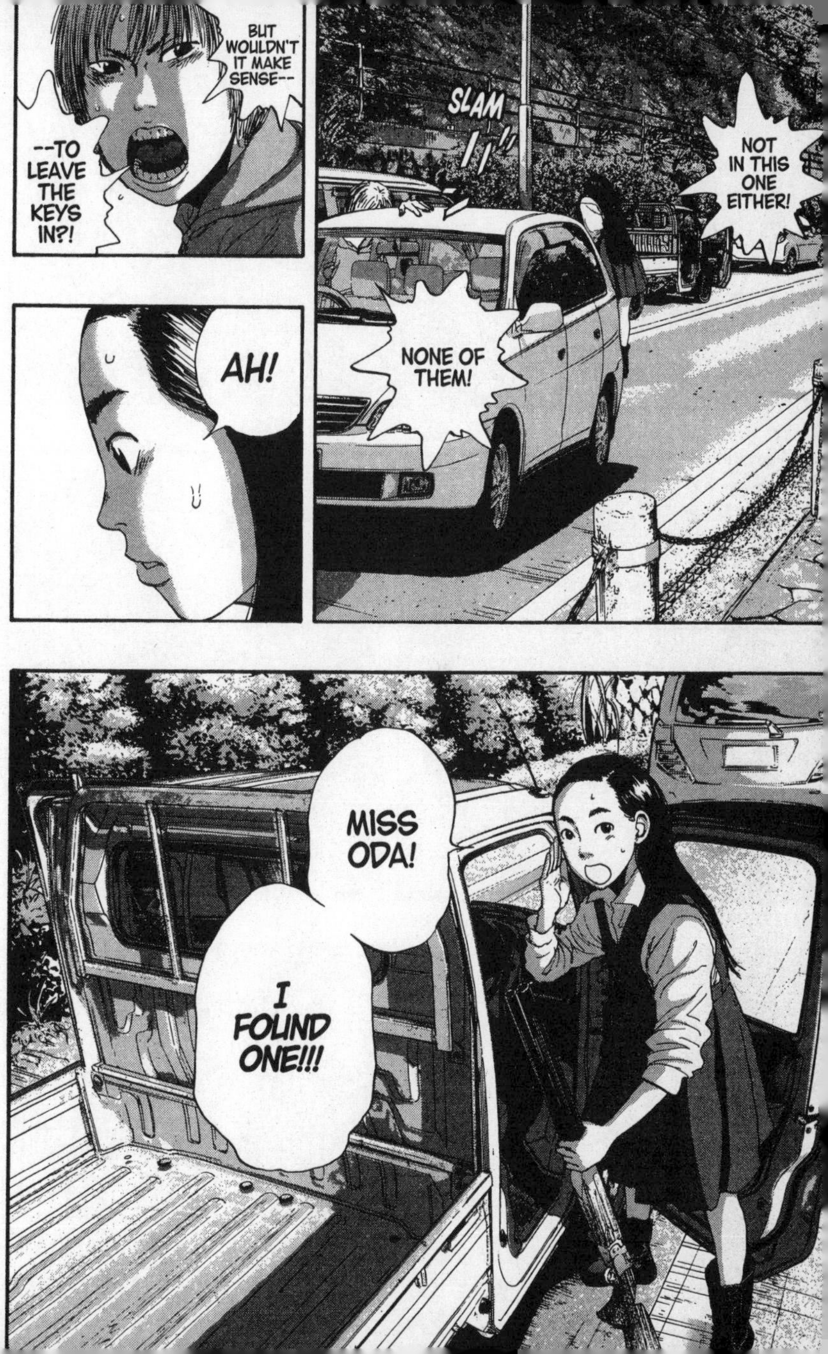
SLAM
NOT IN THIS ONE EITHER!
NONE OF THEM!
BUT WOULDN'T IT MAKE SENSE--
--TO LEAVE THE KEYS IN?!
AH!
MISS ODA!
I FOUND ONE!!!

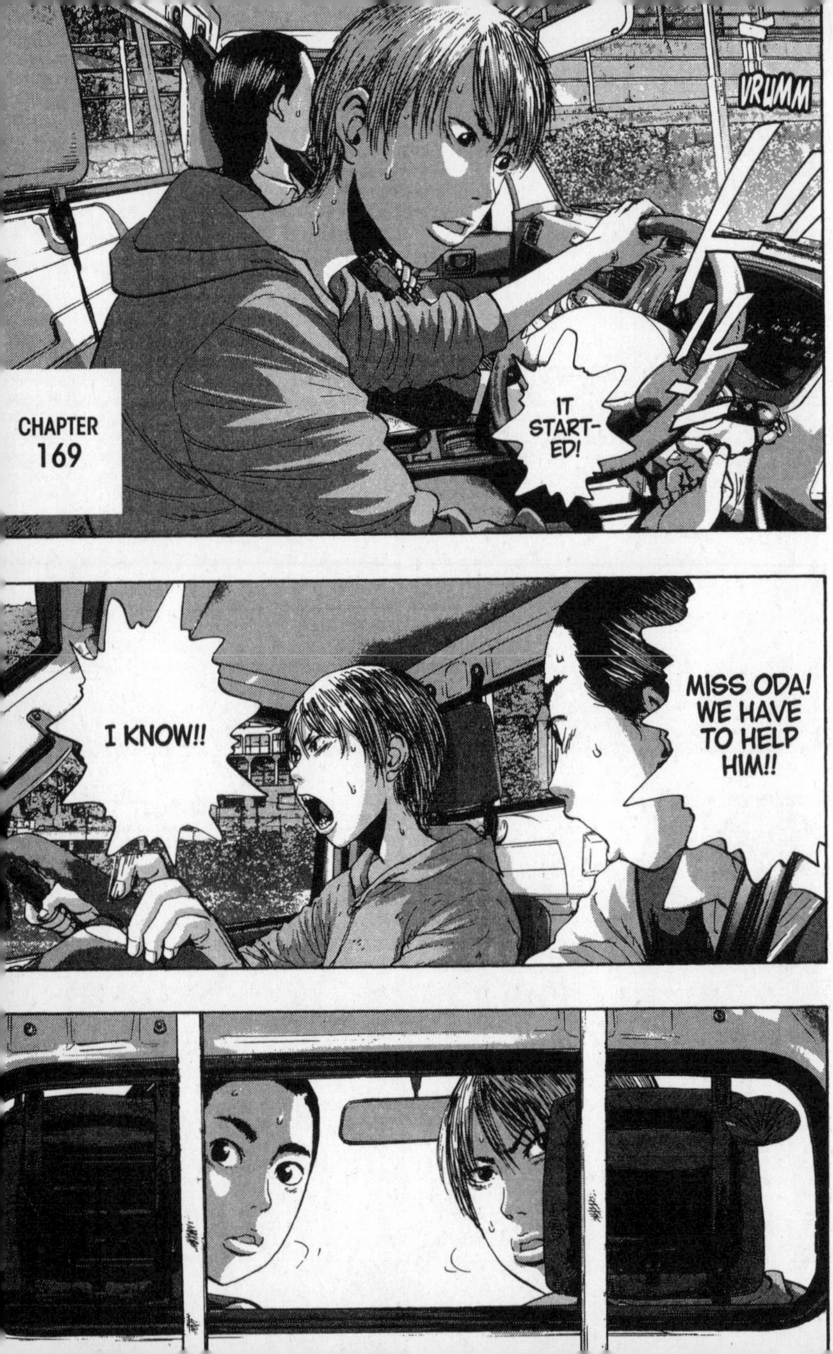
VRUMM
IT STARTED!
CHAPTER 169
MISS ODA! WE HAVE TO HELP HIM!!
I KNOW!!

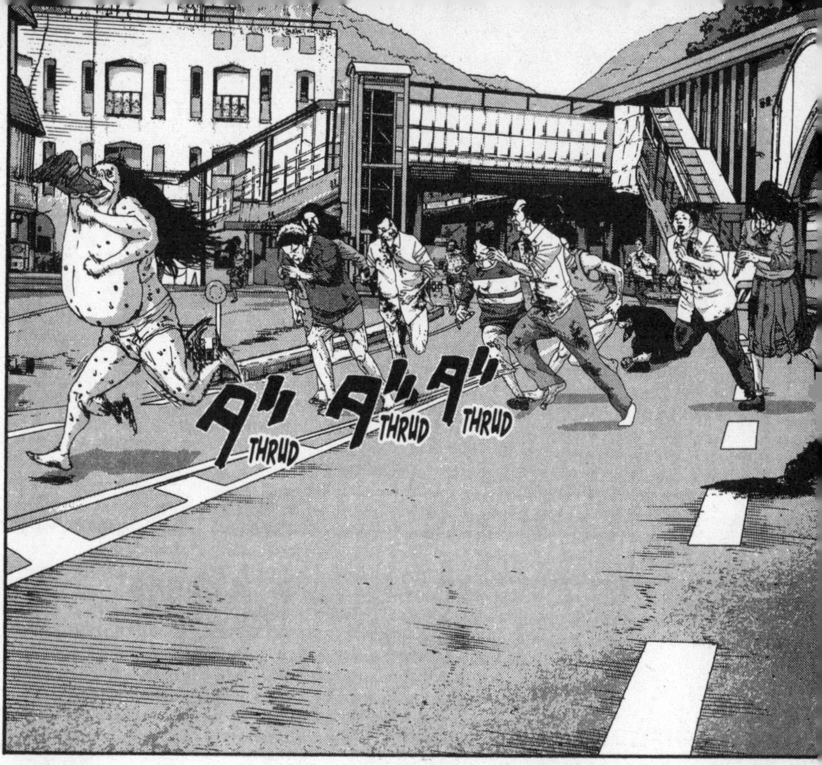
ダッ
THRUD
ダッ
THRUD
ダッ
THRUD
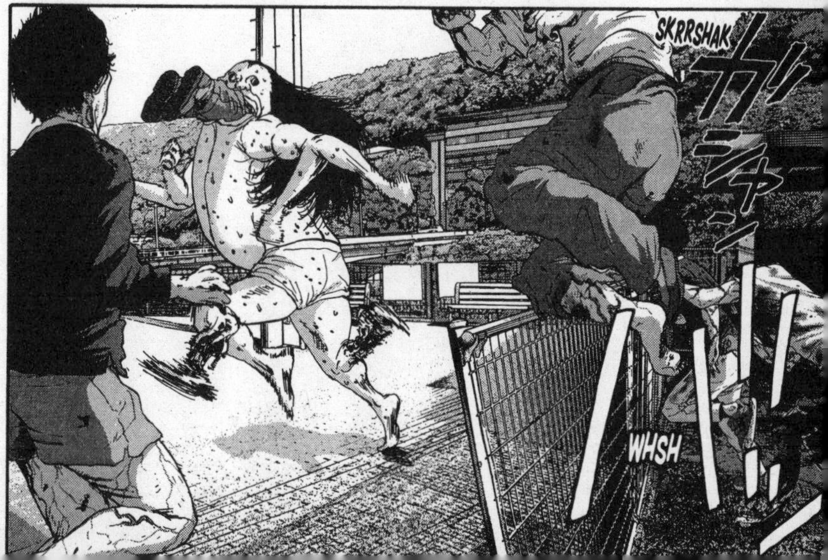
ガシャーン
SKRRSHAK
WHSH

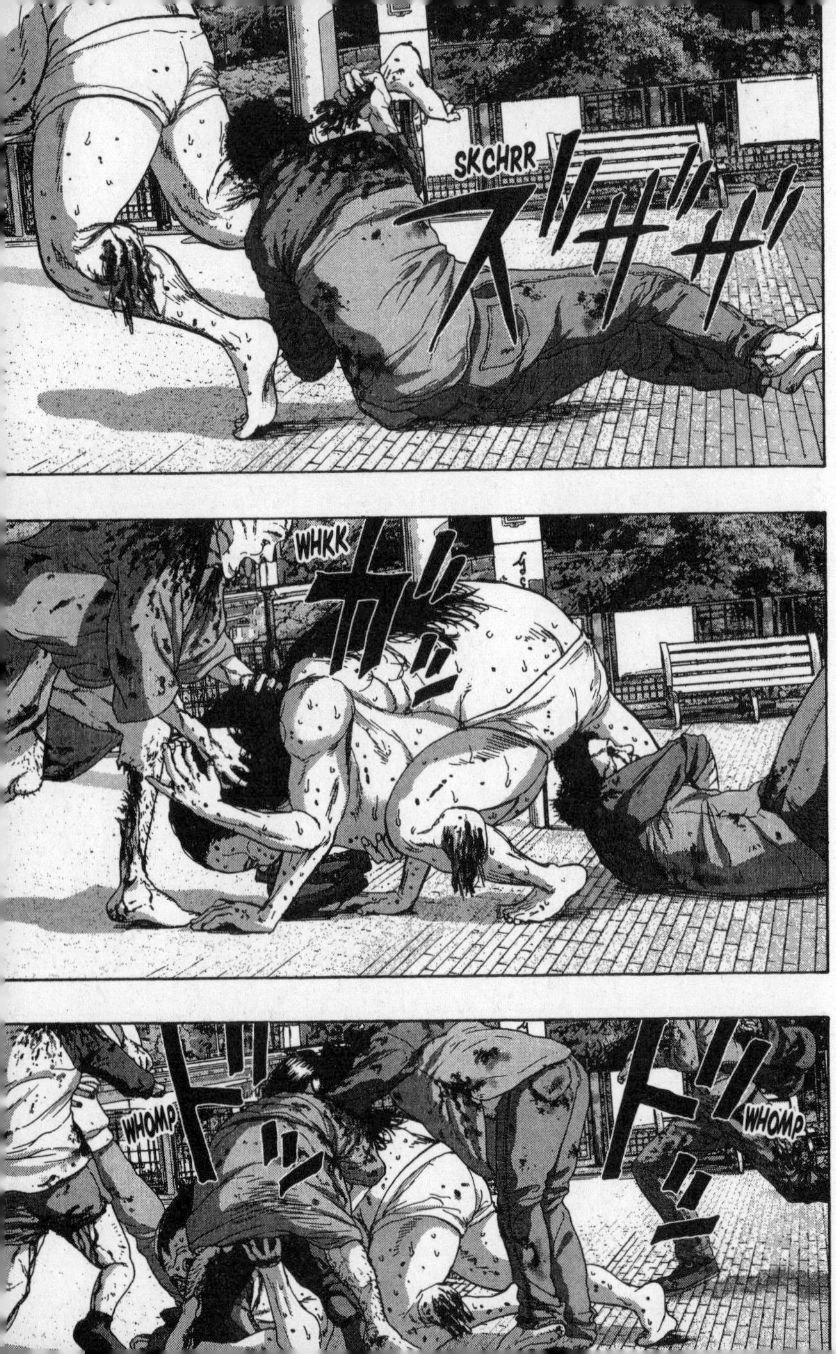
SKCHRR
WHKK
WHOMP
WHOMP

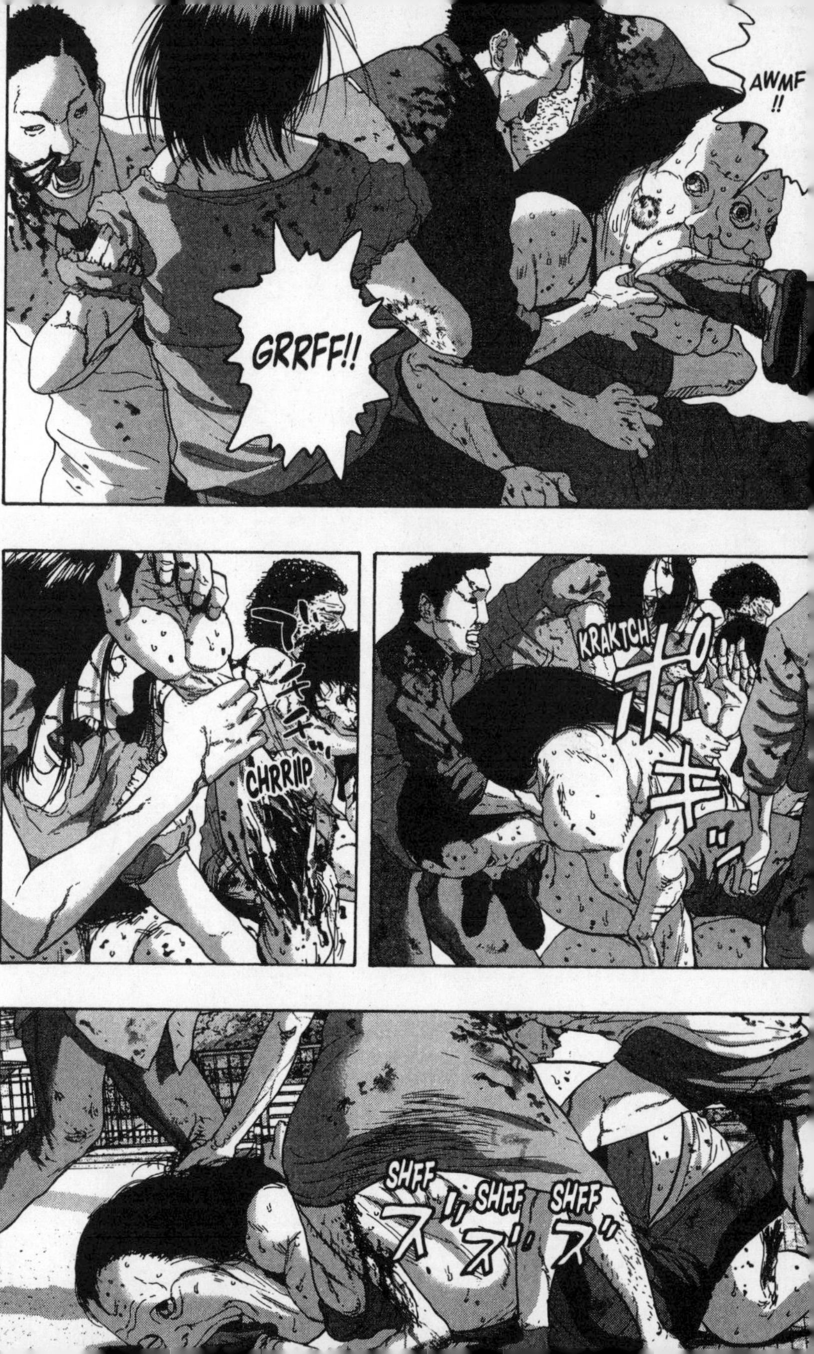
AWMF !!
GRRFF!!
KRAKTCH
CHRRIIP
SHFF
SHFF
SHFF

TOSS

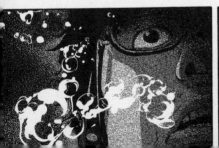

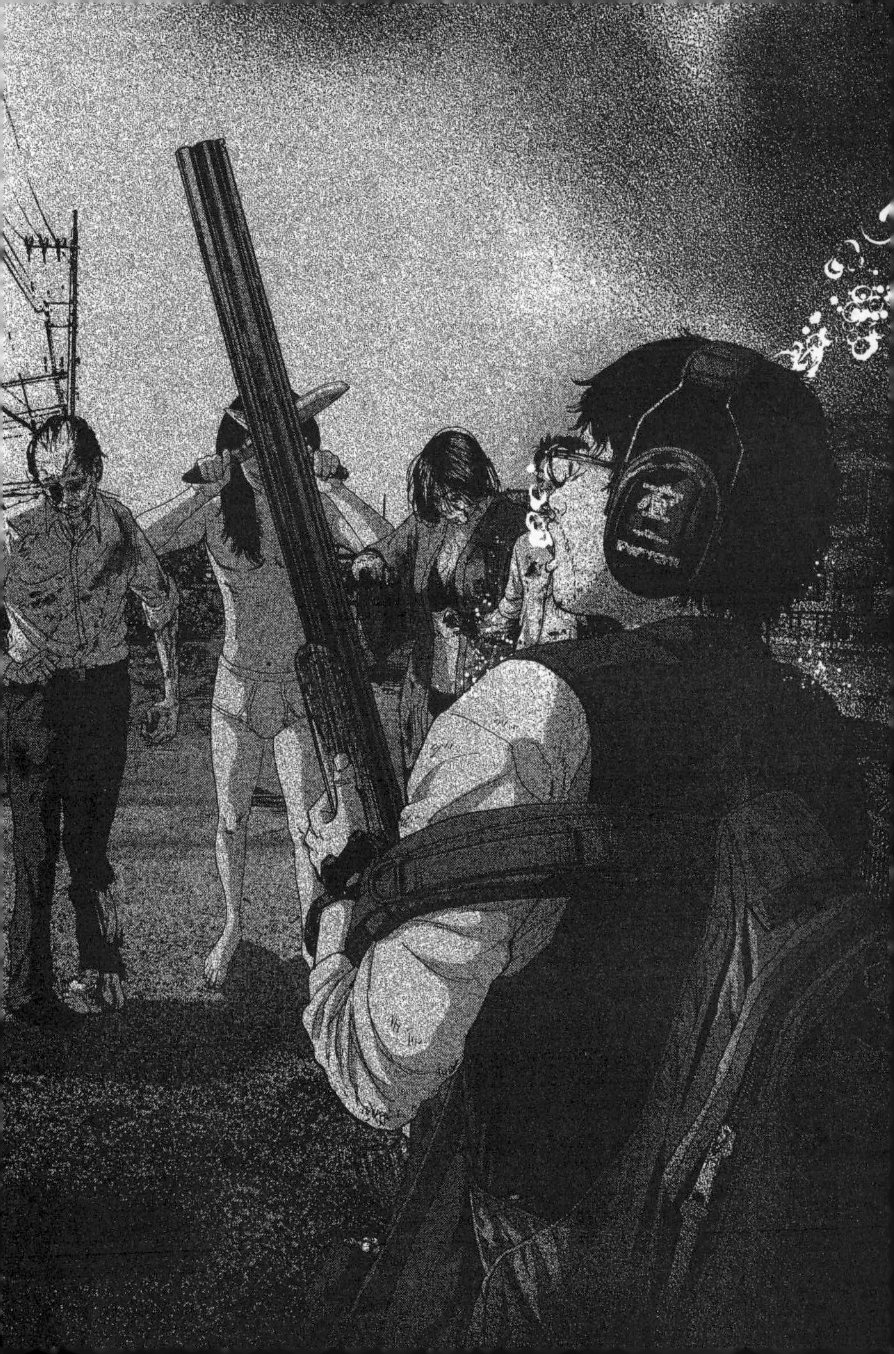

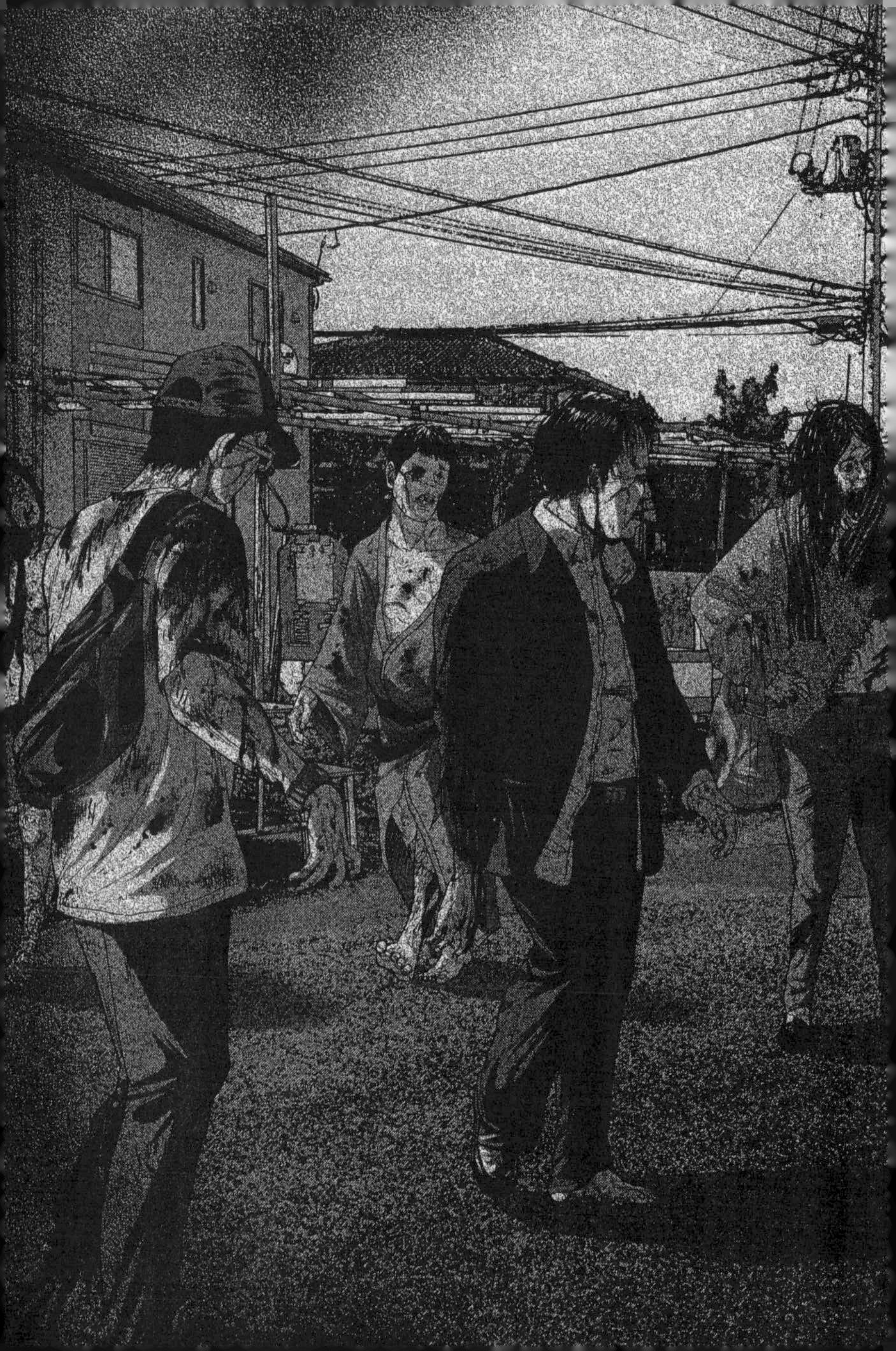

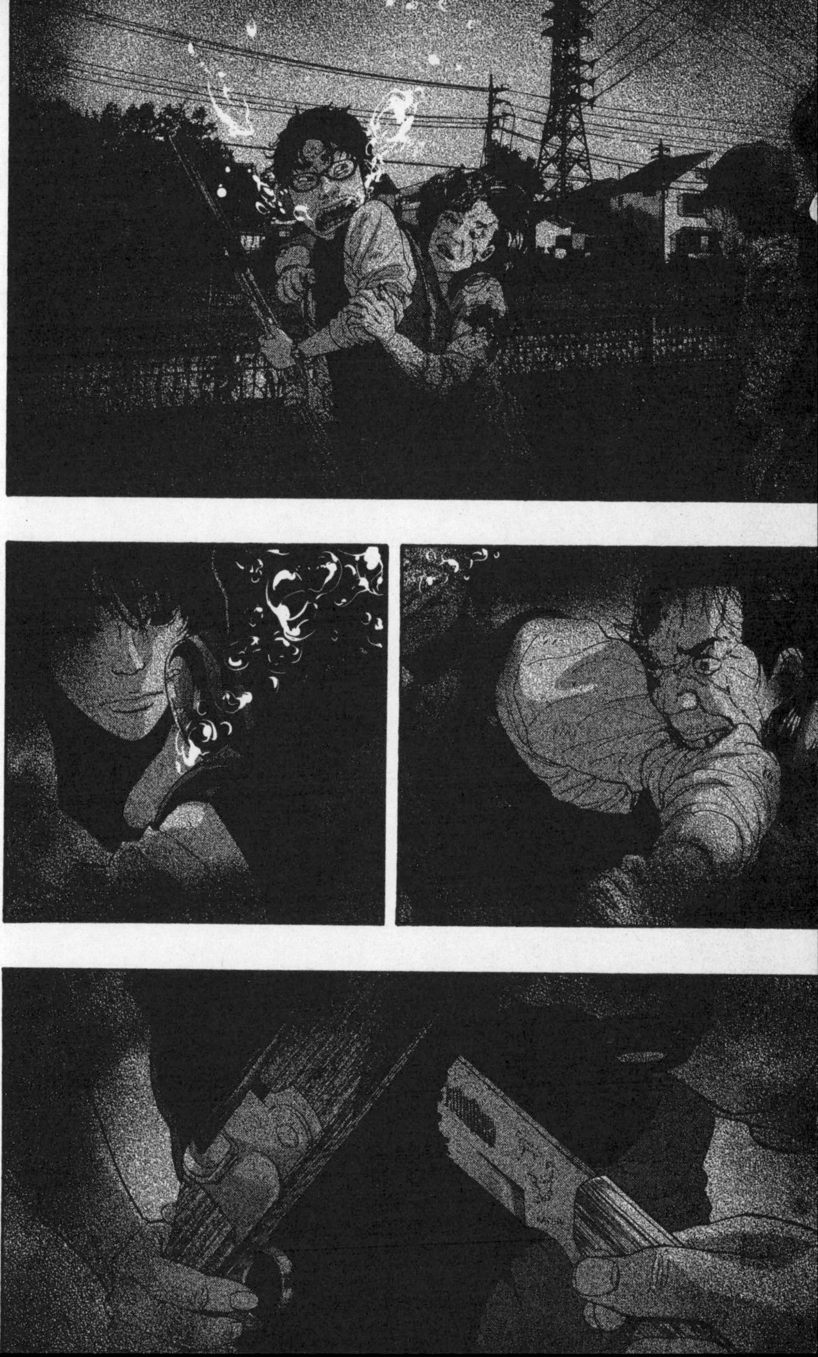

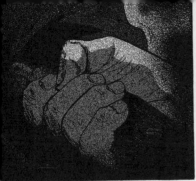

HOW'S THAT?

HURT?

AGON-IZING?

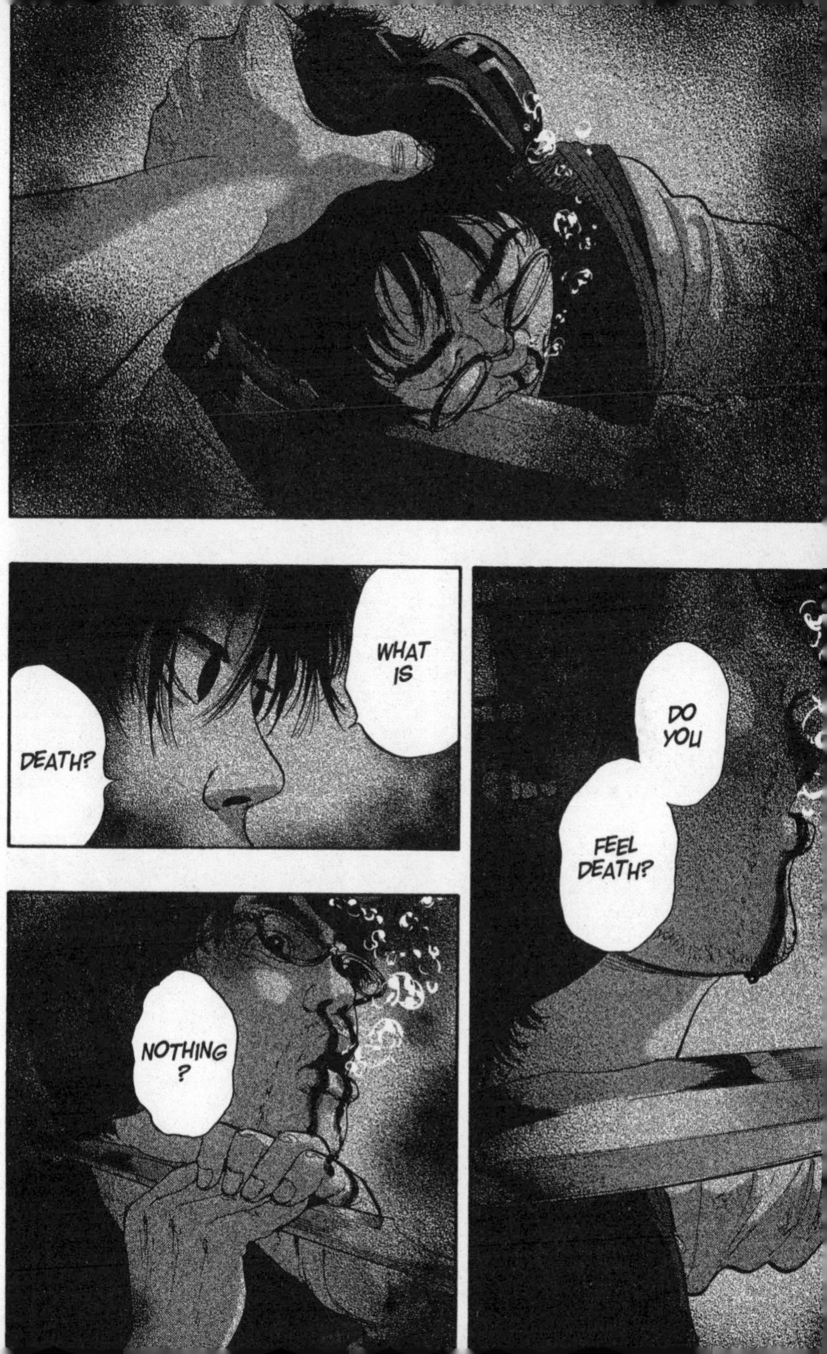
DO YOU
FEEL DEATH?
WHAT IS
DEATH?
NOTHING
?

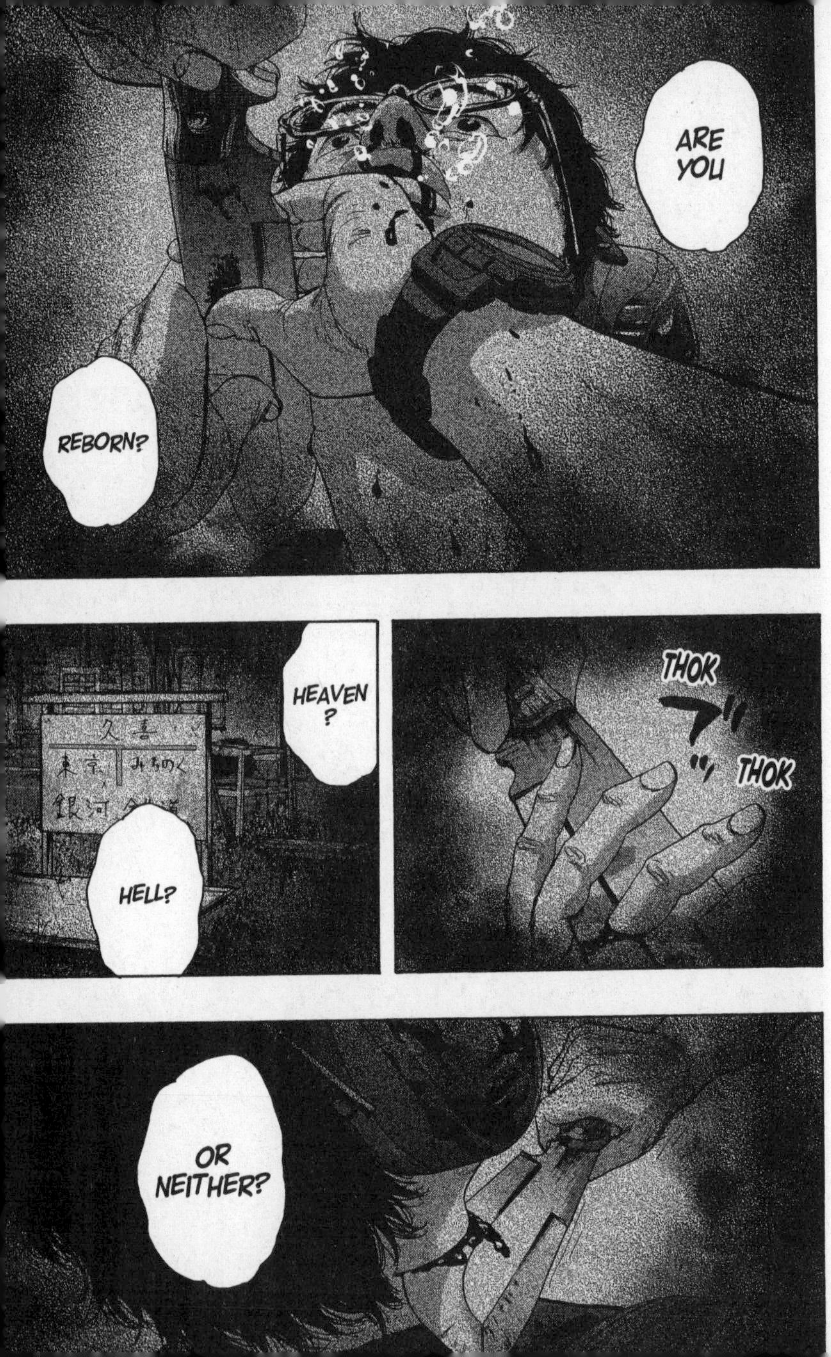
ARE YOU
REBORN?
THOK
THOK
HEAVEN ?
久喜
東京
みちのく
HELL?
OR NEITHER?

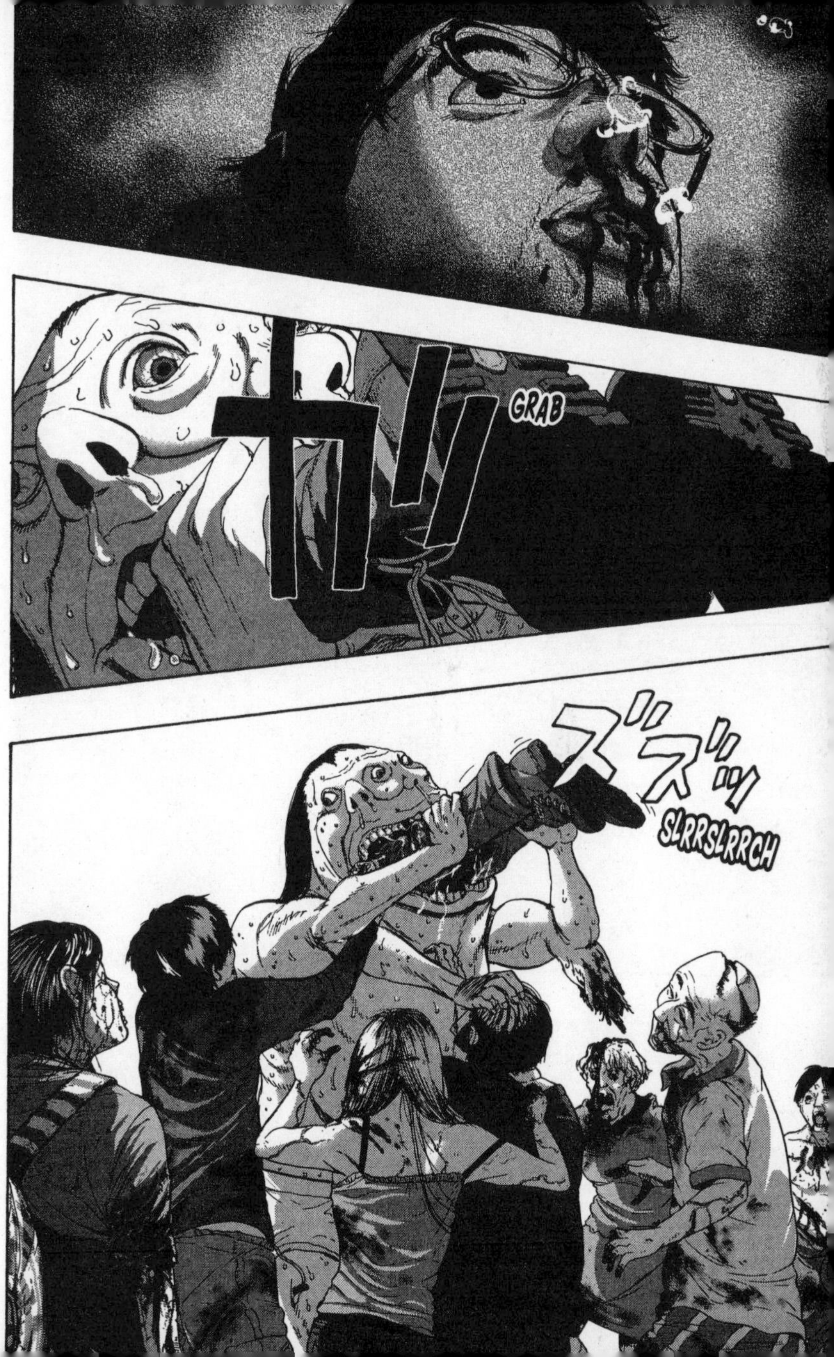
カリ
GRAB
ズズッ
SLRRSLRRCH

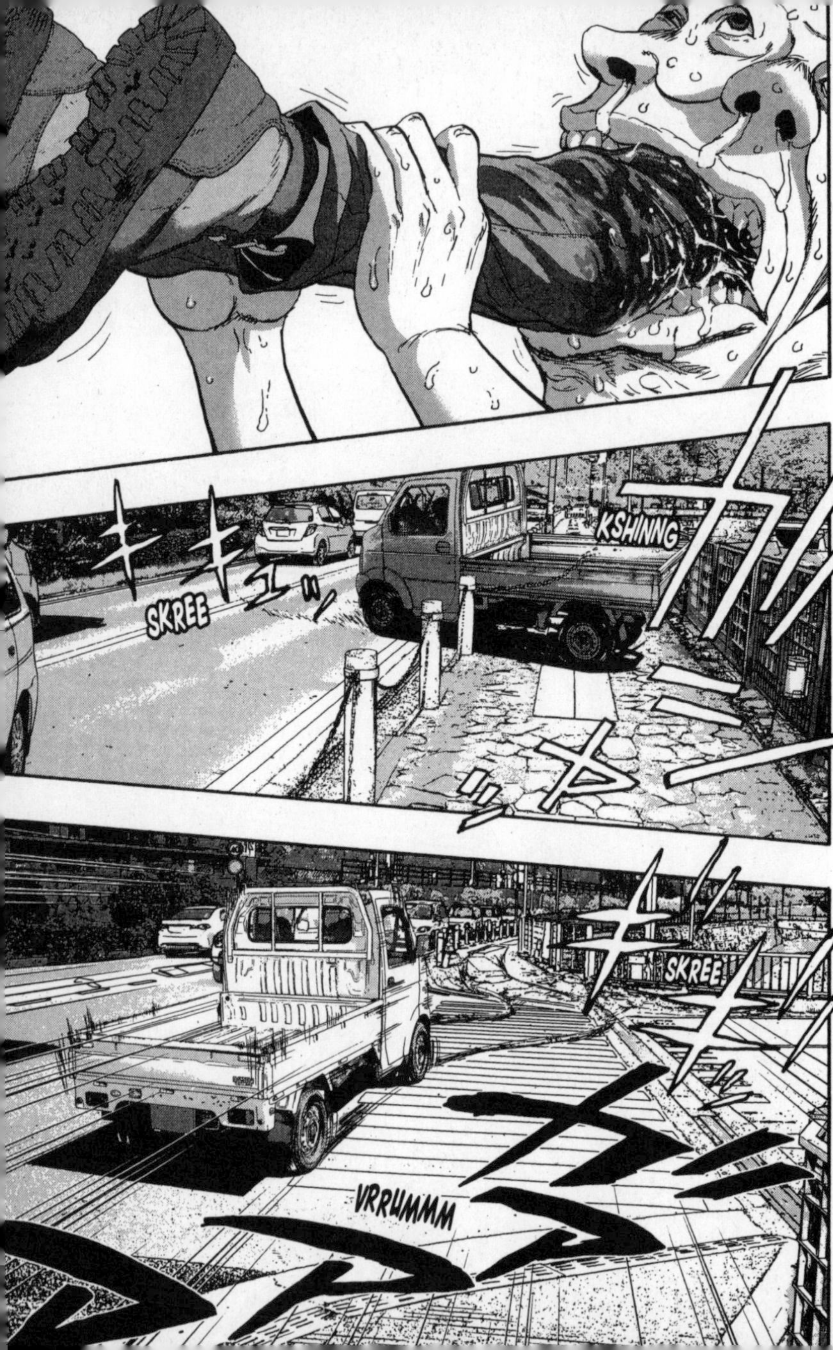
KSHINNG
SKREE
SKREE
VRRUMMM

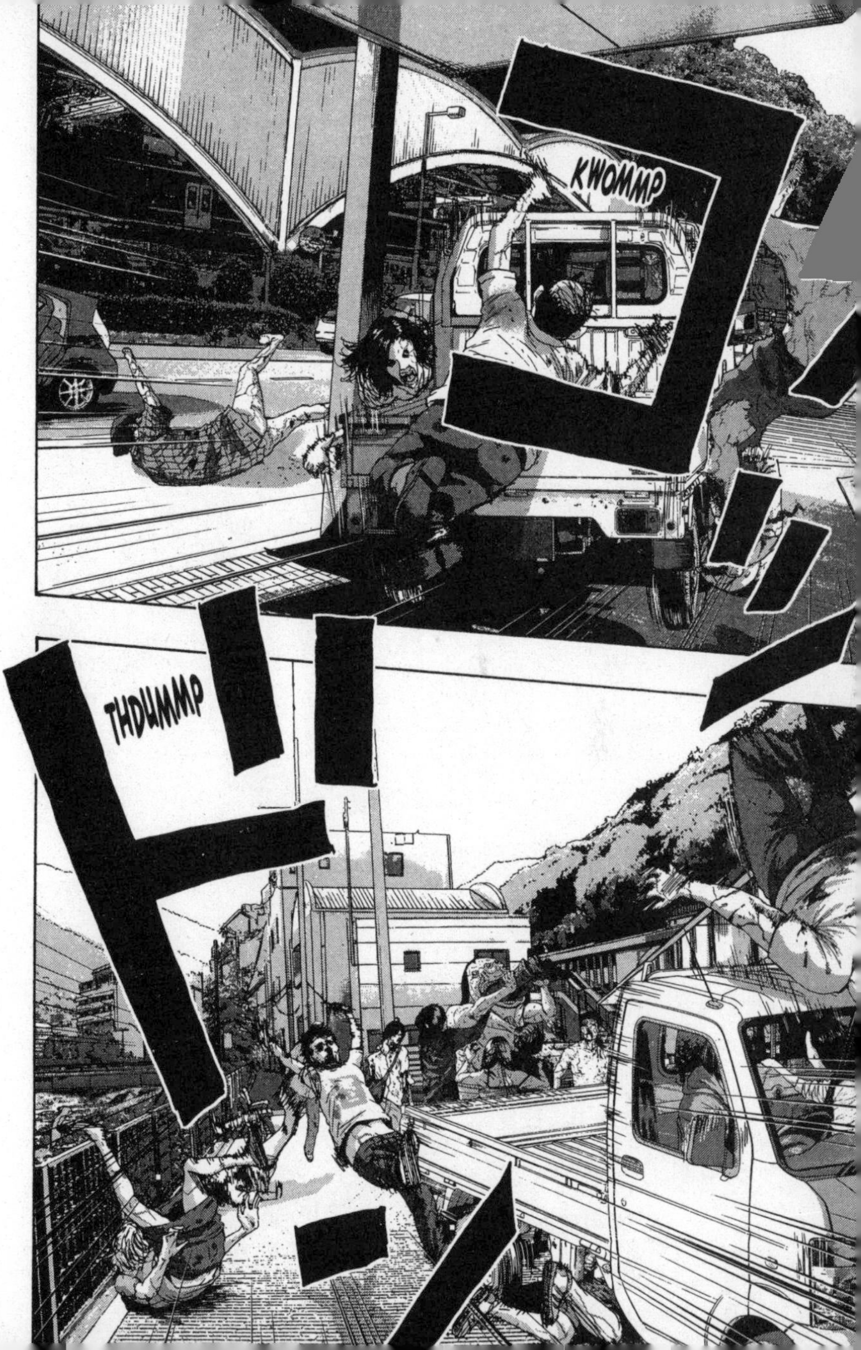
KWOMMP
THDUMMP

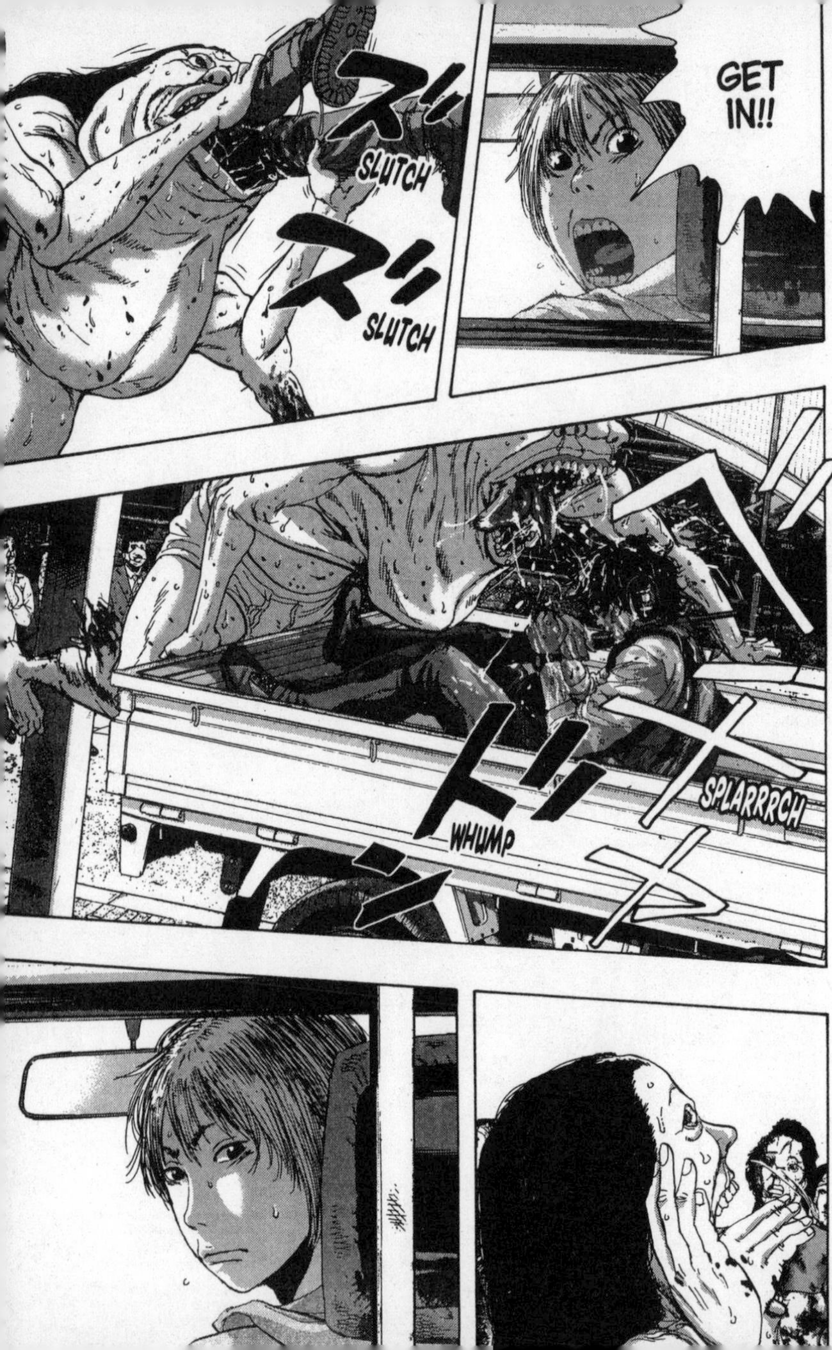

GET IN!!
SLUTCH
SLUTCH
SPLARRRCH
WHUMP

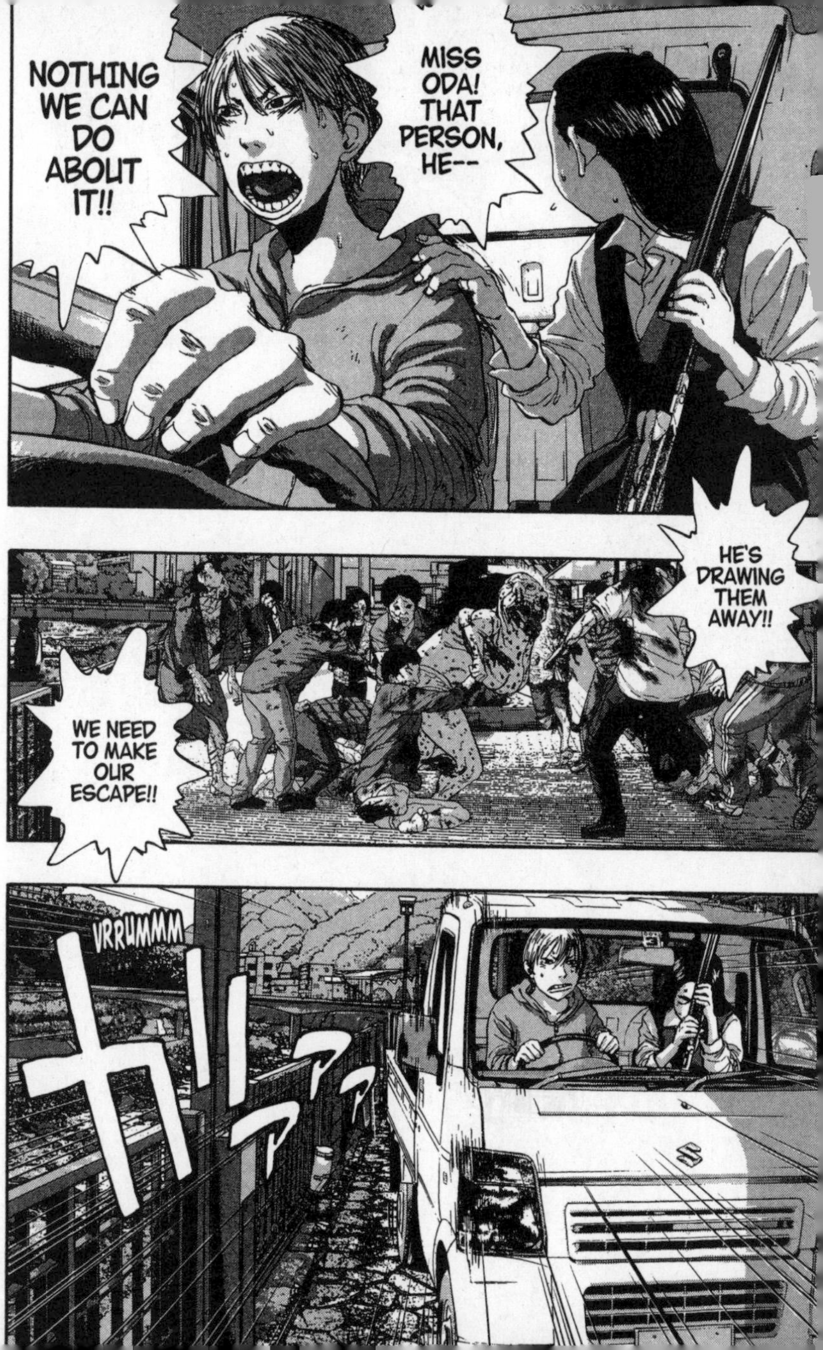
MISS ODA! THAT PERSON, HE--
NOTHING WE CAN DO ABOUT IT!!
HE'S DRAWING THEM AWAY!!
WE NEED TO MAKE OUR ESCAPE!!
VRRUMMM

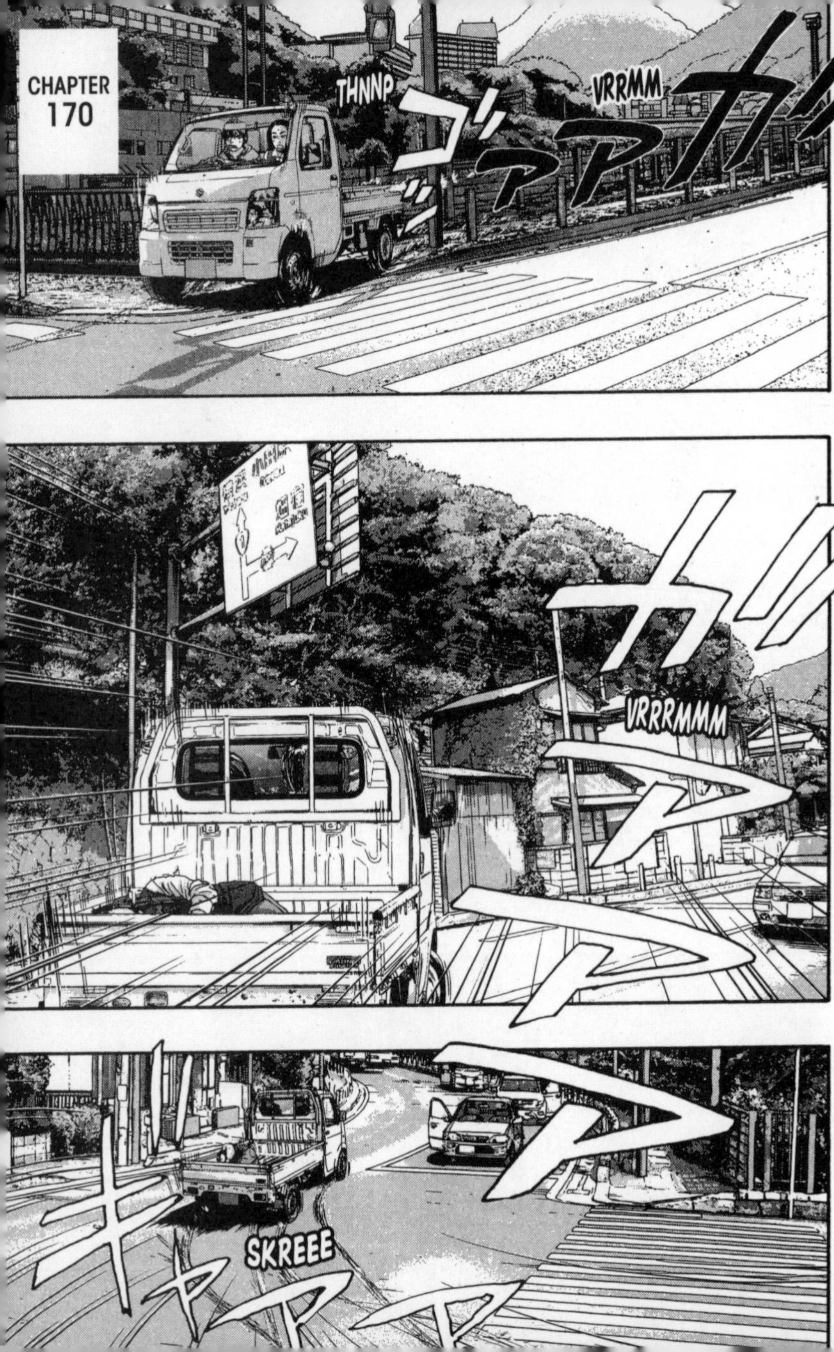
CHAPTER
170
VRRMM
THNNP
VRRRMMM
SKREEE

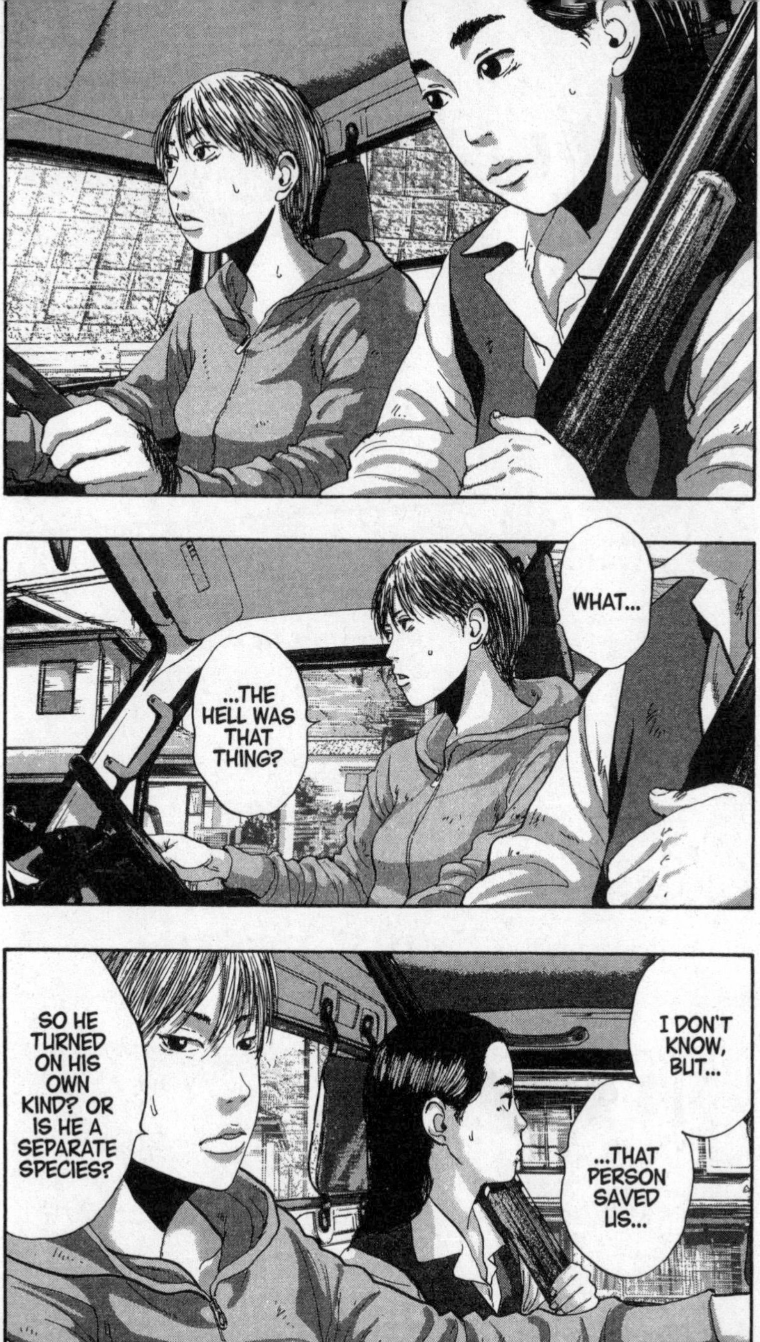
WHAT...
...THE HELL WAS THAT THING?
I DON'T KNOW, BUT...
...THAT PERSON SAVED US...
SO HE TURNED ON HIS OWN KIND? OR IS HE A SEPARATE SPECIES?

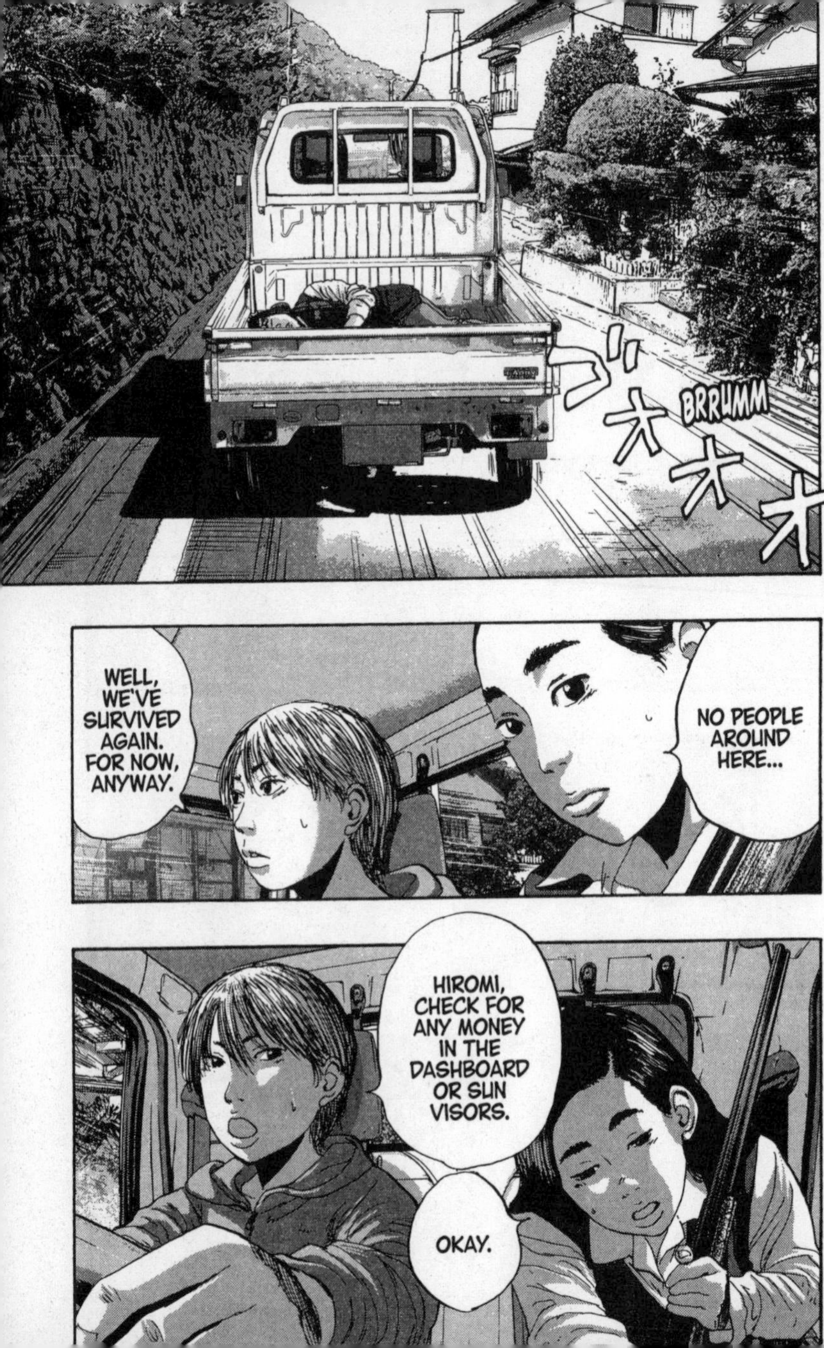
ゴオオオ
BRRUMM
NO PEOPLE AROUND HERE...
WELL, WE'VE SURVIVED AGAIN. FOR NOW, ANYWAY.
HIROMI, CHECK FOR ANY MONEY IN THE DASHBOARD OR SUN VISORS.
OKAY.

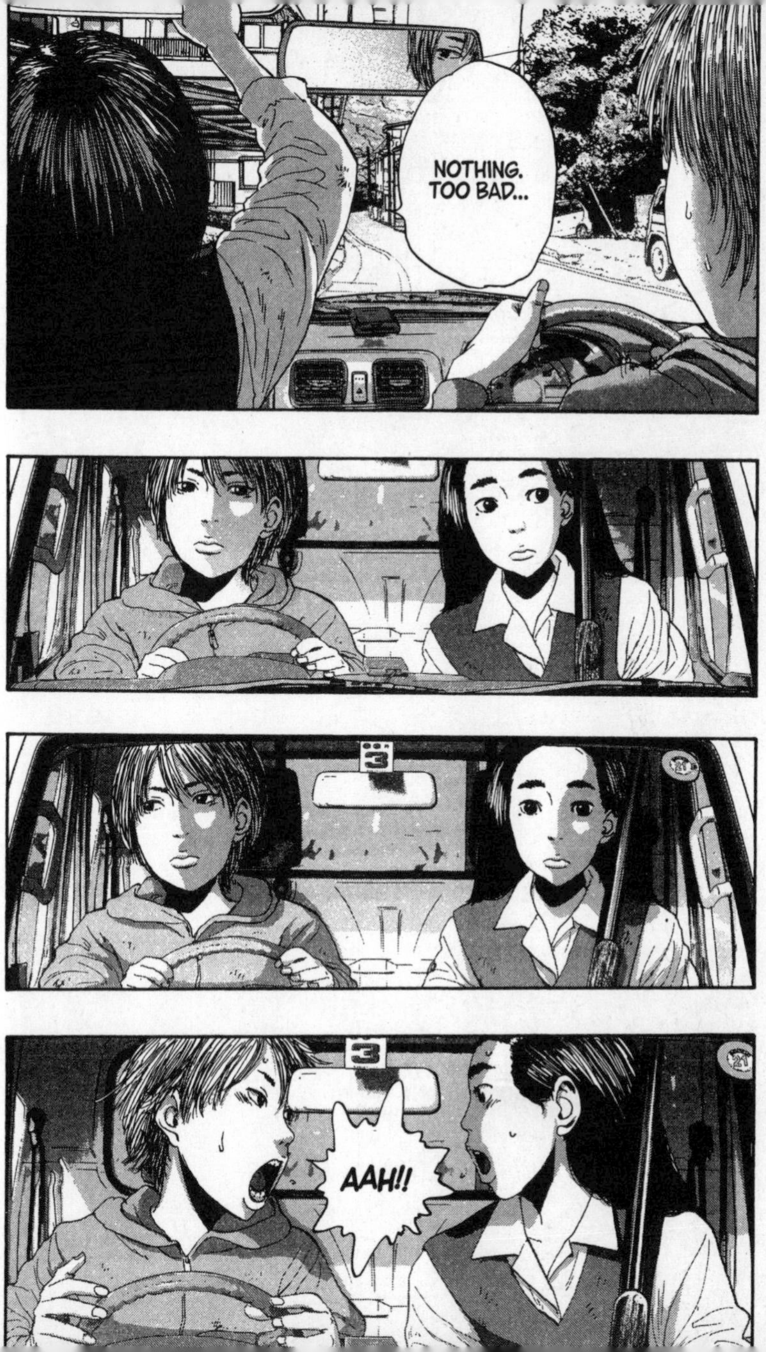
NOTHING.
TOO BAD...
3
21
AAH!!

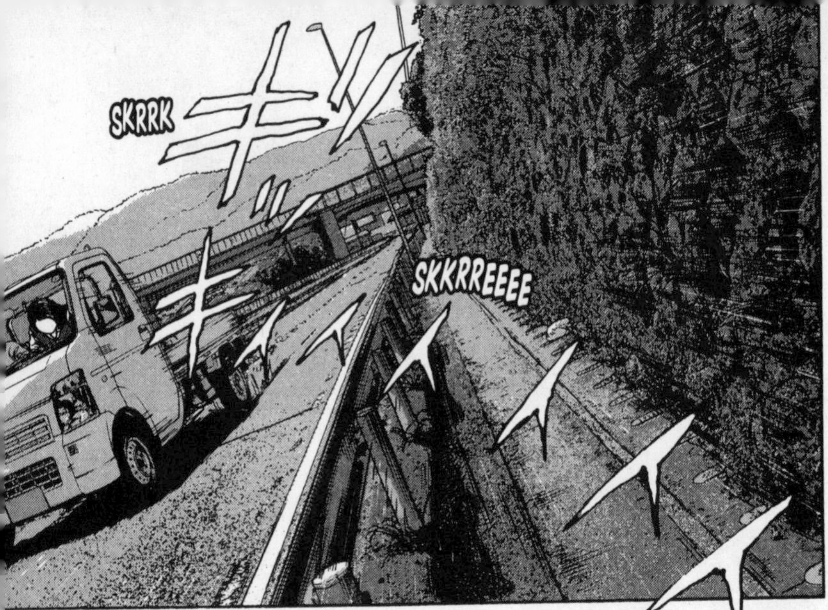
SKRRK
SKKRREEEE
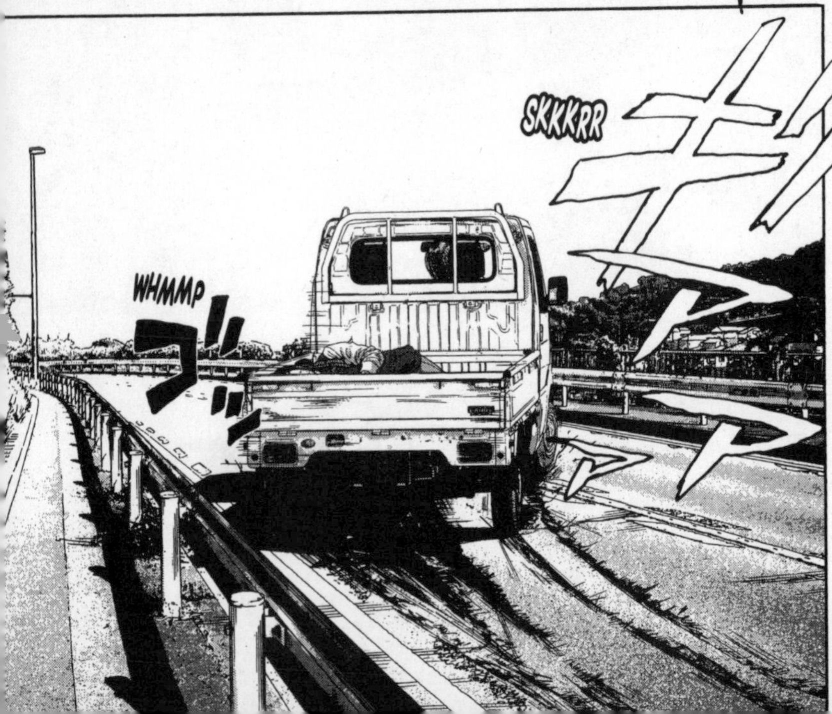
SKKKRR
WHMMP

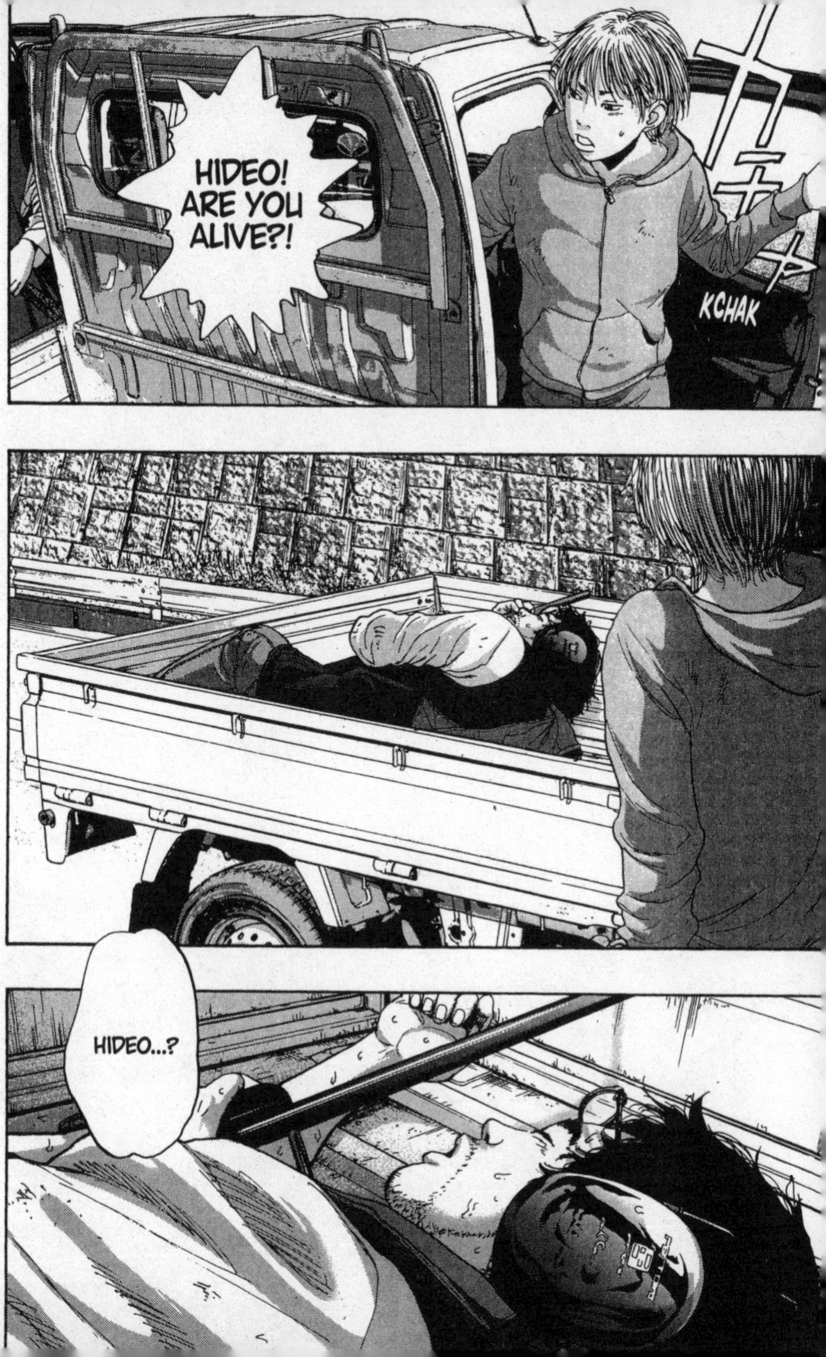
KCHAK
HIDEO! ARE YOU ALIVE?!
HIDEO...?

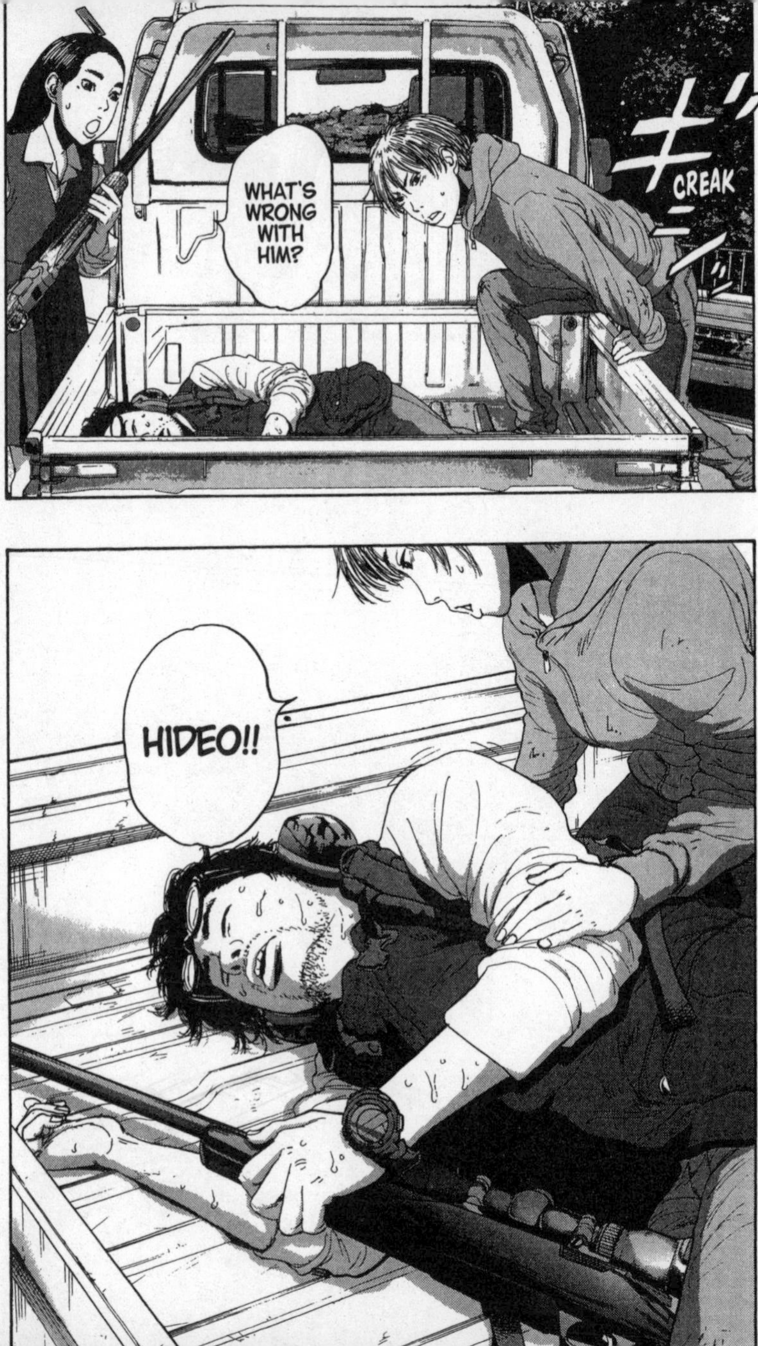
CREAK
WHAT'S WRONG WITH HIM?
HIDEO!!

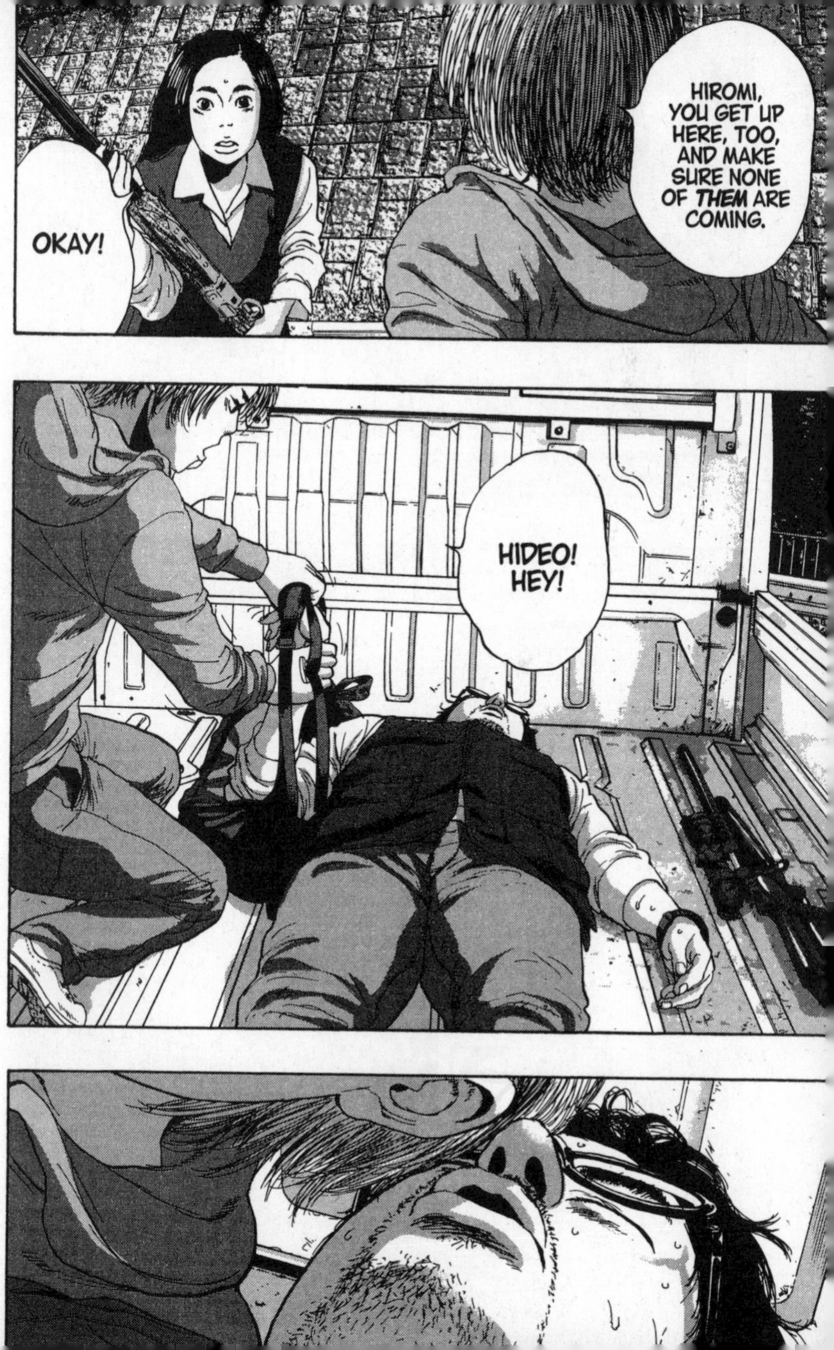
HIROMI, YOU GET UP HERE, TOO, AND MAKE SURE NONE OF *THEM* ARE COMING.
OKAY!
HIDEO! HEY!

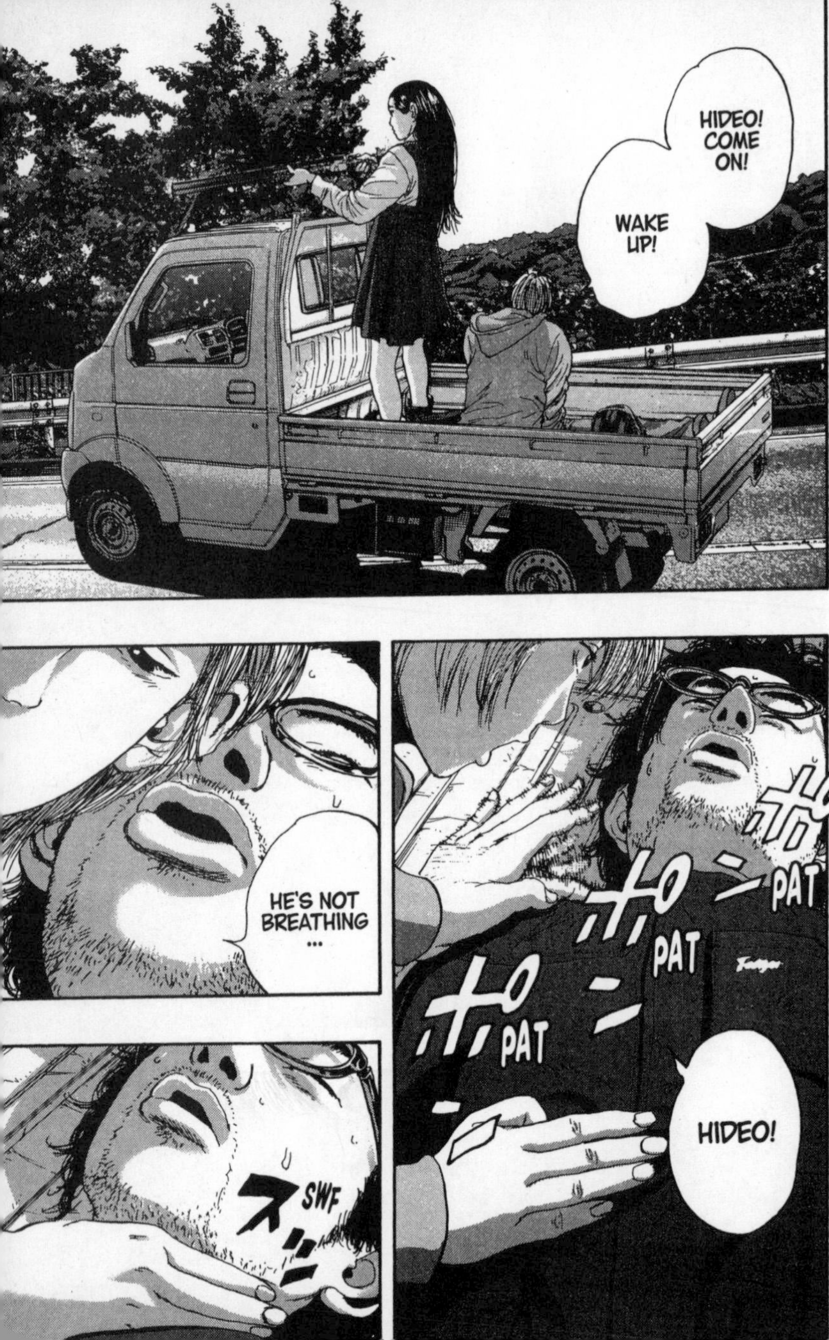
HIDEO! COME ON!
WAKE UP!
PAT
PAT
PAT
HIDEO!
HE'S NOT BREATHING ...
SWF

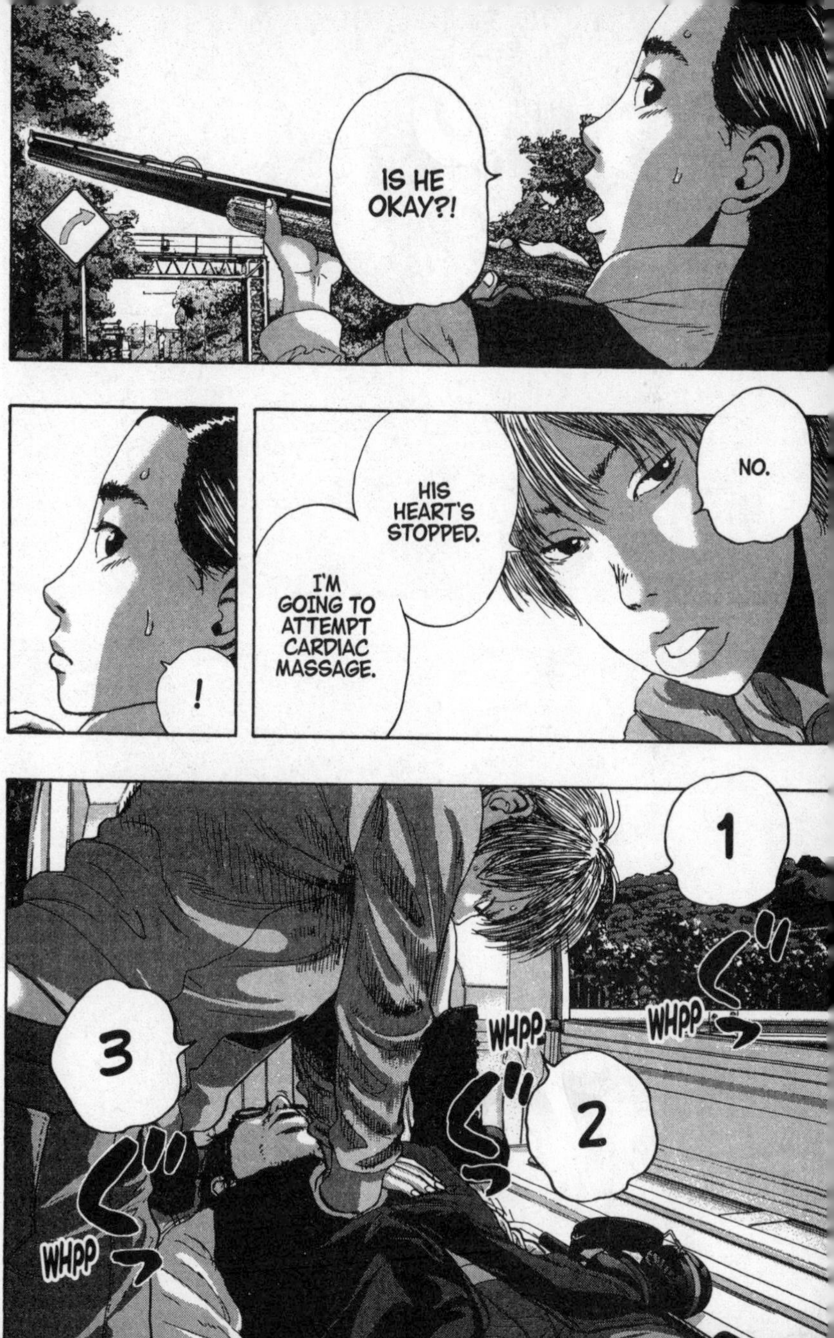
IS HE OKAY?!
NO.
HIS HEART'S STOPPED.
I'M GOING TO ATTEMPT CARDIAC MASSAGE.
!
1
ぐっ
WHPP
WHPP
ぐっ
2
3
ぐっ
WHPP

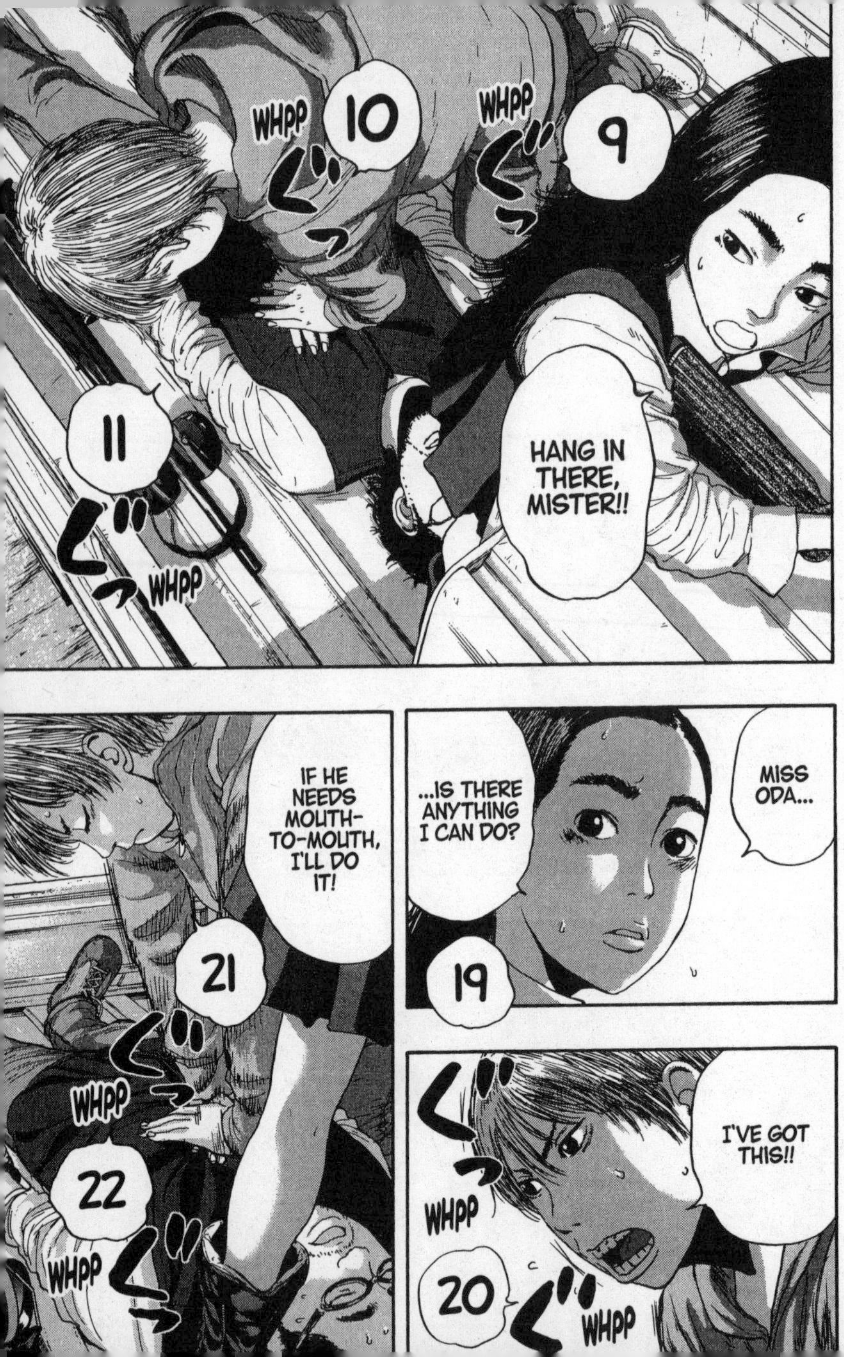
9
WHPP
ぐっ
10
WHPP
ぐっ
HANG IN THERE, MISTER!!
11
ぐっ
WHPP
MISS ODA...
...IS THERE ANYTHING I CAN DO?
19
I'VE GOT THIS!!
ぐっ
WHPP
20
ぐっ
WHPP
IF HE NEEDS MOUTH-TO-MOUTH, I'LL DO IT!
21
ぐっ
WHPP
22
WHPP
ぐっ

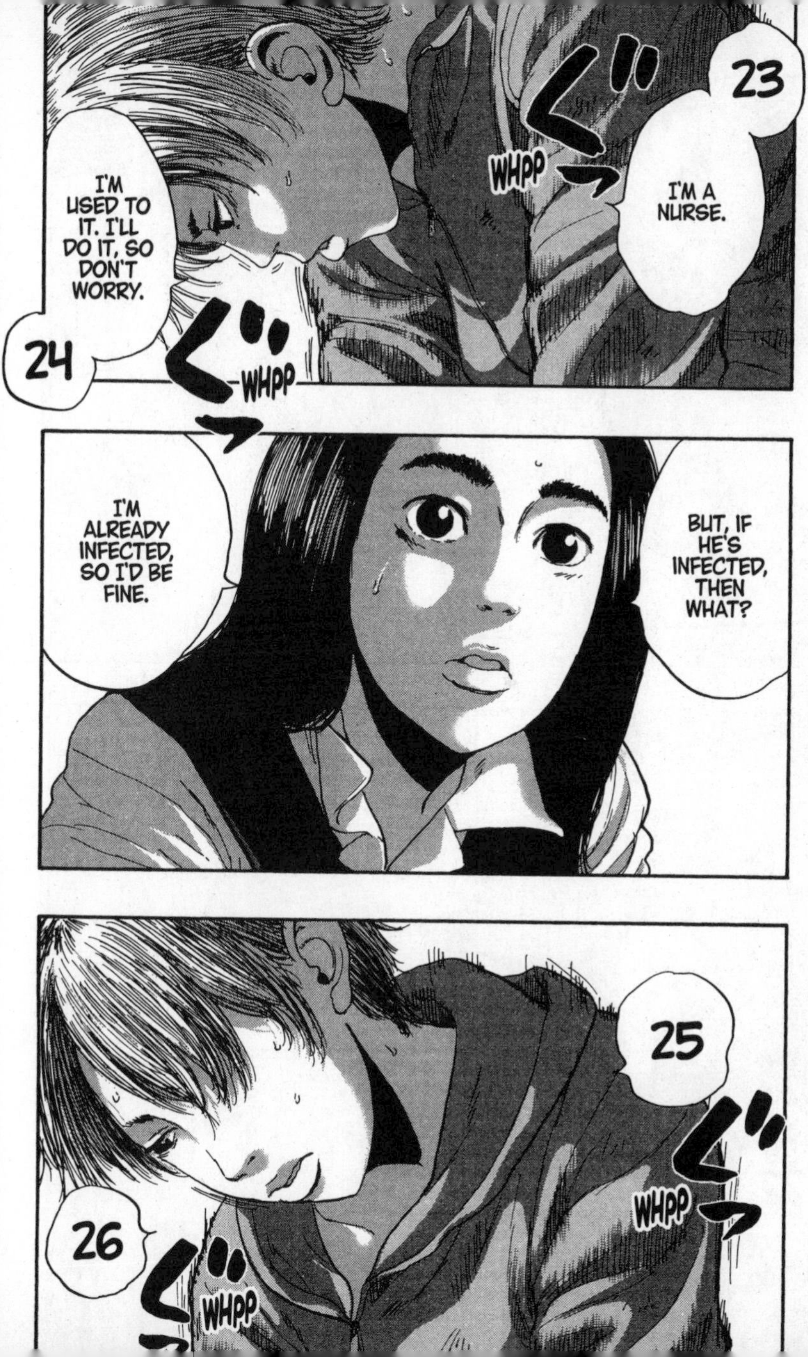
23
ぐ
WHPP
I'M A NURSE.
I'M USED TO IT. I'LL DO IT, SO DON'T WORRY.
24
ぐ
WHPP
BUT, IF HE'S INFECTED, THEN WHAT?
I'M ALREADY INFECTED, SO I'D BE FINE.
25
ぐ
WHPP
26
ぐ
WHPP

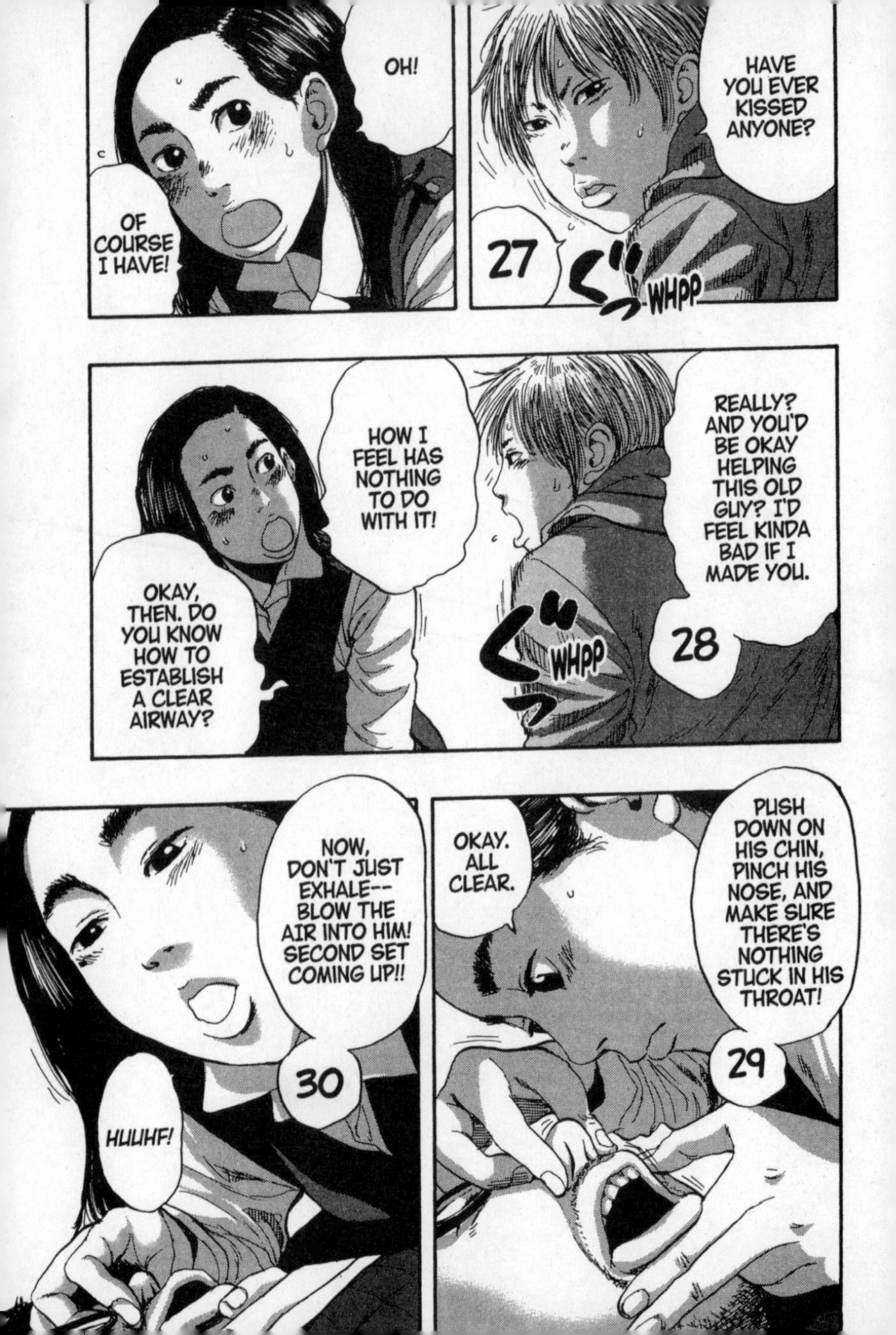
HAVE YOU EVER KISSED ANYONE?
27
WHPP
OH!
OF COURSE I HAVE!
REALLY? AND YOU'D BE OKAY HELPING THIS OLD GUY? I'D FEEL KINDA BAD IF I MADE YOU.
28
WHPP
HOW I FEEL HAS NOTHING TO DO WITH IT!
OKAY, THEN. DO YOU KNOW HOW TO ESTABLISH A CLEAR AIRWAY?
PUSH DOWN ON HIS CHIN, PINCH HIS NOSE, AND MAKE SURE THERE'S NOTHING STUCK IN HIS THROAT!
OKAY. ALL CLEAR.
29
NOW, DON'T JUST EXHALE-- BLOW THE AIR INTO HIM! SECOND SET COMING UP!!
30
HUUHF!

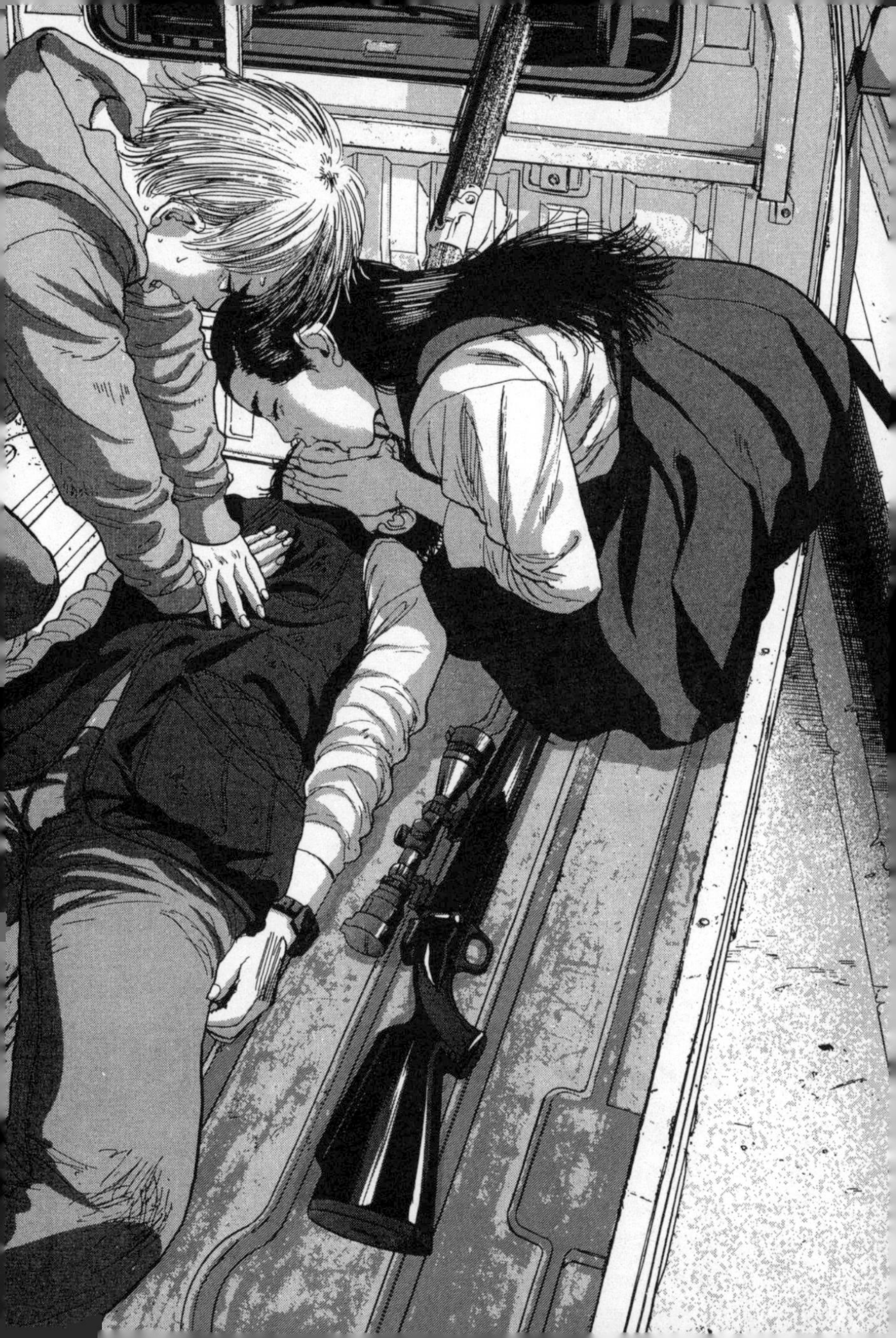

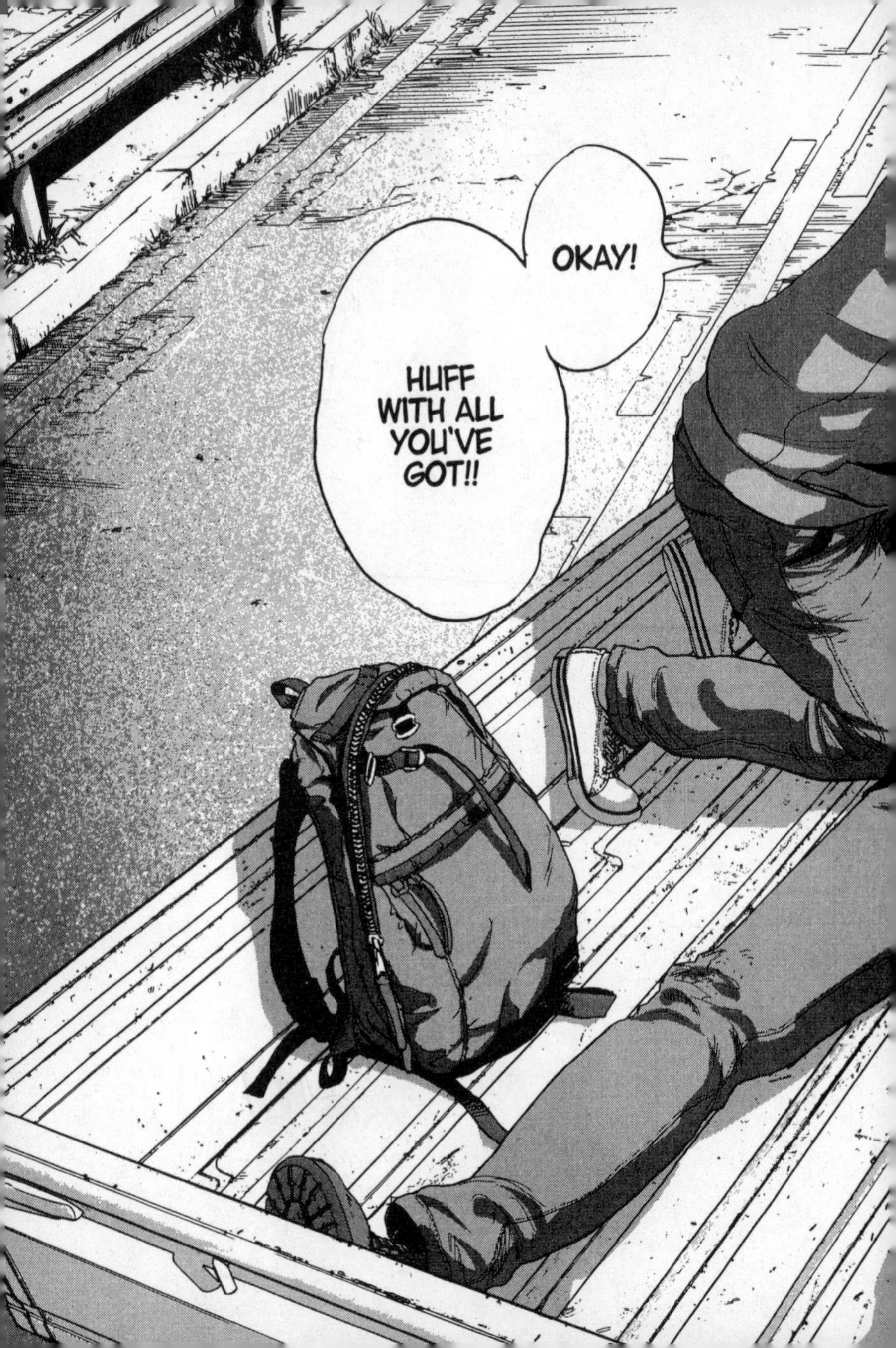

OKAY!
HUFF WITH ALL YOU'VE GOT!!

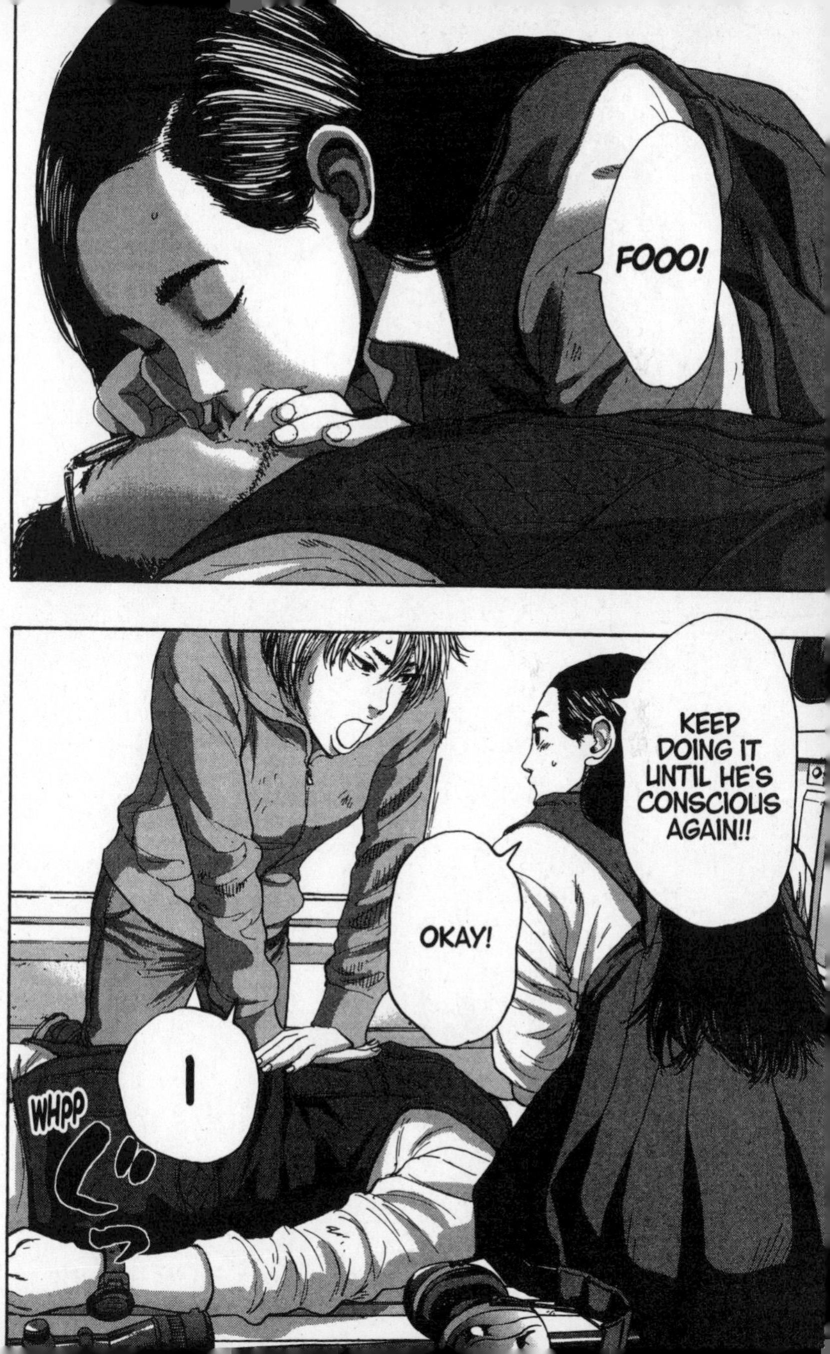
FOOO!
KEEP DOING IT UNTIL HE'S CONSCIOUS AGAIN!!
OKAY!
I
WHPP

CHAPTER
171

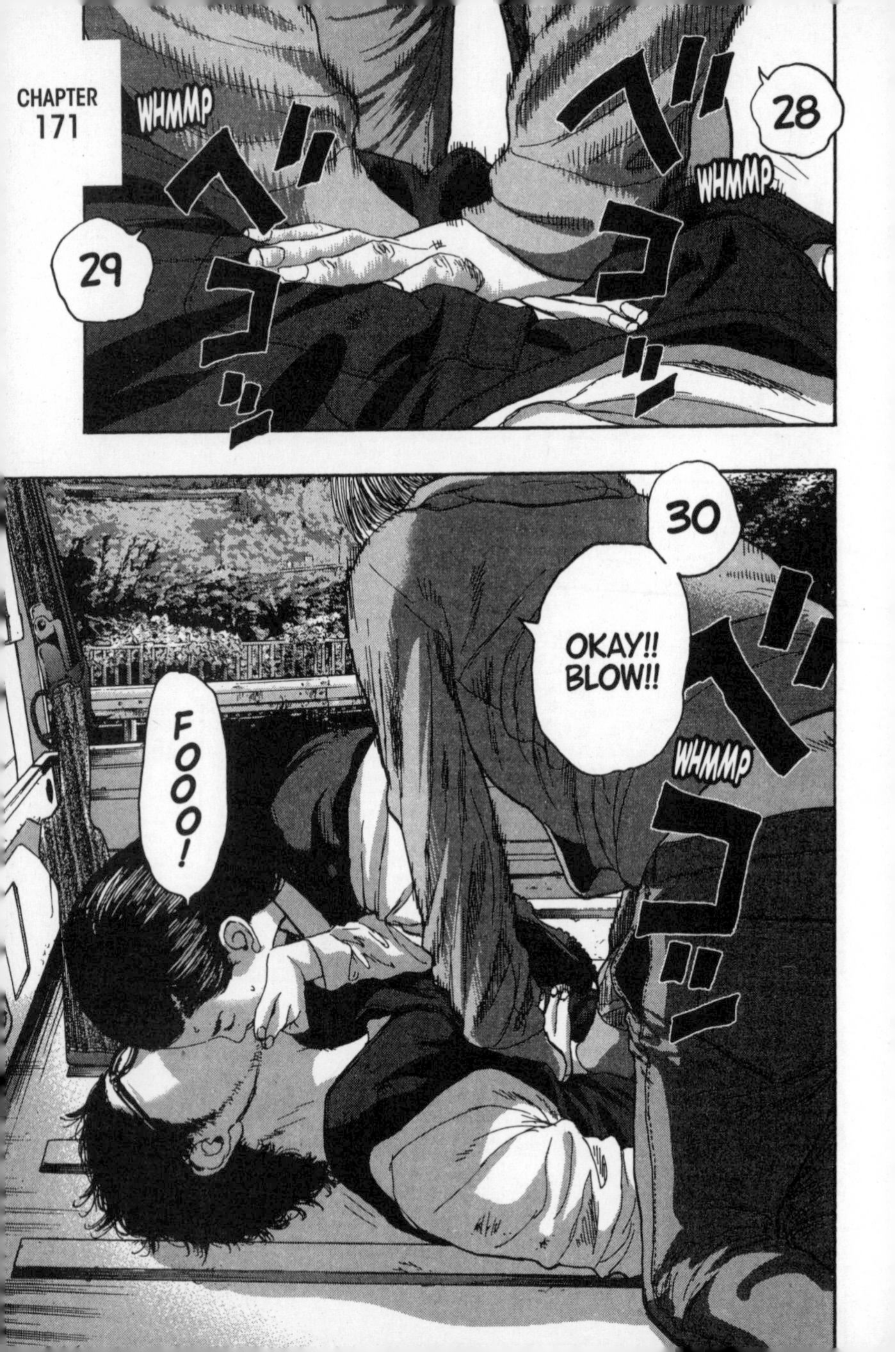
28
WHMMP
29
WHMMP
30
OKAY!! BLOW!!
WHMMP
FOOO!

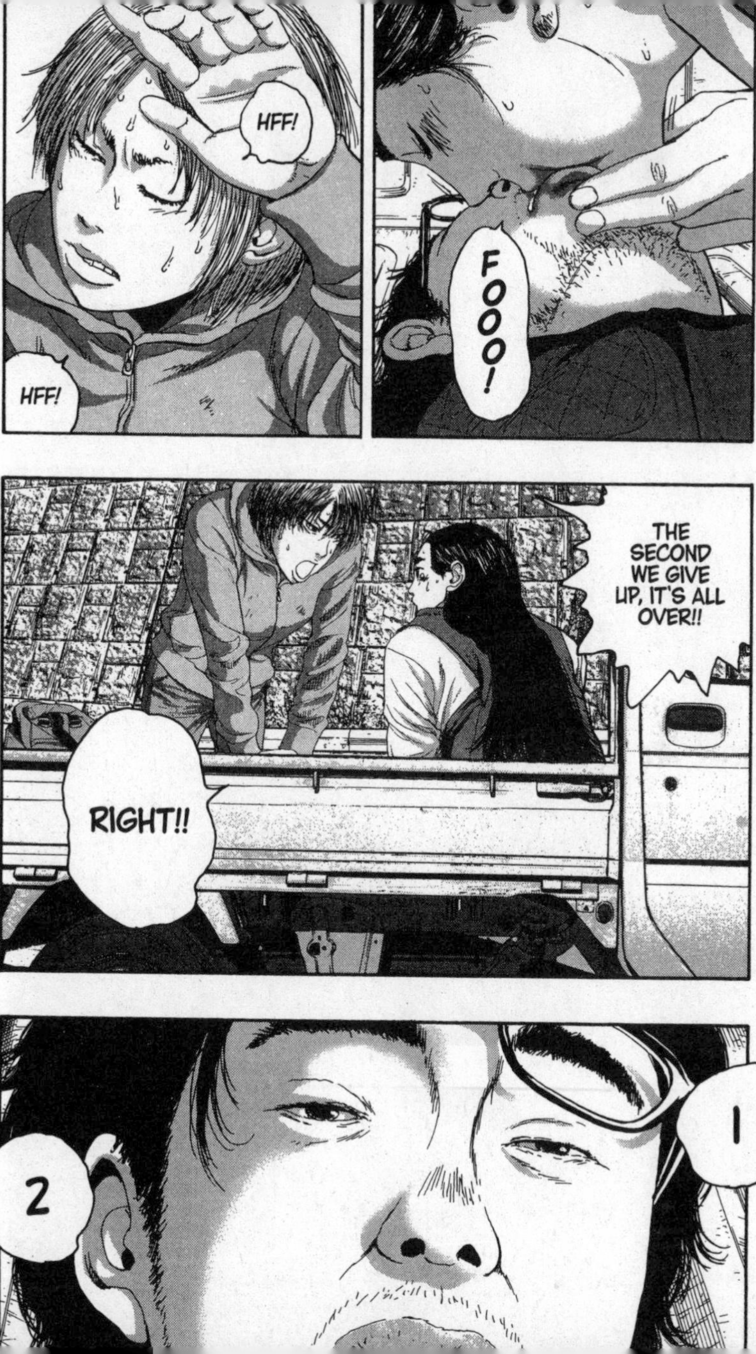
FOOO!
HFF!
HFF!
THE SECOND WE GIVE UP, IT'S ALL OVER!!
RIGHT!!
1
2

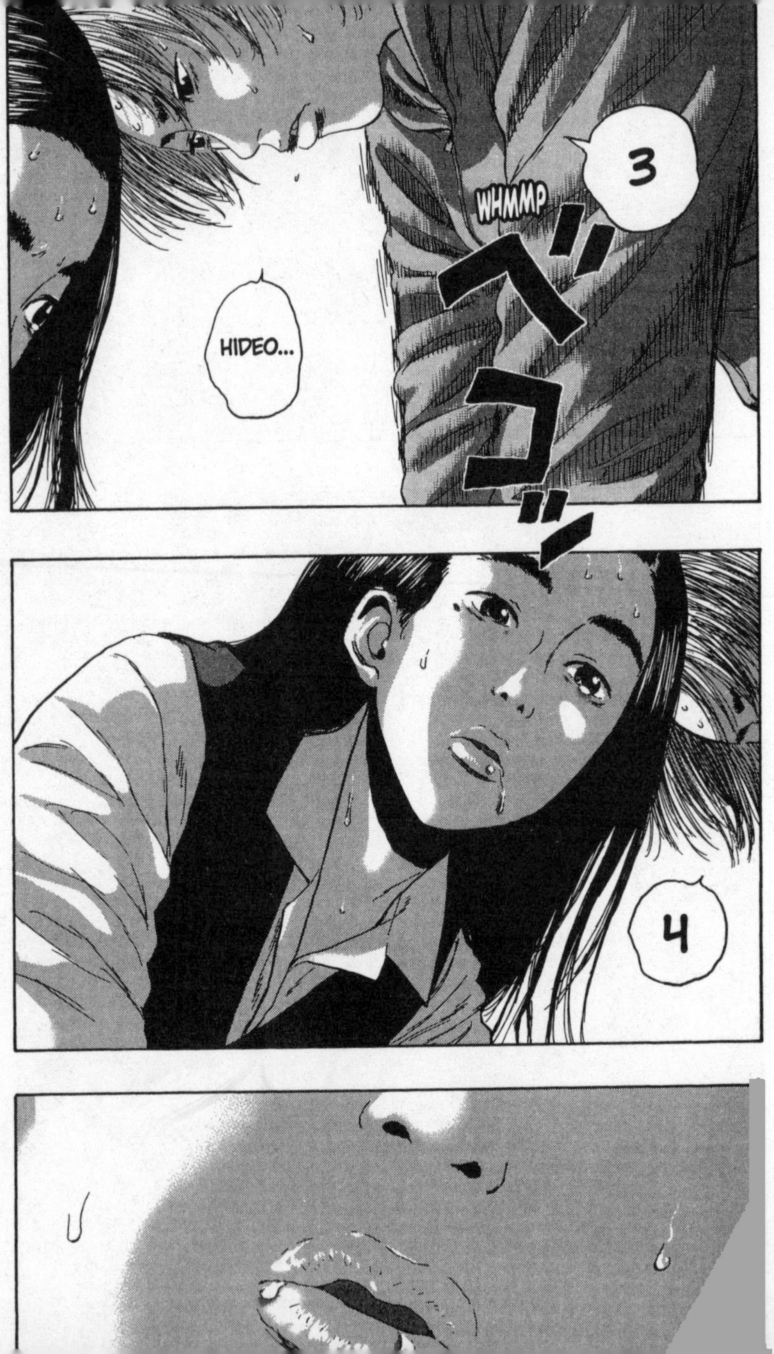
3
WHMMP
ベゴ
HIDEO...
4

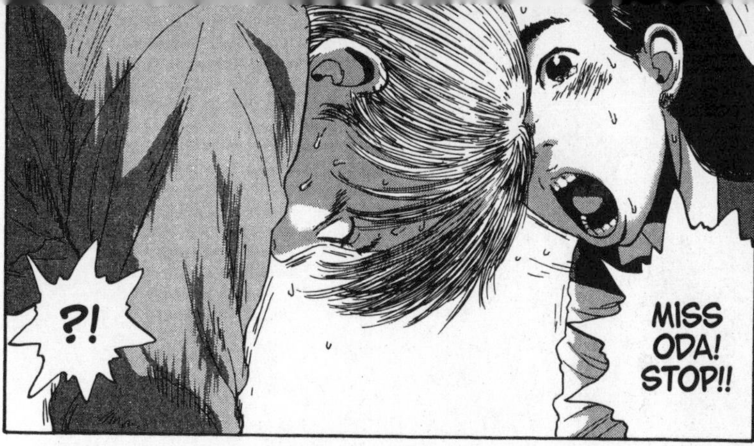
MISS ODA! STOP!!
?!
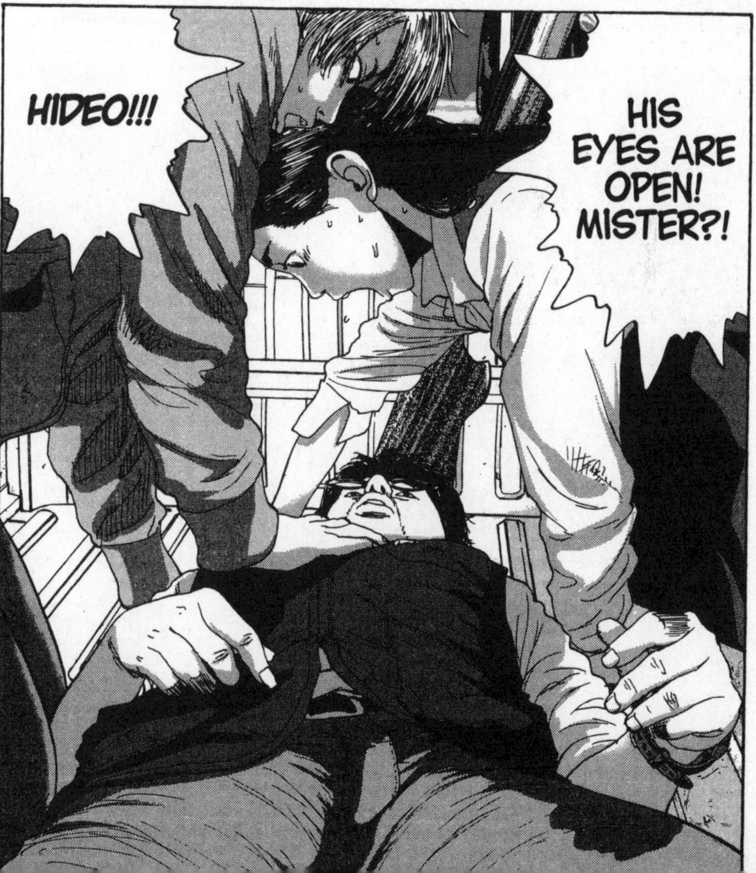
HIS EYES ARE OPEN! MISTER?!
HIDEO!!!

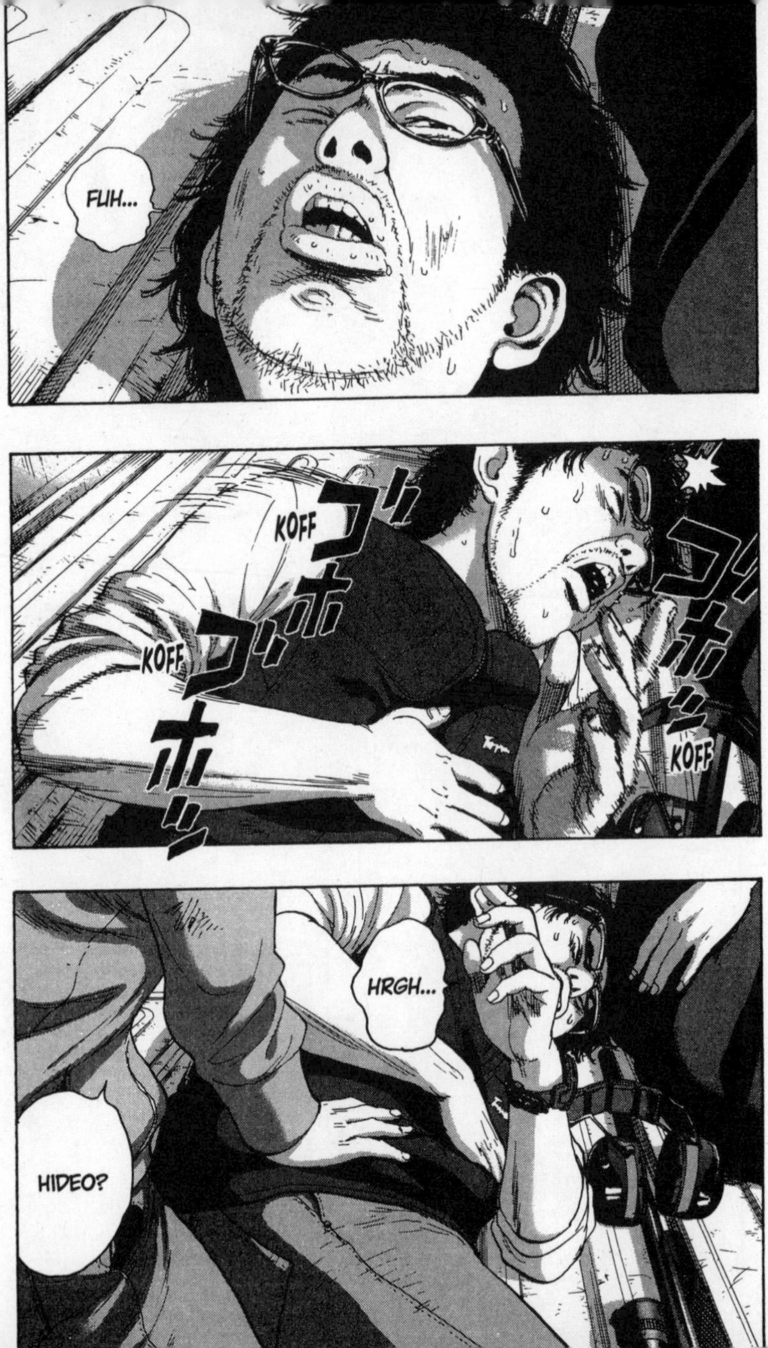
FUH...
ゴホッ
KOFF
ゴホ
KOFF
ゴホッ
KOFF
HRGH...
HIDEO?

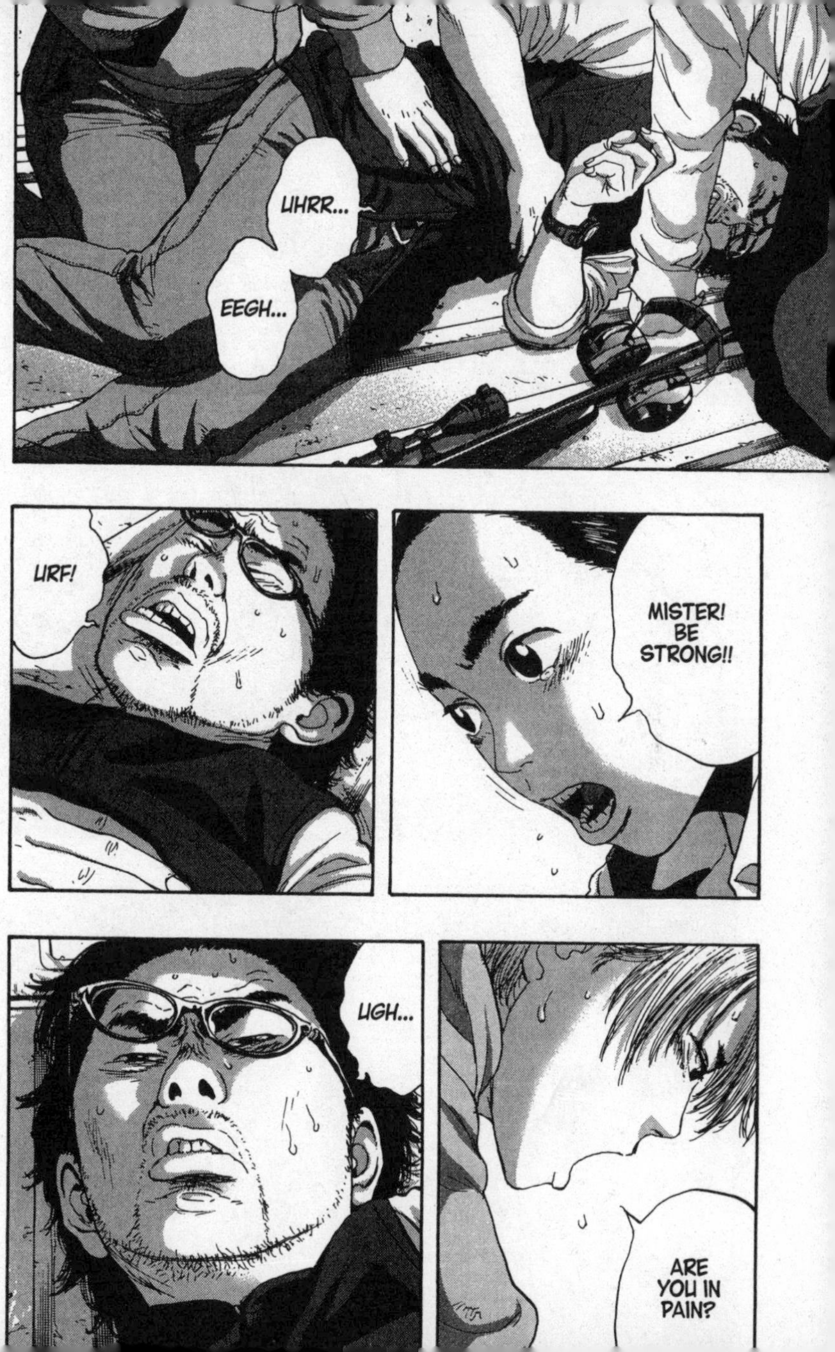
UHRR...
EEGH...
MISTER! BE STRONG!!
URF!
ARE YOU IN PAIN?
UGH...

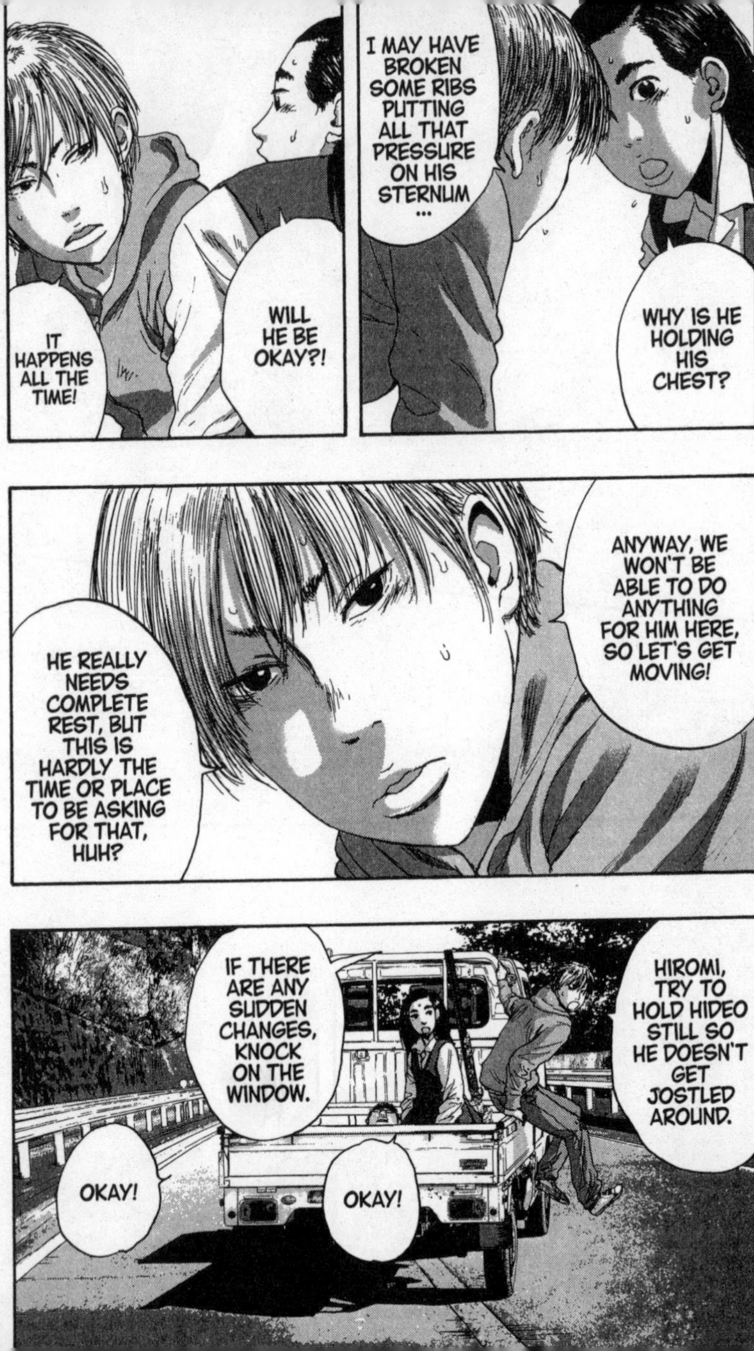
WHY IS HE HOLDING HIS CHEST?
I MAY HAVE BROKEN SOME RIBS PUTTING ALL THAT PRESSURE ON HIS STERNUM ...
WILL HE BE OKAY?!
IT HAPPENS ALL THE TIME!
ANYWAY, WE WON'T BE ABLE TO DO ANYTHING FOR HIM HERE, SO LET'S GET MOVING!
HE REALLY NEEDS COMPLETE REST, BUT THIS IS HARDLY THE TIME OR PLACE TO BE ASKING FOR THAT, HUH?
HIROMI, TRY TO HOLD HIDEO STILL SO HE DOESN'T GET JOSTLED AROUND.
IF THERE ARE ANY SUDDEN CHANGES, KNOCK ON THE WINDOW.
OKAY!
OKAY!

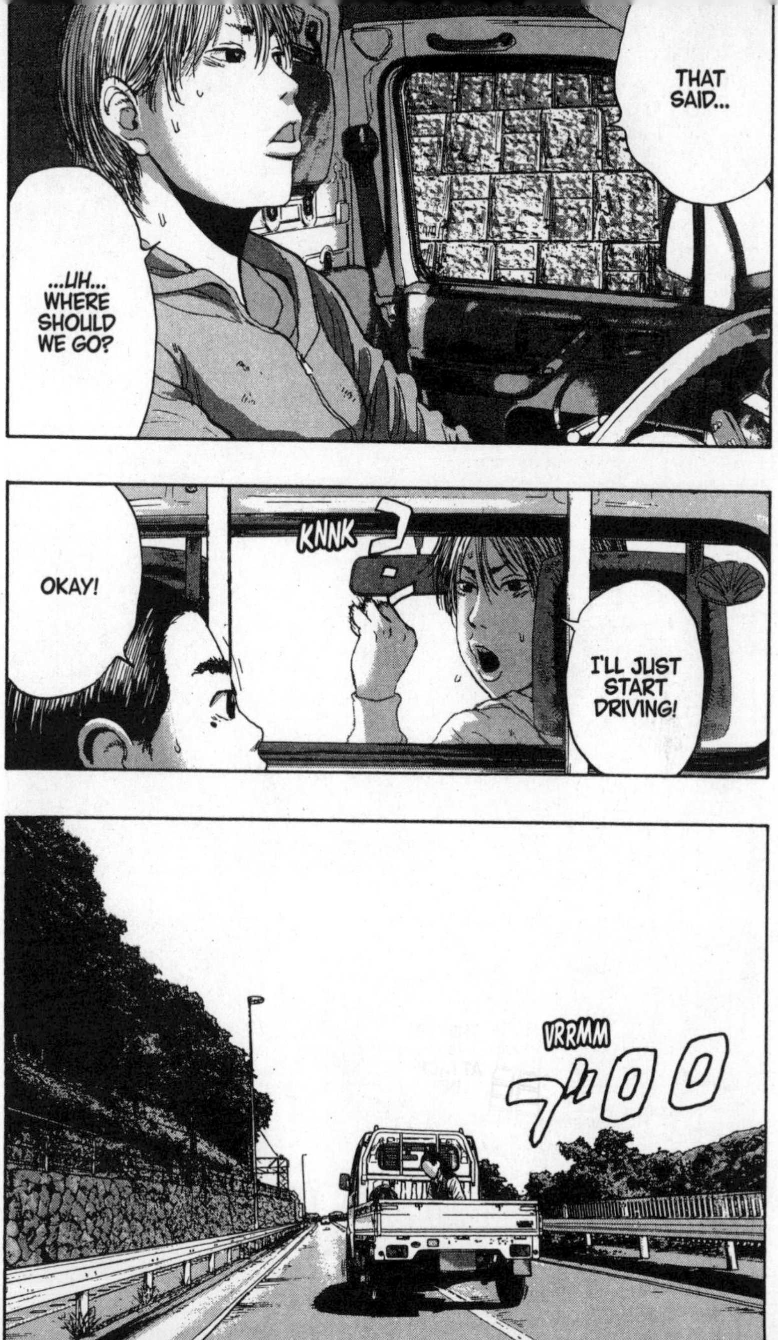
THAT SAID...
...UH... WHERE SHOULD WE GO?
KNNK
I'LL JUST START DRIVING!
OKAY!
VRRMM
ブロロ

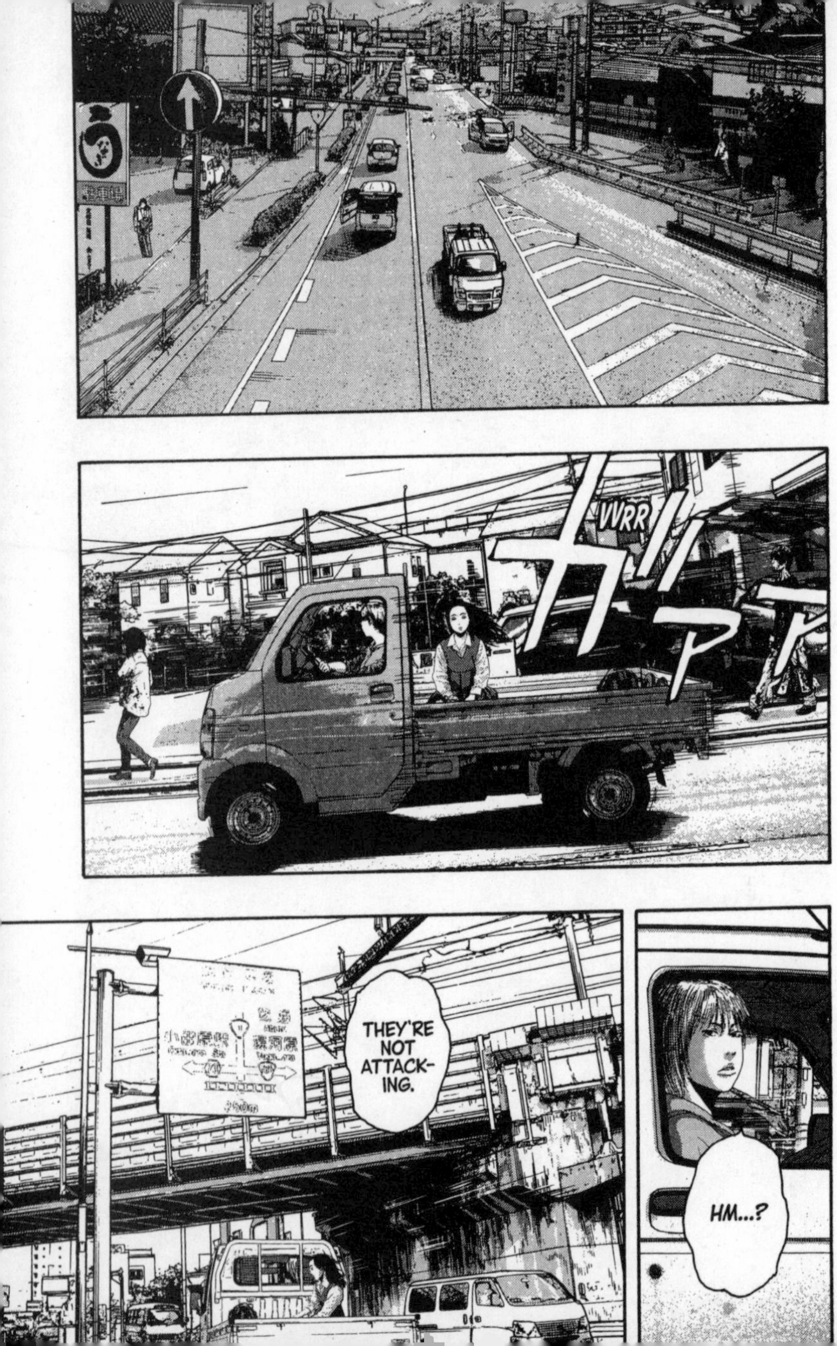
VVRR
HM...?
THEY'RE NOT ATTACKING.

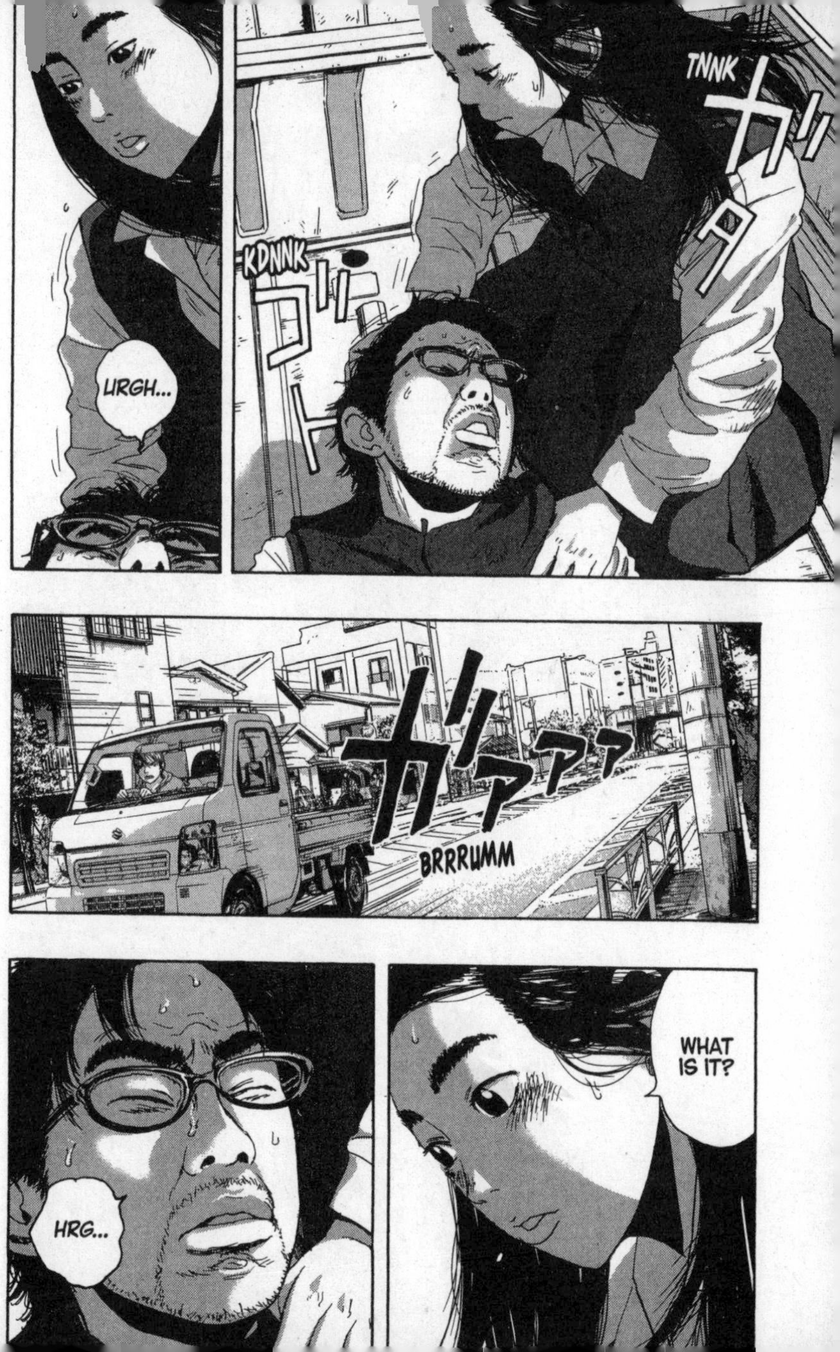
TNNK
KDNNK
URGH...
BRRRUMM
WHAT IS IT?
HRG...

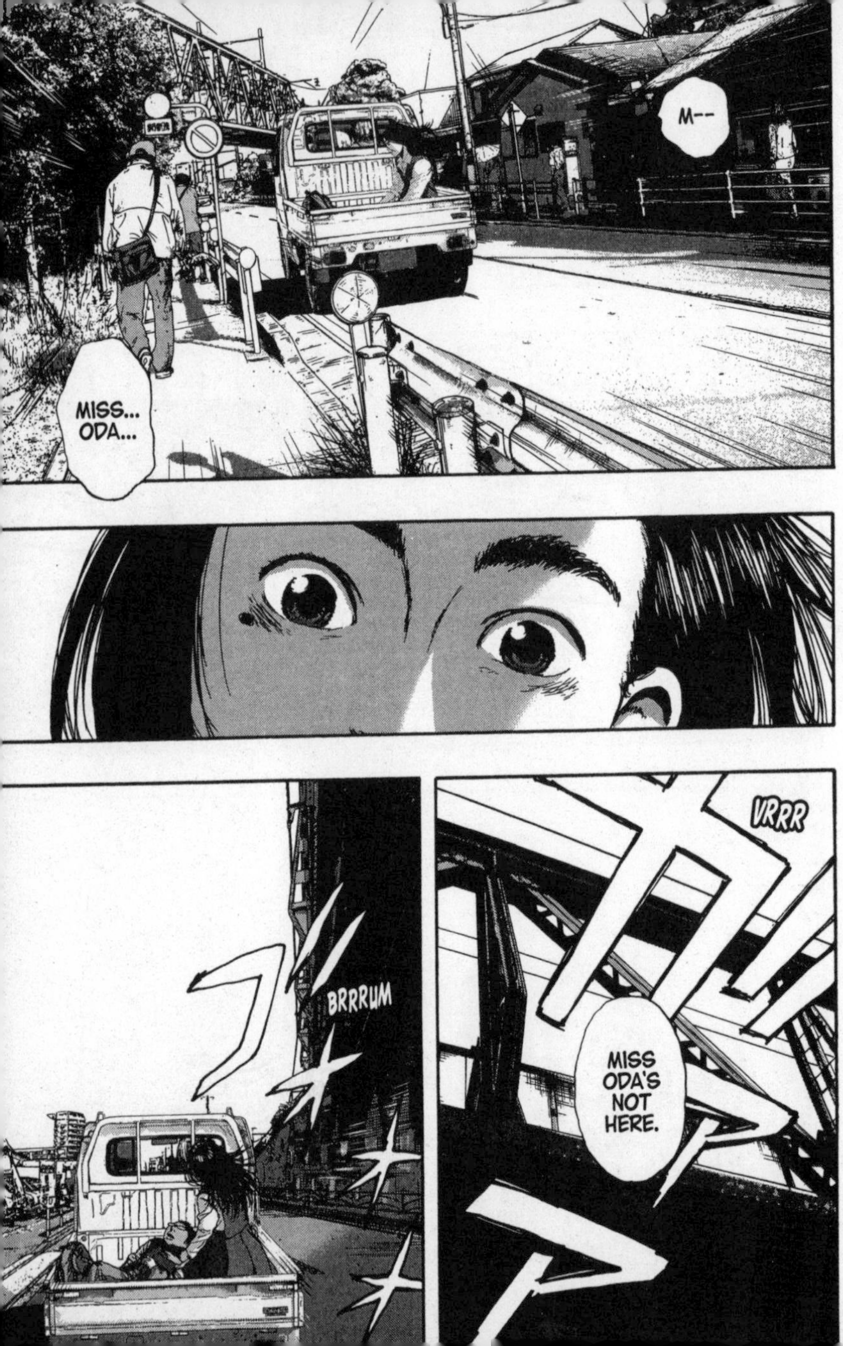
M--
MISS... ODA...
VRRR
MISS ODA'S NOT HERE.
BRRRUM

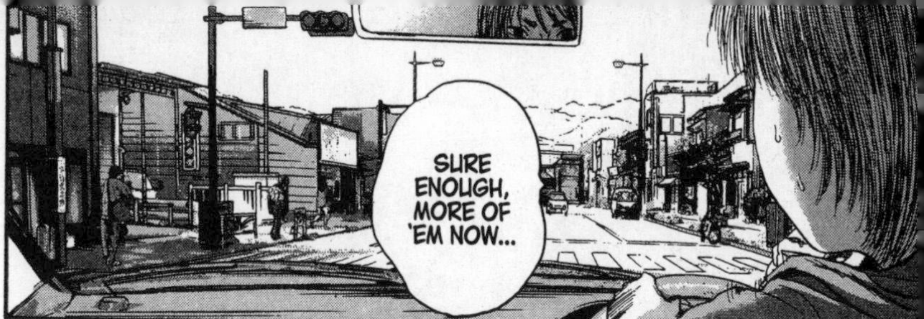
SURE ENOUGH, MORE OF 'EM NOW...

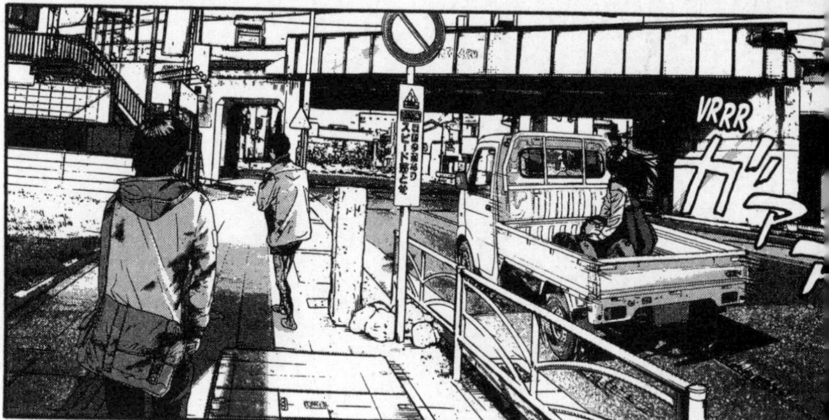
VRRR

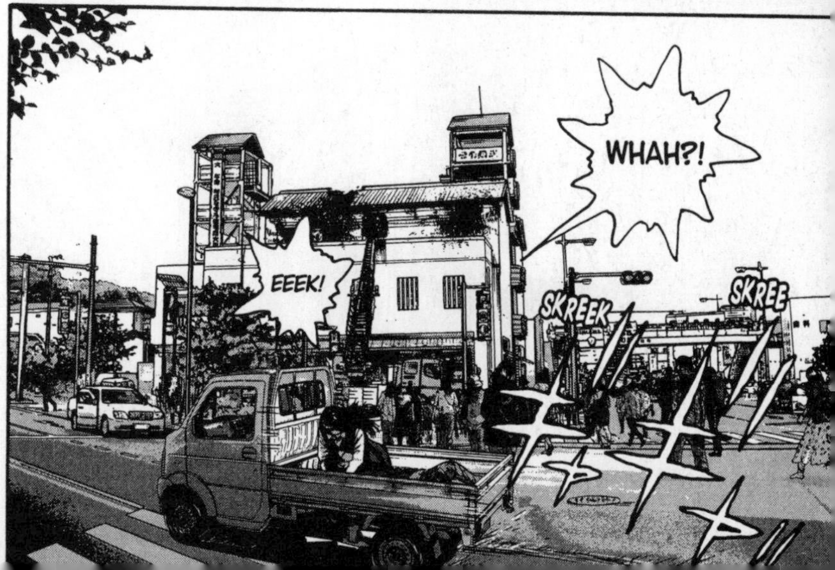
WHAH?!
SKREE
SKREEK
EEEK!

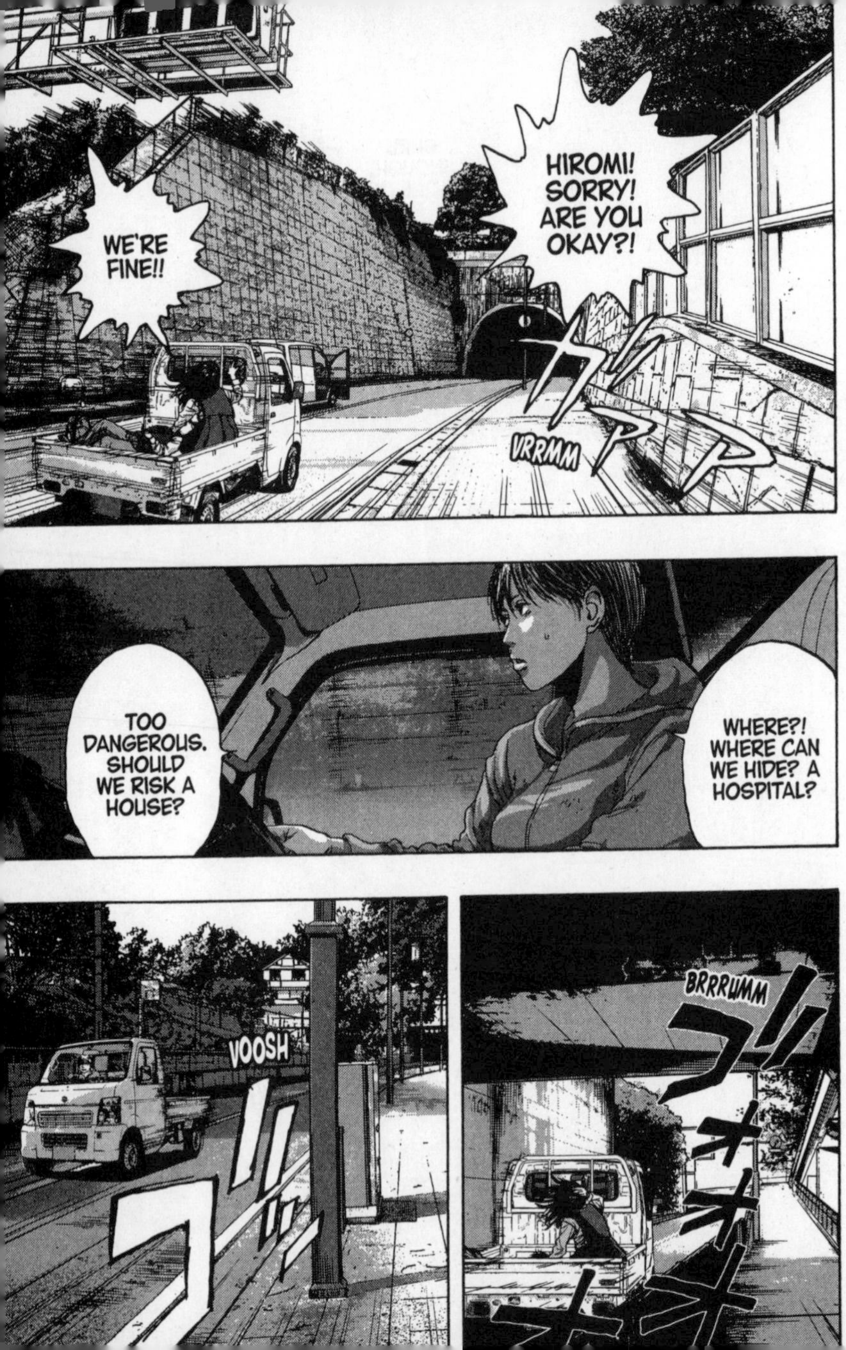
HIROMI! SORRY! ARE YOU OKAY?!
WE'RE FINE!!
VRRMM
WHERE?! WHERE CAN WE HIDE? A HOSPITAL?
TOO DANGEROUS. SHOULD WE RISK A HOUSE?
BRRRUMM
VOOSH

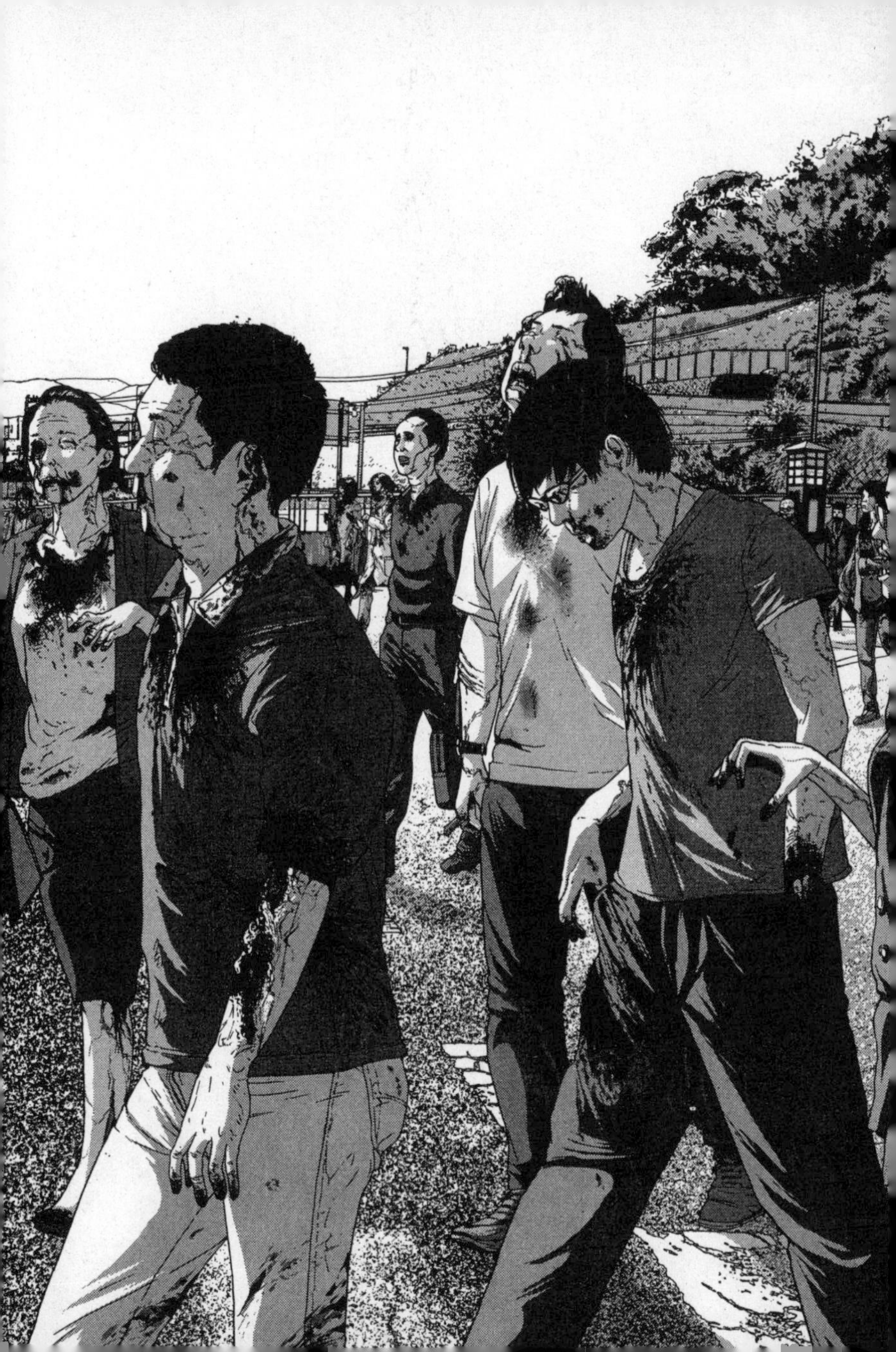

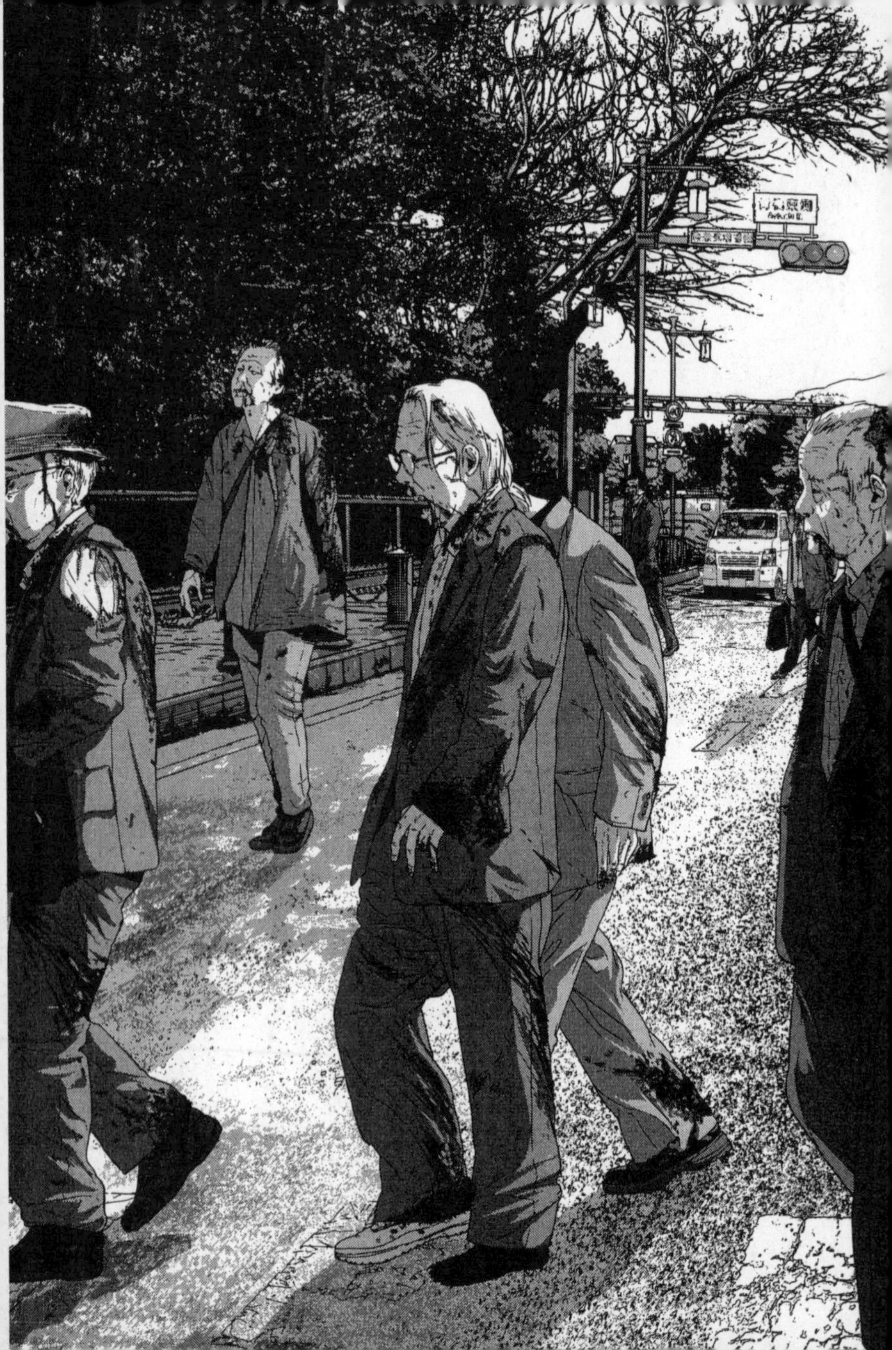

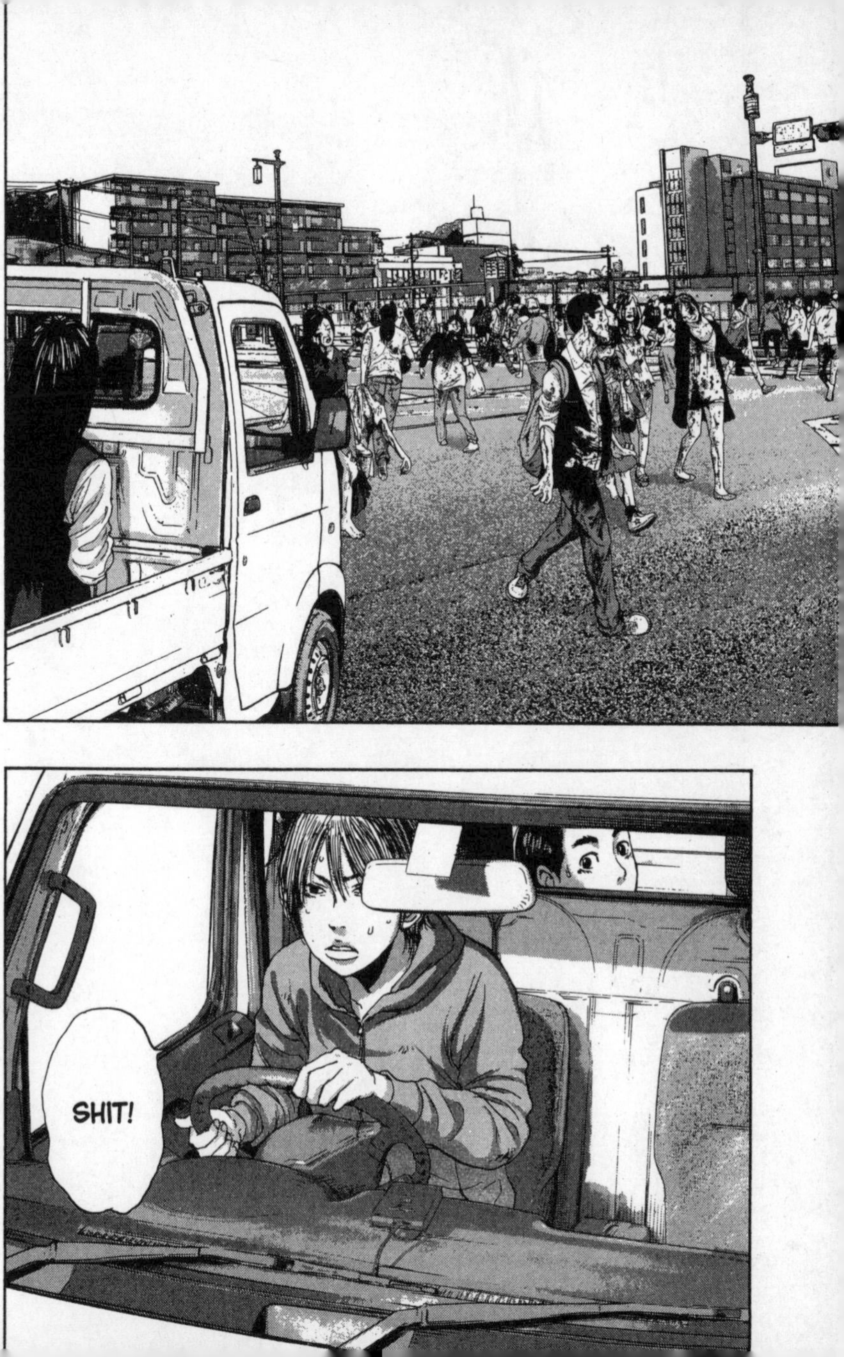
SHIT!

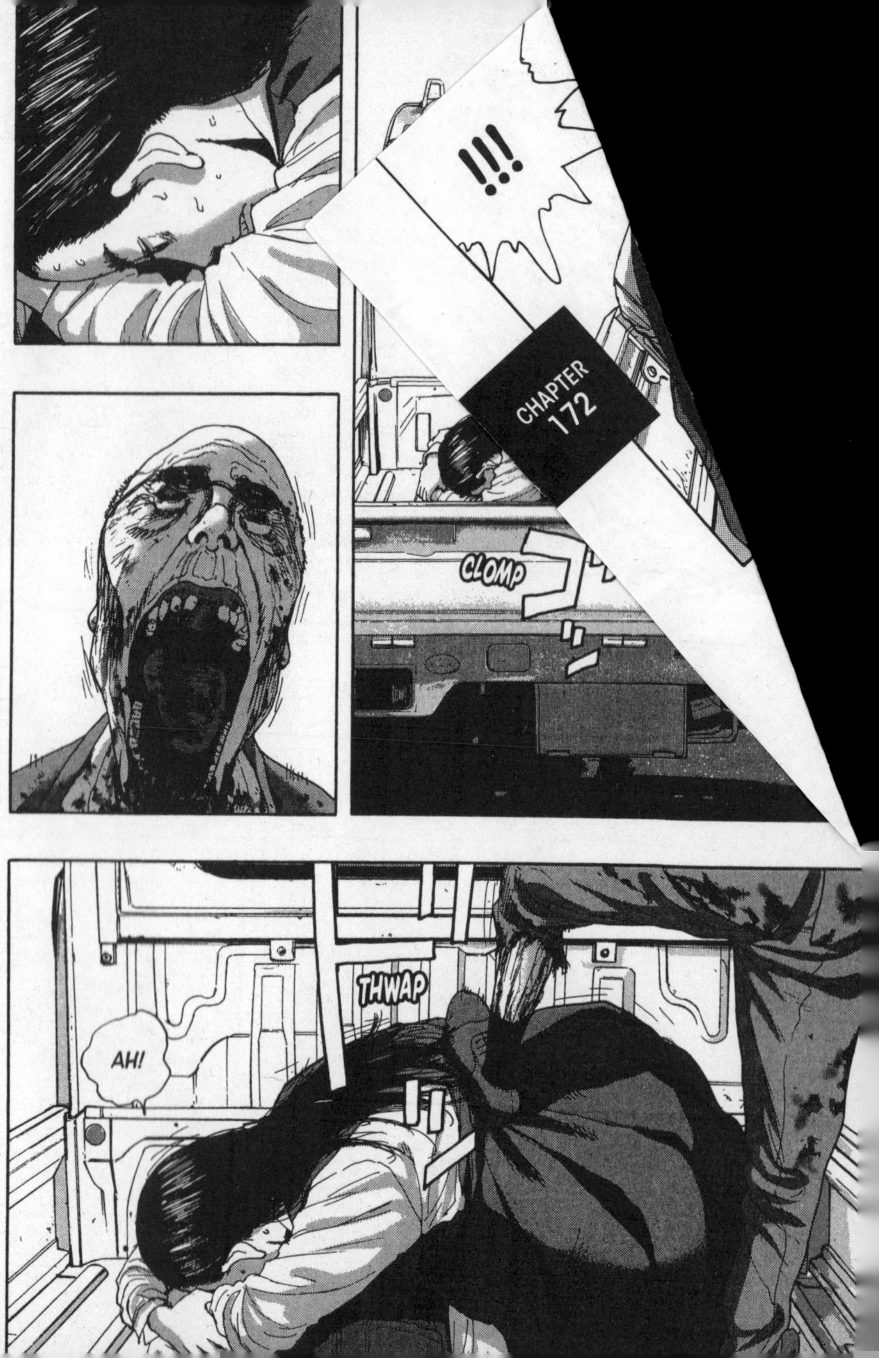
CHAPTER 172
!!!
CLOMP
THWAP
AH!
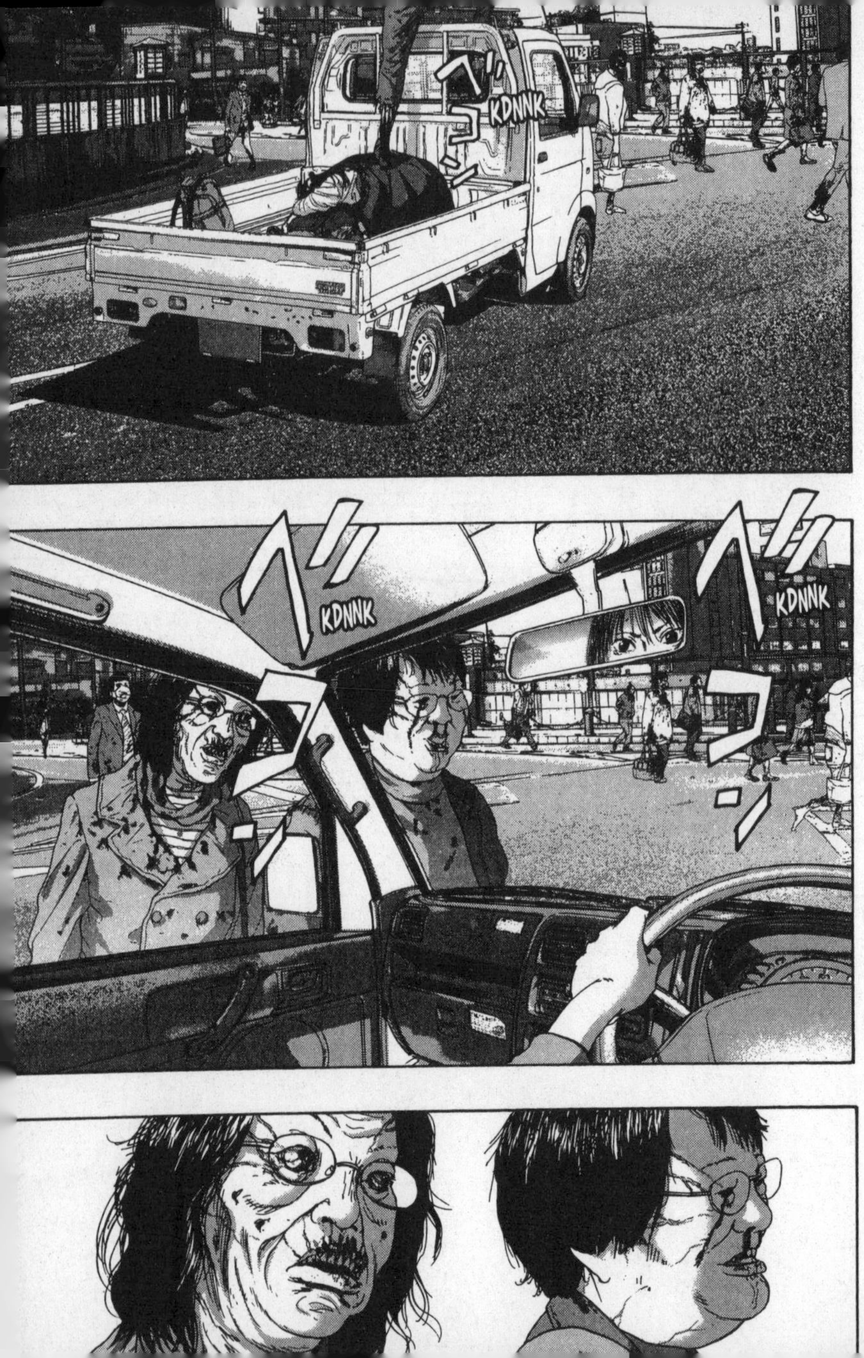
KDNNK
KDNNK
KDNNK

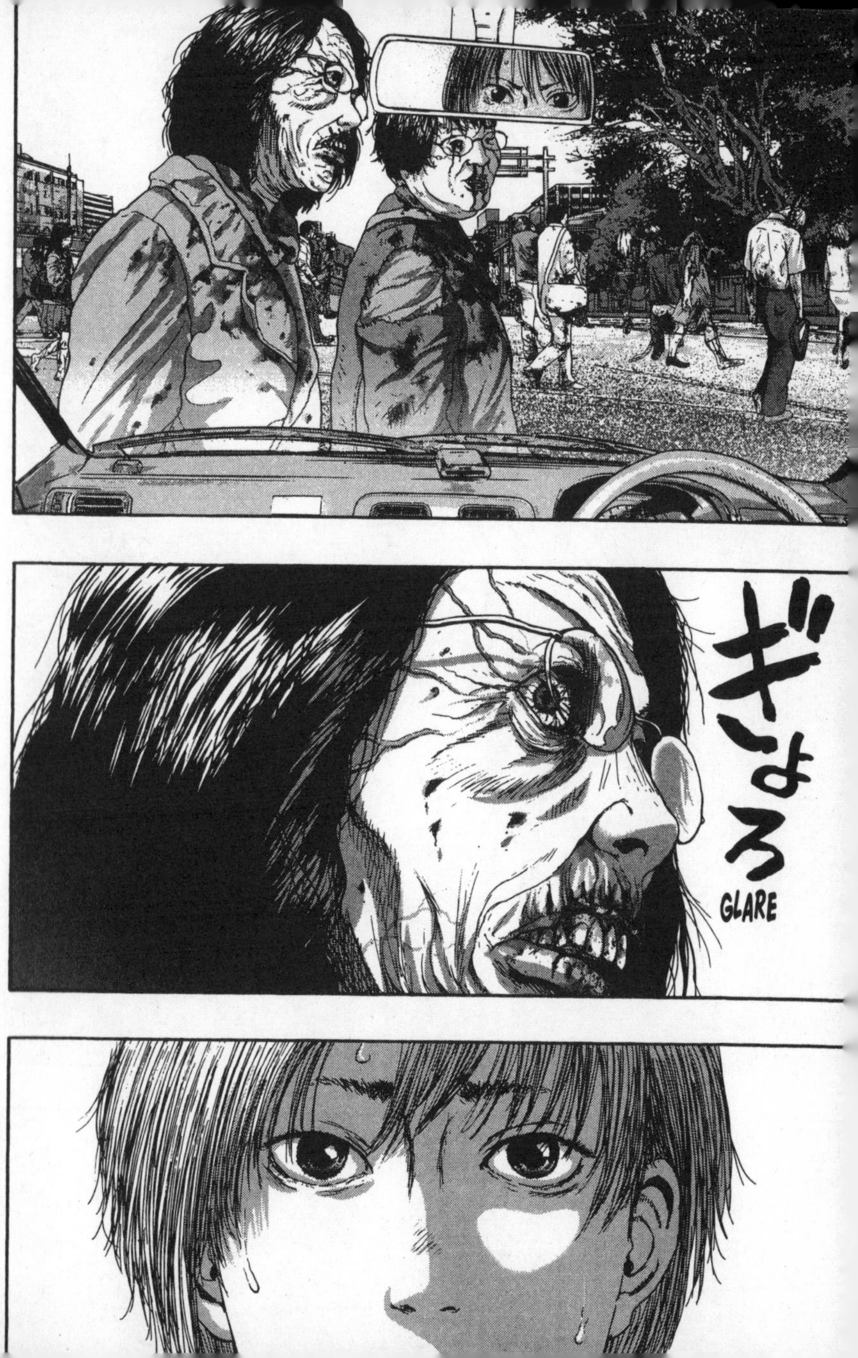
ギょろ
GLARE

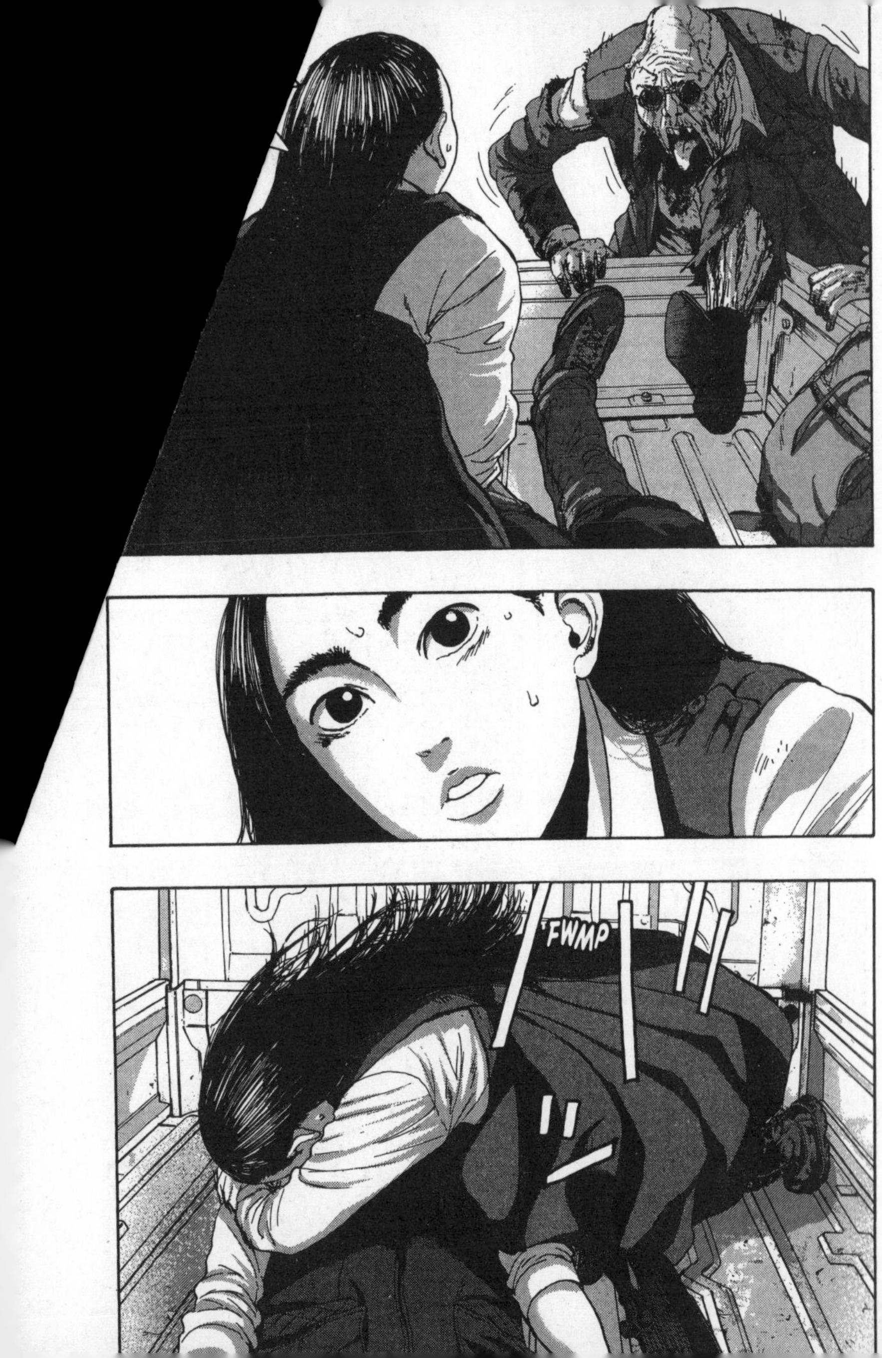
FWMP

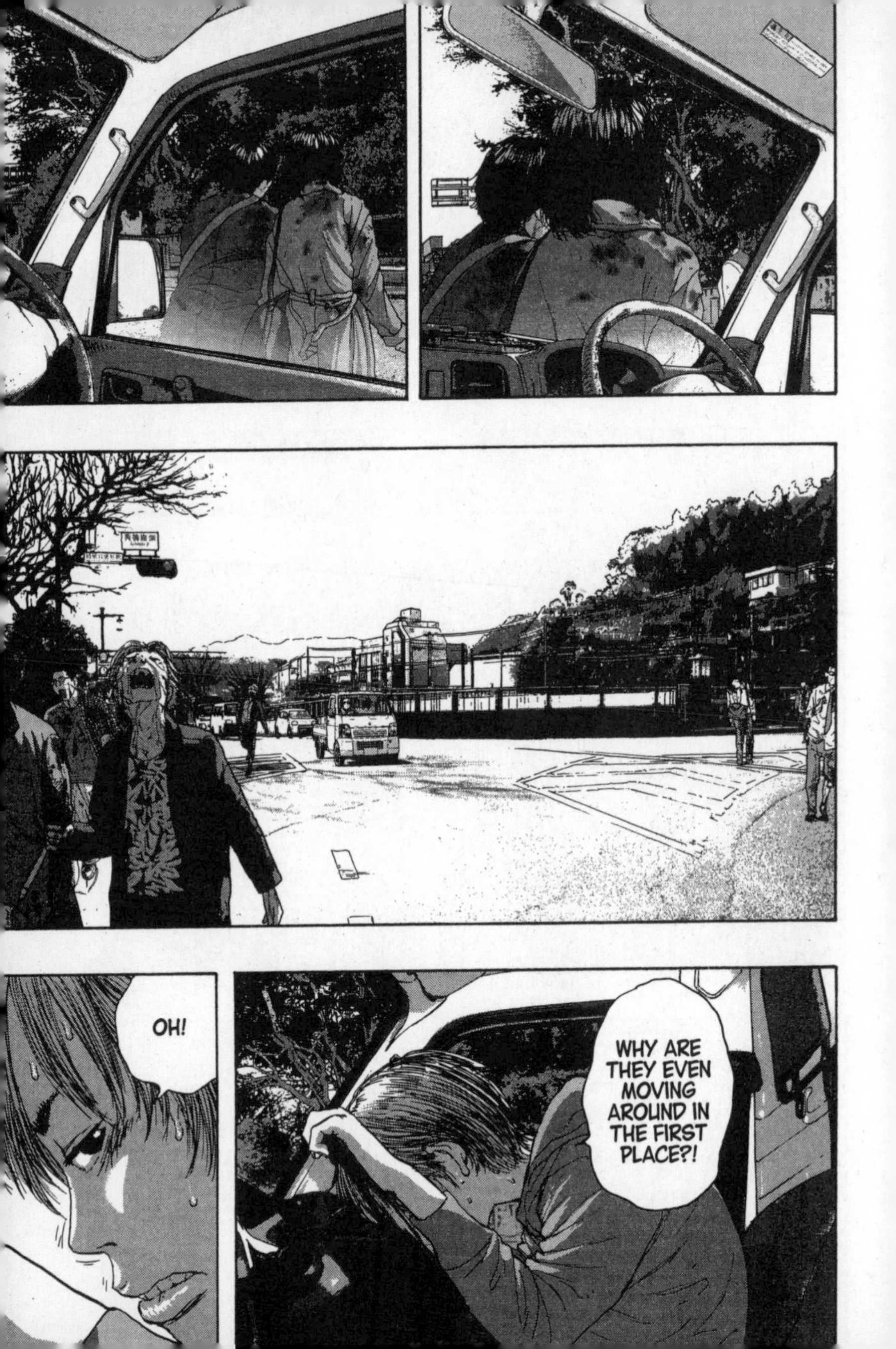
WHY ARE THEY EVEN MOVING AROUND IN THE FIRST PLACE?!
OH!

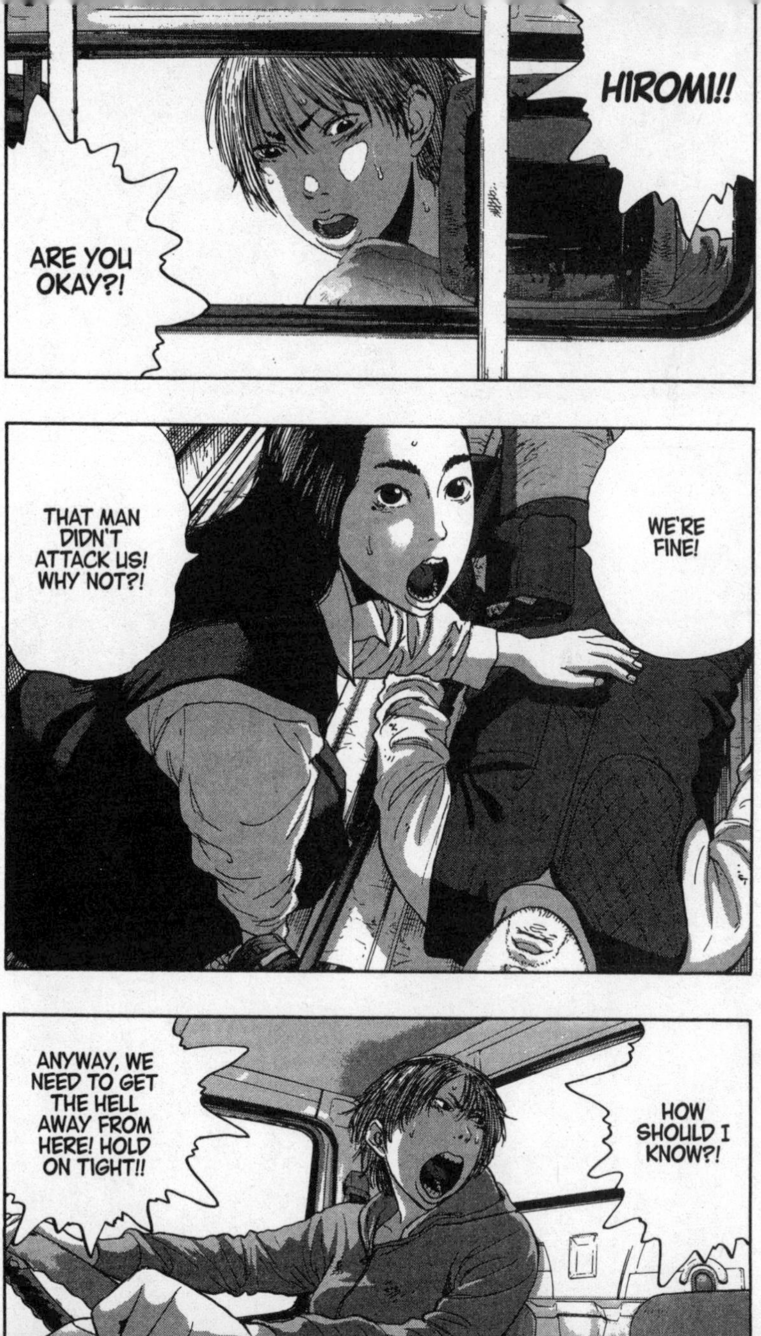
HIROMI!!
ARE YOU OKAY?!
WE'RE FINE!
THAT MAN DIDN'T ATTACK US! WHY NOT?!
HOW SHOULD I KNOW?!
ANYWAY, WE NEED TO GET THE HELL AWAY FROM HERE! HOLD ON TIGHT!!

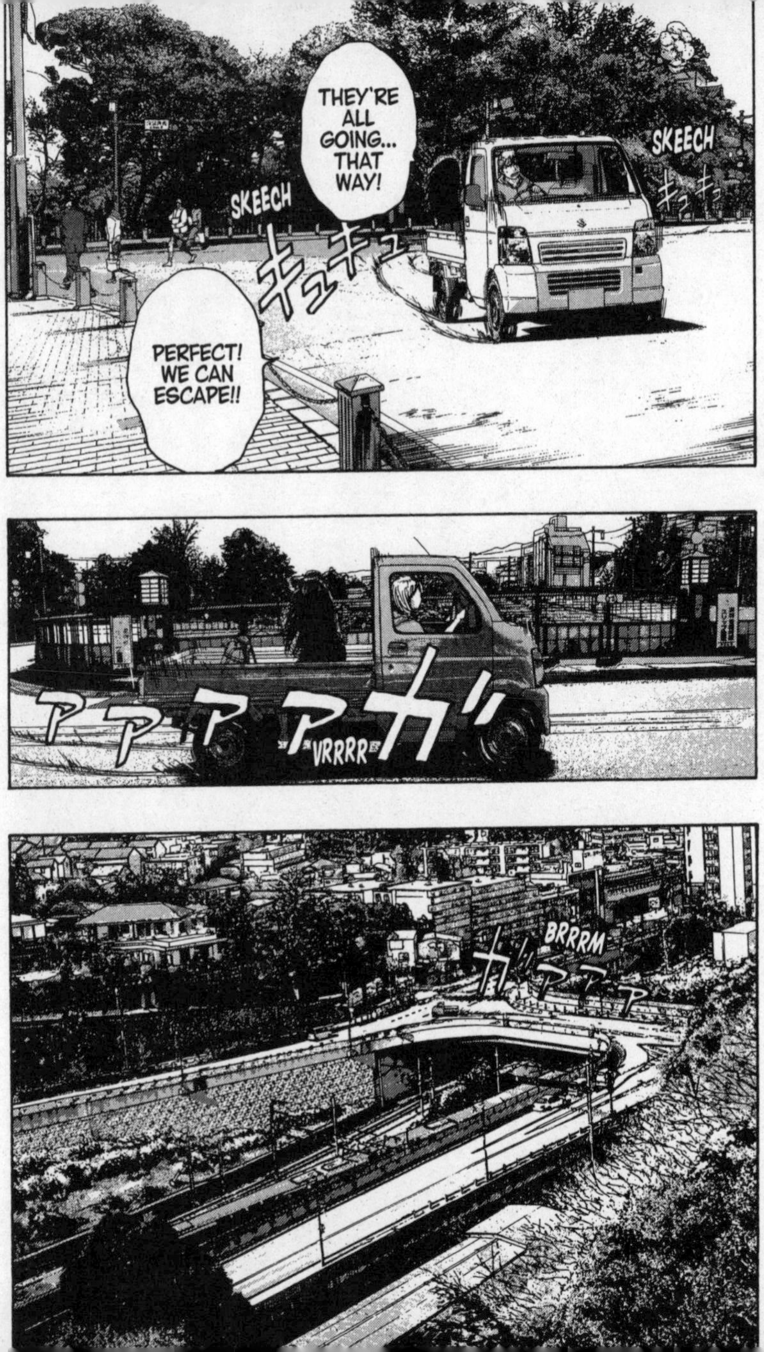
SKEECH
THEY'RE ALL GOING... THAT WAY!
SKEECH
PERFECT! WE CAN ESCAPE!!
VRRRR
BRRRM

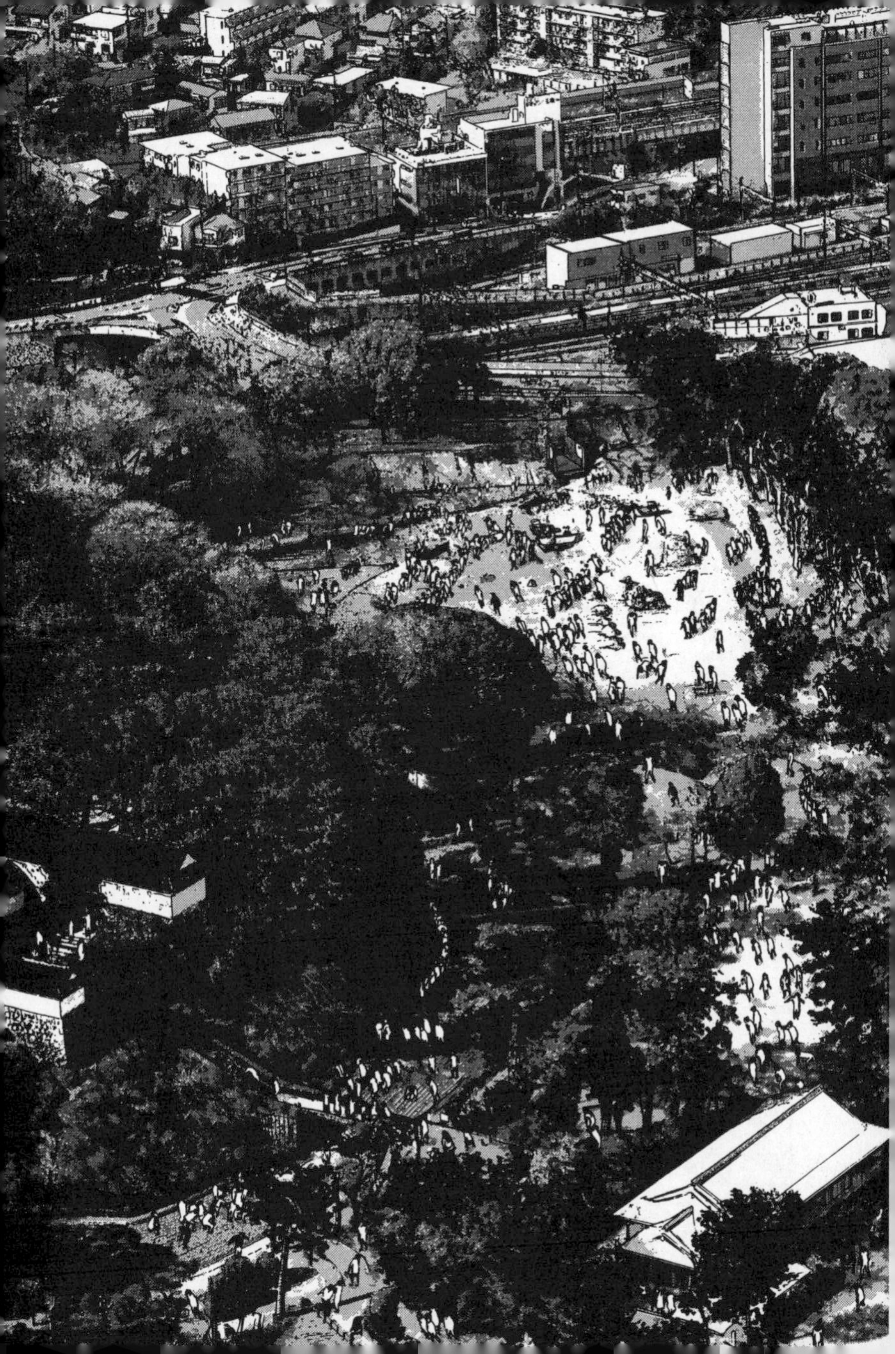

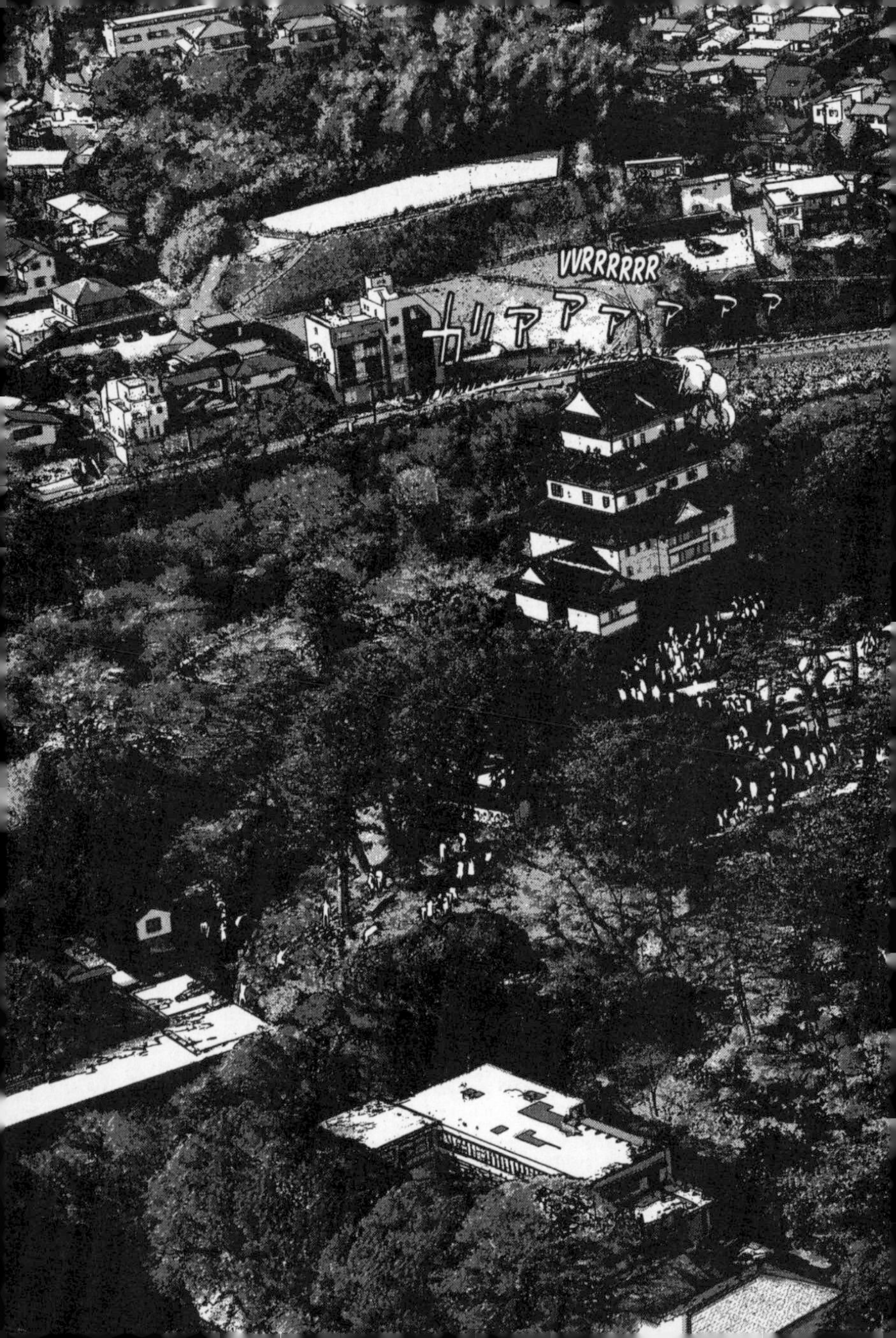
VVRRRRRR

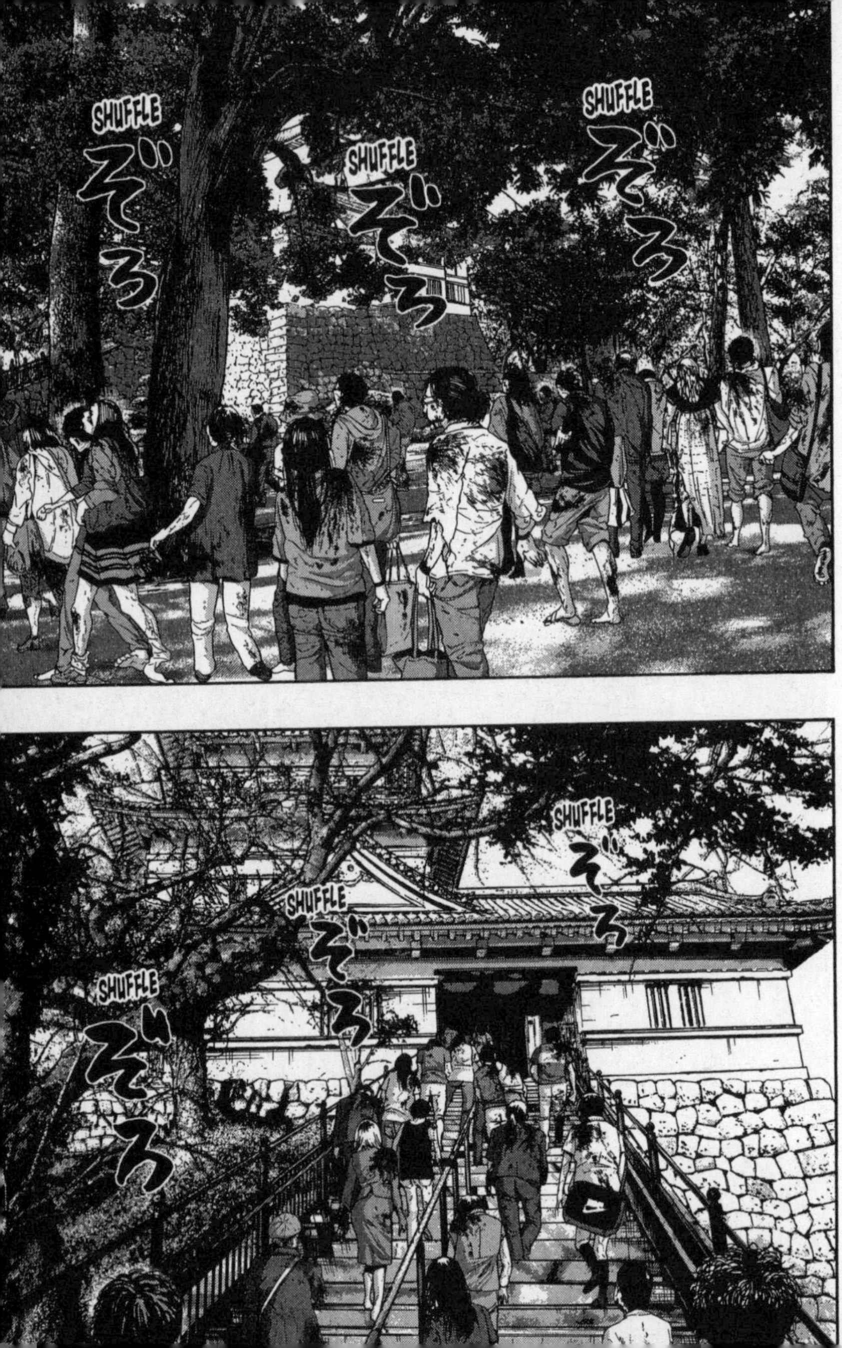
SHUFFLE
ぞろ
SHUFFLE
ぞろ
SHUFFLE
ぞろ
SHUFFLE
ぞろ
SHUFFLE
ぞろ
SHUFFLE
ぞろ

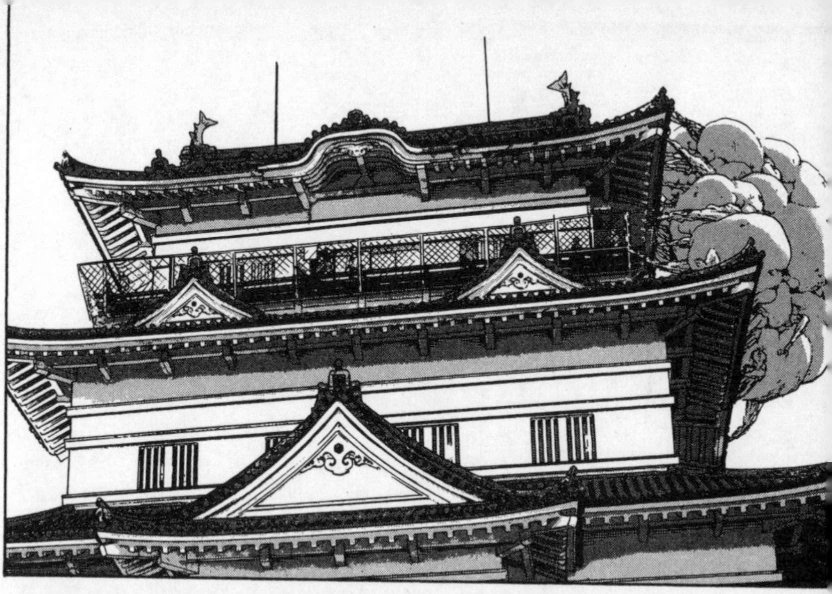

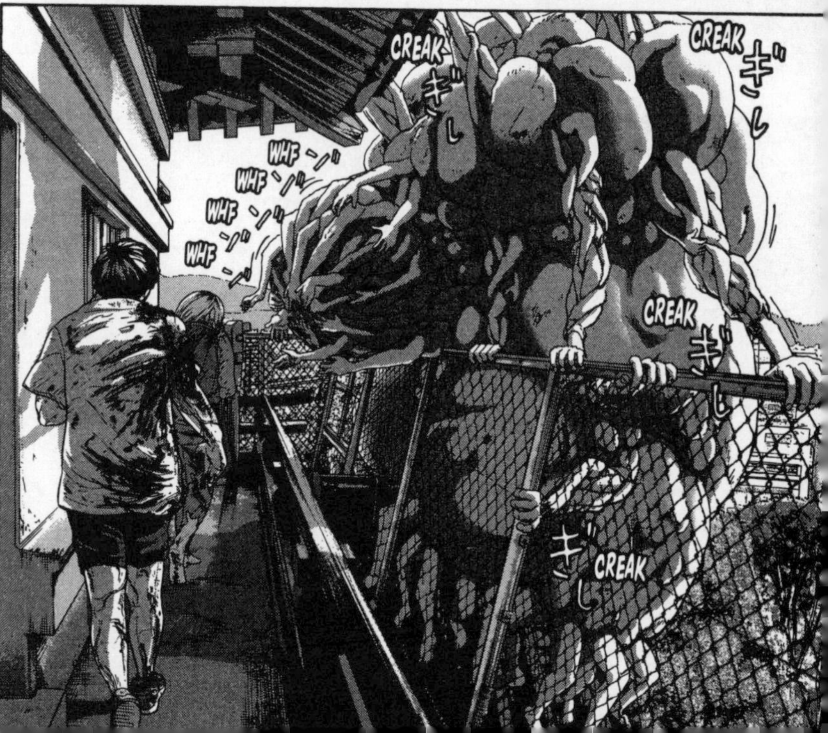
CREAK
ぎし
CREAK
ぎし
WHF
WHF
WHF
WHF
CREAK
ぎし
ぎし
CREAK

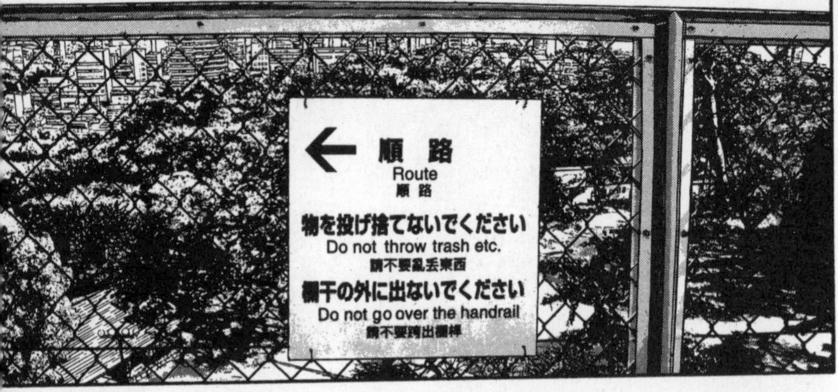

← 順路
Route
順路
物を投げ捨てないでください
Do not throw trash etc.
請不要乱丢東西
欄干の外に出ないでください
Do not go over the handrail
請不要跨出欄桿

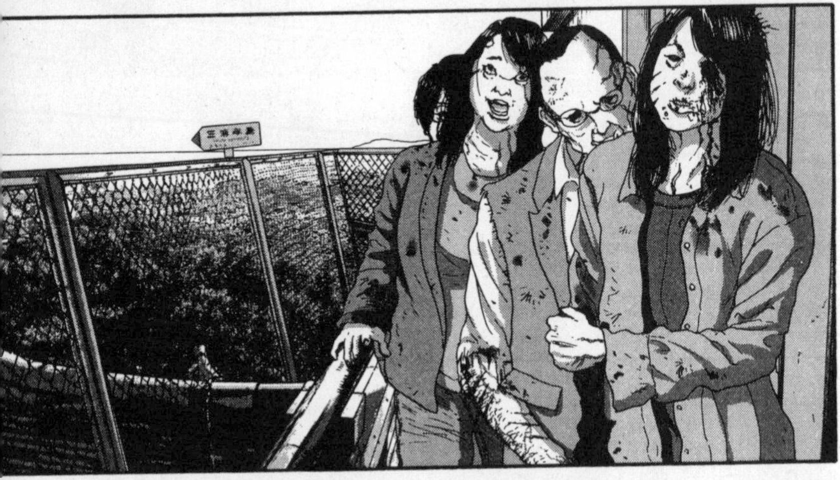

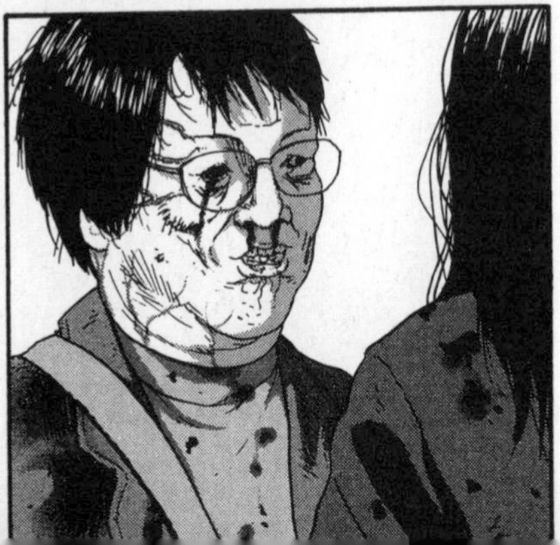

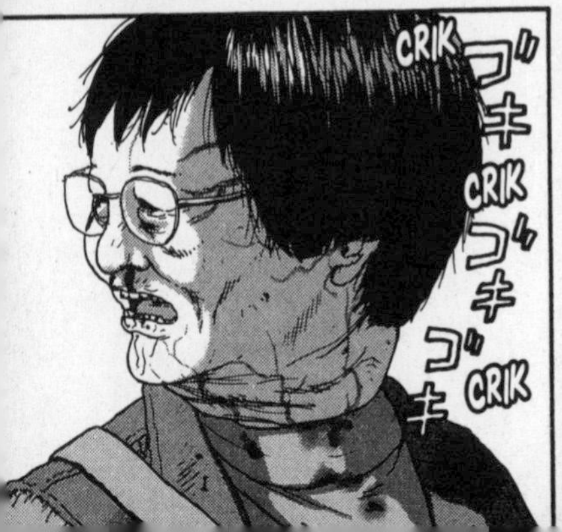

CRIK
ゴキ
CRIK
ゴキ
ゴキ
CRIK

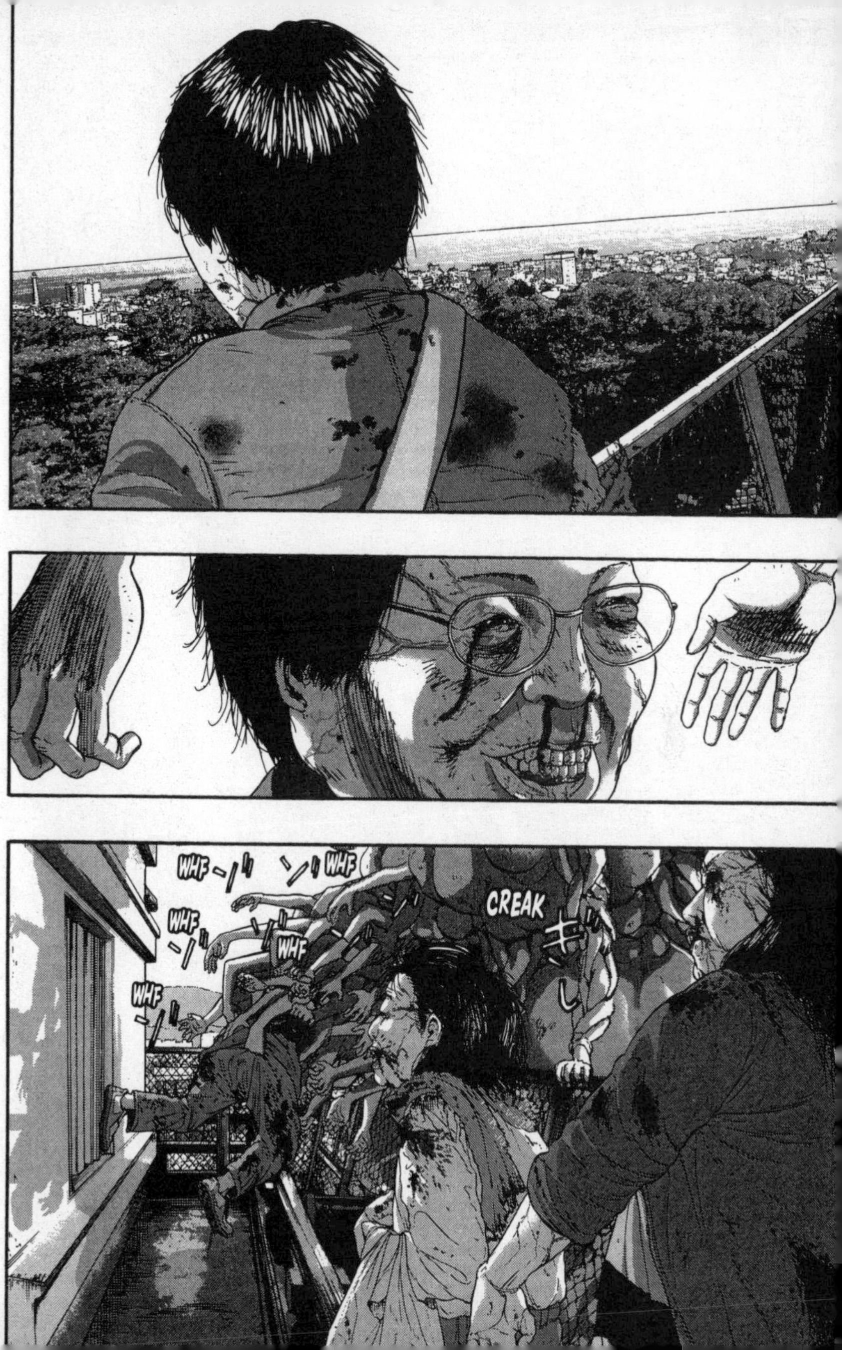
CREAK
WHF
WHF
WHF
WHF
WHF

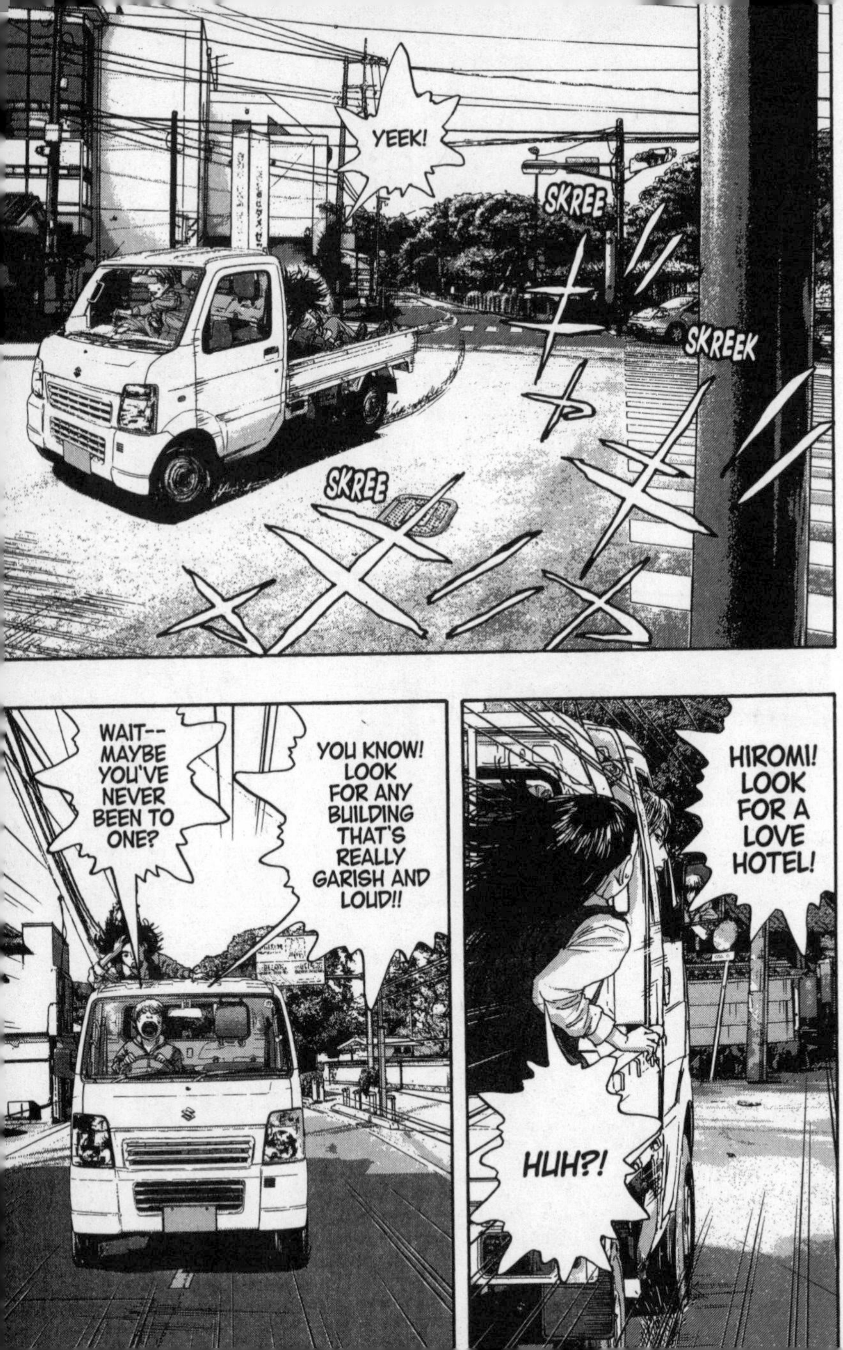
YEEK!
SKREE
SKREEK
SKREE
HIROMI! LOOK FOR A LOVE HOTEL!
HUH?!
YOU KNOW! LOOK FOR ANY BUILDING THAT'S REALLY GARISH AND LOUD!!
WAIT-- MAYBE YOU'VE NEVER BEEN TO ONE?

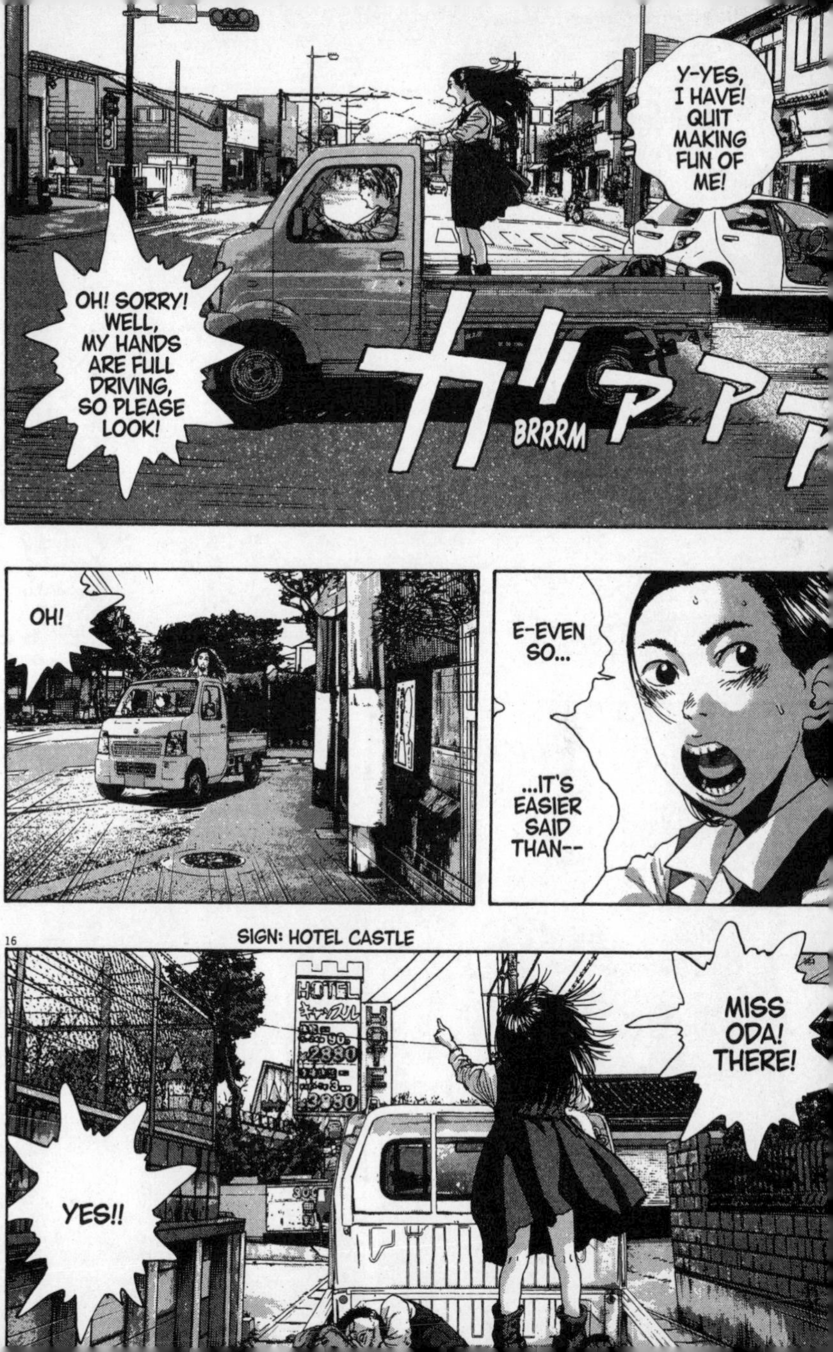

Y-YES, I HAVE! QUIT MAKING FUN OF ME!
OH! SORRY! WELL, MY HANDS ARE FULL DRIVING, SO PLEASE LOOK!
BRRRM
E-EVEN SO...
...IT'S EASIER SAID THAN--
OH!
SIGN: HOTEL CASTLE
HOTEL
MISS ODA! THERE!
YES!!

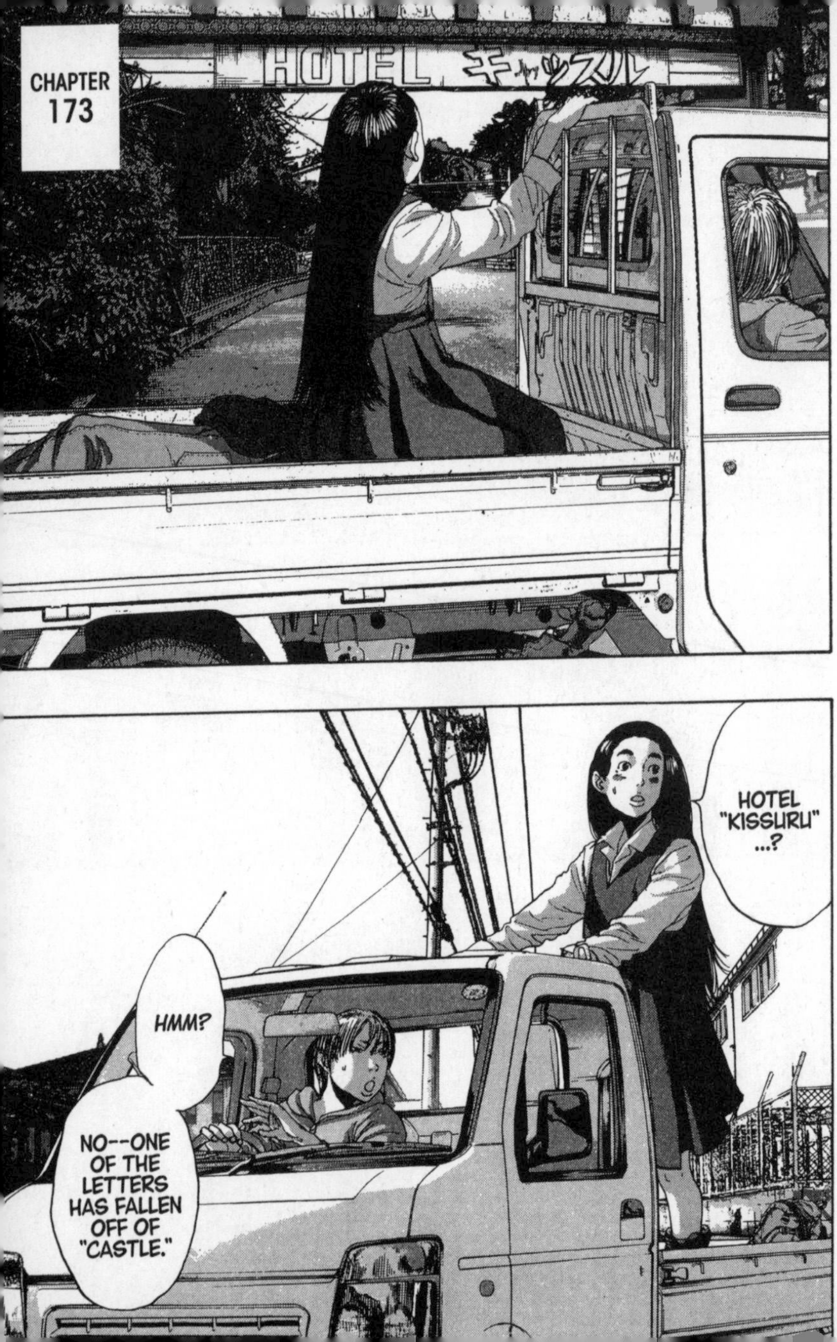
CHAPTER 173
HOTEL キャッスル
HOTEL "KISSURU" ...?
HMM?
NO--ONE OF THE LETTERS HAS FALLEN OFF OF "CASTLE."

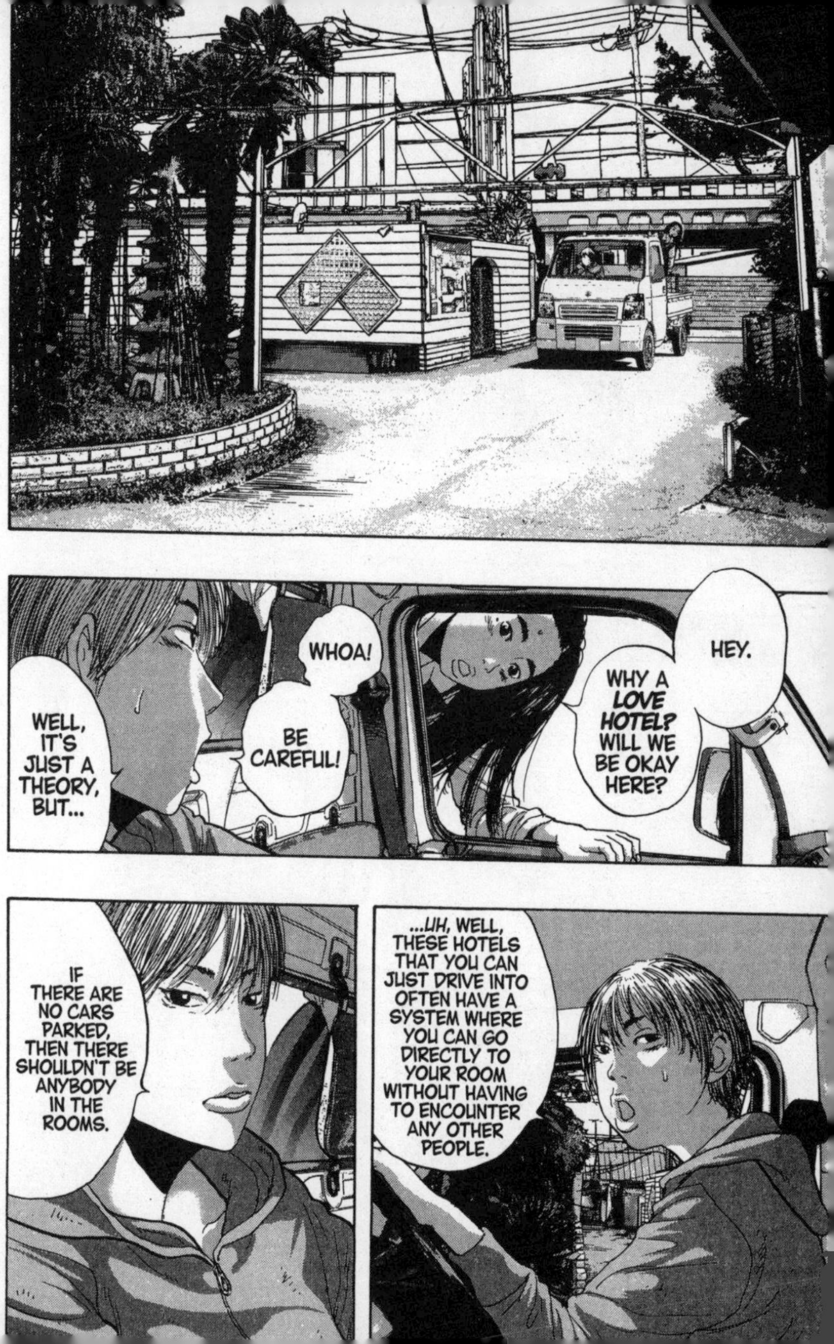
HEY.
WHY A *LOVE HOTEL?* WILL WE BE OKAY HERE?
WHOA!
BE CAREFUL!
WELL, IT'S JUST A THEORY, BUT...
...UH, WELL, THESE HOTELS THAT YOU CAN JUST DRIVE INTO OFTEN HAVE A SYSTEM WHERE YOU CAN GO DIRECTLY TO YOUR ROOM WITHOUT HAVING TO ENCOUNTER ANY OTHER PEOPLE.
IF THERE ARE NO CARS PARKED, THEN THERE SHOULDN'T BE ANYBODY IN THE ROOMS.

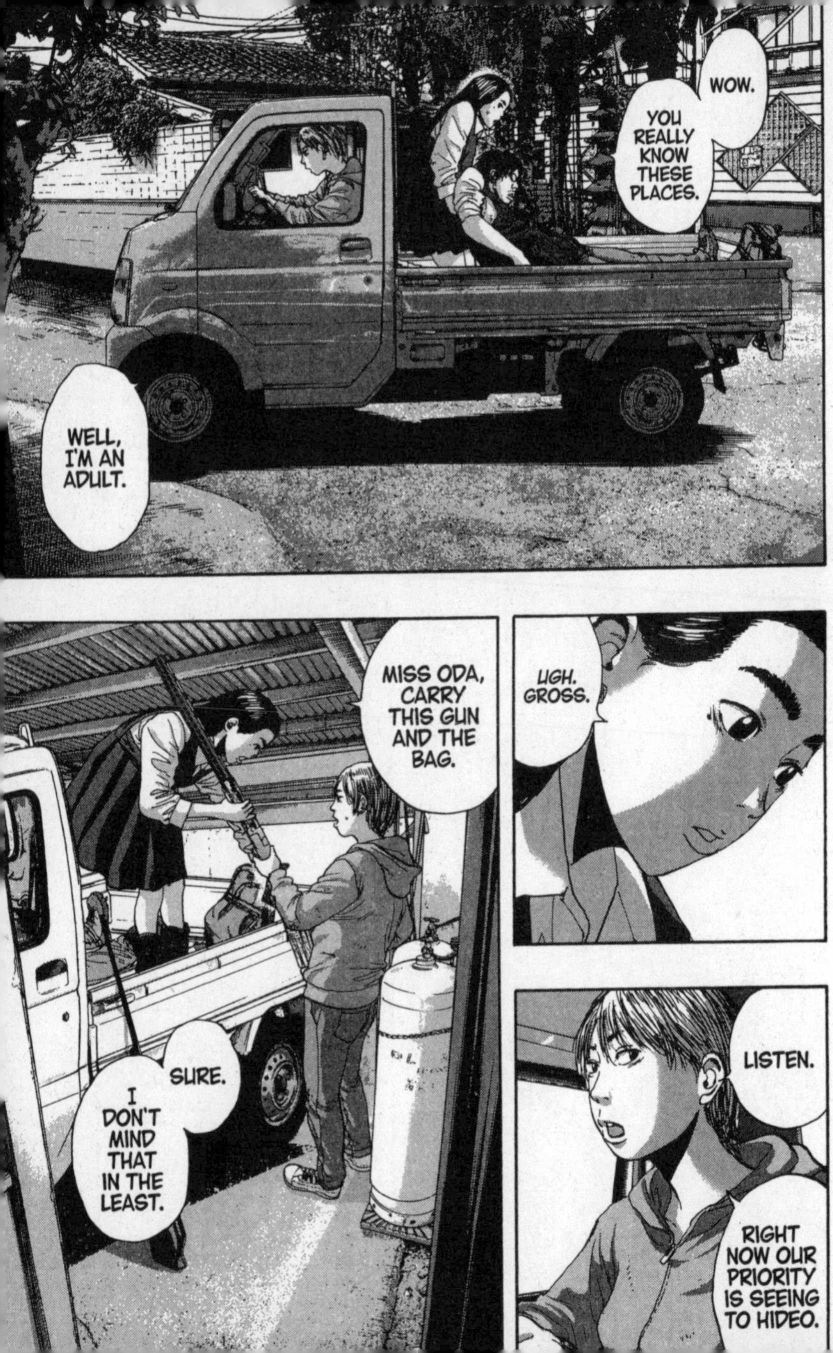
WOW.
YOU REALLY KNOW THESE PLACES.
WELL, I'M AN ADULT.
UGH. GROSS.
LISTEN.
RIGHT NOW OUR PRIORITY IS SEEING TO HIDEO.
MISS ODA, CARRY THIS GUN AND THE BAG.
SURE.
I DON'T MIND THAT IN THE LEAST.

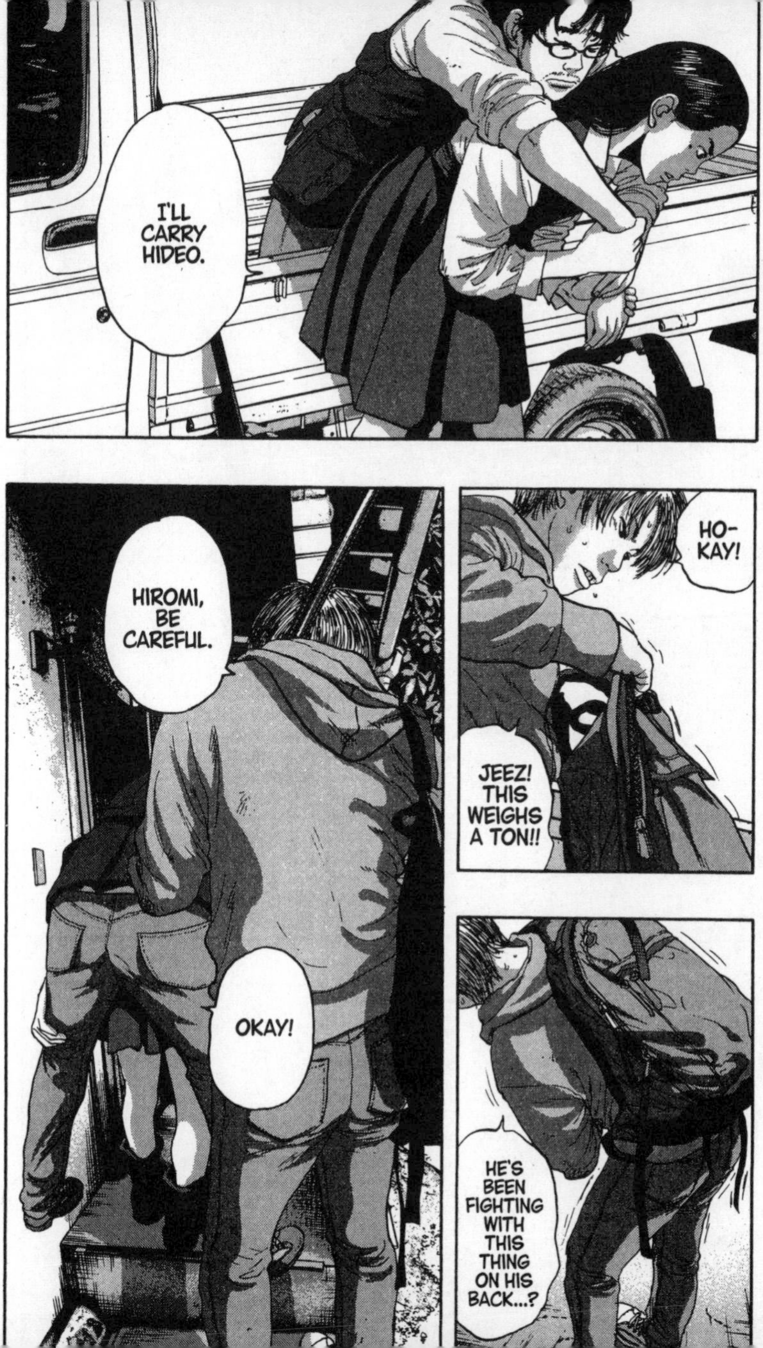
I'LL CARRY HIDEO.
HO-KAY!
JEEZ! THIS WEIGHS A TON!!
HE'S BEEN FIGHTING WITH THIS THING ON HIS BACK...?
HIROMI, BE CAREFUL.
OKAY!

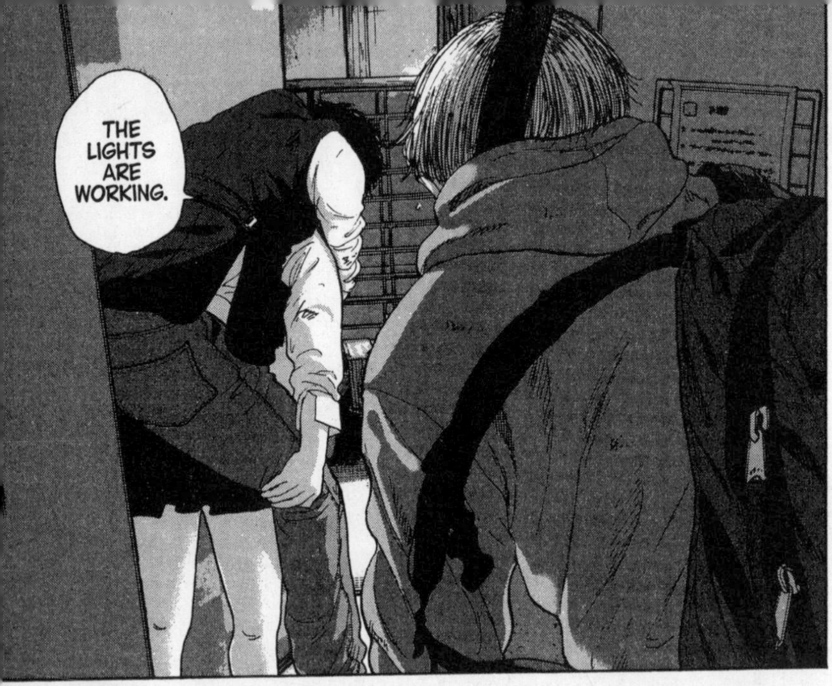
THE LIGHTS ARE WORKING.
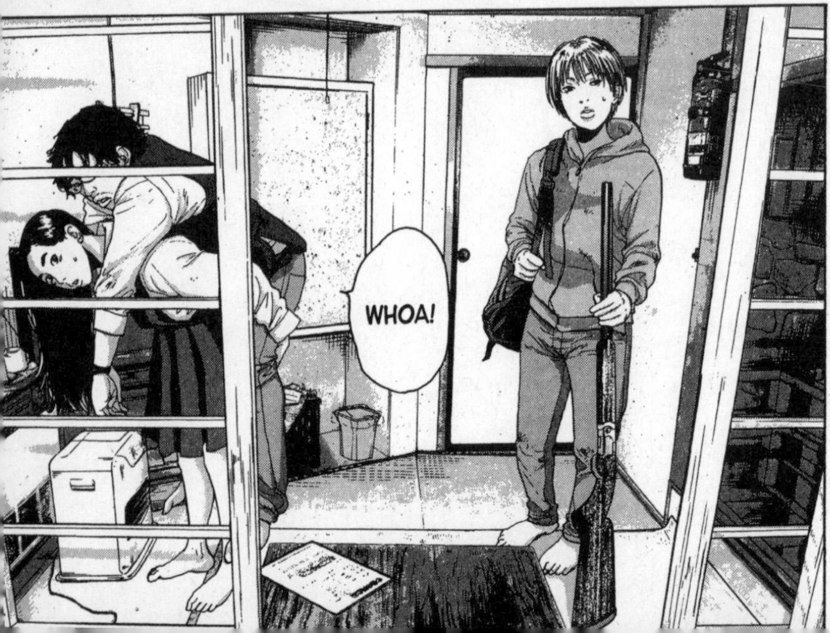
WHOA!

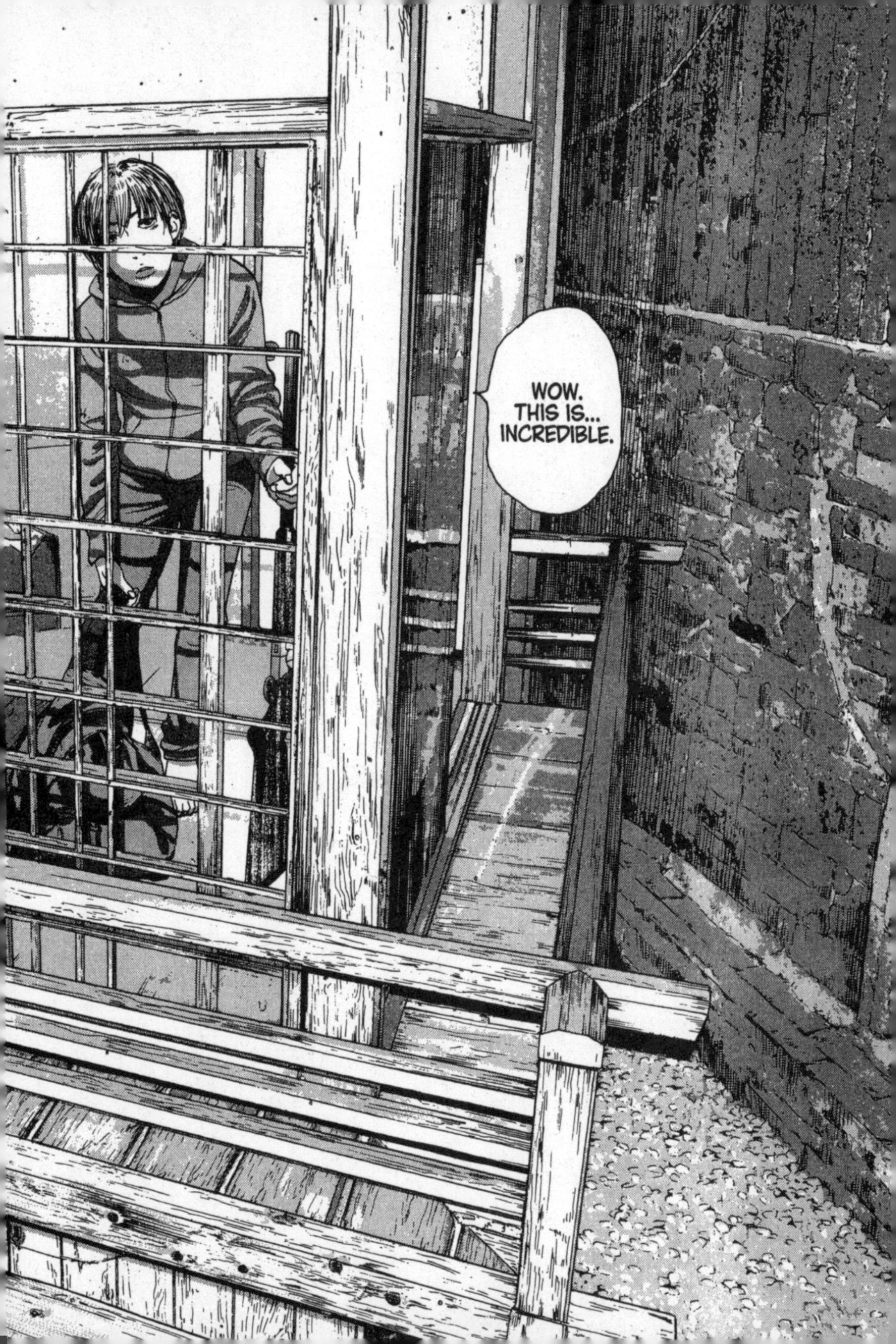
WOW. THIS IS... INCREDIBLE.

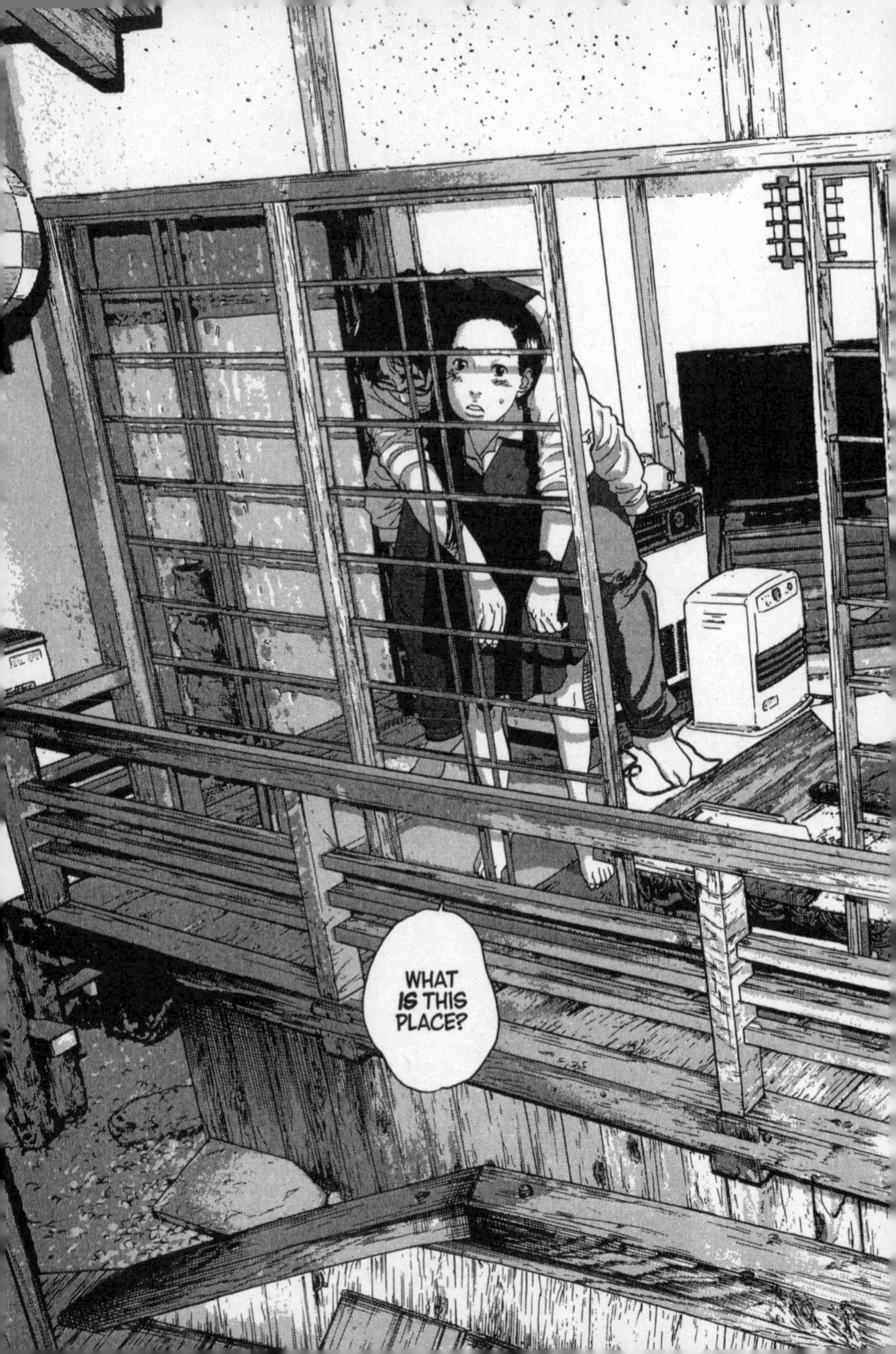
WHAT IS THIS PLACE?

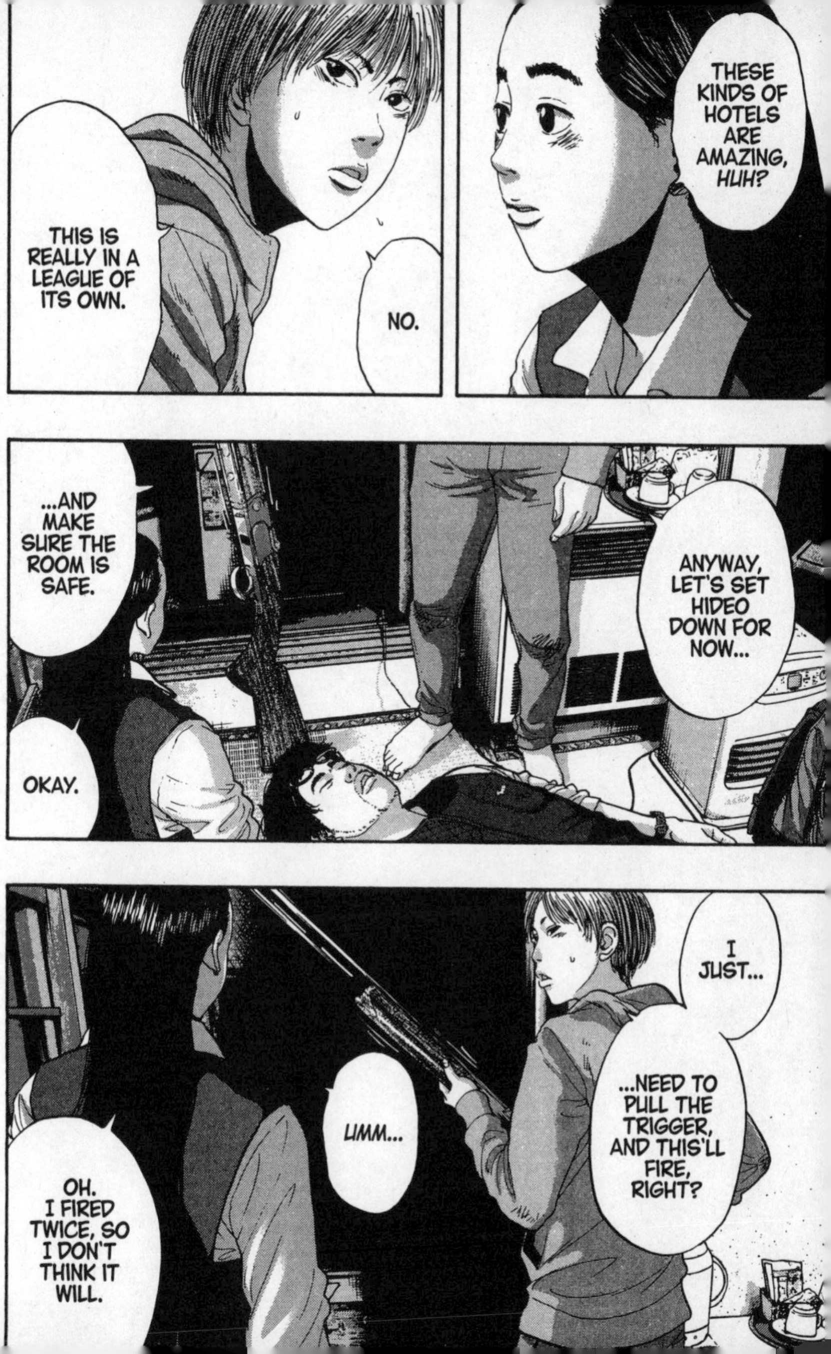
THESE KINDS OF HOTELS ARE AMAZING, HUH?
NO.
THIS IS REALLY IN A LEAGUE OF ITS OWN.
ANYWAY, LET'S SET HIDEO DOWN FOR NOW...
...AND MAKE SURE THE ROOM IS SAFE.
OKAY.
I JUST...
...NEED TO PULL THE TRIGGER, AND THIS'LL FIRE, RIGHT?
UMM...
OH. I FIRED TWICE, SO I DON'T THINK IT WILL.

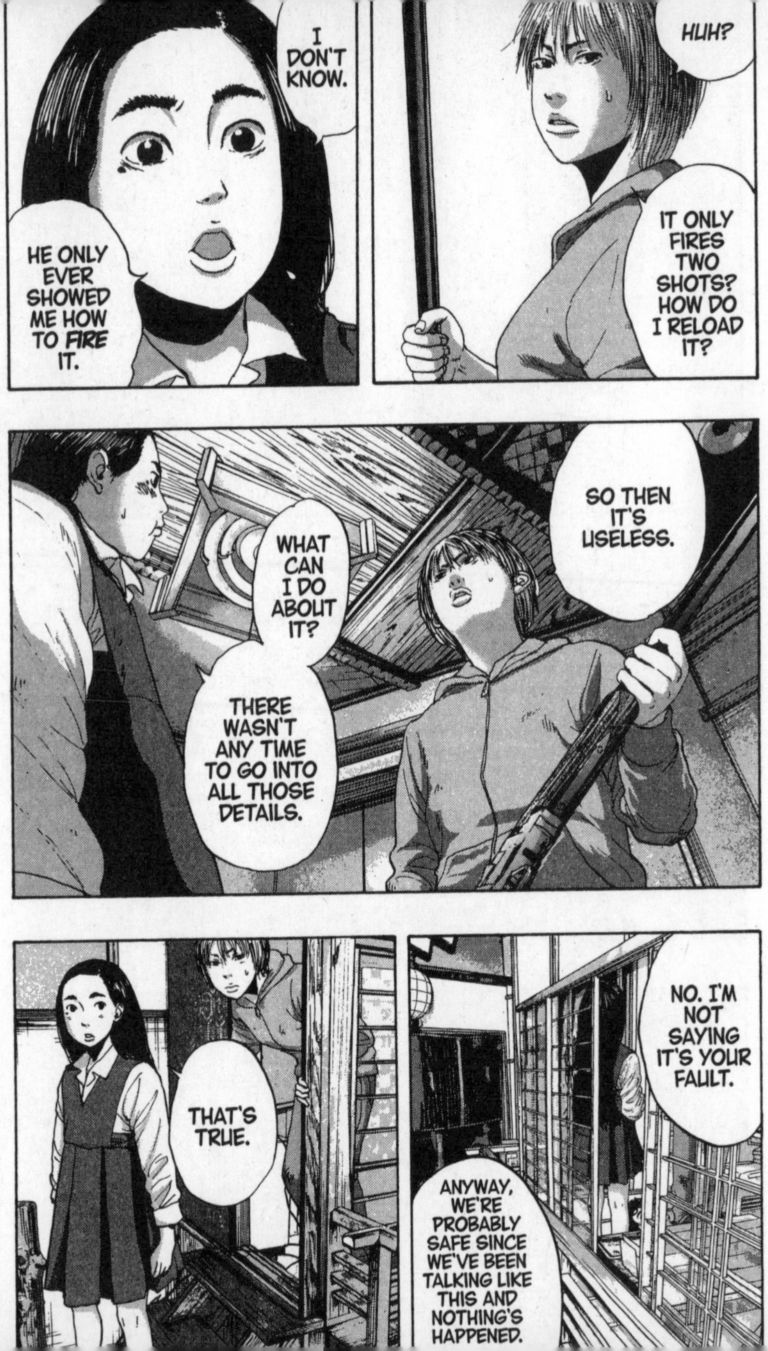
HUH?
IT ONLY FIRES TWO SHOTS? HOW DO I RELOAD IT?
I DON'T KNOW.
HE ONLY EVER SHOWED ME HOW TO *FIRE* IT.
SO THEN IT'S USELESS.
WHAT CAN I DO ABOUT IT?
THERE WASN'T ANY TIME TO GO INTO ALL THOSE DETAILS.
NO. I'M NOT SAYING IT'S YOUR FAULT.
ANYWAY, WE'RE PROBABLY SAFE SINCE WE'VE BEEN TALKING LIKE THIS AND NOTHING'S HAPPENED.
THAT'S TRUE.

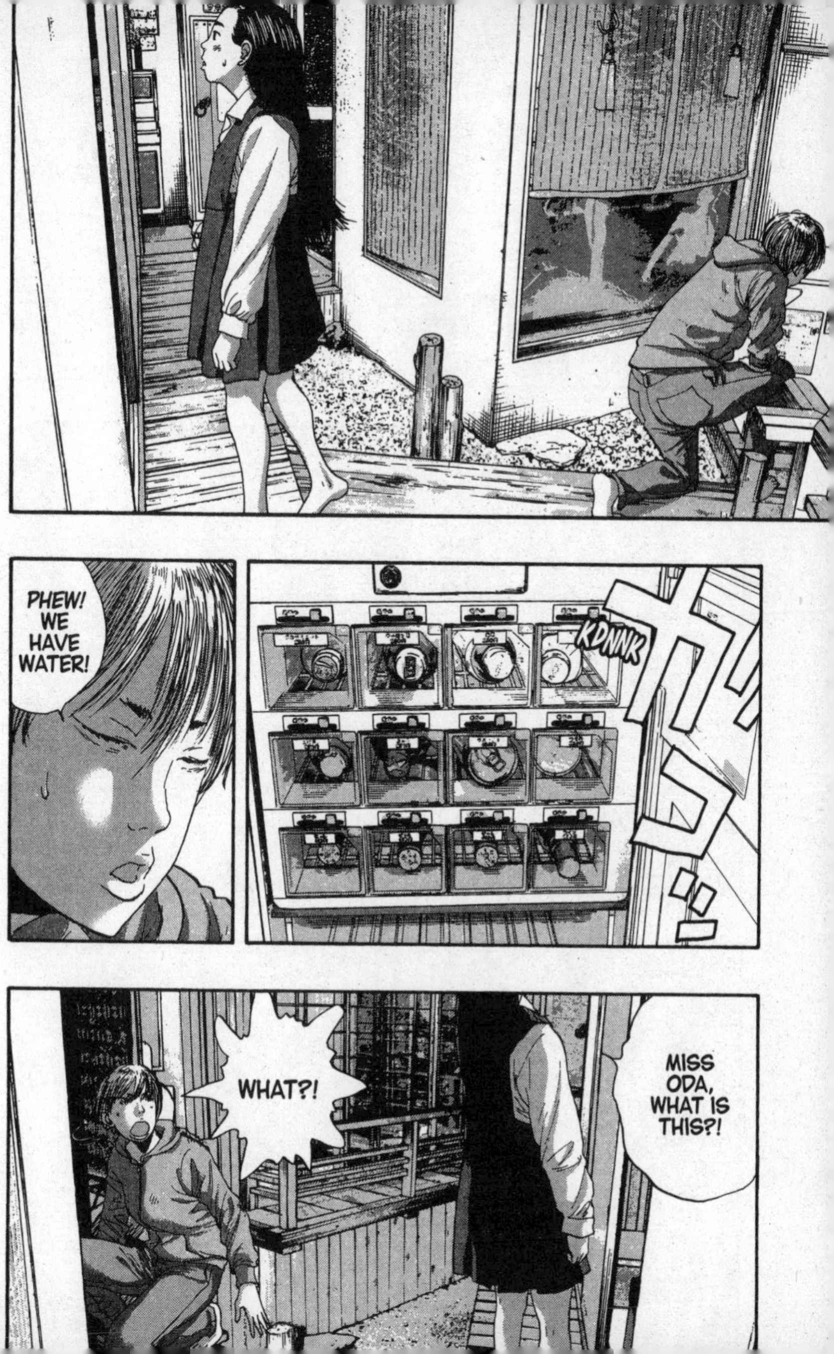
KDNNK
PHEW! WE HAVE WATER!
MISS ODA, WHAT IS THIS?!
WHAT?!

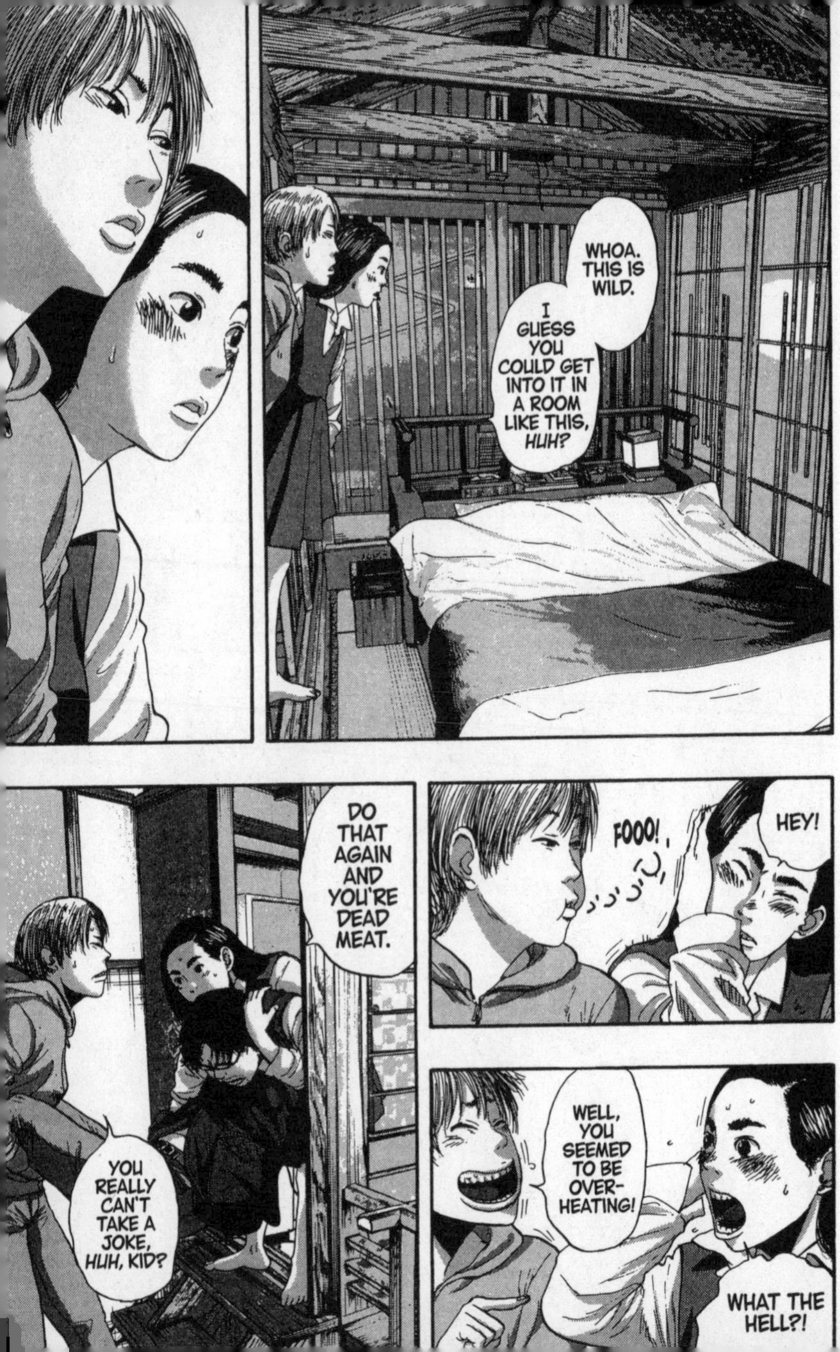
WHOA. THIS IS WILD.
I GUESS YOU COULD GET INTO IT IN A ROOM LIKE THIS, HUH?
HEY!
FOOO!
WELL, YOU SEEMED TO BE OVER-HEATING!
WHAT THE HELL?!
DO THAT AGAIN AND YOU'RE DEAD MEAT.
YOU REALLY CAN'T TAKE A JOKE, HUH, KID?

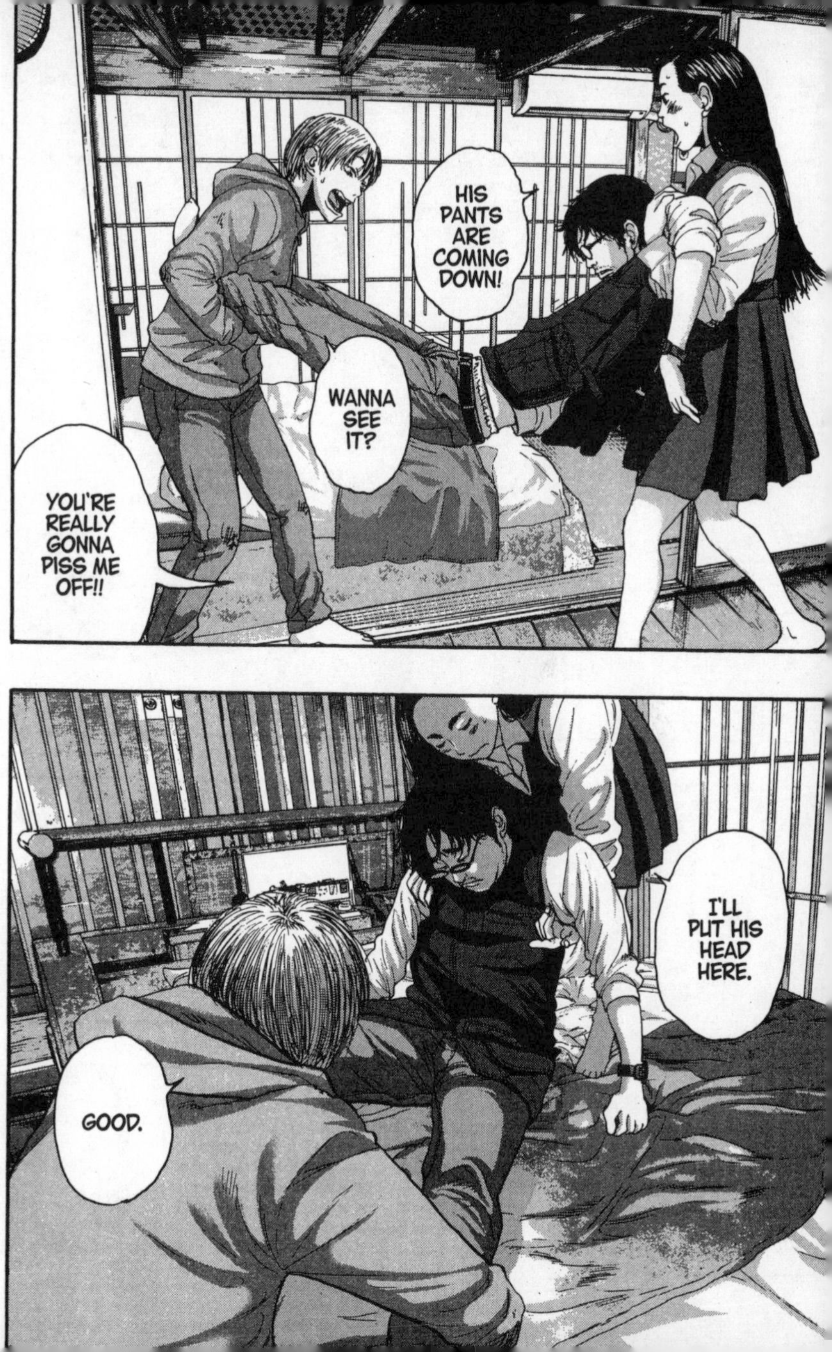
HIS PANTS ARE COMING DOWN!
WANNA SEE IT?
YOU'RE REALLY GONNA PISS ME OFF!!
I'LL PUT HIS HEAD HERE.
GOOD.

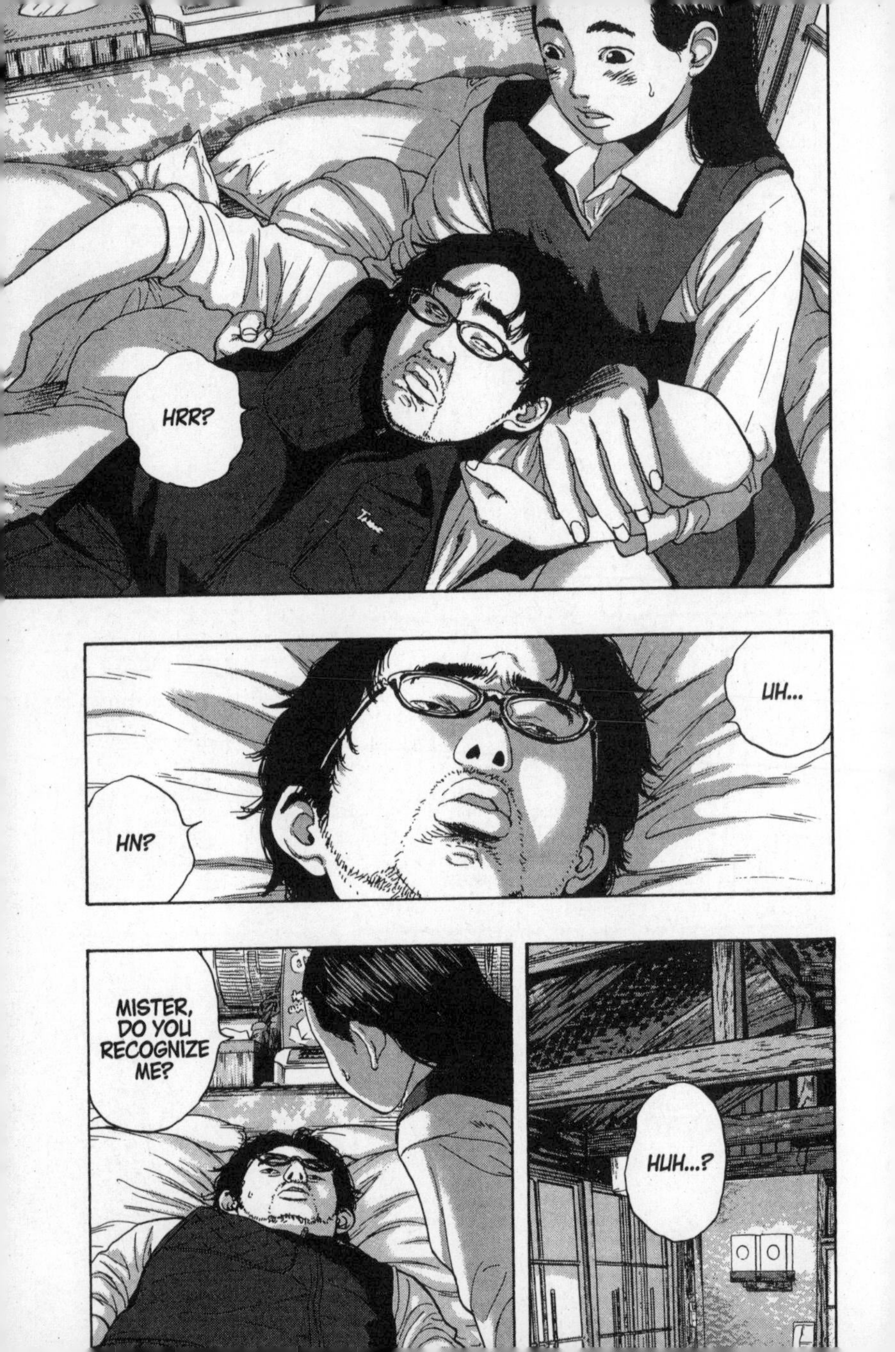
HRR?
UH...
HN?
HUH...?
MISTER, DO YOU RECOGNIZE ME?

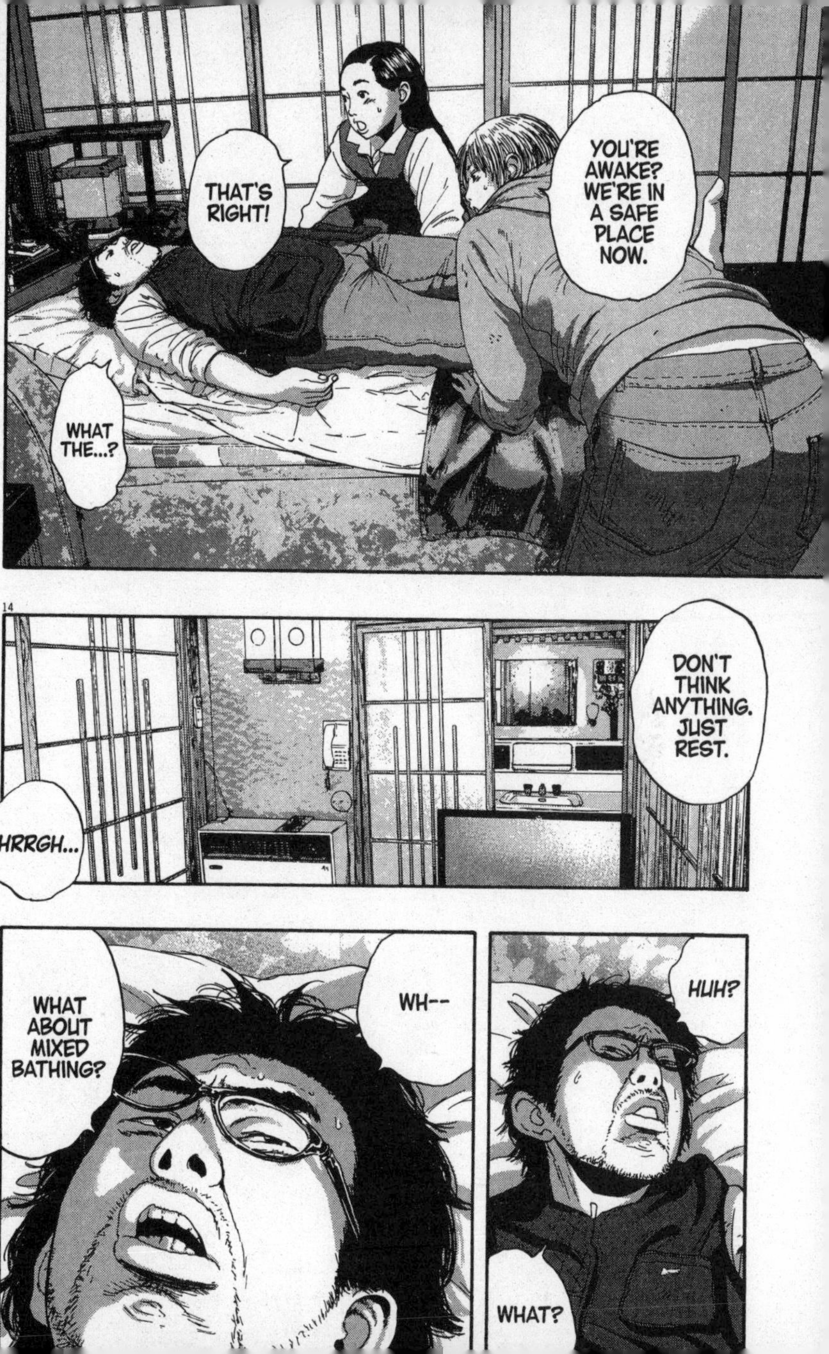
YOU'RE AWAKE? WE'RE IN A SAFE PLACE NOW.
THAT'S RIGHT!
WHAT THE...?
DON'T THINK ANYTHING. JUST REST.
HRRGH...
HUH?
WHAT?
WH--
WHAT ABOUT MIXED BATHING?

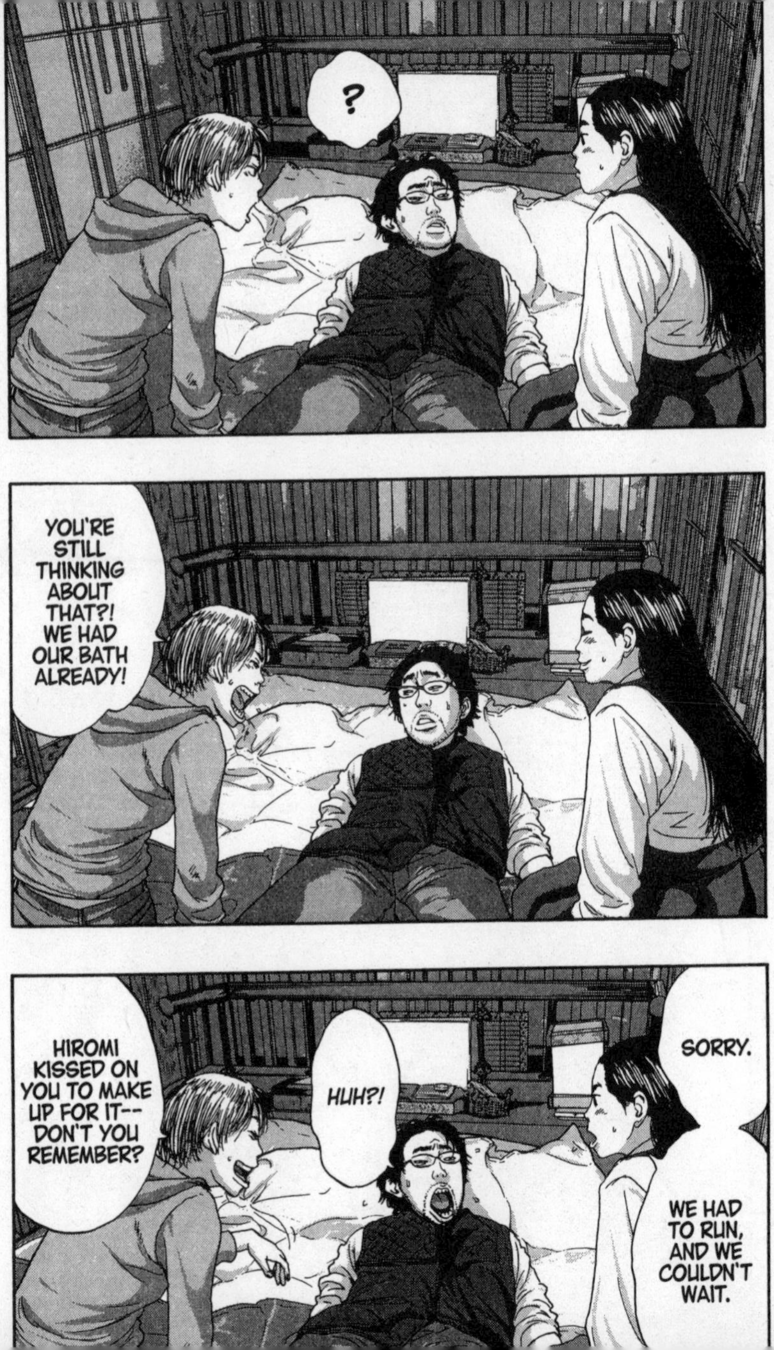
?
YOU'RE STILL THINKING ABOUT THAT?! WE HAD OUR BATH ALREADY!
HIROMI KISSED ON YOU TO MAKE UP FOR IT-- DON'T YOU REMEMBER?
HUH?!
SORRY.
WE HAD TO RUN, AND WE COULDN'T WAIT.

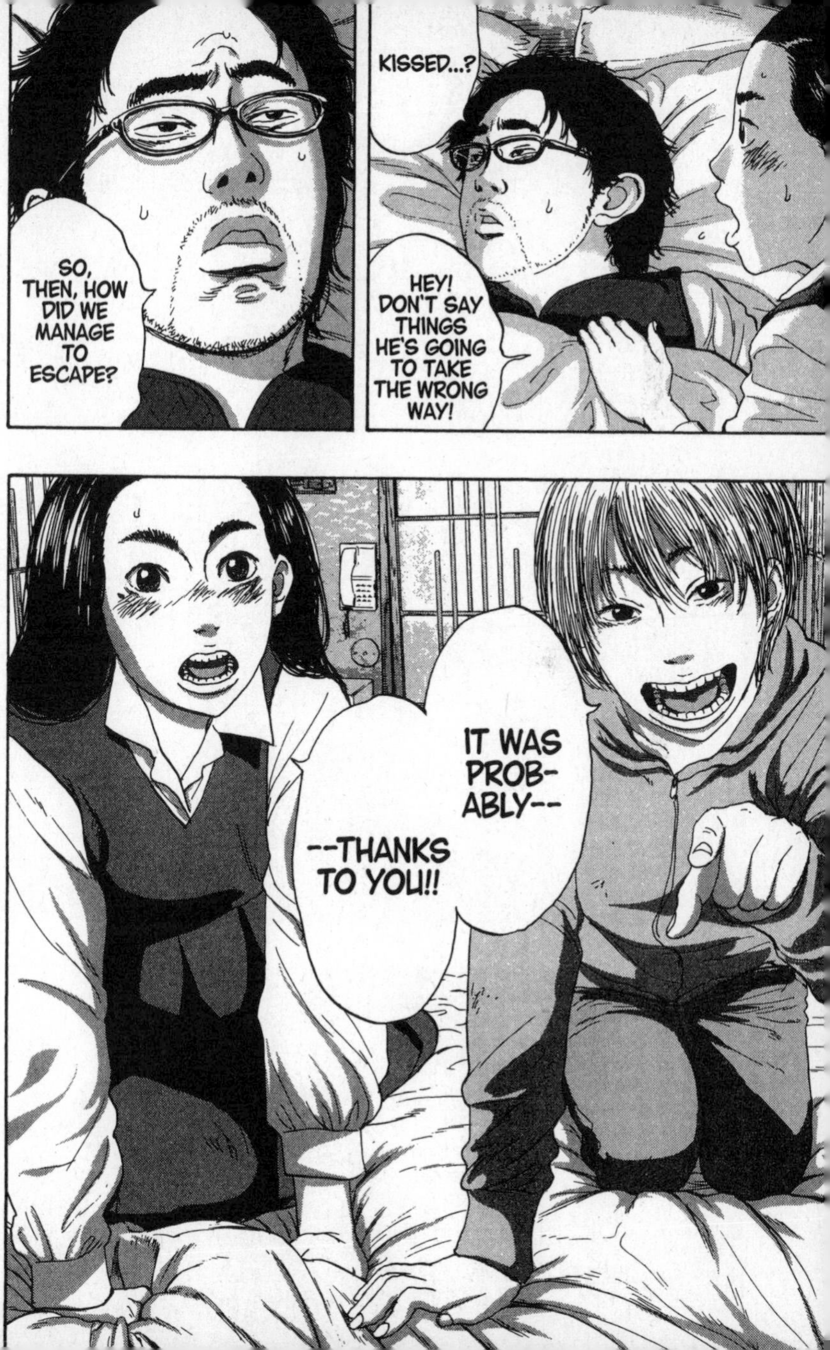
KISSED...?
HEY! DON'T SAY THINGS HE'S GOING TO TAKE THE WRONG WAY!
SO, THEN, HOW DID WE MANAGE TO ESCAPE?
IT WAS PROB-ABLY--
--THANKS TO YOU!!

I AM
A HERO

CHAPTER 174

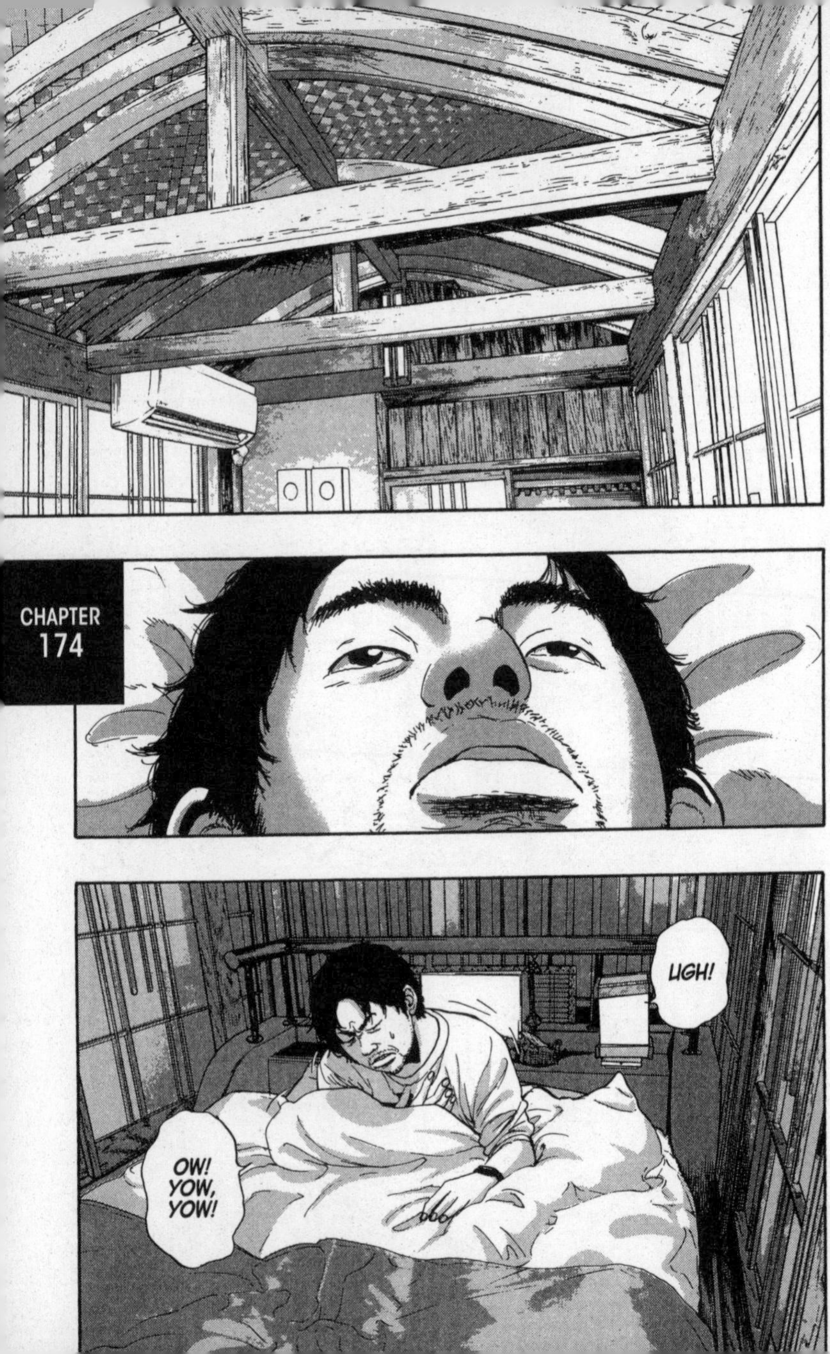
UGH!
OW! YOW, YOW!

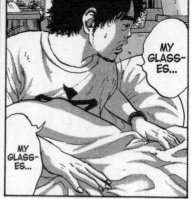

MY GLASS-ES...

MY GLASS-ES...

FOOO!

HUH? NOBODY HERE.

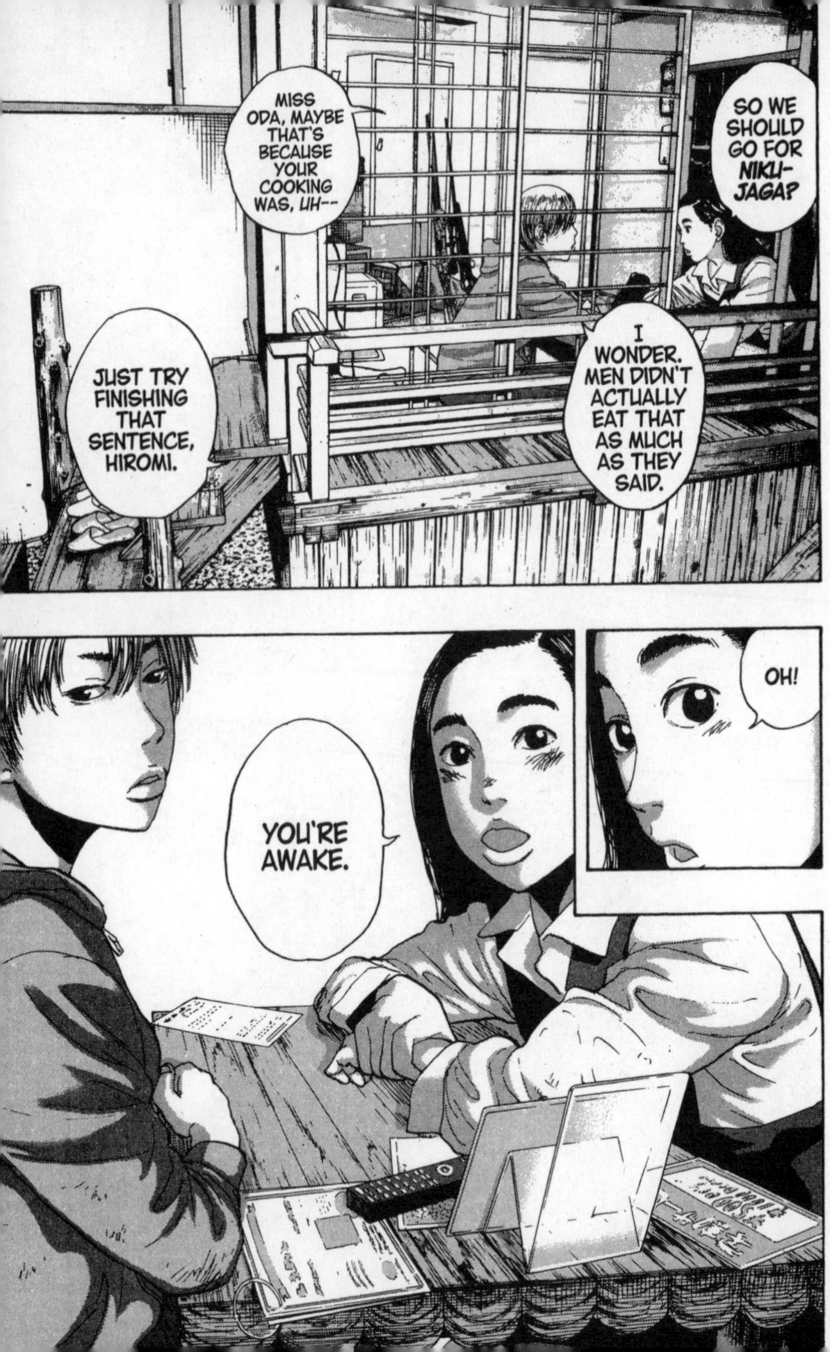
SO WE SHOULD GO FOR NIKU-JAGA?
I WONDER. MEN DIDN'T ACTUALLY EAT THAT AS MUCH AS THEY SAID.
MISS ODA, MAYBE THAT'S BECAUSE YOUR COOKING WAS, UH--
JUST TRY FINISHING THAT SENTENCE, HIROMI.
OH!
YOU'RE AWAKE.

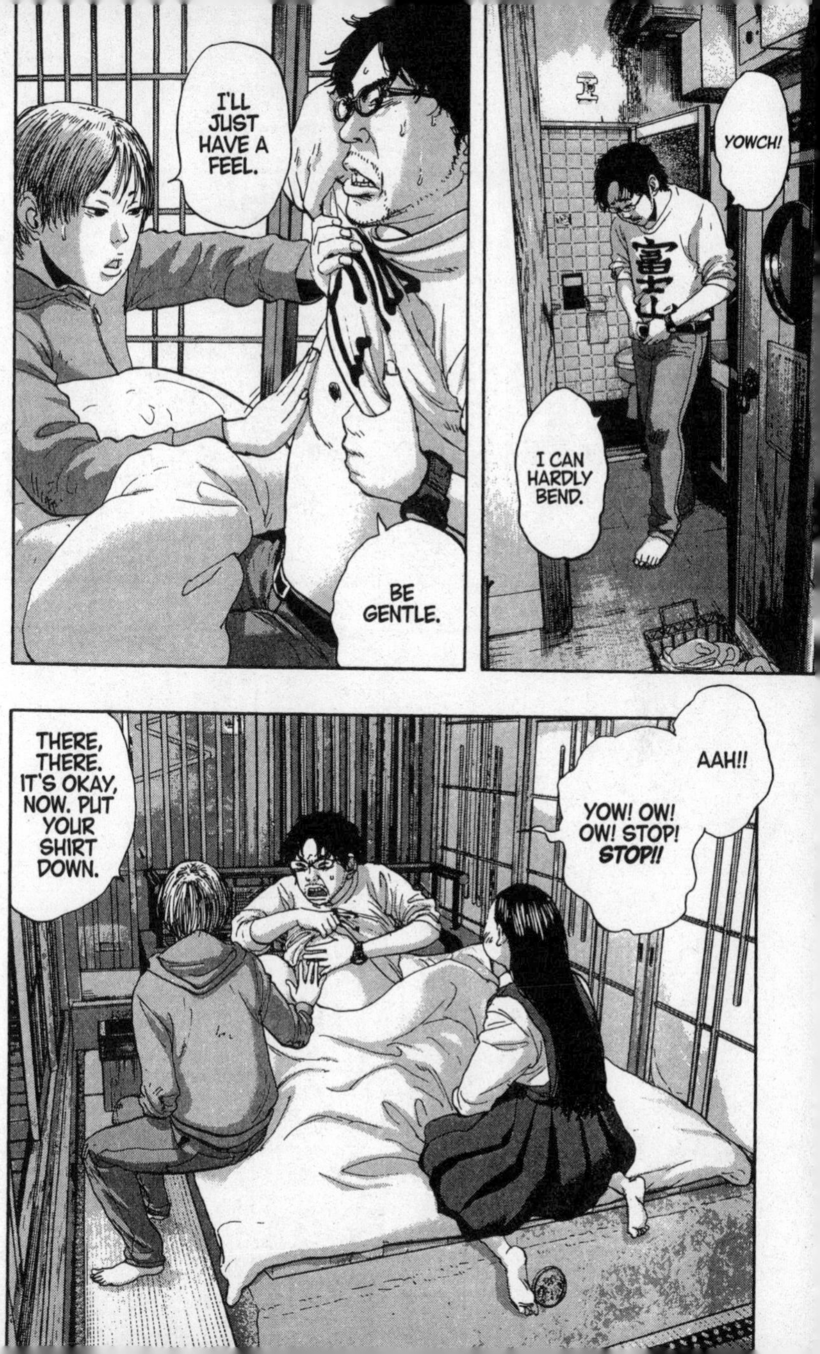
YOWCH!
I CAN HARDLY BEND.
I'LL JUST HAVE A FEEL.
BE GENTLE.
AAH!!
YOW! OW! OW! STOP! **STOP!!**
THERE, THERE. IT'S OKAY, NOW. PUT YOUR SHIRT DOWN.

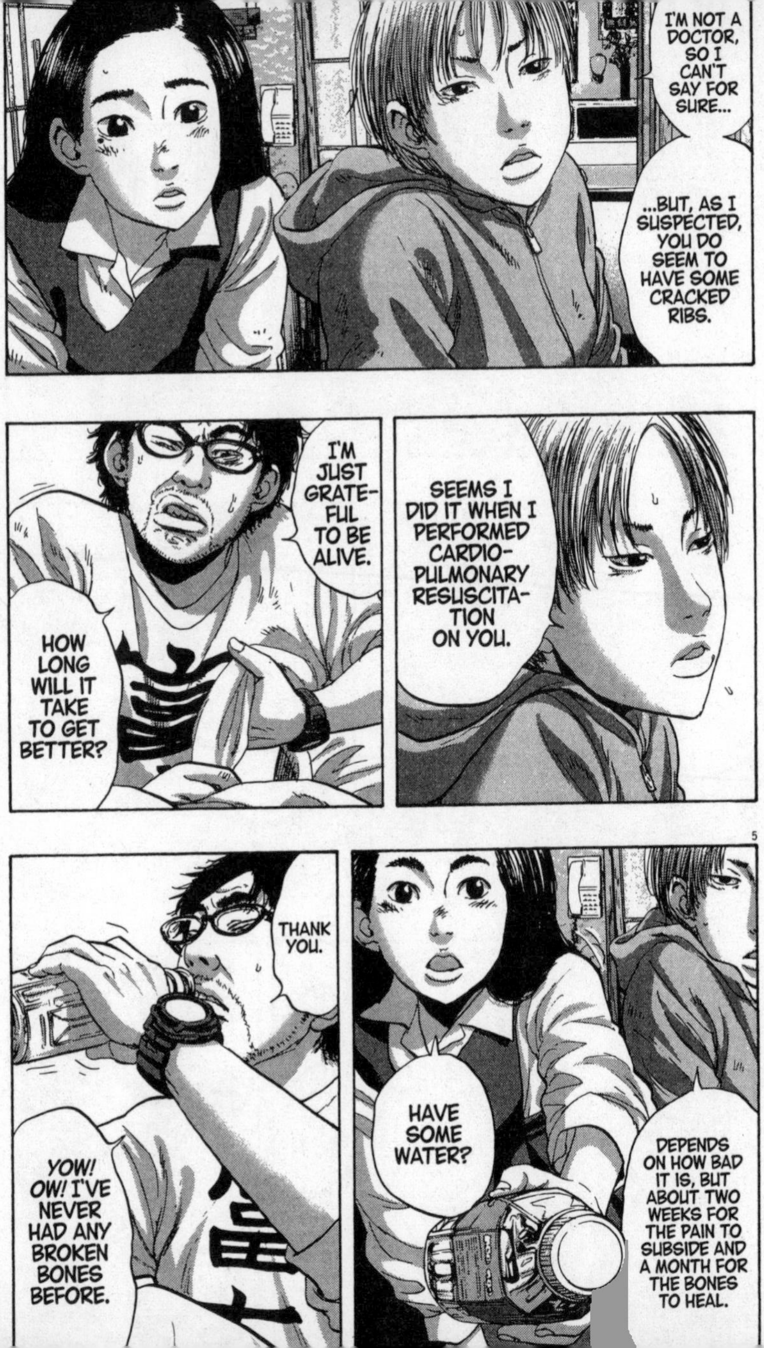
I'M NOT A DOCTOR, SO I CAN'T SAY FOR SURE...
...BUT, AS I SUSPECTED, YOU DO SEEM TO HAVE SOME CRACKED RIBS.
SEEMS I DID IT WHEN I PERFORMED CARDIO-PULMONARY RESUSCITATION ON YOU.
I'M JUST GRATEFUL TO BE ALIVE.
HOW LONG WILL IT TAKE TO GET BETTER?
DEPENDS ON HOW BAD IT IS, BUT ABOUT TWO WEEKS FOR THE PAIN TO SUBSIDE AND A MONTH FOR THE BONES TO HEAL.
HAVE SOME WATER?
THANK YOU.
YOW! OW! I'VE NEVER HAD ANY BROKEN BONES BEFORE.

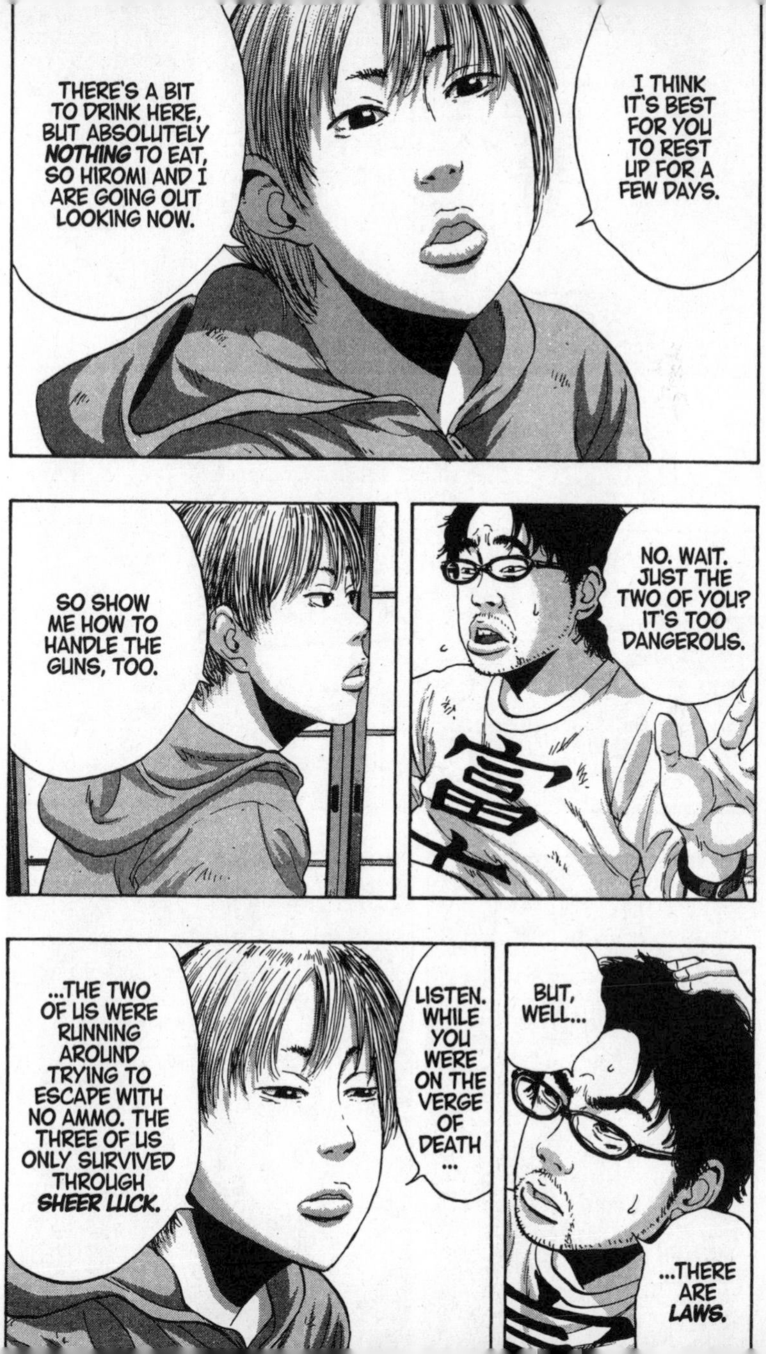
I THINK IT'S BEST FOR YOU TO REST UP FOR A FEW DAYS.
THERE'S A BIT TO DRINK HERE, BUT ABSOLUTELY *NOTHING* TO EAT, SO HIROMI AND I ARE GOING OUT LOOKING NOW.
NO. WAIT. JUST THE TWO OF YOU? IT'S TOO DANGEROUS.
SO SHOW ME HOW TO HANDLE THE GUNS, TOO.
BUT, WELL...
...THERE ARE *LAWS.*
LISTEN. WHILE YOU WERE ON THE VERGE OF DEATH...
...THE TWO OF US WERE RUNNING AROUND TRYING TO ESCAPE WITH NO AMMO. THE THREE OF US ONLY SURVIVED THROUGH *SHEER LUCK.*

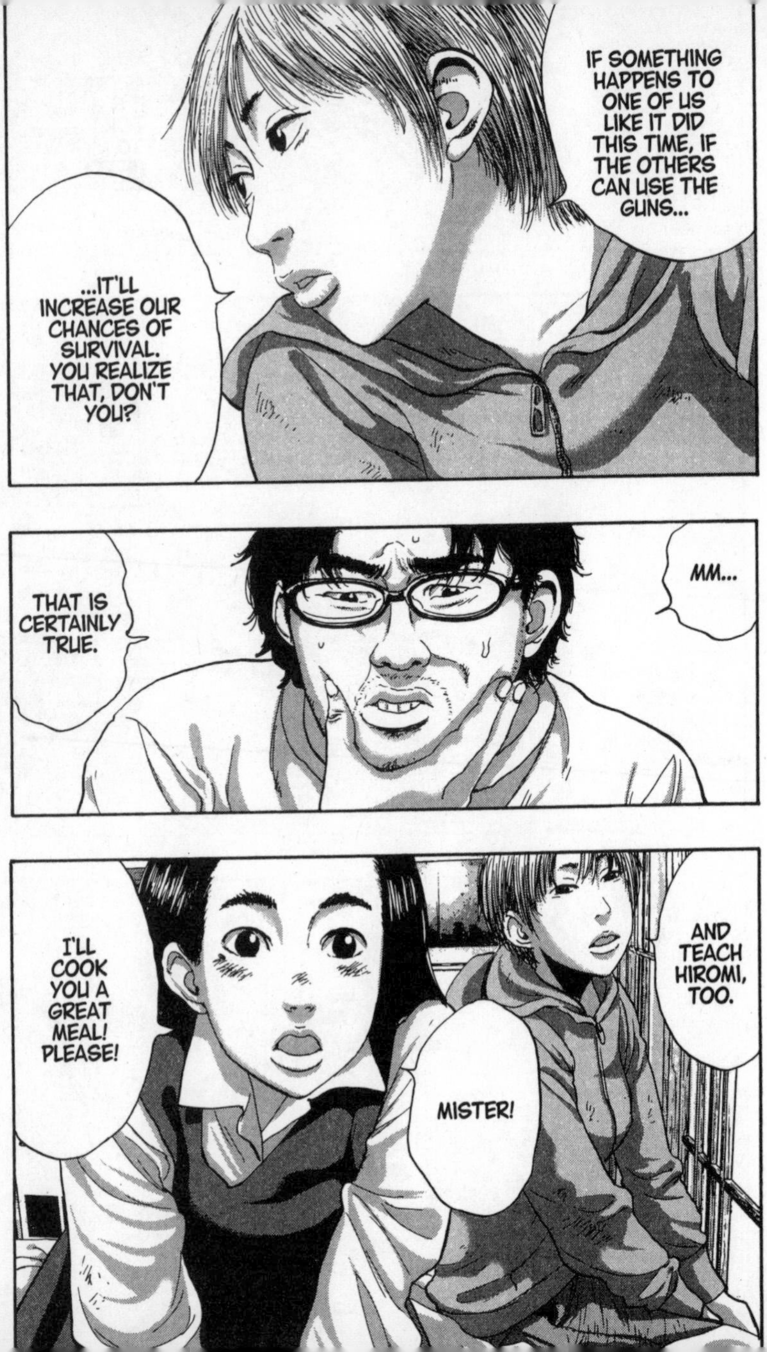
IF SOMETHING HAPPENS TO ONE OF US LIKE IT DID THIS TIME, IF THE OTHERS CAN USE THE GUNS...
...IT'LL INCREASE OUR CHANCES OF SURVIVAL. YOU REALIZE THAT, DON'T YOU?
MM...
THAT IS CERTAINLY TRUE.
AND TEACH HIROMI, TOO.
I'LL COOK YOU A GREAT MEAL! PLEASE!
MISTER!

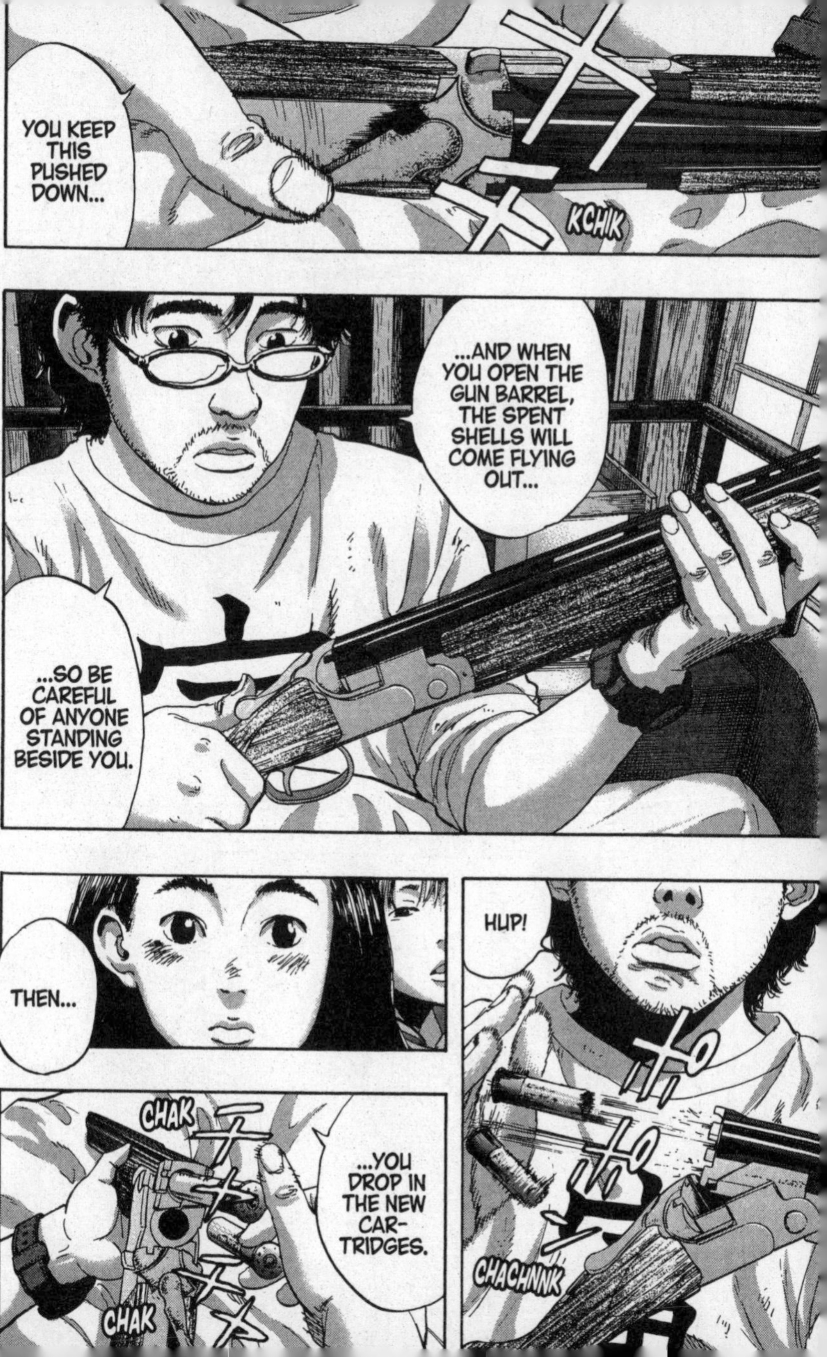
YOU KEEP THIS PUSHED DOWN...
KCHIK
...AND WHEN YOU OPEN THE GUN BARREL, THE SPENT SHELLS WILL COME FLYING OUT...
...SO BE CAREFUL OF ANYONE STANDING BESIDE YOU.
HUP!
CHACHNNK
THEN...
CHAK
...YOU DROP IN THE NEW CAR-TRIDGES.
CHAK

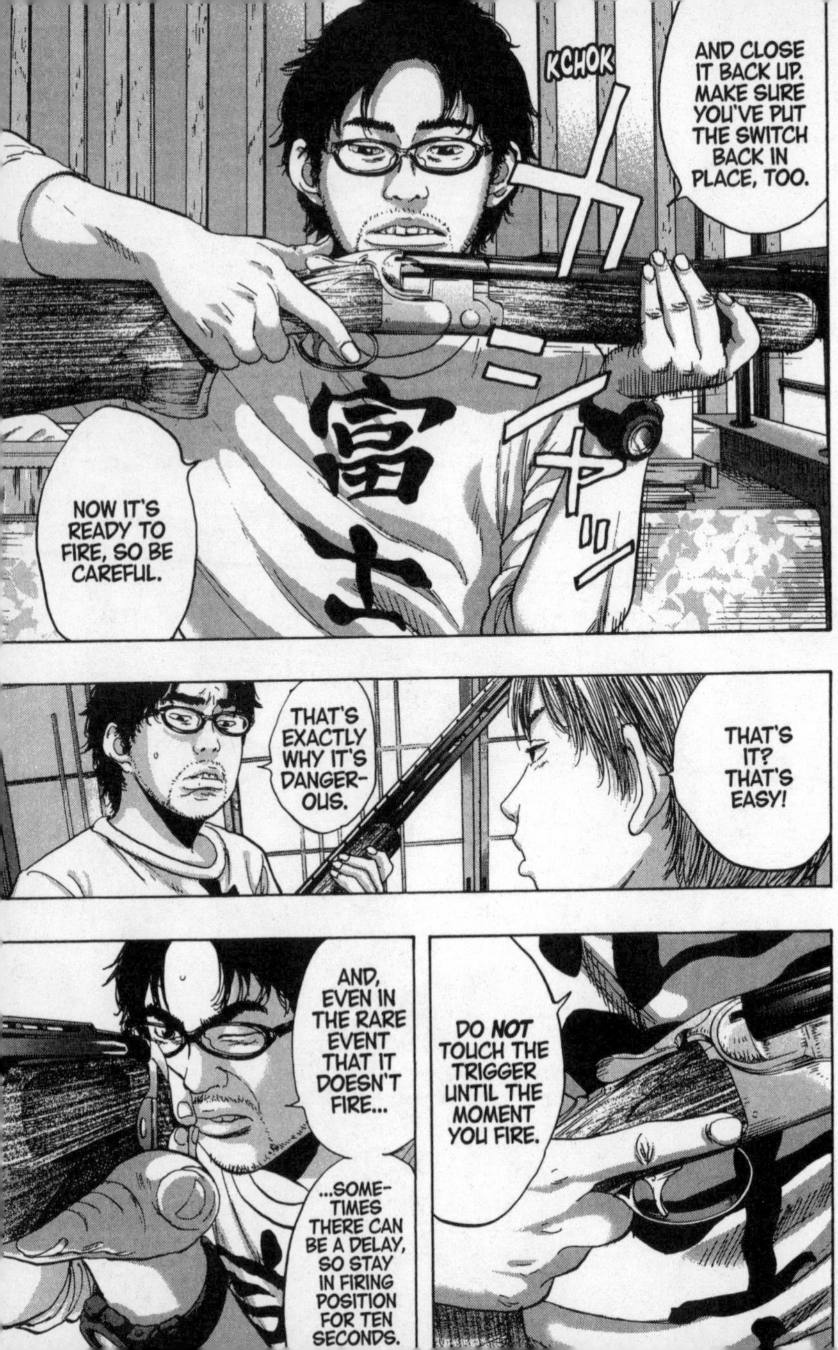
KCHOK
AND CLOSE IT BACK UP. MAKE SURE YOU'VE PUT THE SWITCH BACK IN PLACE, TOO.
富士
NOW IT'S READY TO FIRE, SO BE CAREFUL.
THAT'S IT? THAT'S EASY!
THAT'S EXACTLY WHY IT'S DANGER-OUS.
DO **NOT** TOUCH THE TRIGGER UNTIL THE MOMENT YOU FIRE.
AND, EVEN IN THE RARE EVENT THAT IT DOESN'T FIRE...
...SOME-TIMES THERE CAN BE A DELAY, SO STAY IN FIRING POSITION FOR TEN SECONDS.

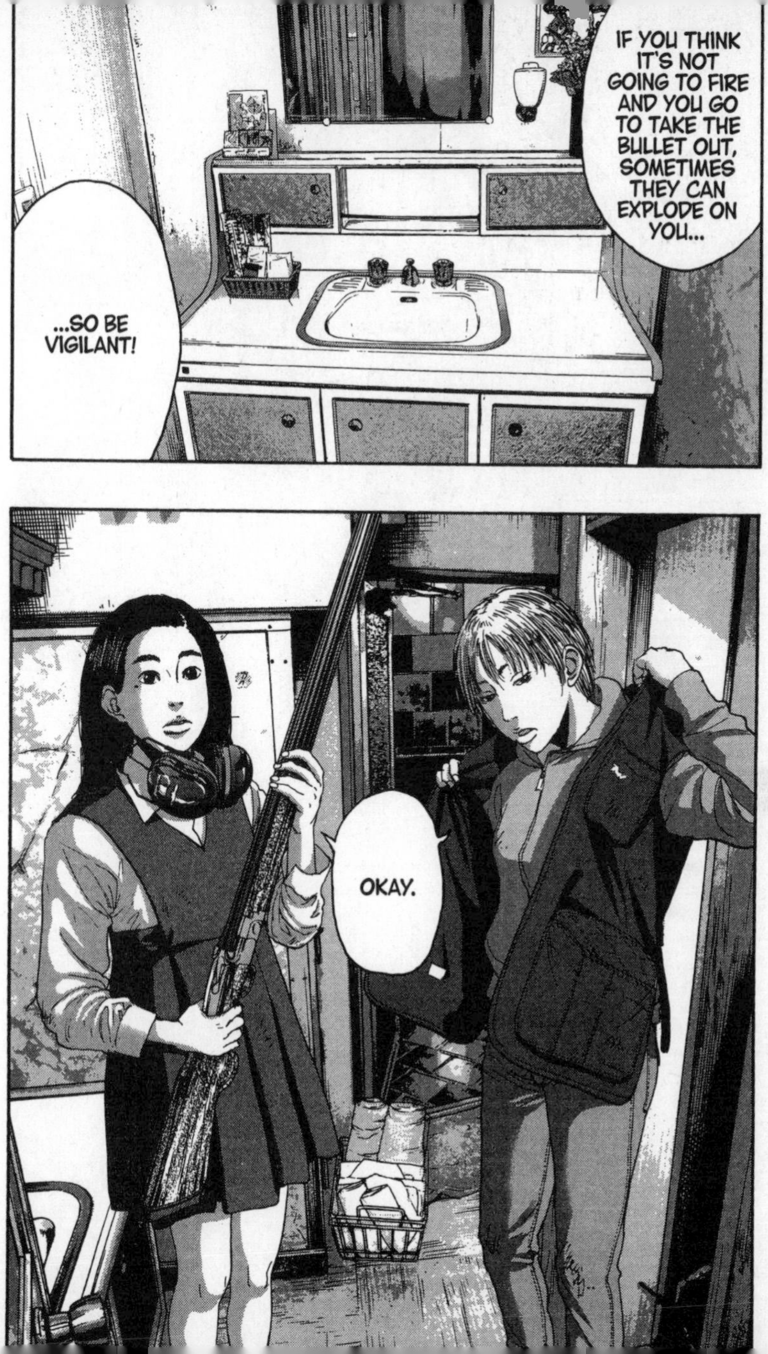
IF YOU THINK IT'S NOT GOING TO FIRE AND YOU GO TO TAKE THE BULLET OUT, SOMETIMES THEY CAN EXPLODE ON YOU...
...SO BE VIGILANT!
OKAY.

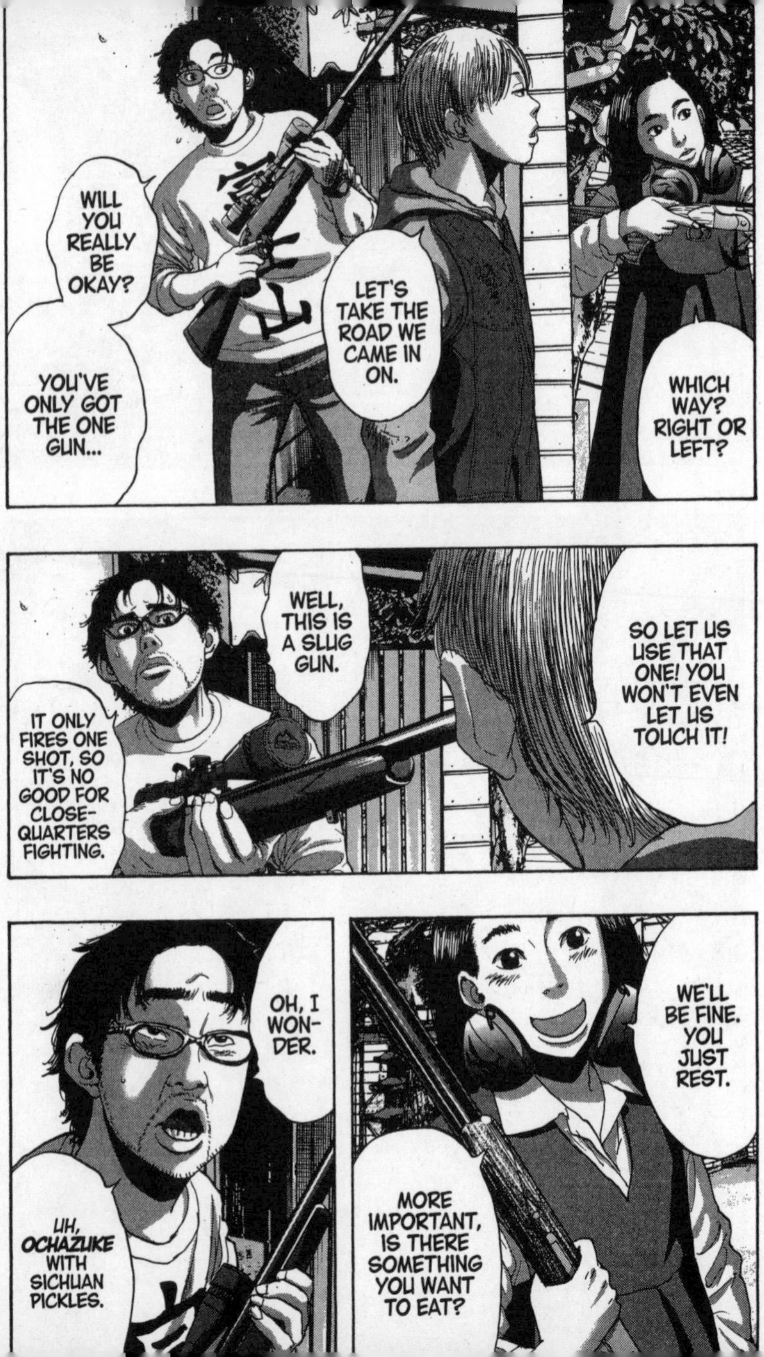
WHICH WAY? RIGHT OR LEFT?
LET'S TAKE THE ROAD WE CAME IN ON.
WILL YOU REALLY BE OKAY?
YOU'VE ONLY GOT THE ONE GUN...
SO LET US USE THAT ONE! YOU WON'T EVEN LET US TOUCH IT!
WELL, THIS IS A SLUG GUN.
IT ONLY FIRES ONE SHOT, SO IT'S NO GOOD FOR CLOSE-QUARTERS FIGHTING.
WE'LL BE FINE. YOU JUST REST.
MORE IMPORTANT, IS THERE SOMETHING YOU WANT TO EAT?
OH, I WONDER.
UH, **OCHAZUKE** WITH SICHUAN PICKLES.

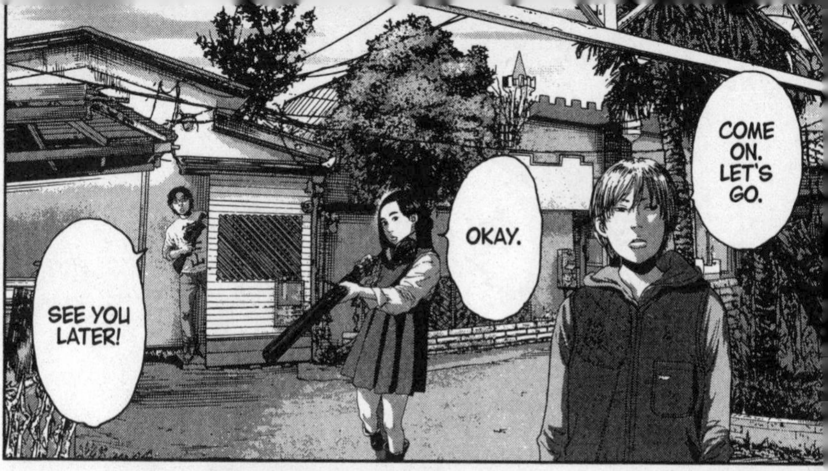
COME ON. LET'S GO.
OKAY.
SEE YOU LATER!

SIGN: HOTEL CASTLE

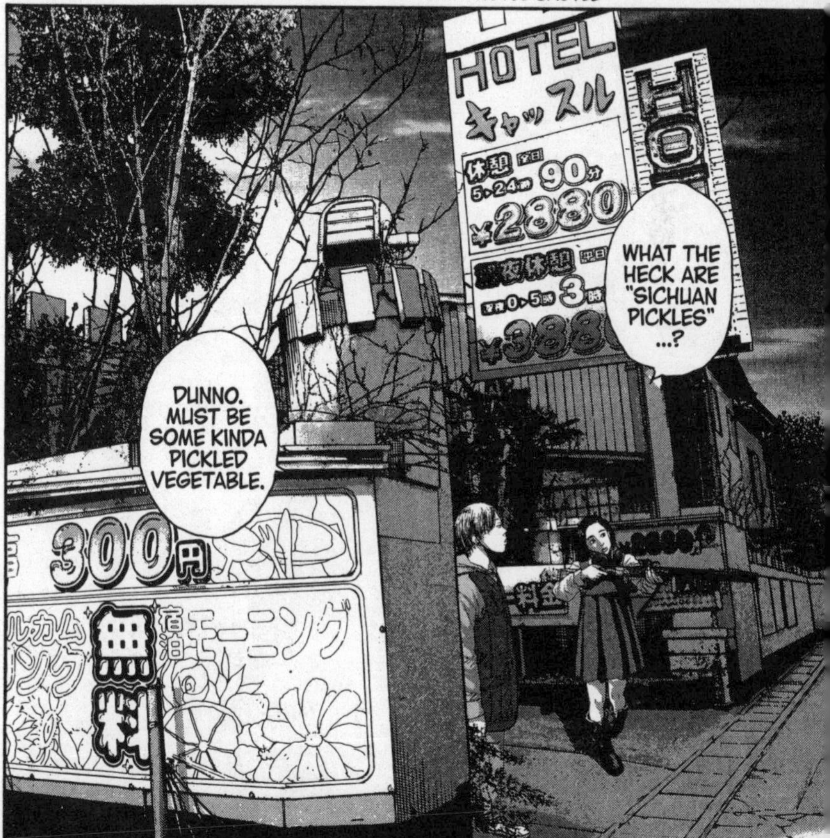
HOTEL
キャッスル
¥2880
WHAT THE HECK ARE "SICHUAN PICKLES" ...?
DUNNO. MUST BE SOME KINDA PICKLED VEGETABLE.
300円
無料

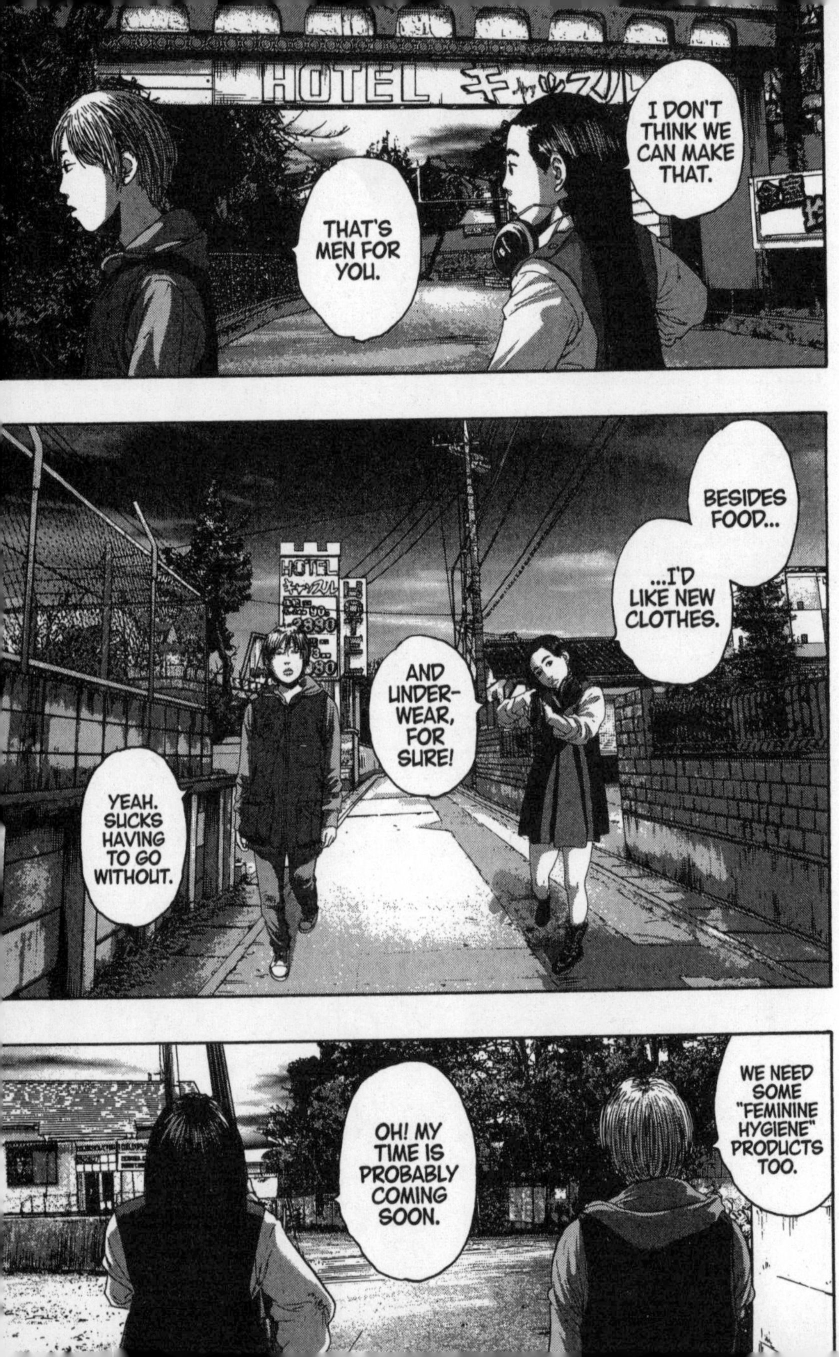
HOTEL
I DON'T THINK WE CAN MAKE THAT.
THAT'S MEN FOR YOU.
BESIDES FOOD...
...I'D LIKE NEW CLOTHES.
AND UNDER-WEAR, FOR SURE!
YEAH. SUCKS HAVING TO GO WITHOUT.
WE NEED SOME "FEMININE HYGIENE" PRODUCTS TOO.
OH! MY TIME IS PROBABLY COMING SOON.

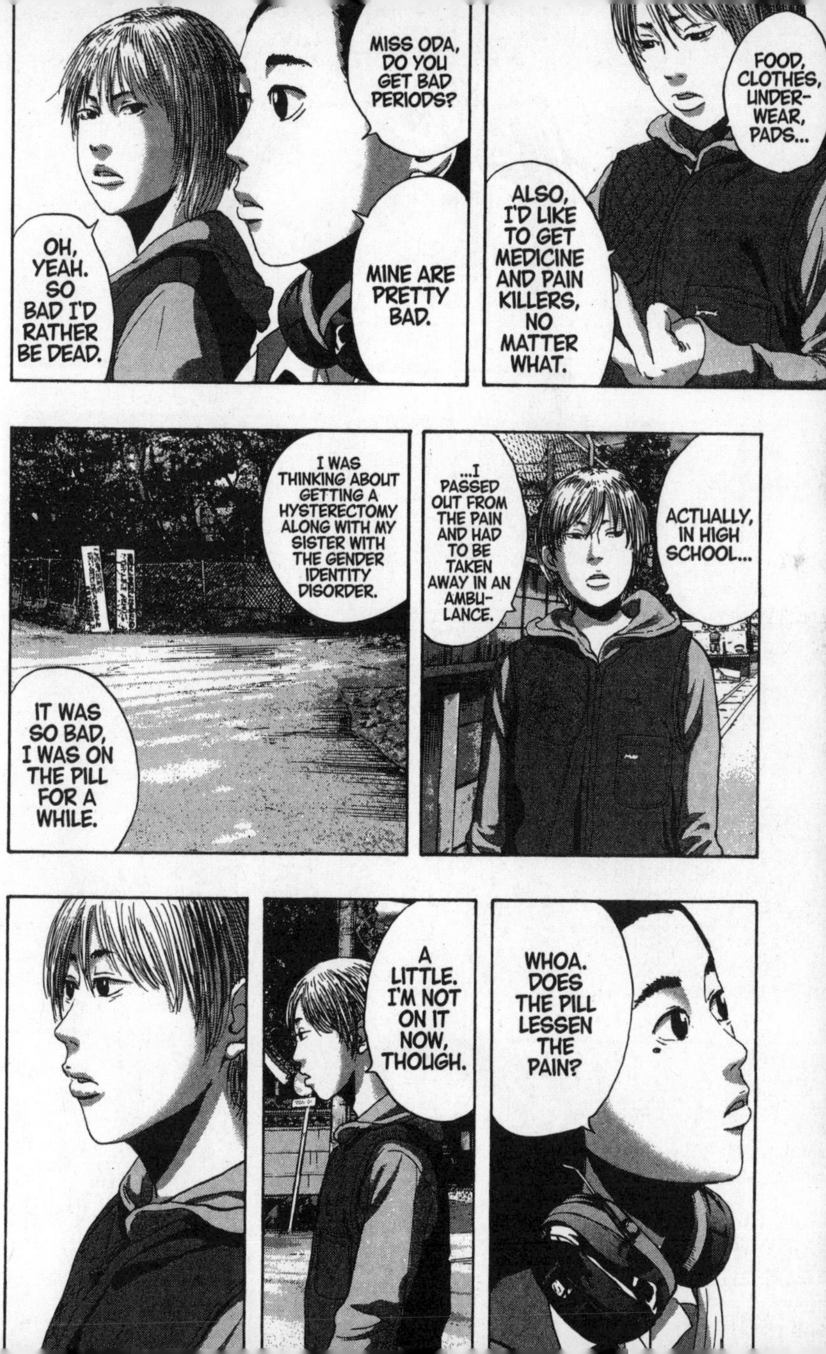
FOOD, CLOTHES, UNDER-WEAR, PADS...
ALSO, I'D LIKE TO GET MEDICINE AND PAIN KILLERS, NO MATTER WHAT.
MISS ODA, DO YOU GET BAD PERIODS?
MINE ARE PRETTY BAD.
OH, YEAH. SO BAD I'D RATHER BE DEAD.
ACTUALLY, IN HIGH SCHOOL...
...I PASSED OUT FROM THE PAIN AND HAD TO BE TAKEN AWAY IN AN AMBU-LANCE.
I WAS THINKING ABOUT GETTING A HYSTERECTOMY ALONG WITH MY SISTER WITH THE GENDER IDENTITY DISORDER.
IT WAS SO BAD, I WAS ON THE PILL FOR A WHILE.
WHOA. DOES THE PILL LESSEN THE PAIN?
A LITTLE. I'M NOT ON IT NOW, THOUGH.

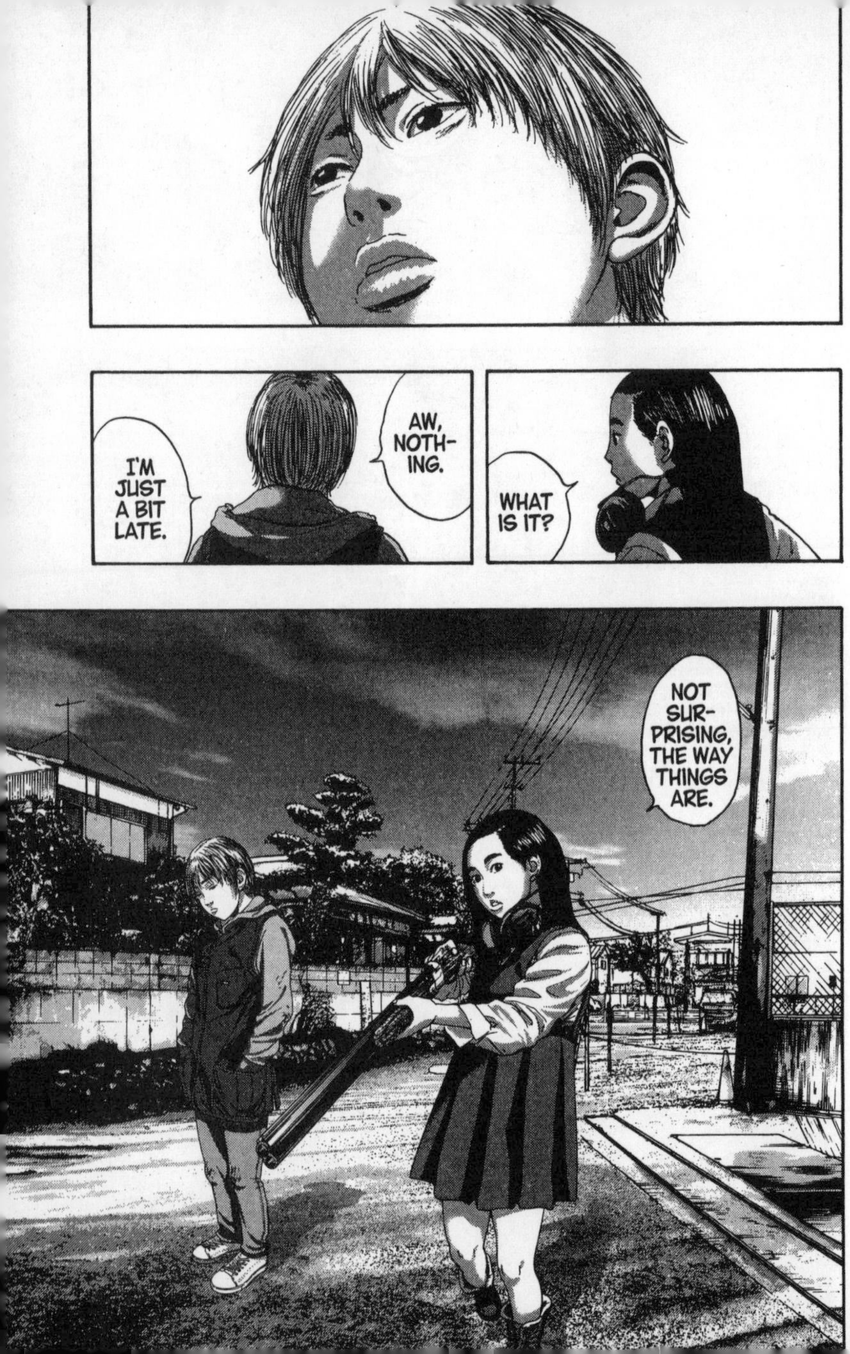
WHAT IS IT?
AW, NOTHING.
I'M JUST A BIT LATE.
NOT SURPRISING, THE WAY THINGS ARE.

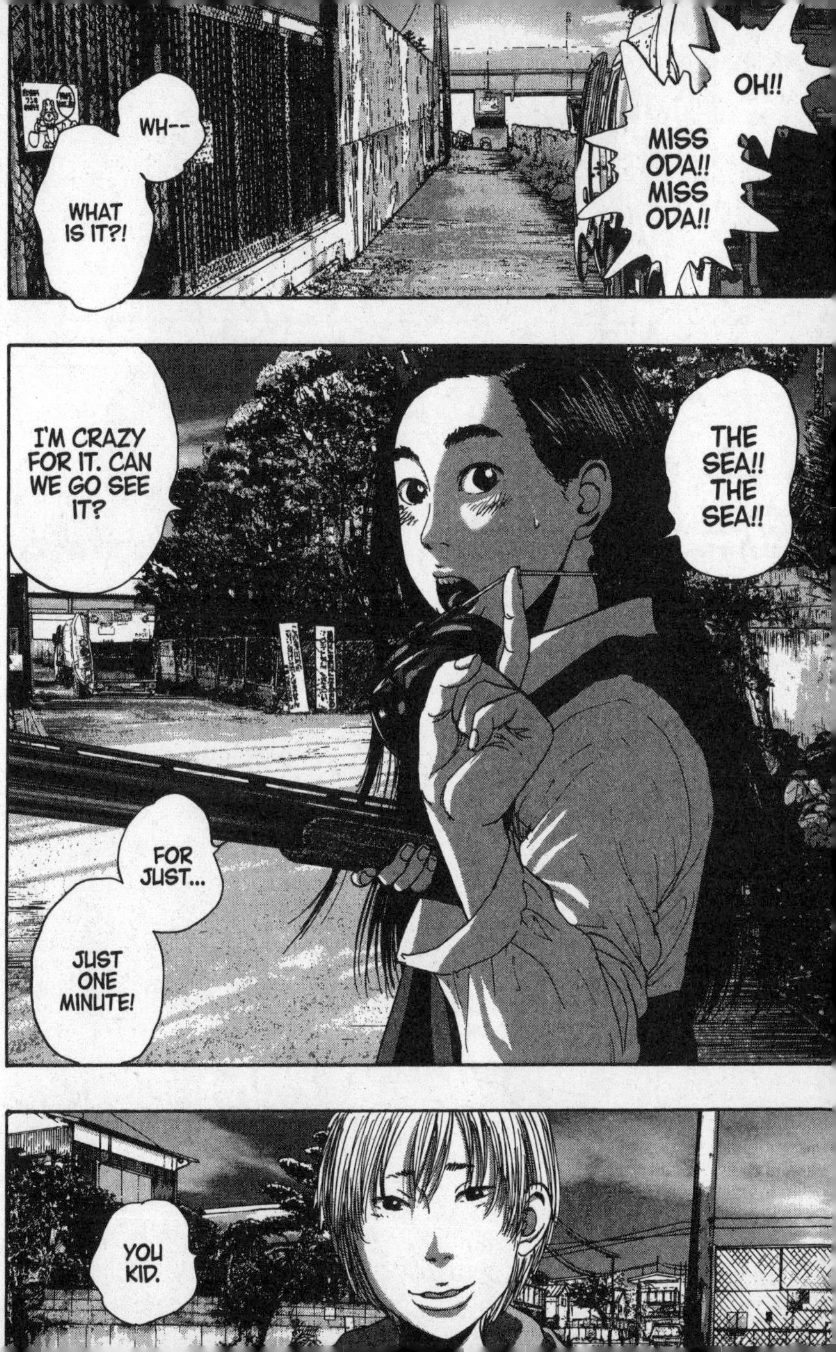
OH!!
MISS ODA!! MISS ODA!!
WH--
WHAT IS IT?!
THE SEA!! THE SEA!!
I'M CRAZY FOR IT. CAN WE GO SEE IT?
FOR JUST...
JUST ONE MINUTE!
YOU KID.

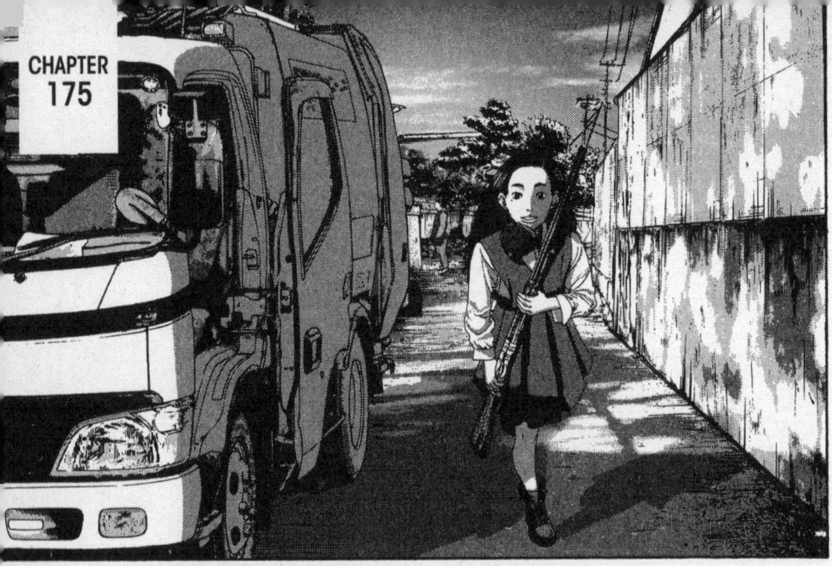
CHAPTER
175

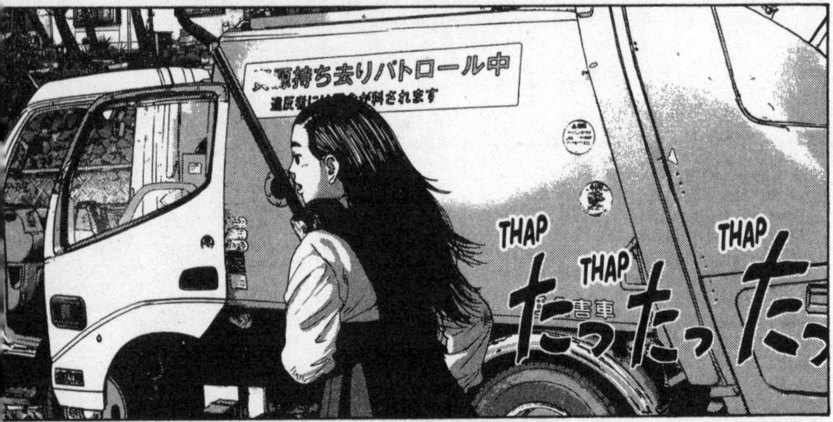
源持ち去りパトロール中
THAP
THAP
THAP
たったったっ

SIGN ON VEHICLE: ON PATROL FOR RESOURCES

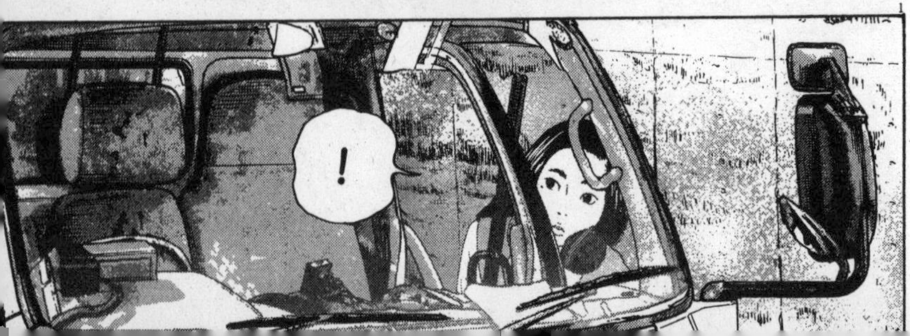
!

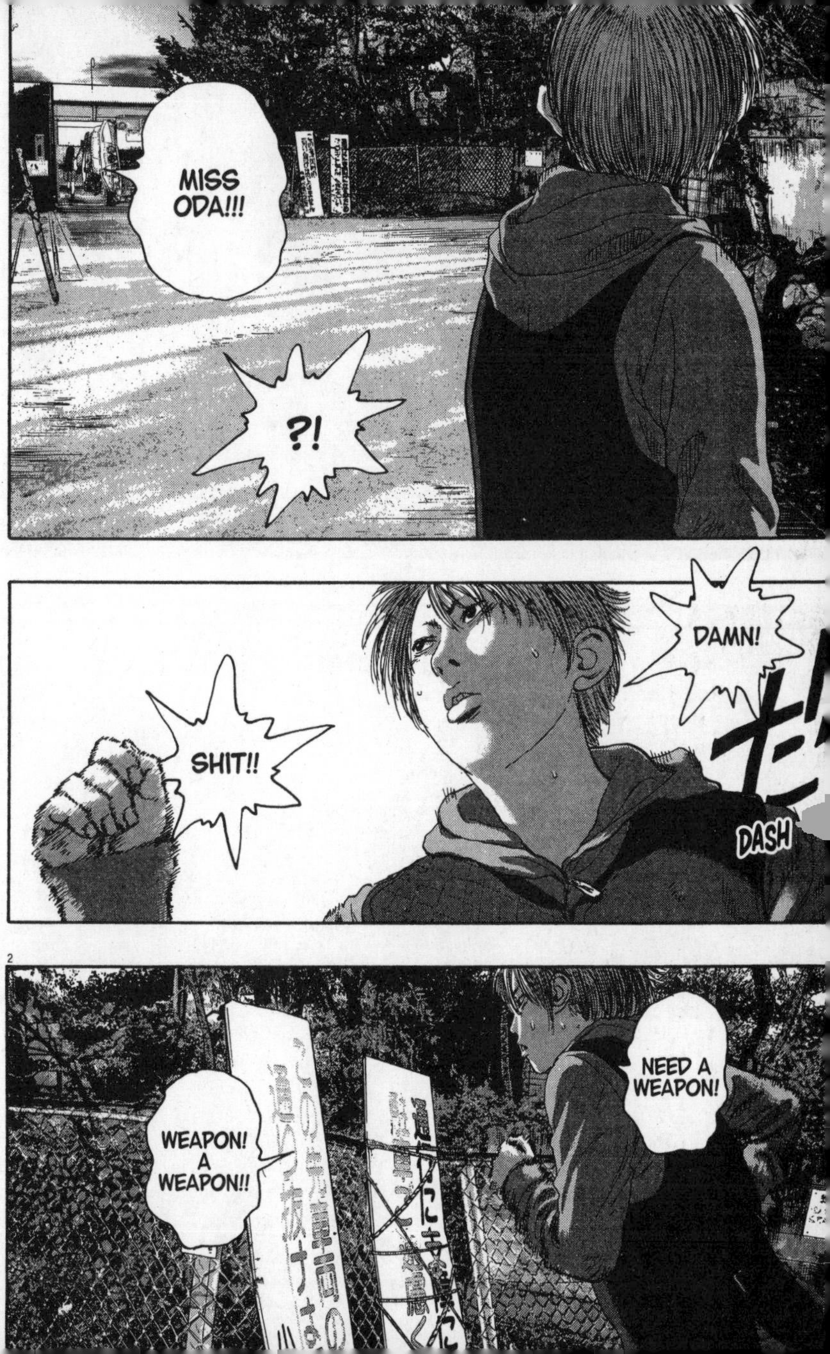
MISS ODA!!!
?!
DAMN!
DASH
SHIT!!
NEED A WEAPON!
WEAPON! A WEAPON!!

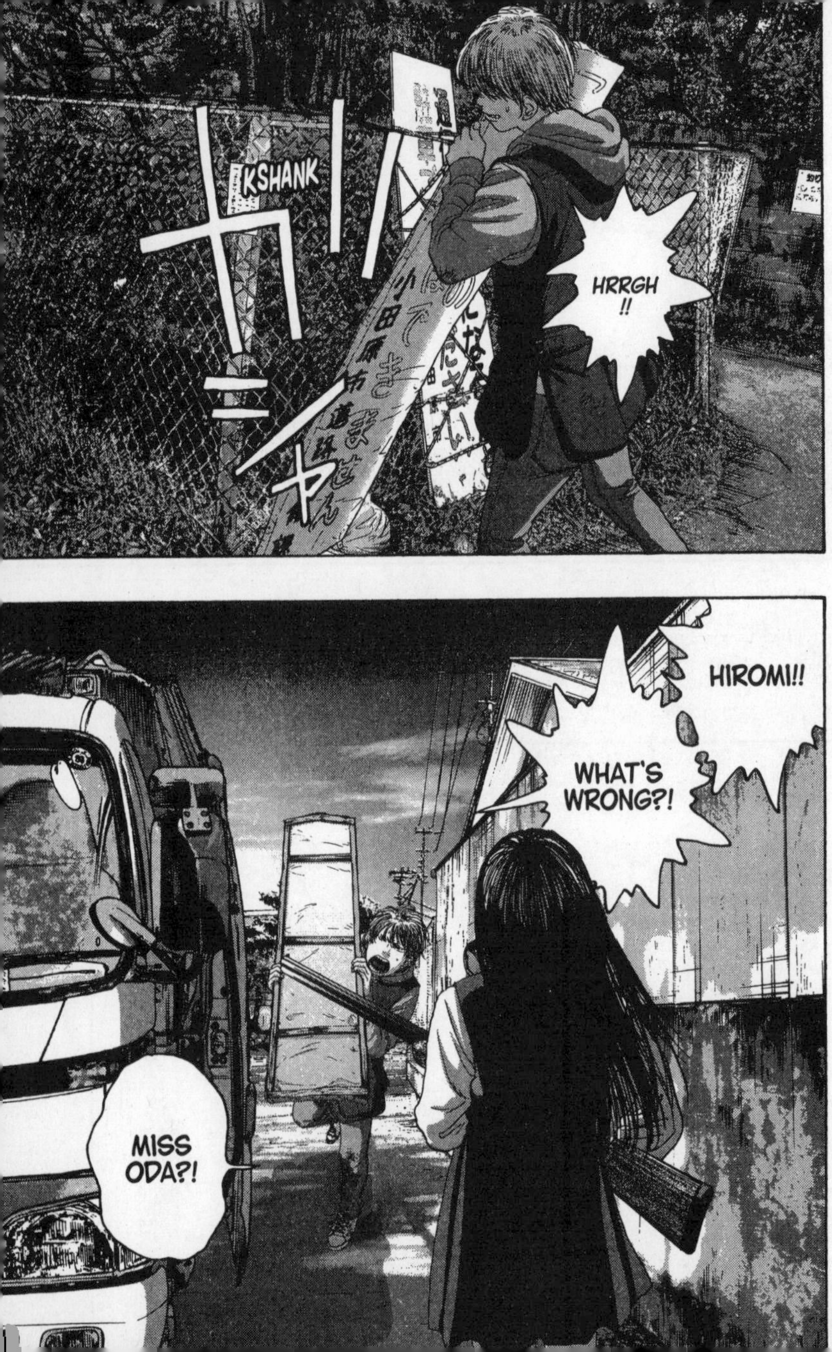
KSHANK
HRRGH!!
HIROMI!!
WHAT'S WRONG?!
MISS ODA?!

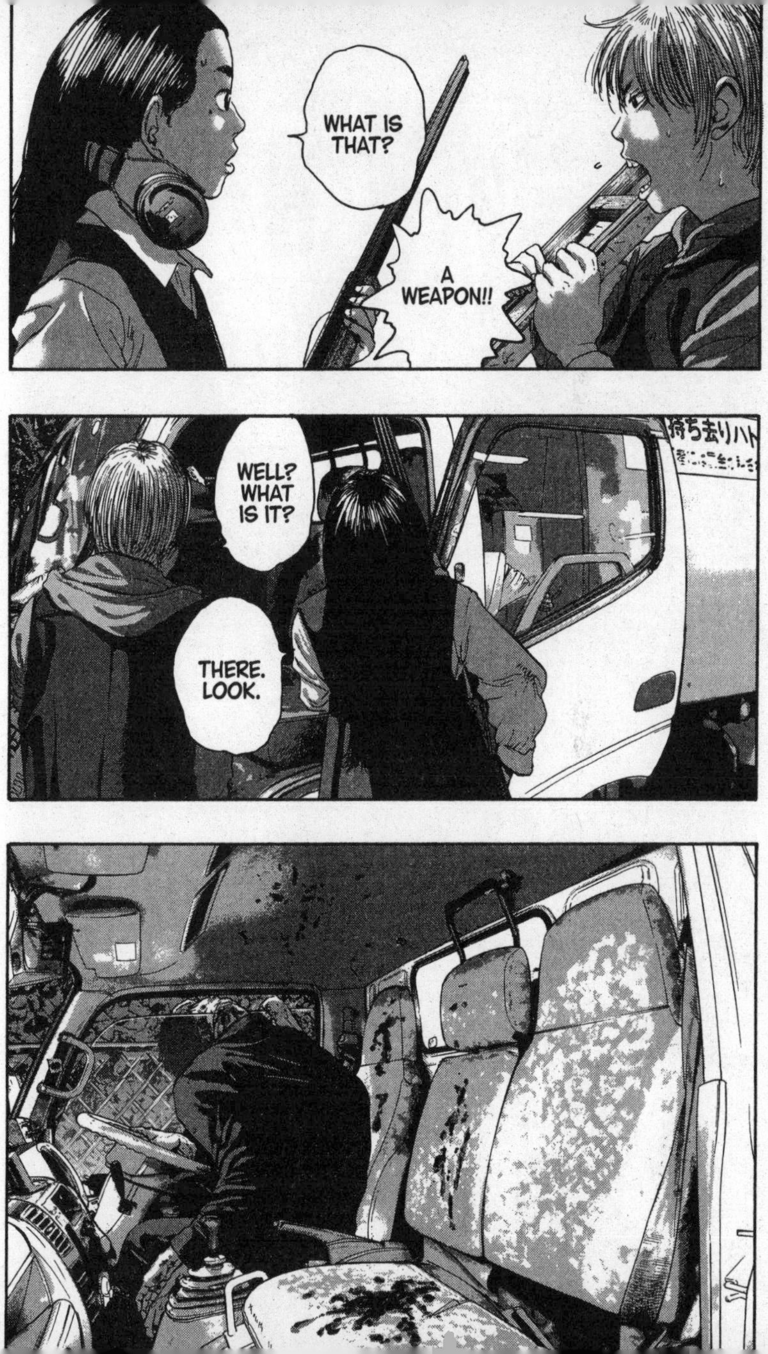
WHAT IS THAT?
A WEAPON!!
持ち去りハト
WELL? WHAT IS IT?
THERE. LOOK.

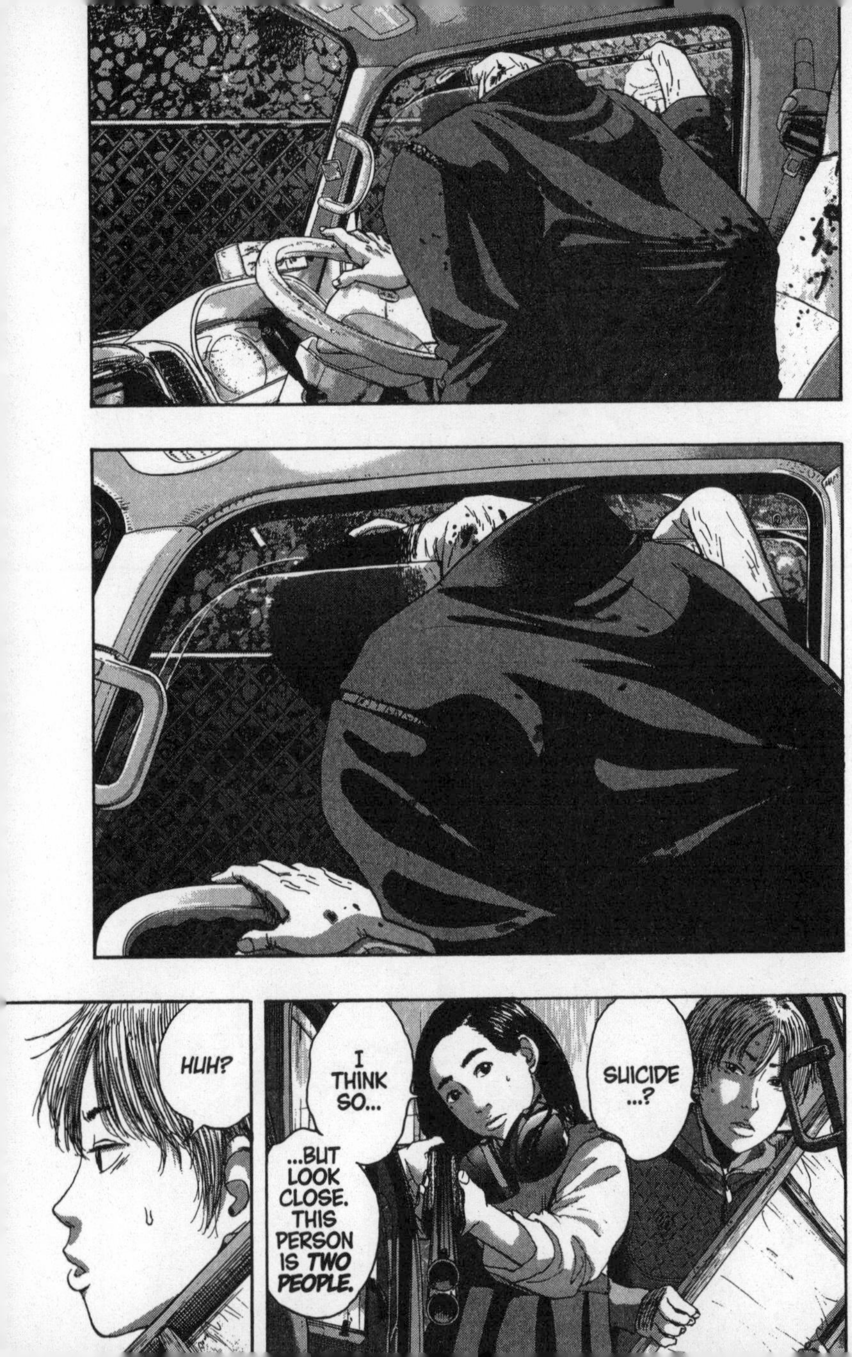
SUICIDE ...?
I THINK SO...
...BUT LOOK CLOSE. THIS PERSON IS *TWO PEOPLE.*
HUH?

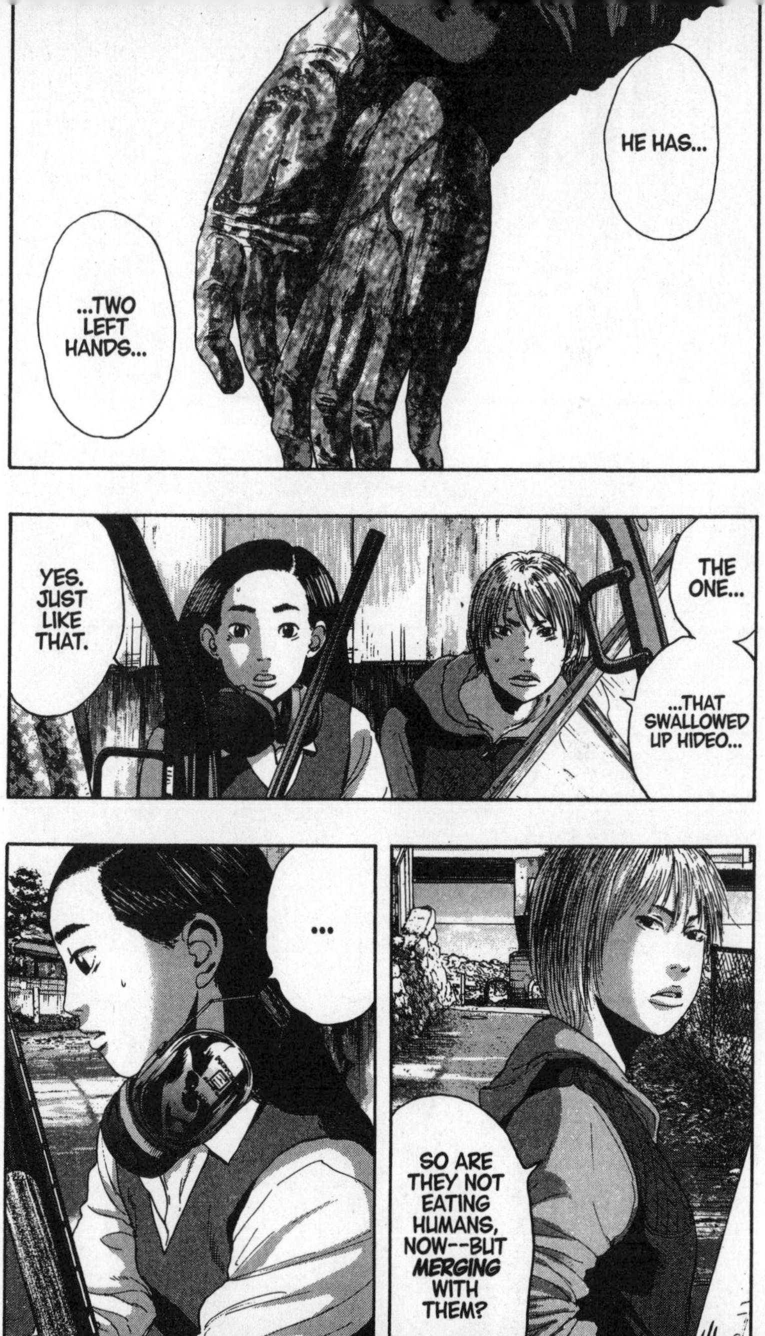
HE HAS...
...TWO LEFT HANDS...
THE ONE...
...THAT SWALLOWED UP HIDEO...
YES. JUST LIKE THAT.
SO ARE THEY NOT EATING HUMANS, NOW--BUT *MERGING* WITH THEM?
...

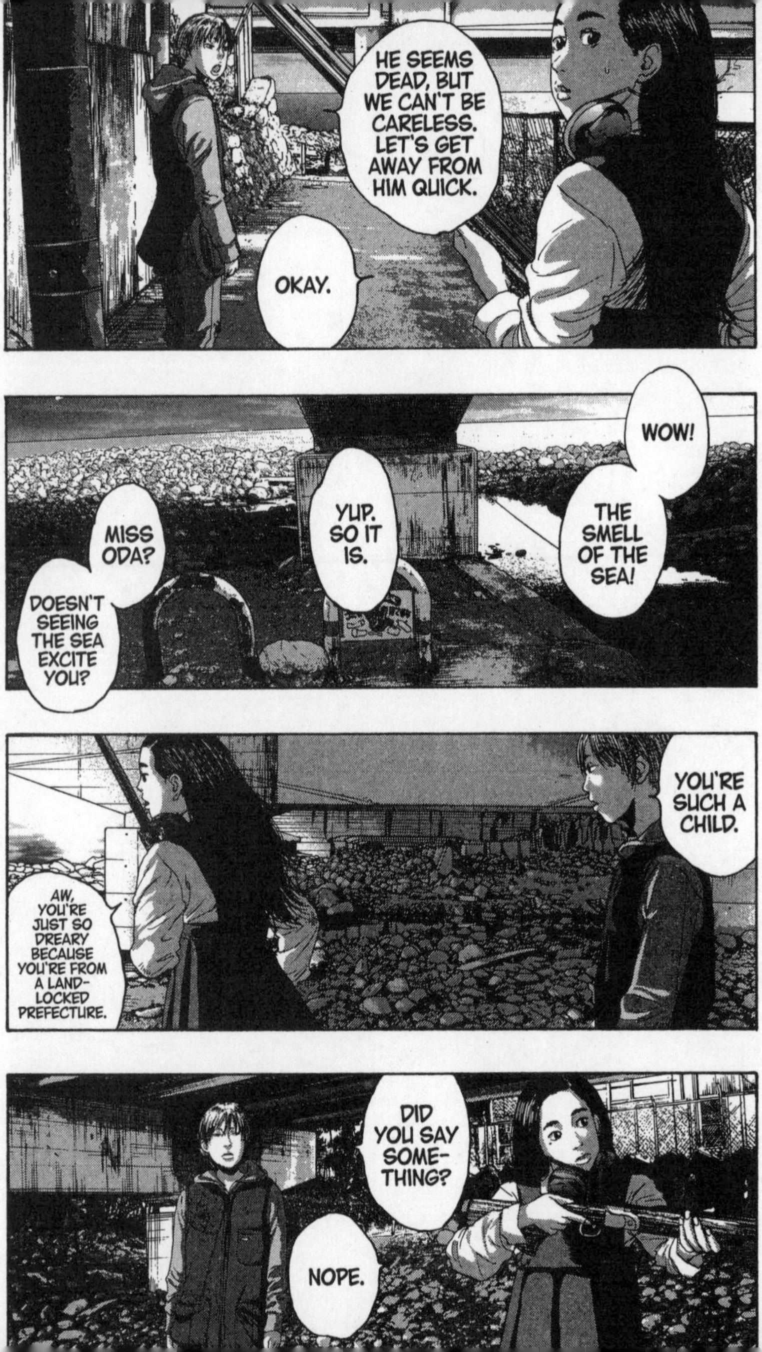
HE SEEMS DEAD, BUT WE CAN'T BE CARELESS. LET'S GET AWAY FROM HIM QUICK.
OKAY.
WOW!
THE SMELL OF THE SEA!
YUP. SO IT IS.
MISS ODA?
DOESN'T SEEING THE SEA EXCITE YOU?
YOU'RE SUCH A CHILD.
AW, YOU'RE JUST SO DREARY BECAUSE YOU'RE FROM A LAND-LOCKED PREFECTURE.
DID YOU SAY SOME-THING?
NOPE.

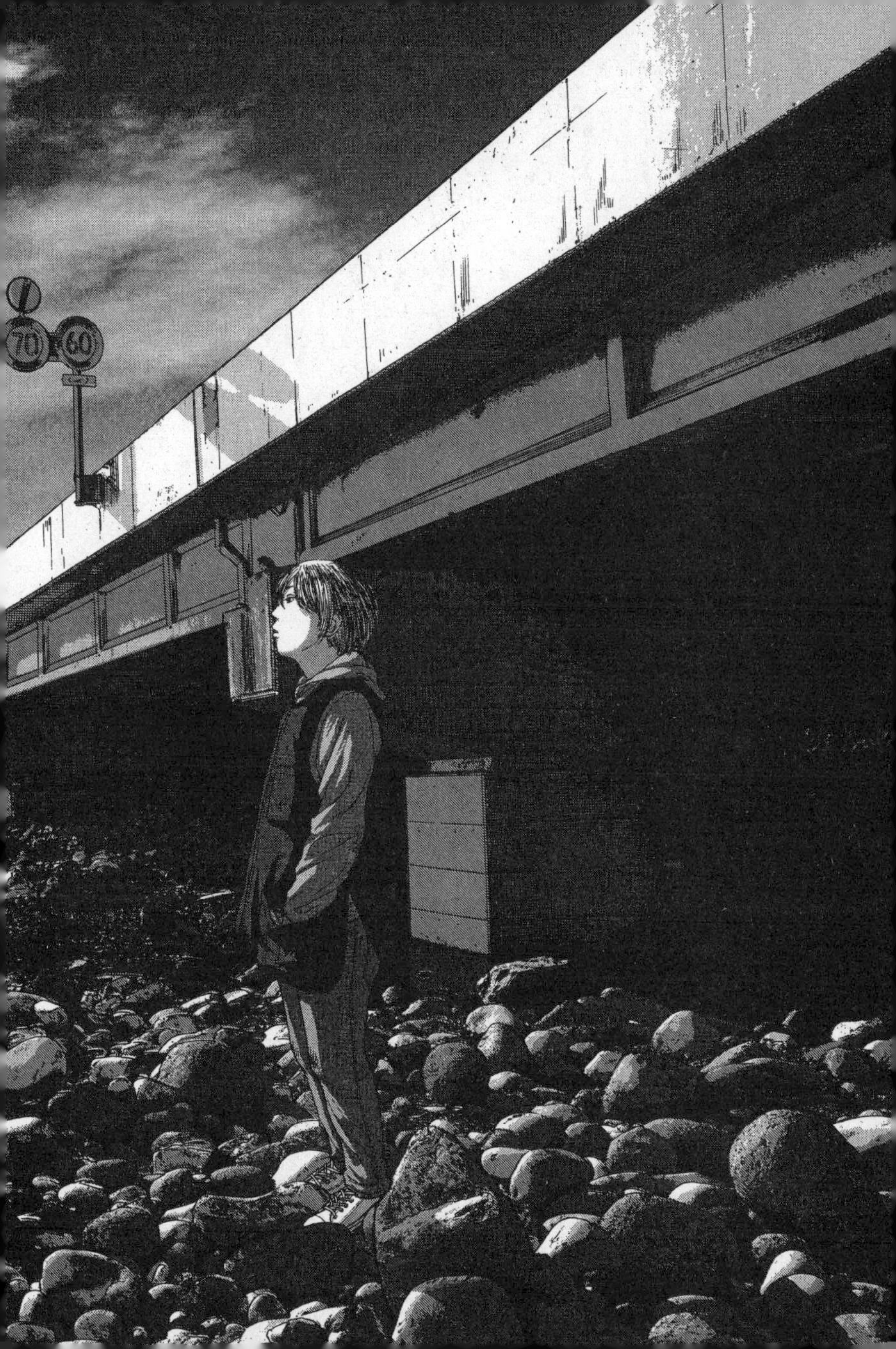
70
60

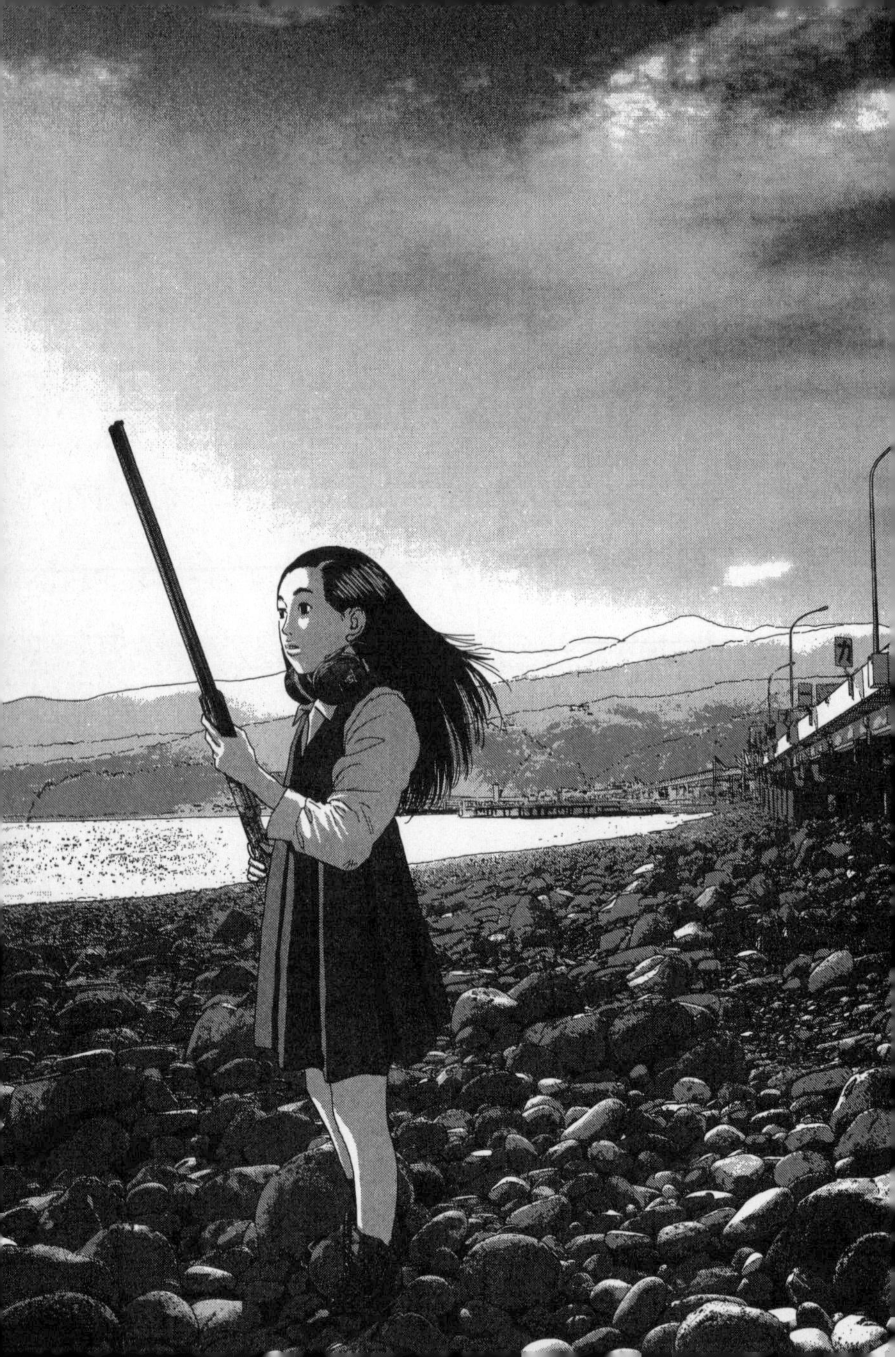

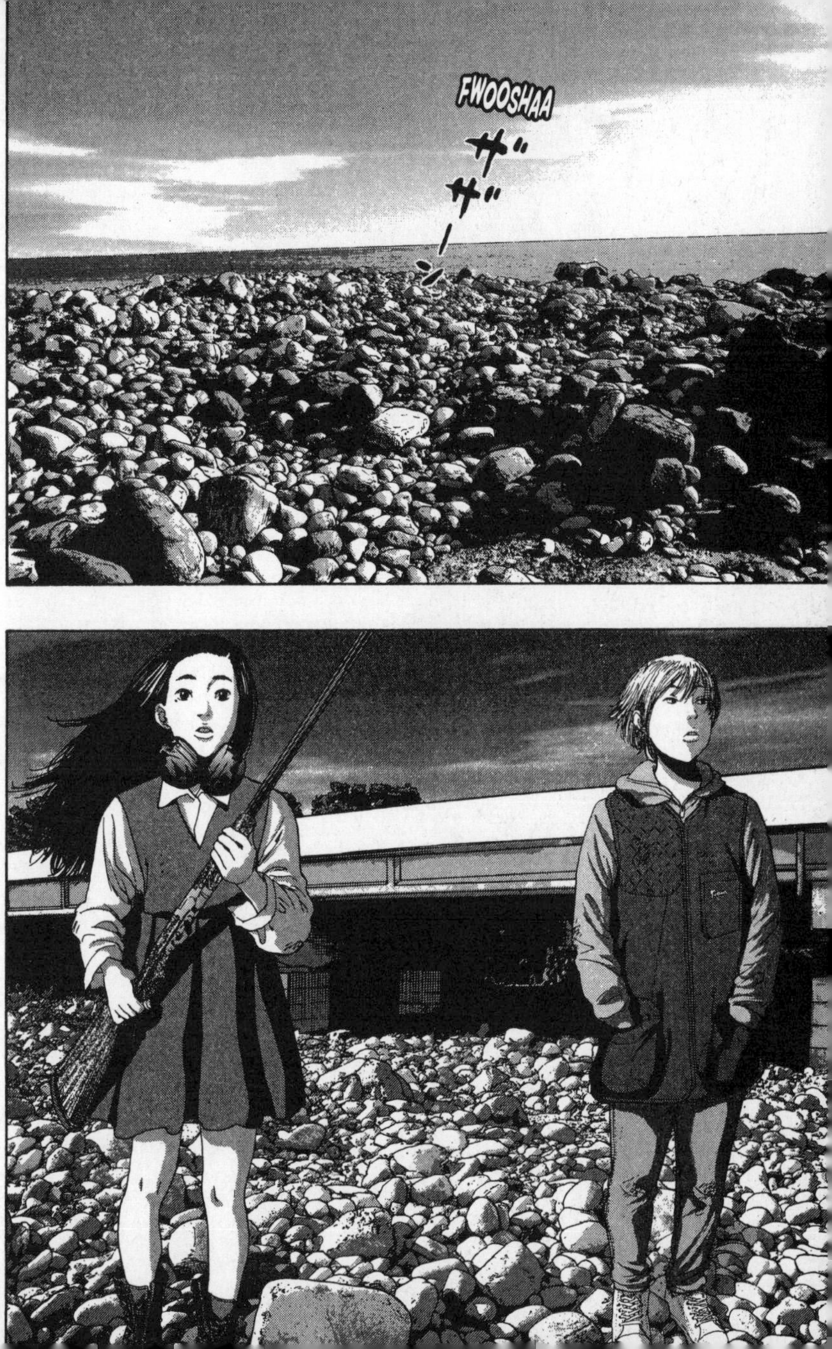
FWOOSHAA
ザザーッ

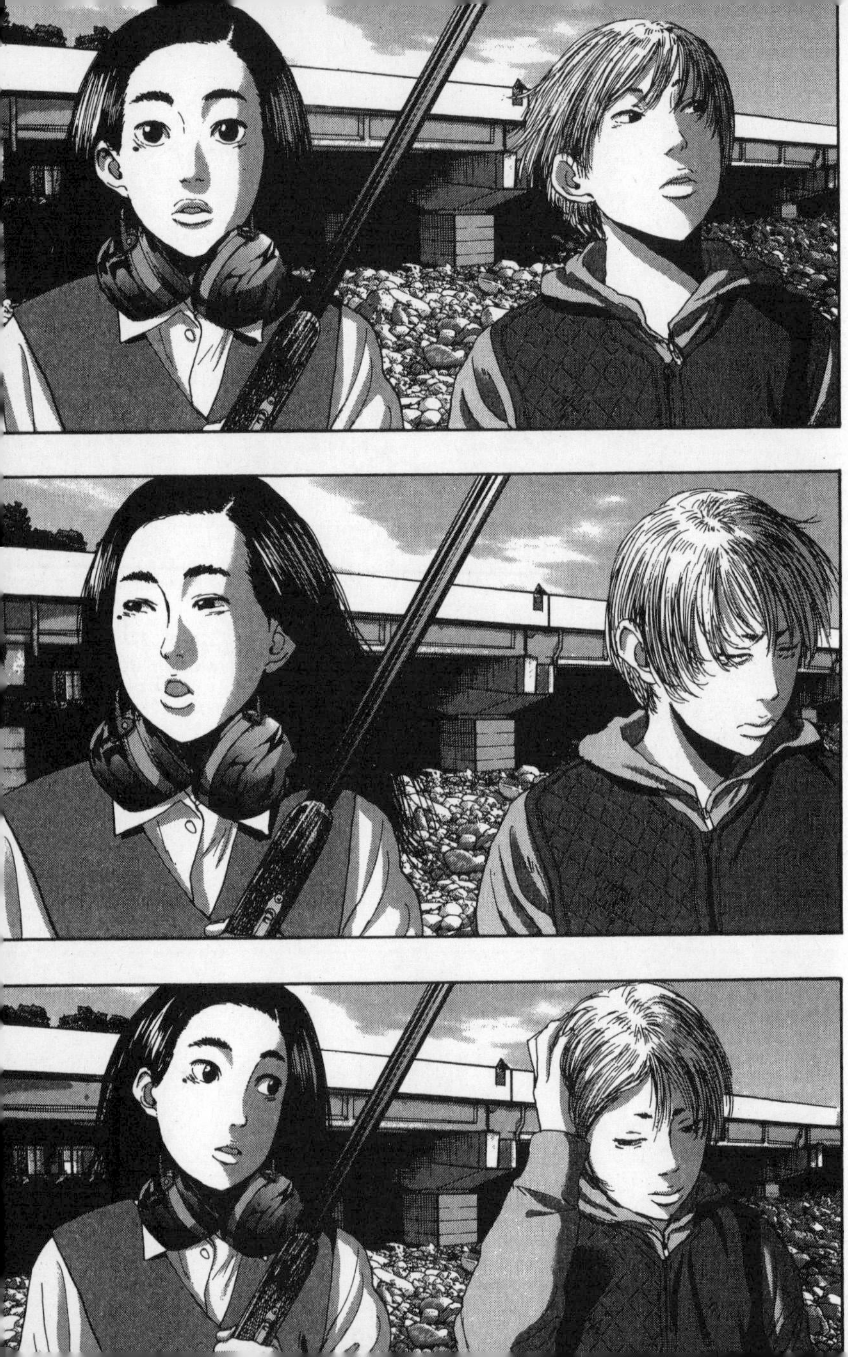

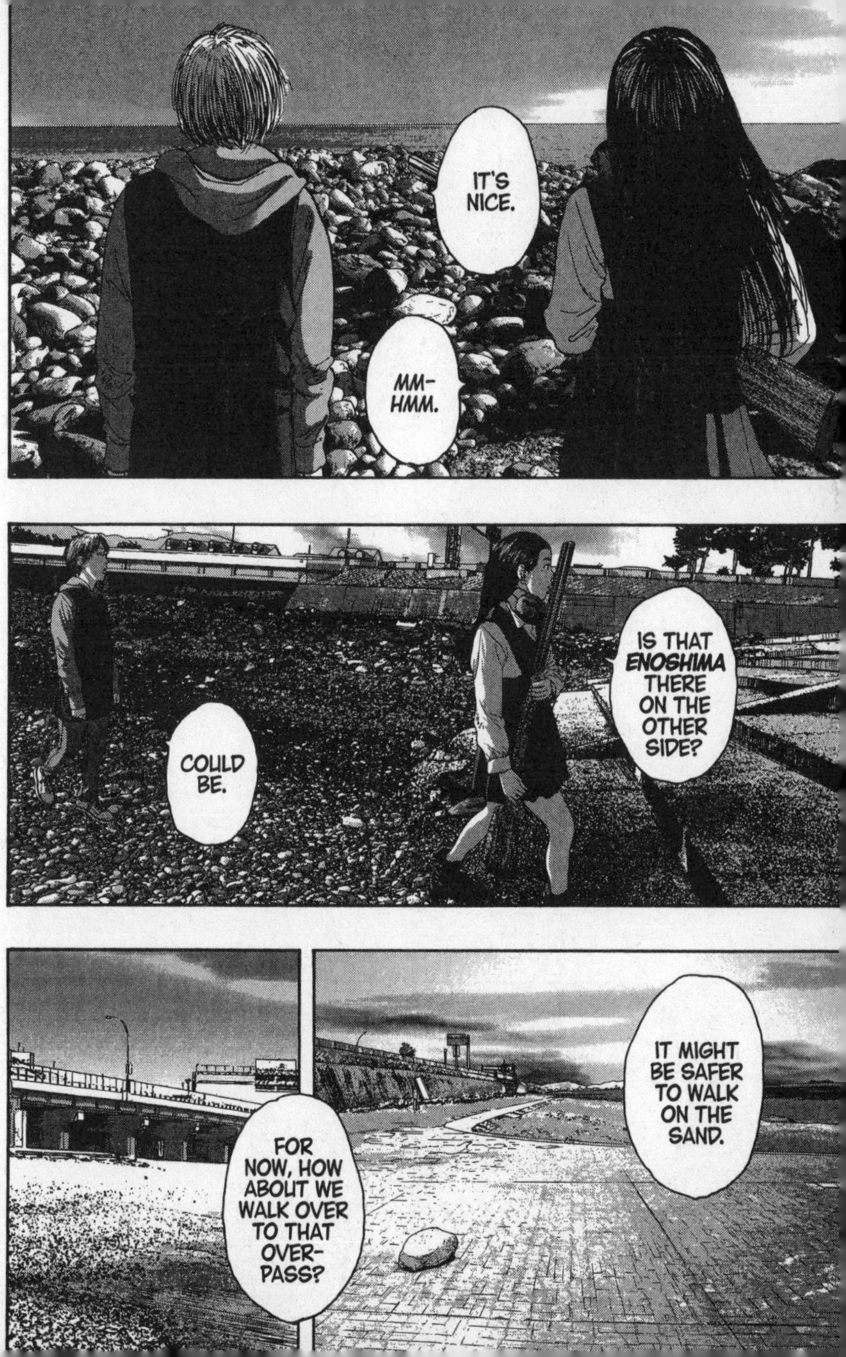
IT'S NICE.
MM-HMM.
IS THAT ENOSHIMA THERE ON THE OTHER SIDE?
COULD BE.
IT MIGHT BE SAFER TO WALK ON THE SAND.
FOR NOW, HOW ABOUT WE WALK OVER TO THAT OVER-PASS?

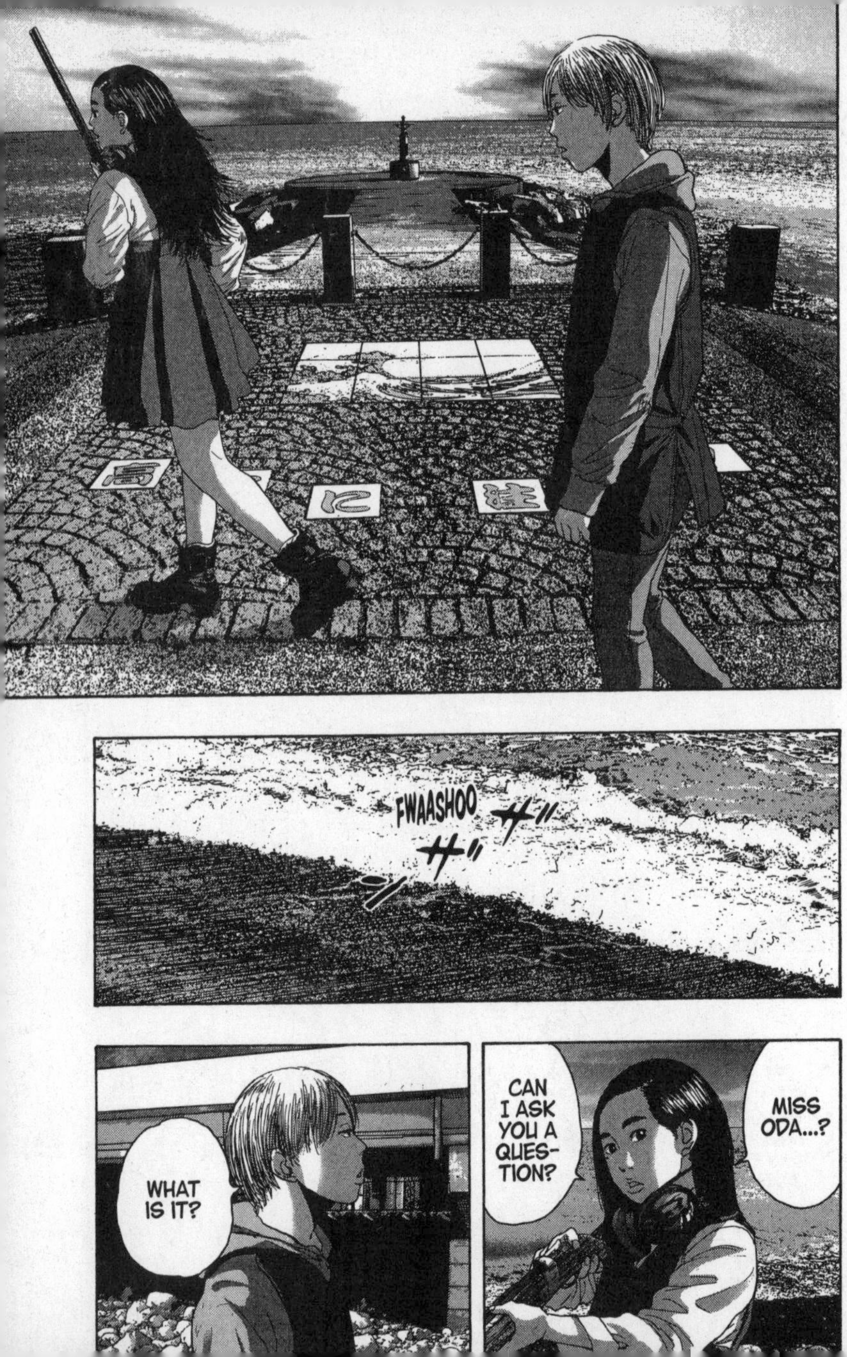
FWAASHOO
MISS ODA...?
CAN I ASK YOU A QUESTION?
WHAT IS IT?

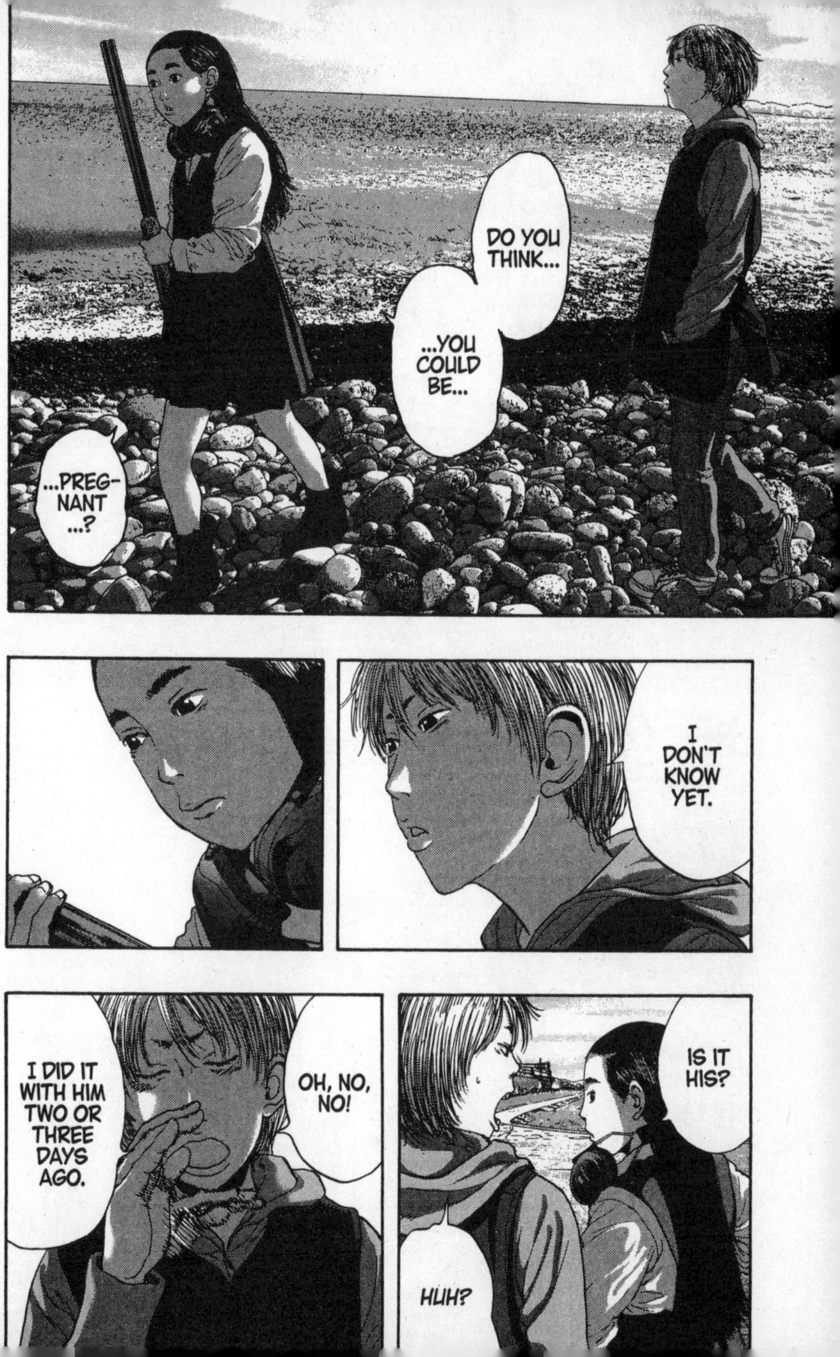
DO YOU THINK...
...YOU COULD BE...
...PREG-NANT ...?
I DON'T KNOW YET.
IS IT HIS?
HUH?
OH, NO, NO!
I DID IT WITH HIM TWO OR THREE DAYS AGO.

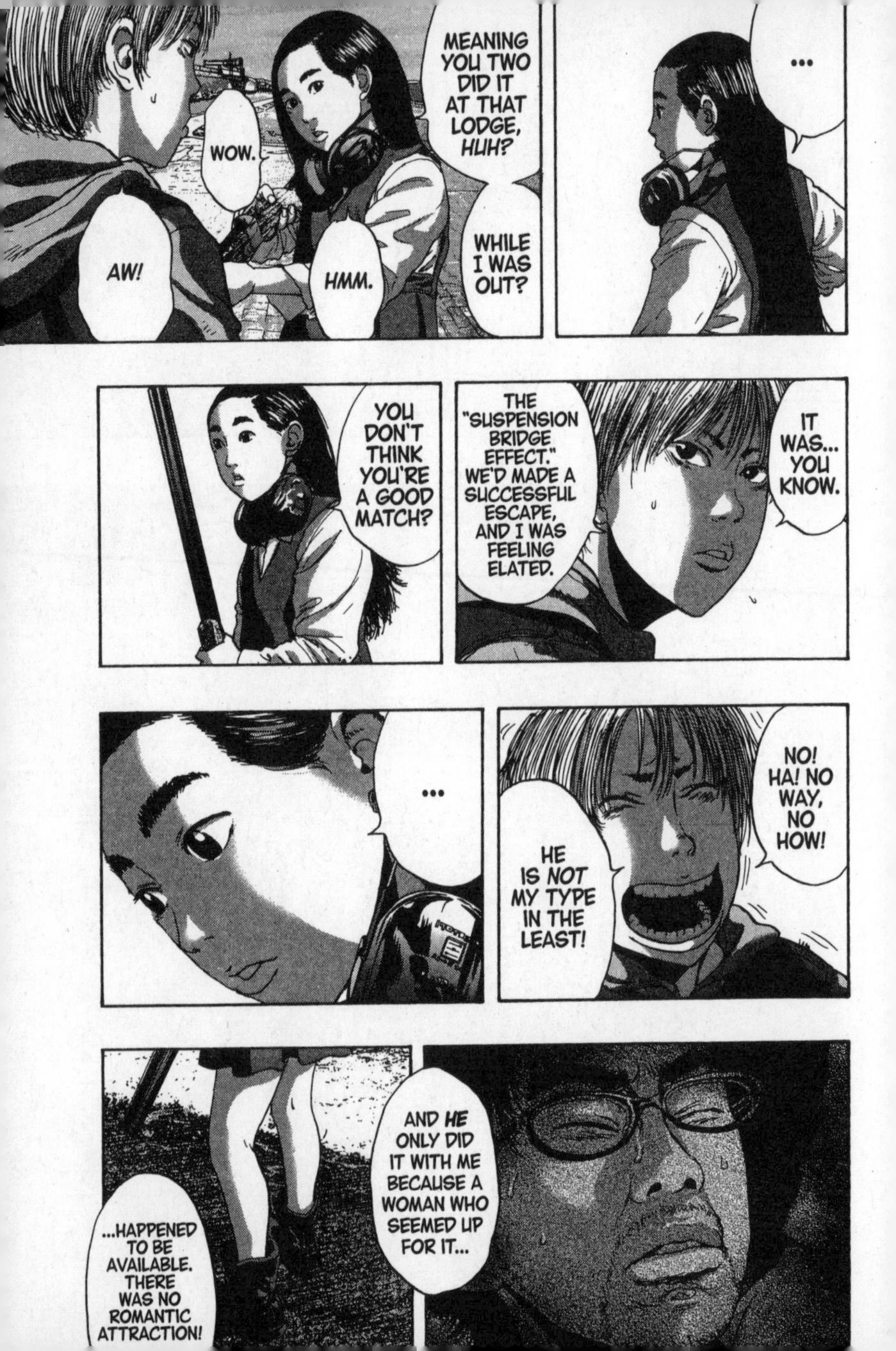
...
MEANING YOU TWO DID IT AT THAT LODGE, HUH?
WOW.
WHILE I WAS OUT?
HMM.
AW!
IT WAS... YOU KNOW.
THE "SUSPENSION BRIDGE EFFECT." WE'D MADE A SUCCESSFUL ESCAPE, AND I WAS FEELING ELATED.
YOU DON'T THINK YOU'RE A GOOD MATCH?
NO! HA! NO WAY, NO HOW!
HE IS *NOT* MY TYPE IN THE LEAST!
...
AND *HE* ONLY DID IT WITH ME BECAUSE A WOMAN WHO SEEMED UP FOR IT...
...HAPPENED TO BE AVAILABLE. THERE WAS NO ROMANTIC ATTRACTION!

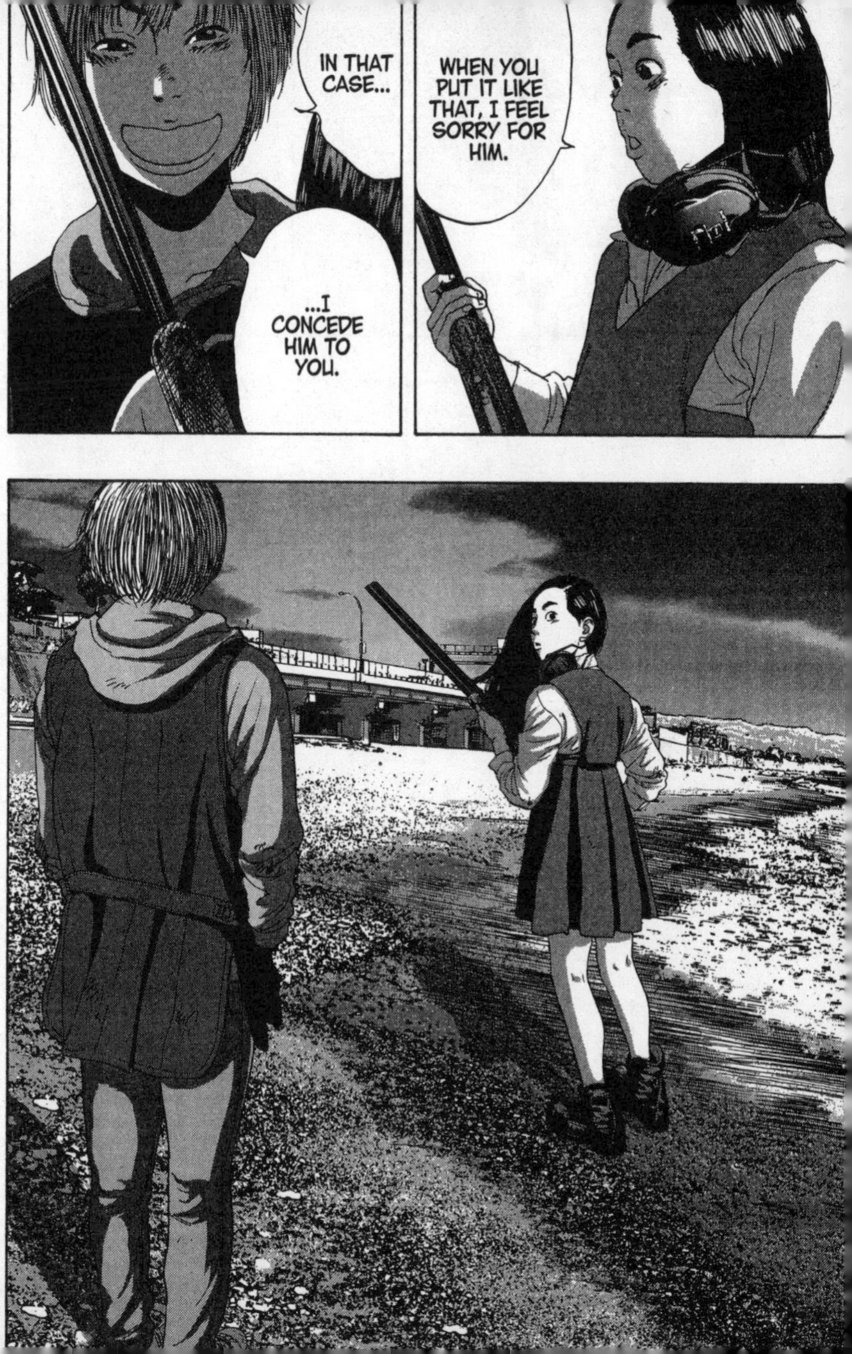
WHEN YOU PUT IT LIKE THAT, I FEEL SORRY FOR HIM.
IN THAT CASE...
...I CONCEDE HIM TO YOU.

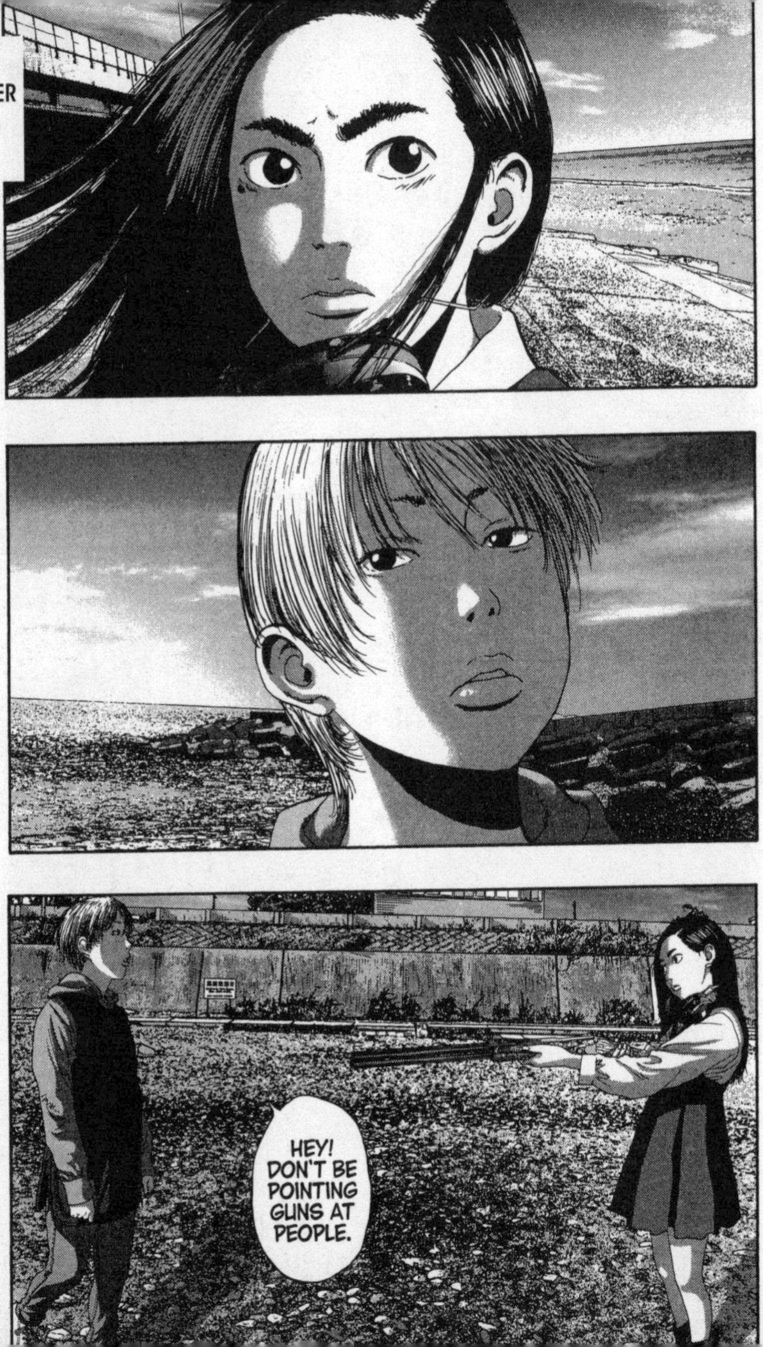
CHAPTER 176
HEY! DON'T BE POINTING GUNS AT PEOPLE.

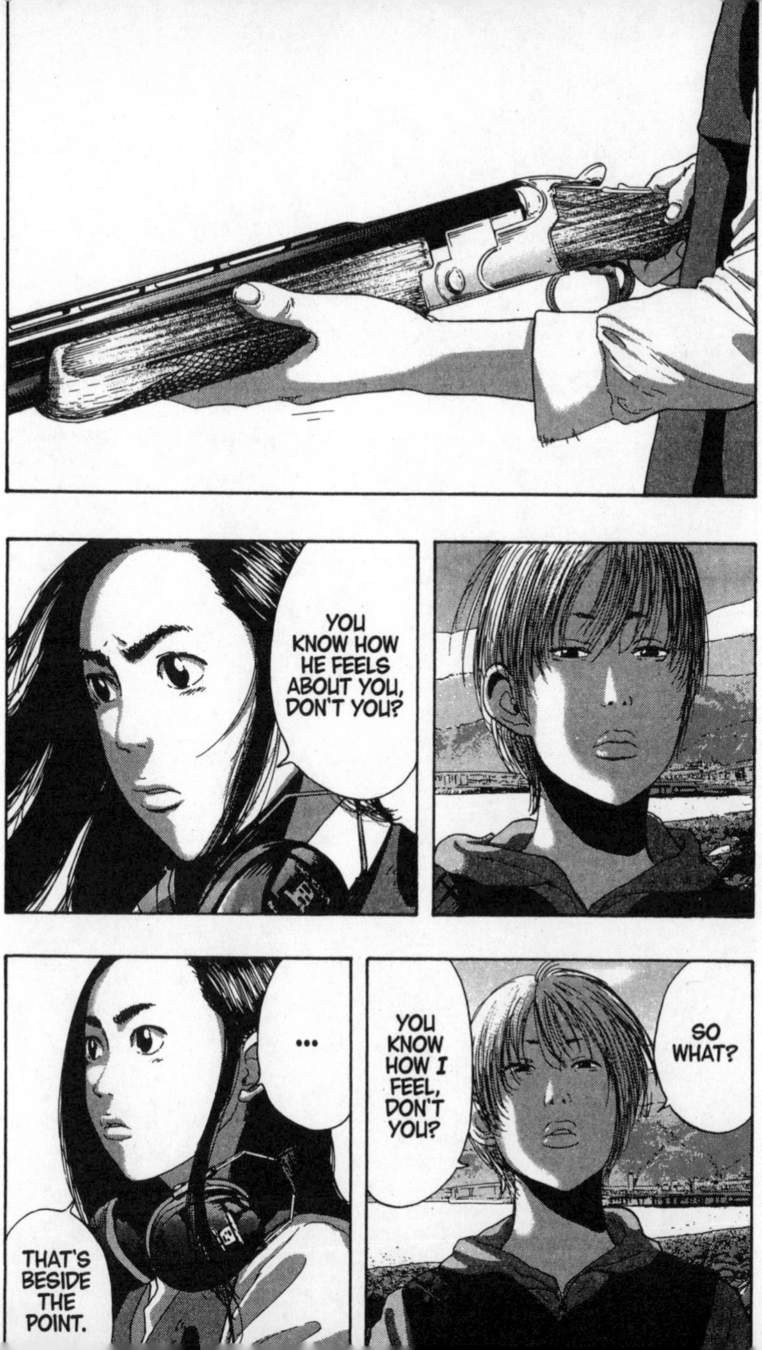
YOU KNOW HOW HE FEELS ABOUT YOU, DON'T YOU?
SO WHAT?
YOU KNOW HOW I FEEL, DON'T YOU?
...
THAT'S BESIDE THE POINT.

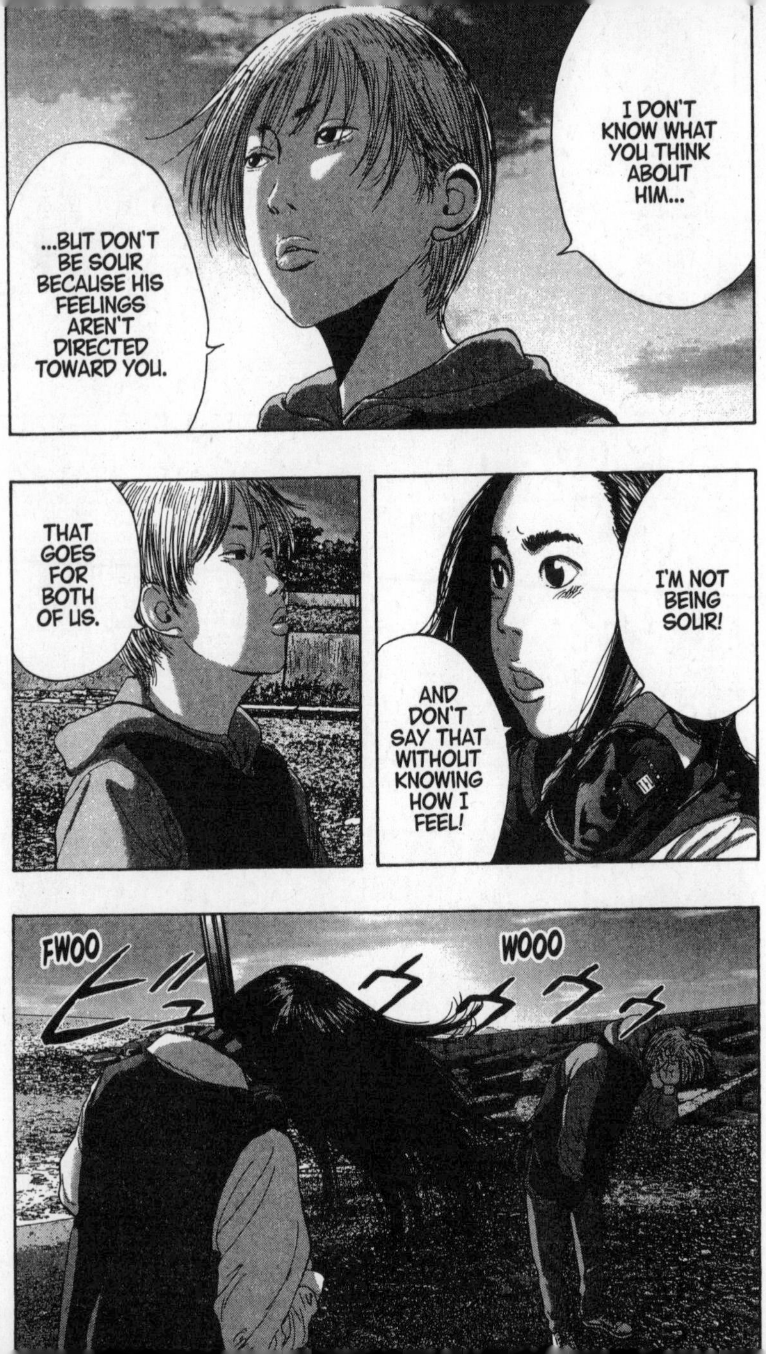
I DON'T KNOW WHAT YOU THINK ABOUT HIM...
...BUT DON'T BE SOUR BECAUSE HIS FEELINGS AREN'T DIRECTED TOWARD YOU.
I'M NOT BEING SOUR!
AND DON'T SAY THAT WITHOUT KNOWING HOW I FEEL!
THAT GOES FOR BOTH OF US.
FWOO WOOO

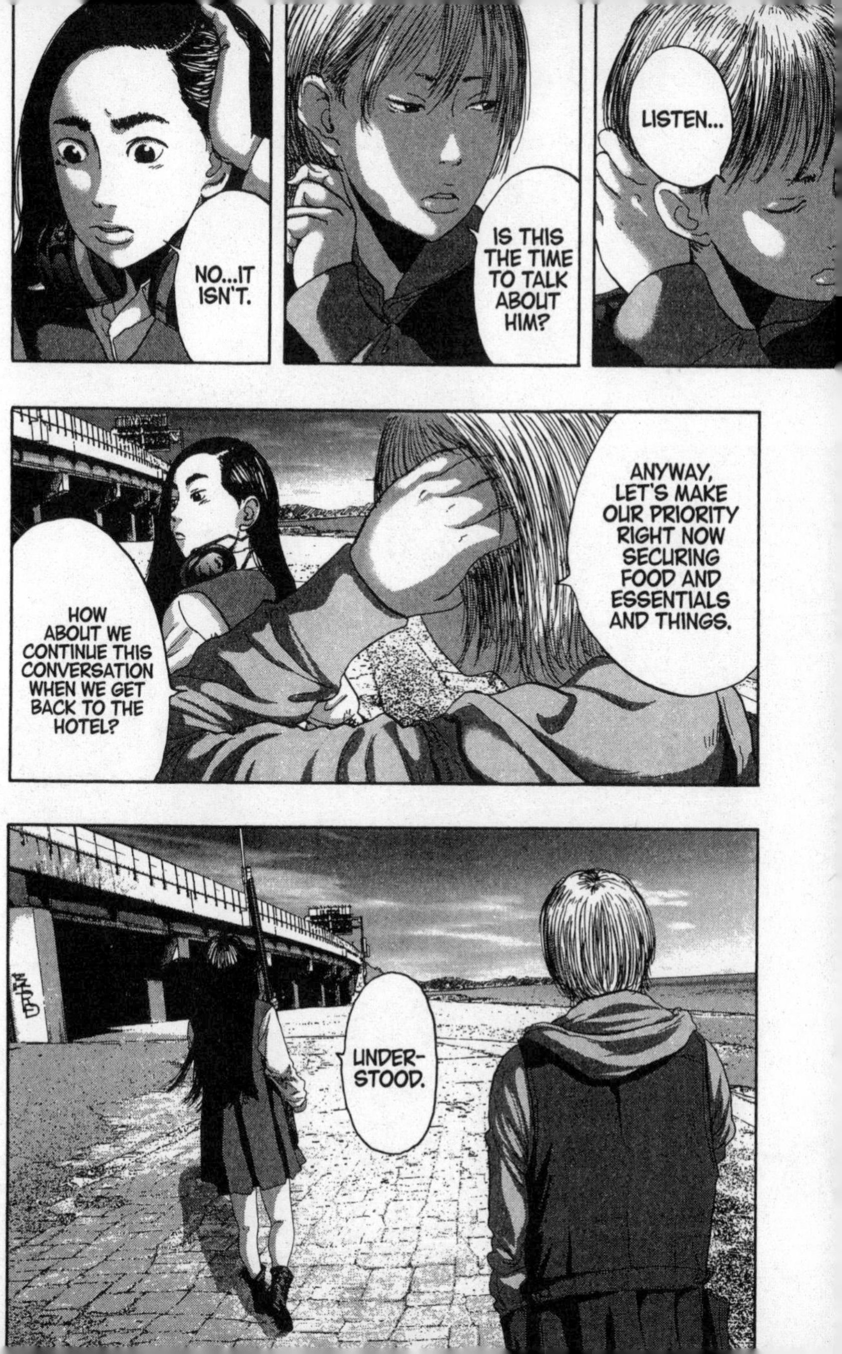
LISTEN...
IS THIS THE TIME TO TALK ABOUT HIM?
NO...IT ISN'T.
ANYWAY, LET'S MAKE OUR PRIORITY RIGHT NOW SECURING FOOD AND ESSENTIALS AND THINGS.
HOW ABOUT WE CONTINUE THIS CONVERSATION WHEN WE GET BACK TO THE HOTEL?
UNDER-STOOD.

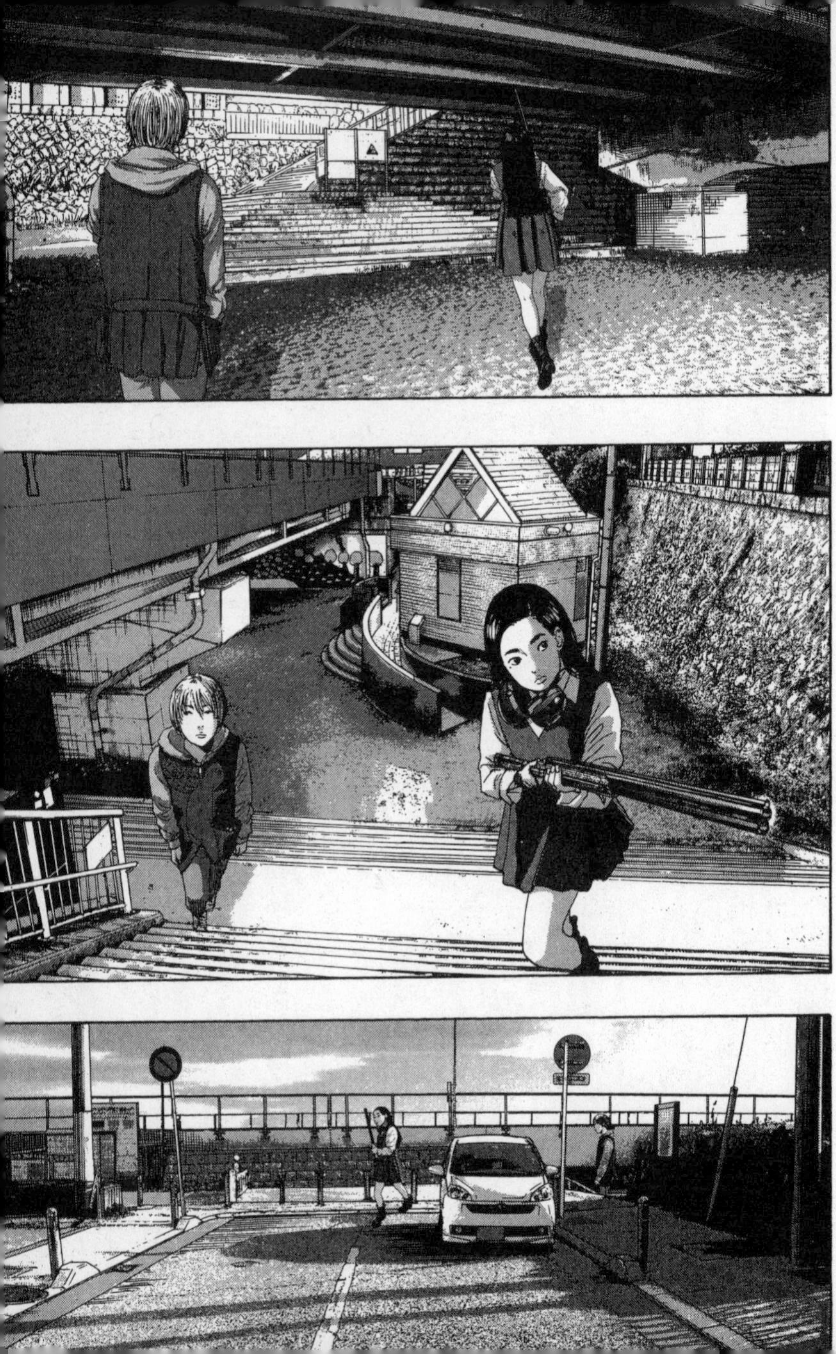

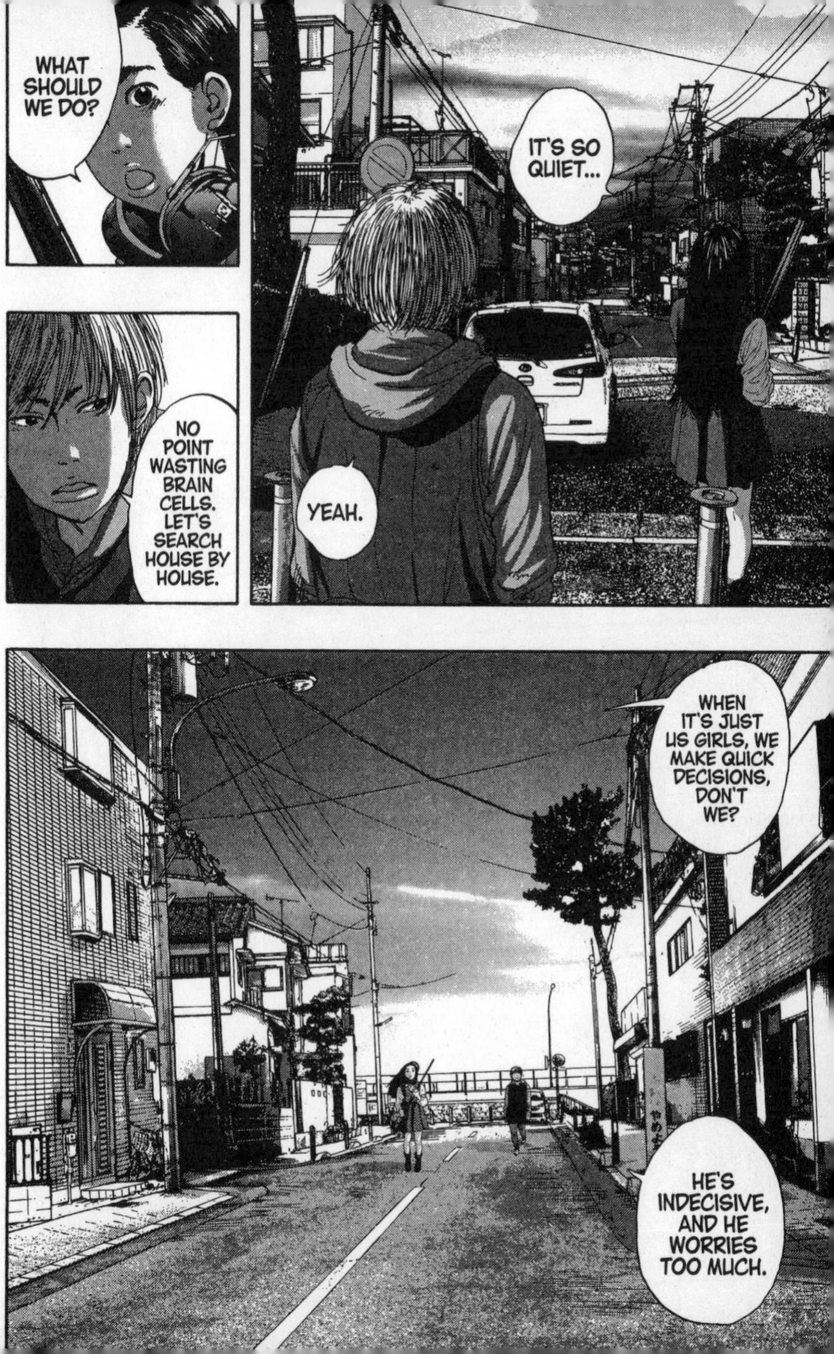
IT'S SO QUIET...
YEAH.
WHAT SHOULD WE DO?
NO POINT WASTING BRAIN CELLS. LET'S SEARCH HOUSE BY HOUSE.
WHEN IT'S JUST US GIRLS, WE MAKE QUICK DECISIONS, DON'T WE?
HE'S INDECISIVE, AND HE WORRIES TOO MUCH.

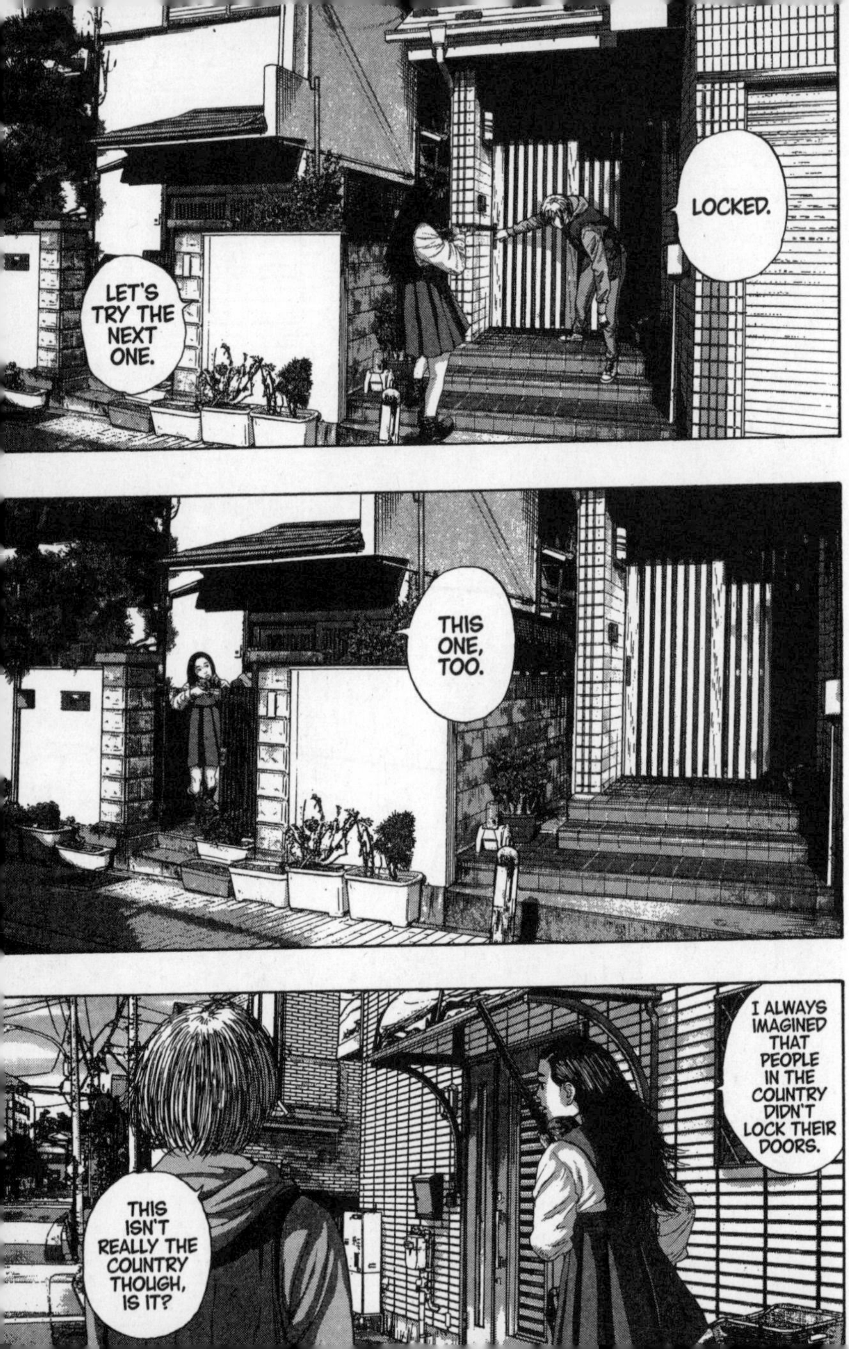
LOCKED.
LET'S TRY THE NEXT ONE.
THIS ONE, TOO.
I ALWAYS IMAGINED THAT PEOPLE IN THE COUNTRY DIDN'T LOCK THEIR DOORS.
THIS ISN'T REALLY THE COUNTRY THOUGH, IS IT?

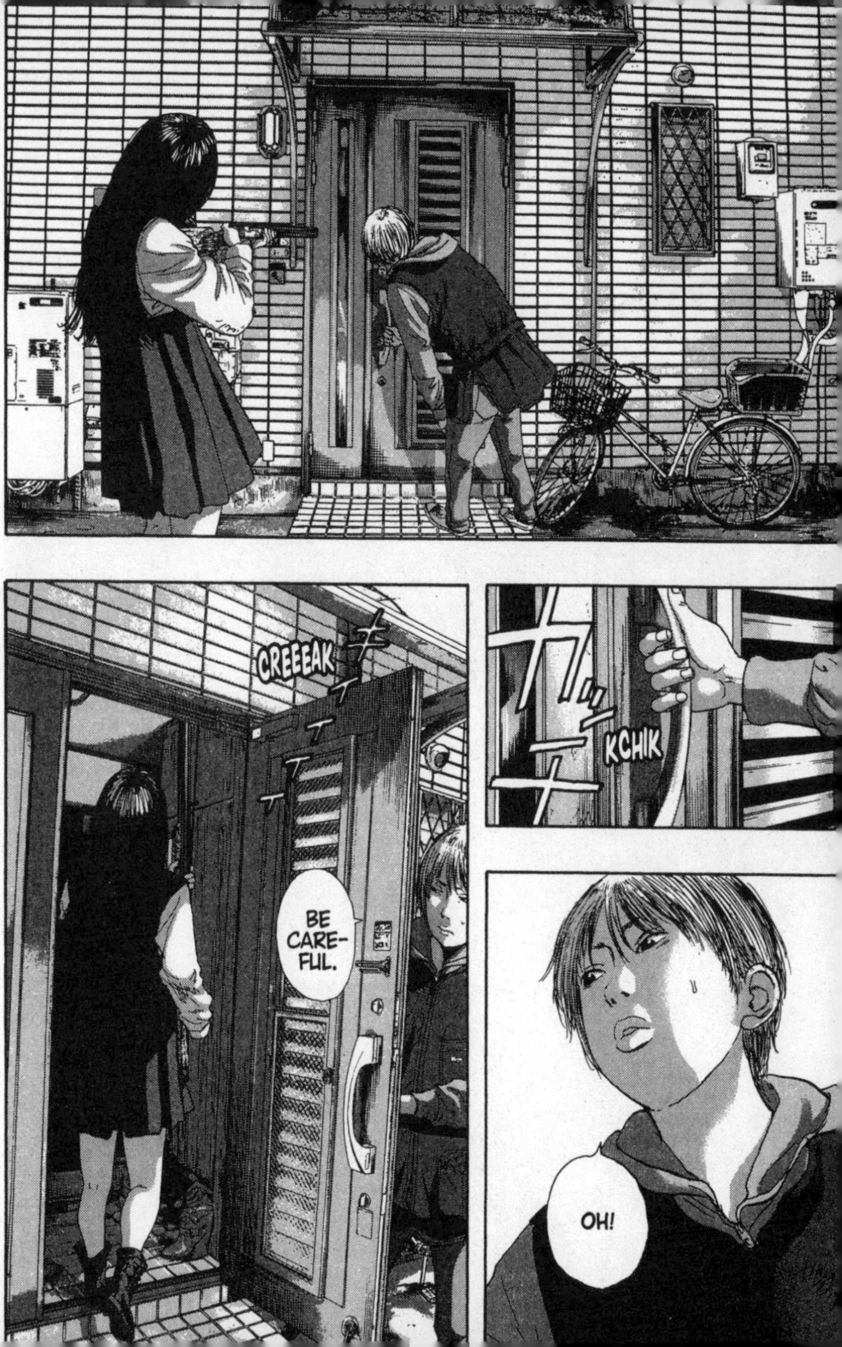
KCHIK
OH!
CREEEAK
BE CAREFUL.

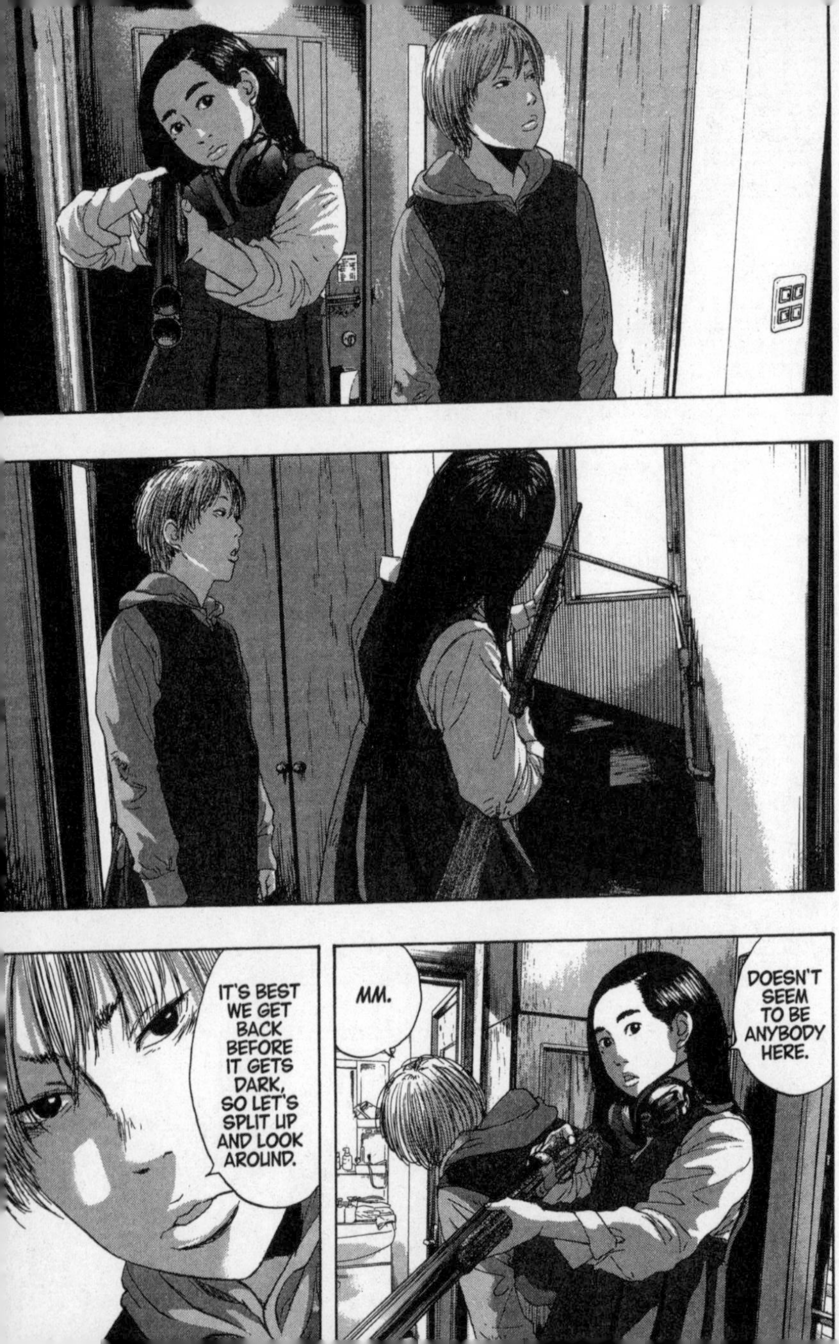
DOESN'T SEEM TO BE ANYBODY HERE.
MM.
IT'S BEST WE GET BACK BEFORE IT GETS DARK, SO LET'S SPLIT UP AND LOOK AROUND.

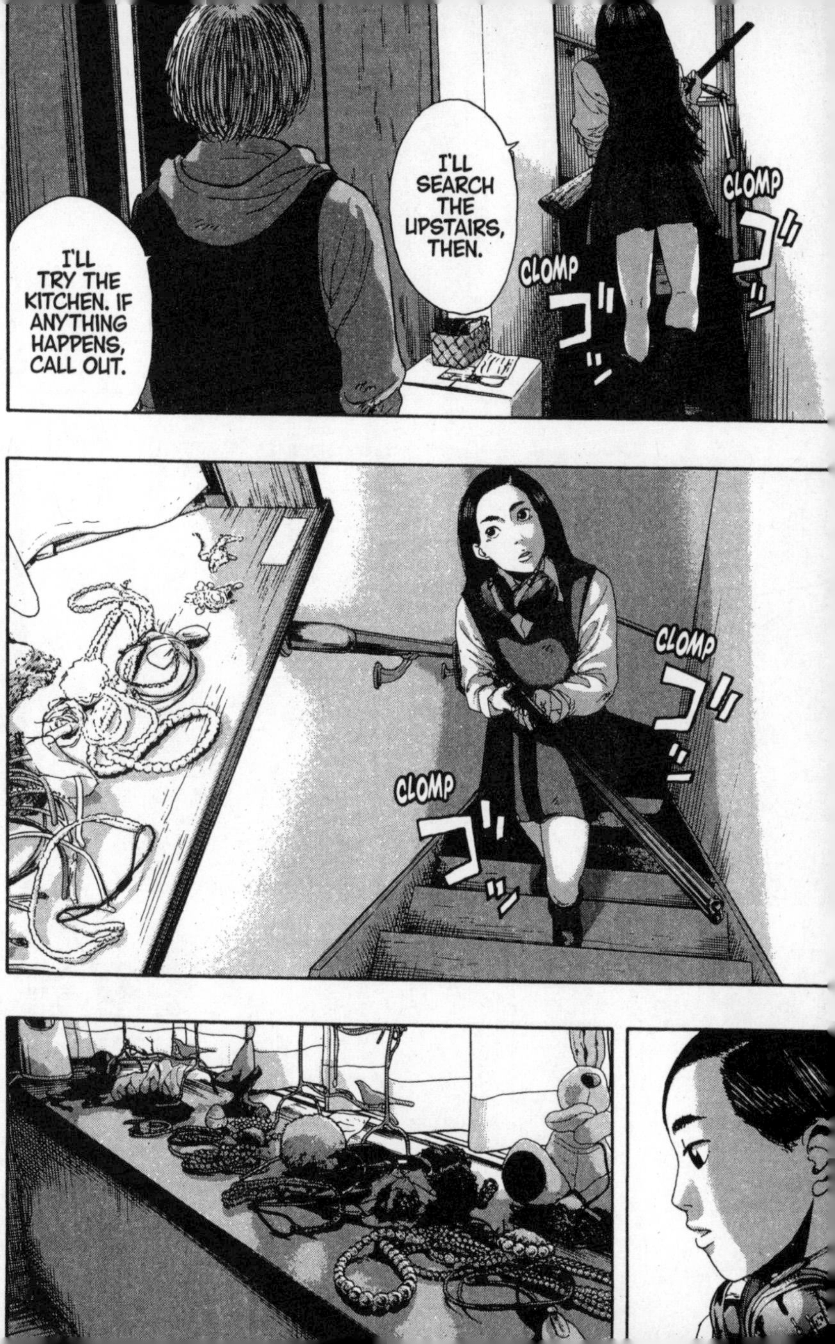
CLOMP
I'LL SEARCH THE UPSTAIRS, THEN.
CLOMP
I'LL TRY THE KITCHEN. IF ANYTHING HAPPENS, CALL OUT.
CLOMP
CLOMP

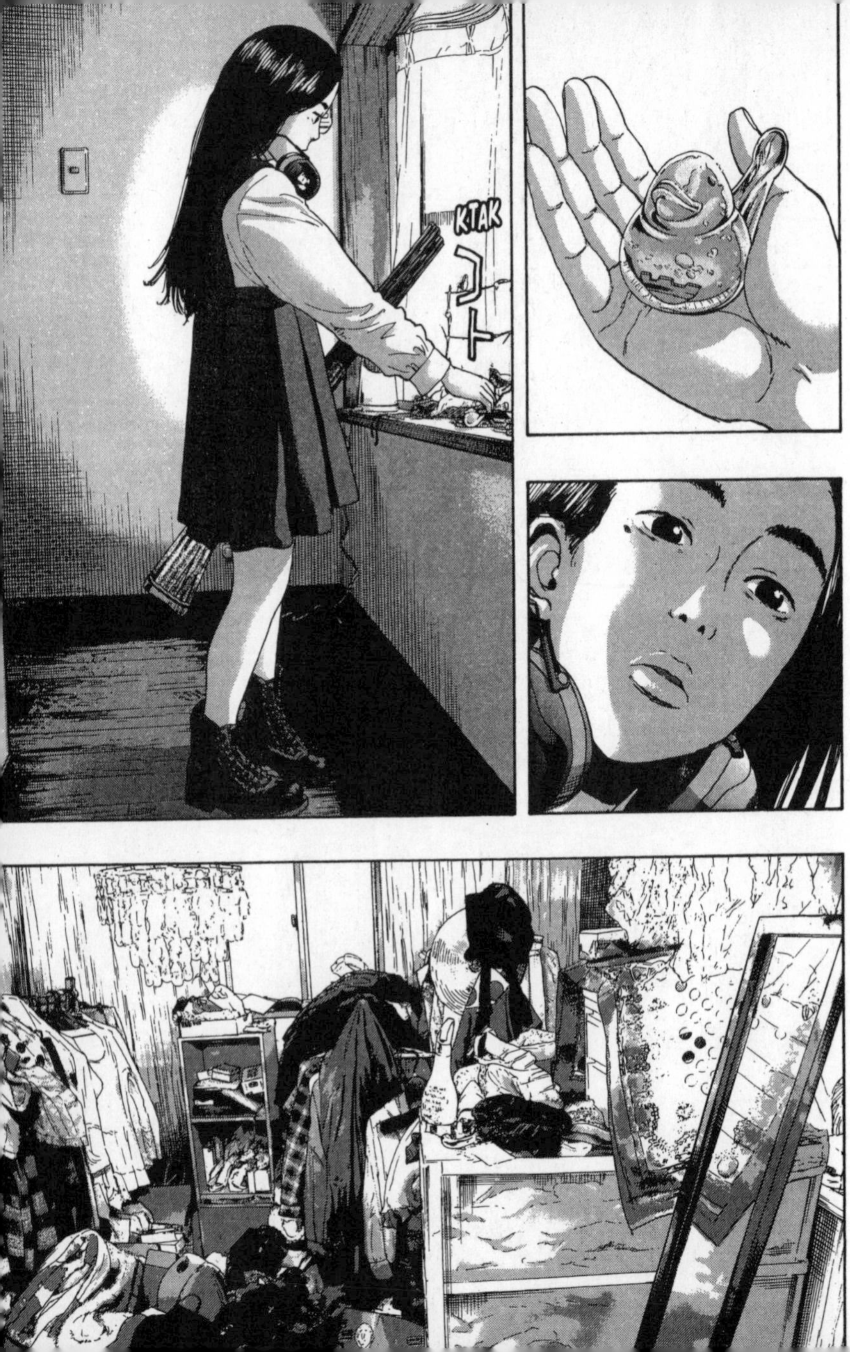
KTAK
コト

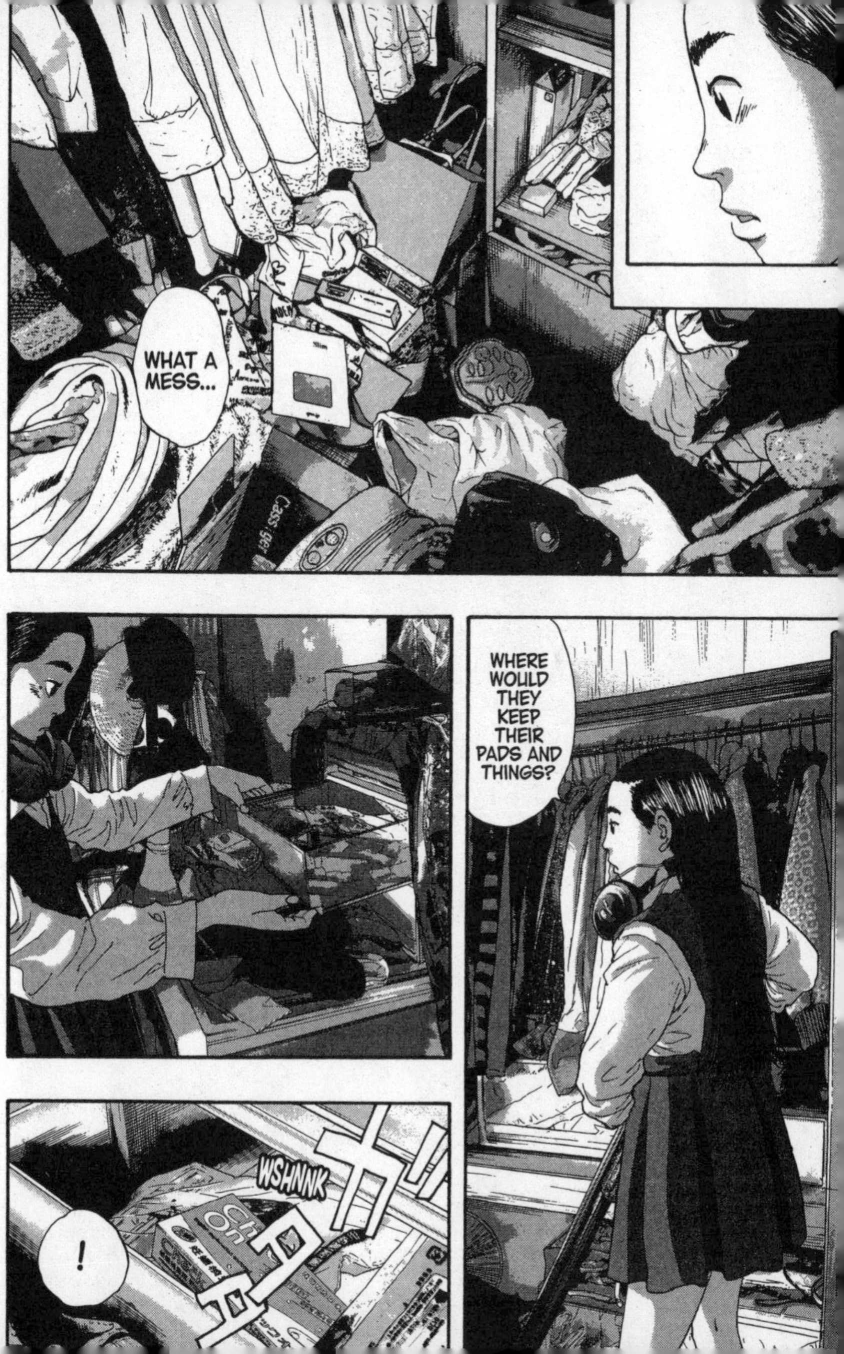
WHAT A MESS...
WHERE WOULD THEY KEEP THEIR PADS AND THINGS?
WSHNNK
!

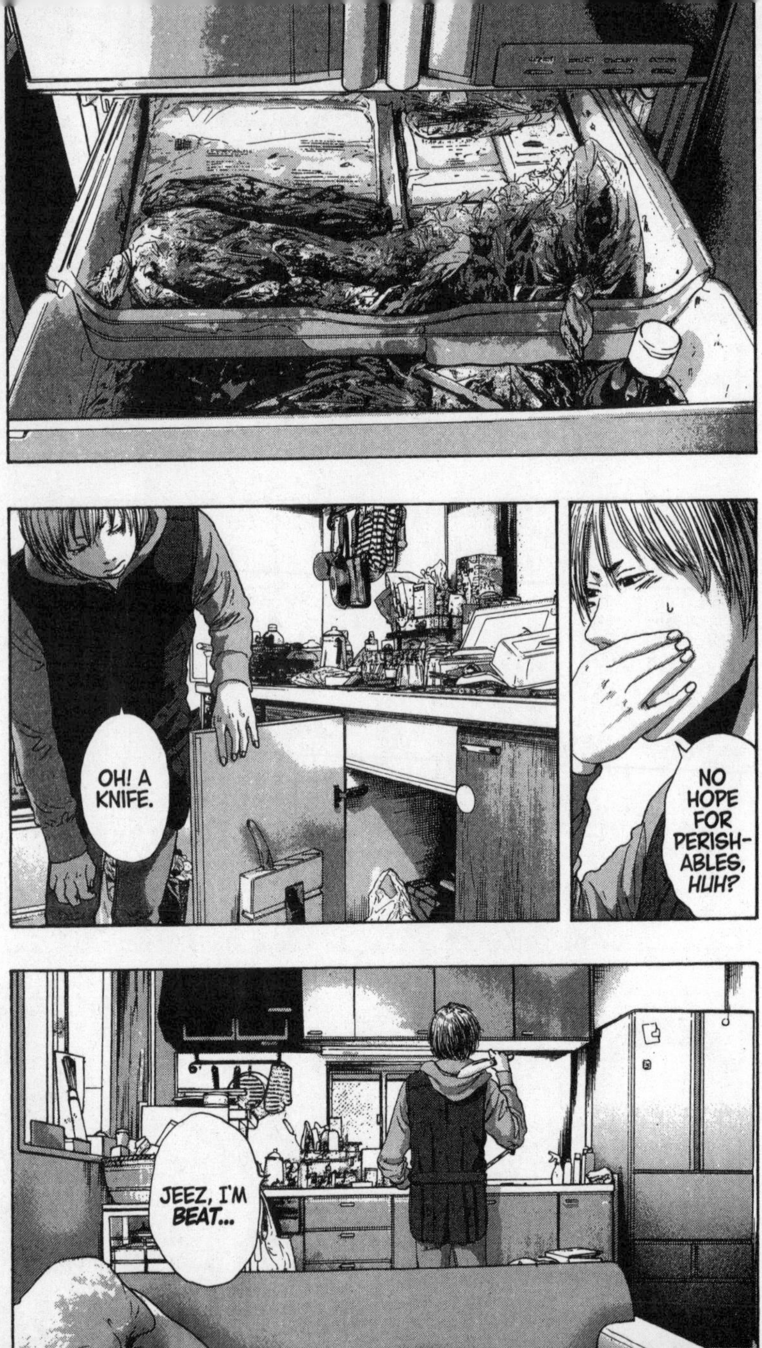
NO HOPE FOR PERISH-ABLES, HUH?
OH! A KNIFE.
JEEZ, I'M BEAT...

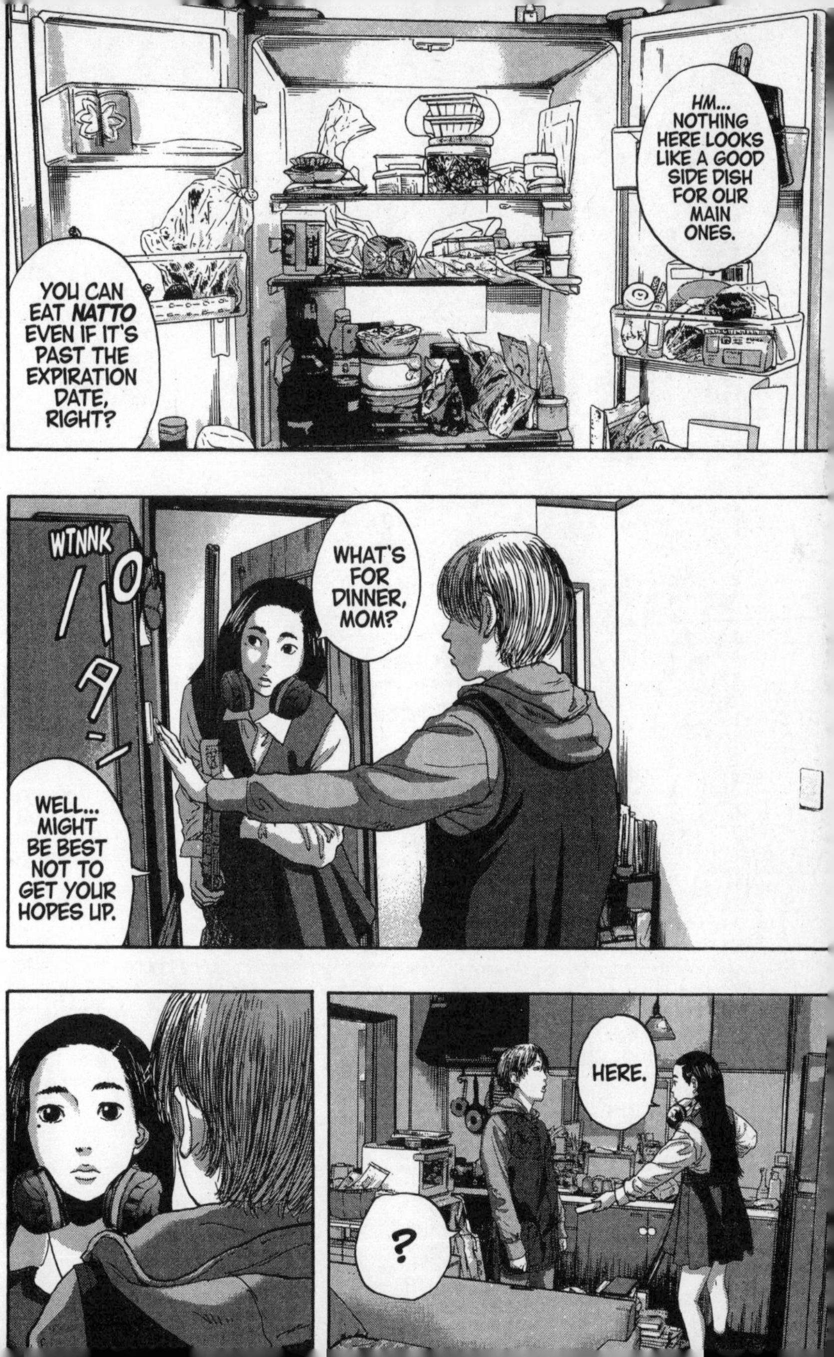
HM... NOTHING HERE LOOKS LIKE A GOOD SIDE DISH FOR OUR MAIN ONES.
YOU CAN EAT NATTO EVEN IF IT'S PAST THE EXPIRATION DATE, RIGHT?
WHAT'S FOR DINNER, MOM?
WTNNK
WELL... MIGHT BE BEST NOT TO GET YOUR HOPES UP.
HERE.
?

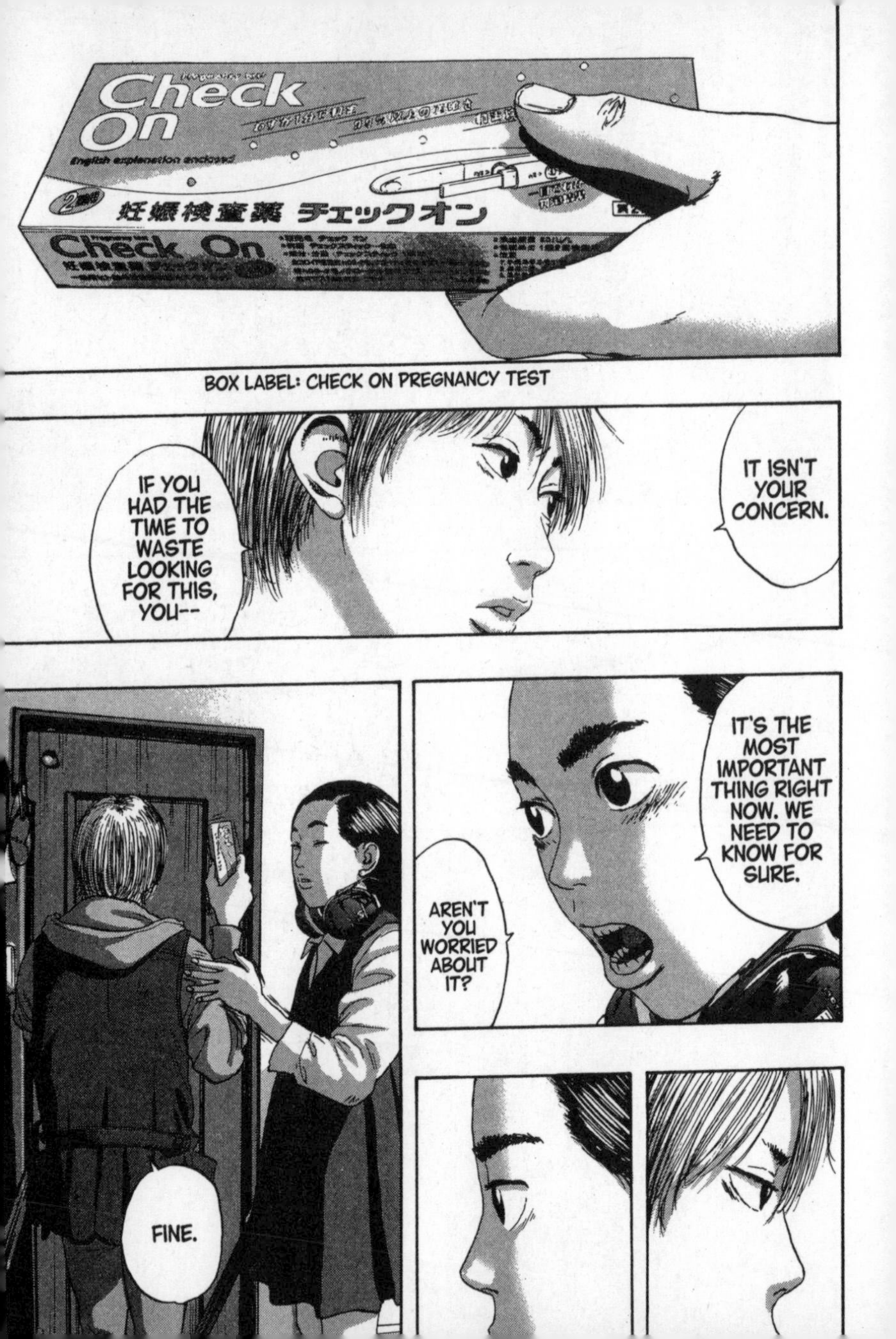
Check On
English explanation enclosed
妊娠検査薬 チェックオン
Check On
BOX LABEL: CHECK ON PREGNANCY TEST
IT ISN'T YOUR CONCERN.
IF YOU HAD THE TIME TO WASTE LOOKING FOR THIS, YOU--
IT'S THE MOST IMPORTANT THING RIGHT NOW. WE NEED TO KNOW FOR SURE.
AREN'T YOU WORRIED ABOUT IT?
FINE.

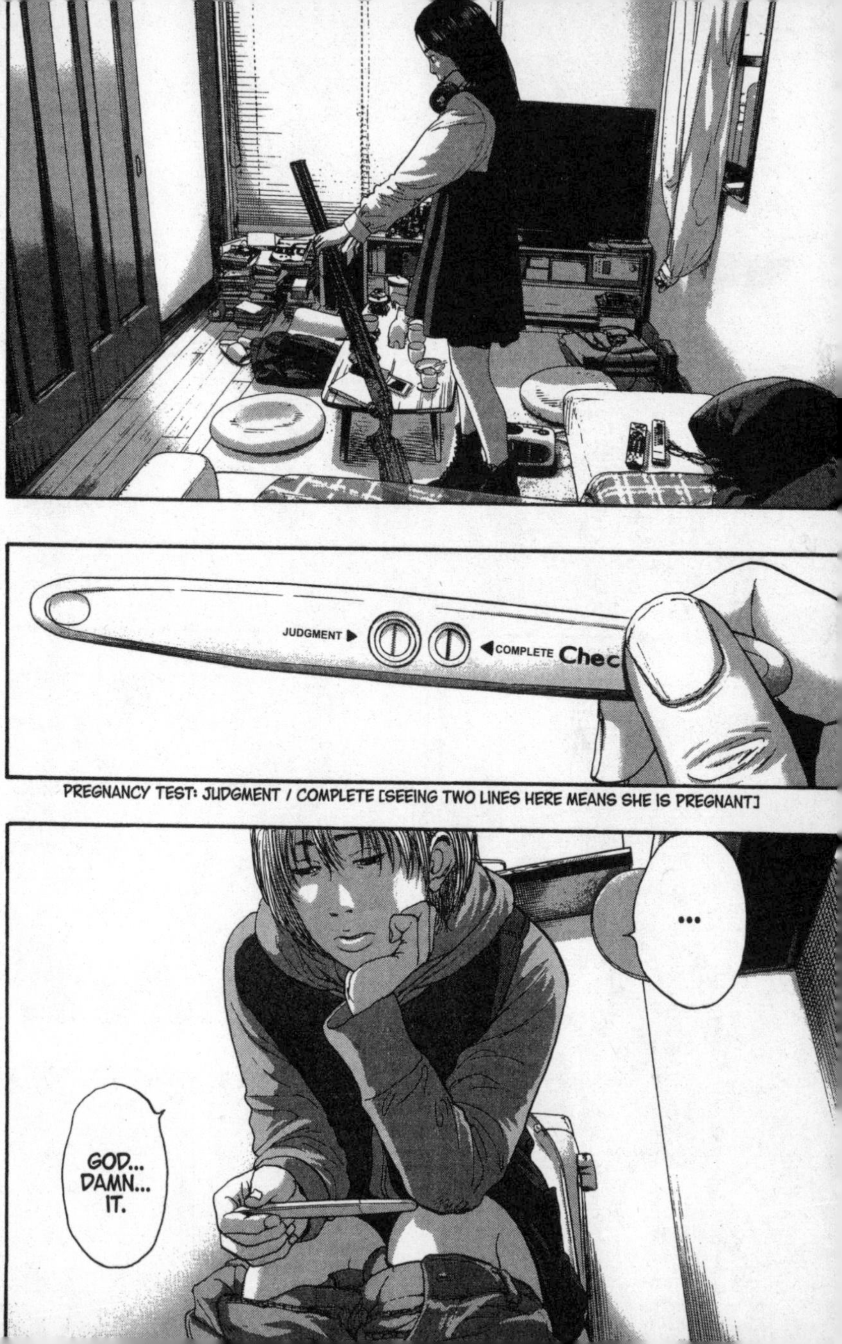
JUDGMENT ▶
◀ COMPLETE
Chec
PREGNANCY TEST: JUDGMENT / COMPLETE [SEEING TWO LINES HERE MEANS SHE IS PREGNANT]
...
GOD... DAMN... IT.

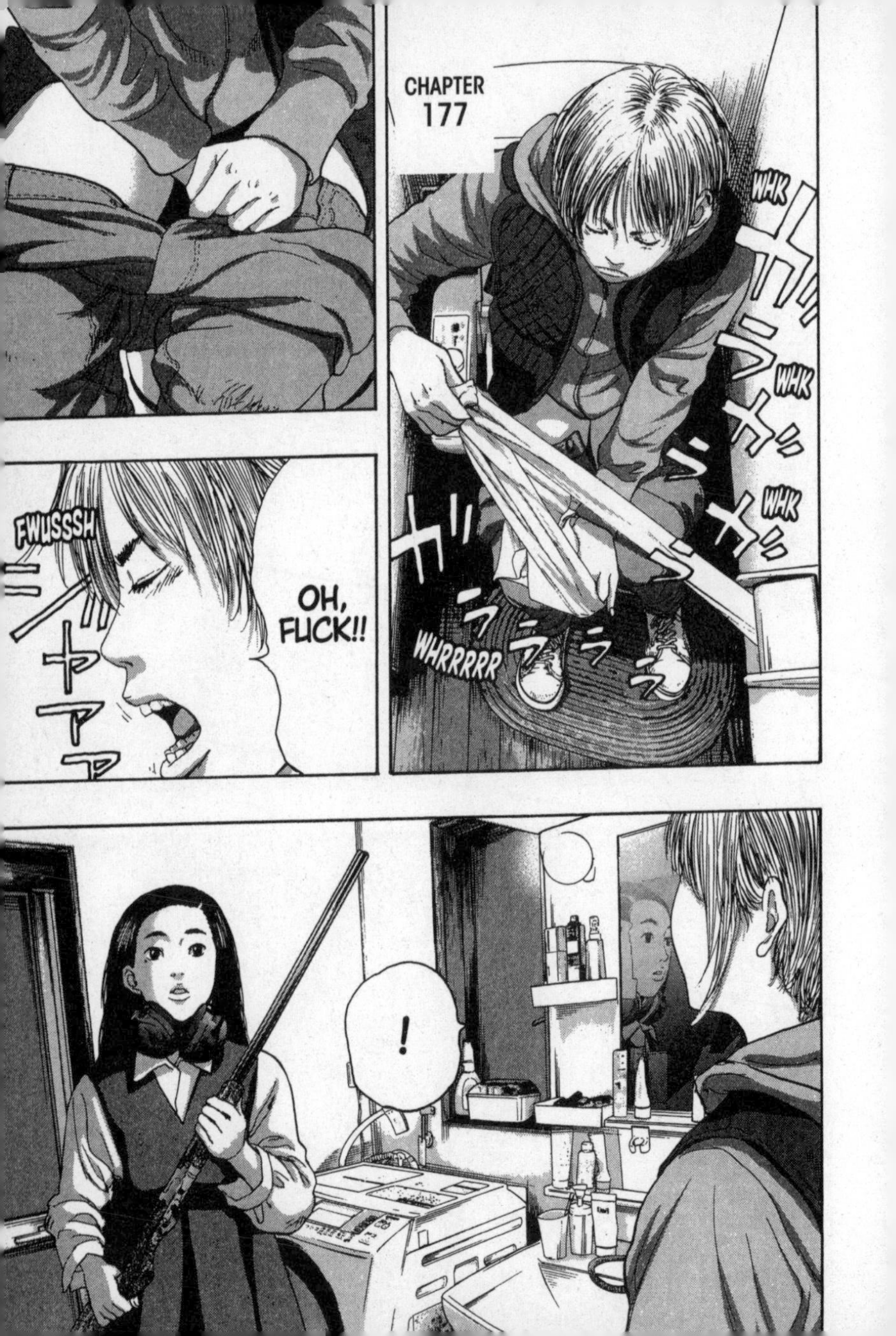
CHAPTER
177
WHK
WHK
WHK
WHRRRRR
FWUSSSH
OH, FUCK!!
!

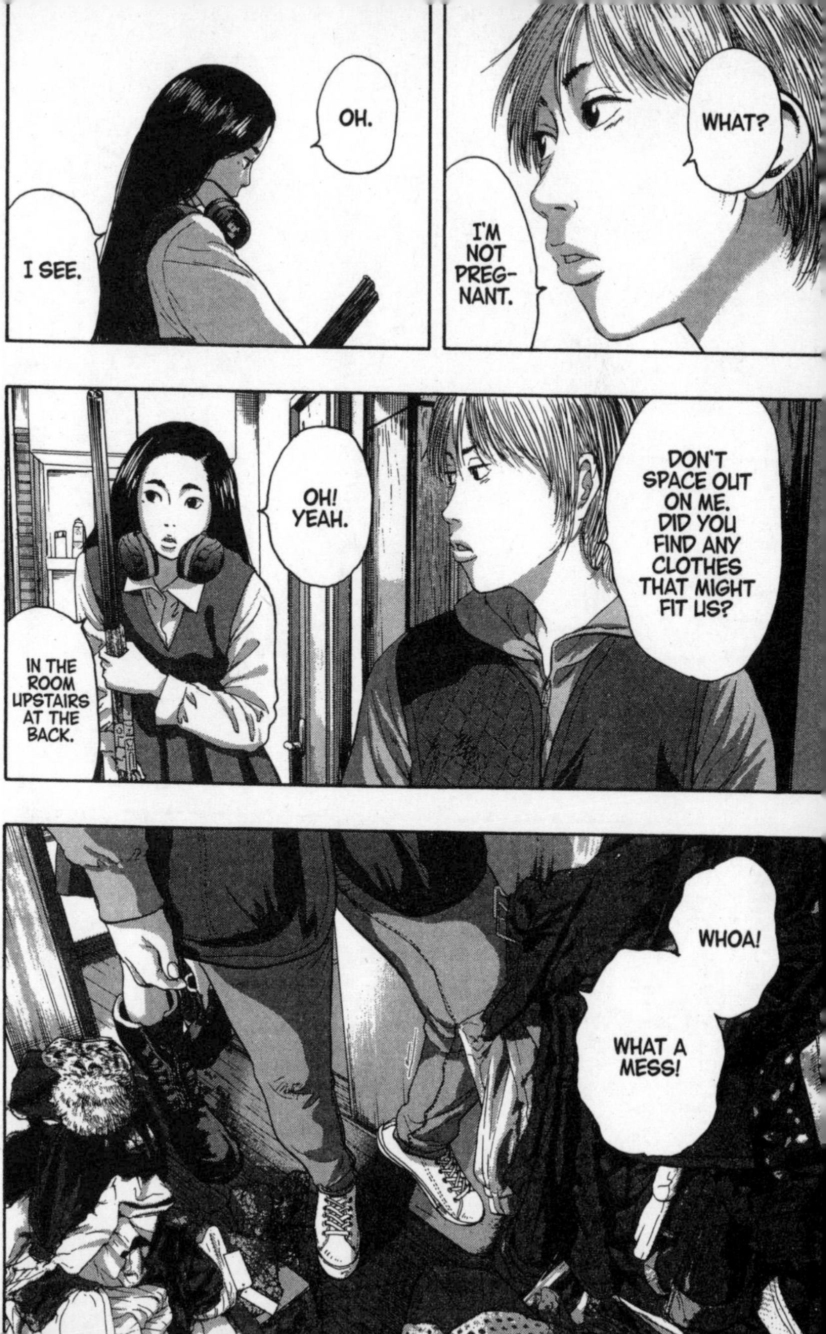
WHAT?
I'M NOT PREGNANT.
OH.
I SEE.
DON'T SPACE OUT ON ME. DID YOU FIND ANY CLOTHES THAT MIGHT FIT US?
OH! YEAH.
IN THE ROOM UPSTAIRS AT THE BACK.
WHOA!
WHAT A MESS!

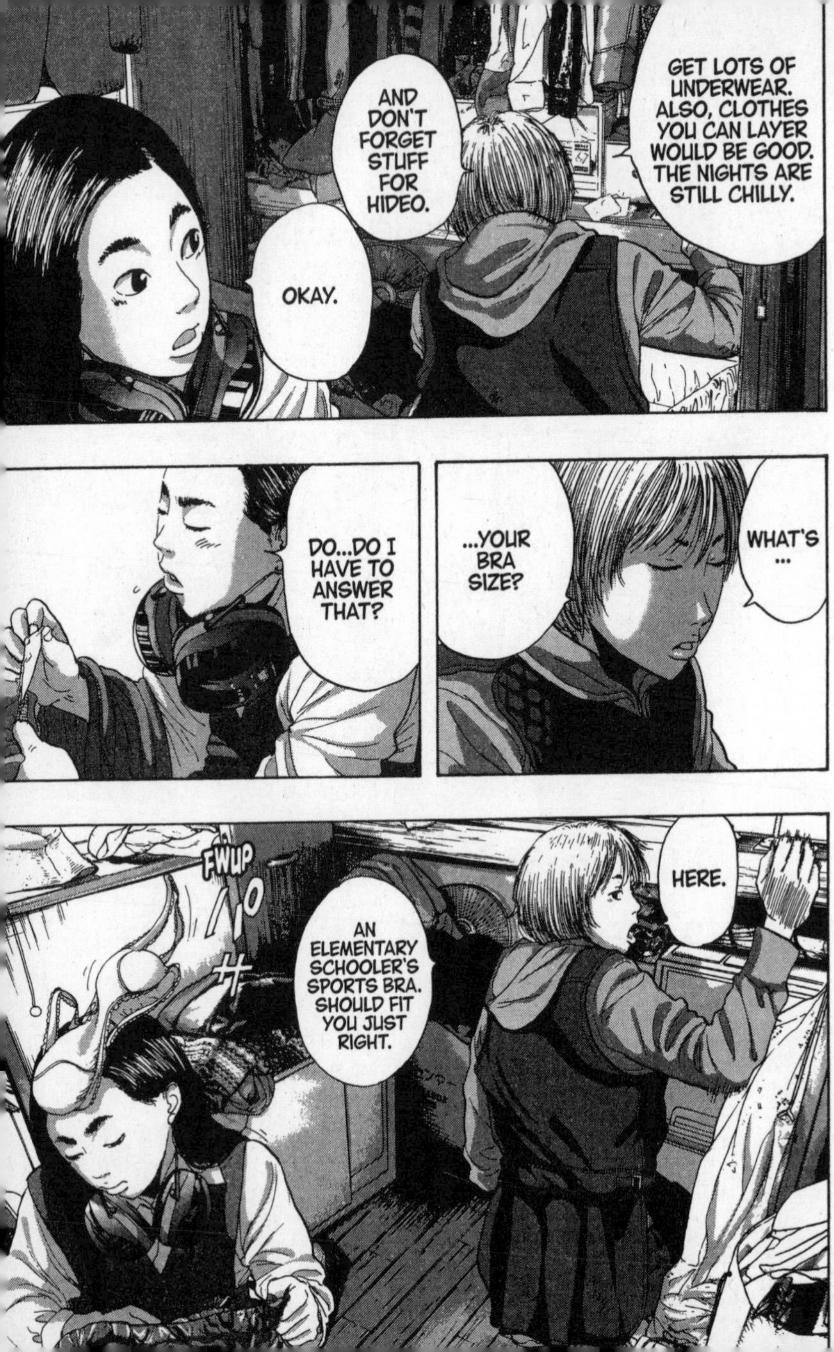
GET LOTS OF UNDERWEAR. ALSO, CLOTHES YOU CAN LAYER WOULD BE GOOD. THE NIGHTS ARE STILL CHILLY.
AND DON'T FORGET STUFF FOR HIDEO.
OKAY.
WHAT'S ...
...YOUR BRA SIZE?
DO...DO I HAVE TO ANSWER THAT?
HERE.
AN ELEMENTARY SCHOOLER'S SPORTS BRA. SHOULD FIT YOU JUST RIGHT.
FWUP

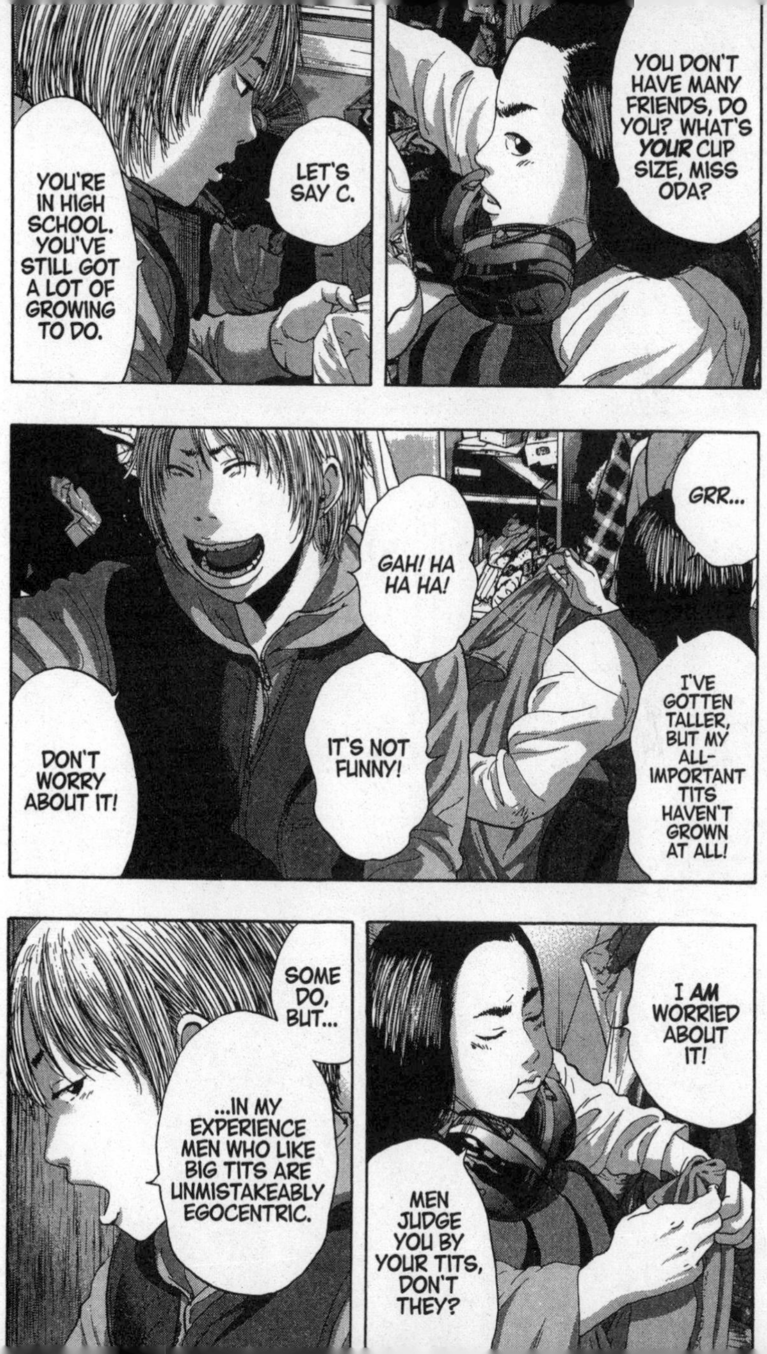
YOU DON'T HAVE MANY FRIENDS, DO YOU? WHAT'S *YOUR* CUP SIZE, MISS ODA?
LET'S SAY C.
YOU'RE IN HIGH SCHOOL. YOU'VE STILL GOT A LOT OF GROWING TO DO.
GRR...
GAH! HA HA HA!
I'VE GOTTEN TALLER, BUT MY ALL-IMPORTANT TITS HAVEN'T GROWN AT ALL!
IT'S NOT FUNNY!
DON'T WORRY ABOUT IT!
I *AM* WORRIED ABOUT IT!
MEN JUDGE YOU BY YOUR TITS, DON'T THEY?
SOME DO, BUT...
...IN MY EXPERIENCE MEN WHO LIKE BIG TITS ARE UNMISTAKEABLY EGOCENTRIC.

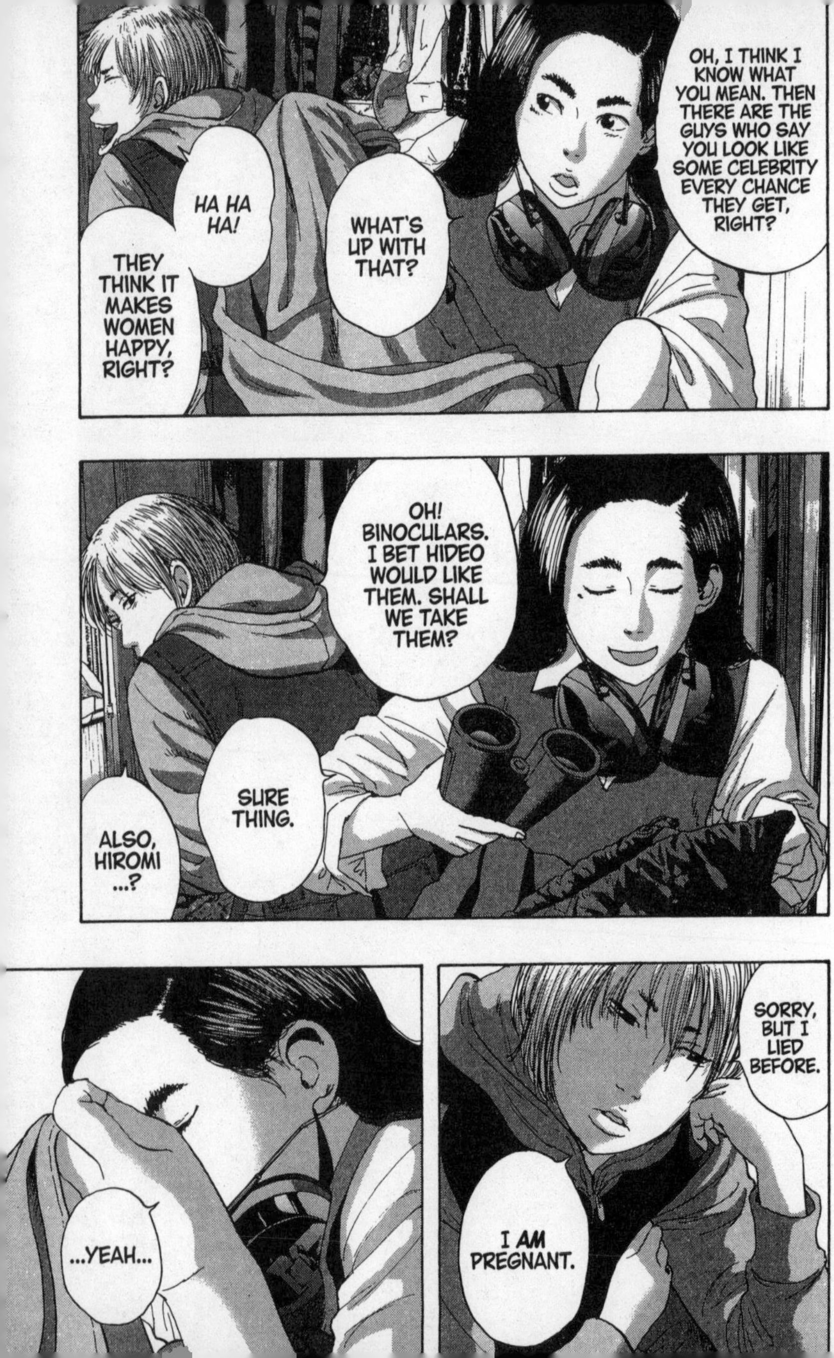
OH, I THINK I KNOW WHAT YOU MEAN. THEN THERE ARE THE GUYS WHO SAY YOU LOOK LIKE SOME CELEBRITY EVERY CHANCE THEY GET, RIGHT?
WHAT'S UP WITH THAT?
HA HA HA!
THEY THINK IT MAKES WOMEN HAPPY, RIGHT?
OH! BINOCULARS. I BET HIDEO WOULD LIKE THEM. SHALL WE TAKE THEM?
SURE THING.
ALSO, HIROMI ...?
SORRY, BUT I LIED BEFORE.
I AM PREGNANT.
...YEAH...

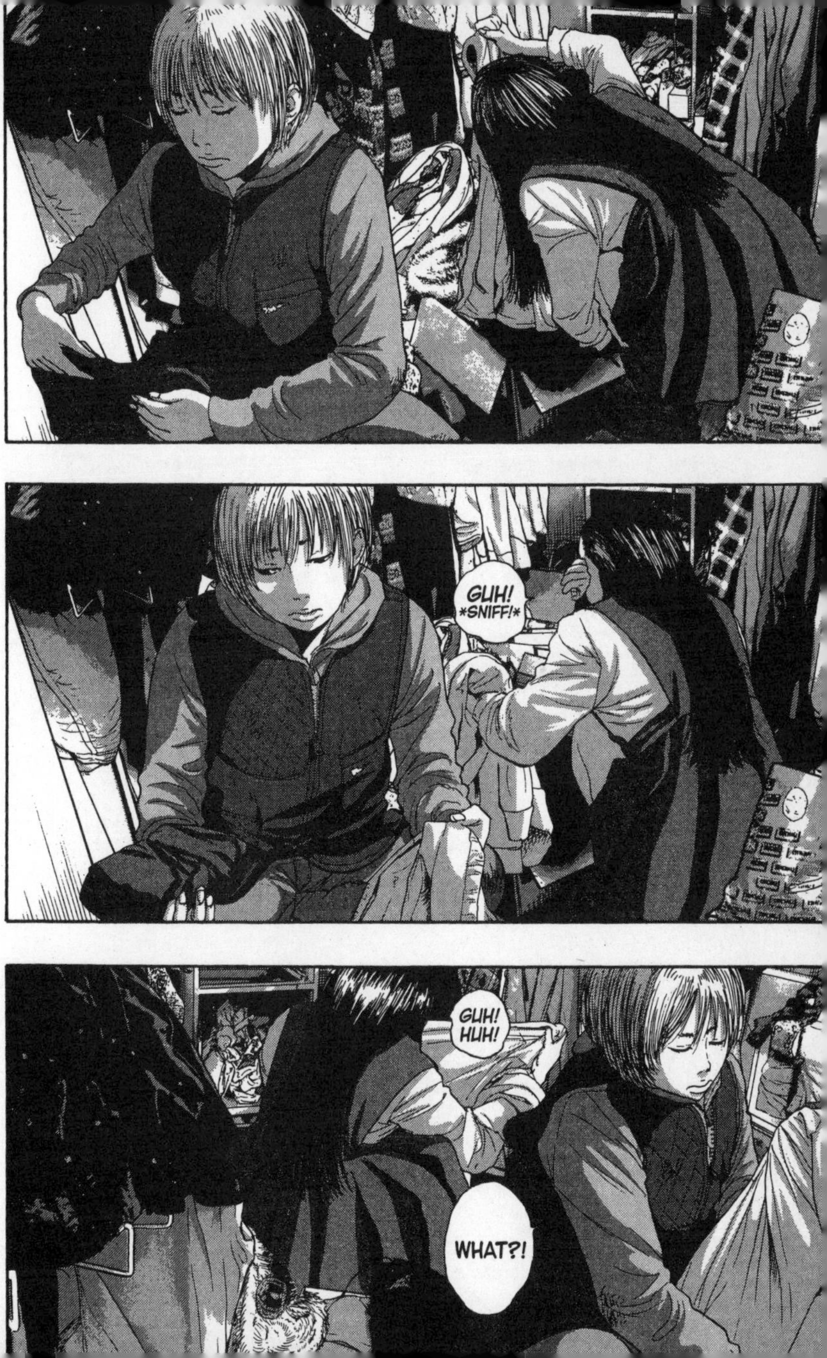
GUH!
SNIFF!
GUH!
HUH!
WHAT?!

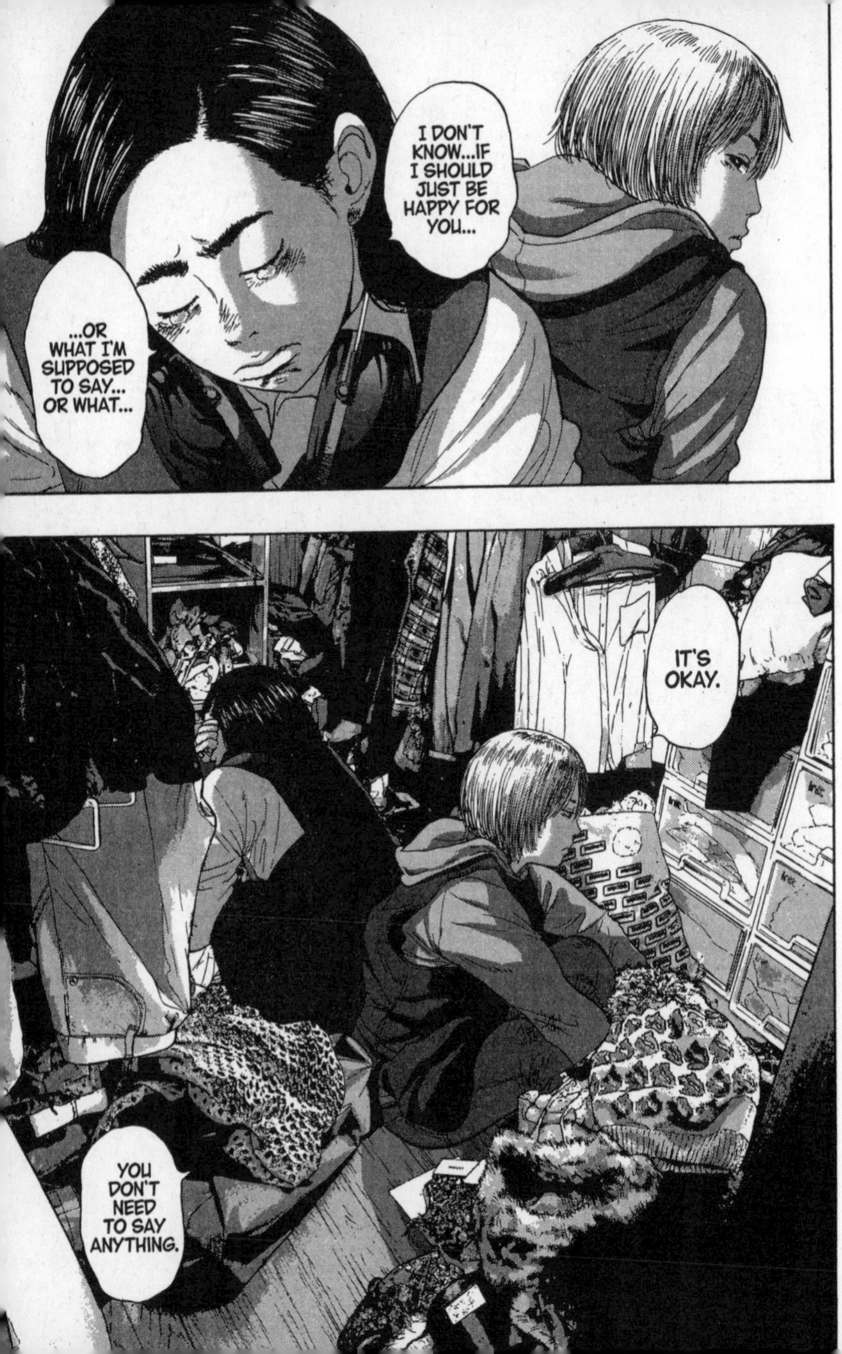
I DON'T KNOW...IF I SHOULD JUST BE HAPPY FOR YOU...
...OR WHAT I'M SUPPOSED TO SAY... OR WHAT...
IT'S OKAY.
YOU DON'T NEED TO SAY ANYTHING.

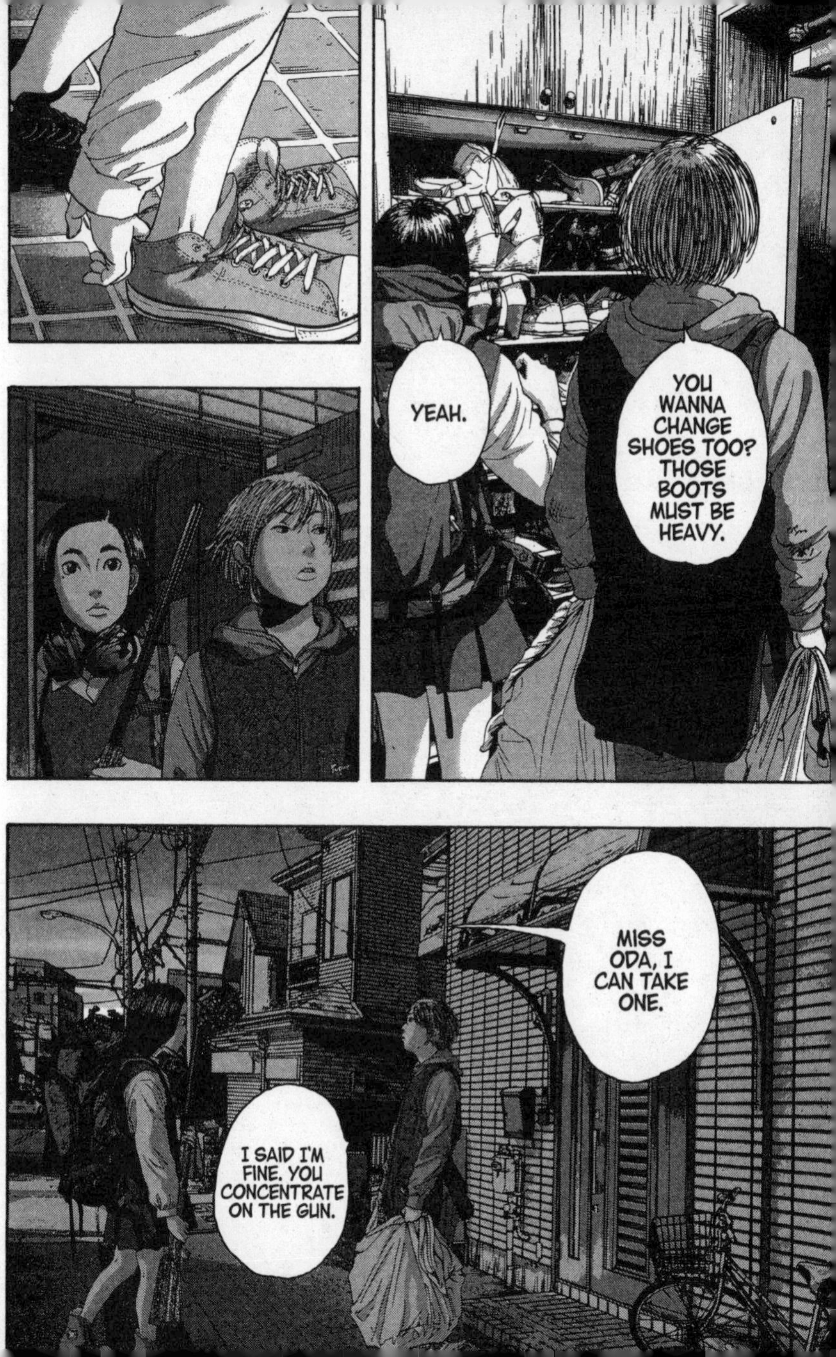
YOU WANNA CHANGE SHOES TOO? THOSE BOOTS MUST BE HEAVY.
YEAH.
MISS ODA, I CAN TAKE ONE.
I SAID I'M FINE. YOU CONCENTRATE ON THE GUN.

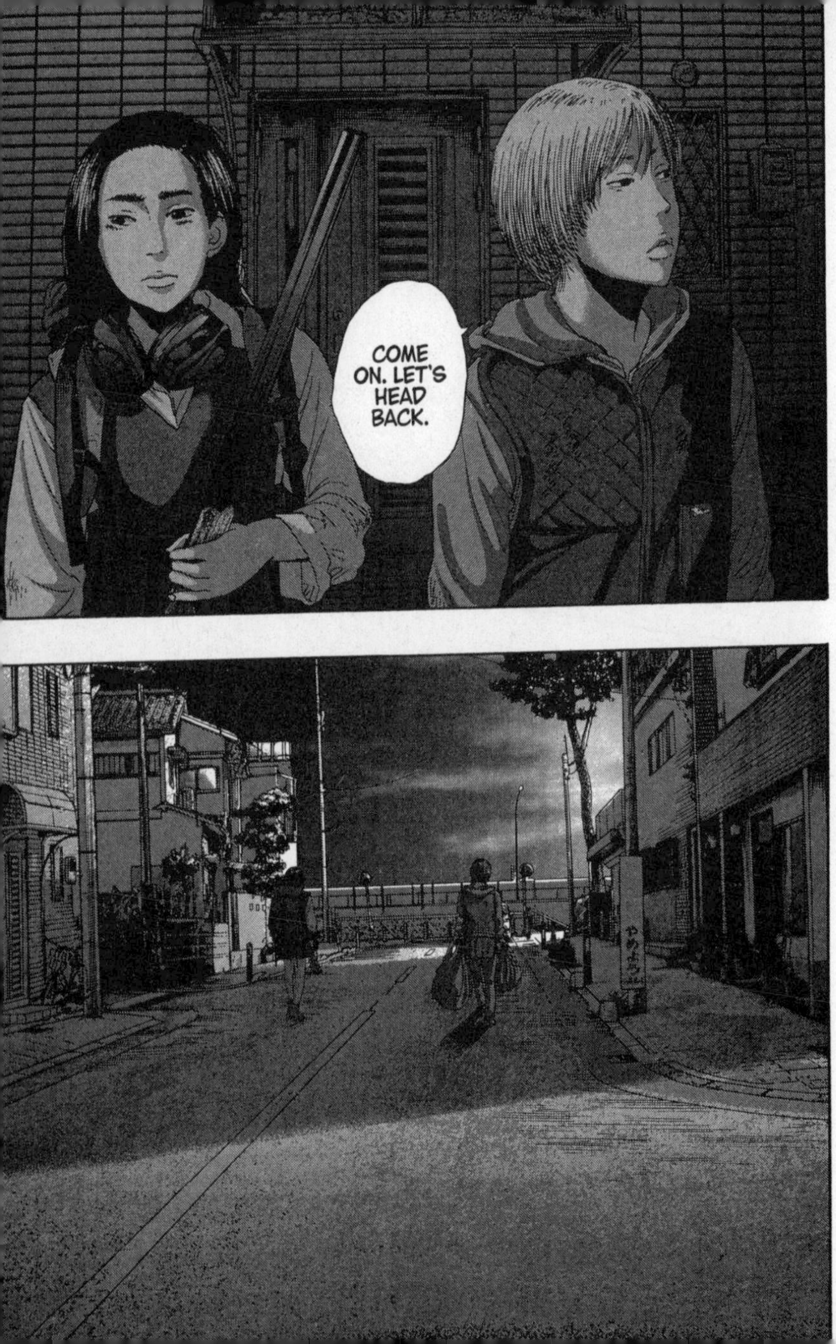
COME ON. LET'S HEAD BACK.

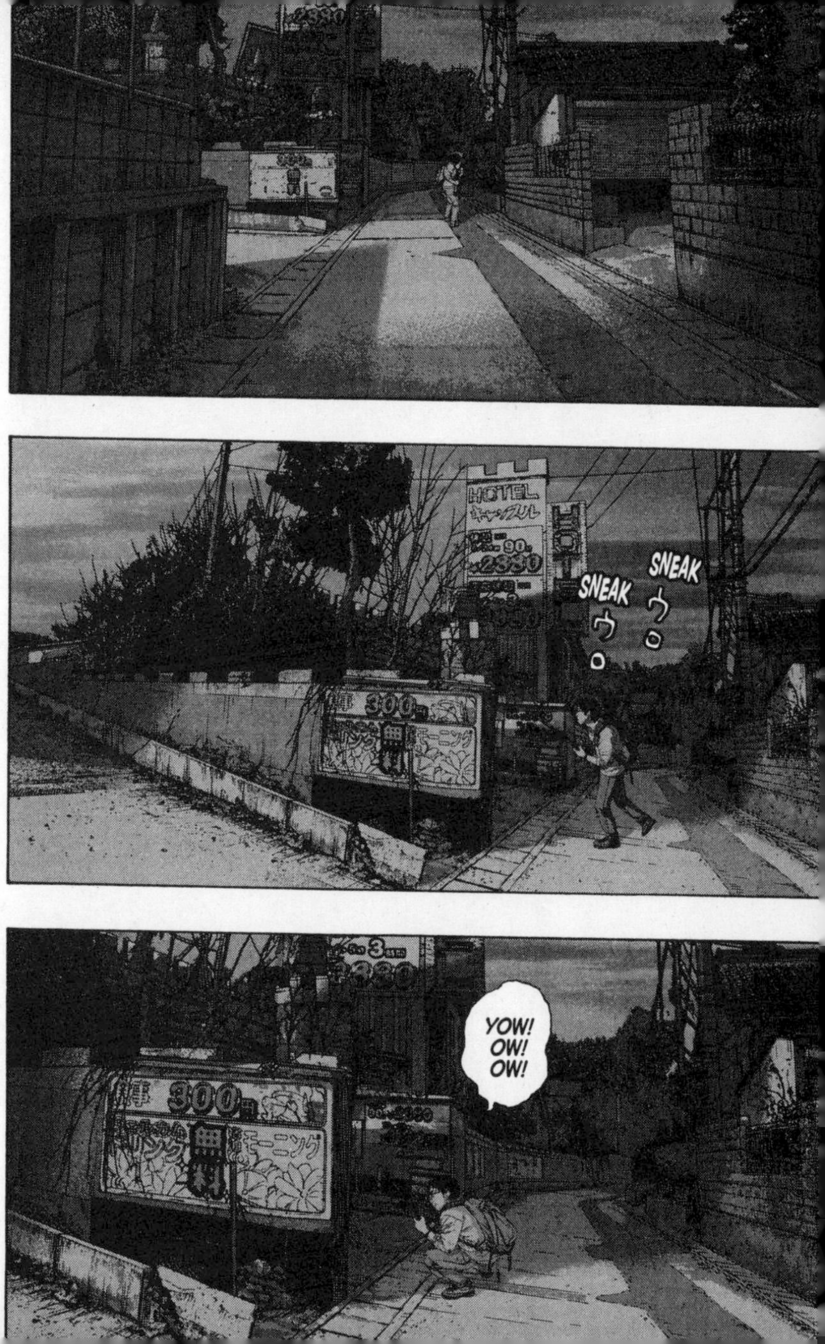
HOTEL
SNEAK ウロ
SNEAK ウロ
300
YOW! OW! OW!

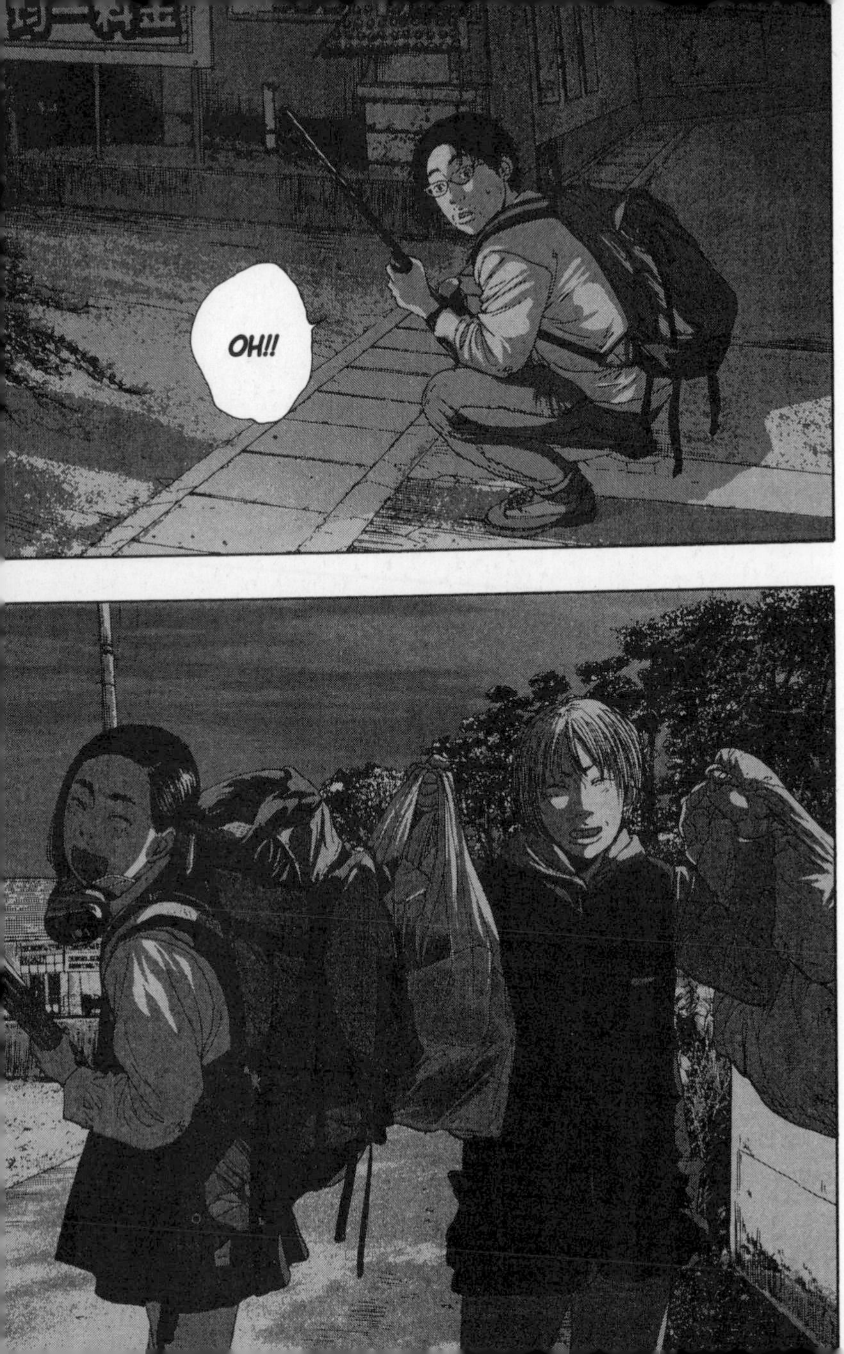
OH!!

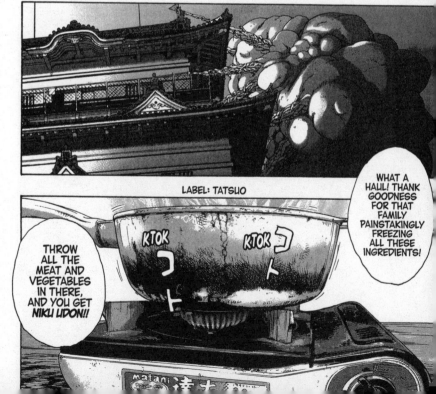

LABEL: TATSUO

WHAT A HAUL! THANK GOODNESS FOR THAT FAMILY PAINSTAKINGLY FREEZING ALL THESE INGREDIENTS!

THROW ALL THE MEAT AND VEGETABLES IN THERE, AND YOU GET *NIKU UDON!!*

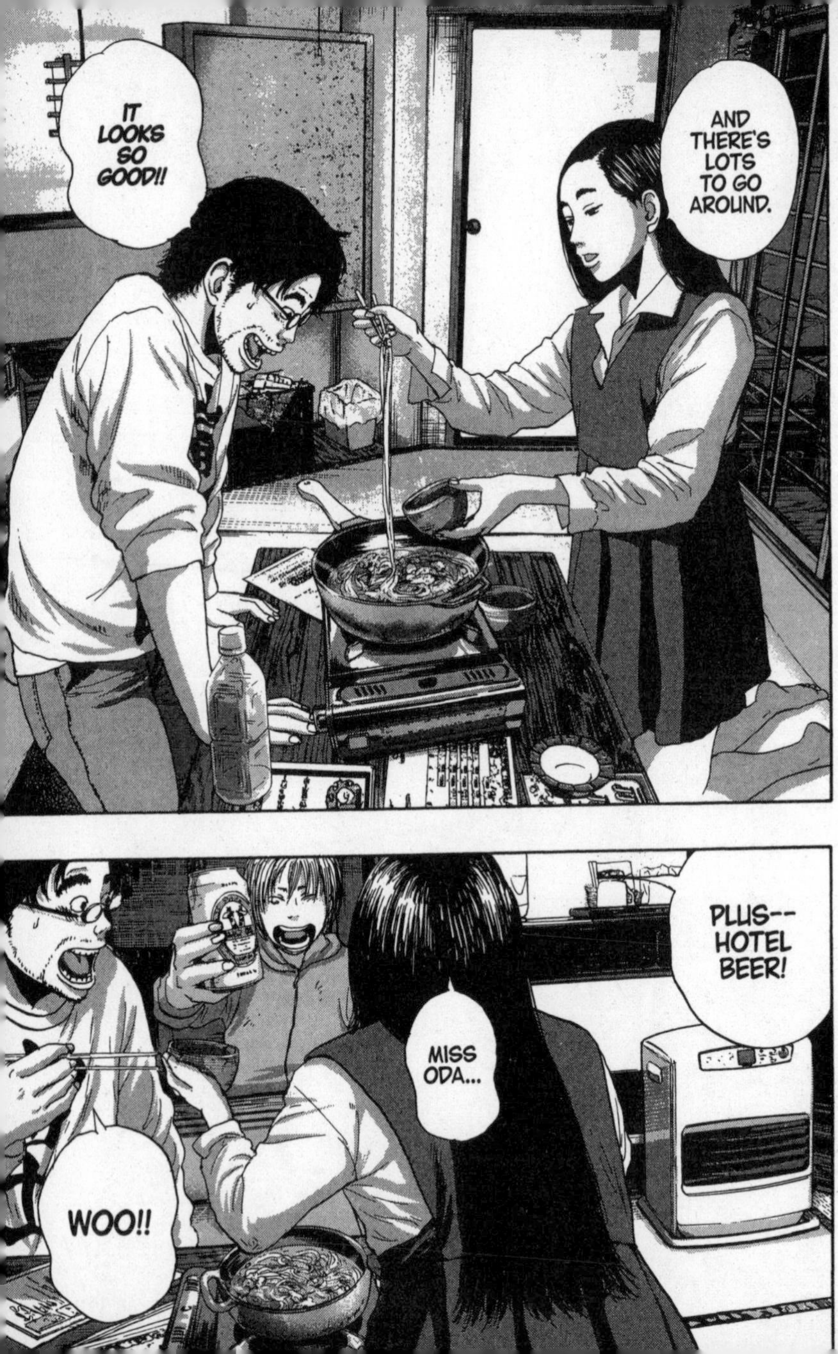
AND THERE'S LOTS TO GO AROUND.
IT LOOKS SO GOOD!!
PLUS-- HOTEL BEER!
MISS ODA...
WOO!!

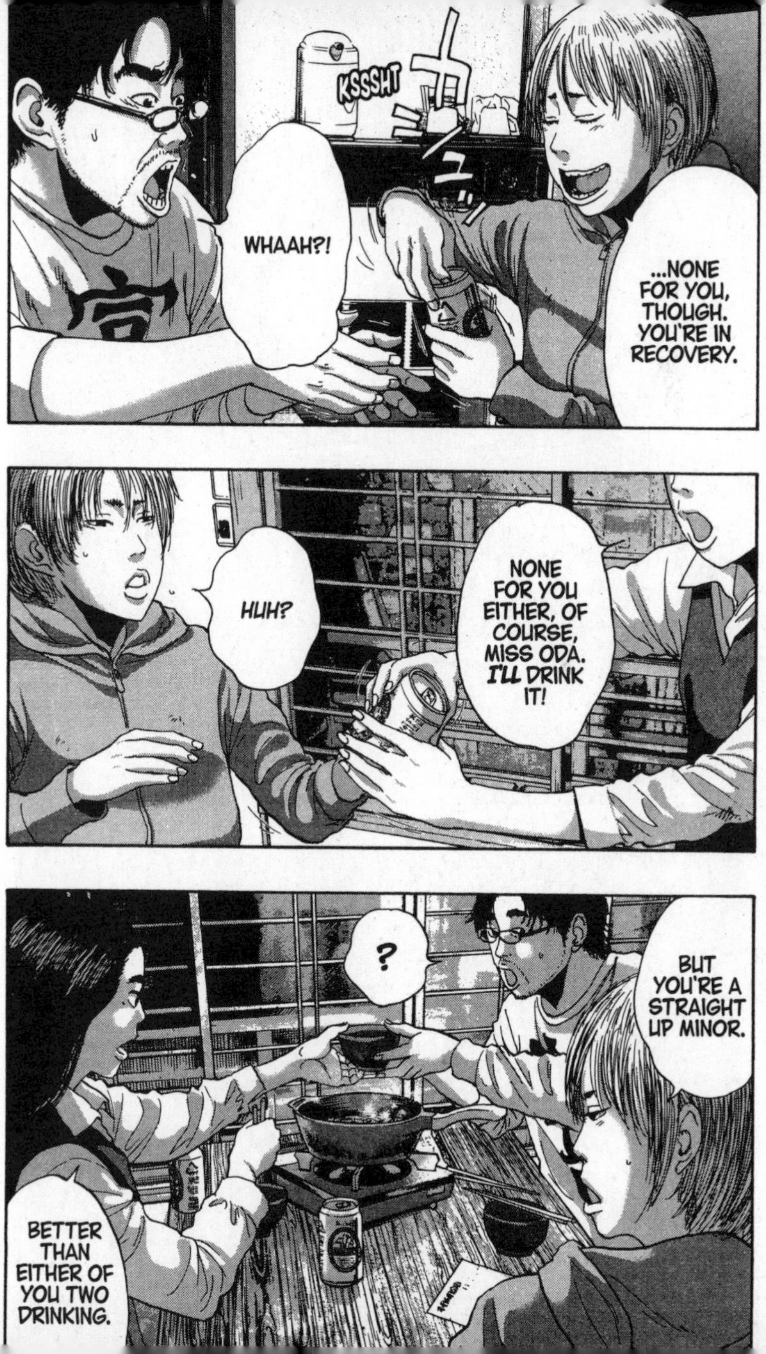
KSSSHT
...NONE FOR YOU, THOUGH. YOU'RE IN RECOVERY.
WHAAH?!
NONE FOR YOU EITHER, OF COURSE, MISS ODA. *I'LL* DRINK IT!
HUH?
BUT YOU'RE A STRAIGHT UP MINOR.
?
BETTER THAN EITHER OF YOU TWO DRINKING.

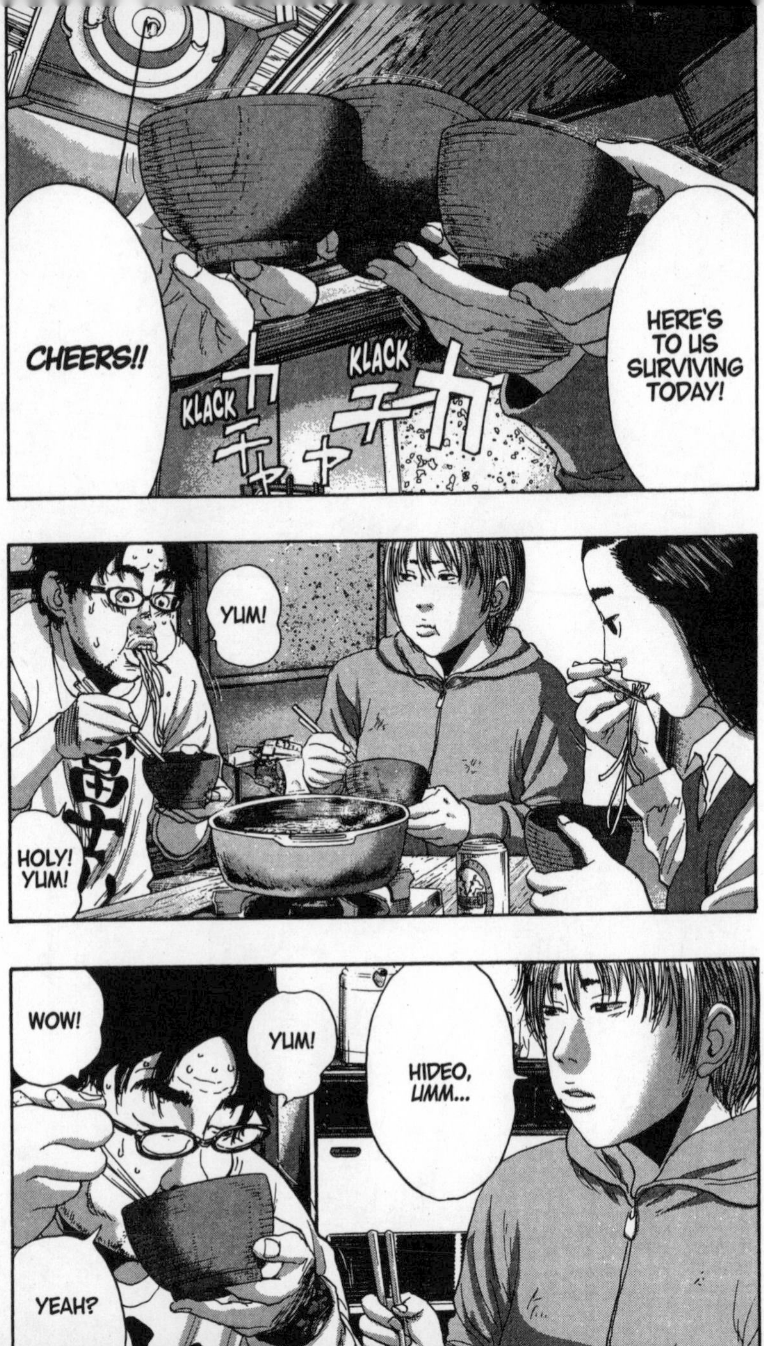
HERE'S TO US SURVIVING TODAY!
KLACK
KLACK
CHEERS!!
YUM!
HOLY! YUM!
HIDEO, UMM...
YUM!
WOW!
YEAH?

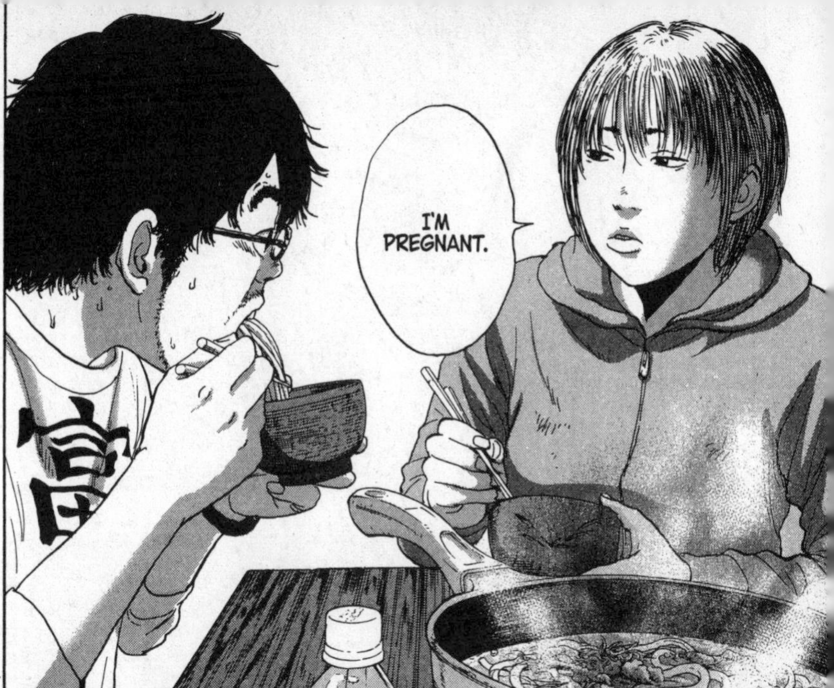
I'M PREGNANT.
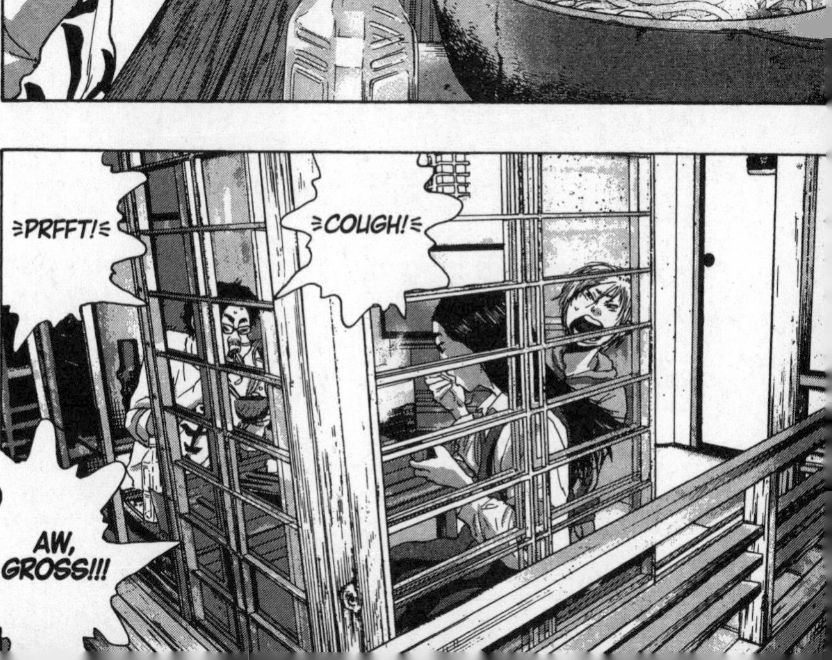
PRFFT!
COUGH!
AW, GROSS!!!

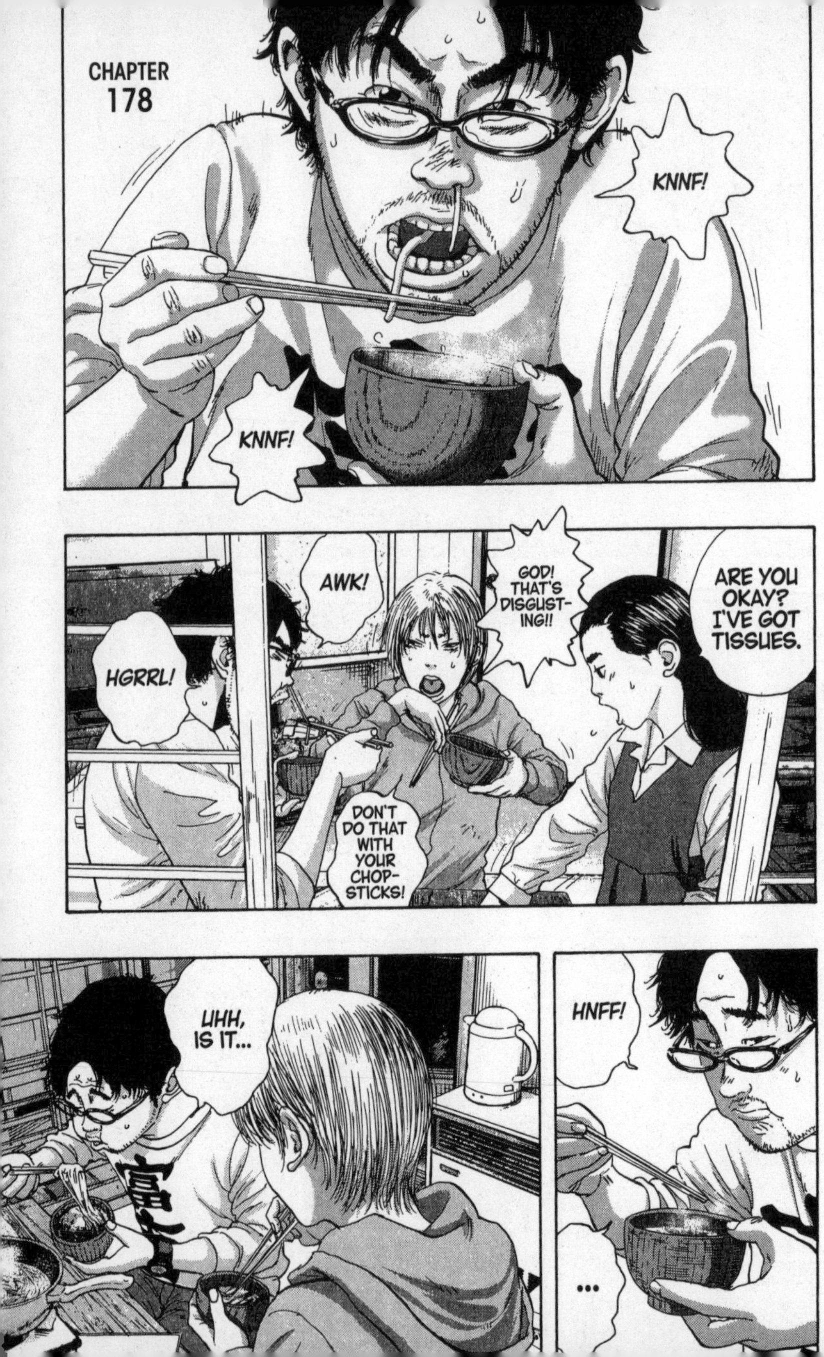
CHAPTER 178
KNNF!
KNNF!
ARE YOU OKAY? I'VE GOT TISSUES.
GOD! THAT'S DISGUSTING!!
AWK!
HGRRL!
DON'T DO THAT WITH YOUR CHOPSTICKS!
HNFF!
...
UHH, IS IT...

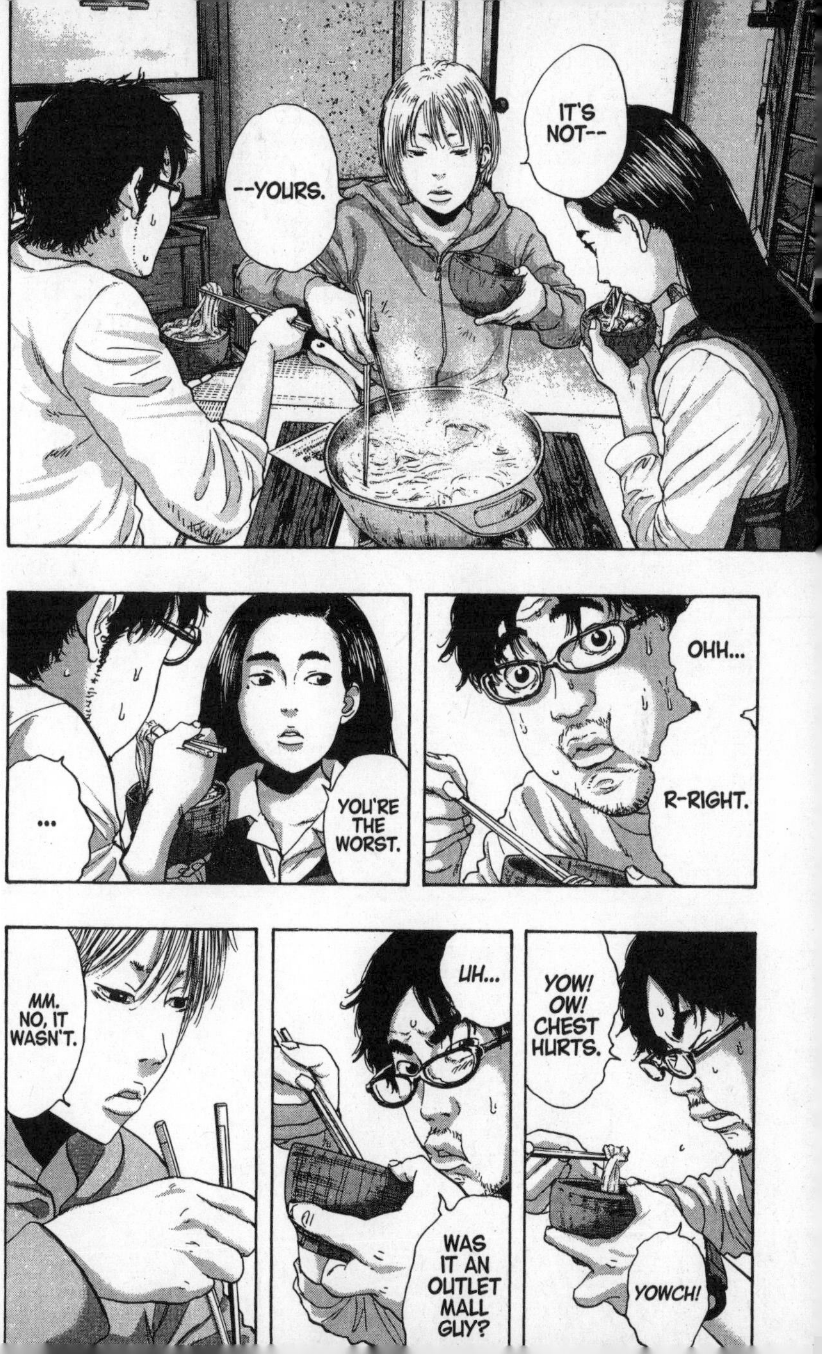
IT'S NOT--
--YOURS.
OHH...
R-RIGHT.
YOU'RE THE WORST.
...
YOW! OW! CHEST HURTS.
YOWCH!
UH...
WAS IT AN OUTLET MALL GUY?
MM. NO, IT WASN'T.

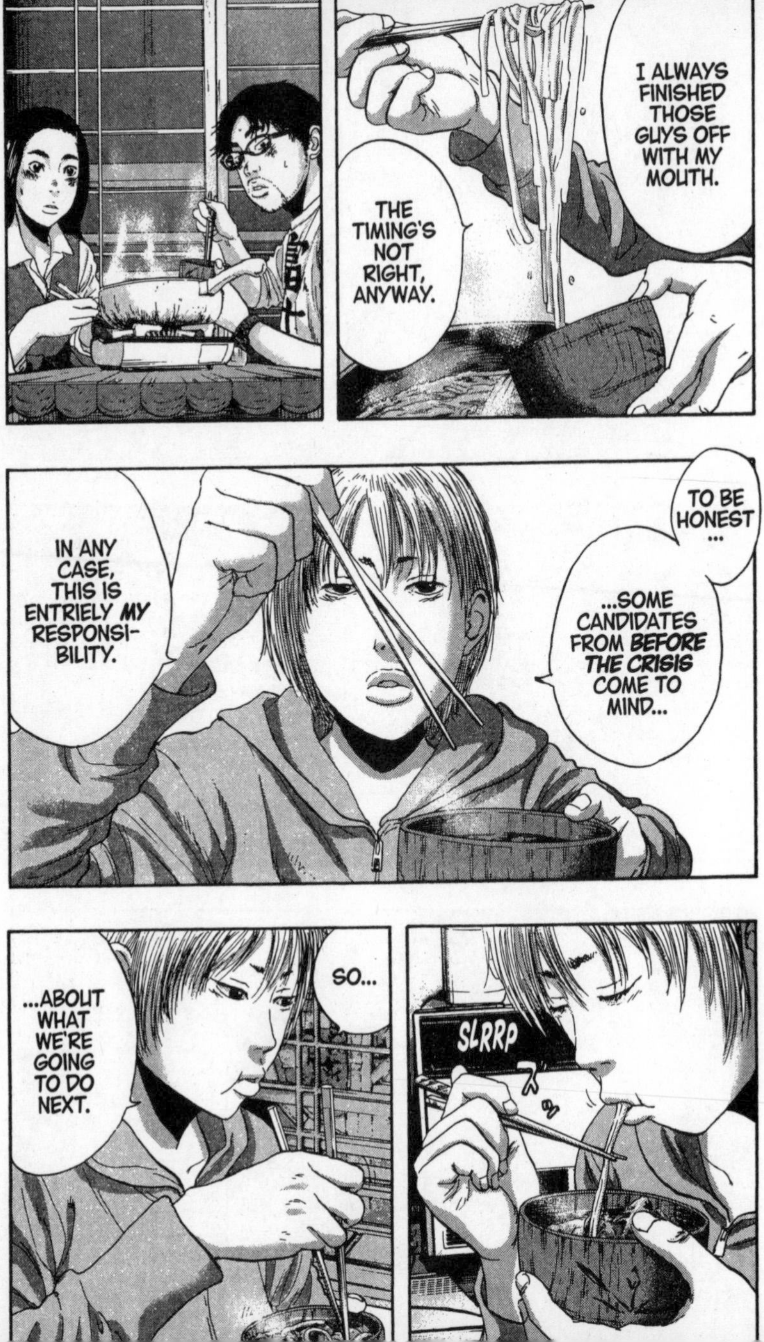
I ALWAYS FINISHED THOSE GUYS OFF WITH MY MOUTH.
THE TIMING'S NOT RIGHT, ANYWAY.
TO BE HONEST ...
...SOME CANDIDATES FROM BEFORE THE CRISIS COME TO MIND...
IN ANY CASE, THIS IS ENTRIELY MY RESPONSI-BILITY.
SLRRP
SO...
...ABOUT WHAT WE'RE GOING TO DO NEXT.

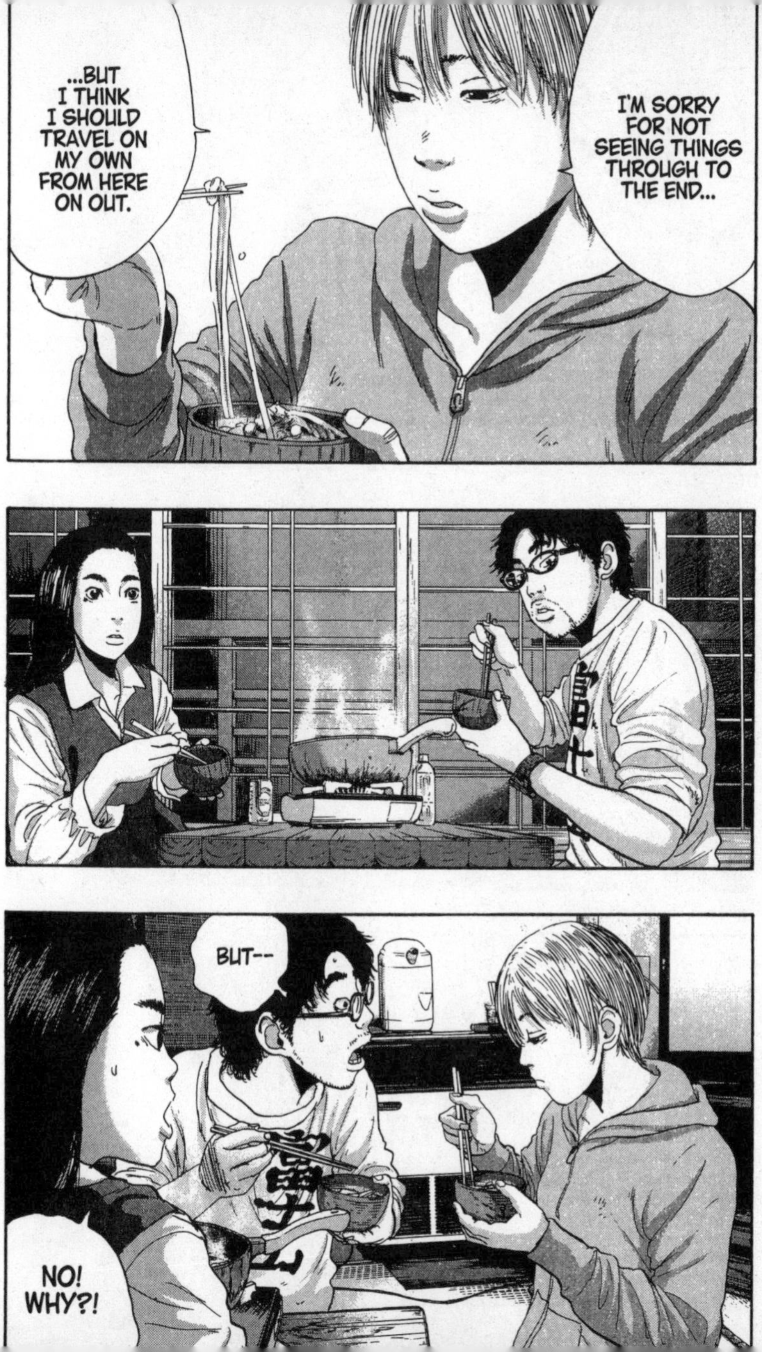
I'M SORRY FOR NOT SEEING THINGS THROUGH TO THE END...
...BUT I THINK I SHOULD TRAVEL ON MY OWN FROM HERE ON OUT.
BUT--
NO! WHY?!

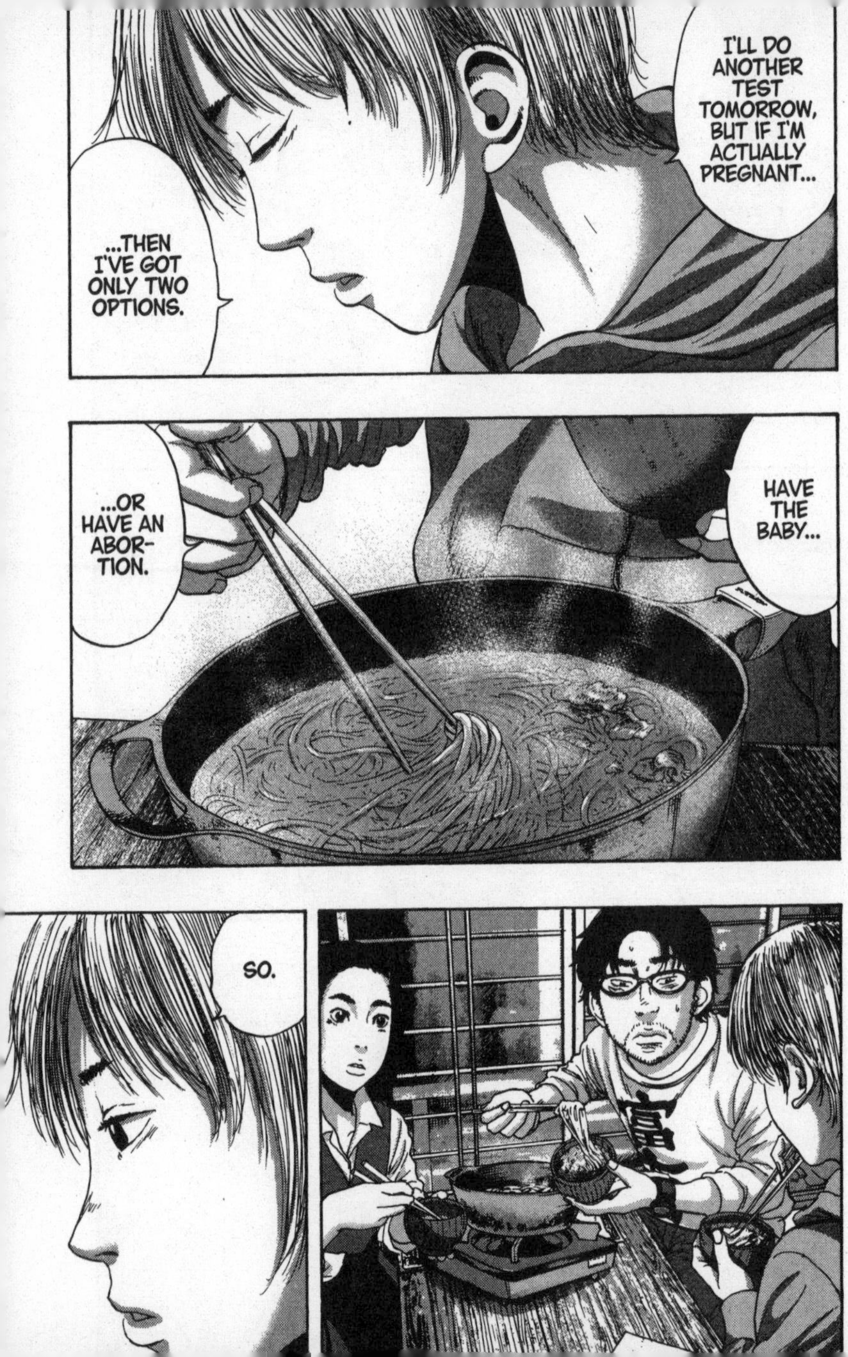
I'LL DO ANOTHER TEST TOMORROW, BUT IF I'M ACTUALLY PREGNANT...
...THEN I'VE GOT ONLY TWO OPTIONS.
HAVE THE BABY...
...OR HAVE AN ABOR-TION.
SO.

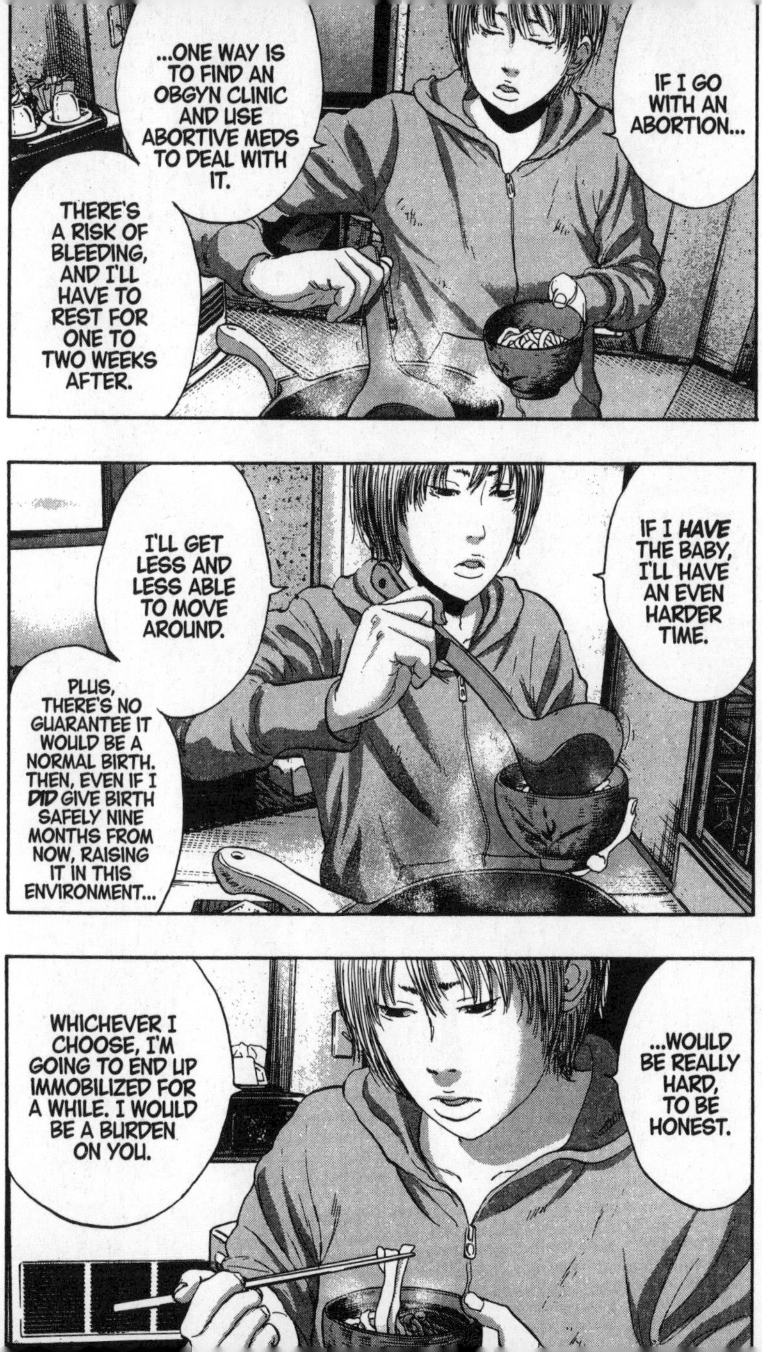
IF I GO WITH AN ABORTION...
...ONE WAY IS TO FIND AN OBGYN CLINIC AND USE ABORTIVE MEDS TO DEAL WITH IT.
THERE'S A RISK OF BLEEDING, AND I'LL HAVE TO REST FOR ONE TO TWO WEEKS AFTER.
IF I *HAVE* THE BABY, I'LL HAVE AN EVEN HARDER TIME.
I'LL GET LESS AND LESS ABLE TO MOVE AROUND.
PLUS, THERE'S NO GUARANTEE IT WOULD BE A NORMAL BIRTH. THEN, EVEN IF I *DID* GIVE BIRTH SAFELY NINE MONTHS FROM NOW, RAISING IT IN THIS ENVIRONMENT...
...WOULD BE REALLY HARD, TO BE HONEST.
WHICHEVER I CHOOSE, I'M GOING TO END UP IMMOBILIZED FOR A WHILE. I WOULD BE A BURDEN ON YOU.

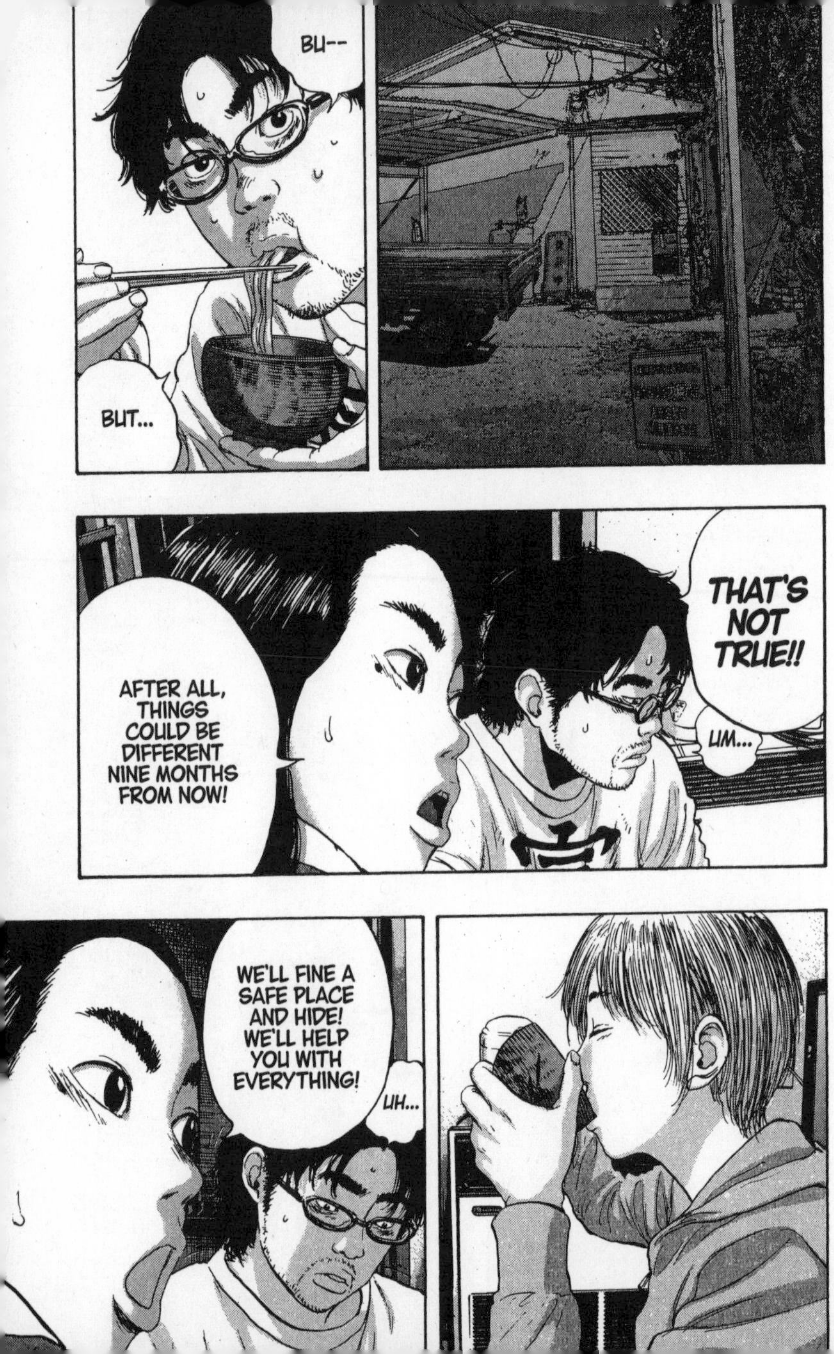
BU--
BUT...
THAT'S NOT TRUE!!
UM...
AFTER ALL, THINGS COULD BE DIFFERENT NINE MONTHS FROM NOW!
WE'LL FINE A SAFE PLACE AND HIDE! WE'LL HELP YOU WITH EVERYTHING!
UH...

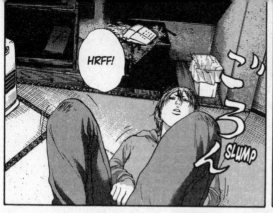

...
HRFF!
SLUMP
NINE MONTHS FROM NOW...?
I WASN'T EXPECTING LIFE TO RETURN TO NORMAL.
I-I'LL GO...
...TO A HOSPITAL AND GET ANY MEDICINES YOU NEED.
YOU SAW THE HOSPITALS. THEY'RE CRAWLING WITH THOSE THINGS.

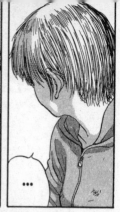

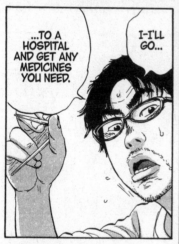

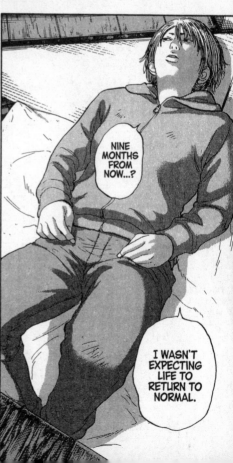

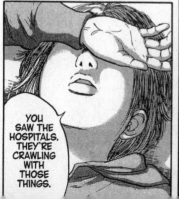

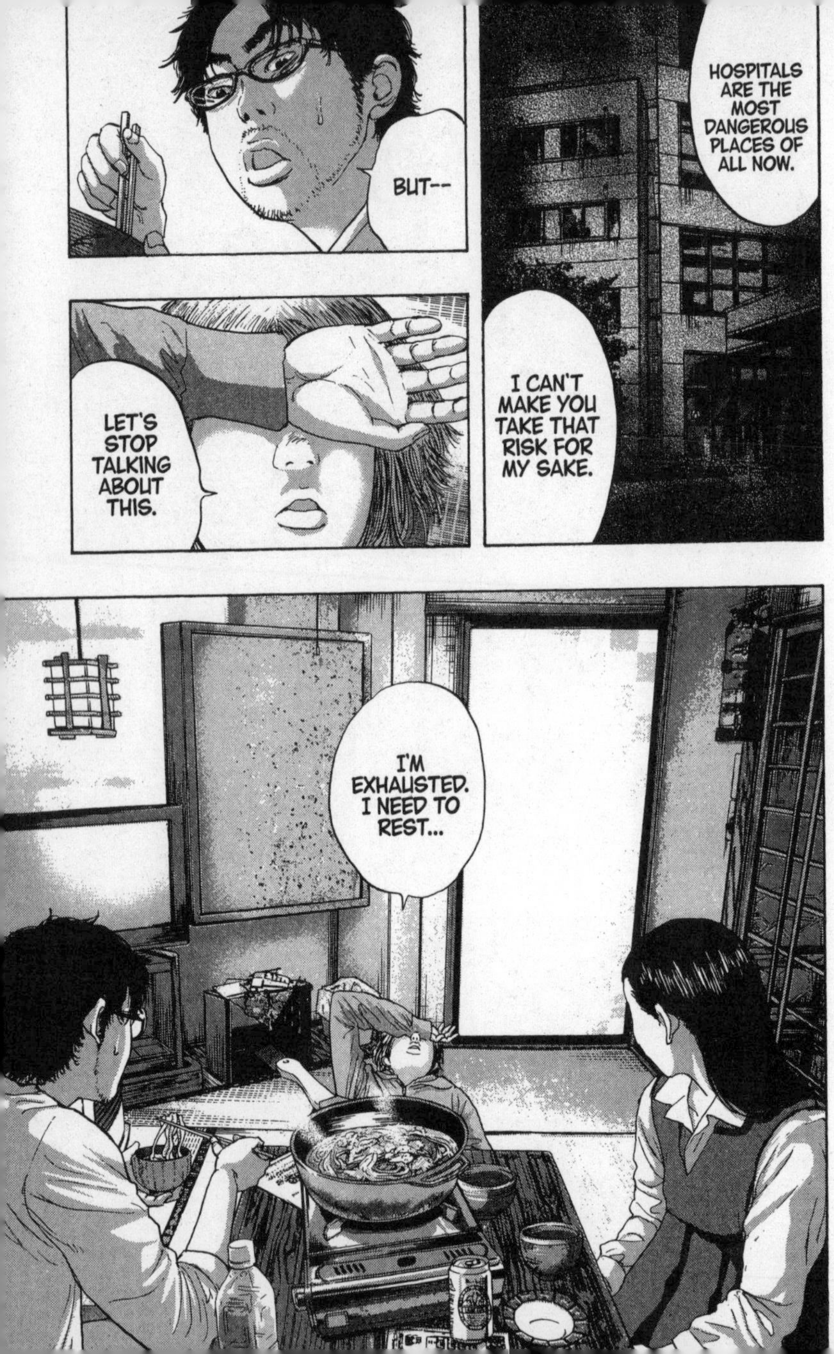
HOSPITALS ARE THE MOST DANGEROUS PLACES OF ALL NOW.
I CAN'T MAKE YOU TAKE THAT RISK FOR MY SAKE.
BUT--
LET'S STOP TALKING ABOUT THIS.
I'M EXHAUSTED. I NEED TO REST...

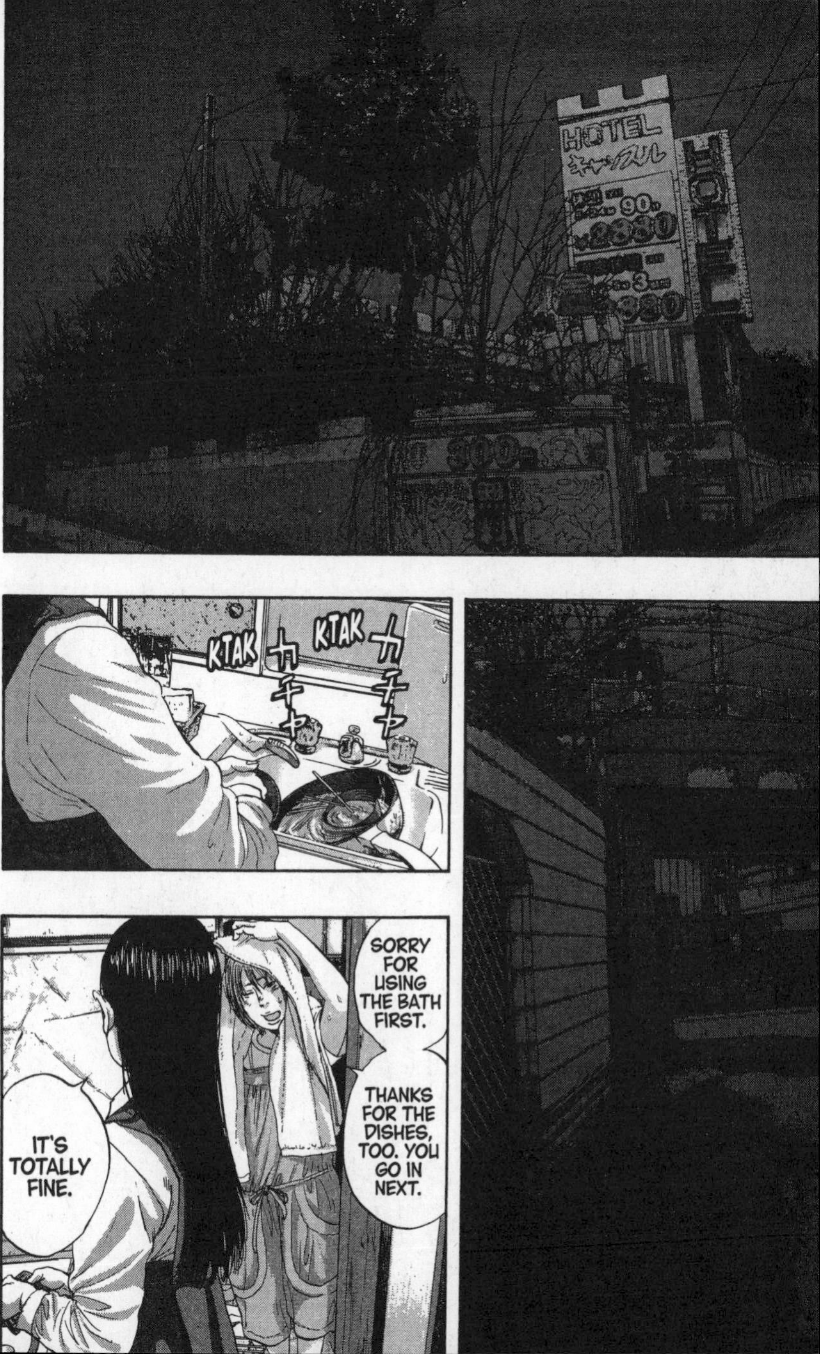
HOTEL
KTAK
カチャ
KTAK
カチャ
SORRY FOR USING THE BATH FIRST.
THANKS FOR THE DISHES, TOO. YOU GO IN NEXT.
IT'S TOTALLY FINE.

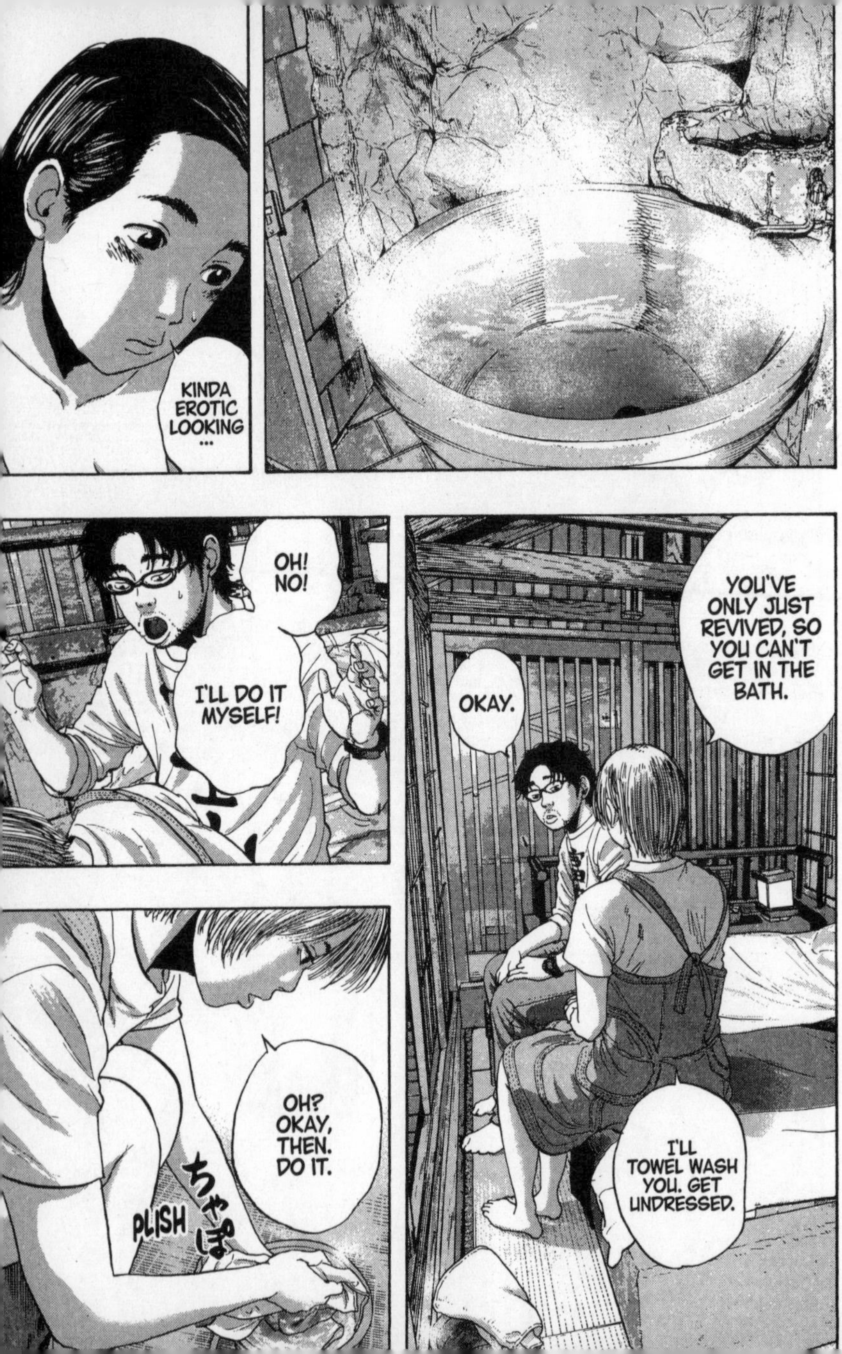
KINDA EROTIC LOOKING ...
YOU'VE ONLY JUST REVIVED, SO YOU CAN'T GET IN THE BATH.
OKAY.
I'LL TOWEL WASH YOU. GET UNDRESSED.
OH! NO!
I'LL DO IT MYSELF!
OH? OKAY, THEN. DO IT.
ちゃぽ
PLISH

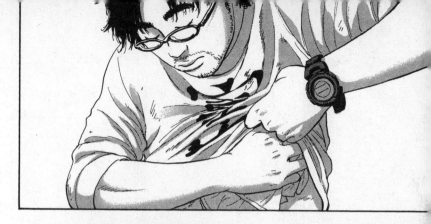

HERE.
I'LL DO YOUR BACK. GIVE ME THE TOWEL.
TH-THANK YOU. I'LL TAKE YOU UP ON THAT...
SPASH SPISH
しゃばば
MISS ODA, UM...

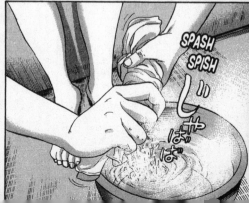

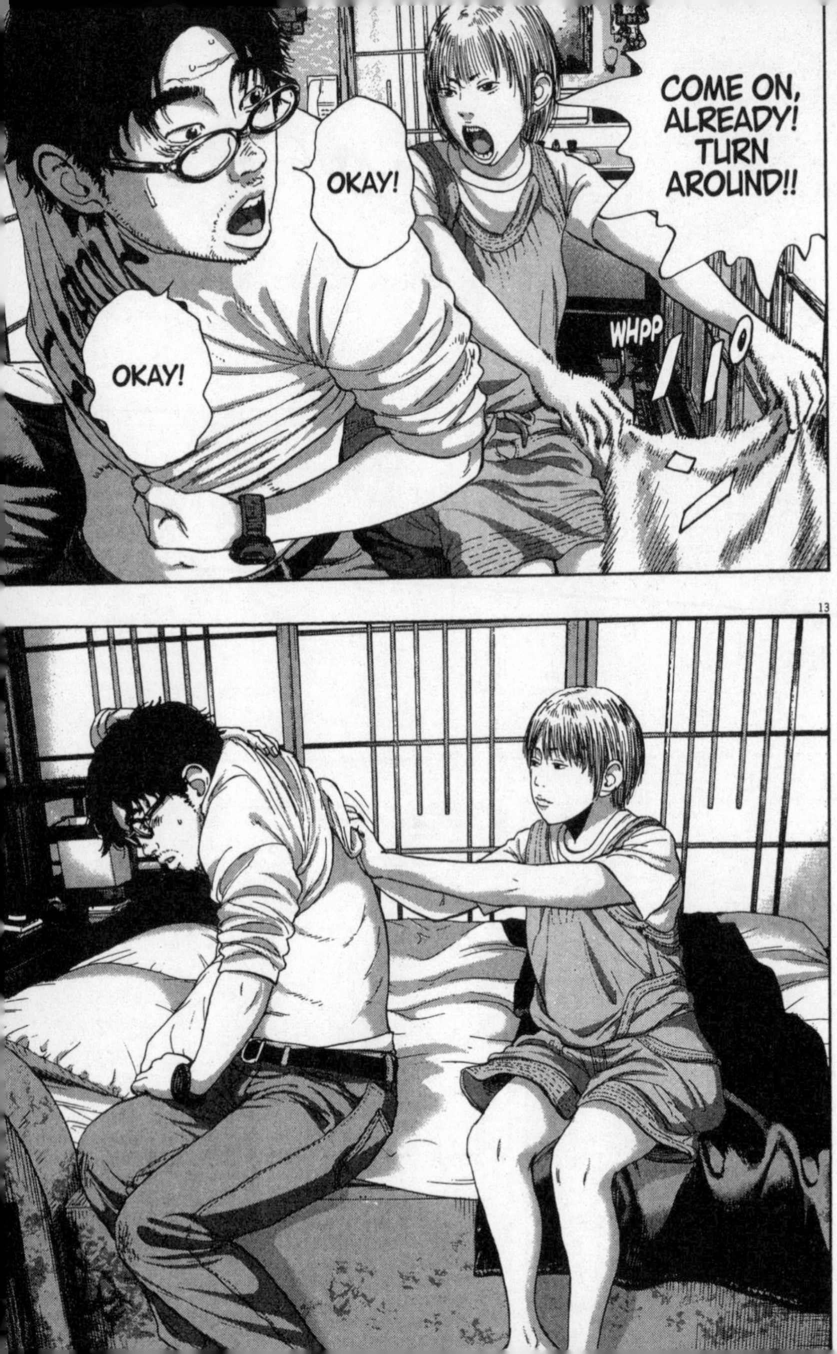
COME ON, ALREADY! TURN AROUND!!
WHPP
OKAY!
OKAY!

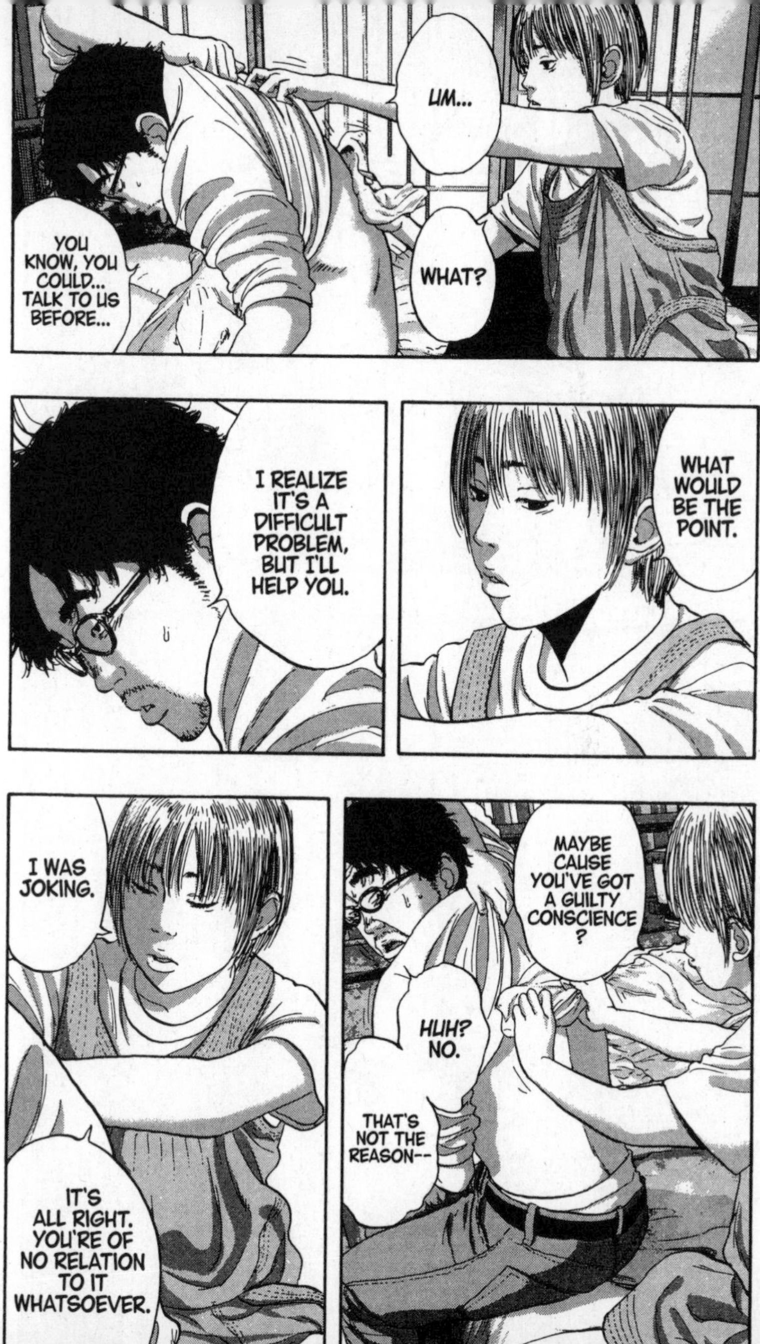
UM...
WHAT?
YOU KNOW, YOU COULD... TALK TO US BEFORE...
WHAT WOULD BE THE POINT.
I REALIZE IT'S A DIFFICULT PROBLEM, BUT I'LL HELP YOU.
MAYBE CAUSE YOU'VE GOT A GUILTY CONSCIENCE ?
HUH? NO.
THAT'S NOT THE REASON--
I WAS JOKING.
IT'S ALL RIGHT. YOU'RE OF NO RELATION TO IT WHATSOEVER.

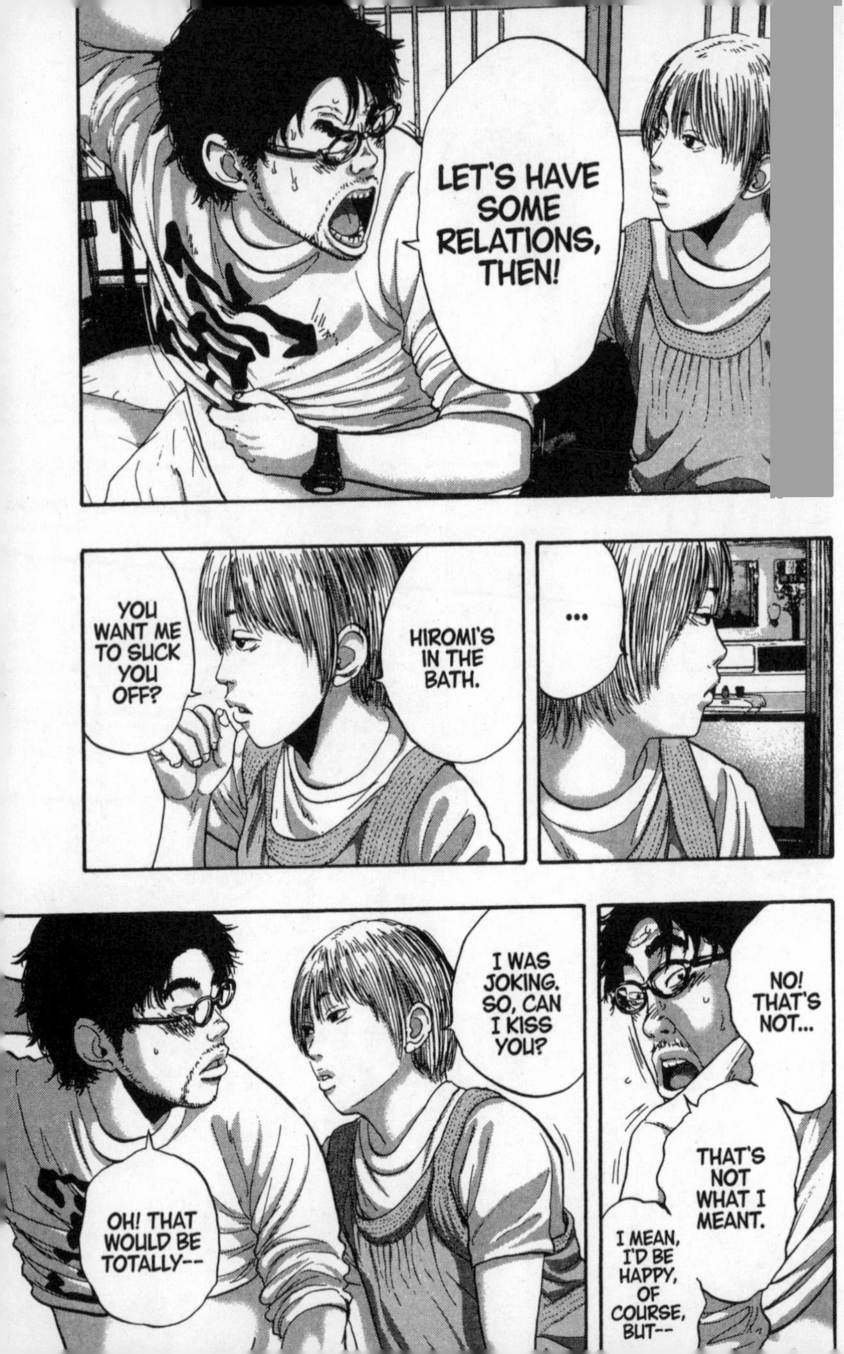
LET'S HAVE SOME RELATIONS, THEN!
...
HIROMI'S IN THE BATH.
YOU WANT ME TO SUCK YOU OFF?
NO! THAT'S NOT...
THAT'S NOT WHAT I MEANT.
I MEAN, I'D BE HAPPY, OF COURSE, BUT--
I WAS JOKING. SO, CAN I KISS YOU?
OH! THAT WOULD BE TOTALLY--

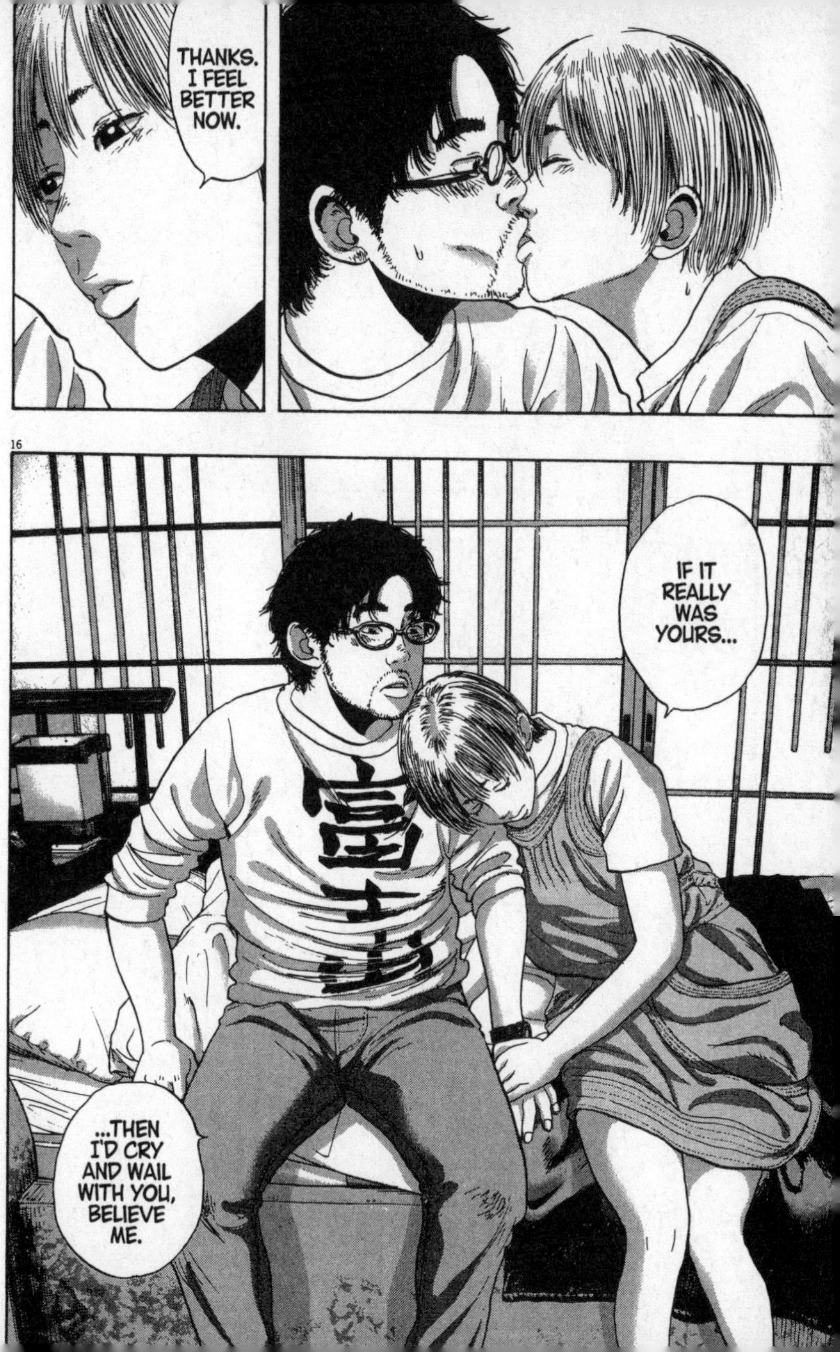
THANKS. I FEEL BETTER NOW.
IF IT REALLY WAS YOURS...
...THEN I'D CRY AND WAIL WITH YOU, BELIEVE ME.

CHAPTER
179

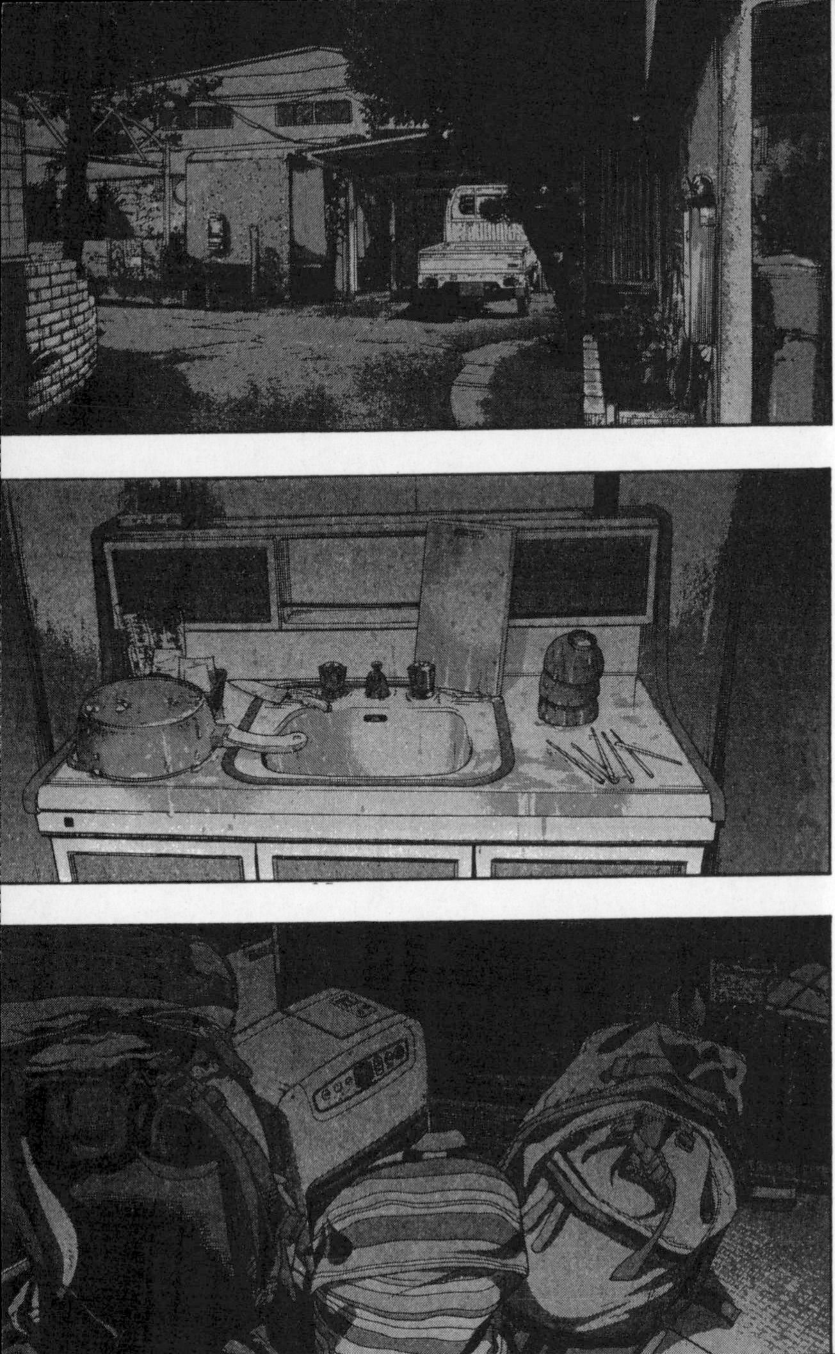

HNNF!

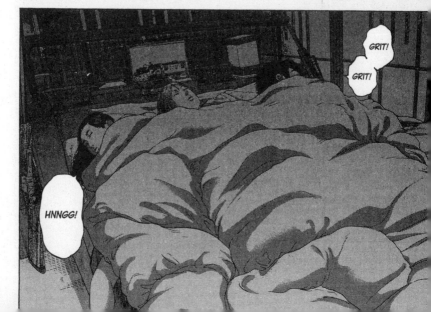

GRIT!

GRIT!

HNNGG!

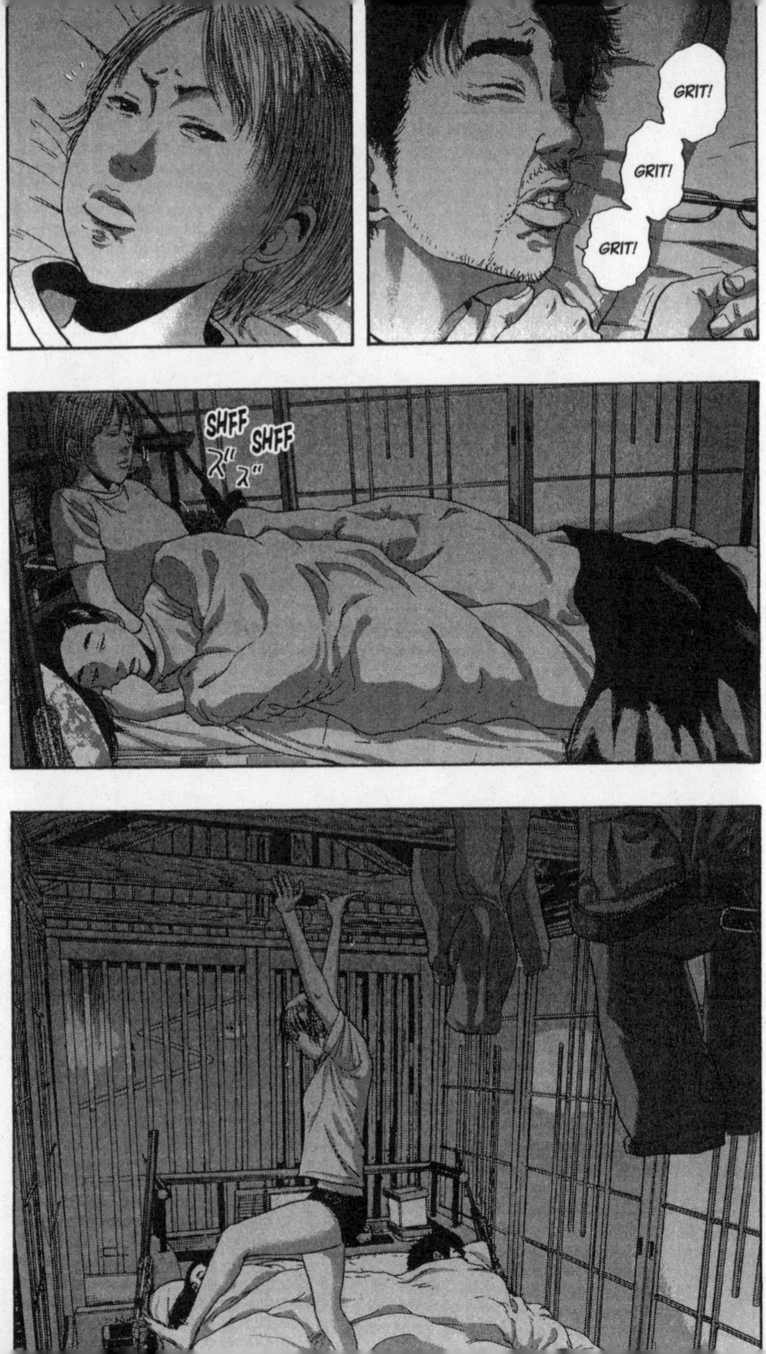
GRIT!
GRIT!
GRIT!
SHFF
SHFF
ズ
ズ

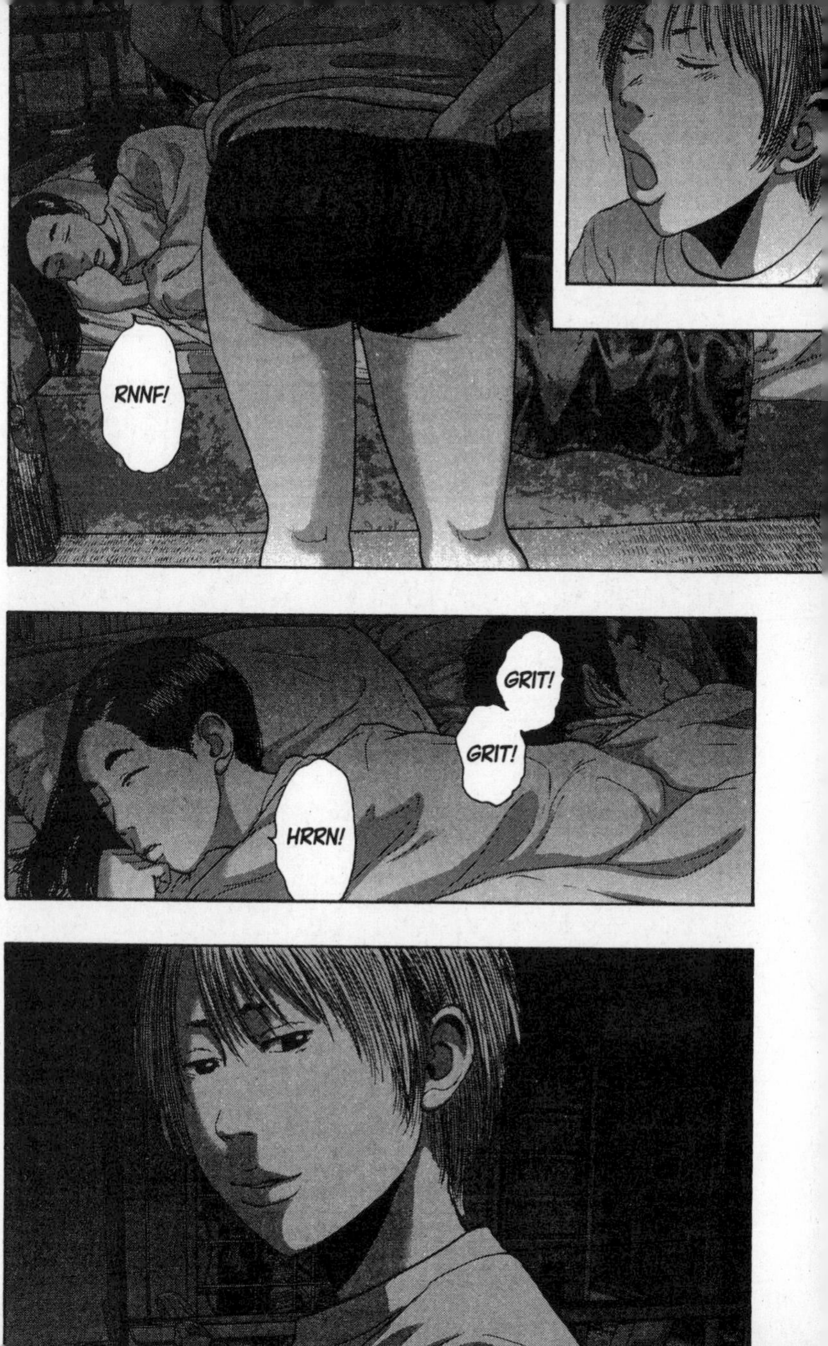
RNNF!
GRIT!
GRIT!
HRRN!

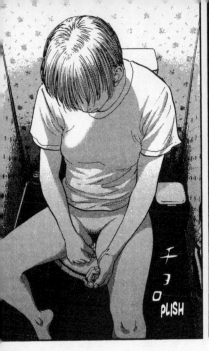

PLISH

CREAK

CREAK

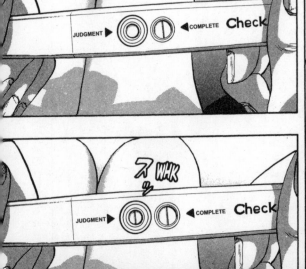

JUDGMENT ▶ ◀ COMPLETE Check

WHK

JUDGMENT ▶ ◀ COMPLETE Check

SPLISHAA

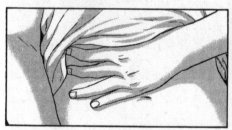

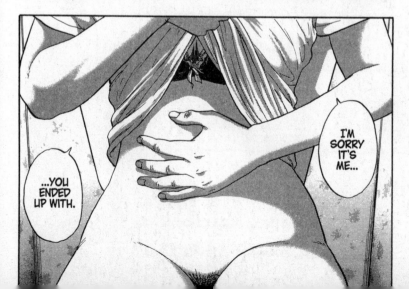

I'M
SORRY
IT'S
ME...

...YOU
ENDED
UP WITH.

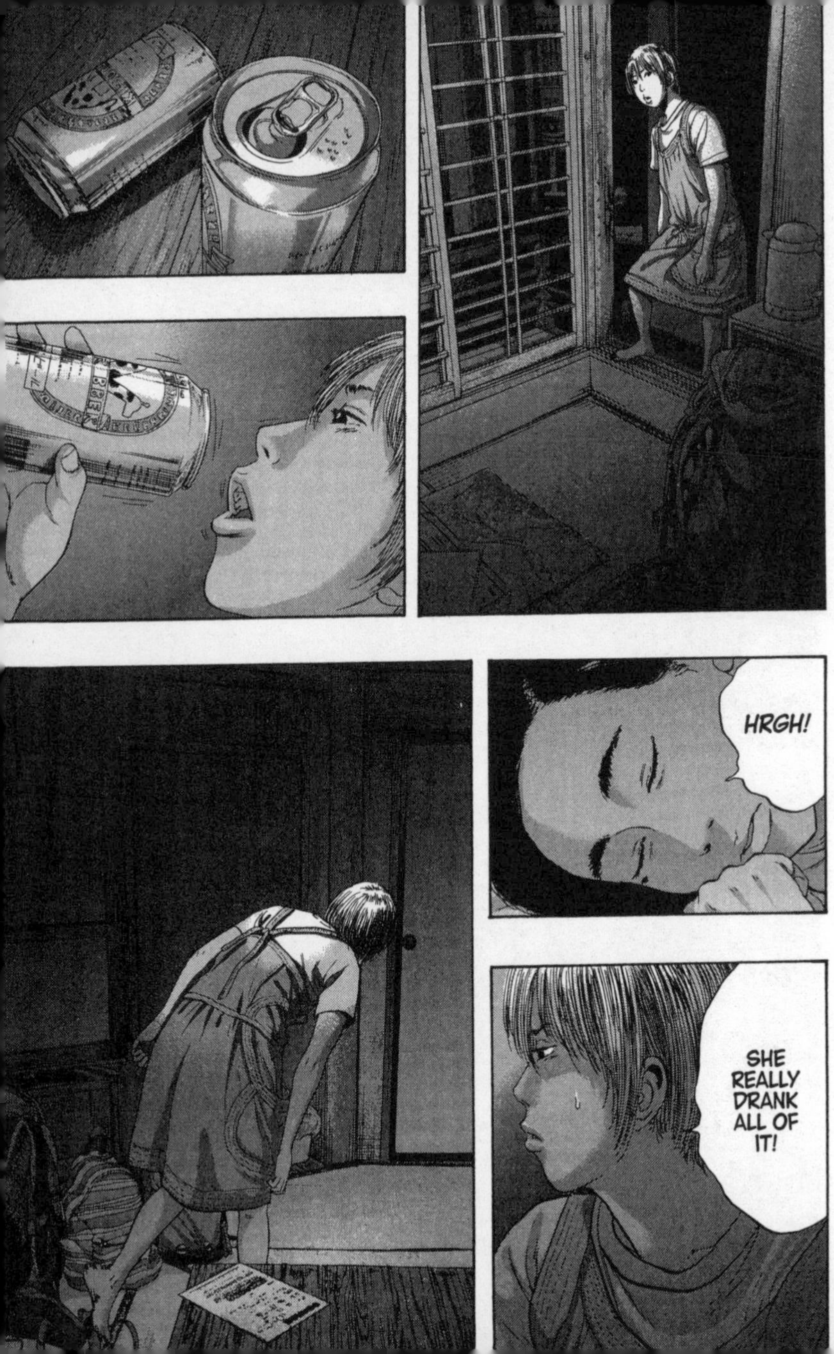
HRGH!
SHE REALLY DRANK ALL OF IT!

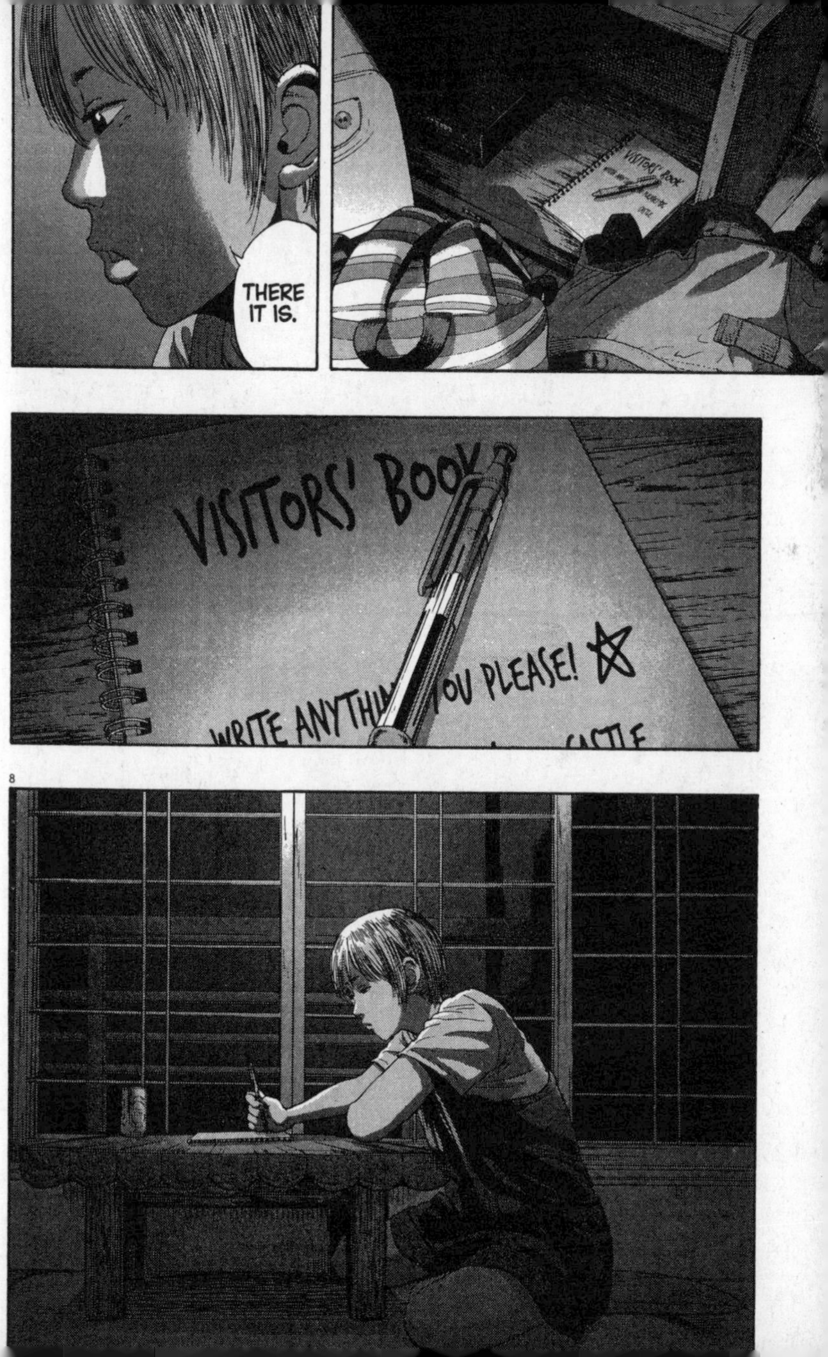
THERE IT IS.
VISITORS'

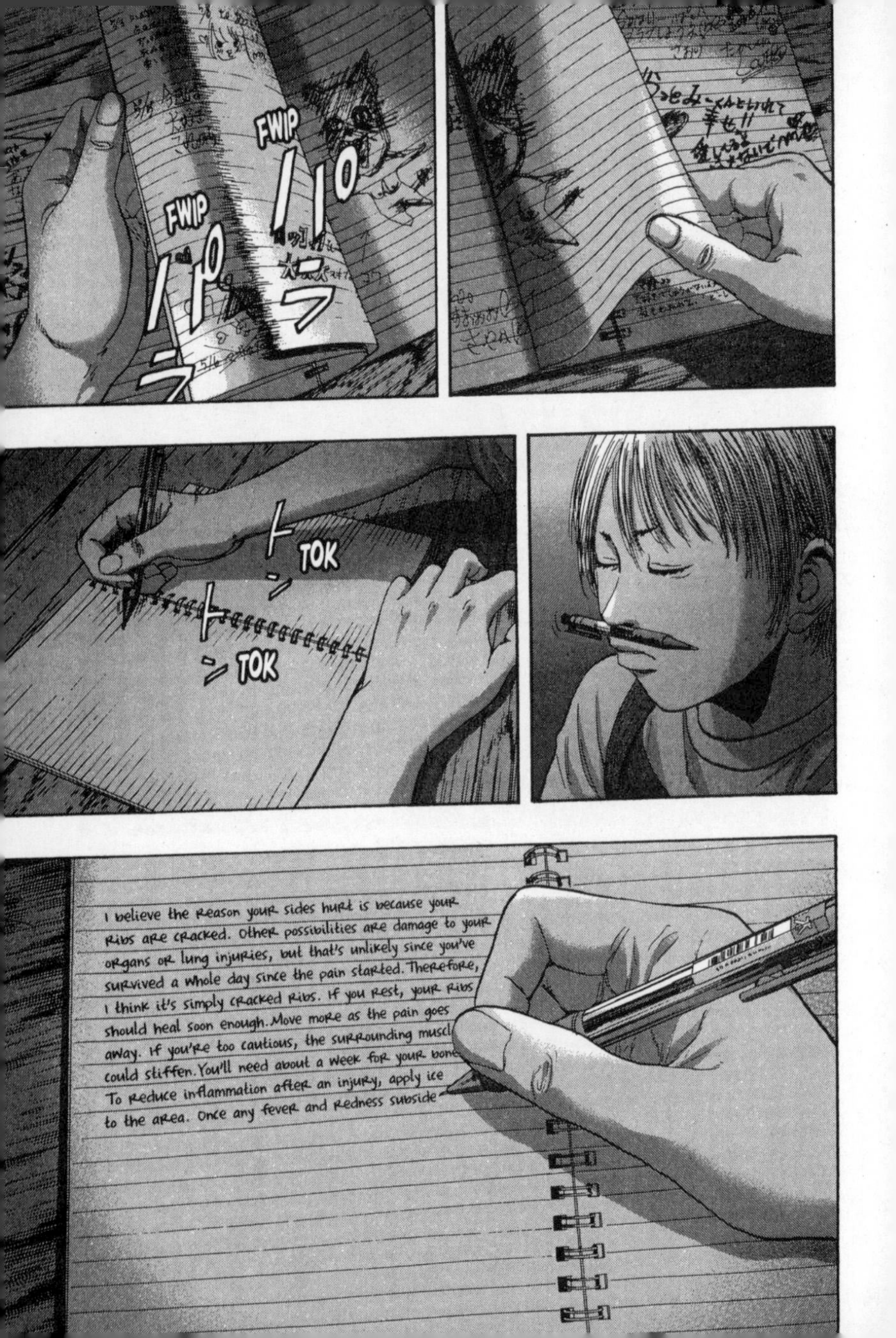

FWIP
パラ
FWIP
パラ
トン
TOK
トン
TOK
I believe the reason your sides hurt is because your ribs are cracked. Other possibilities are damage to your organs or lung injuries, but that's unlikely since you've survived a whole day since the pain started. Therefore, I think it's simply cracked ribs. If you rest, your ribs should heal soon enough. Move more as the pain goes away. If you're too cautious, the surrounding muscl could stiffen. You'll need about a week for your bone To reduce inflammation after an injury, apply ice to the area. Once any fever and redness subside

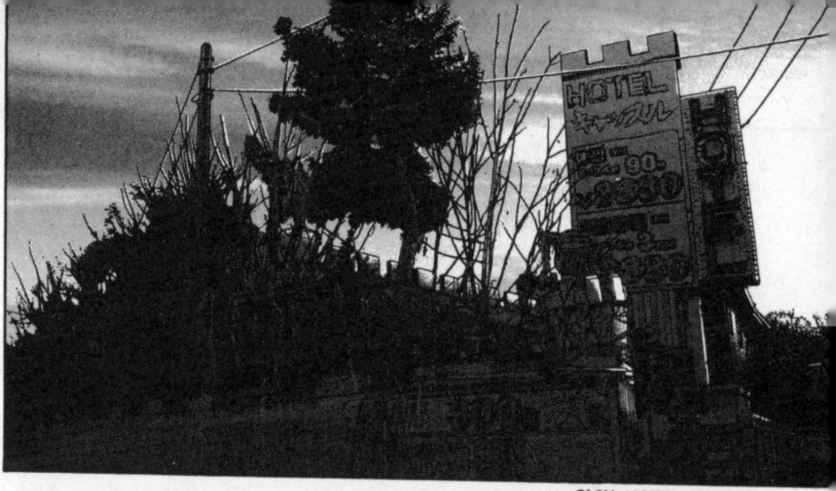
HOTEL

SIGN: HOTEL CASTLE

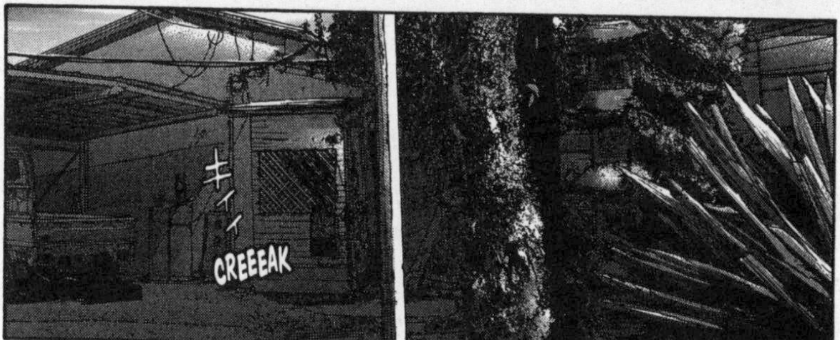
キイイ
CREEEAK

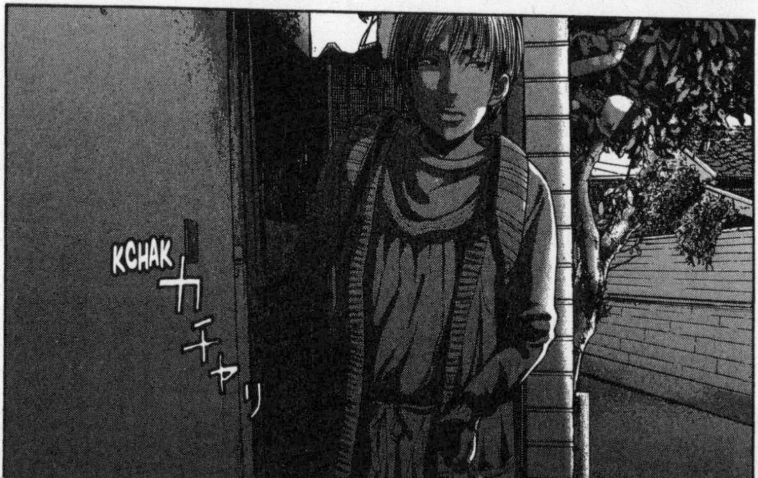
KCHAK
カチャリ

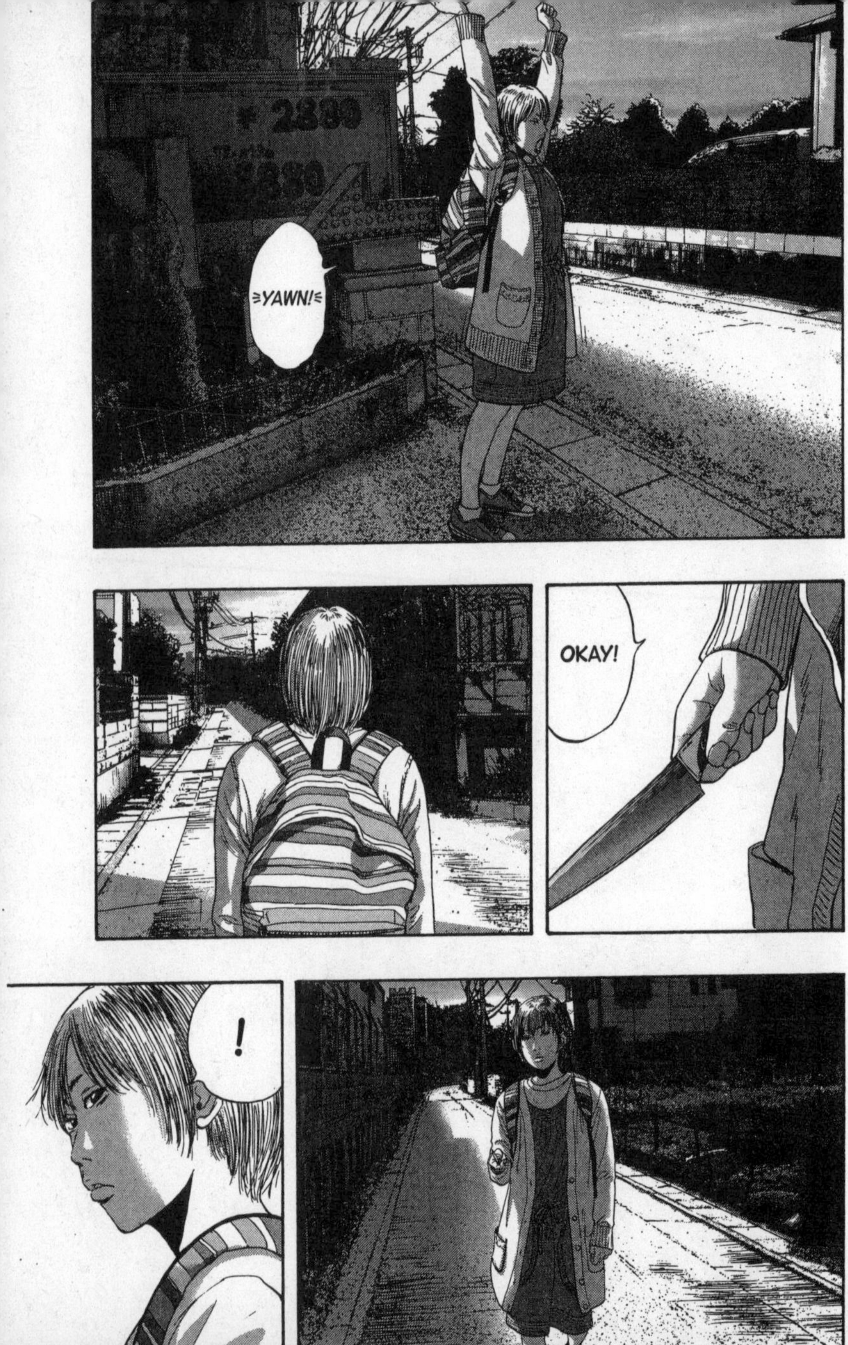
≈YAWN!≈
OKAY!
!

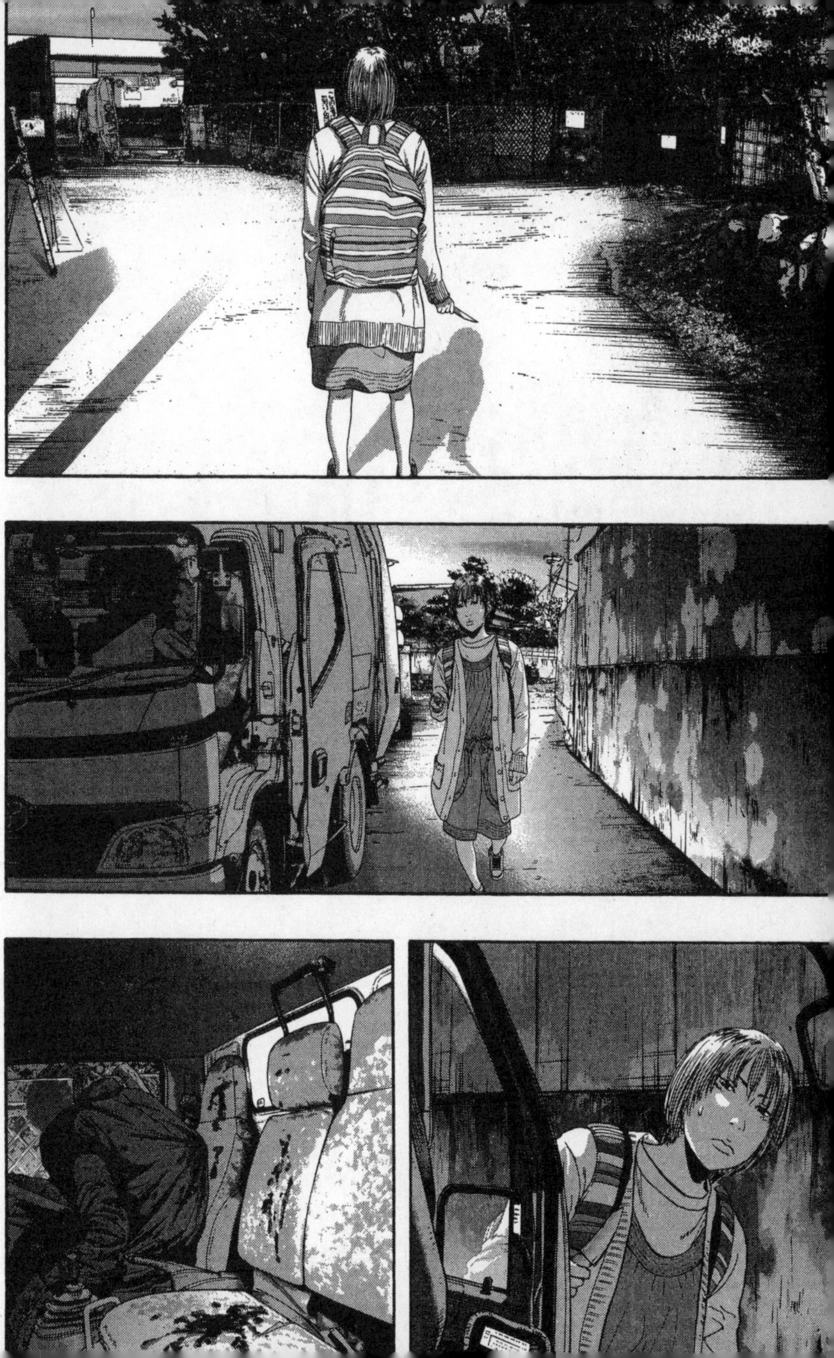

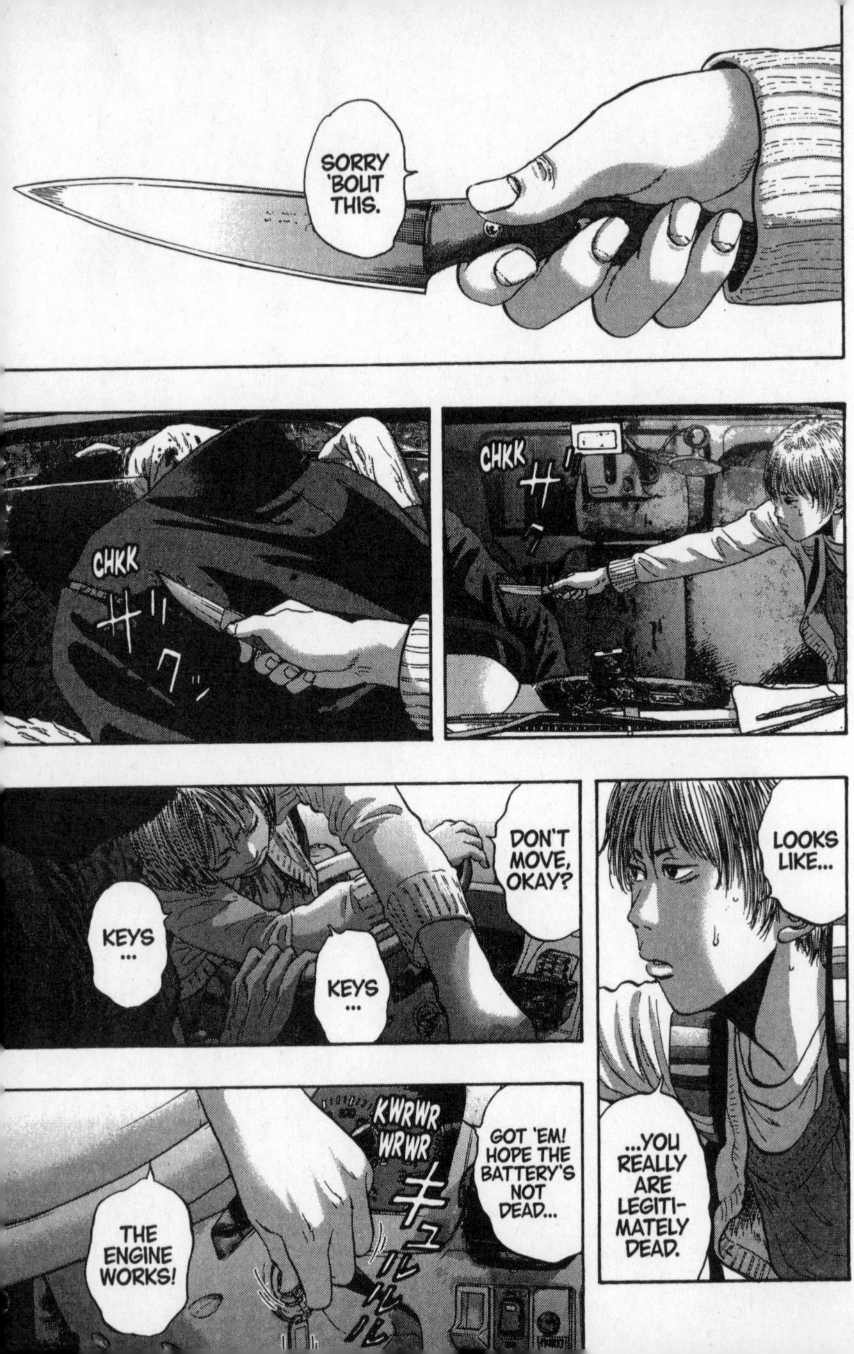
SORRY 'BOUT THIS.
CHKK
CHKK
LOOKS LIKE...
...YOU REALLY ARE LEGITI-MATELY DEAD.
DON'T MOVE, OKAY?
KEYS...
KEYS...
GOT 'EM! HOPE THE BATTERY'S NOT DEAD...
KWRWR WRWR
キュルルル
THE ENGINE WORKS!

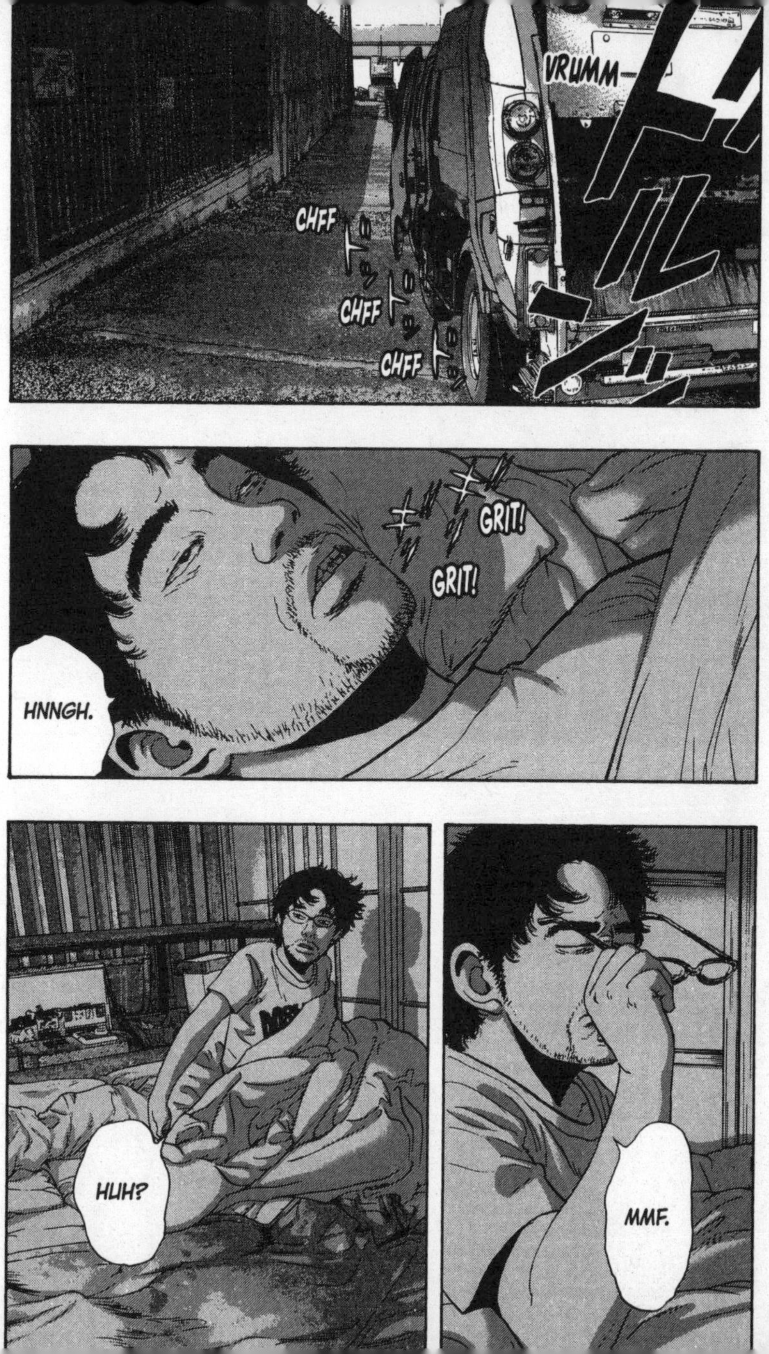
VRUMM
CHFF
CHFF
CHFF
GRIT!
GRIT!
HNNGH.
MMF.
HUH?

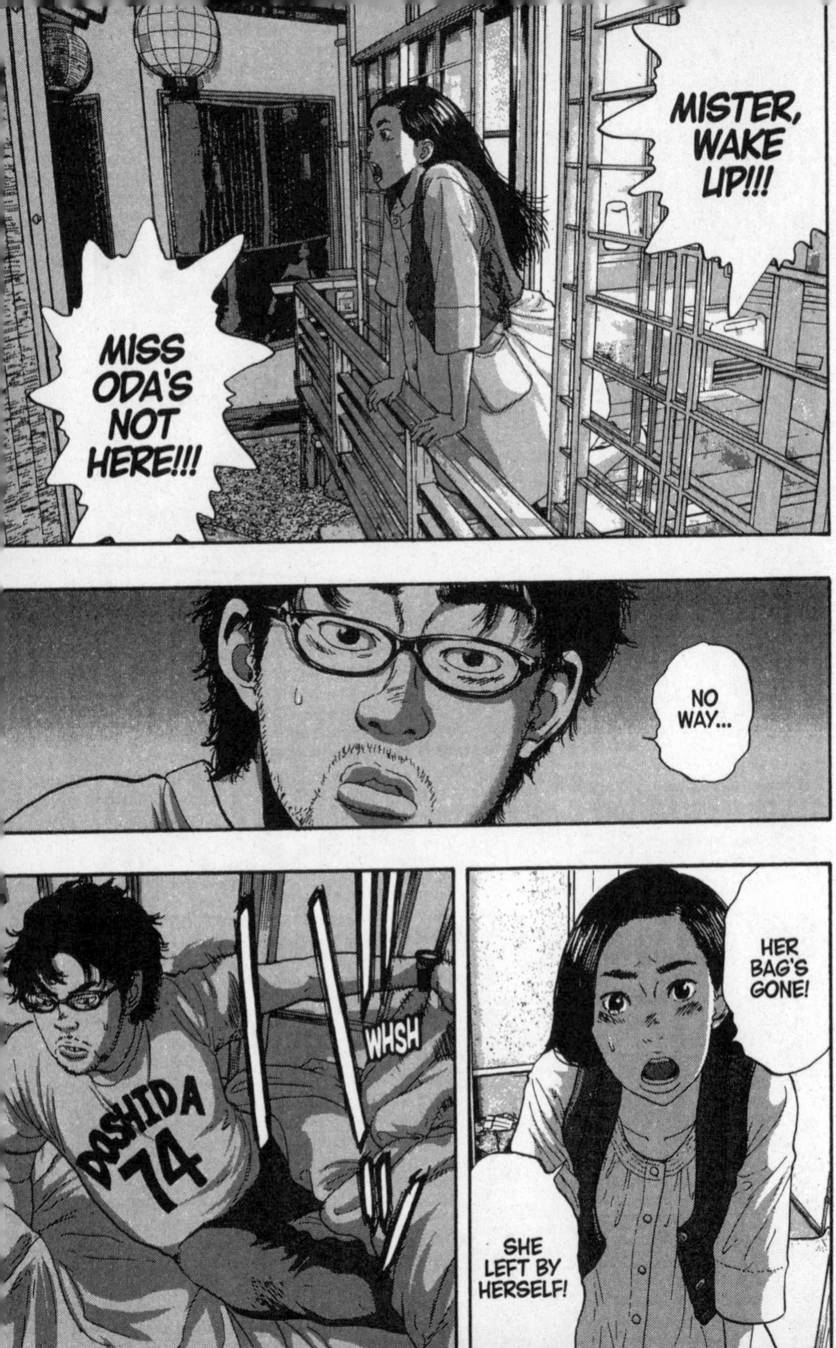
MISTER, WAKE UP!!!
MISS ODA'S NOT HERE!!!
NO WAY...
HER BAG'S GONE!
SHE LEFT BY HERSELF!
WHSH
DOSHIDA 74

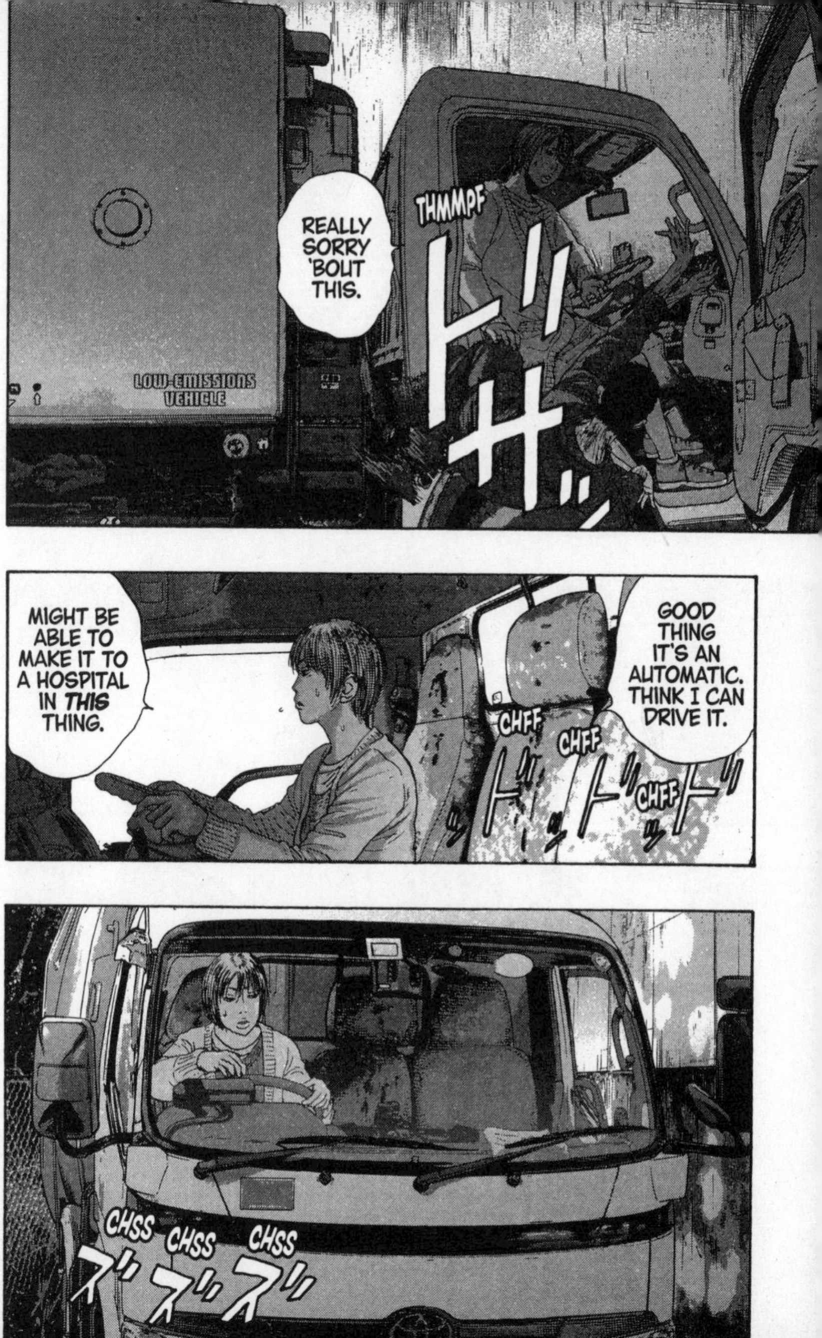
REALLY SORRY 'BOUT THIS.
THMMPF
LOW-EMISSIONS VEHICLE
GOOD THING IT'S AN AUTOMATIC. THINK I CAN DRIVE IT.
CHFF
CHFF
CHFF
MIGHT BE ABLE TO MAKE IT TO A HOSPITAL IN *THIS* THING.
CHSS
CHSS
CHSS

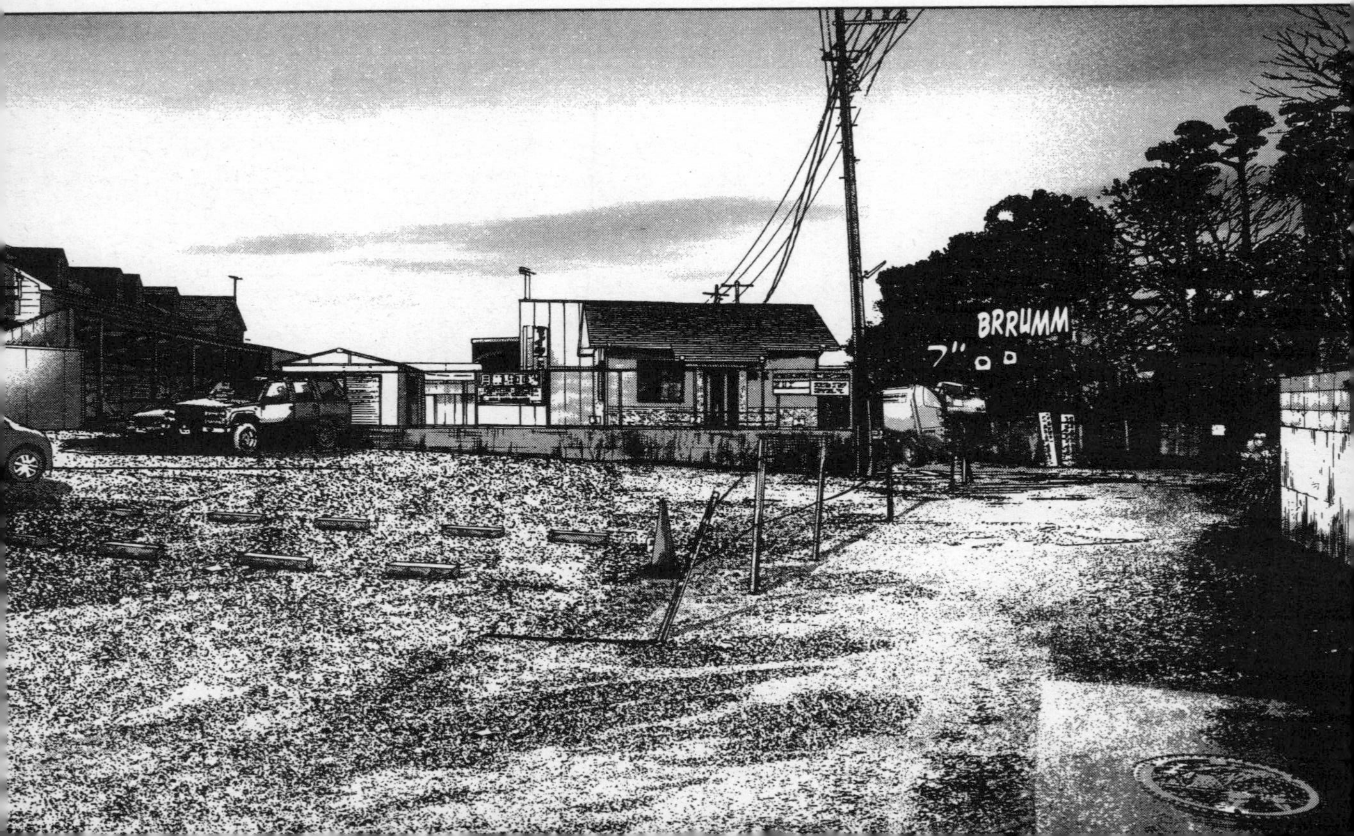
BRRUMM
ブロロ

CHAPTER 180

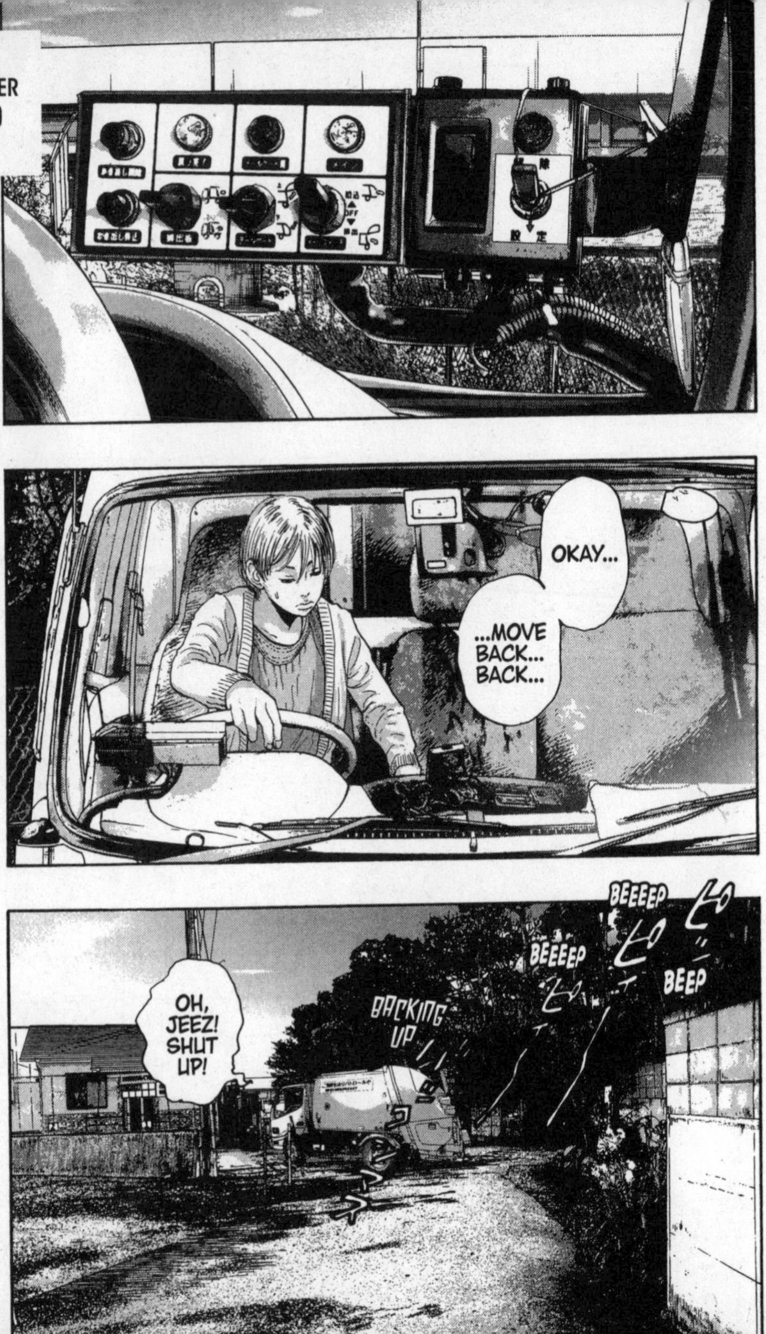
OKAY...
...MOVE BACK... BACK...
BEEEEP
BEEP
BEEEEP
BACKING UP
OH, JEEZ! SHUT UP!

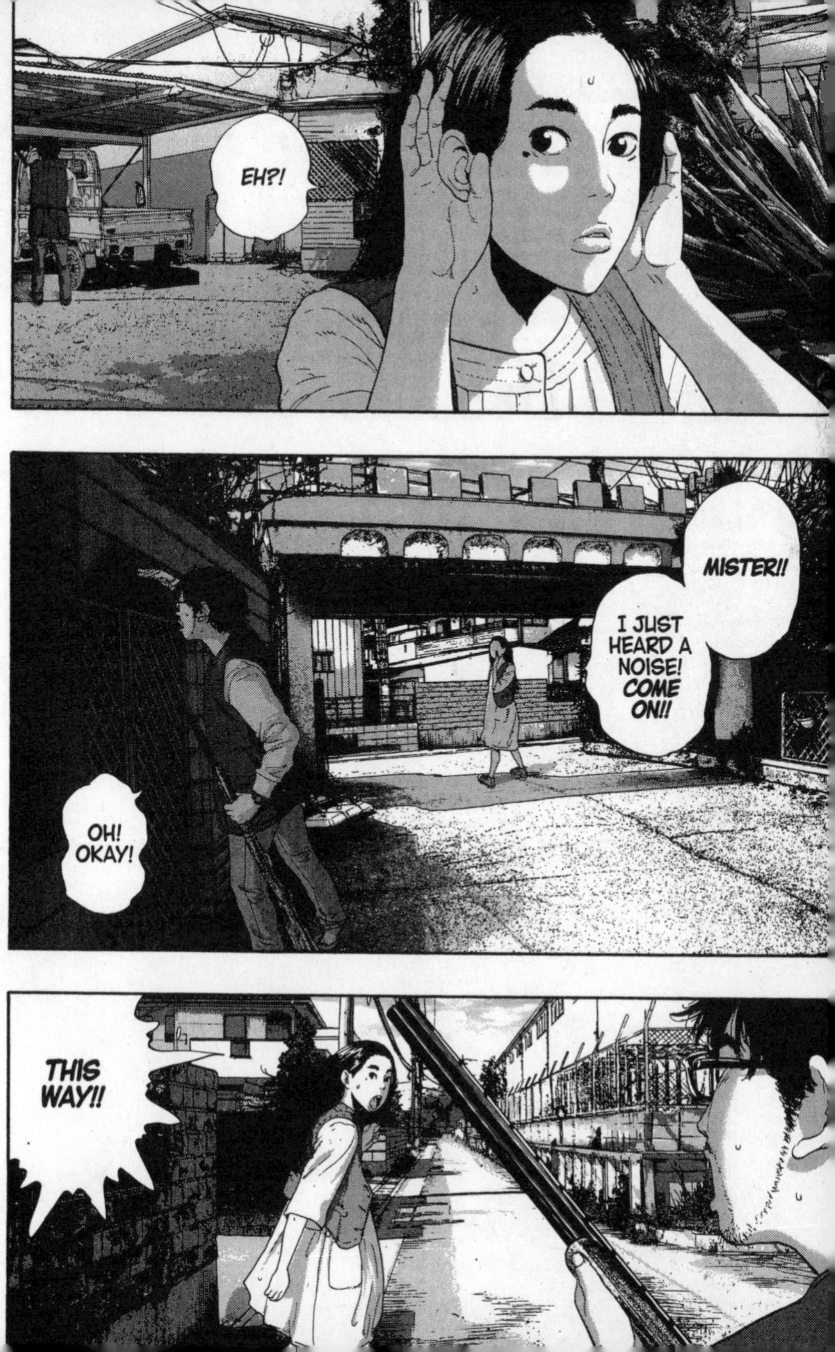
EH?!
MISTER!!
I JUST HEARD A NOISE! COME ON!!
OH! OKAY!
THIS WAY!!

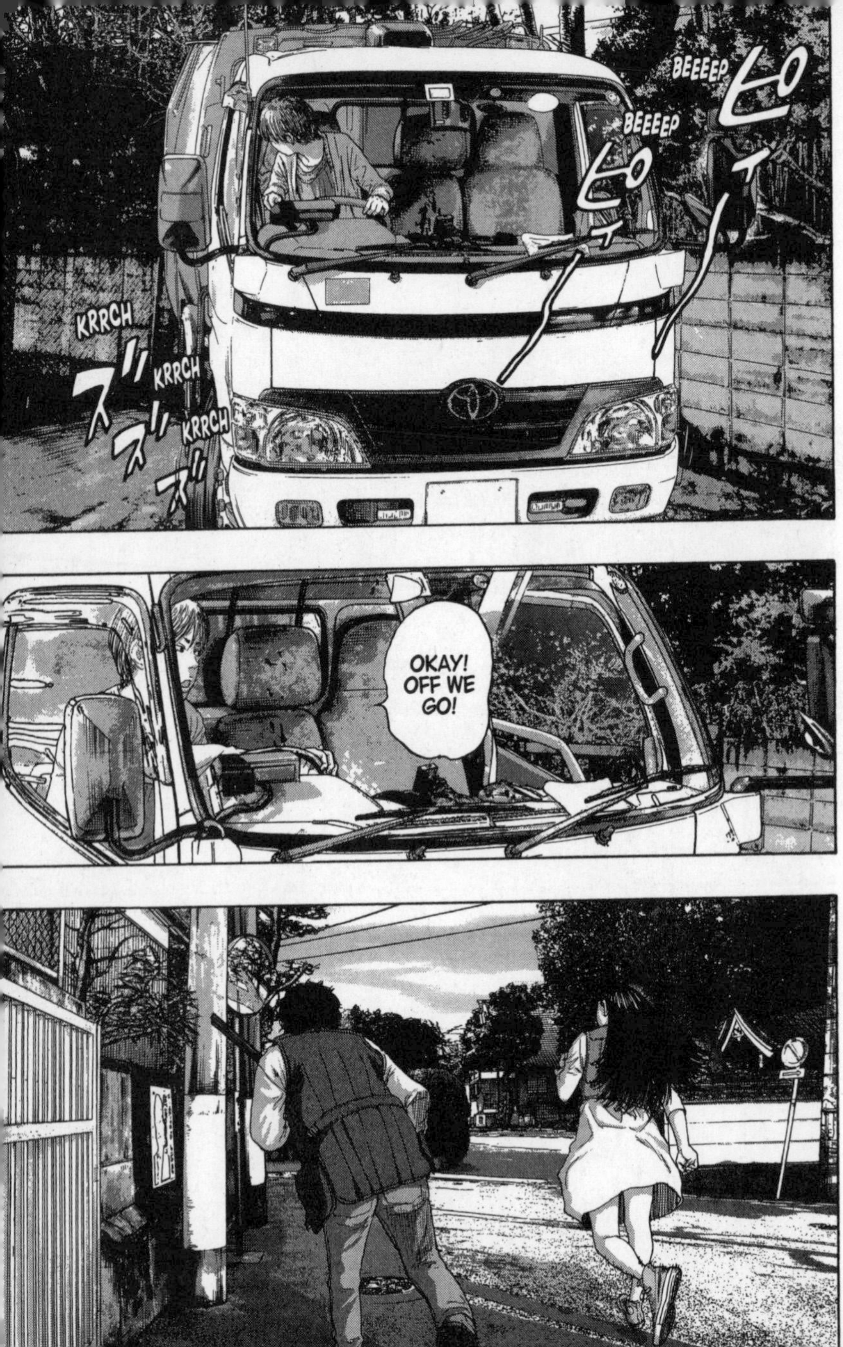
BEEEEP
ピィー
BEEEEP
ピィー
KRRCH
ズ
KRRCH
ズ
KRRCH
ズ
OKAY! OFF WE GO!

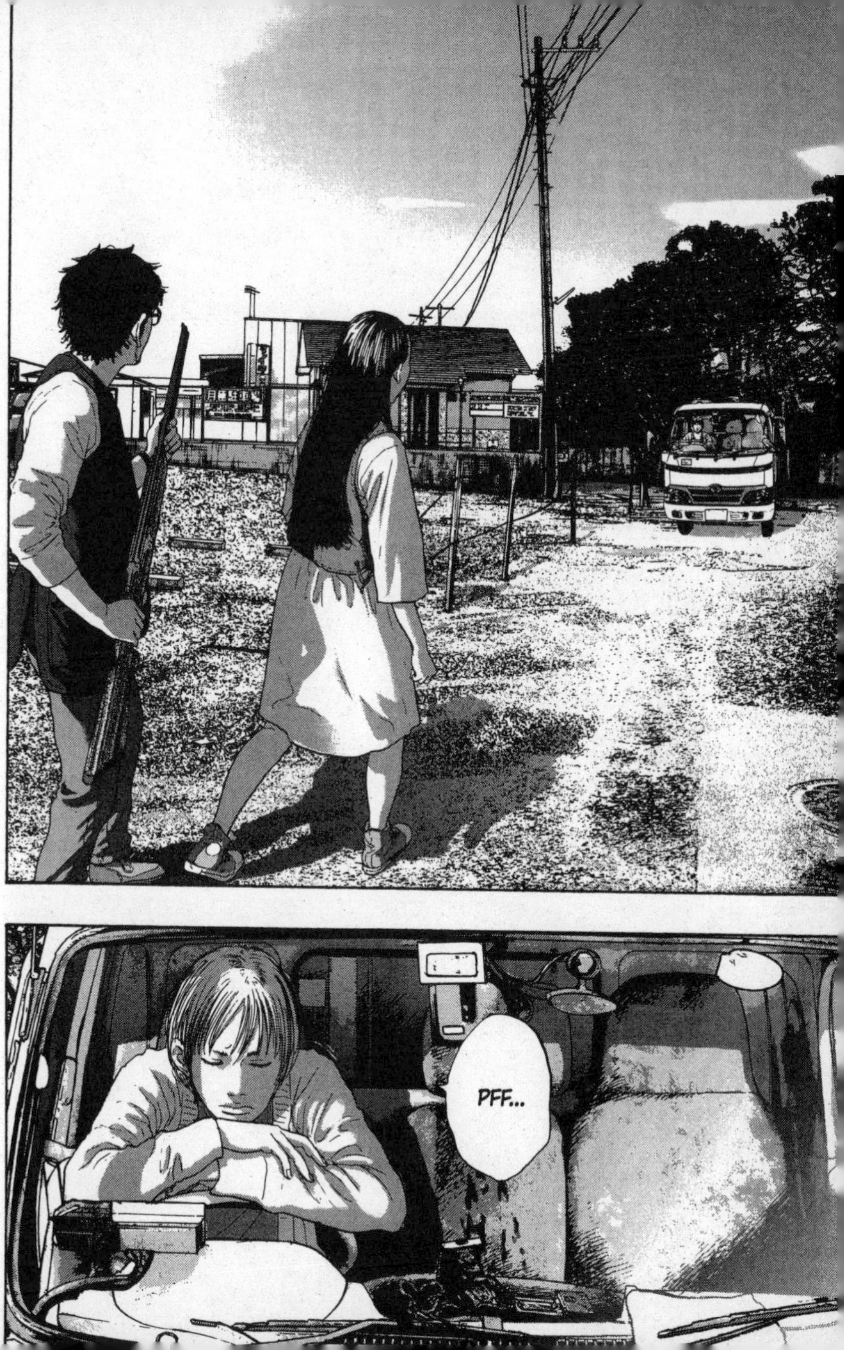
PFF...

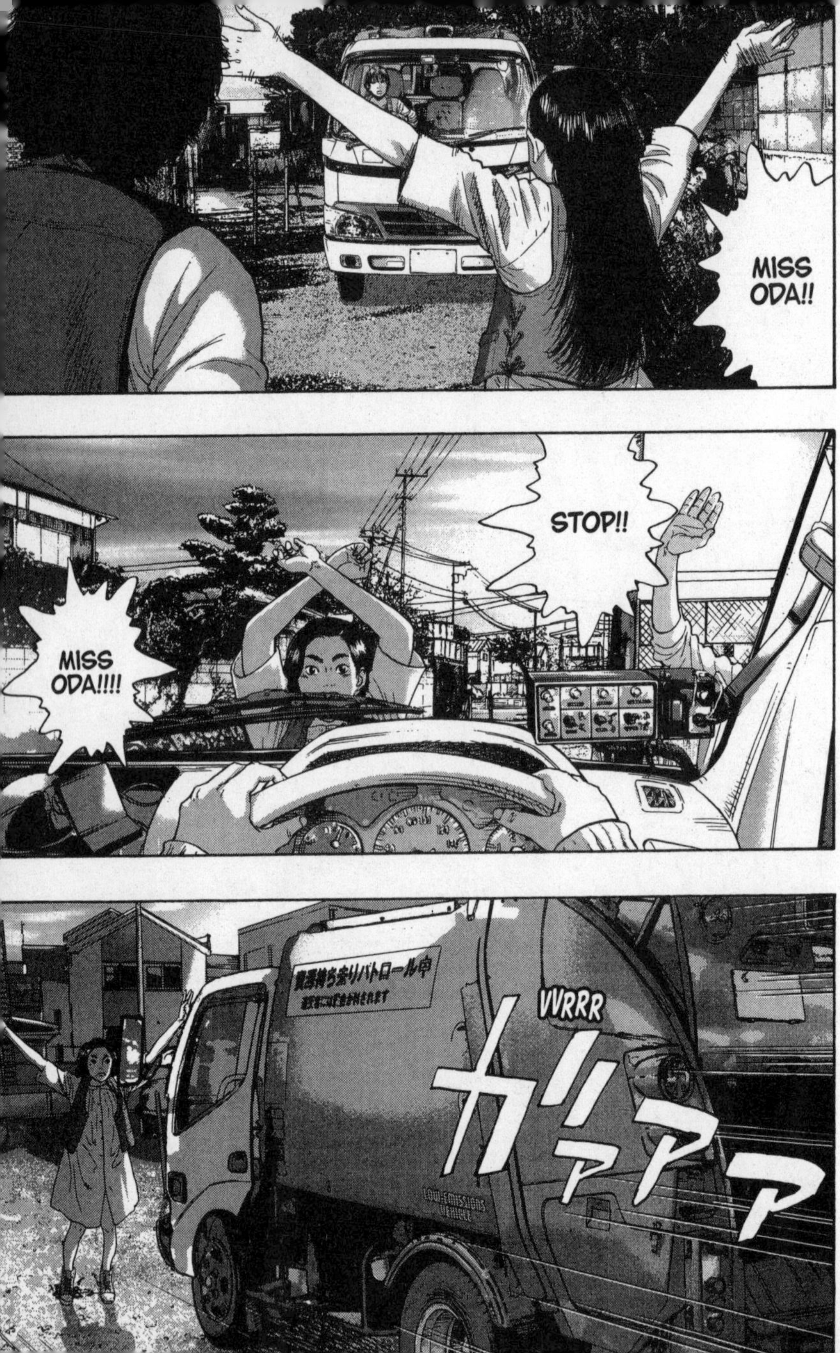
MISS ODA!!
STOP!!
MISS ODA!!!!
VVRRR
ガァアア

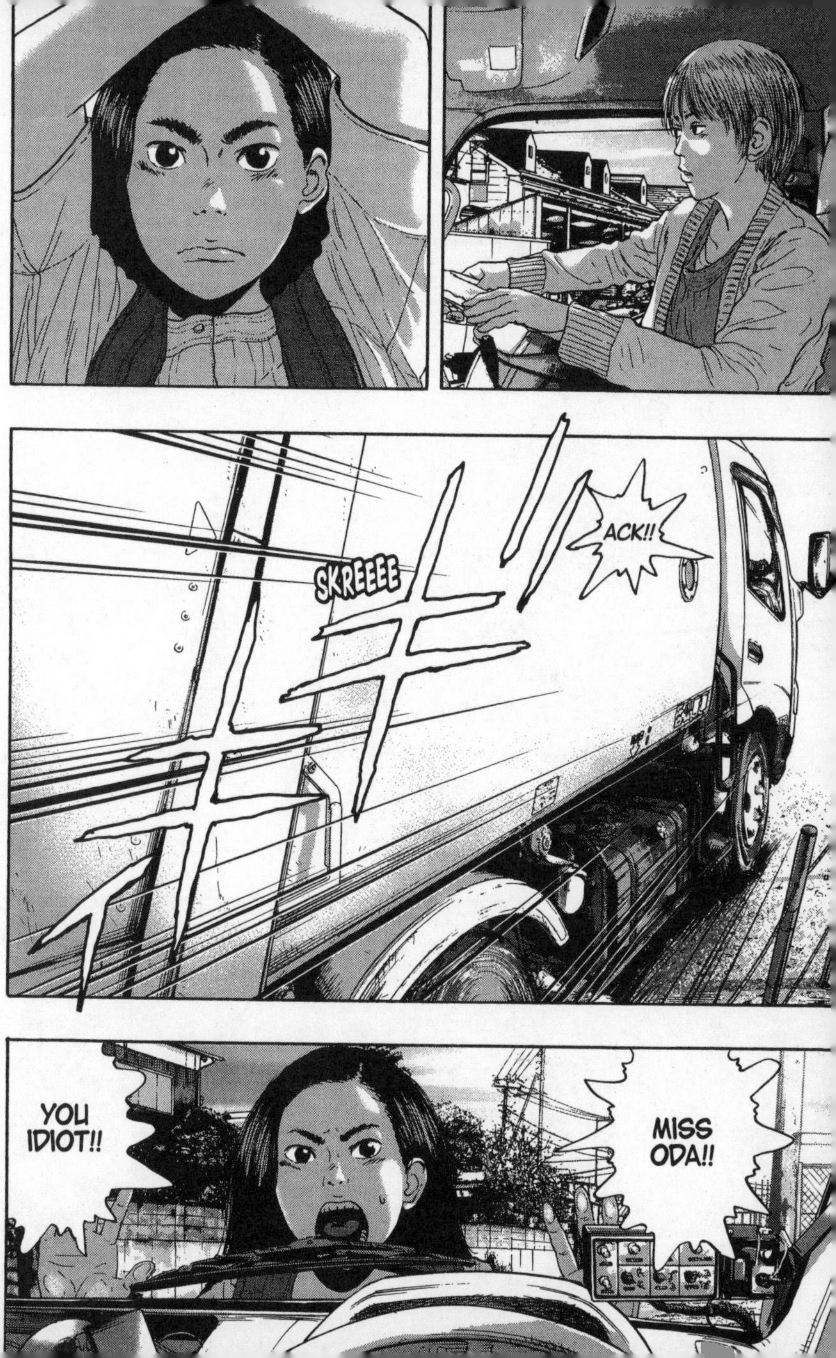
ACK!!
SKREEEE
MISS ODA!!
YOU IDIOT!!

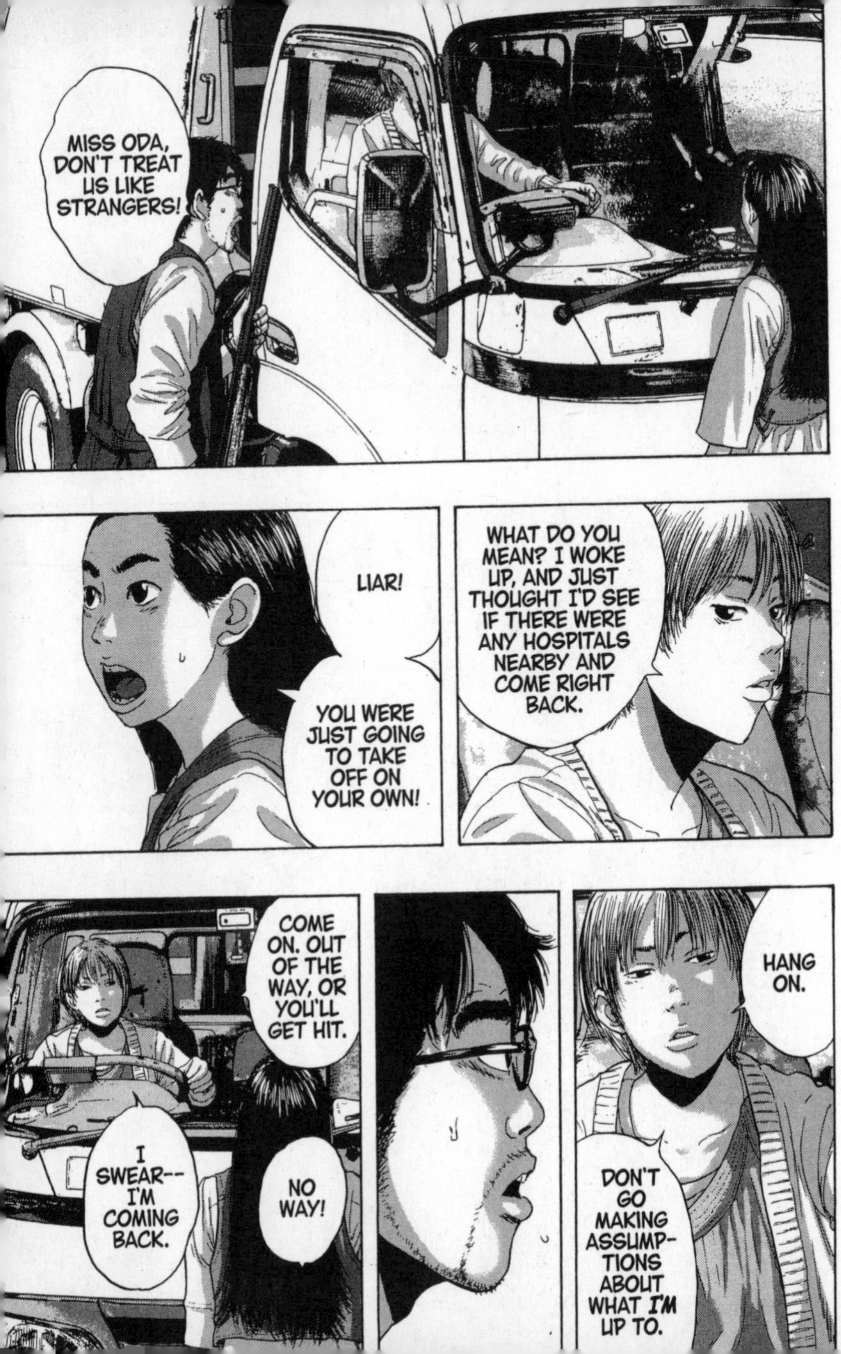
MISS ODA, DON'T TREAT US LIKE STRANGERS!
WHAT DO YOU MEAN? I WOKE UP, AND JUST THOUGHT I'D SEE IF THERE WERE ANY HOSPITALS NEARBY AND COME RIGHT BACK.
LIAR!
YOU WERE JUST GOING TO TAKE OFF ON YOUR OWN!
HANG ON.
DON'T GO MAKING ASSUMPTIONS ABOUT WHAT *I'M* UP TO.
NO WAY!
COME ON. OUT OF THE WAY, OR YOU'LL GET HIT.
I SWEAR-- I'M COMING BACK.

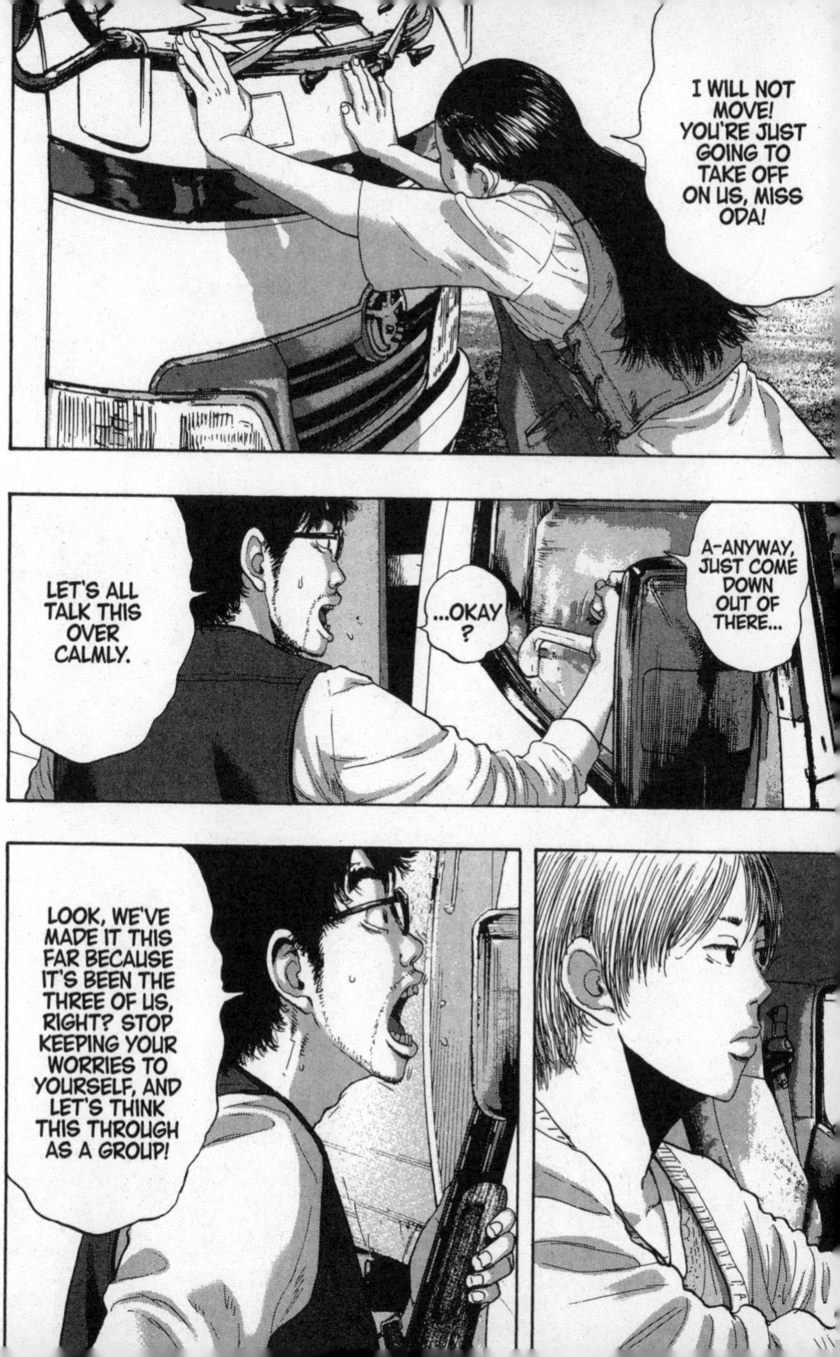
I WILL NOT MOVE! YOU'RE JUST GOING TO TAKE OFF ON US, MISS ODA!
A-ANYWAY, JUST COME DOWN OUT OF THERE...
...OKAY?
LET'S ALL TALK THIS OVER CALMLY.
LOOK, WE'VE MADE IT THIS FAR BECAUSE IT'S BEEN THE THREE OF US, RIGHT? STOP KEEPING YOUR WORRIES TO YOURSELF, AND LET'S THINK THIS THROUGH AS A GROUP!

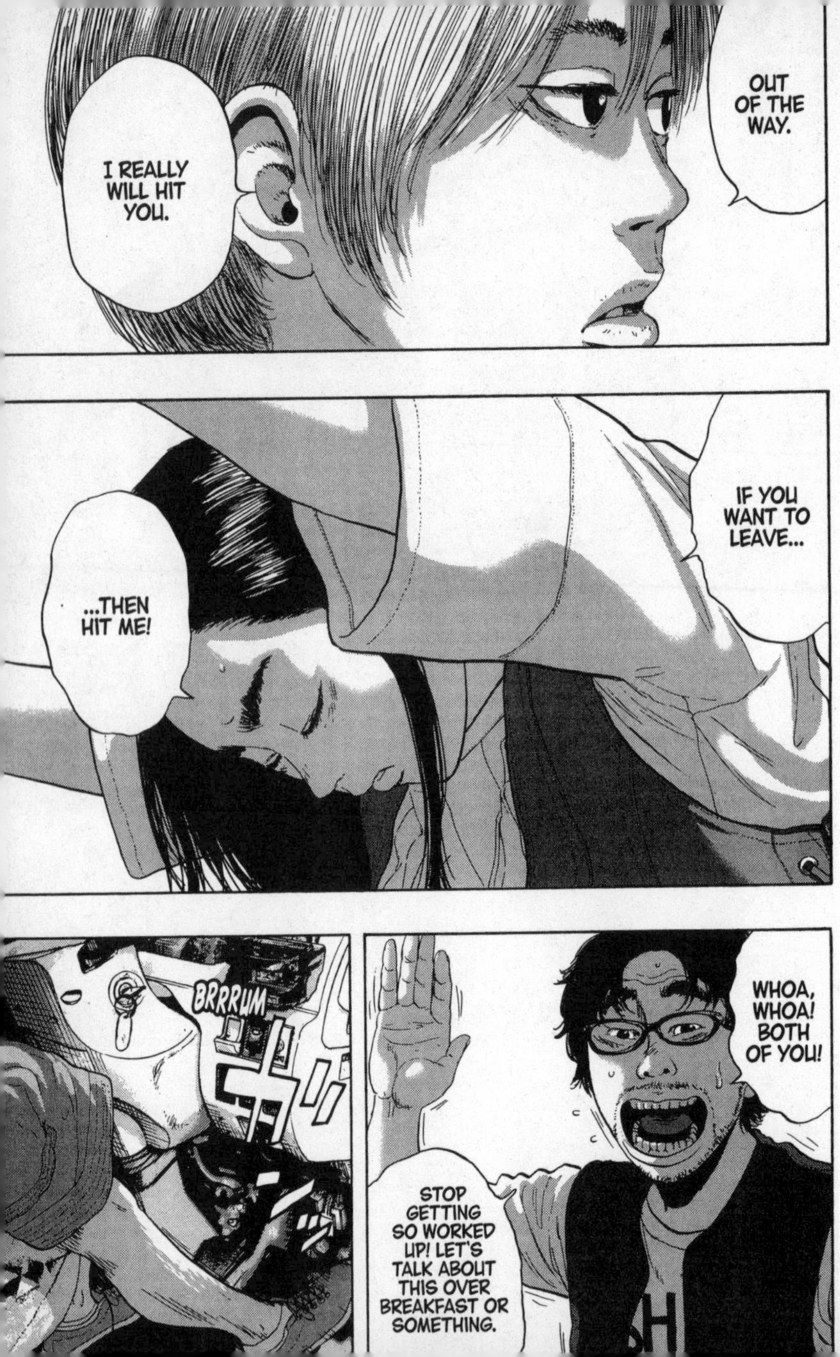
OUT OF THE WAY.
I REALLY WILL HIT YOU.
IF YOU WANT TO LEAVE...
...THEN HIT ME!
WHOA, WHOA! BOTH OF YOU!
STOP GETTING SO WORKED UP! LET'S TALK ABOUT THIS OVER BREAKFAST OR SOMETHING.
BRRRUM

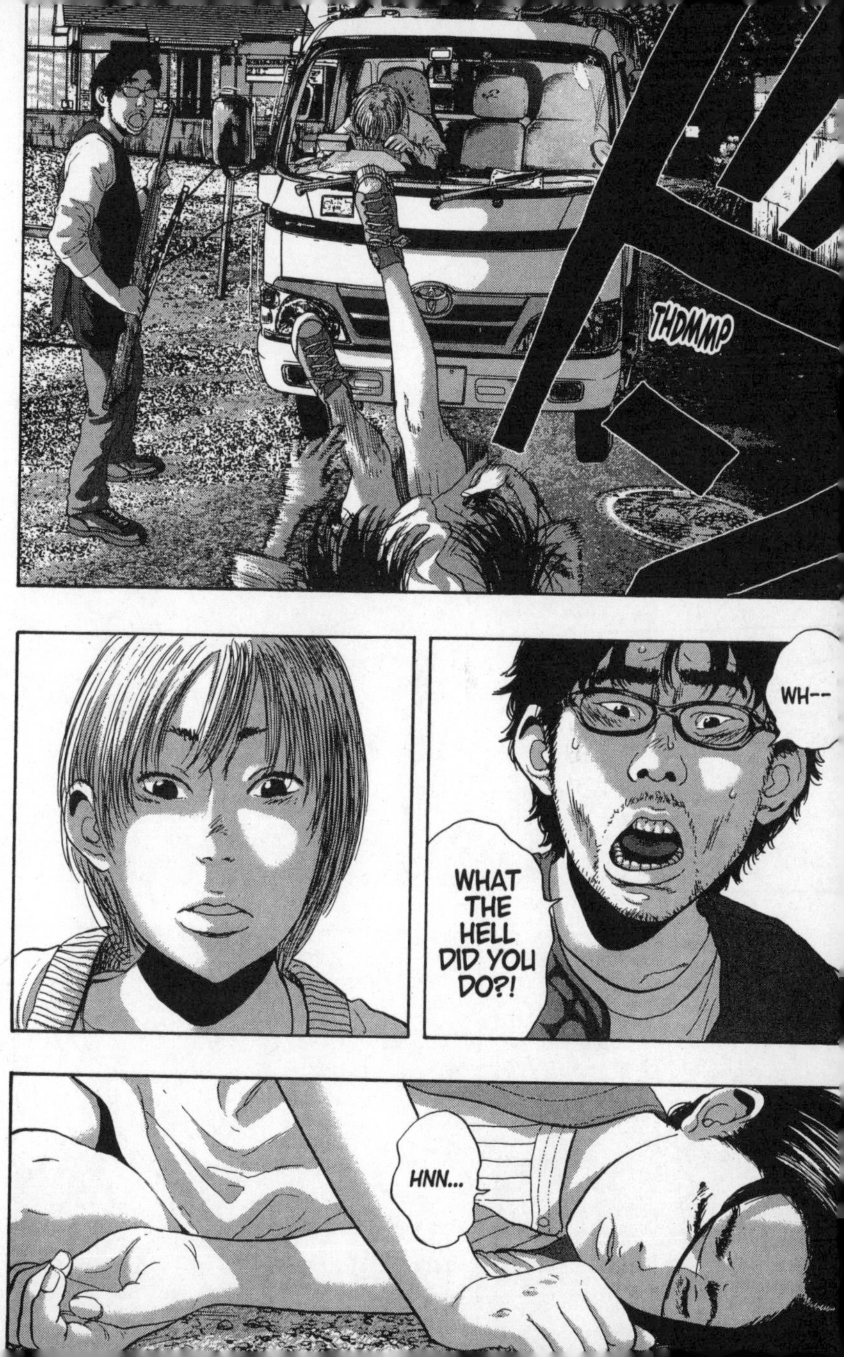
THDMMP
WH--
WHAT THE HELL DID YOU DO?!
HNN...

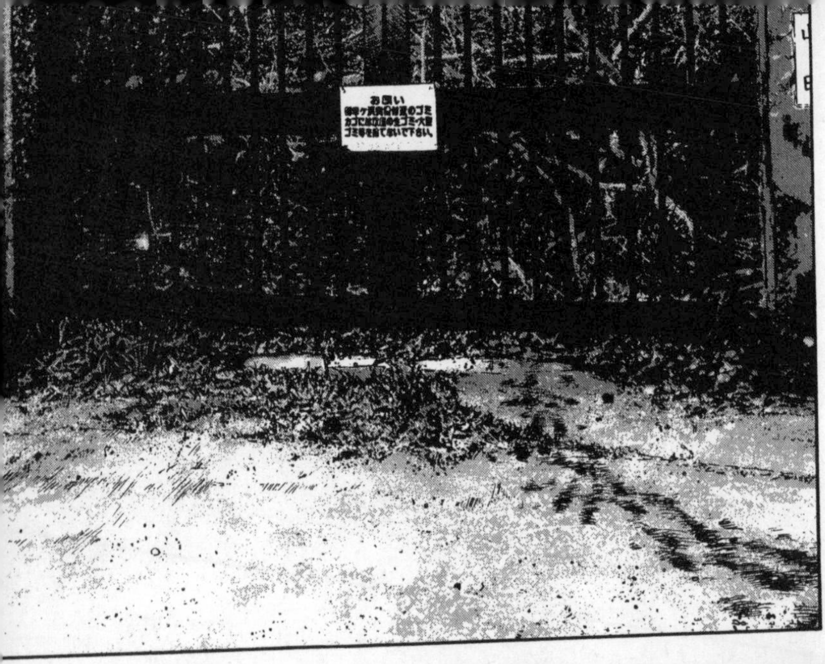
お願い
ゴミ等を捨てないで下さい、
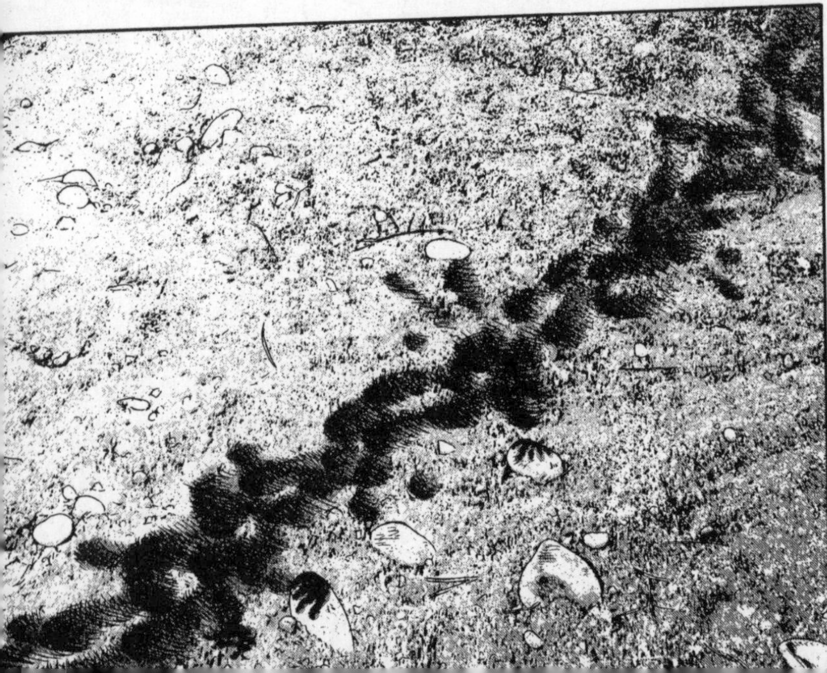

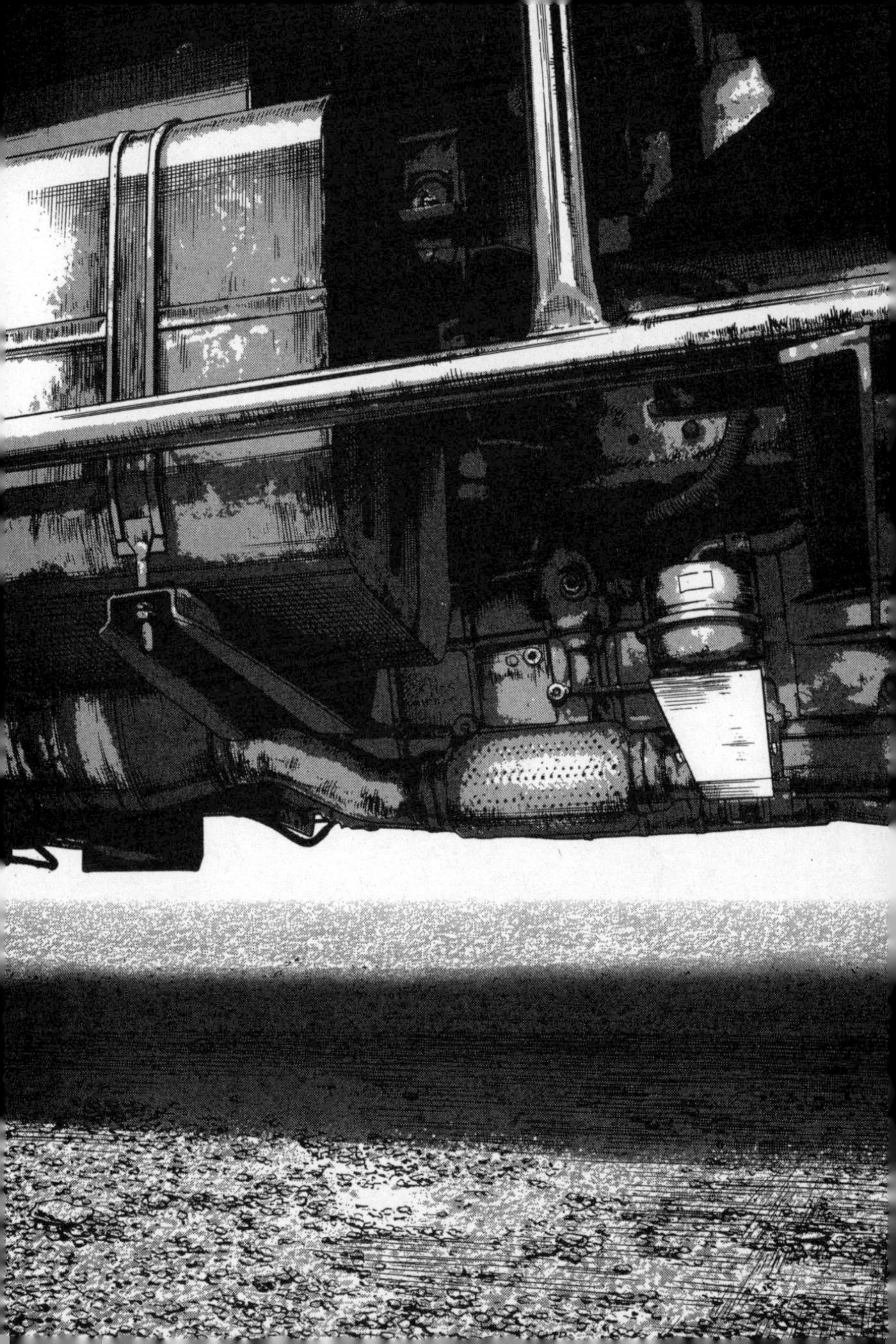

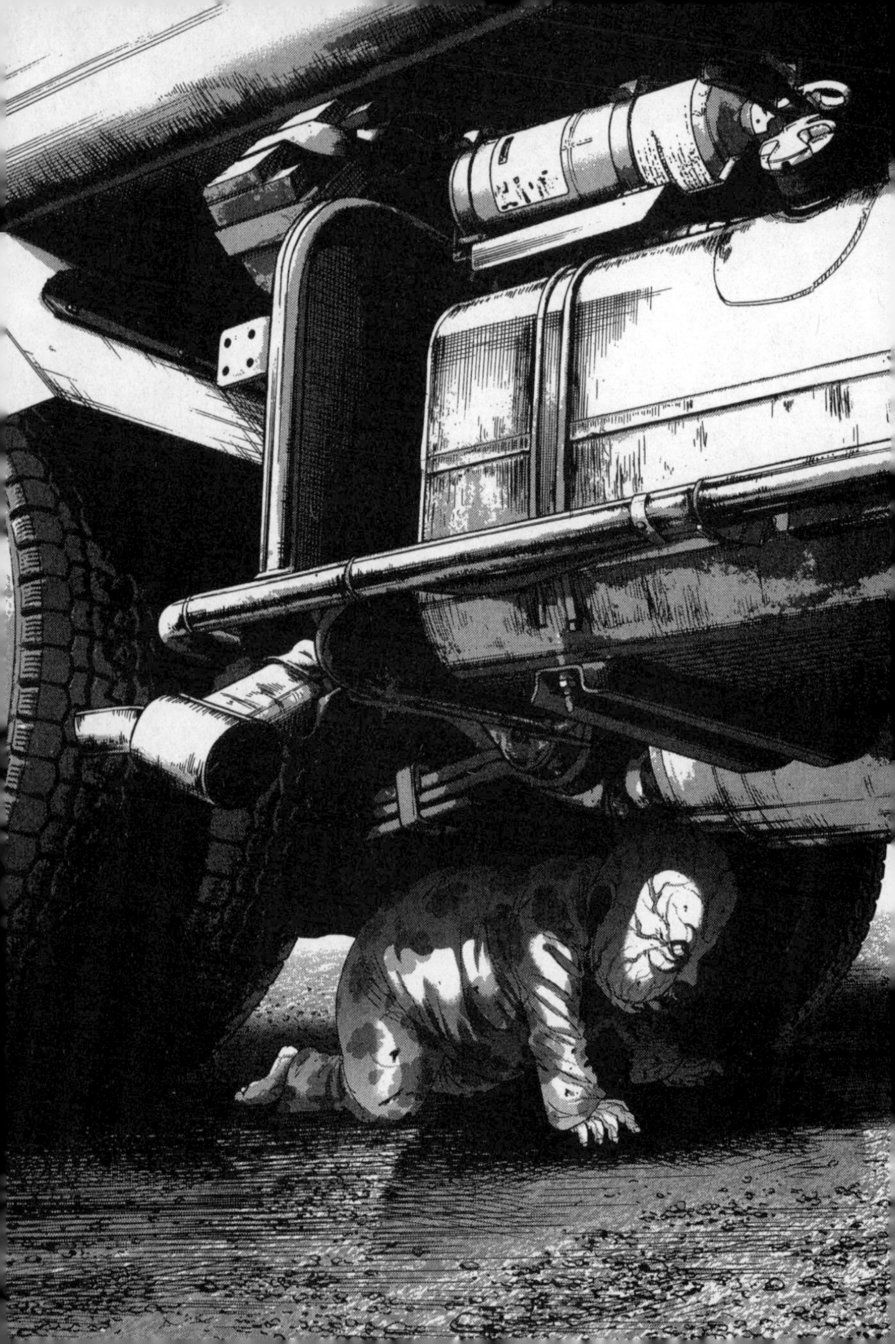

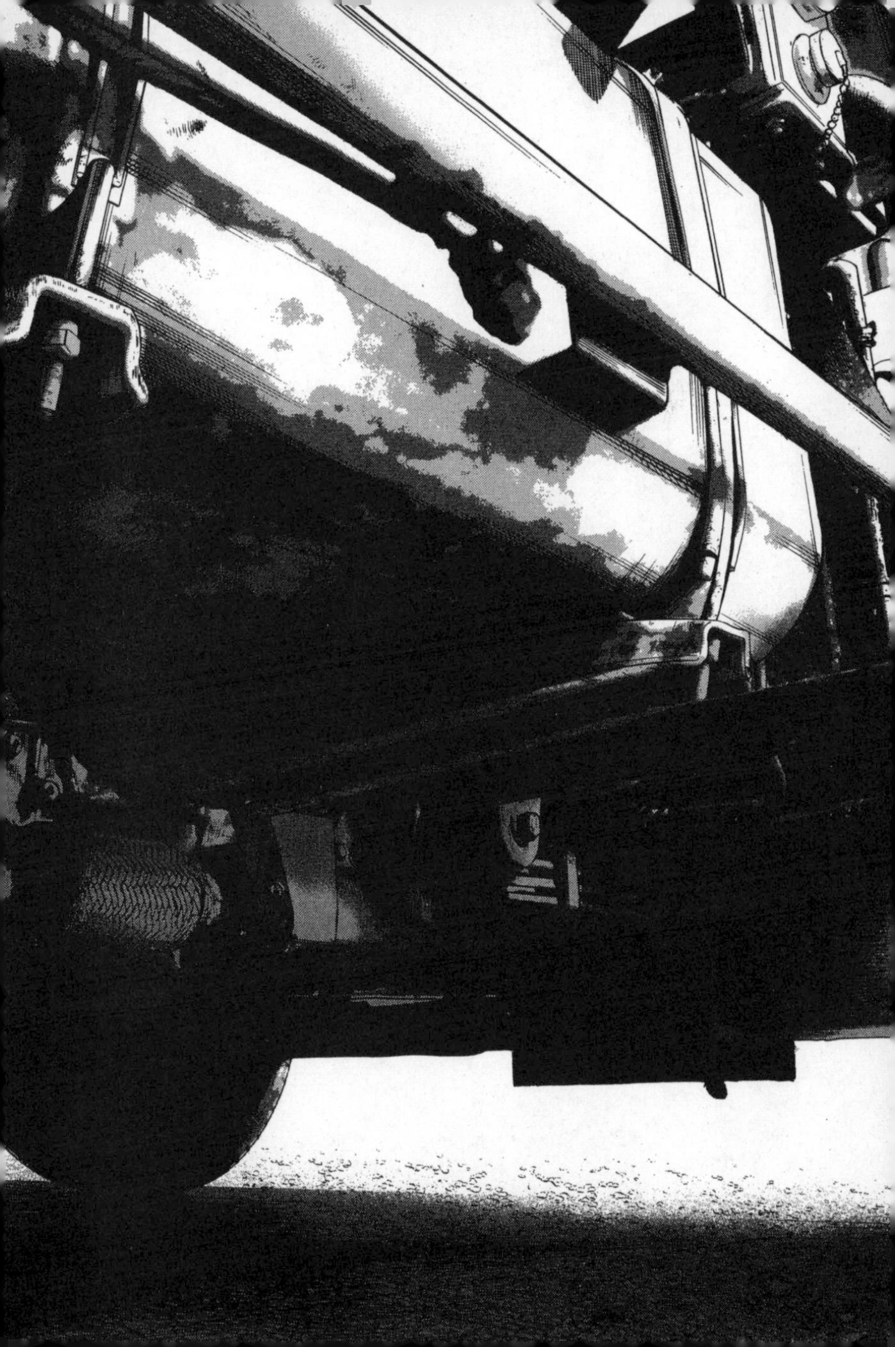

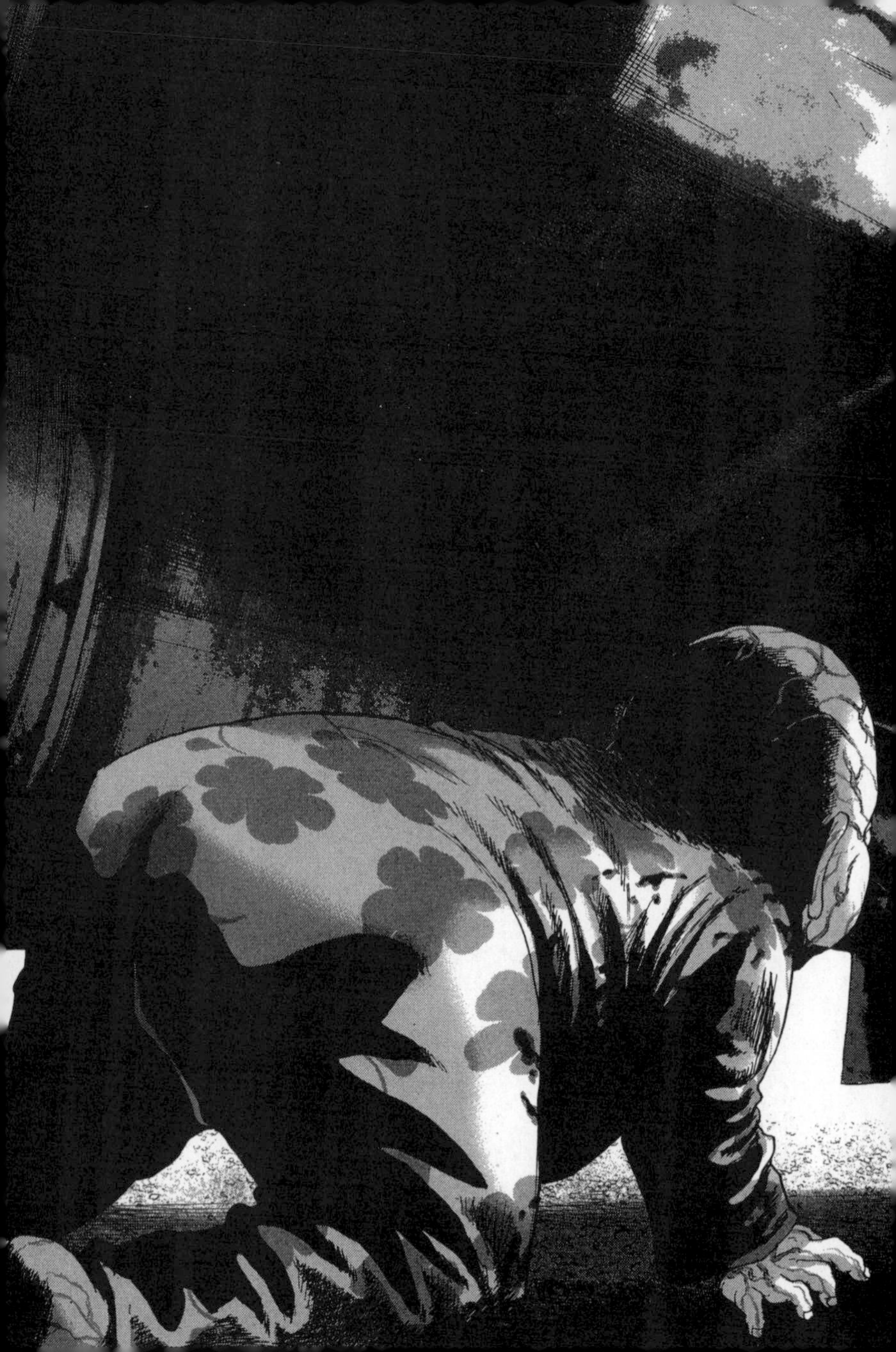

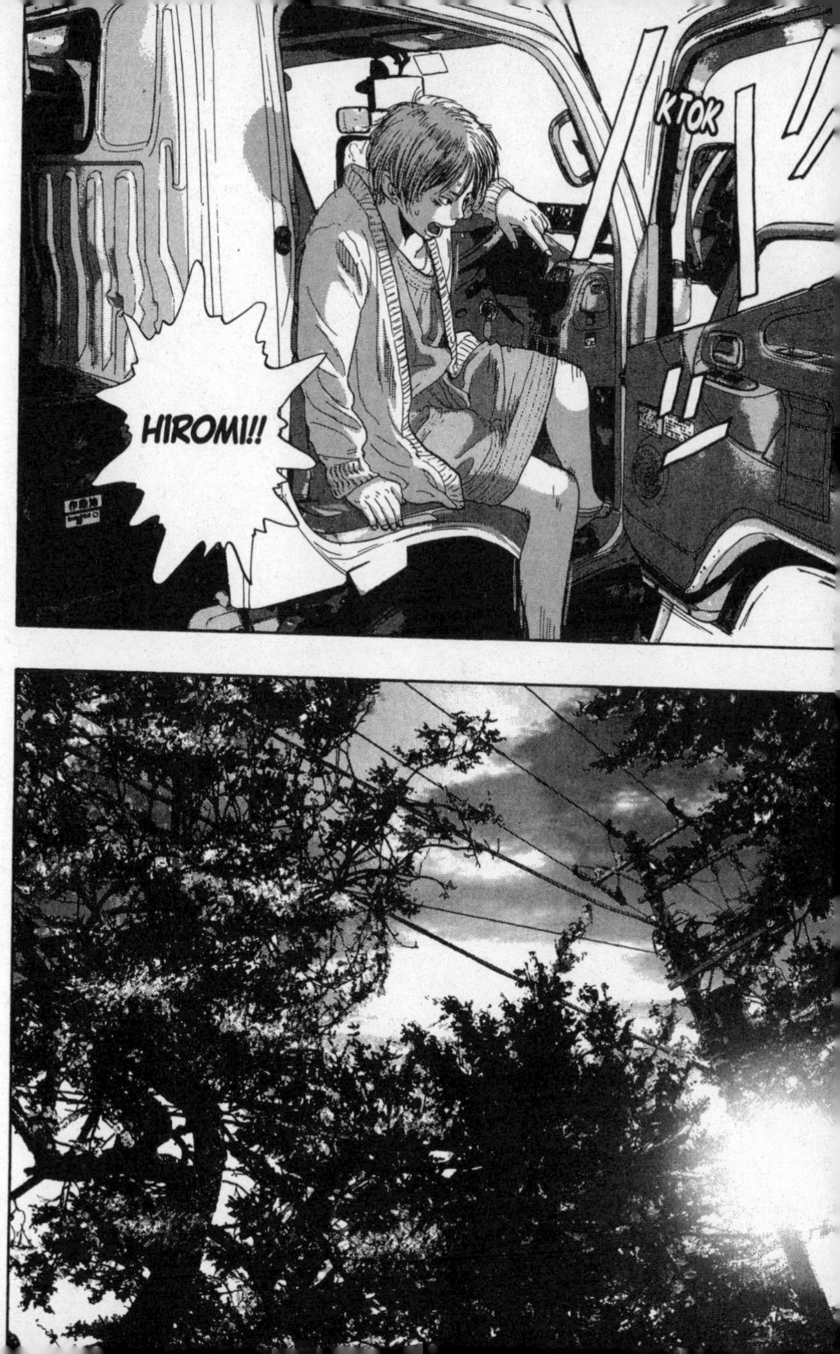
K TOK
HIROMI!!

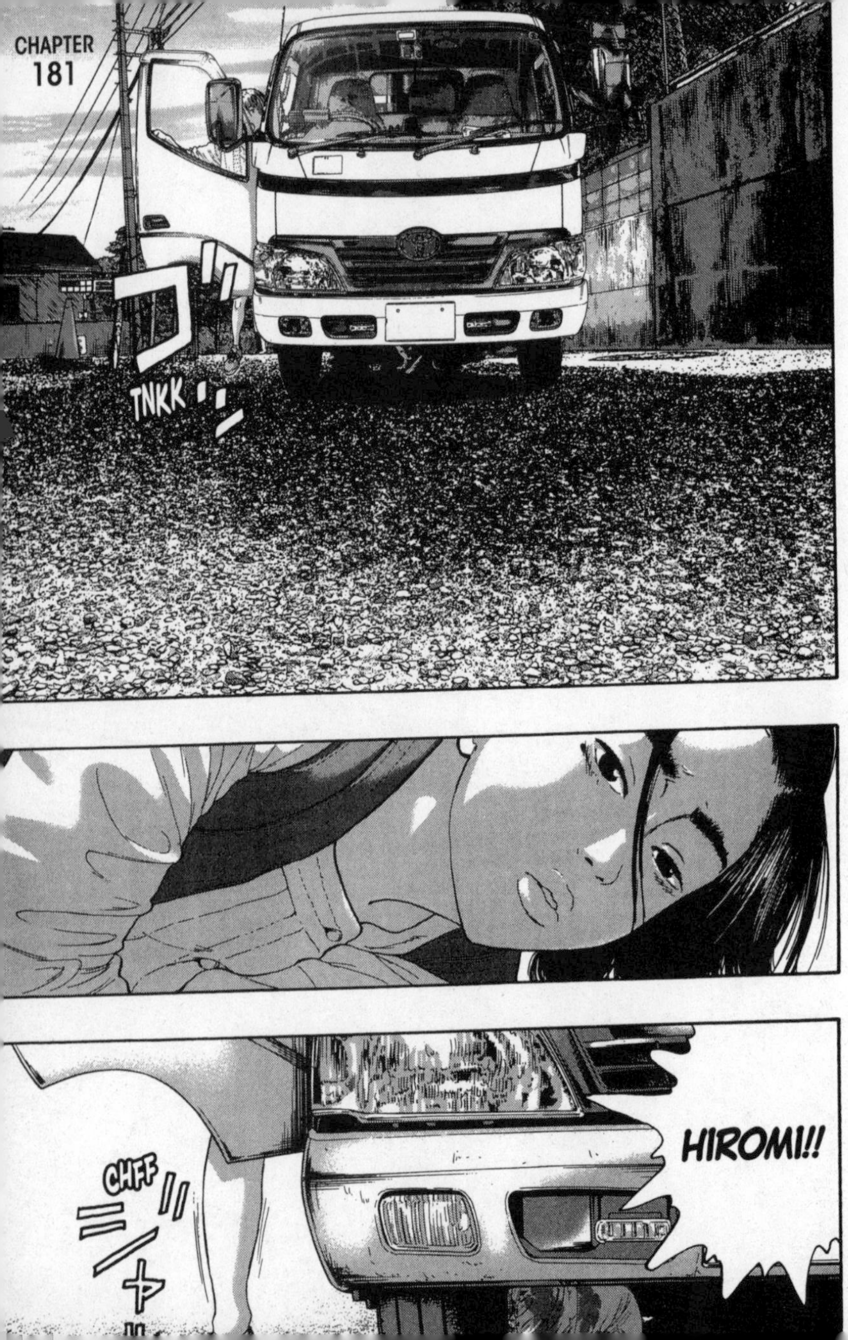
CHAPTER
181
TNKK
HIROMI!!
CHFF

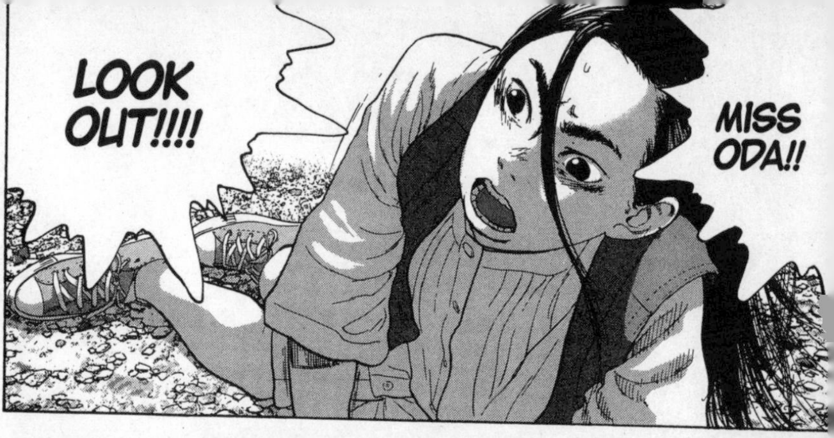
MISS ODA!!
LOOK OUT!!!!
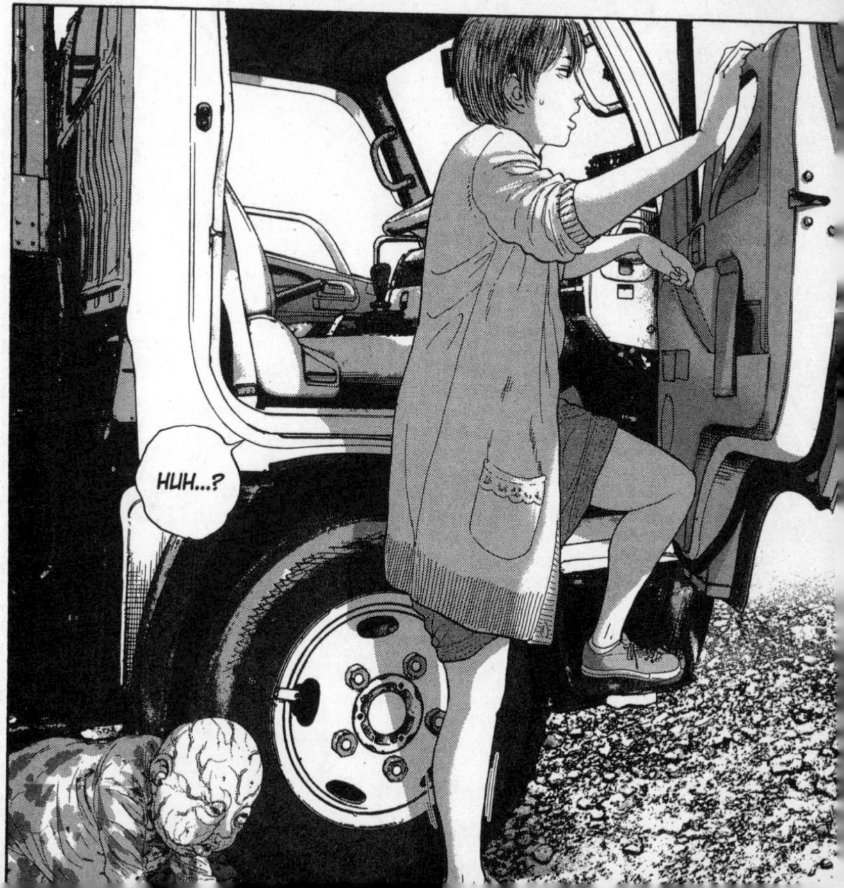
HUH...?

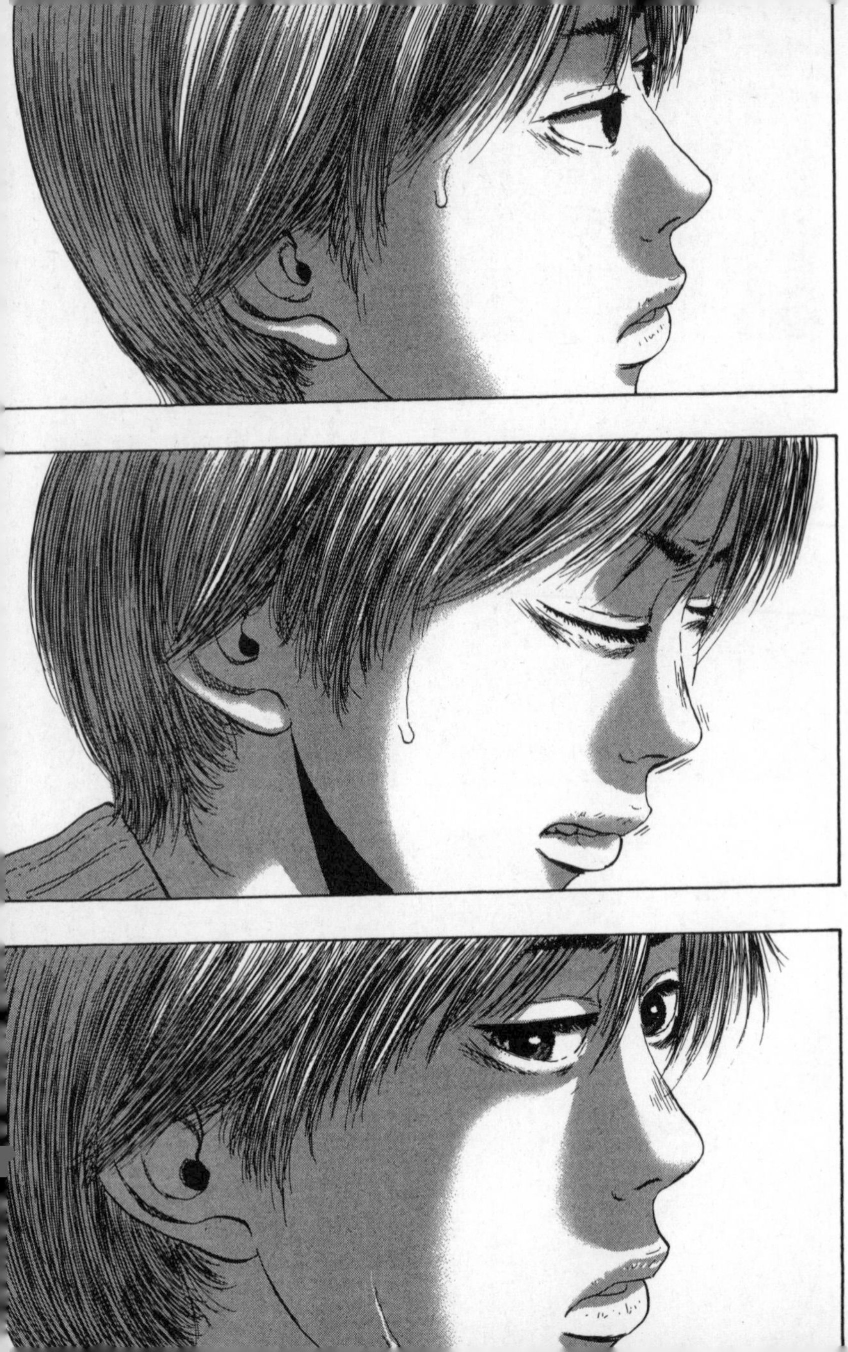

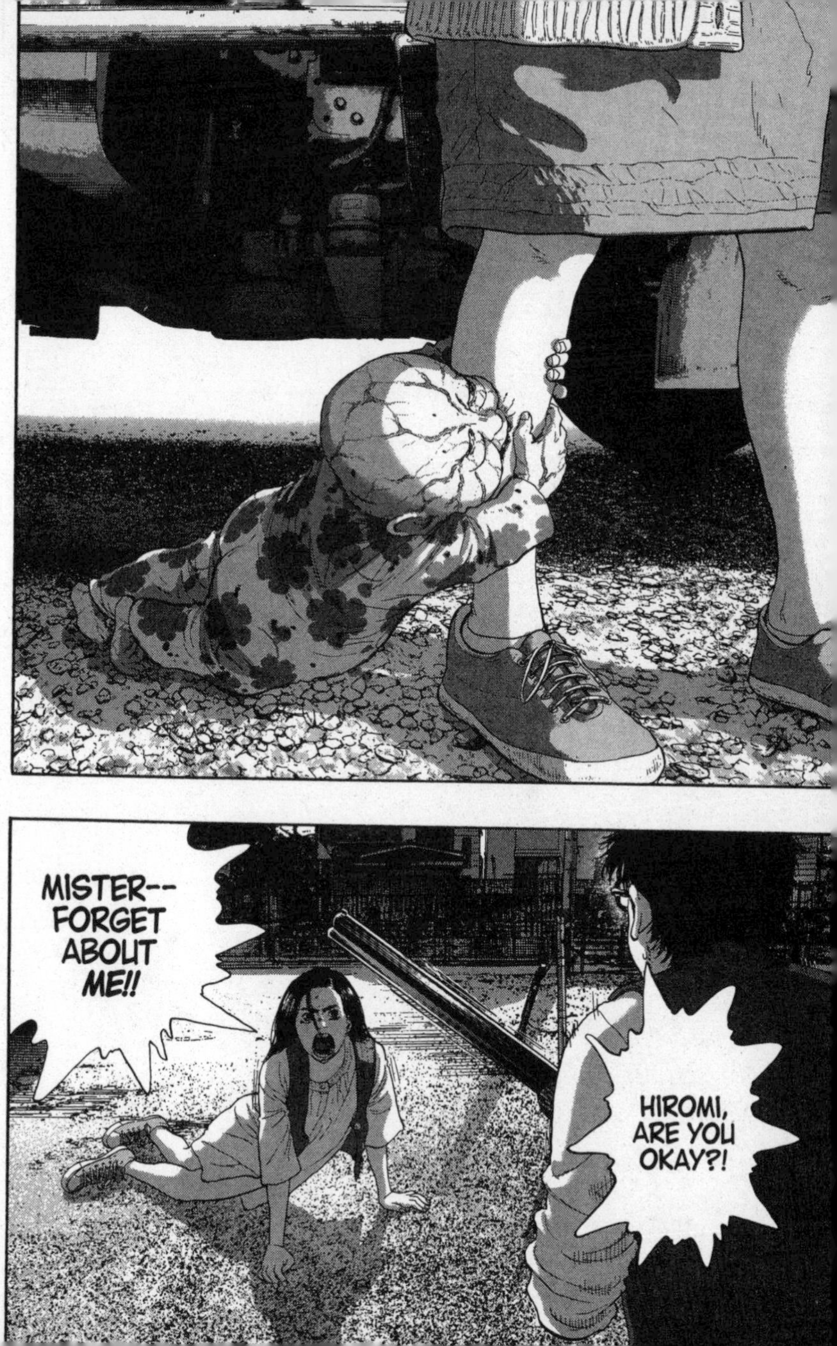
HIROMI, ARE YOU OKAY?!
MISTER-- FORGET ABOUT ME!!

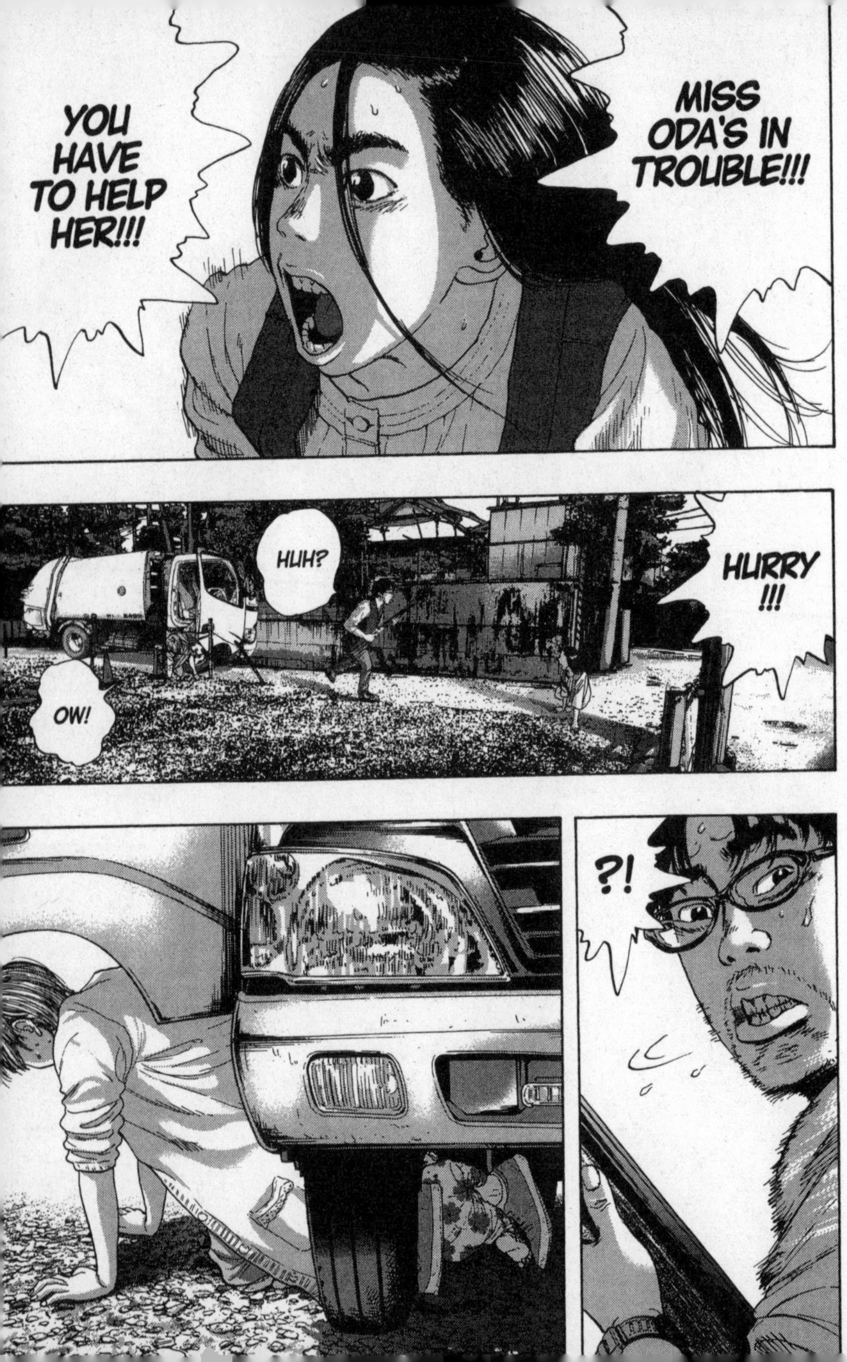
MISS ODA'S IN TROUBLE!!!
YOU HAVE TO HELP HER!!!
HURRY !!!
HUH?
OW!
?!

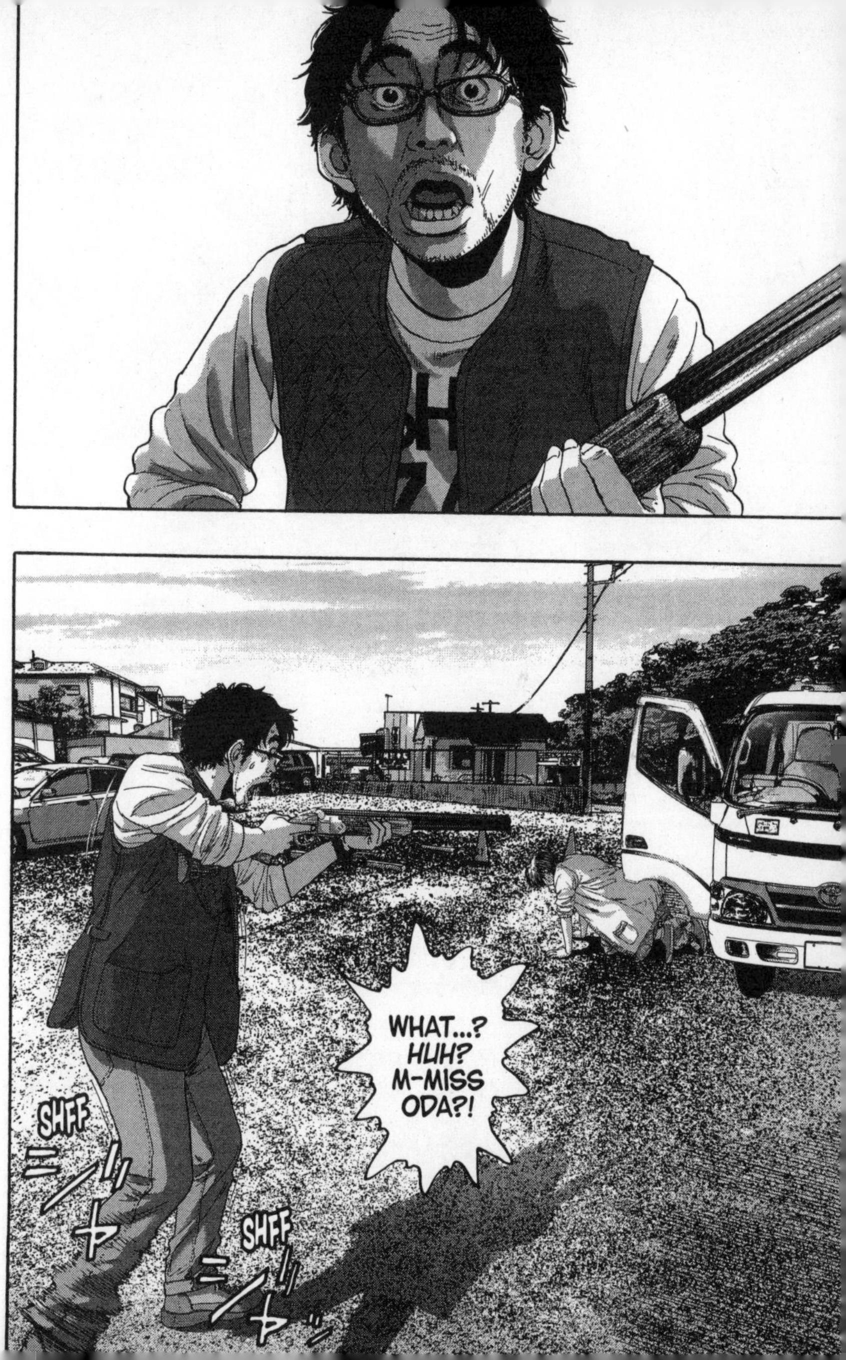
WHAT...? HUH? M-MISS ODA?!
SHFF
SHFF

STAY
BACK!!
BOTH OF
YOU!!

HRRG!

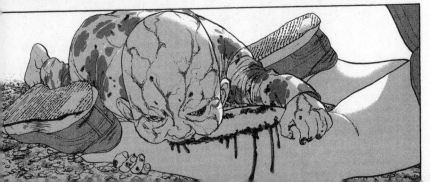

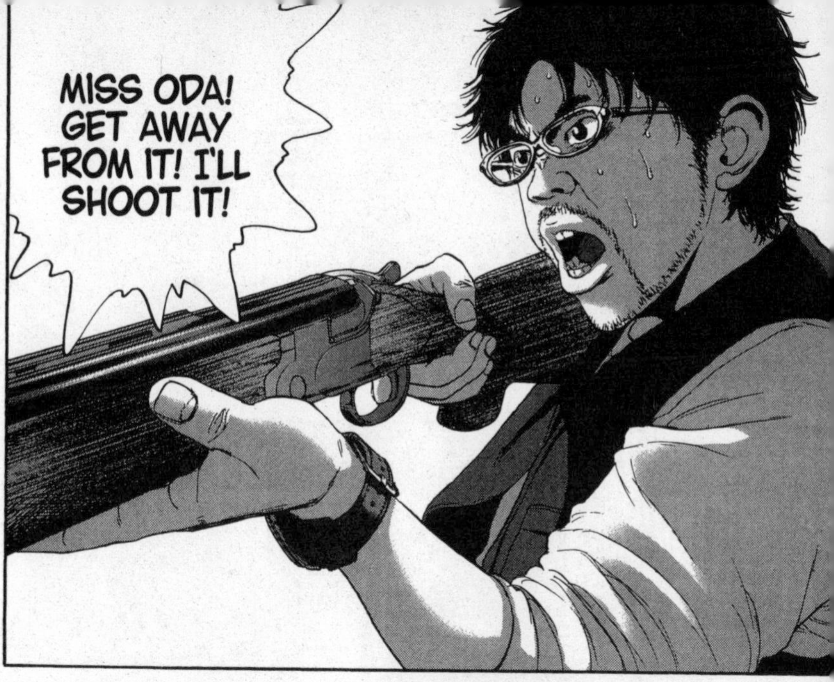
MISS ODA! GET AWAY FROM IT! I'LL SHOOT IT!

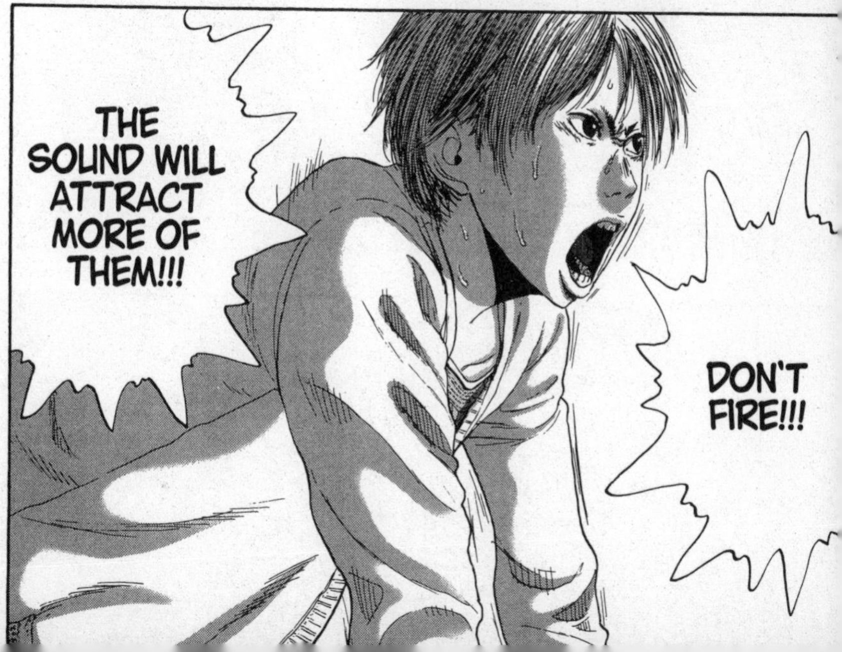
DON'T FIRE!!!
THE SOUND WILL ATTRACT MORE OF THEM!!!

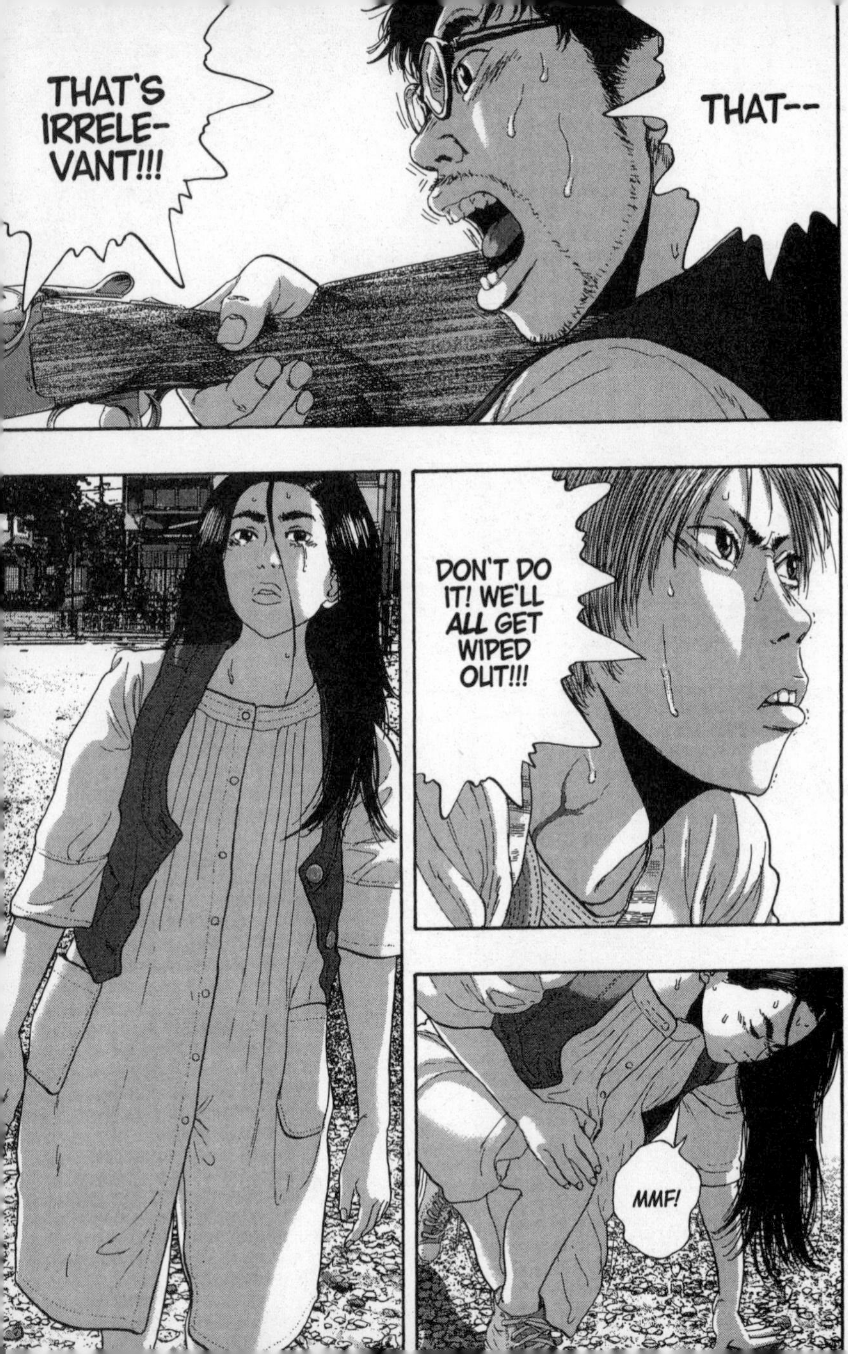
THAT--
THAT'S IRRELE-VANT!!!
DON'T DO IT! WE'LL ALL GET WIPED OUT!!!
MMF!

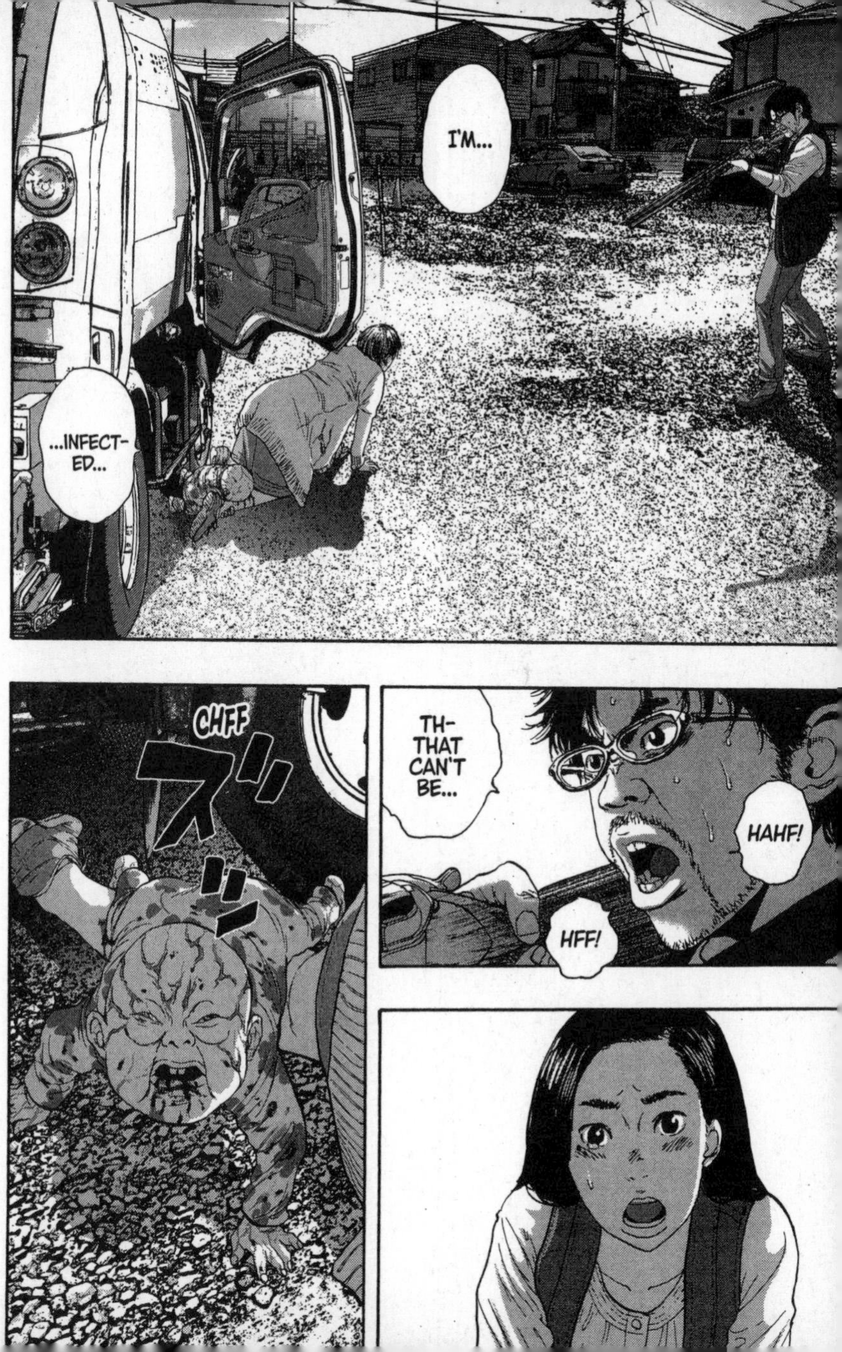
I'M...
...INFECTED-
ED...
TH-
THAT
CAN'T
BE...
HAHF!
HFF!
CHFF
ズッ

WHY, YOU--!

?!

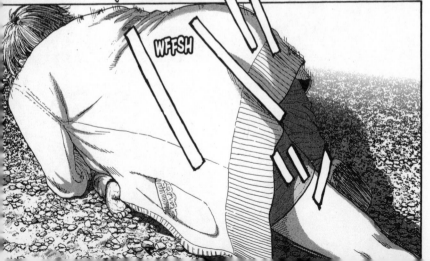

WFFSH

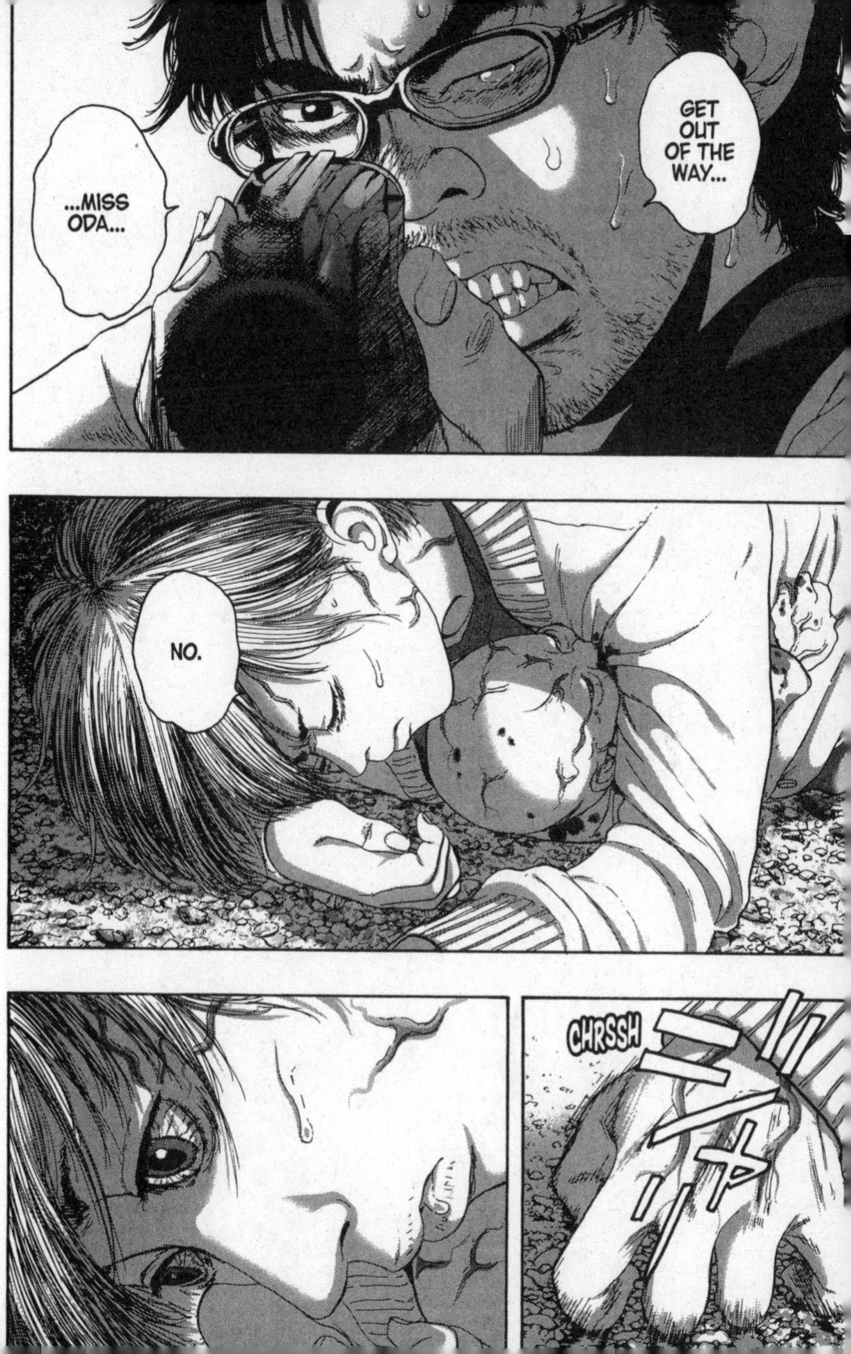
GET OUT OF THE WAY...
...MISS ODA...
NO.
CHRSSH

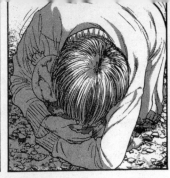

SQUITCH
SQUITCH
SQUITCH
じゅっ
じゅっ
じゅっ

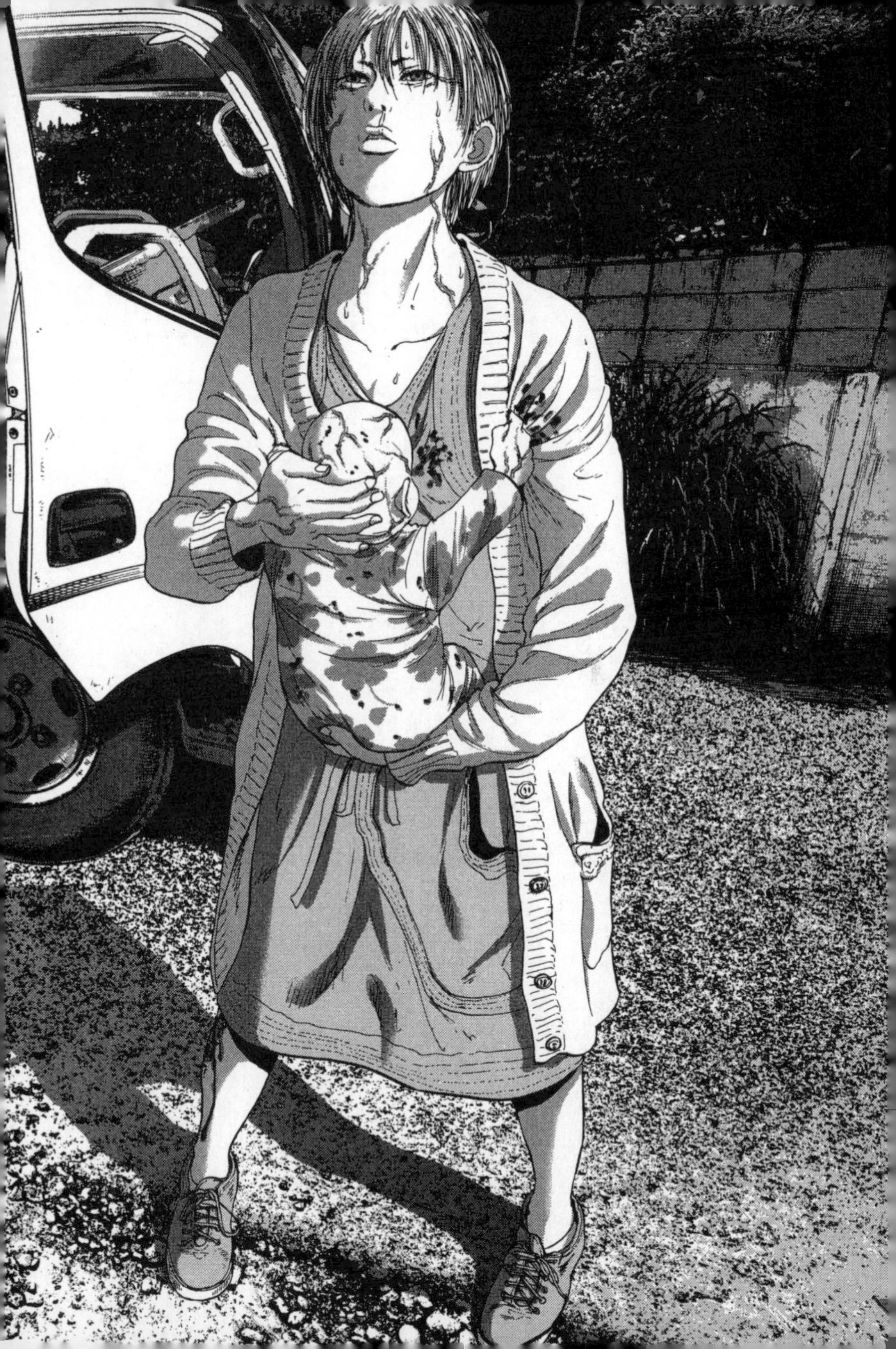

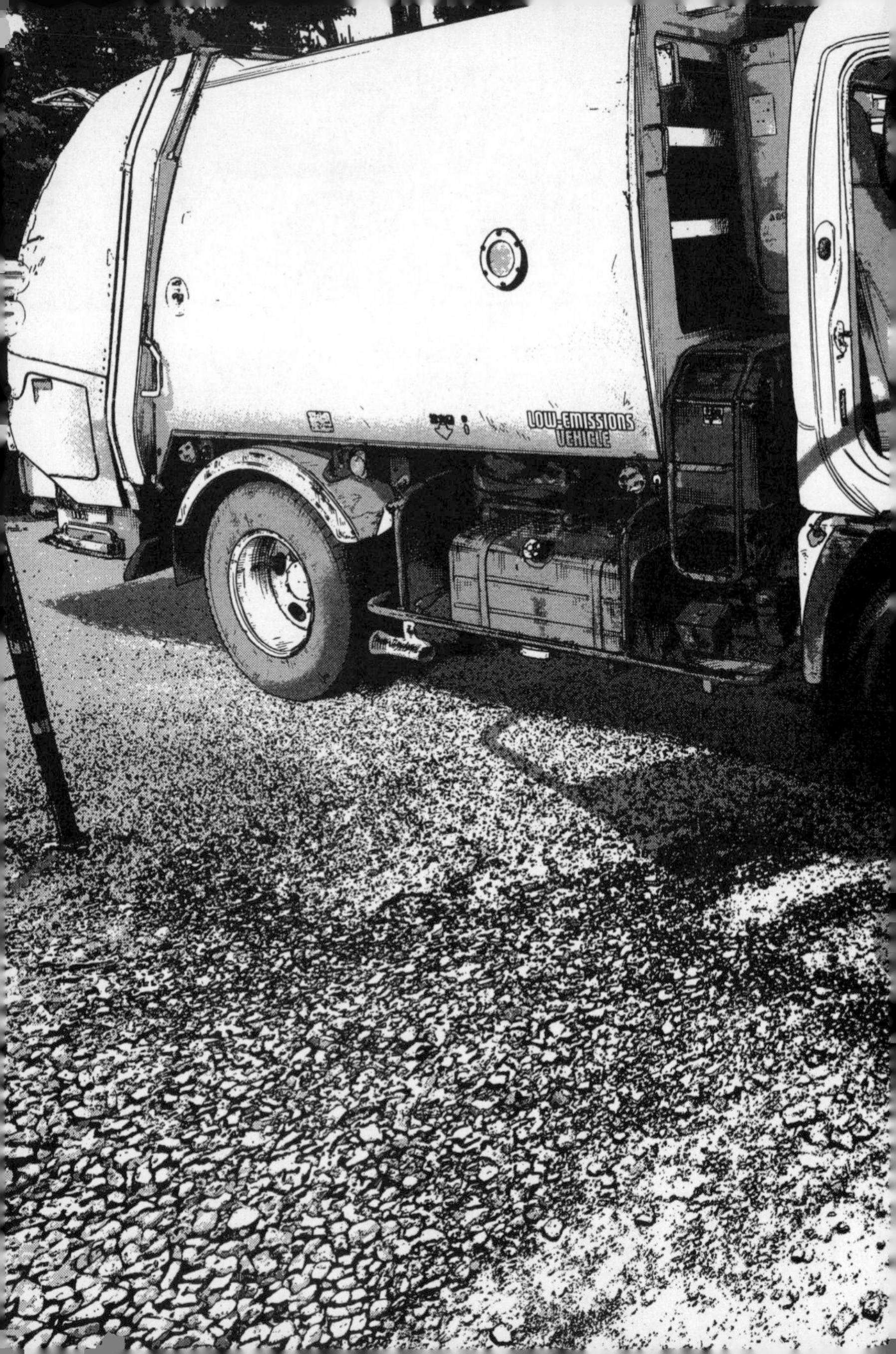
LOW-EMISSIONS
VEHICLE

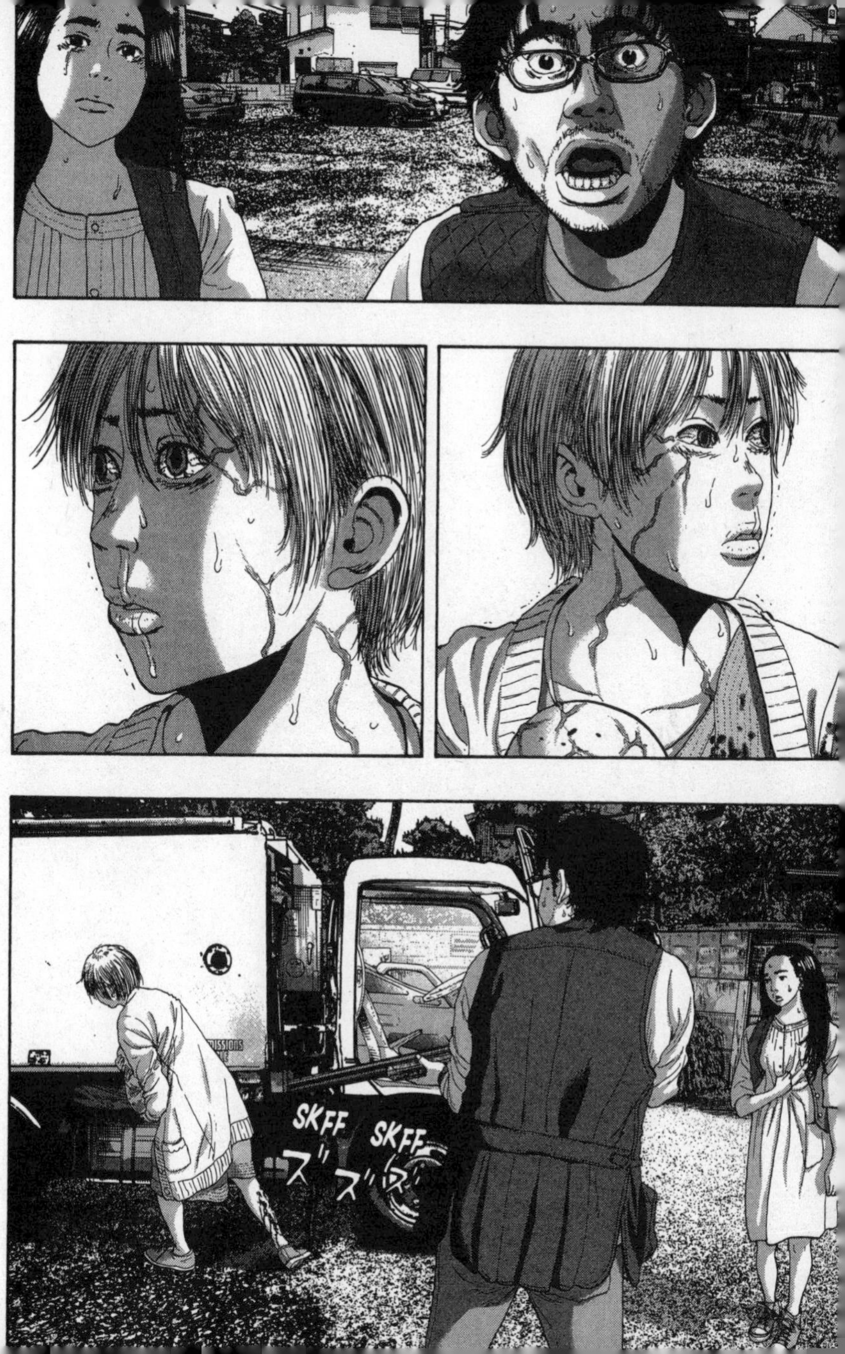
SKFF
SKFF
ズズズ

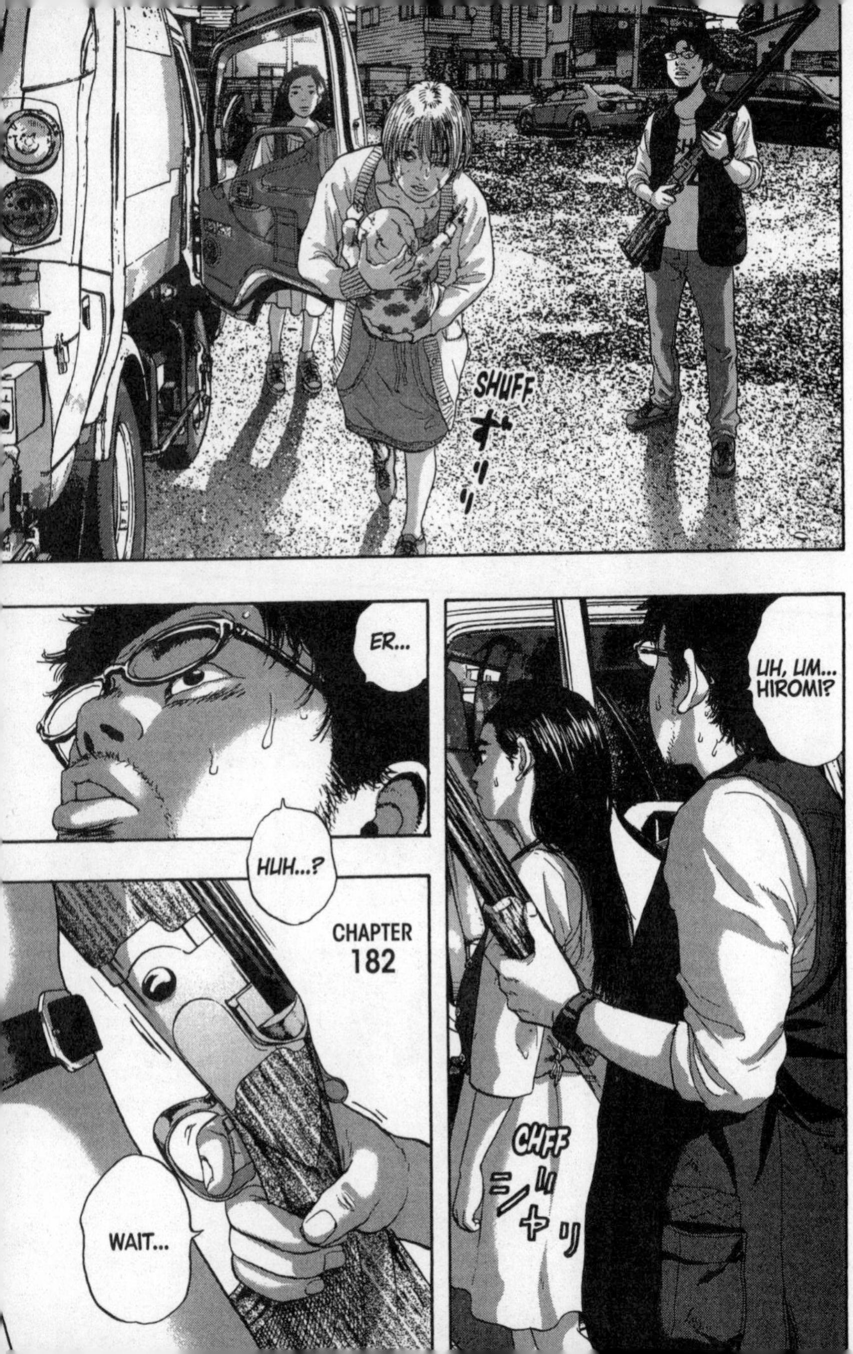
SHUFF
ずりり
UH, UM... HIROMI?
CHFF
ER...
HUH...?
CHAPTER 182
WAIT...

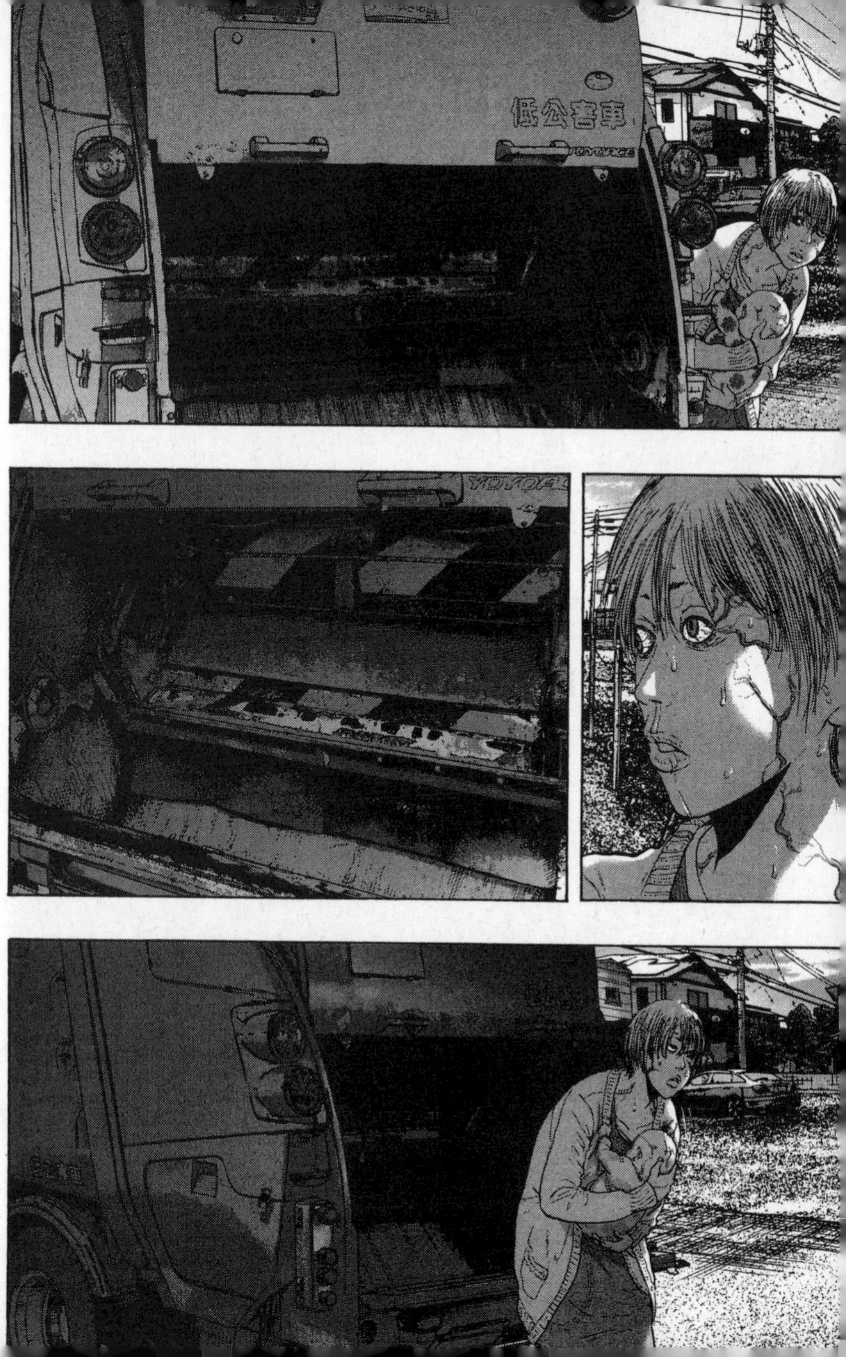
低公害車

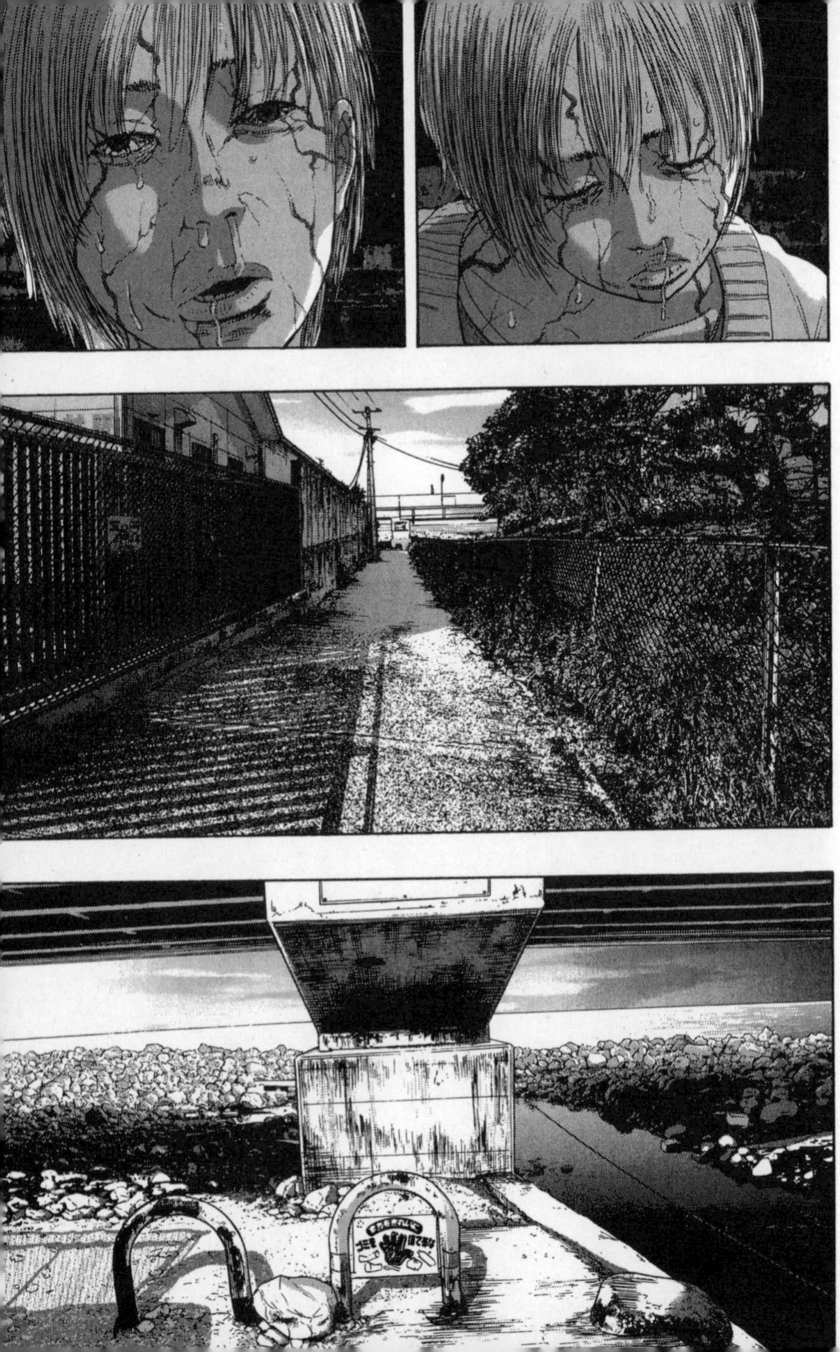
まちをきれいに
ゴミを 捨てるな

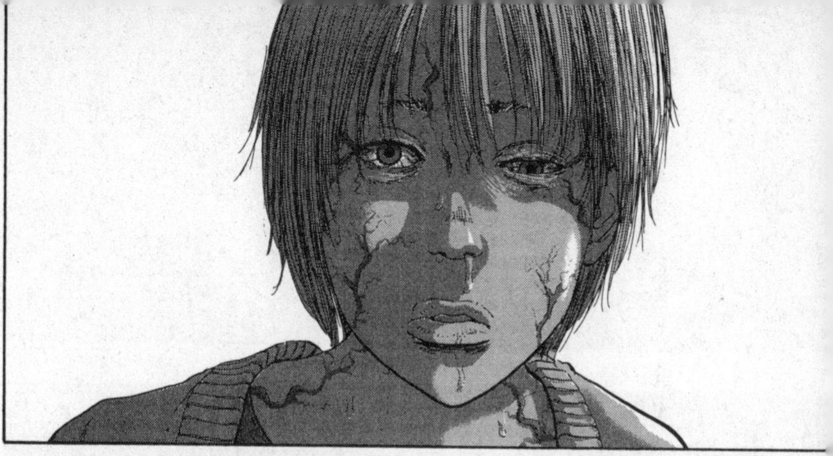

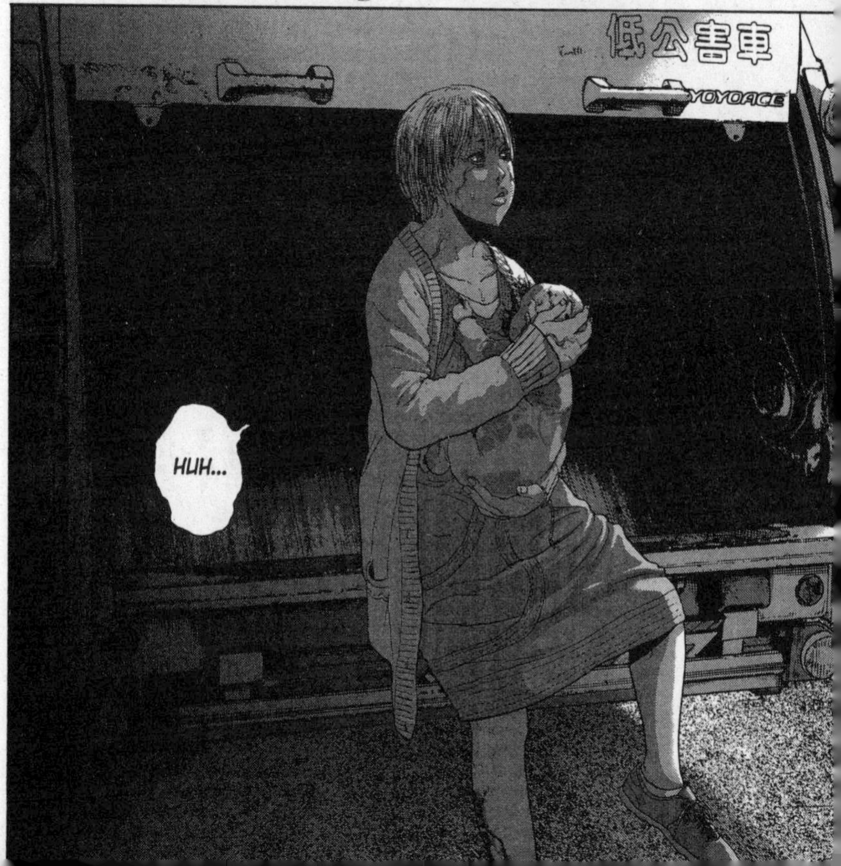
低公害車
YOYOACE
HUH...

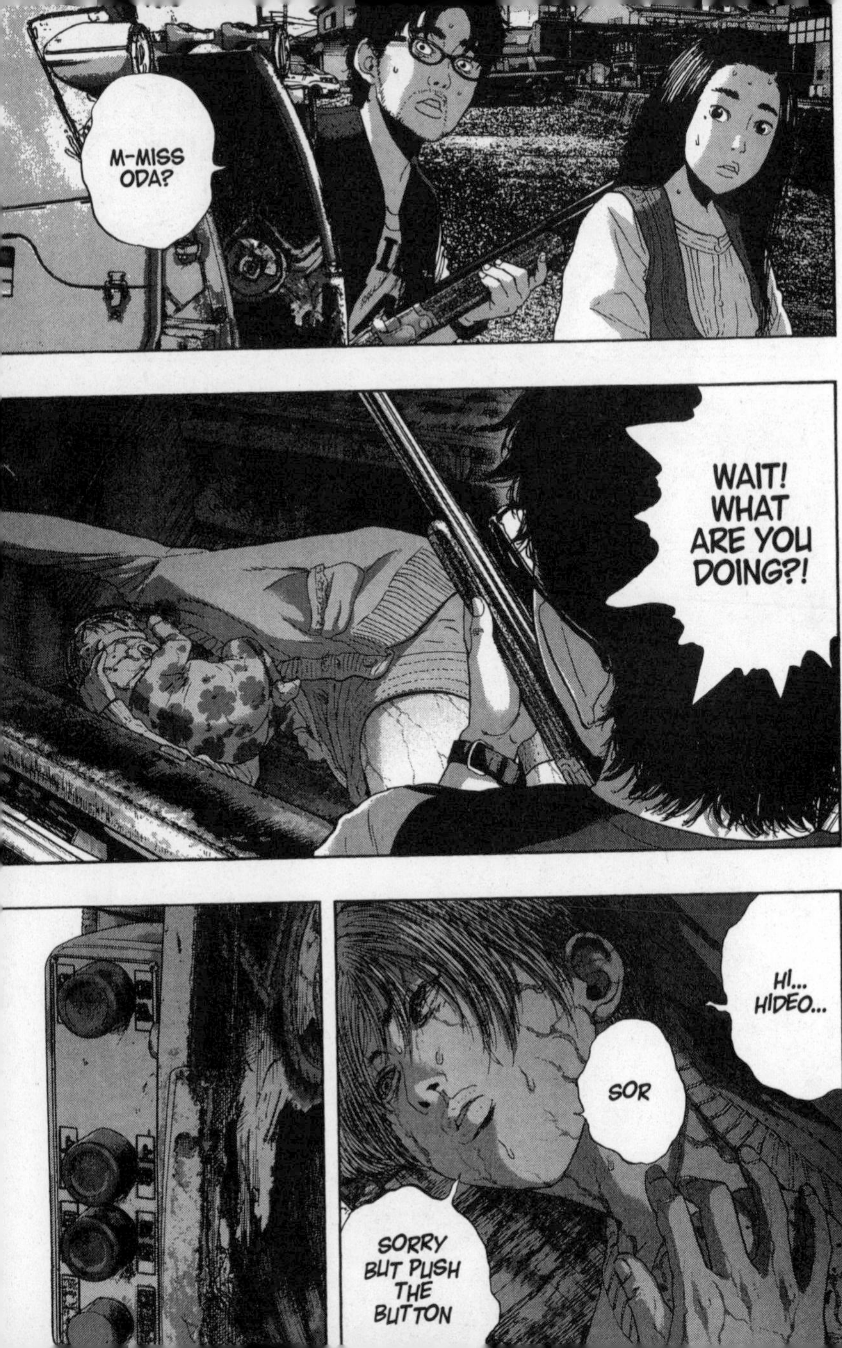
M-MISS ODA?
WAIT! WHAT ARE YOU DOING?!
HI... HIDEO...
SOR
SORRY BUT PUSH THE BUTTON

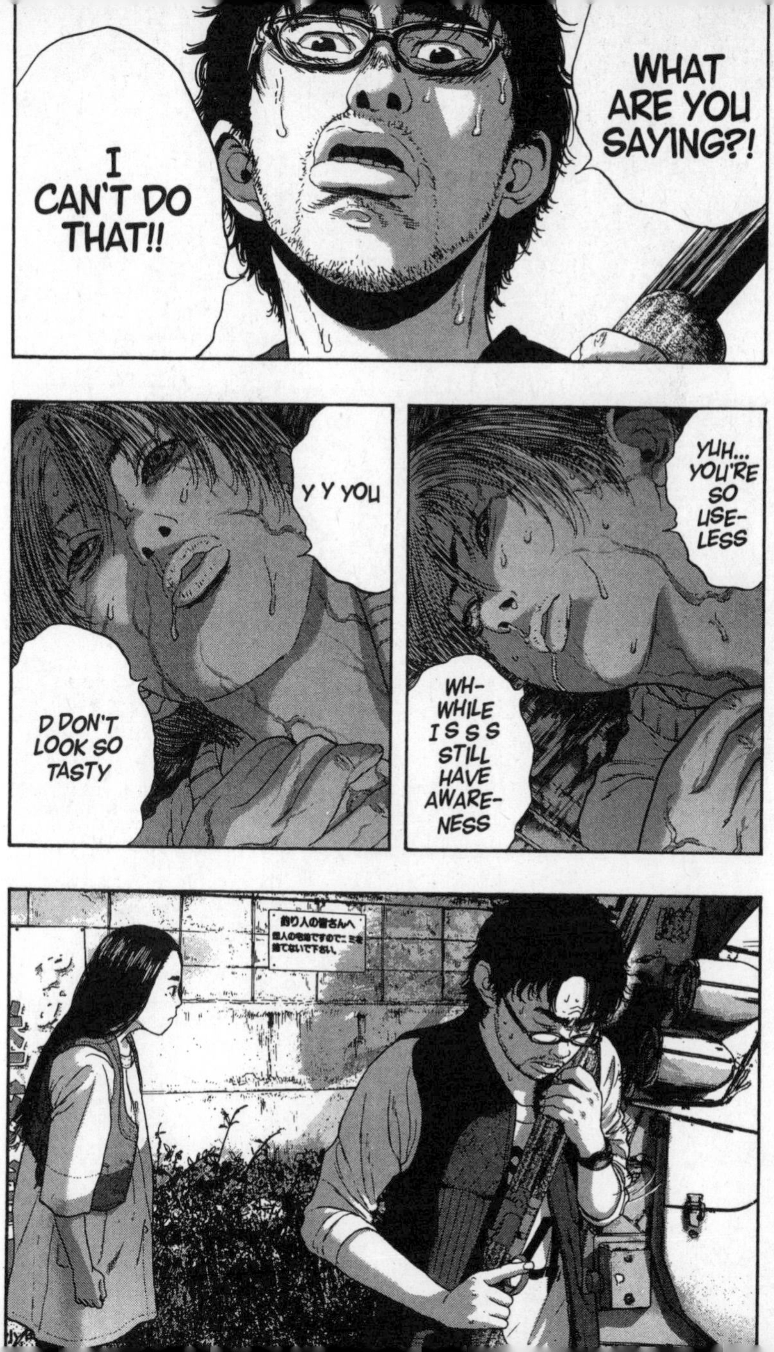
WHAT ARE YOU SAYING?!
I CAN'T DO THAT!!
YUH... YOU'RE SO USE-LESS
WH- WHILE I S S S STILL HAVE AWARE-NESS
Y Y YOU
D DON'T LOOK SO TASTY
釣り人の皆さんへ
個人の宅地ですのでゴミを捨てないで下さい。

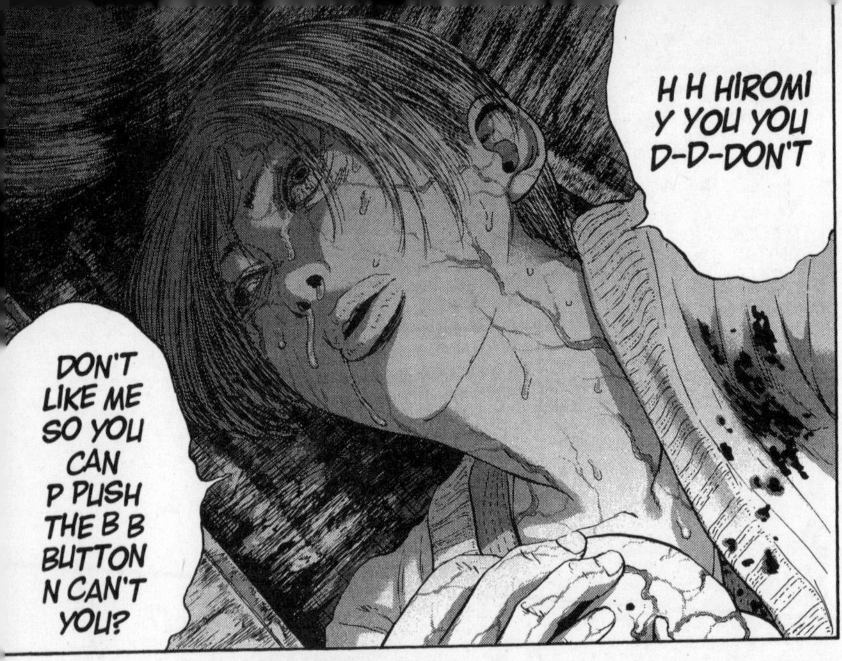
H H HIROMI Y YOU YOU D-D-DON'T
DON'T LIKE ME SO YOU CAN P PUSH THE B B BUTTON N CAN'T YOU?

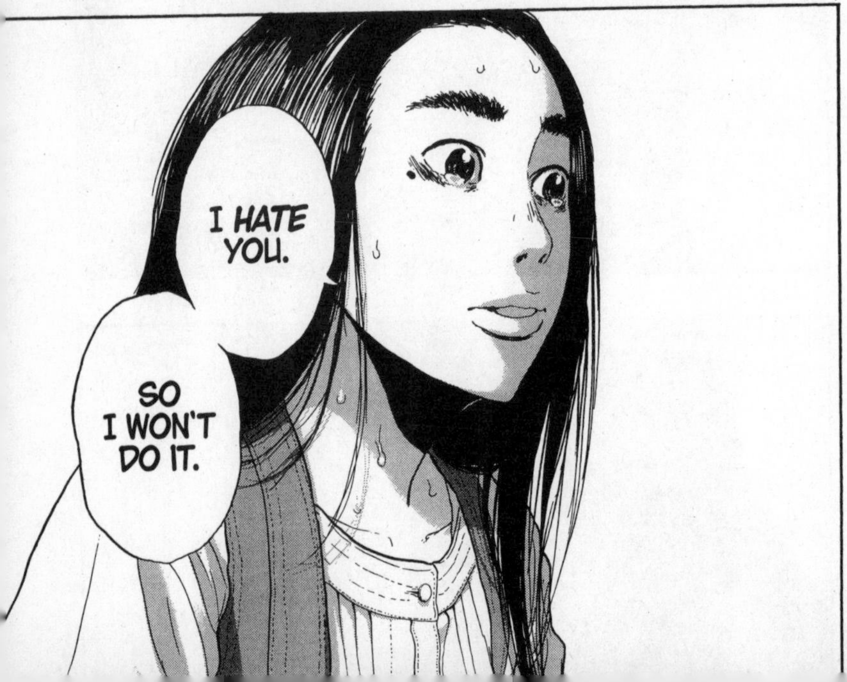
I HATE YOU.
SO I WON'T DO IT.

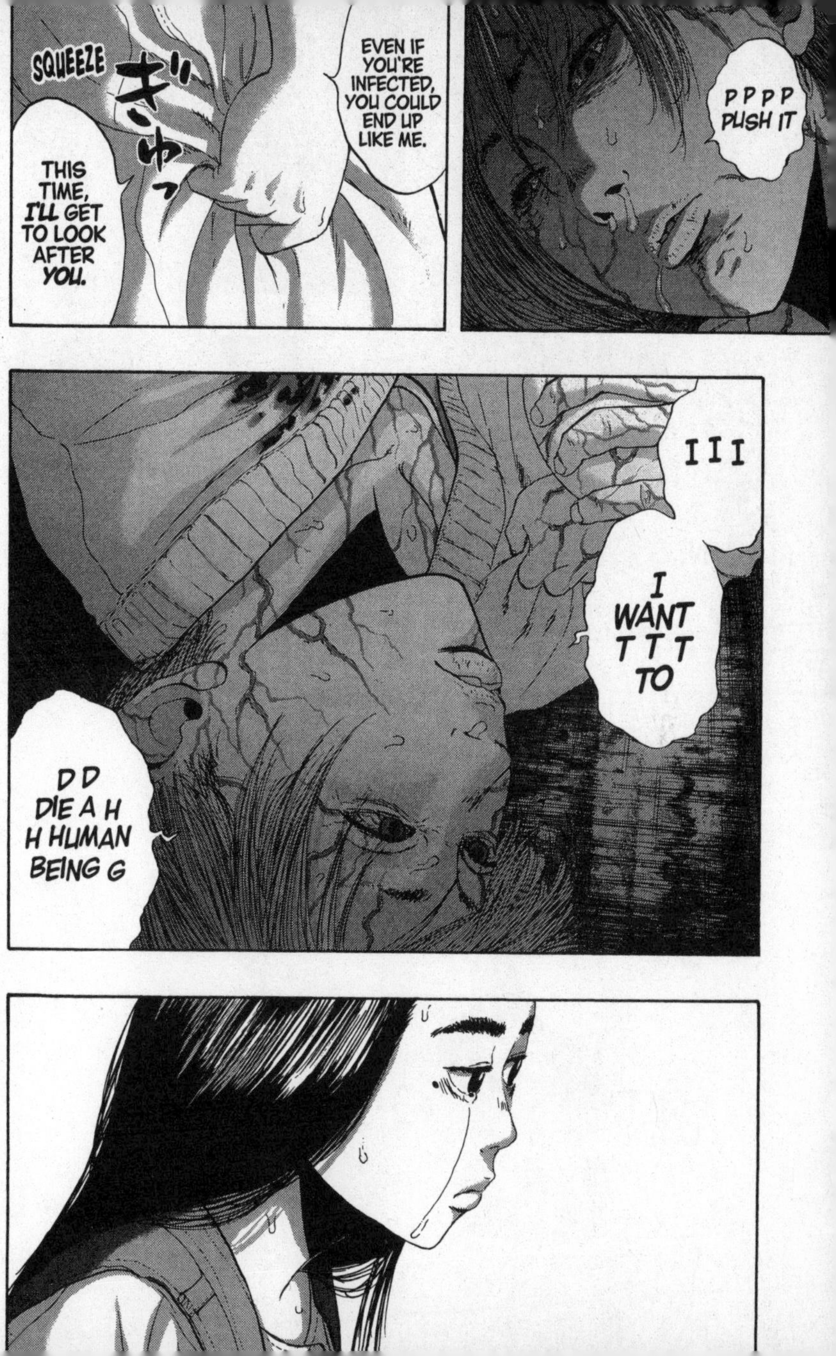
P P P P PUSH IT
EVEN IF YOU'RE INFECTED, YOU COULD END UP LIKE ME.
SQUEEZE
ぎゅっ
THIS TIME, I'LL GET TO LOOK AFTER YOU.
I I I
I WANT T T T TO
D D DIE A H H HUMAN BEING G

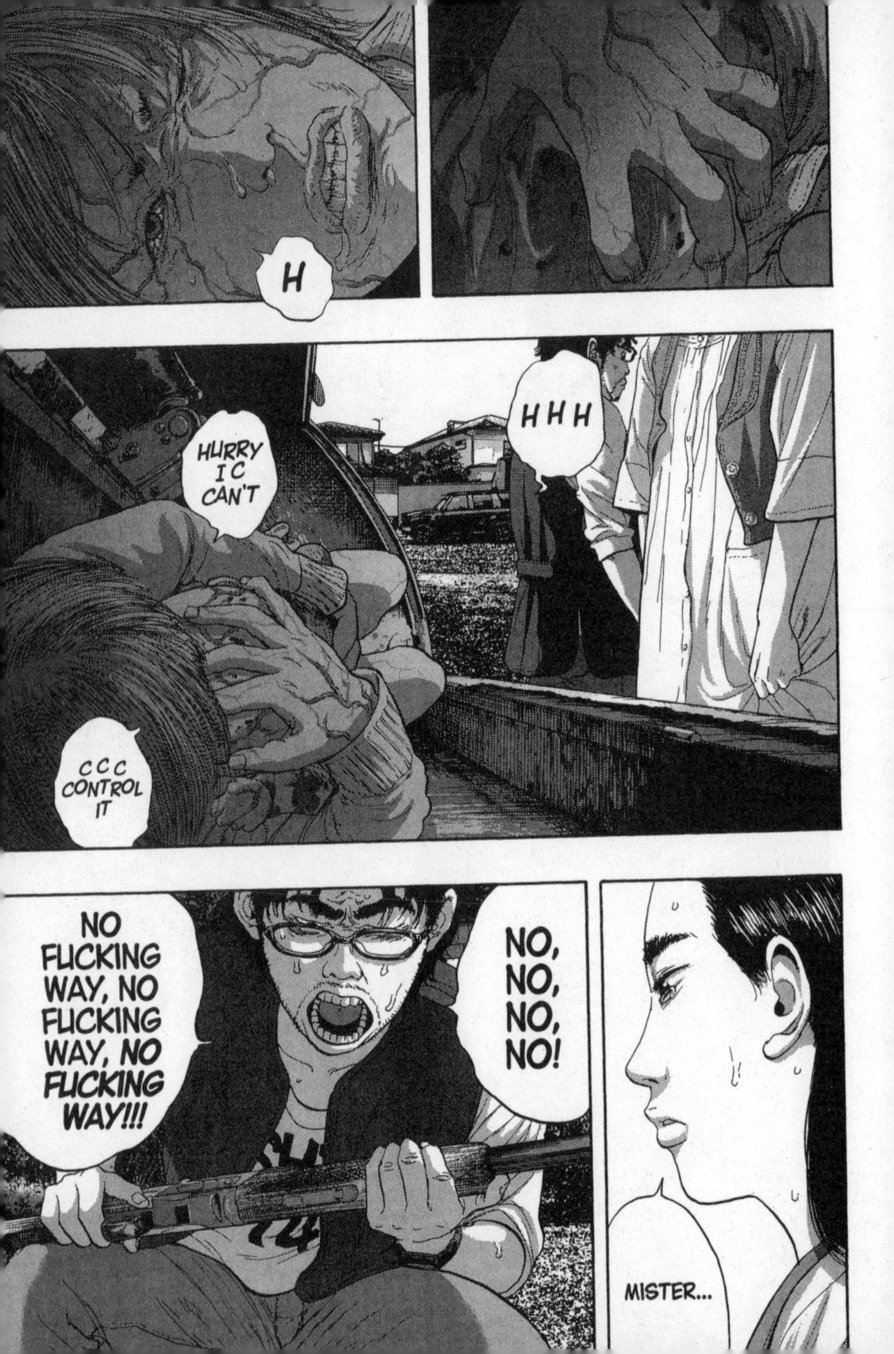
H
HHH
HURRY I C CAN'T
CCC CONTROL IT
MISTER...
NO, NO, NO, NO!
NO FUCKING WAY, NO FUCKING WAY, NO FUCKING WAY!!!

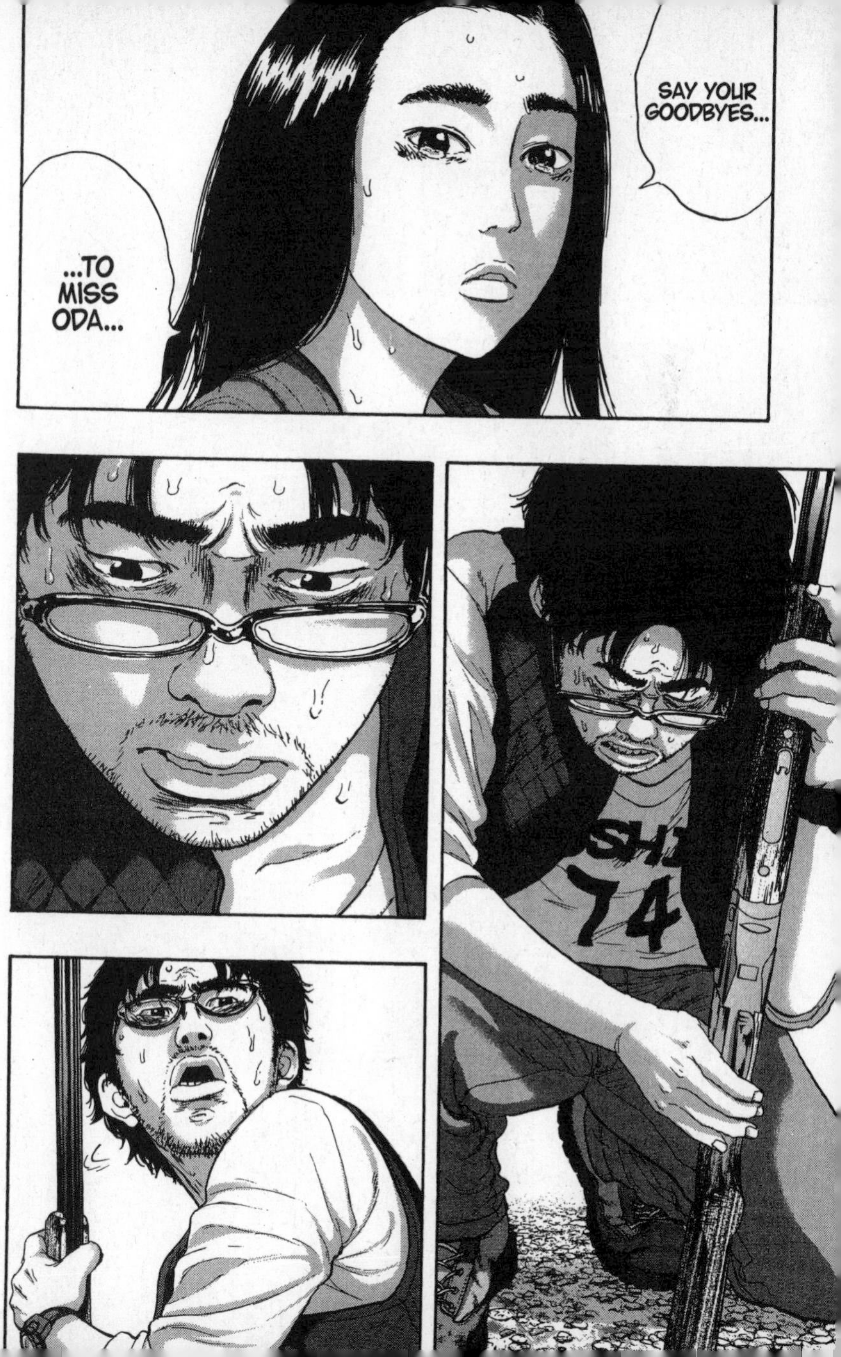
SAY YOUR GOODBYES...
...TO MISS ODA...

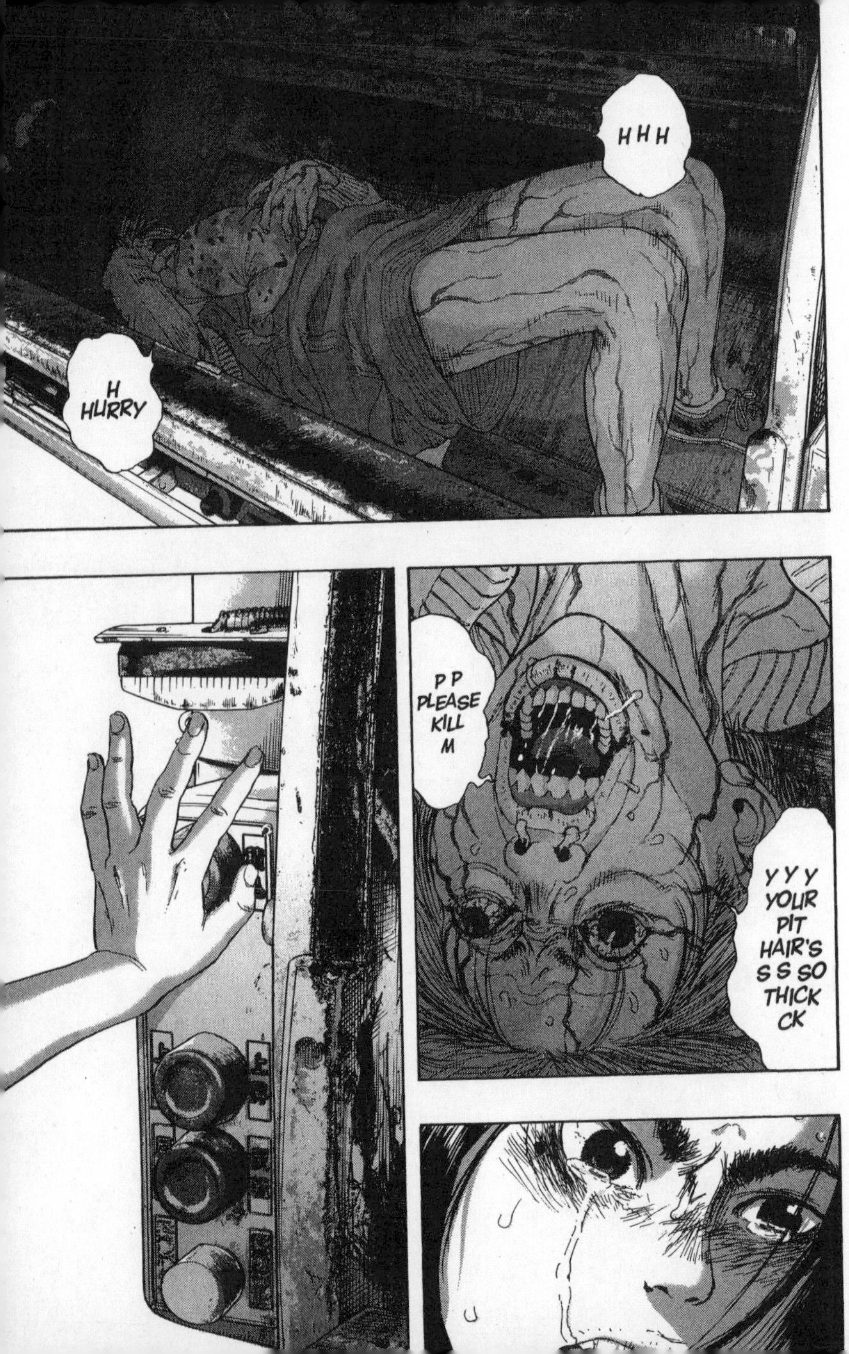
HHH
H HURRY
Y Y Y YOUR PIT HAIR'S S S SO THICK CK
P P PLEASE KILL M

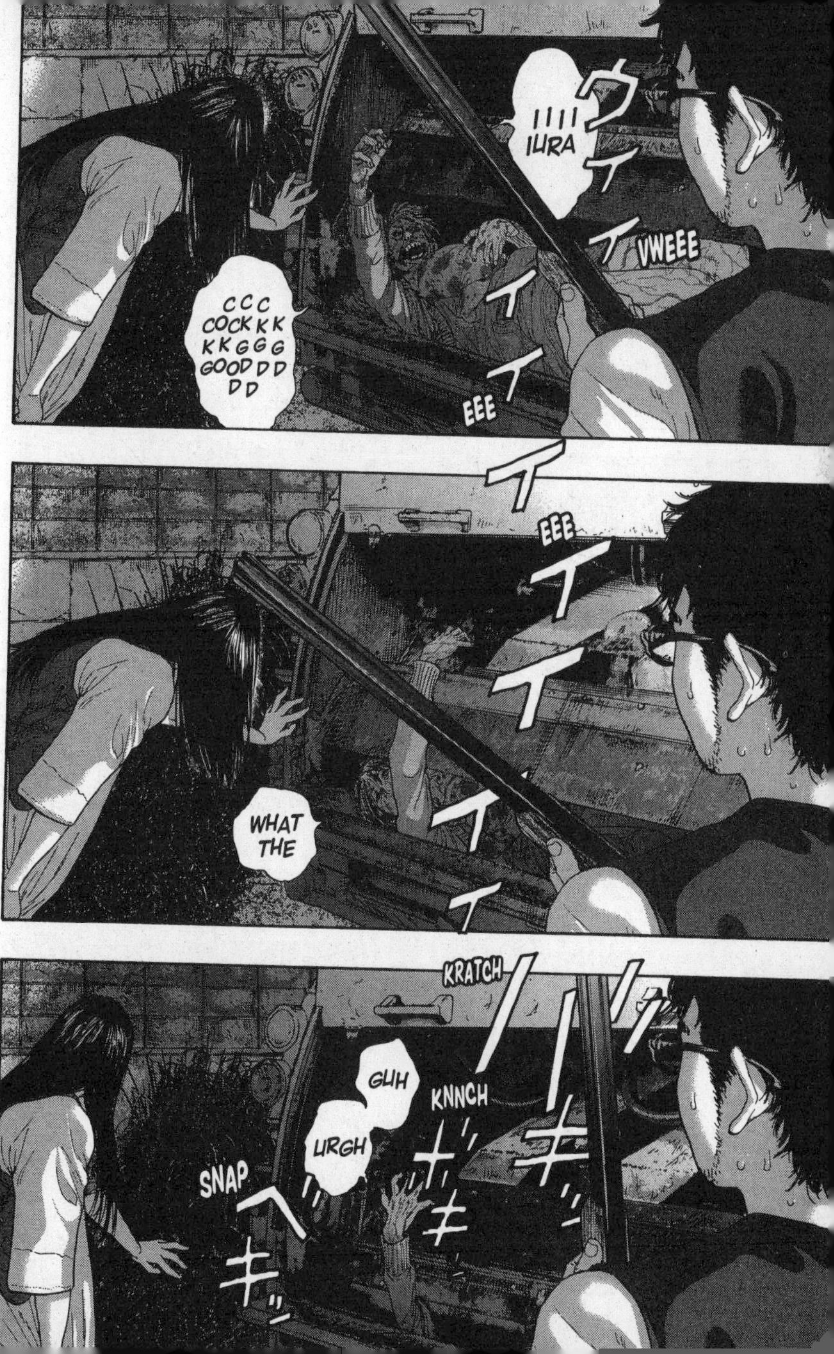

IIII IURA
VWEEE
CCC COCKKK KKGGG GOODDD DD
EEE
EEE
WHAT THE
KRATCH
KNNCH
GUH
URGH
SNAP

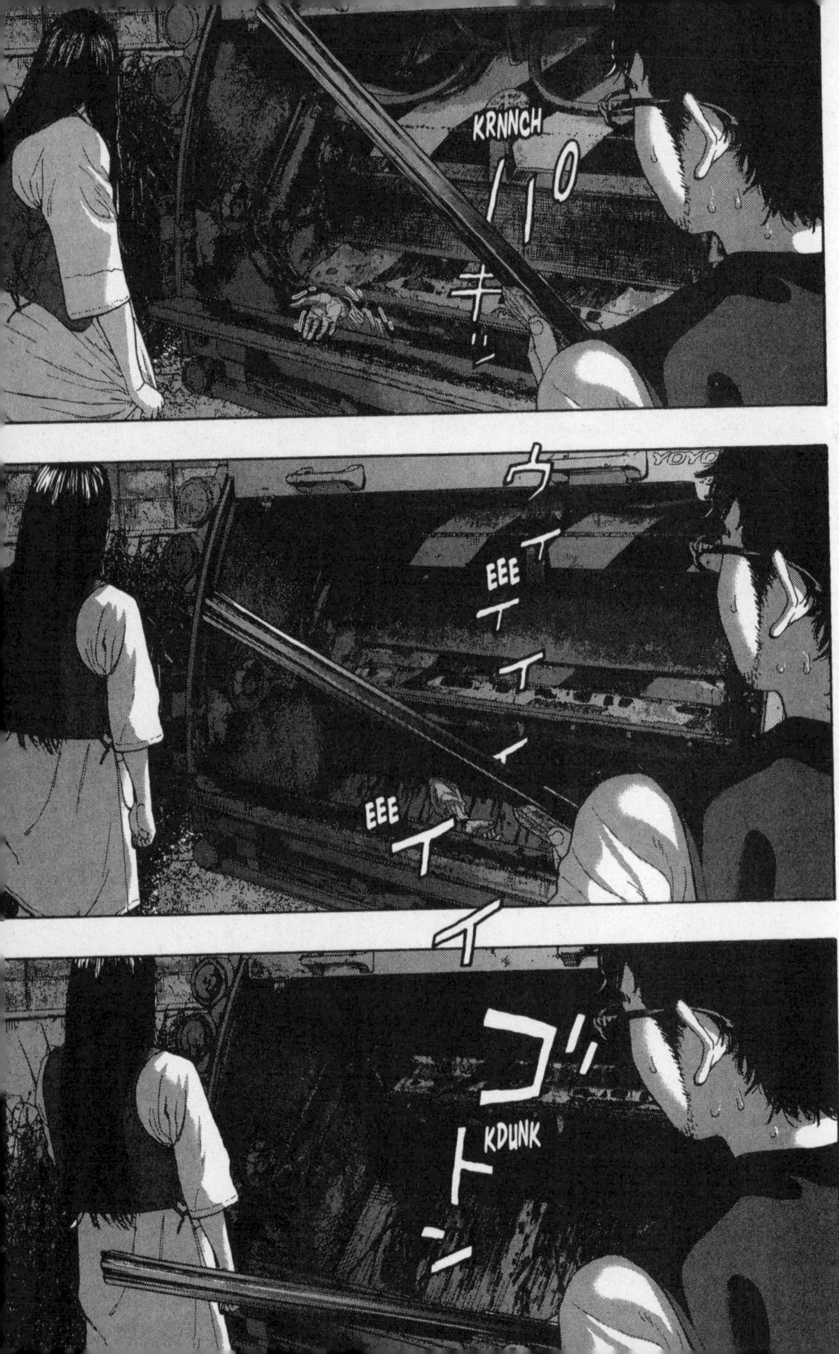
KRNNCH
EEE
EEE
KDUNK

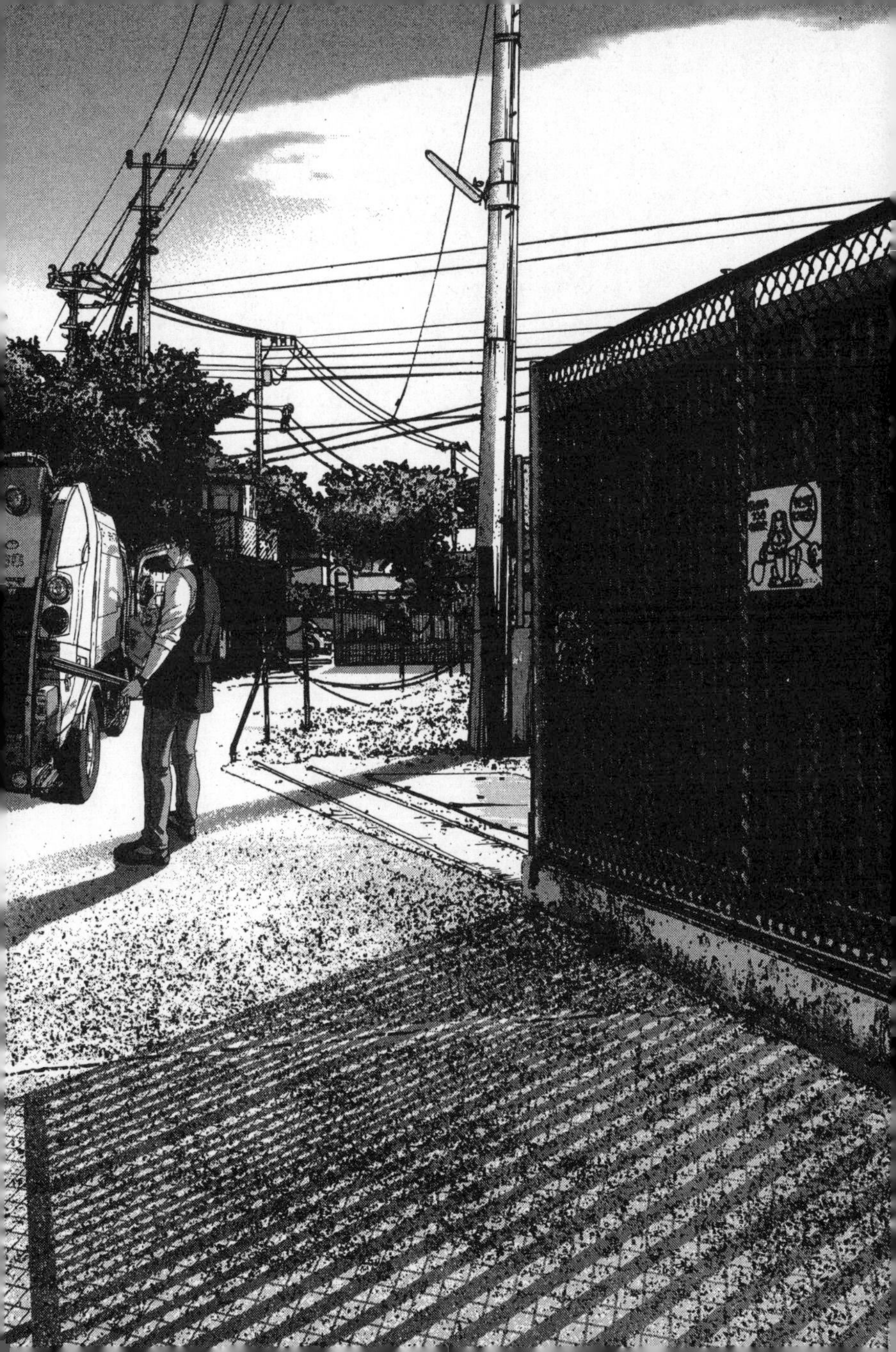

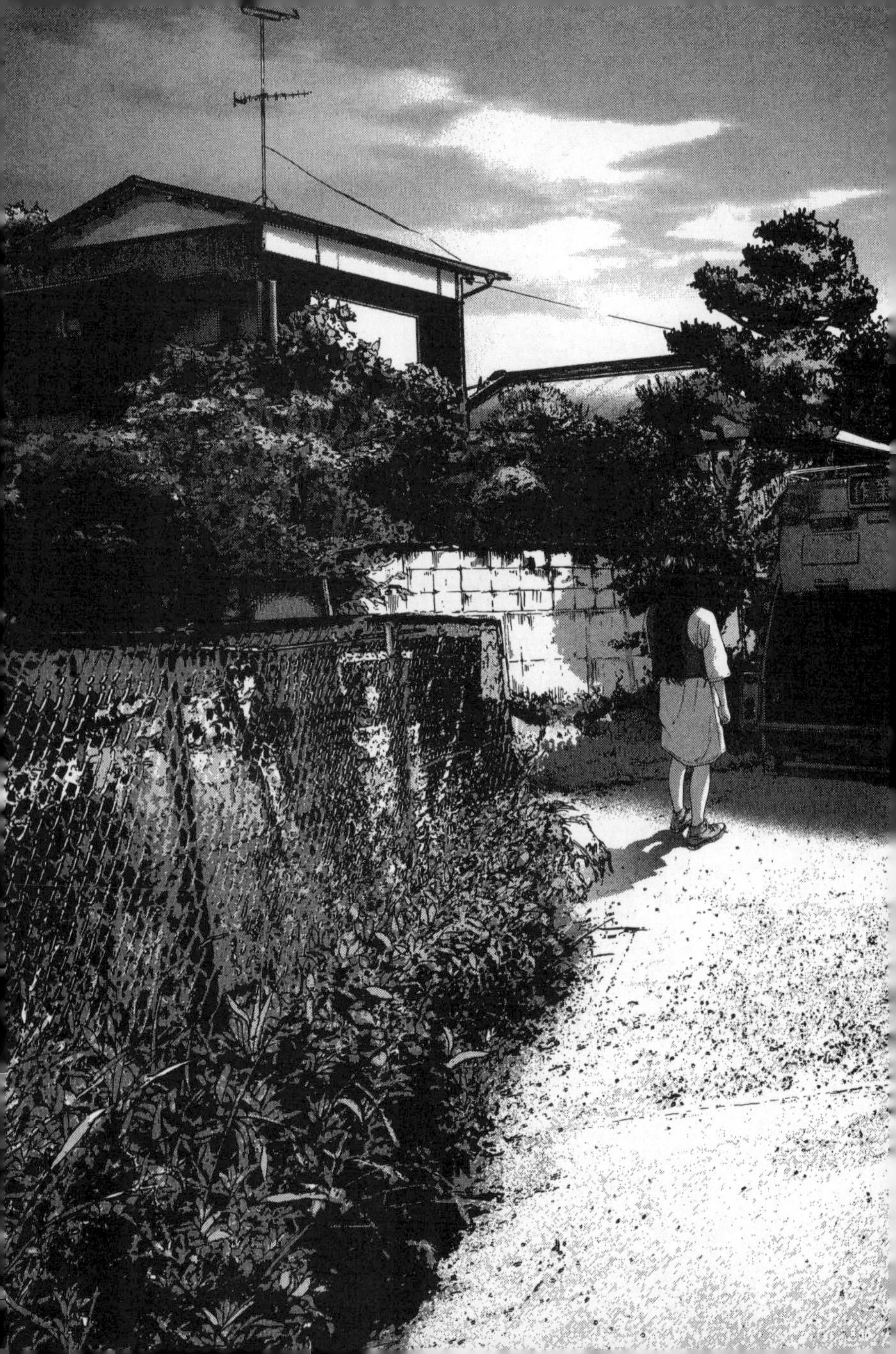

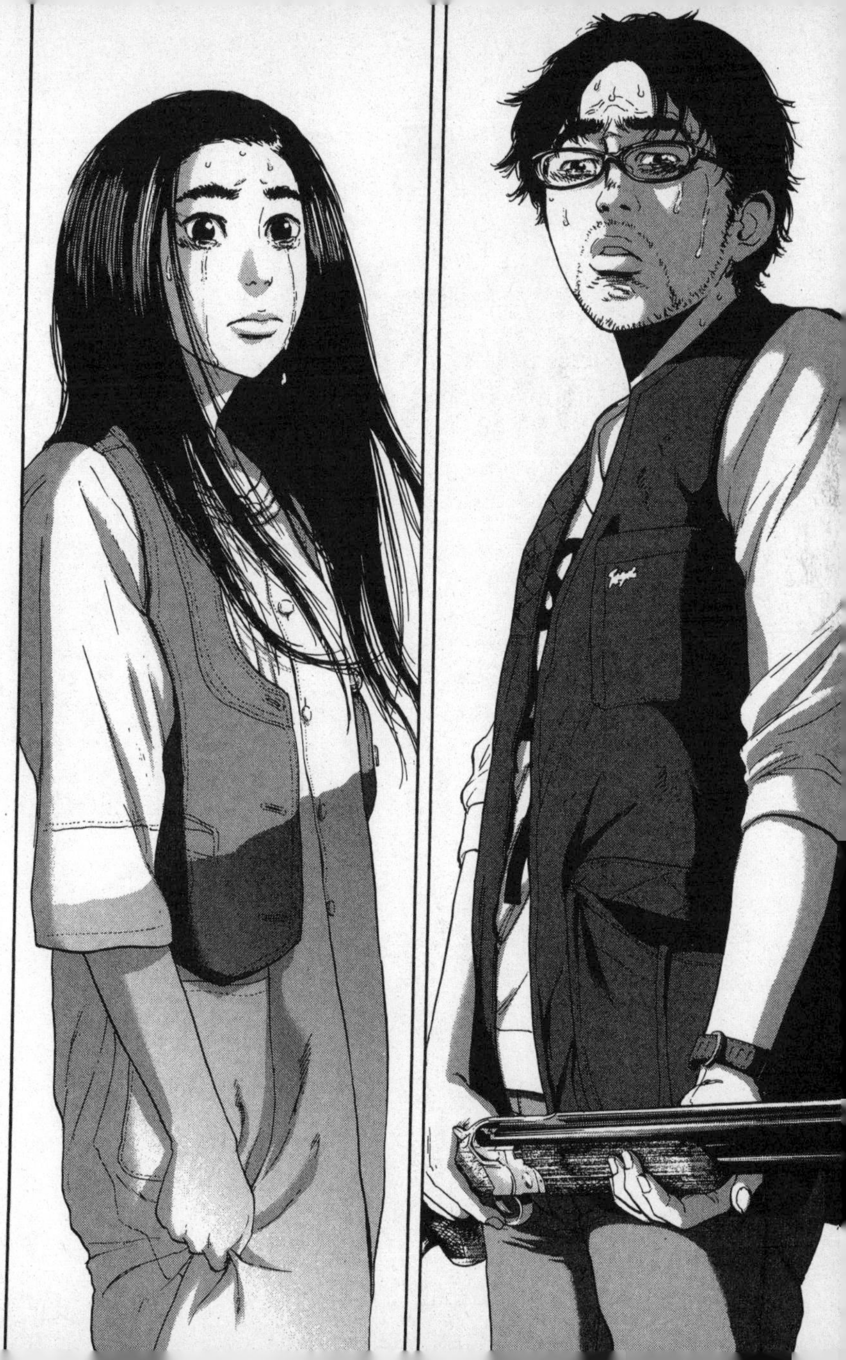

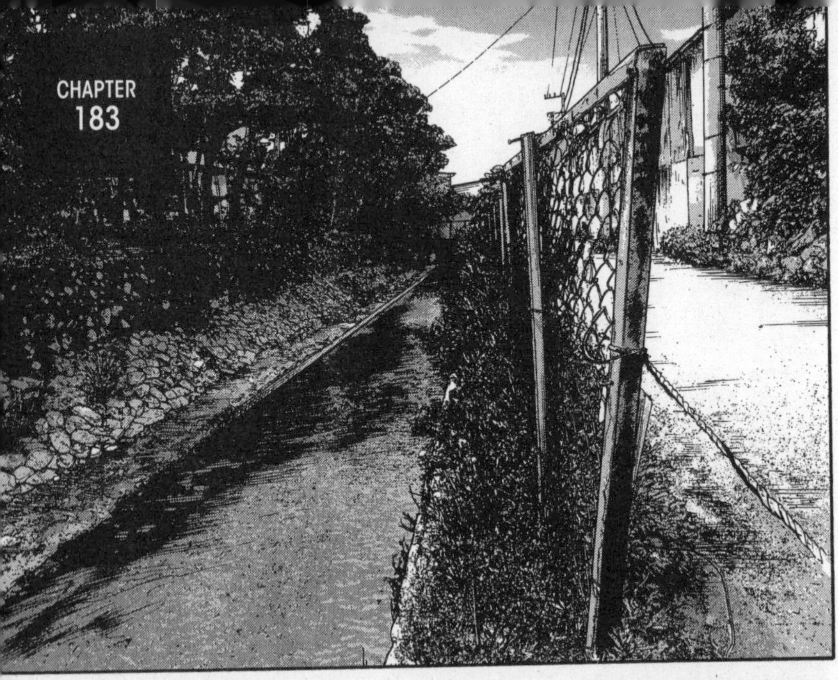
CHAPTER
183

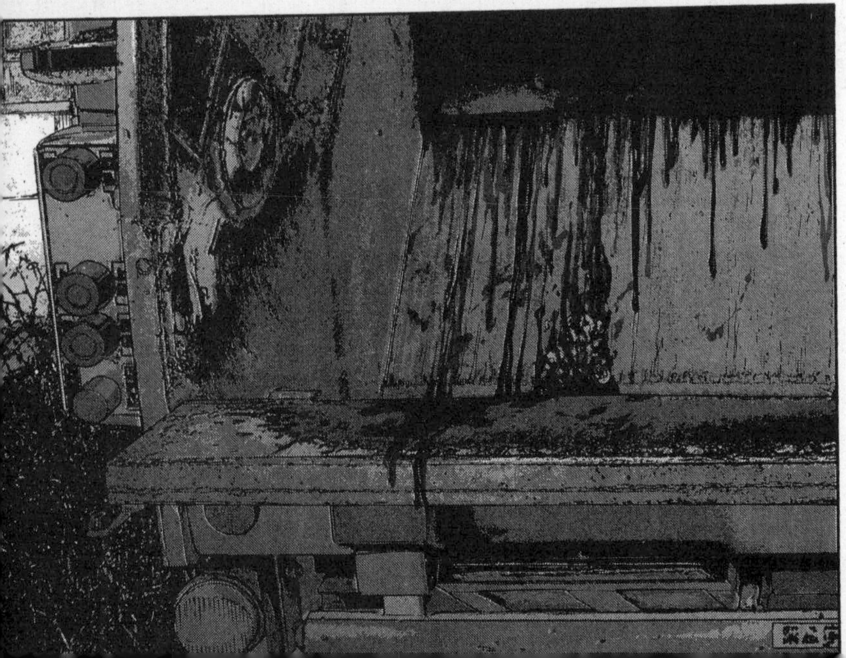

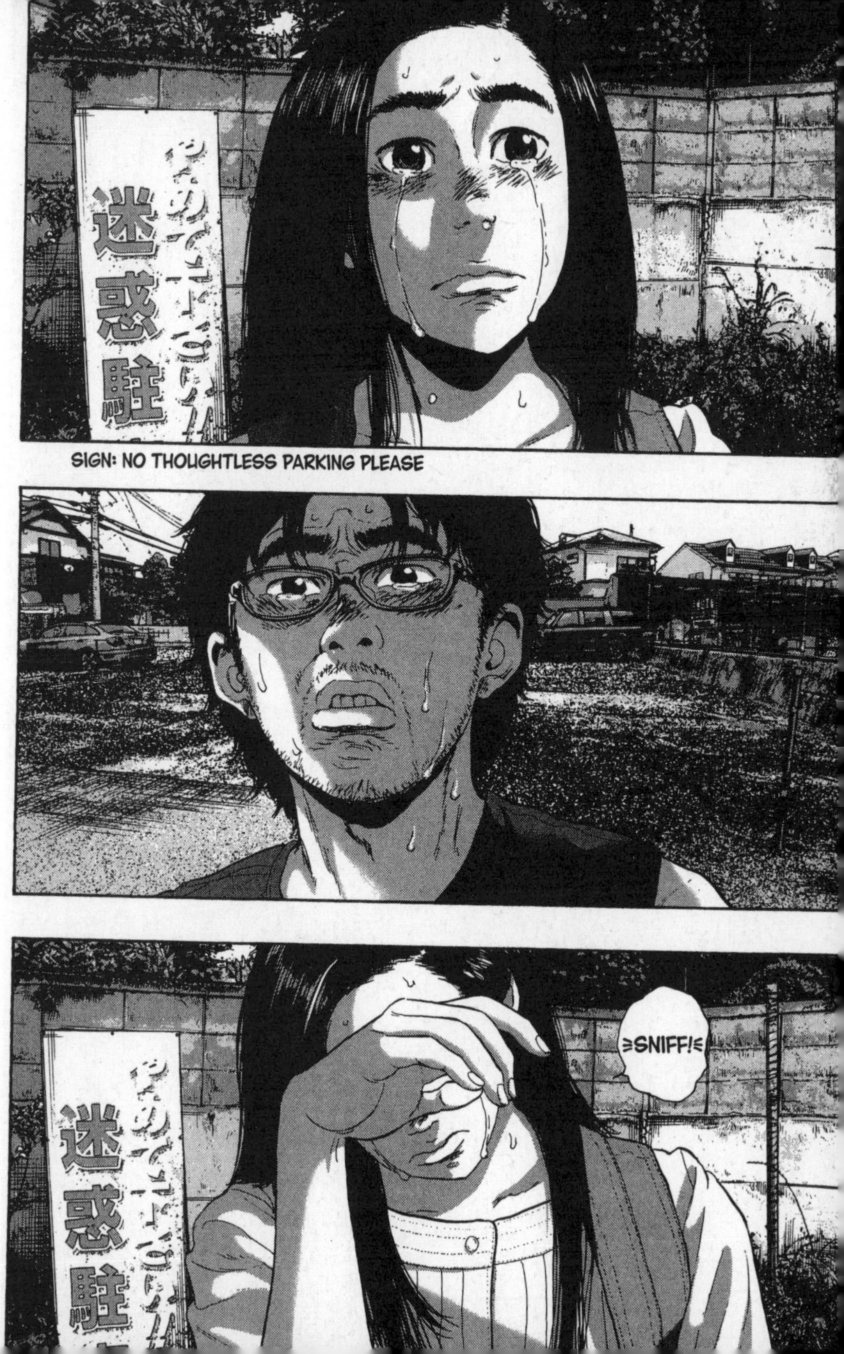
SIGN: NO THOUGHTLESS PARKING PLEASE
SNIFF!

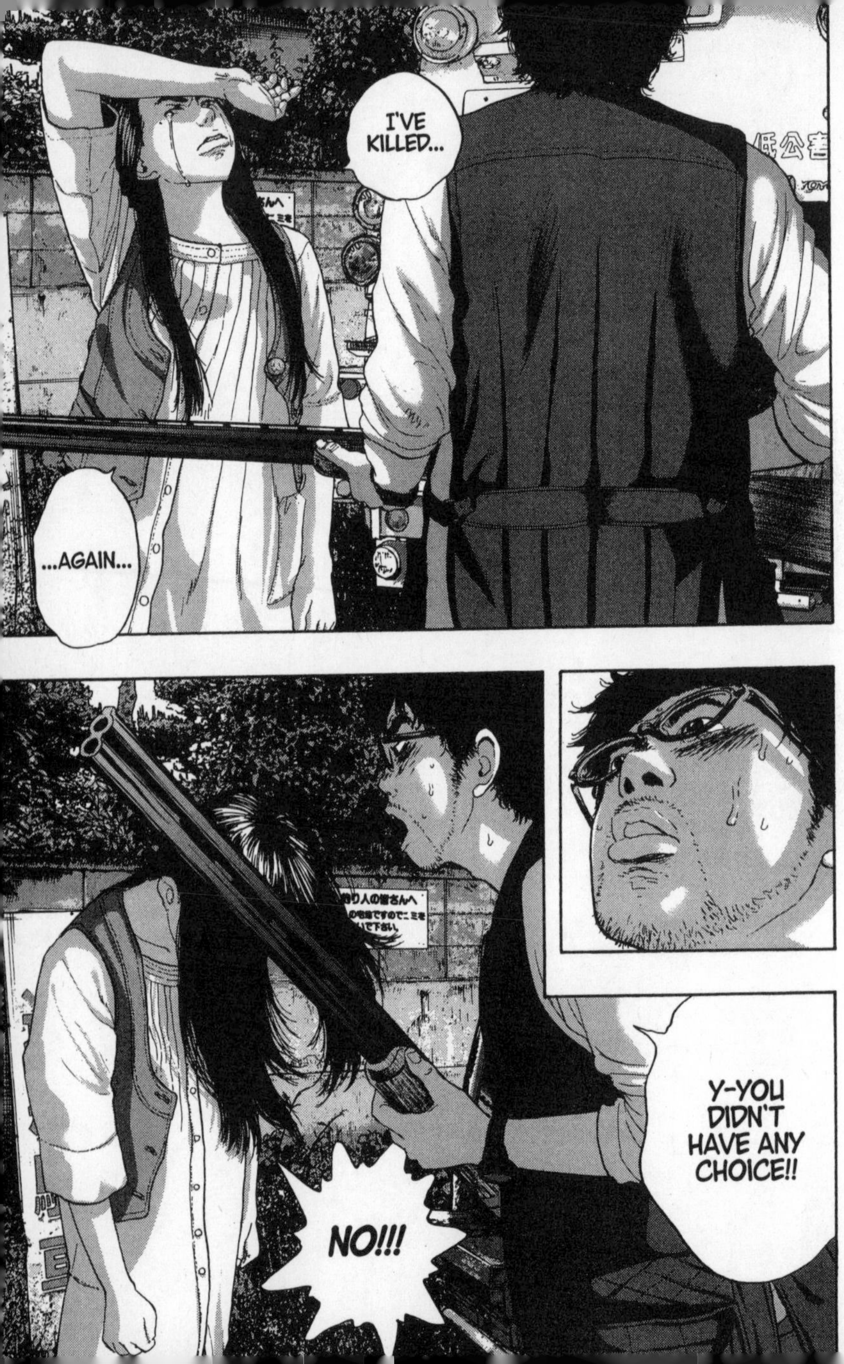
I'VE KILLED...
...AGAIN...
Y-YOU DIDN'T HAVE ANY CHOICE!!
NO!!!

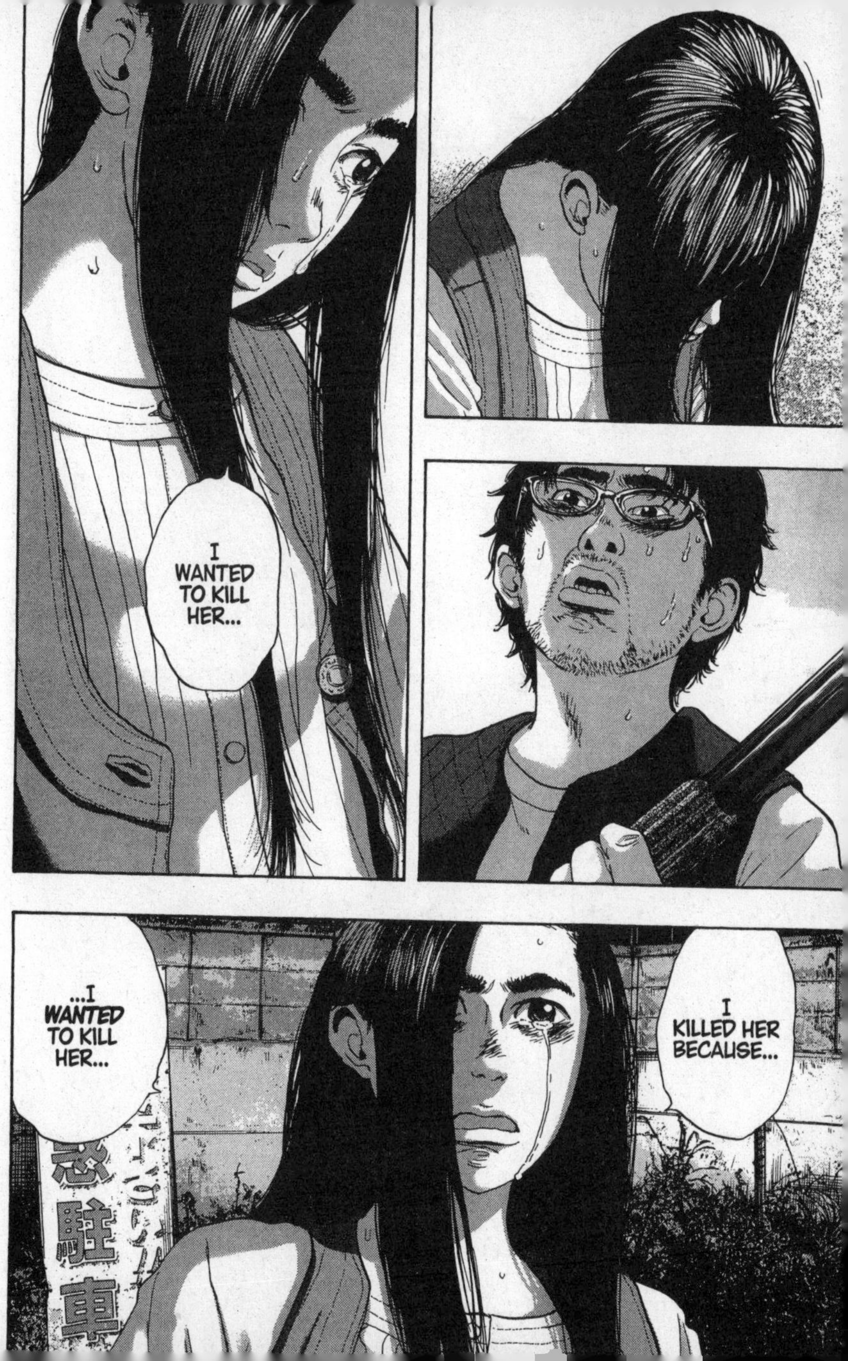
I WANTED TO KILL HER...
I KILLED HER BECAUSE...
...I WANTED TO KILL HER...

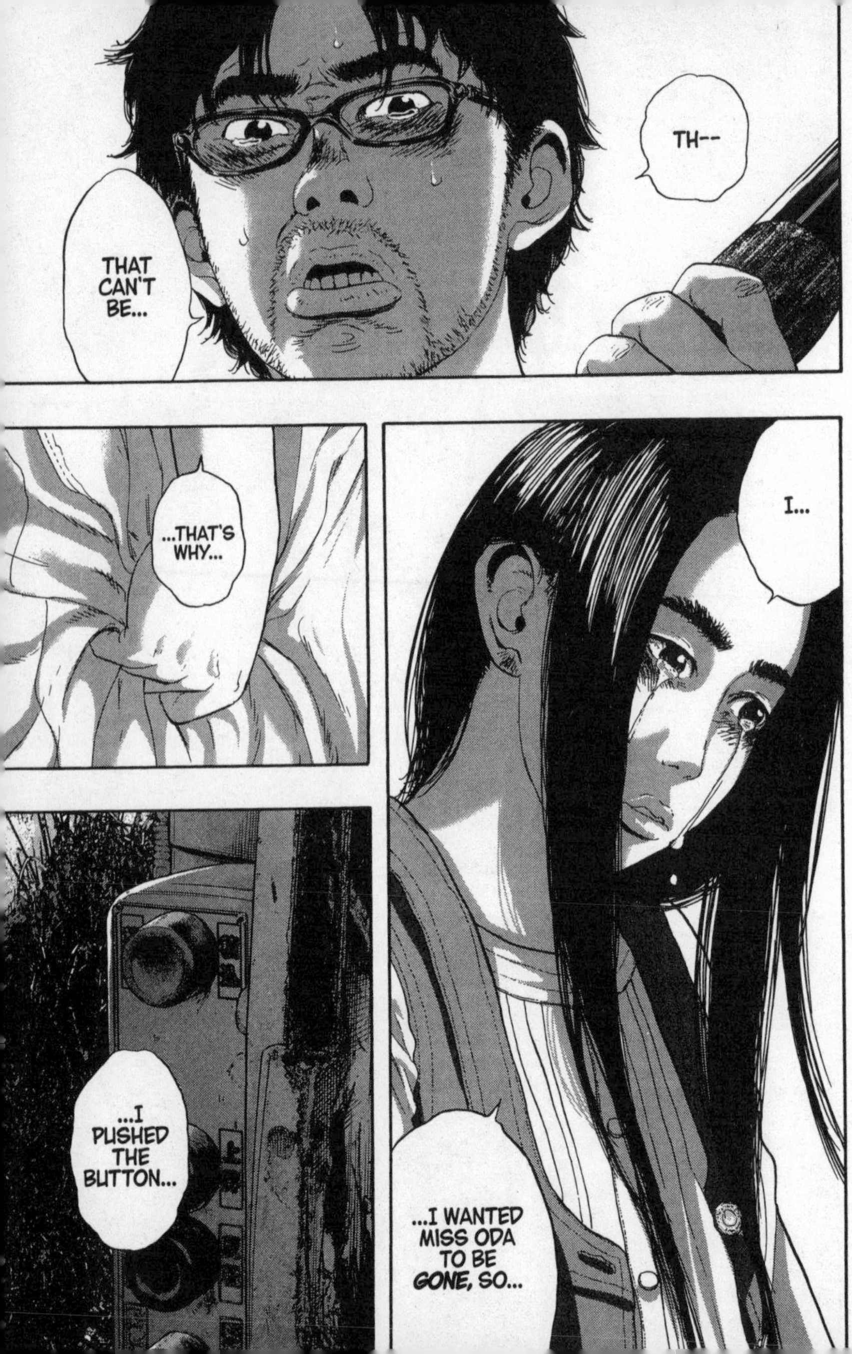
TH--
THAT CAN'T BE...
I...
...I WANTED MISS ODA TO BE GONE, SO...
...THAT'S WHY...
...I PUSHED THE BUTTON...

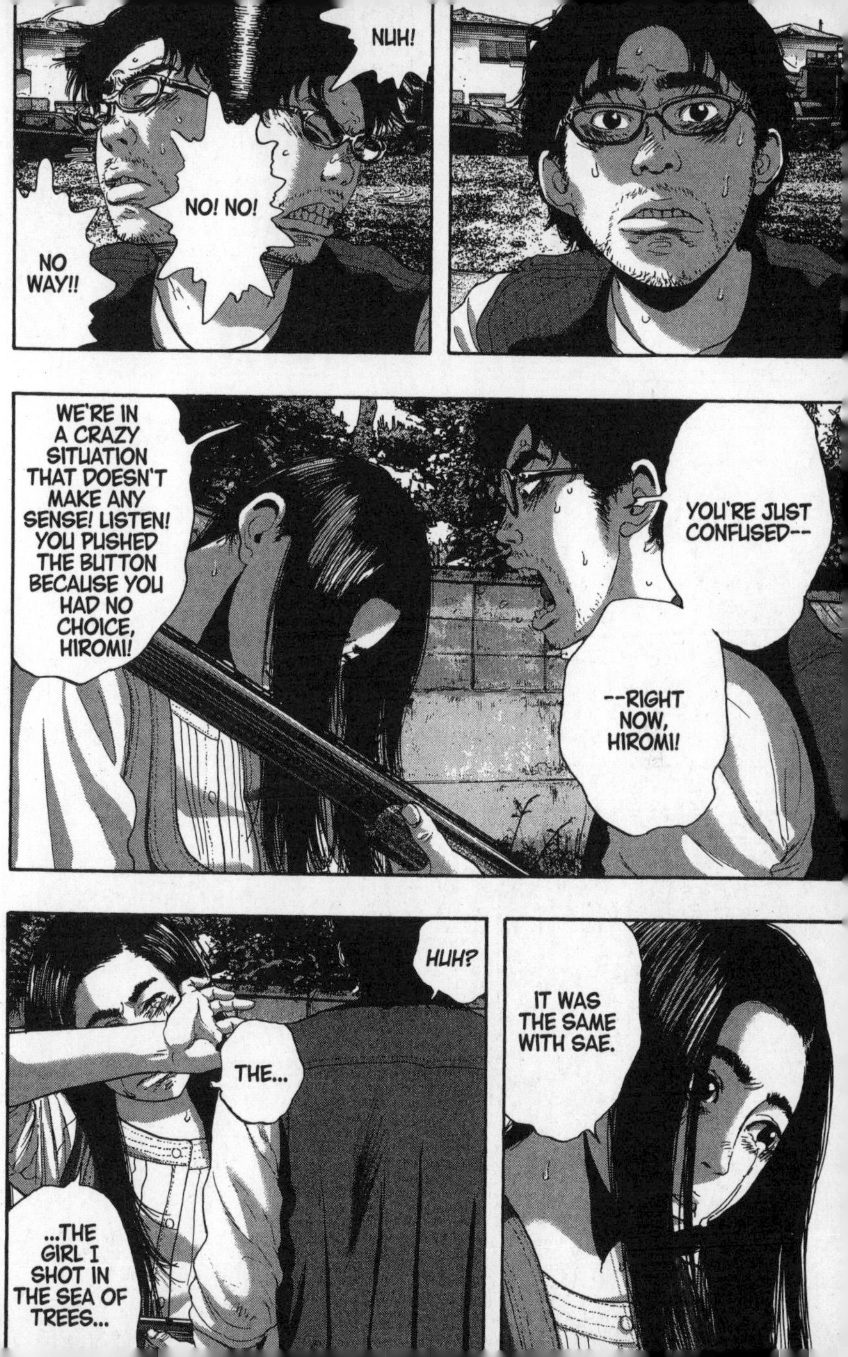
NUH!
NO! NO!
NO WAY!!
YOU'RE JUST CONFUSED--
--RIGHT NOW, HIROMI!
WE'RE IN A CRAZY SITUATION THAT DOESN'T MAKE ANY SENSE! LISTEN! YOU PUSHED THE BUTTON BECAUSE YOU HAD NO CHOICE, HIROMI!
IT WAS THE SAME WITH SAE.
HUH?
THE...
...THE GIRL I SHOT IN THE SEA OF TREES...

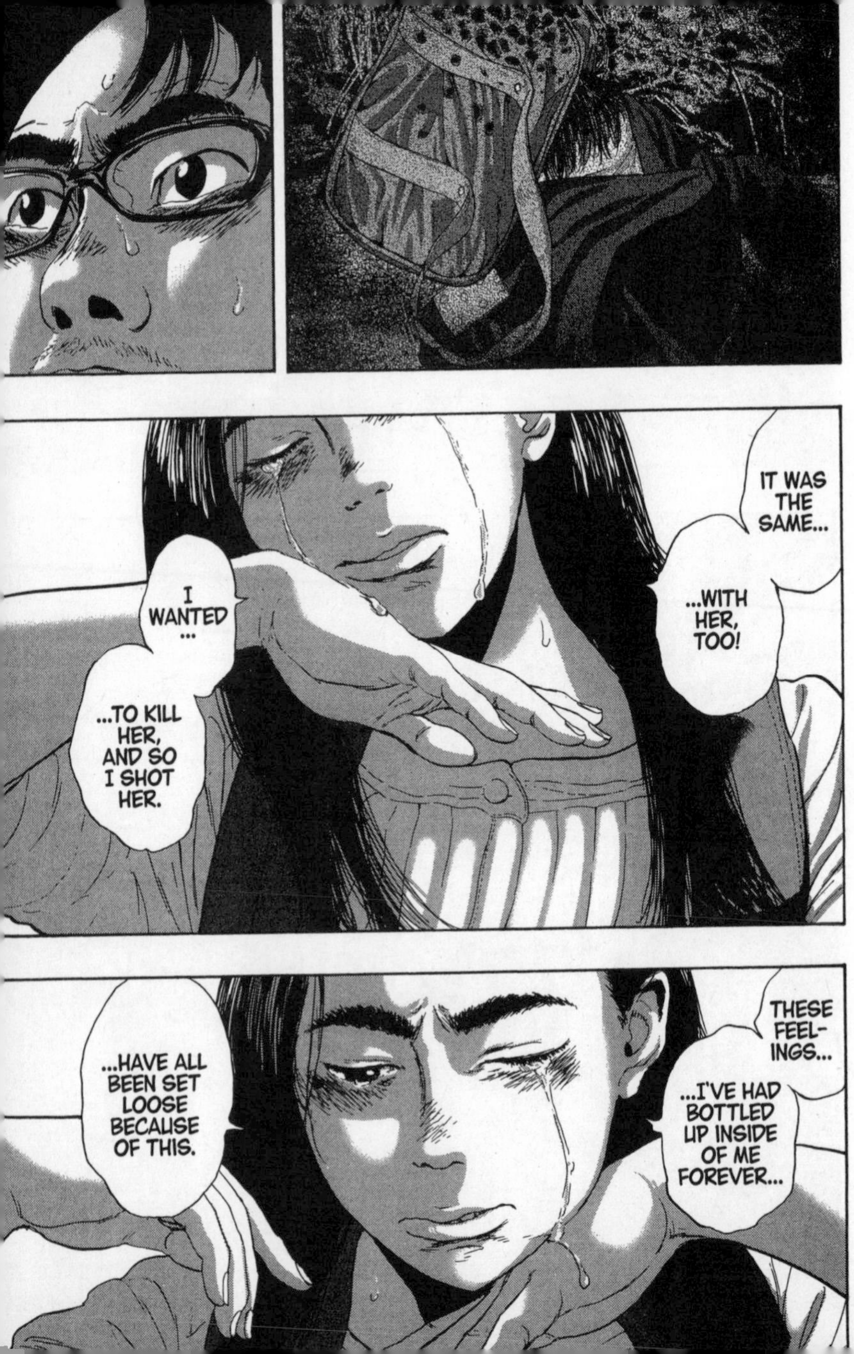
IT WAS THE SAME...
...WITH HER, TOO!
I WANTED...
...TO KILL HER, AND SO I SHOT HER.
THESE FEEL-INGS...
...I'VE HAD BOTTLED UP INSIDE OF ME FOREVER...
...HAVE ALL BEEN SET LOOSE BECAUSE OF THIS.

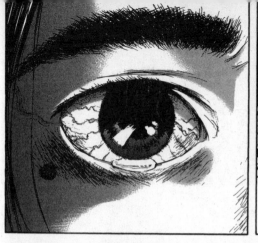

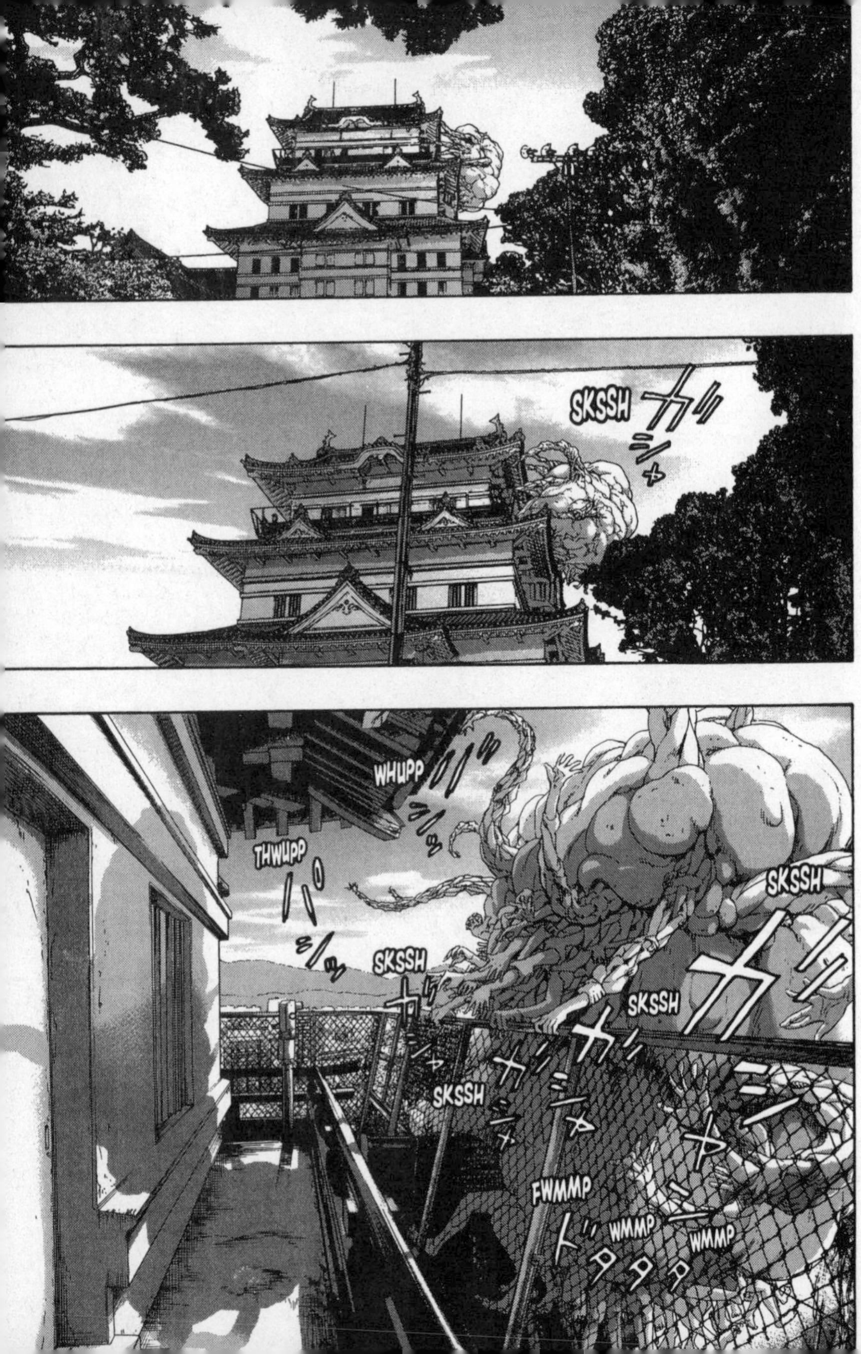
SKSSH
WHUPP
THWUPP
SKSSH
SKSSH
SKSSH
SKSSH
FWMMP
WMMP
WMMP

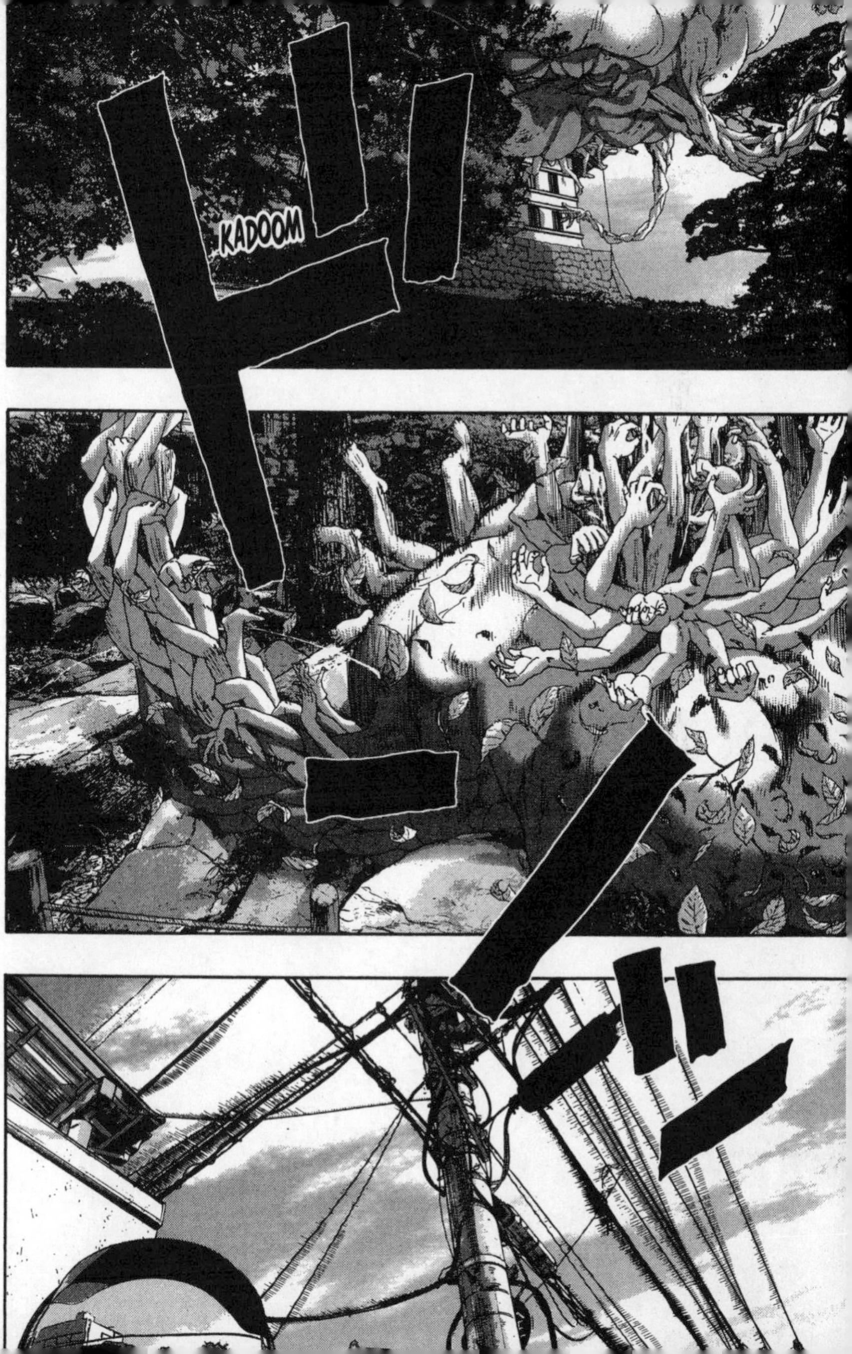
KADOOM

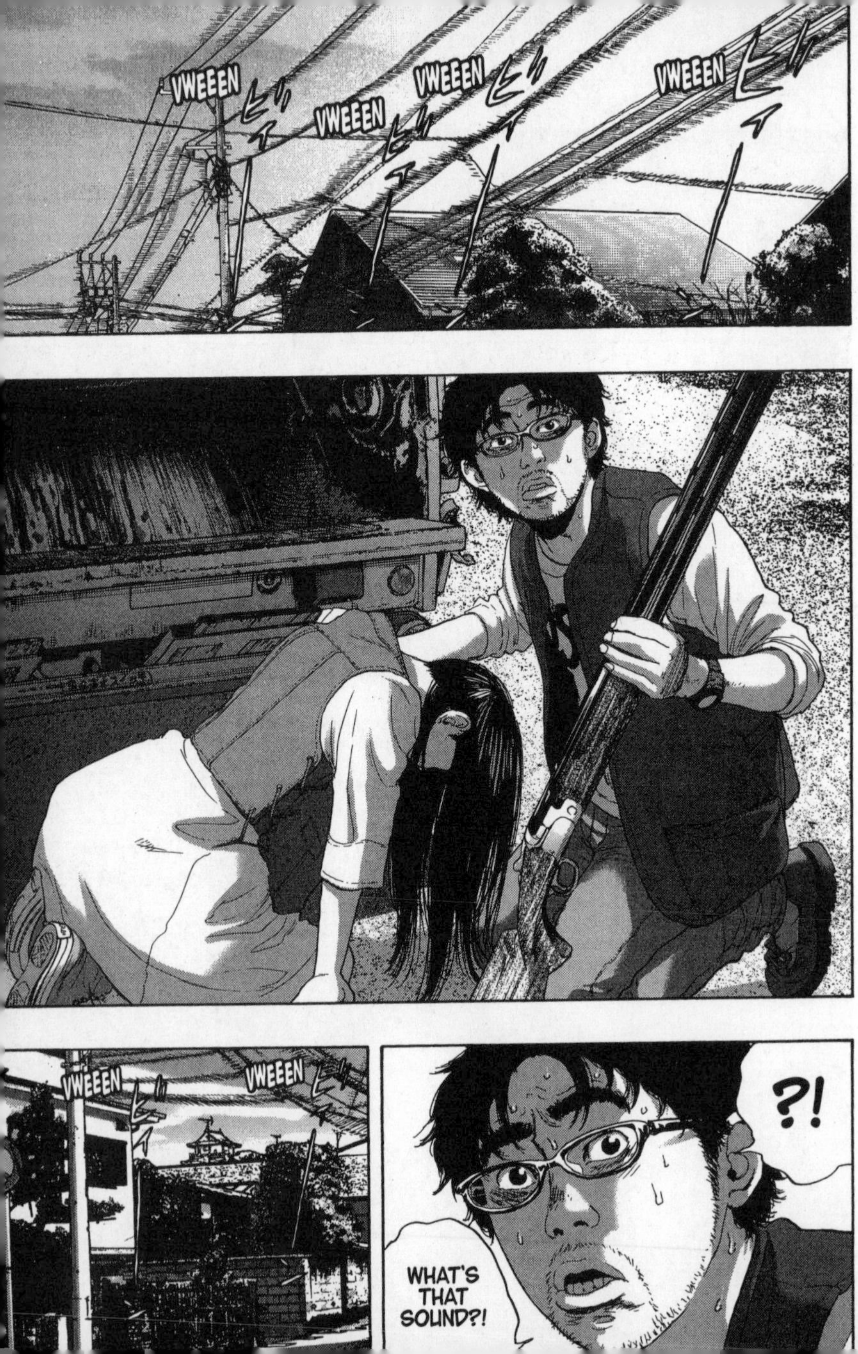
VWEEEN
VWEEEN
VWEEEN
VWEEEN
?!
WHAT'S THAT SOUND?!
VWEEEN
VWEEEN

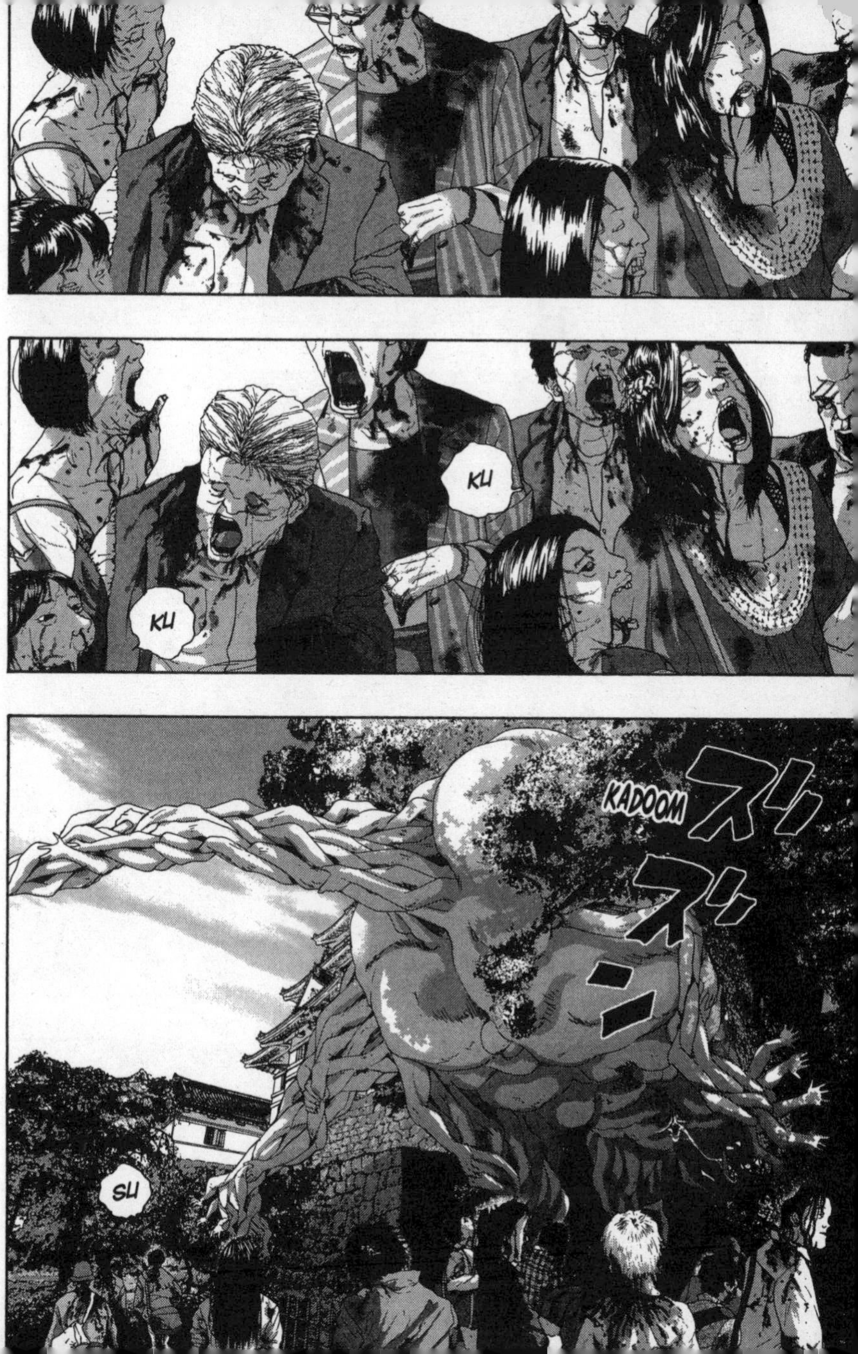
KU
KU
KADOOM
SU

THOOM

THOOM

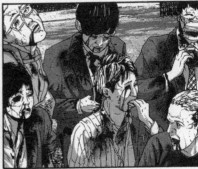

SU

KU

KU

KU

KU

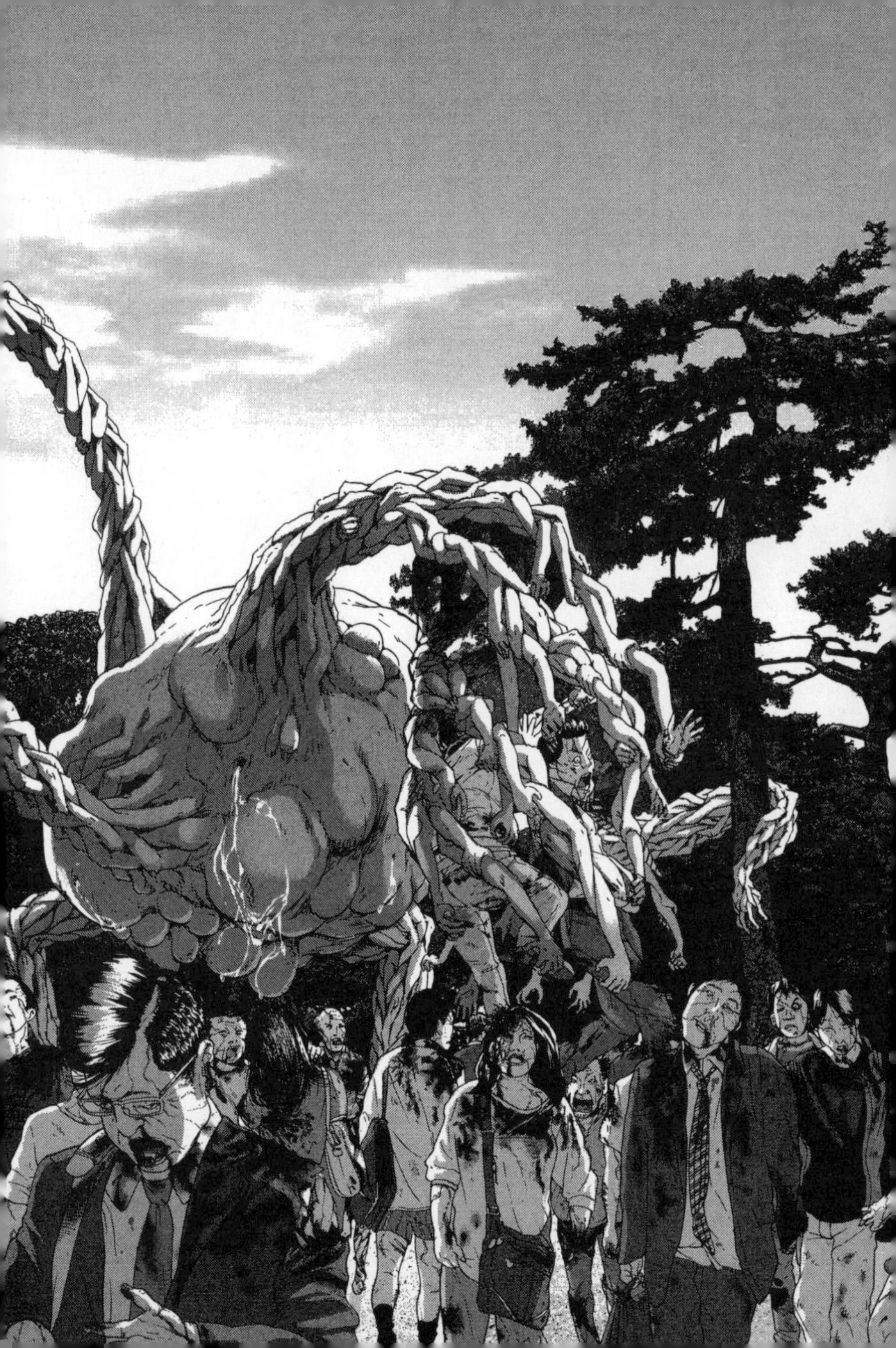

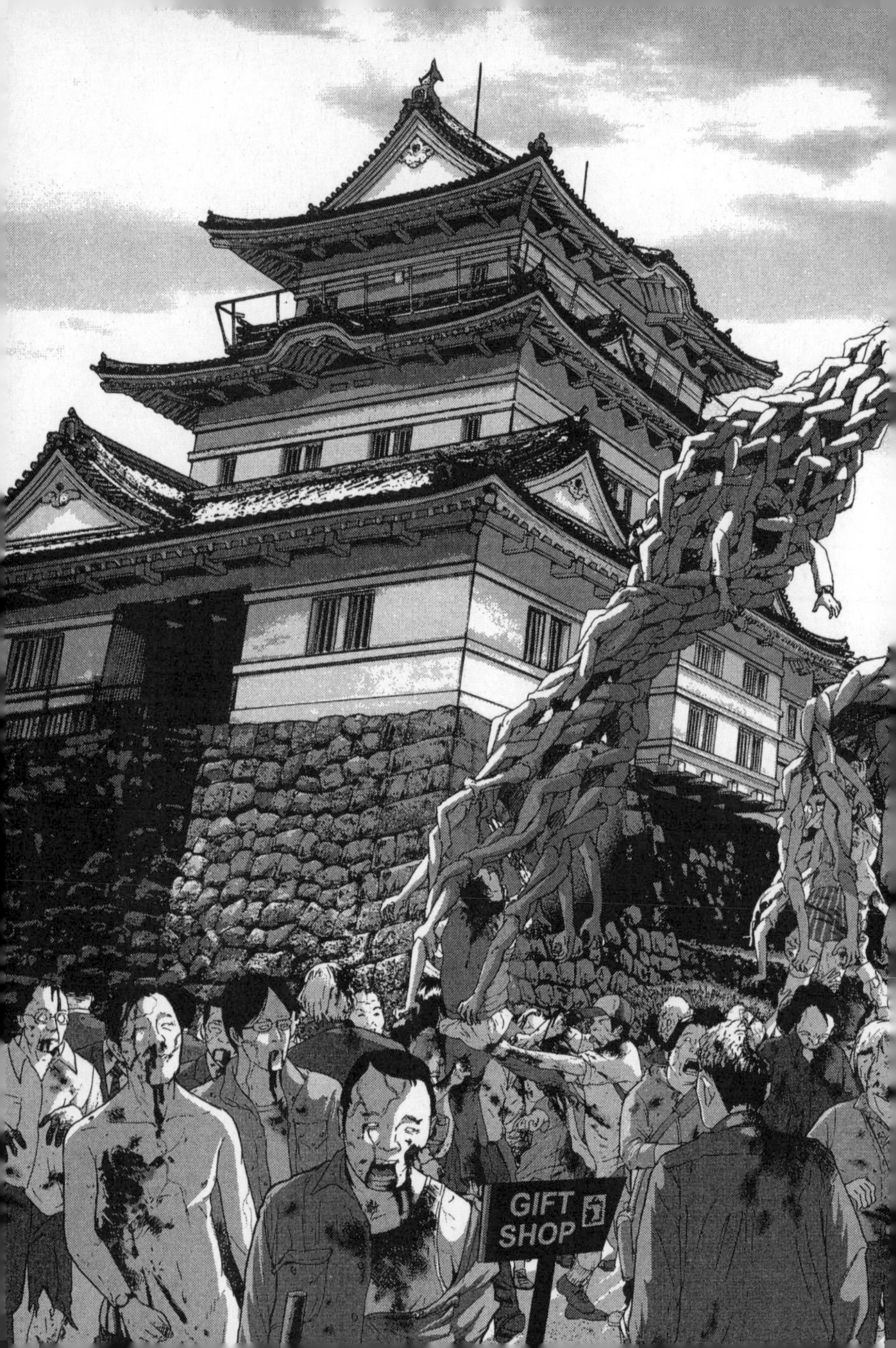
GIFT SHOP

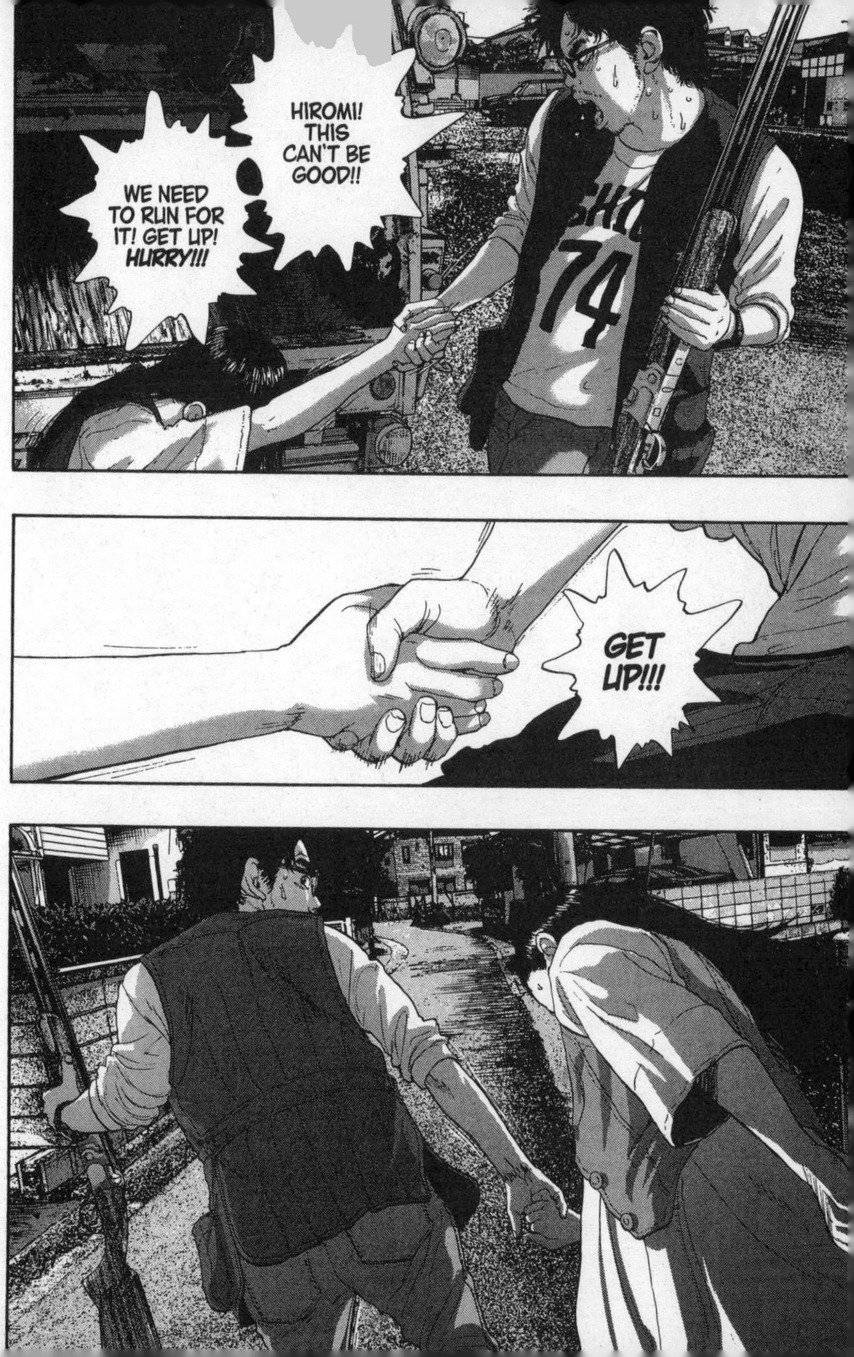
HIROMI! THIS CAN'T BE GOOD!!
WE NEED TO RUN FOR IT! GET UP! HURRY!!!
GET UP!!!

RUN!!!

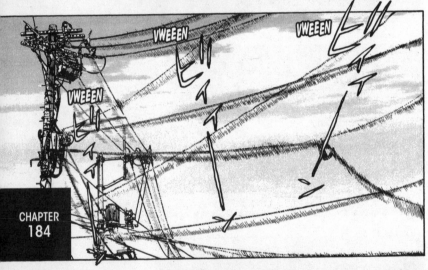

VWEEN

VWEEN

VWEEN

CHAPTER
184

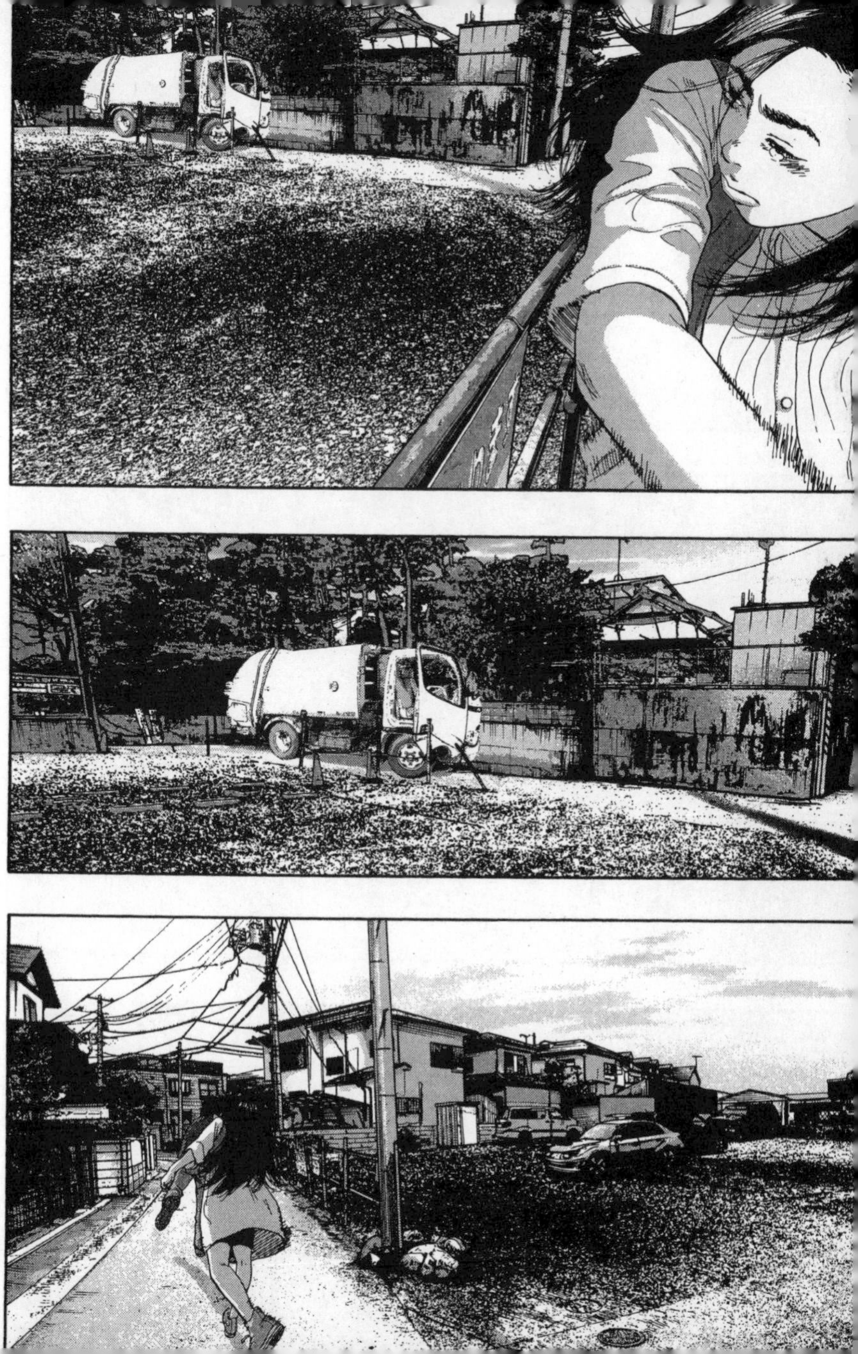

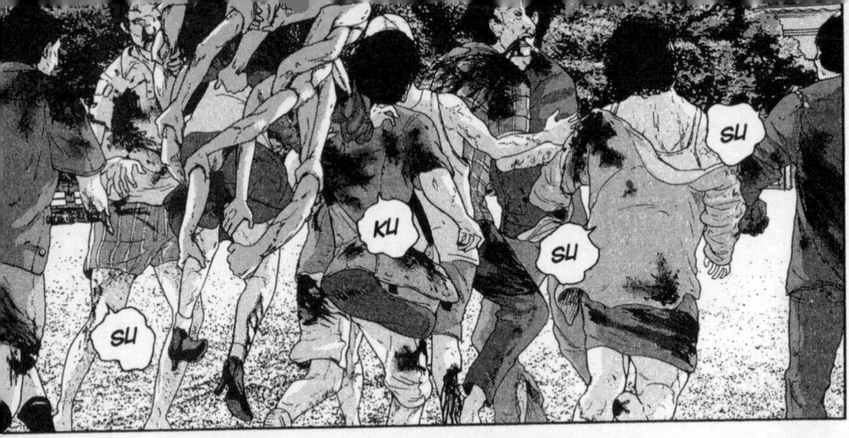
SU
SU
KU
SU

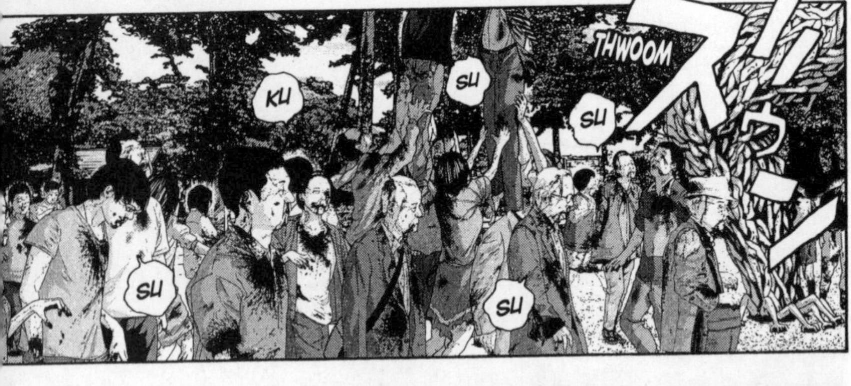
THWOOM
ズゥーン
SU
SU
KU
SU
SU

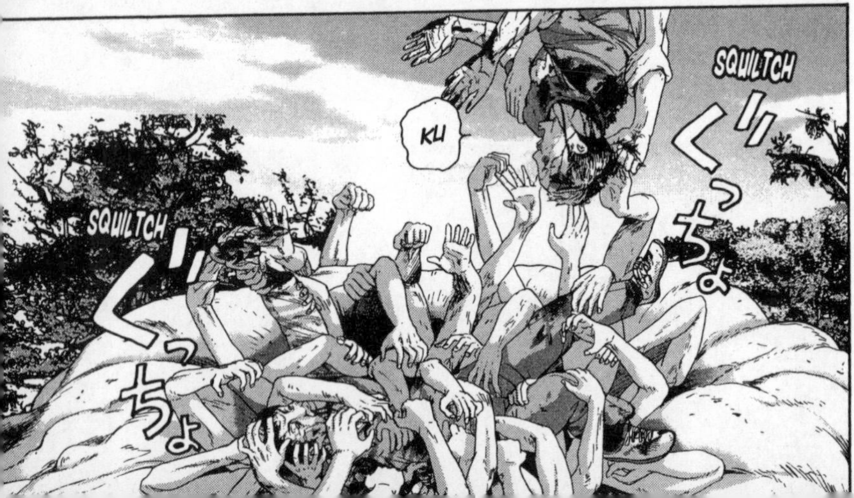
SQUILTCH
ぐっちょ
KU
SQUILTCH
ぐっちょ

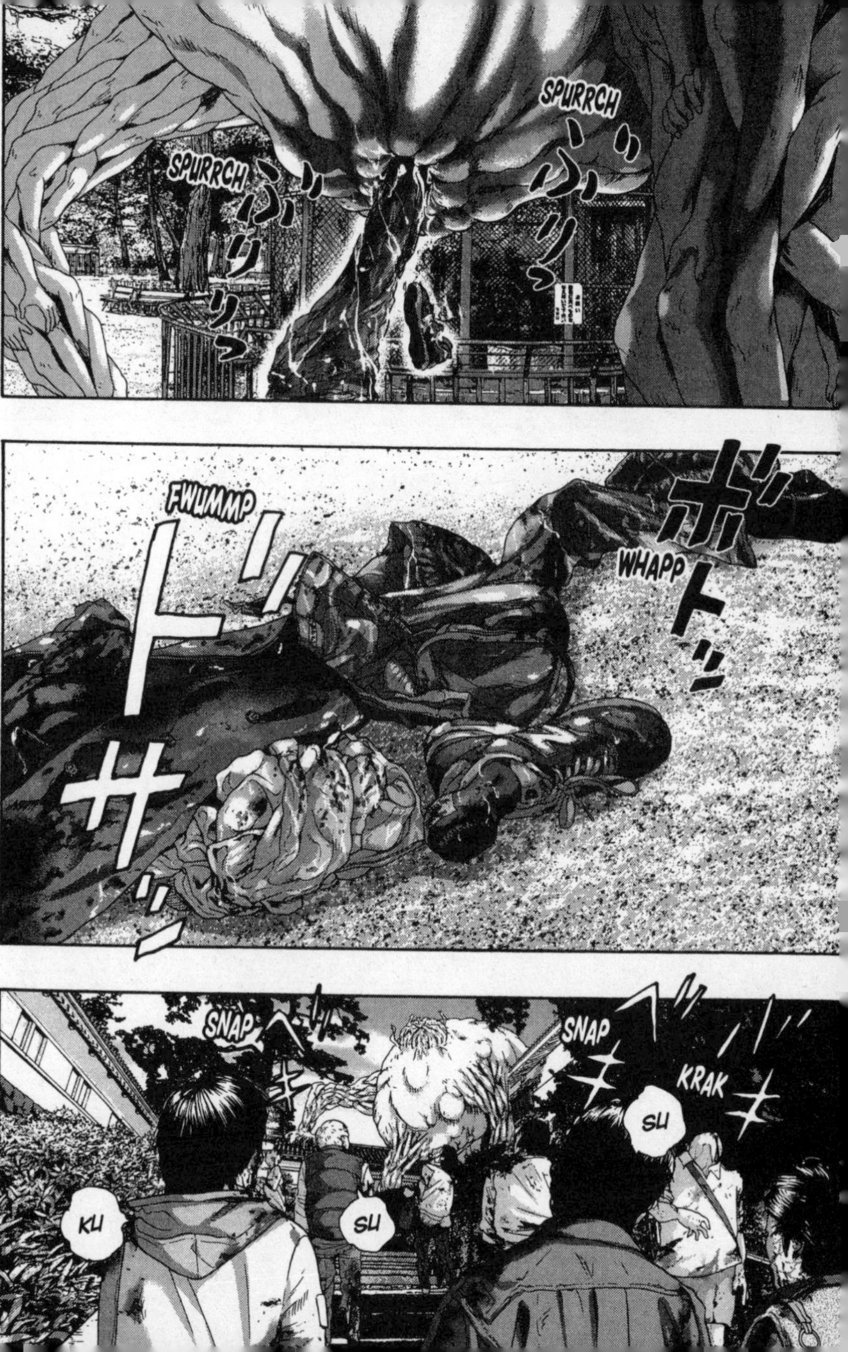
SPURRCH
SPURRCH
ボトッ
WHAPP
FWUMMP
ドサッ
SNAP
KRAK
SU
SNAP
SU
KU

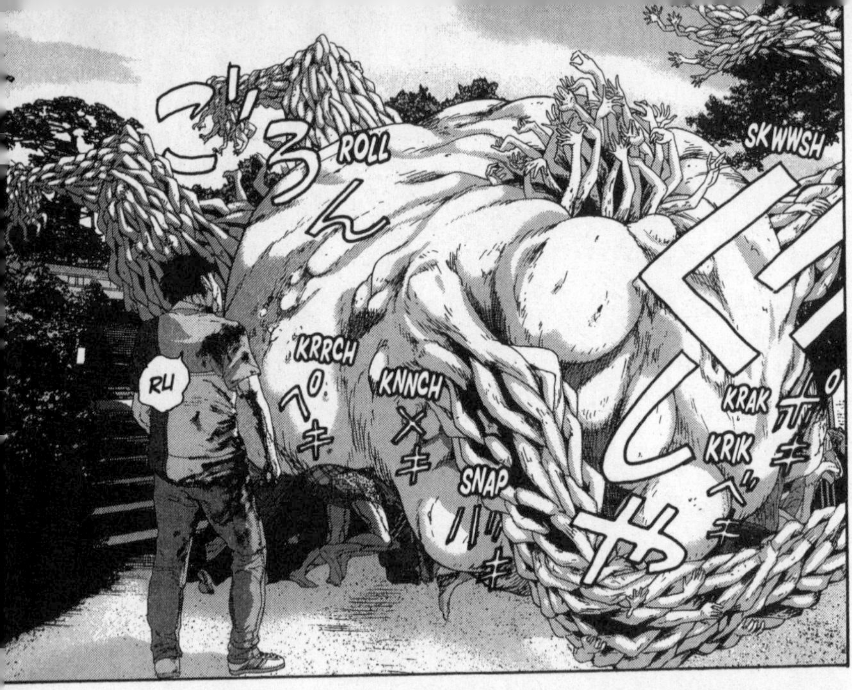
SKWWSH
ぐしゃ
KRAK
ポキ
KRIK
ベキ
SNAP
バキ
KNNCH
メキ
KRRCH
ペキ
ごろん
ROLL
RU

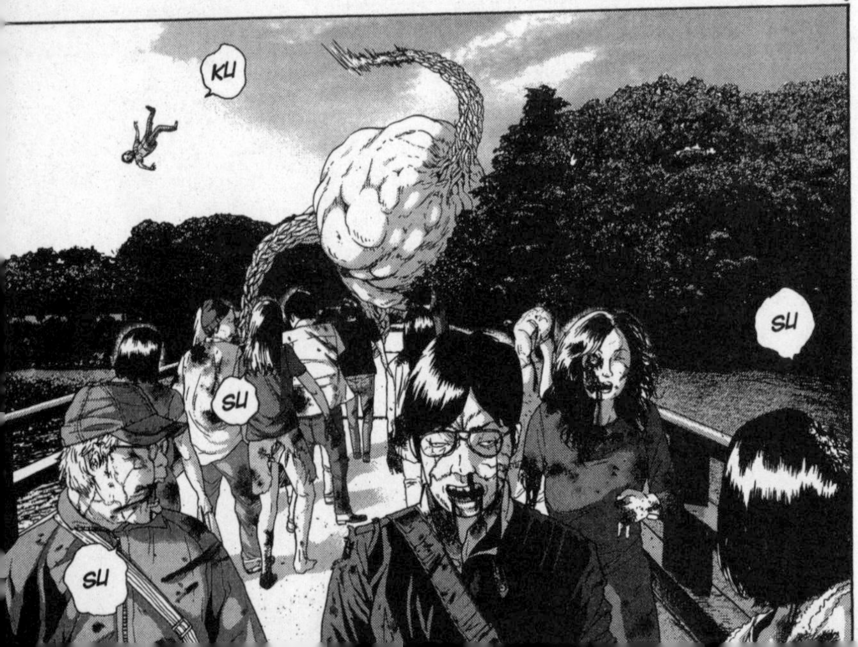
SU
KU
SU
SU

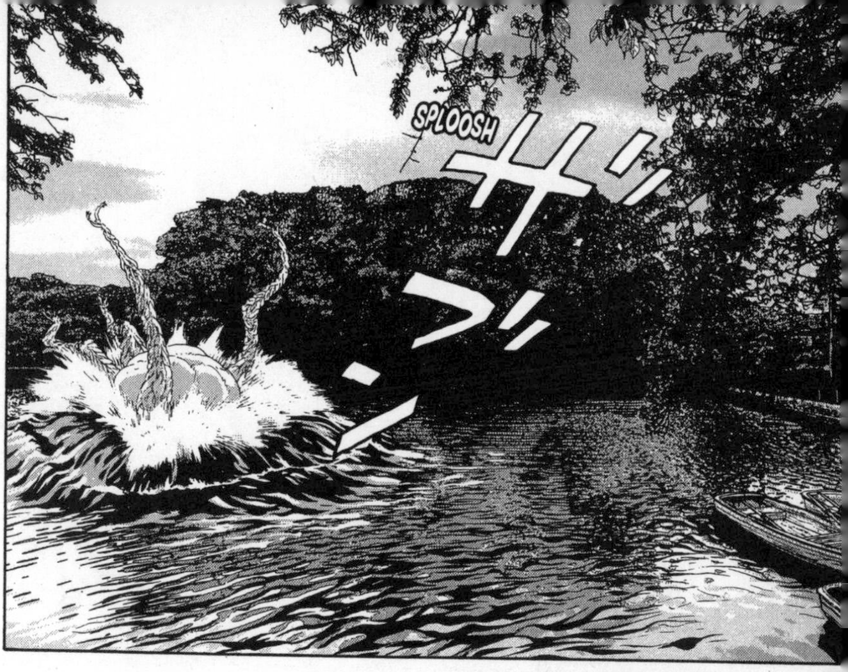
SPLOOSH
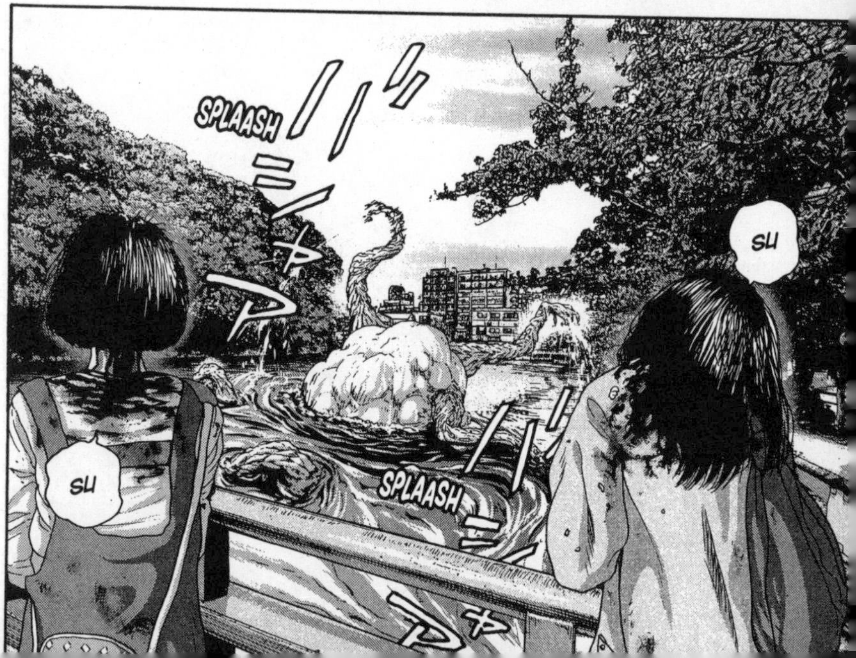
SPLAASH
SU
SPLAASH
SU

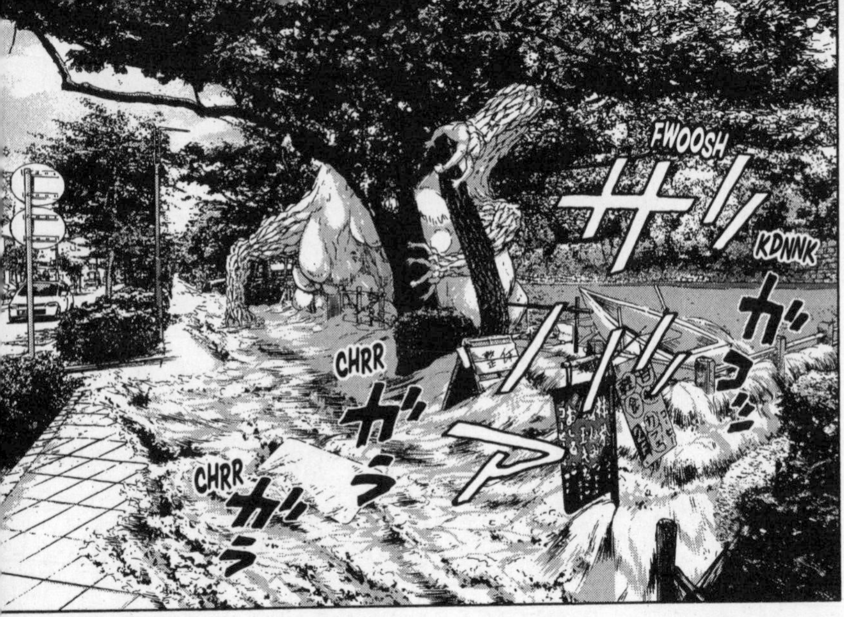
KDNNK
ガコッ
FWOOSH
CHRR
ガラ
CHRR
ガラ
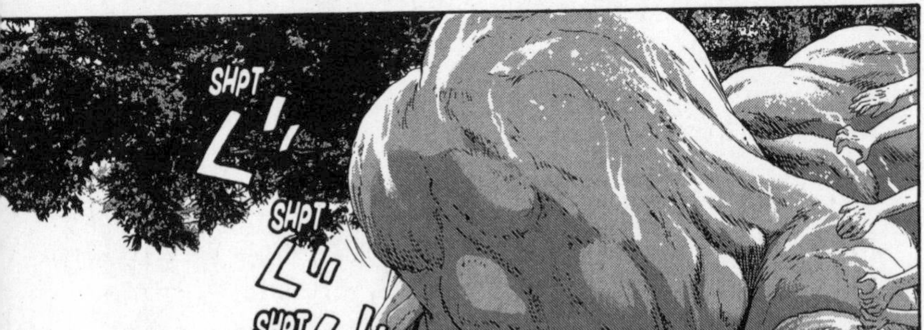
SHPT
SHPT
SHPT
SHPT
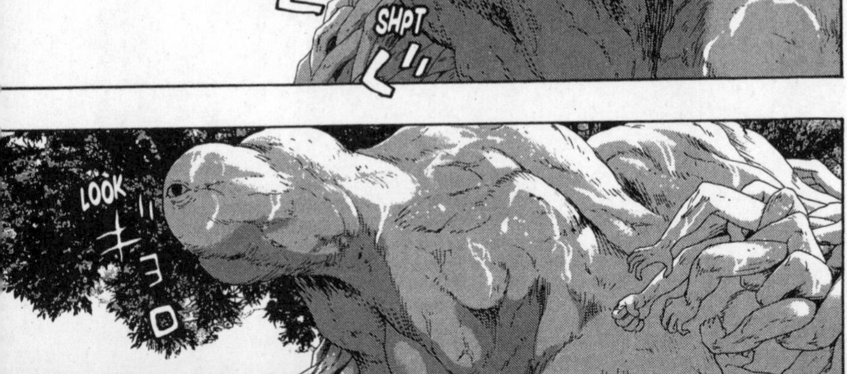
LOOK
キョロ

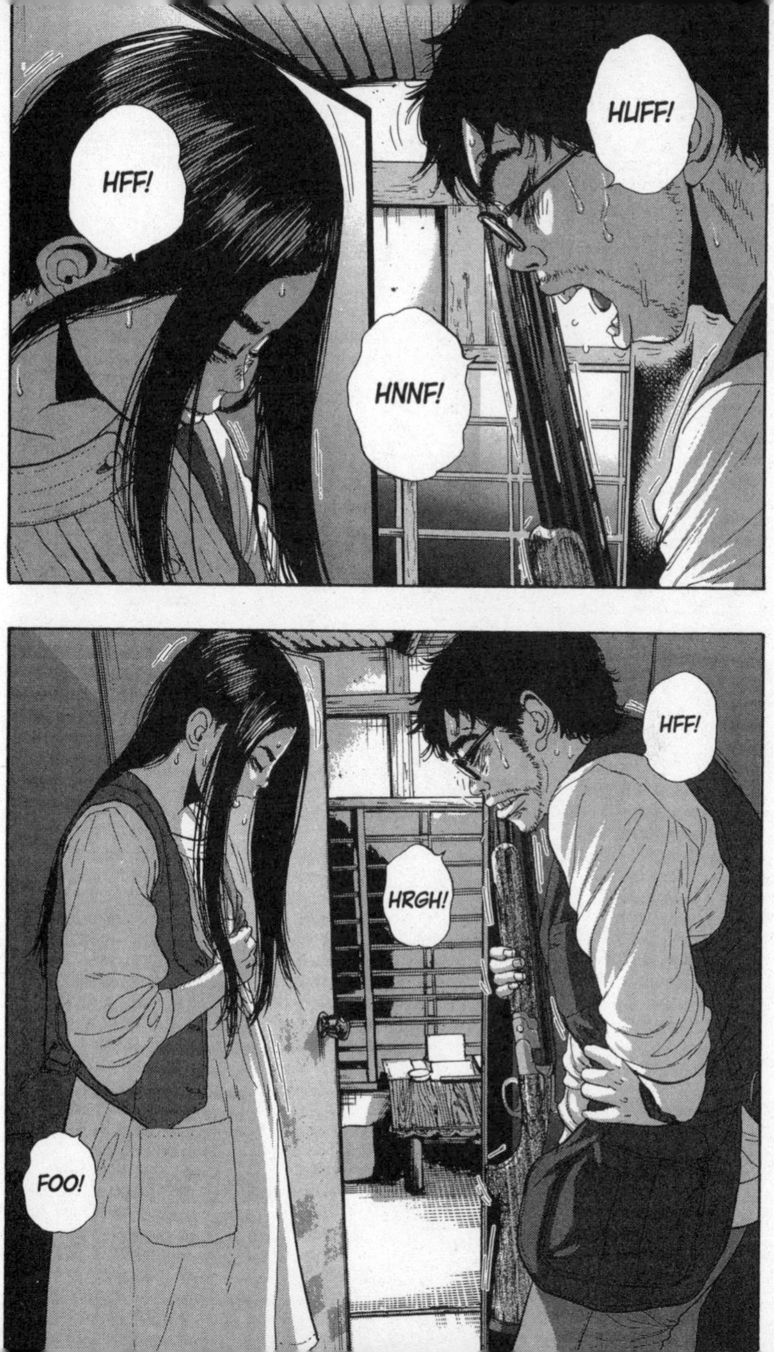

HUFF!
HFF!
HNNF!
HFF!
HRGH!
FOO!

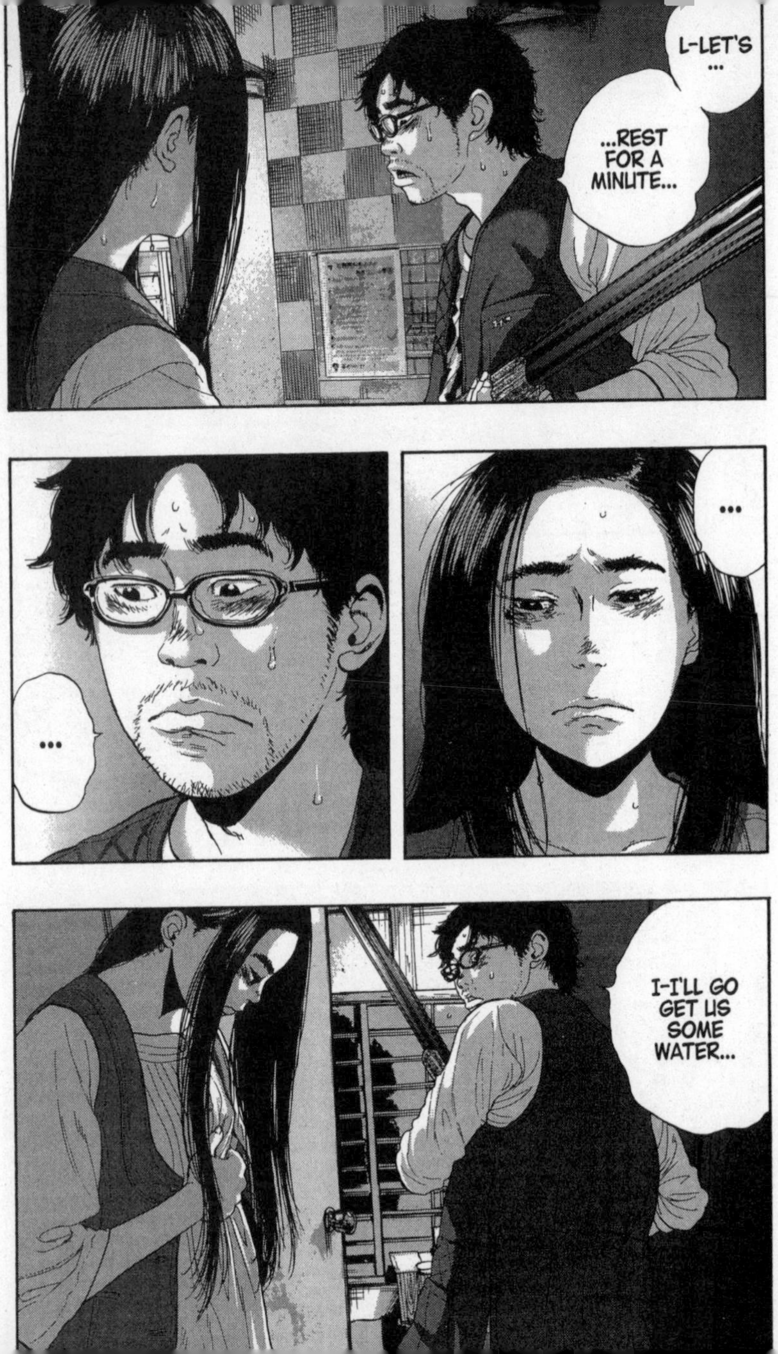
L-LET'S ...
...REST FOR A MINUTE...
...
...
I-I'LL GO GET US SOME WATER...

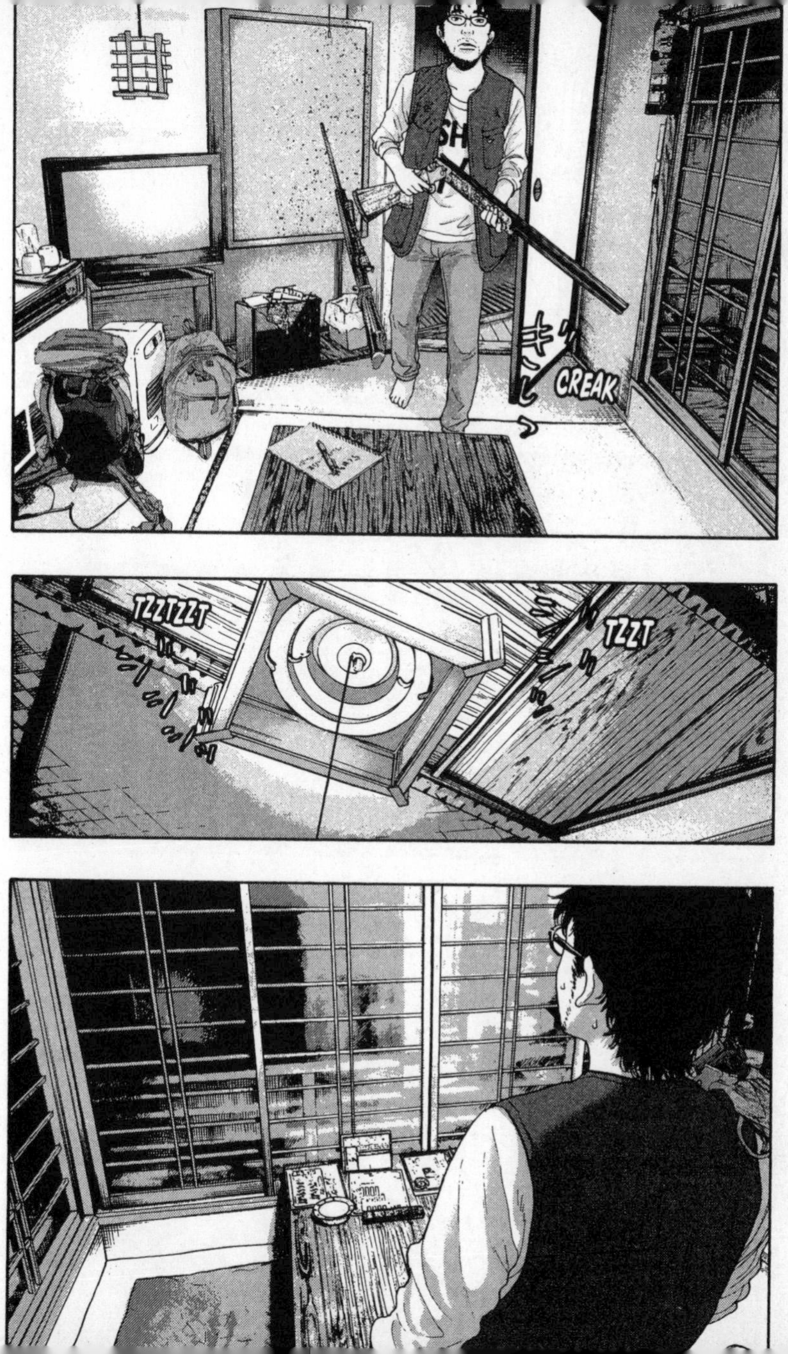
CREAK
TZZT
TZZTZZT

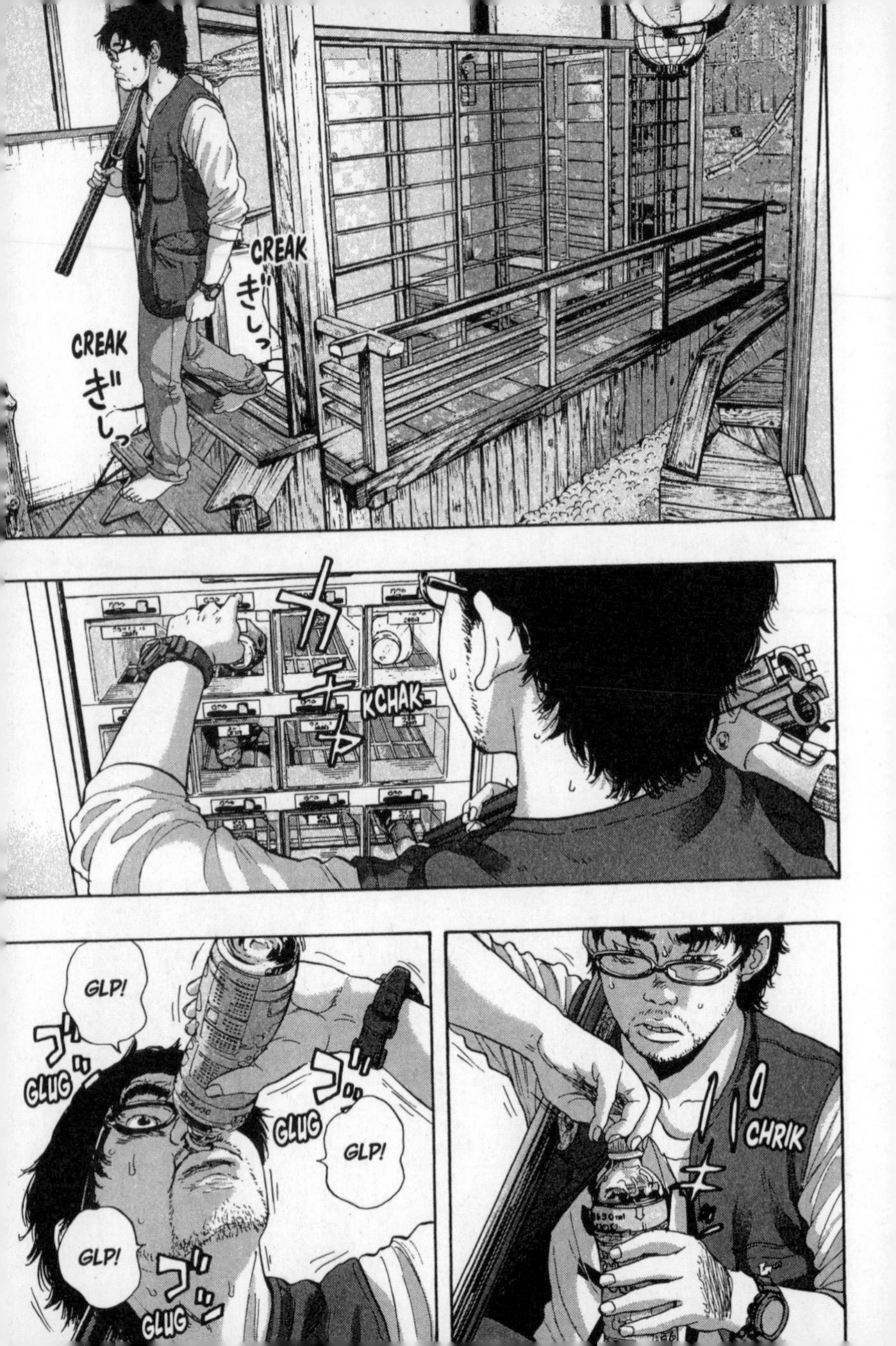
CREAK
ぎしっ
CREAK
ぎしっ
カチャ
KCHAK
CHRIK
GLP!
ゴッ
GLUG
ゴッ
GLUG
GLP!
GLP!
ゴッ
GLUG

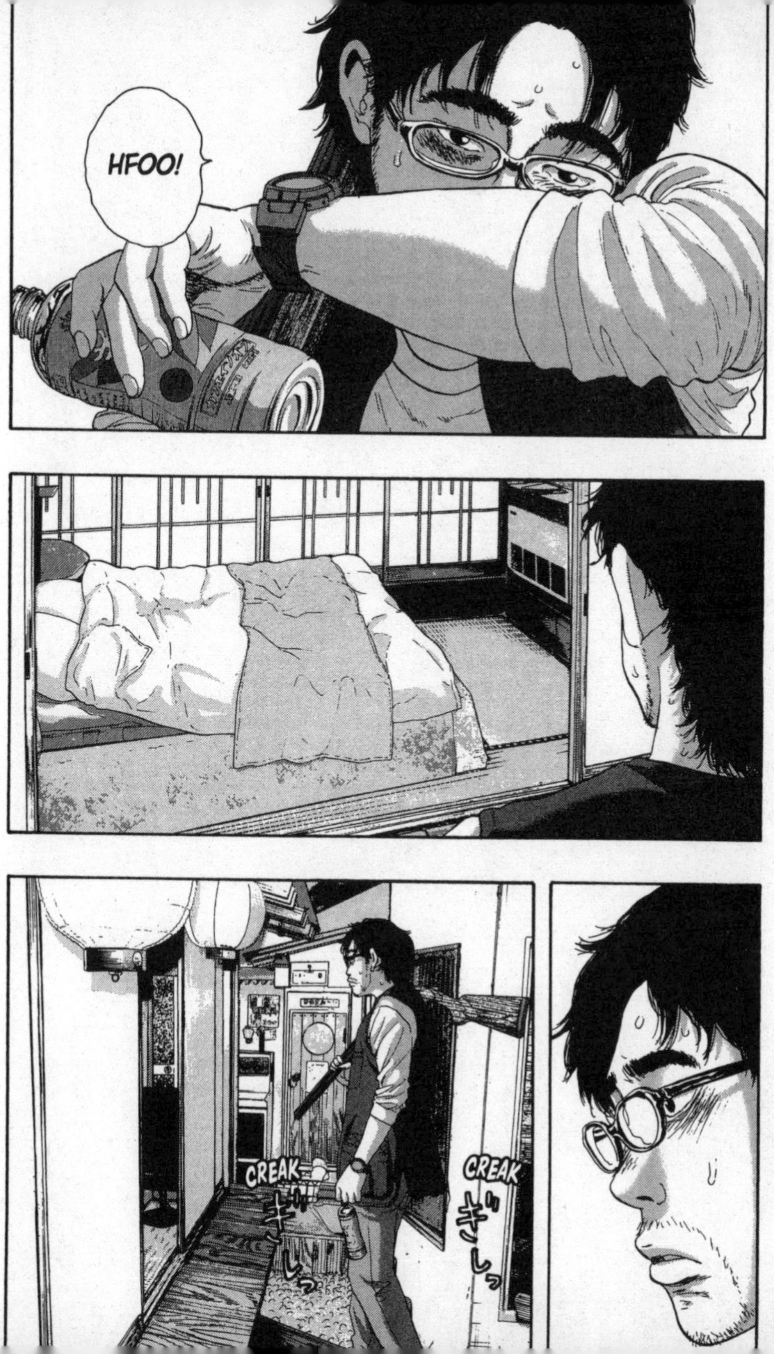
HFOO!
CREAK
ぎしっ
CREAK
ぎしっ

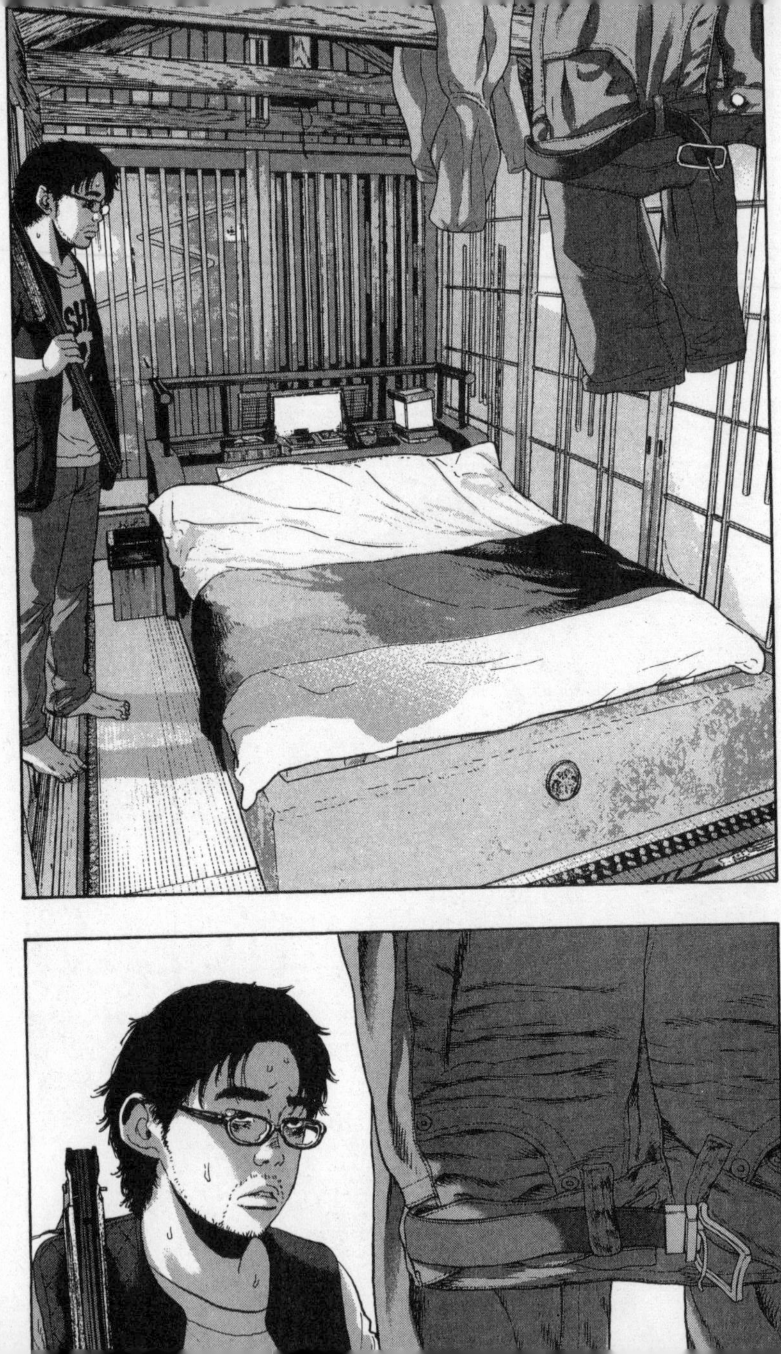

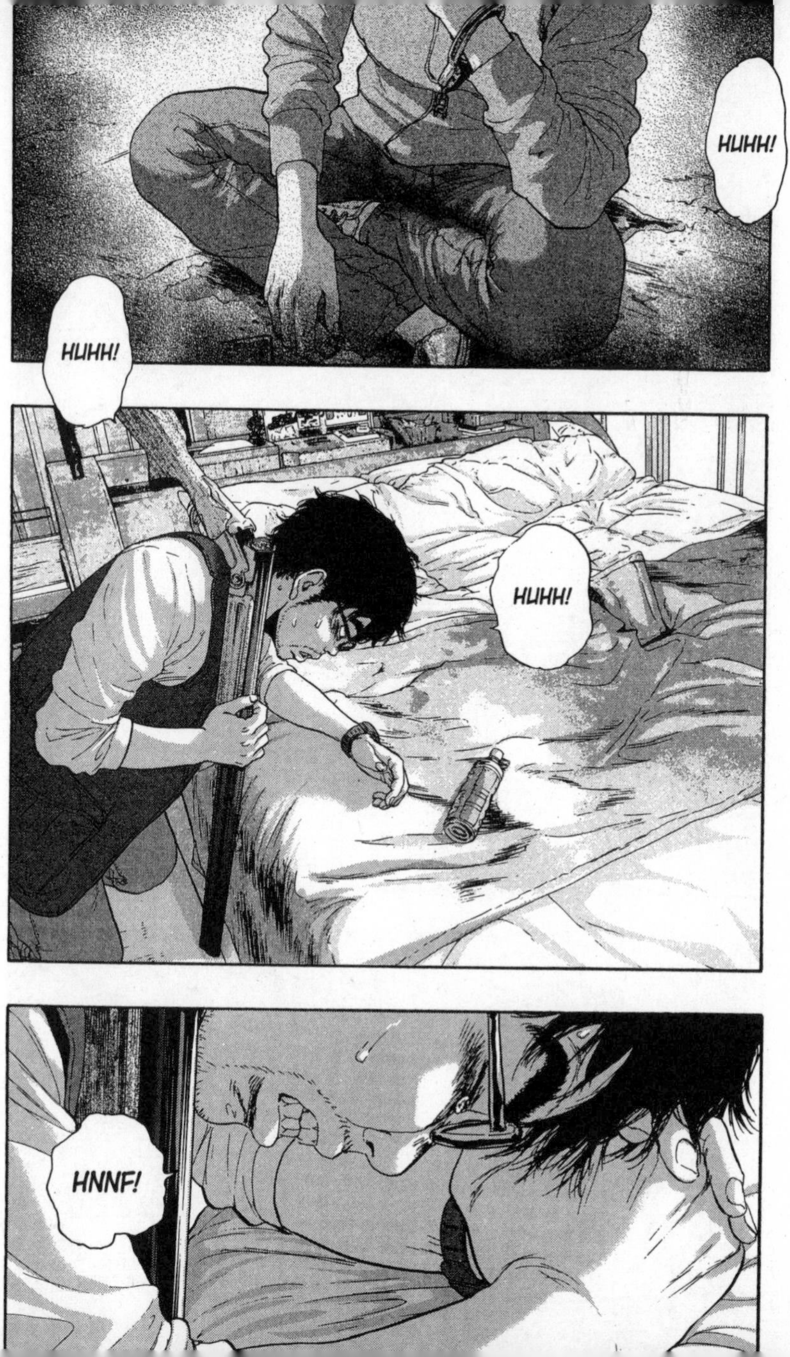
HUHH!
HUHH!
HUHH!
HNNF!

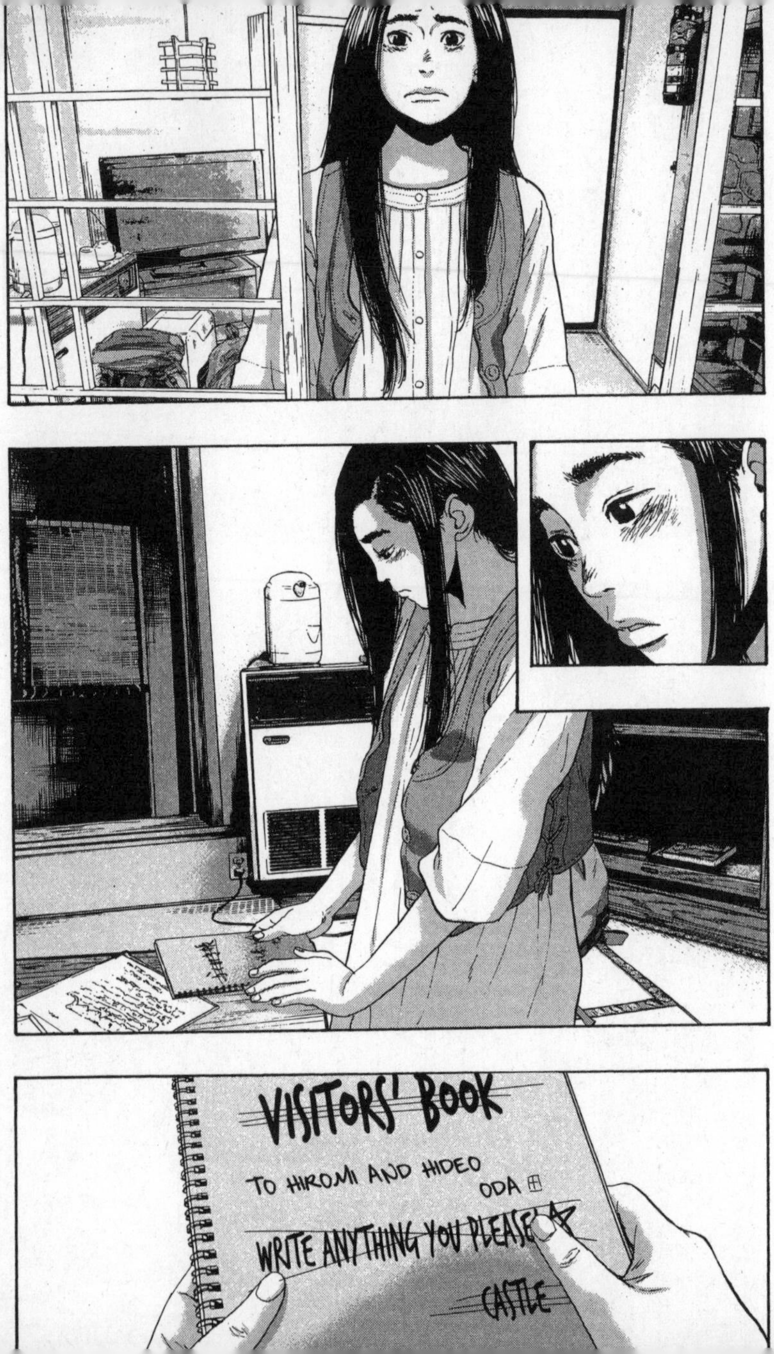
VISITORS' BOOK
TO HIROMI AND HIDEO
ODA
WRITE ANYTHING YOU PLEASE
CASTLE

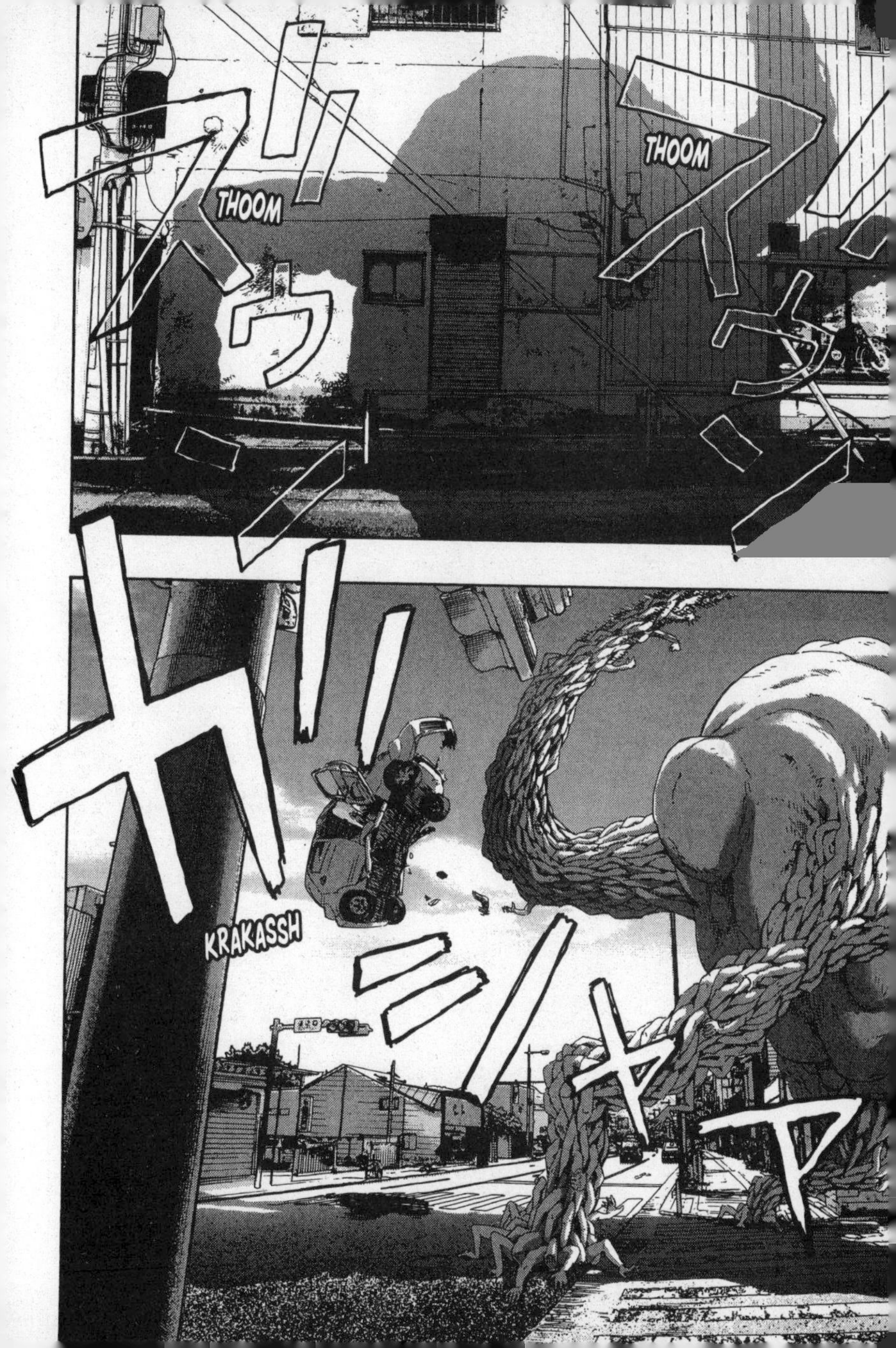
THOOM
THOOM
KRAKASSH

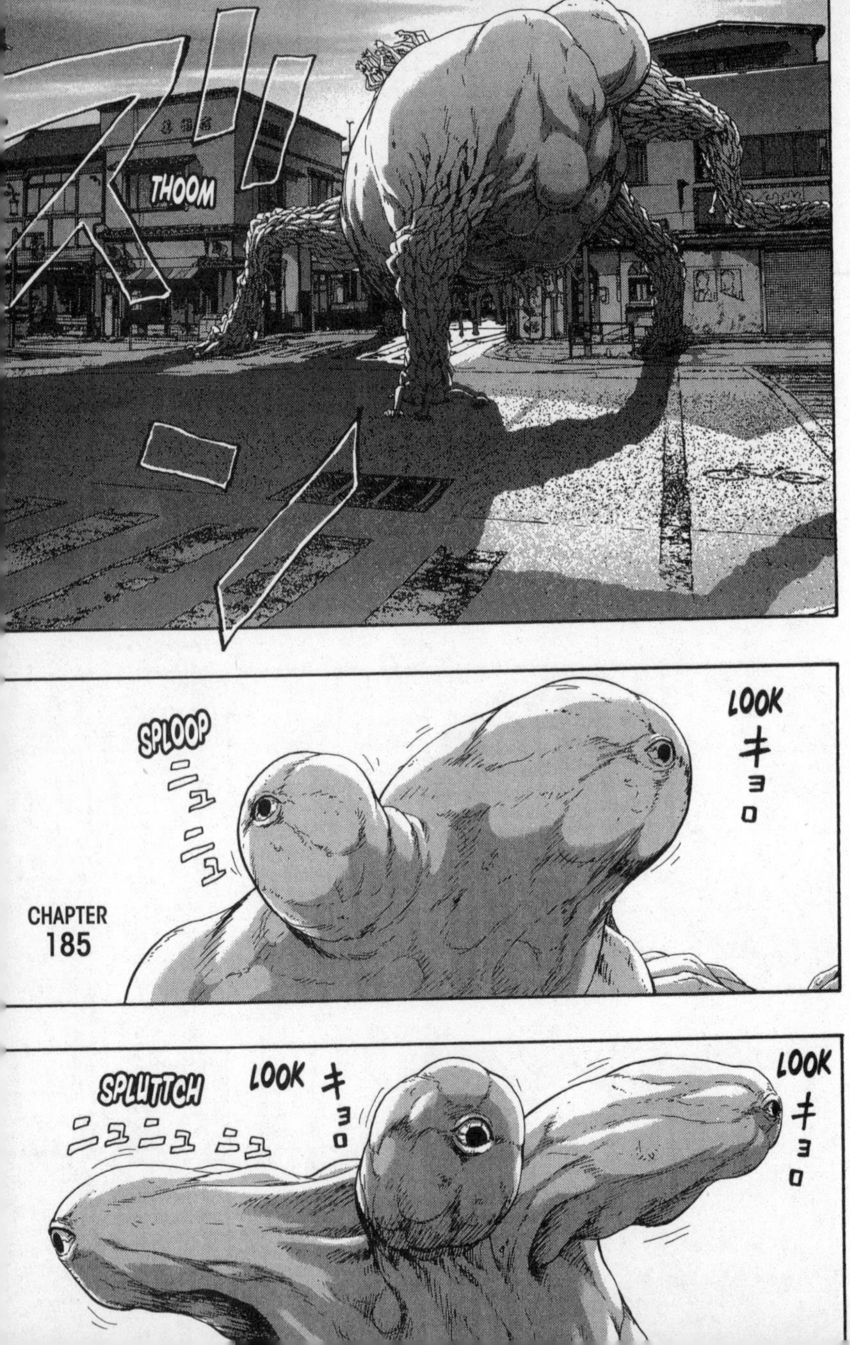
THOOM
LOOK
キョロ
SPLOOP
ニュニュ
CHAPTER 185
LOOK
キョロ
LOOK
キョロ
SPLUTTCH
ニュニュニュ ニュ

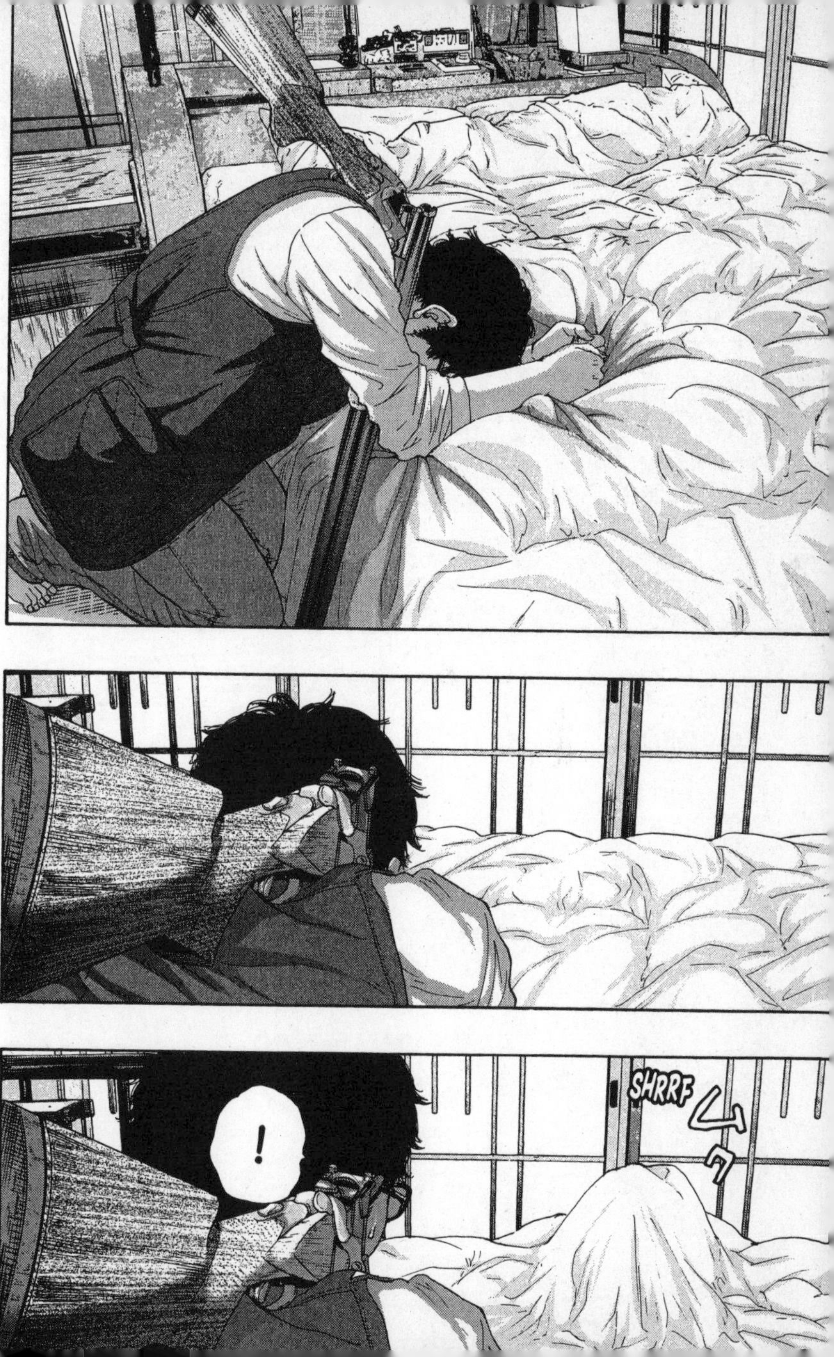
SHRRF
ムク
!

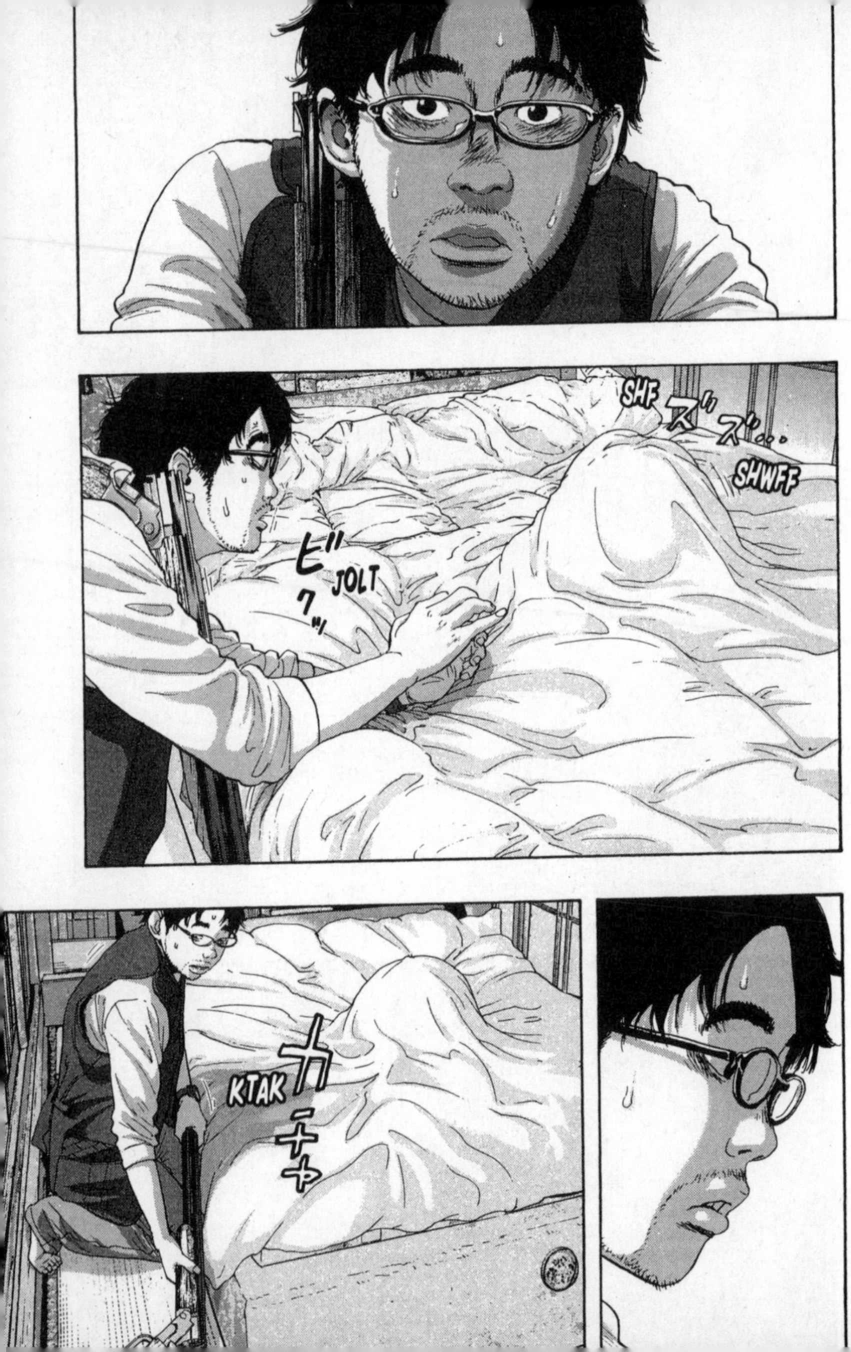
SHF
ズズ…
SHWFF
ビクッ
JOLT
カチャ
KTAK

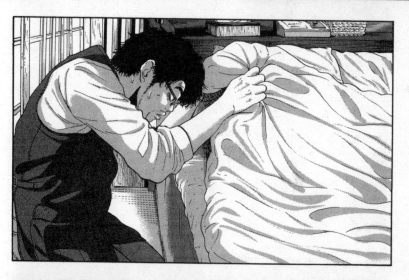

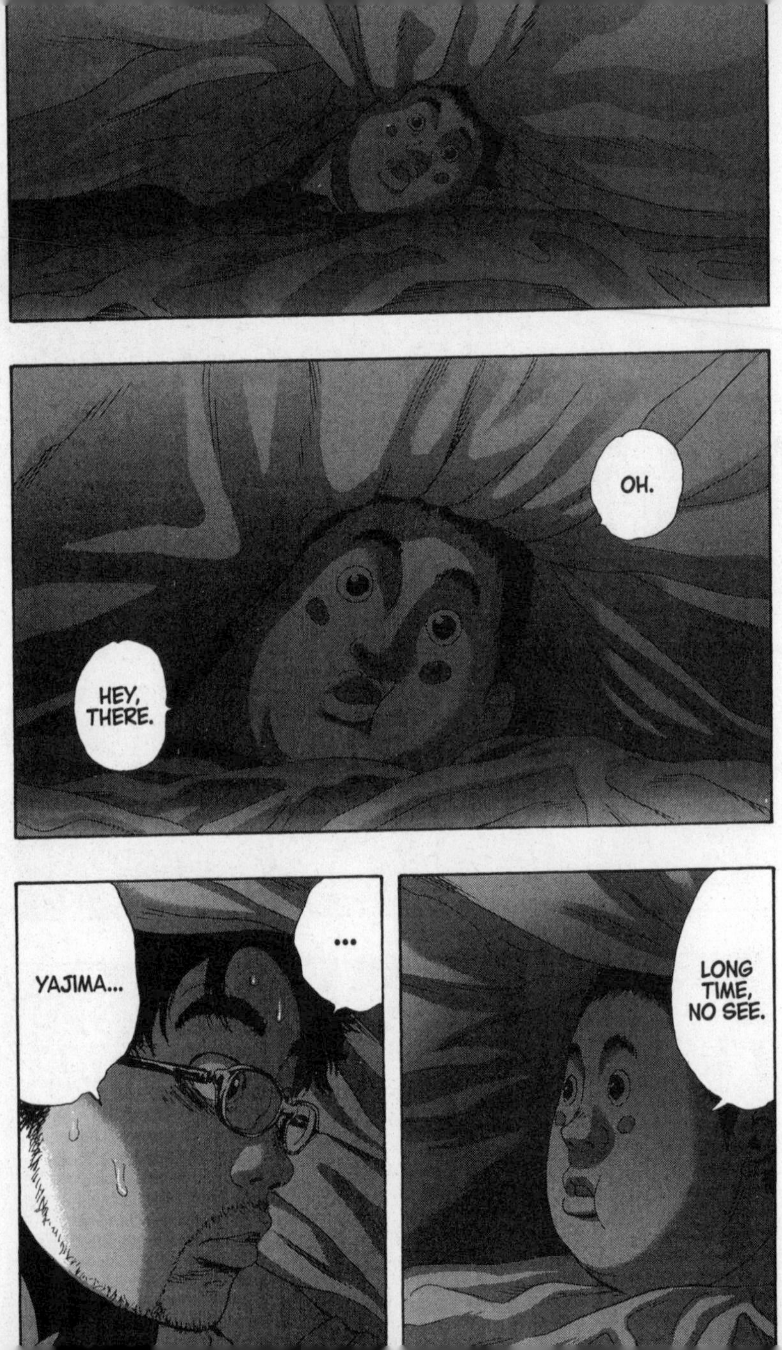
OH.
HEY, THERE.
LONG TIME, NO SEE.
...
YAJIMA...

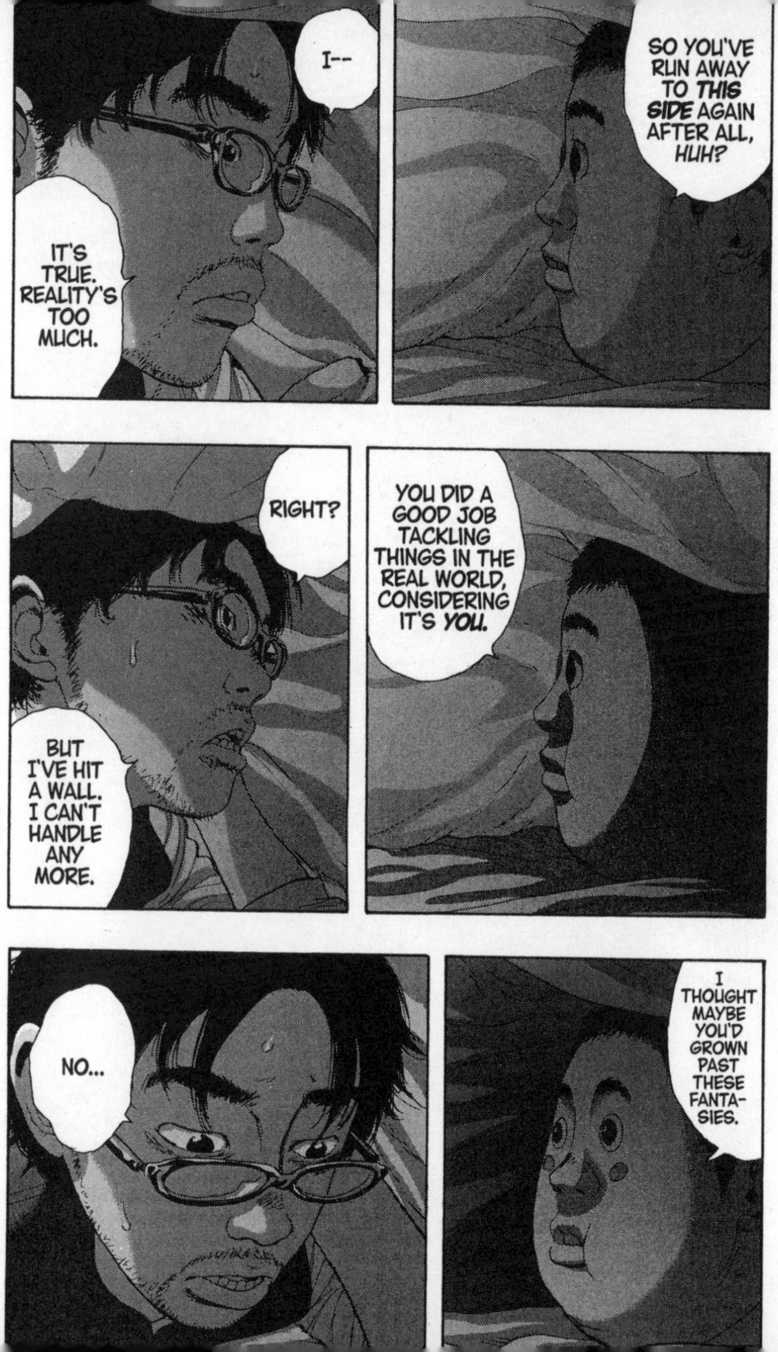
SO YOU'VE RUN AWAY TO THIS SIDE AGAIN AFTER ALL, HUH?
I--
IT'S TRUE. REALITY'S TOO MUCH.
YOU DID A GOOD JOB TACKLING THINGS IN THE REAL WORLD, CONSIDERING IT'S YOU.
RIGHT?
BUT I'VE HIT A WALL. I CAN'T HANDLE ANY MORE.
I THOUGHT MAYBE YOU'D GROWN PAST THESE FANTASIES.
NO...

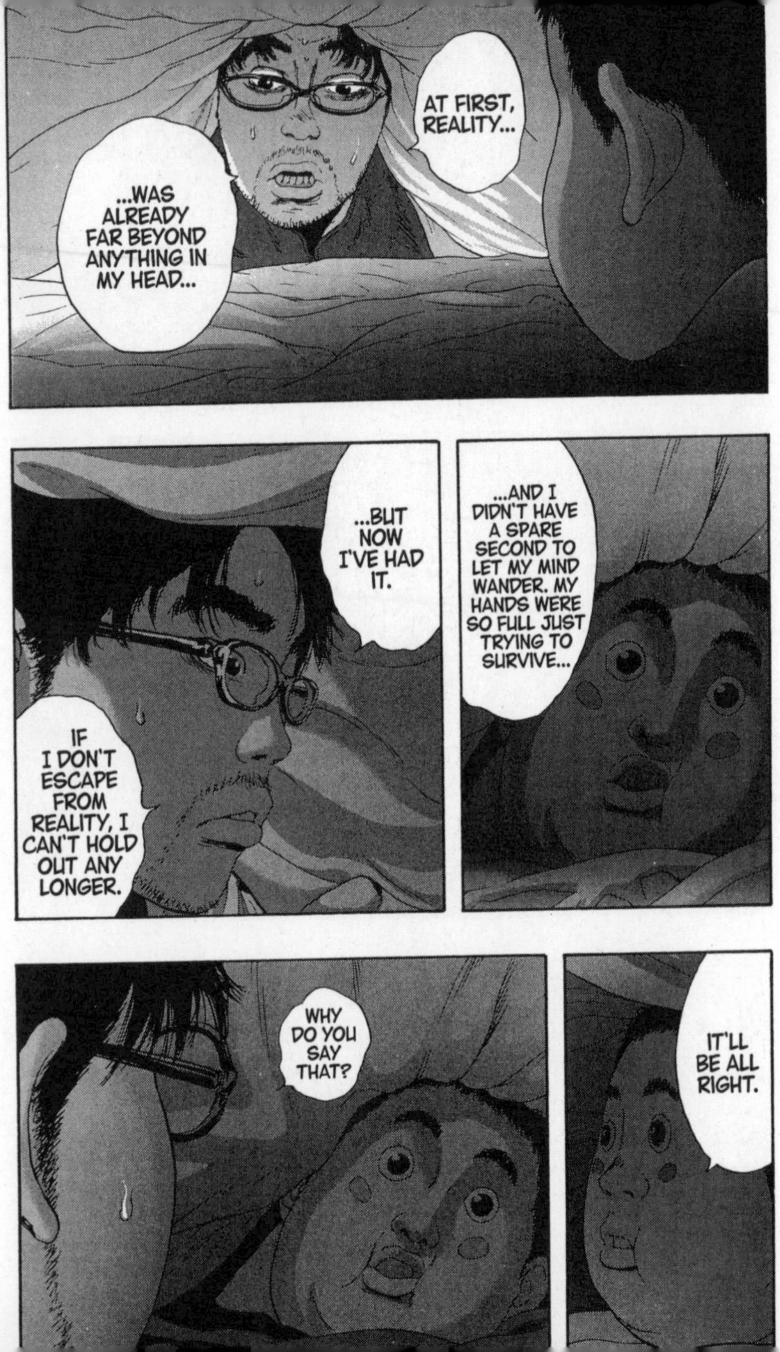
AT FIRST, REALITY...
...WAS ALREADY FAR BEYOND ANYTHING IN MY HEAD...
...AND I DIDN'T HAVE A SPARE SECOND TO LET MY MIND WANDER. MY HANDS WERE SO FULL JUST TRYING TO SURVIVE...
...BUT NOW I'VE HAD IT.
IF I DON'T ESCAPE FROM REALITY, I CAN'T HOLD OUT ANY LONGER.
IT'LL BE ALL RIGHT.
WHY DO YOU SAY THAT?

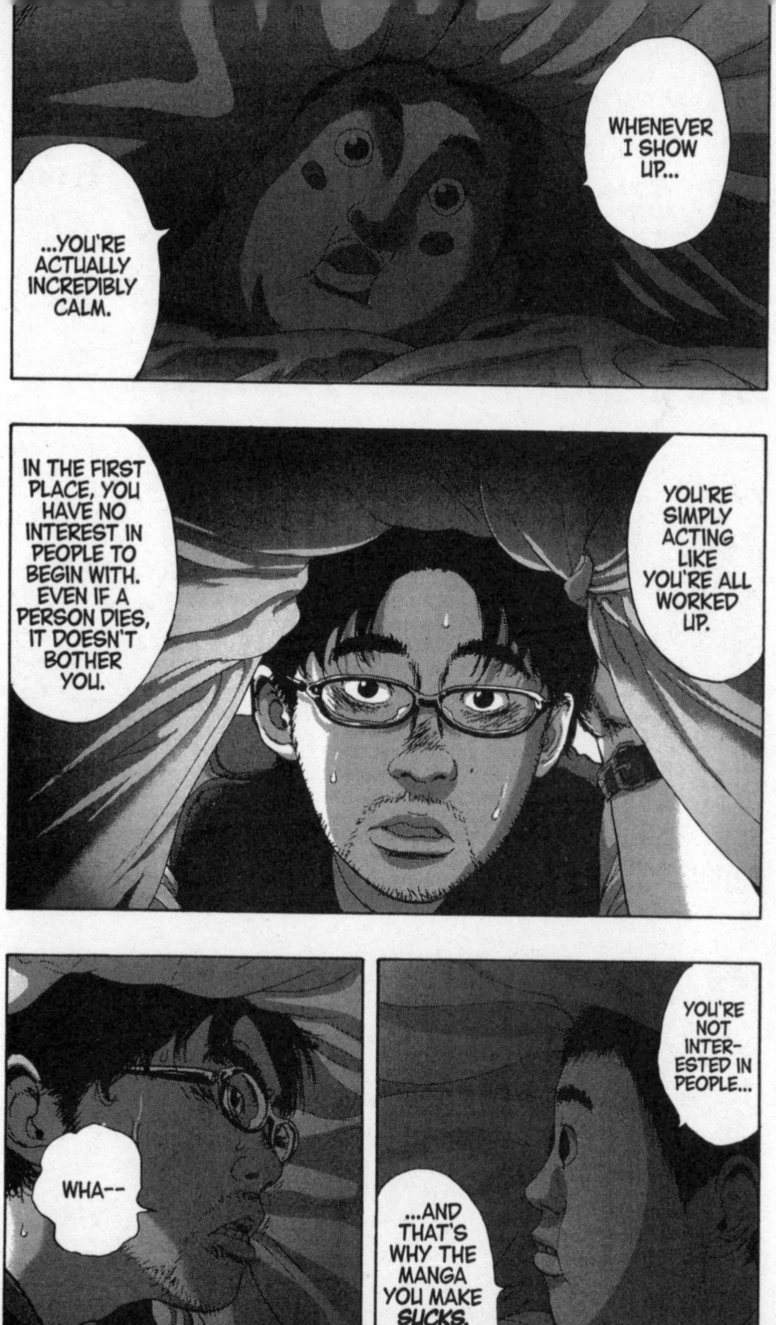
WHENEVER I SHOW UP...
...YOU'RE ACTUALLY INCREDIBLY CALM.
YOU'RE SIMPLY ACTING LIKE YOU'RE ALL WORKED UP.
IN THE FIRST PLACE, YOU HAVE NO INTEREST IN PEOPLE TO BEGIN WITH. EVEN IF A PERSON DIES, IT DOESN'T BOTHER YOU.
YOU'RE NOT INTER-ESTED IN PEOPLE...
...AND THAT'S WHY THE MANGA YOU MAKE **SUCKS.**
WHA--

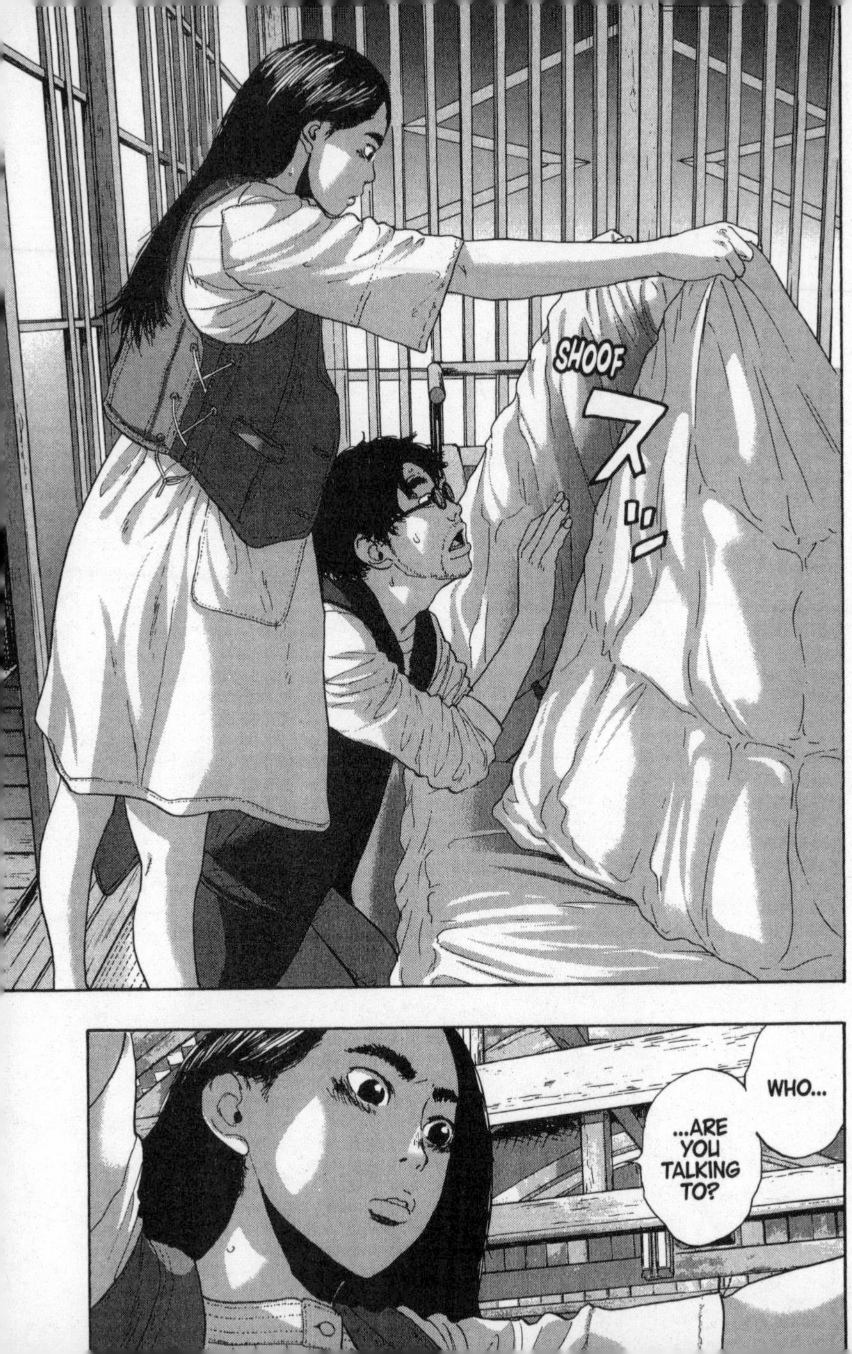
SHOOF
WHO...
...ARE YOU TALKING TO?

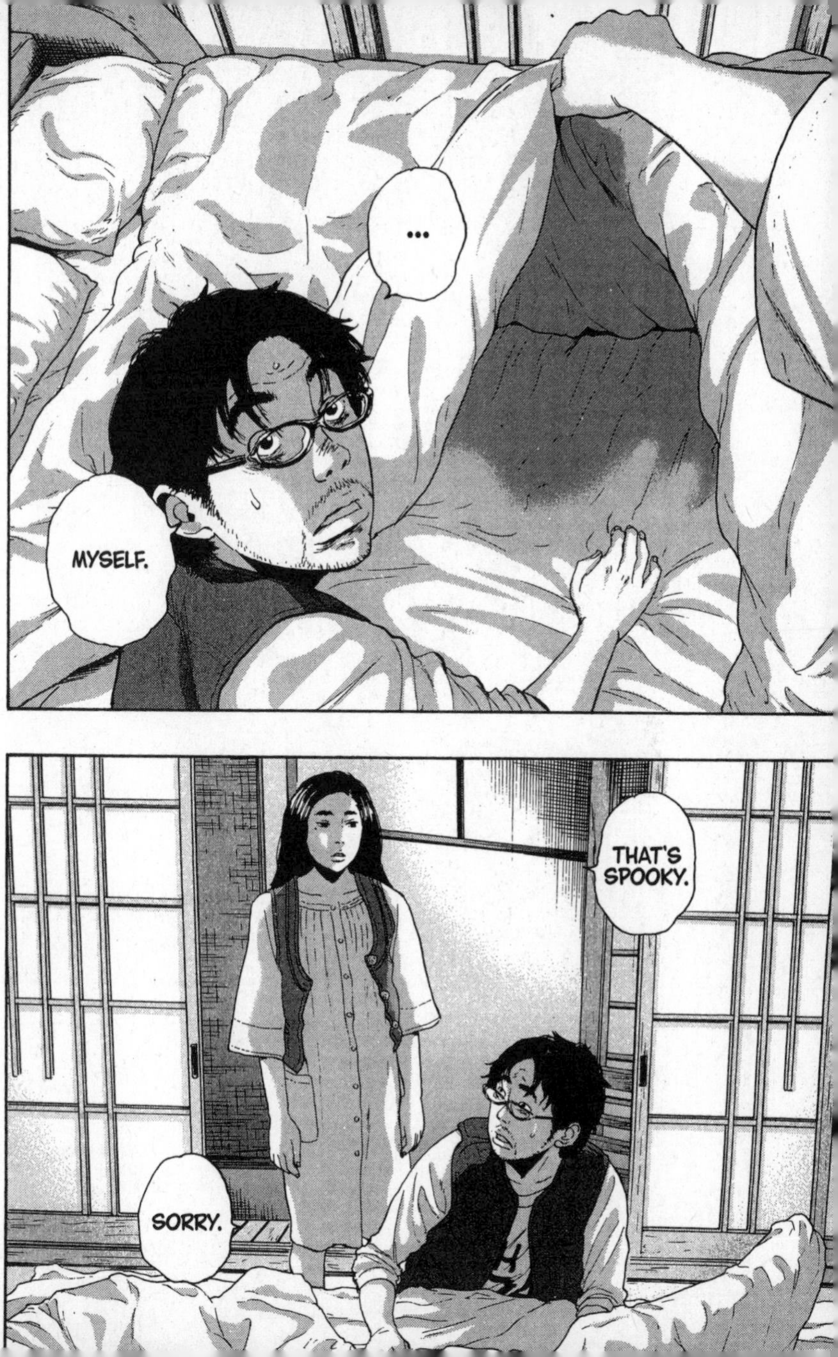
...
MYSELF.
THAT'S SPOOKY.
SORRY.

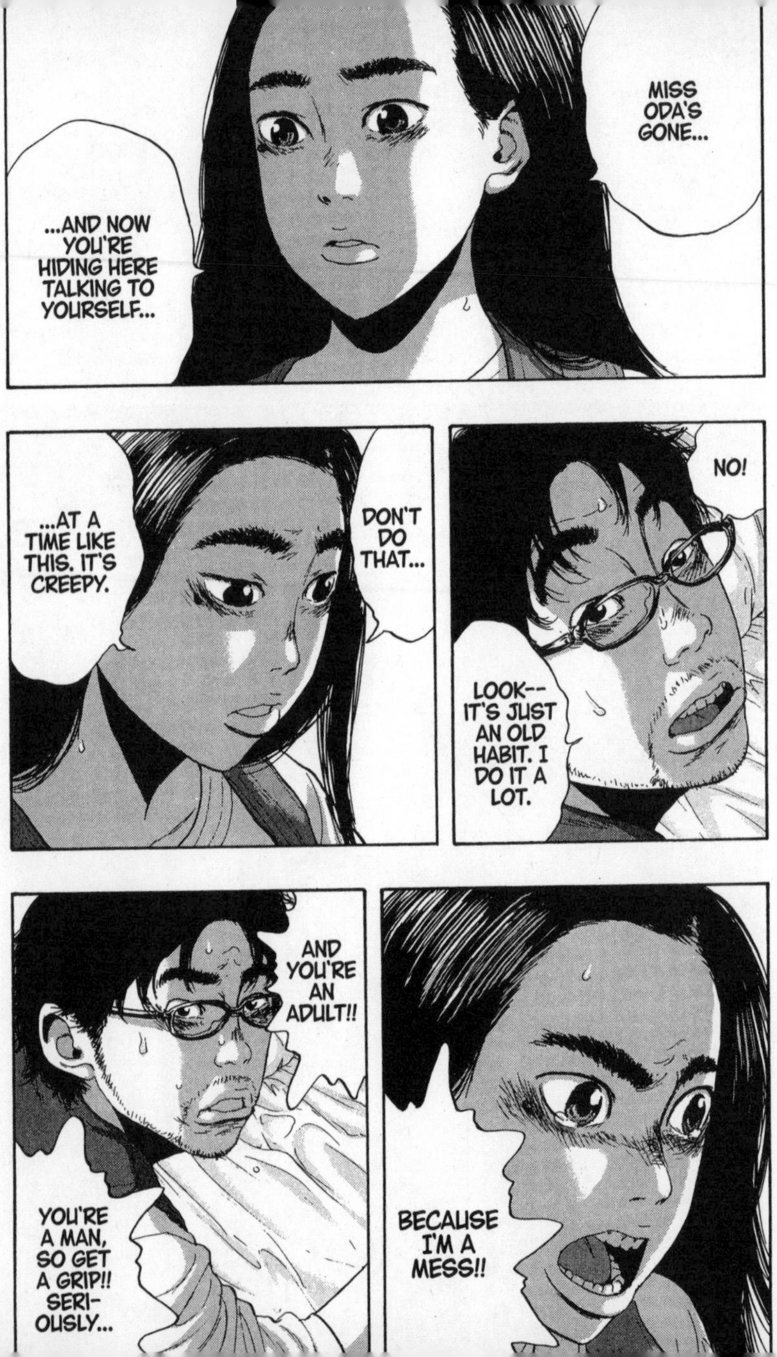
MISS ODA'S GONE...
...AND NOW YOU'RE HIDING HERE TALKING TO YOURSELF...
NO!
LOOK-- IT'S JUST AN OLD HABIT. I DO IT A LOT.
DON'T DO THAT...
...AT A TIME LIKE THIS. IT'S CREEPY.
BECAUSE I'M A MESS!!
AND YOU'RE AN ADULT!!
YOU'RE A MAN, SO GET A GRIP!! SERI-OUSLY...

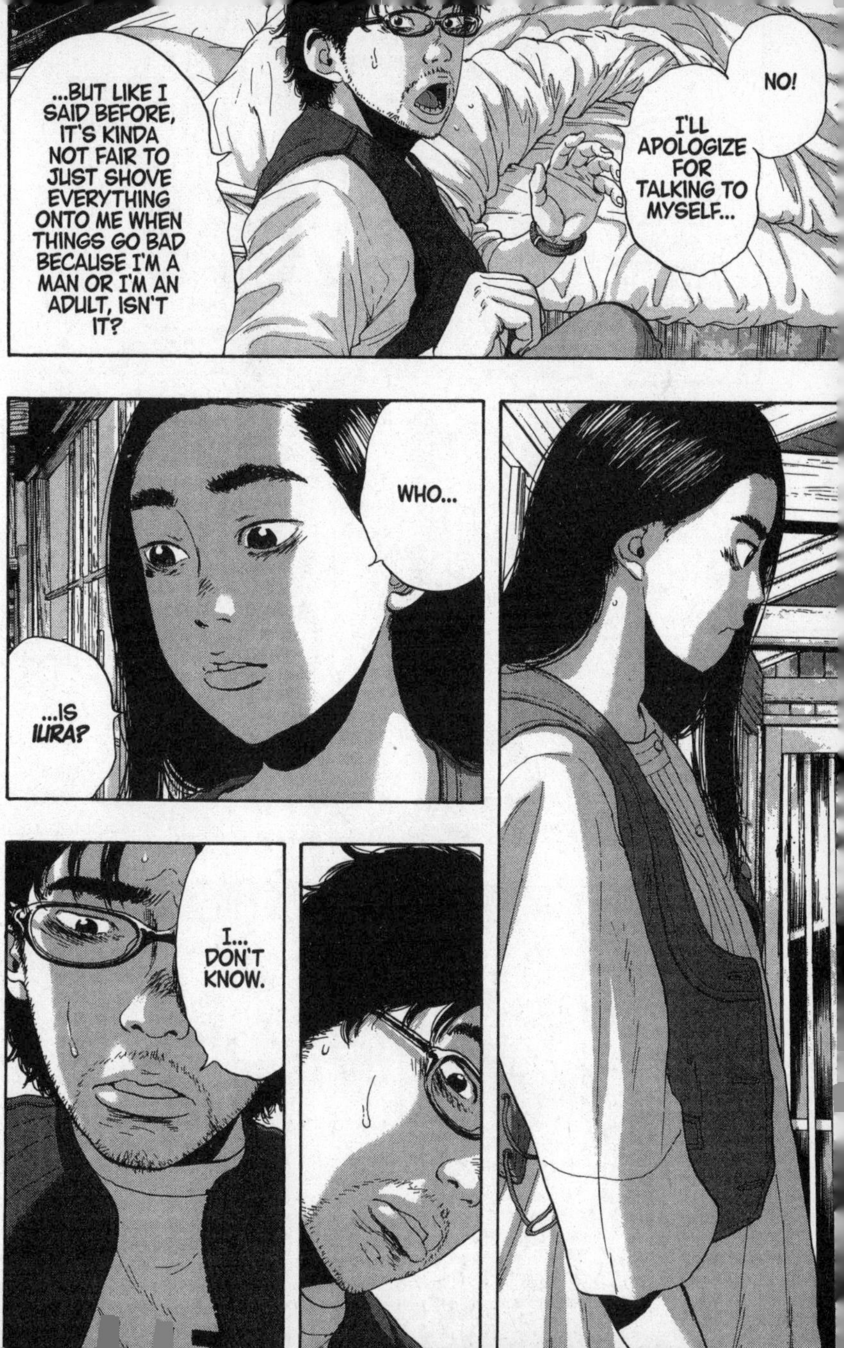
NO!
I'LL APOLOGIZE FOR TALKING TO MYSELF...
...BUT LIKE I SAID BEFORE, IT'S KINDA NOT FAIR TO JUST SHOVE EVERYTHING ONTO ME WHEN THINGS GO BAD BECAUSE I'M A MAN OR I'M AN ADULT, ISN'T IT?
WHO...
...IS IURA?
I... DON'T KNOW.

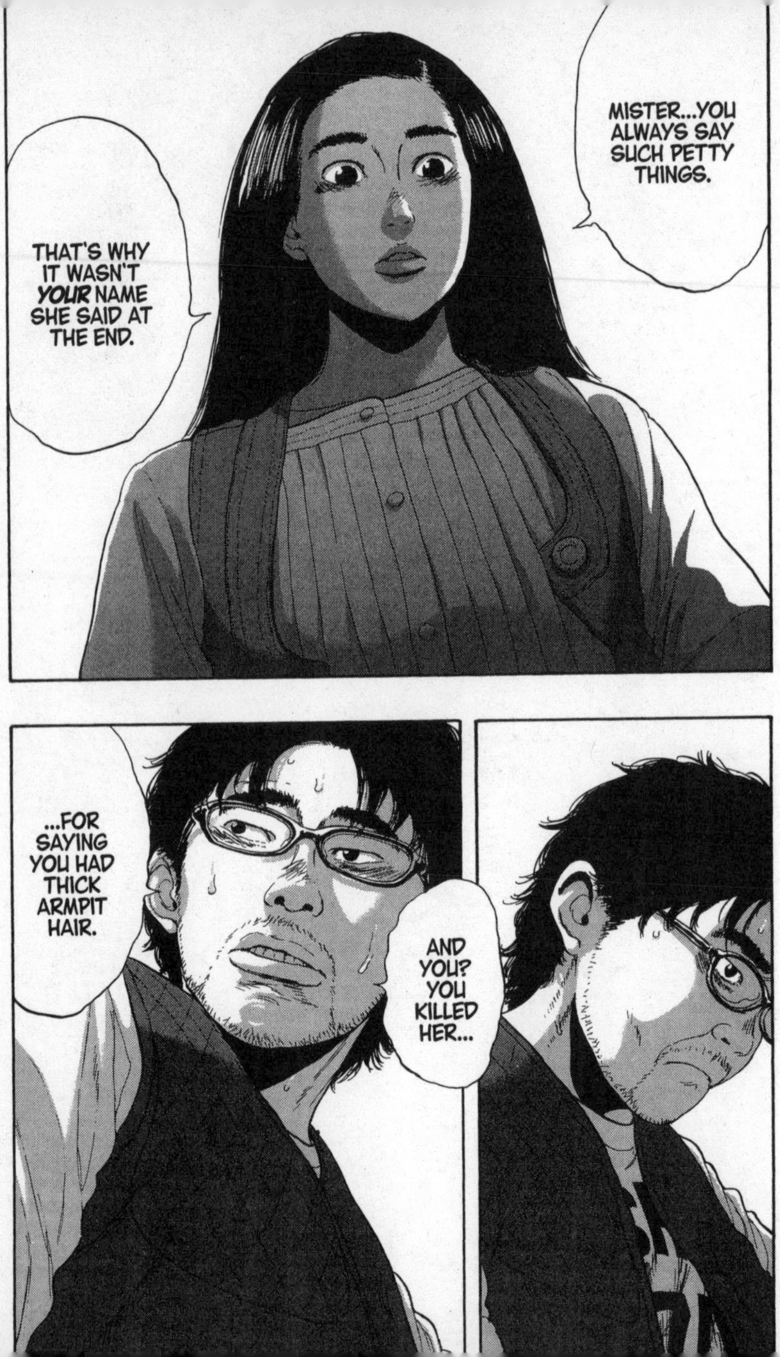
MISTER...YOU ALWAYS SAY SUCH PETTY THINGS.
THAT'S WHY IT WASN'T *YOUR* NAME SHE SAID AT THE END.
AND YOU? YOU KILLED HER...
...FOR SAYING YOU HAD THICK ARMPIT HAIR.

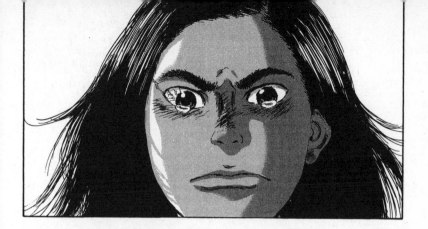

SHUT
UP, YOU
LOSER
!!!

GRAB

I PUSHED
THE
BUTTON
BECAUSE
YOU
WOULDN'T!

OW!

IT'S NOT
THICK
'CAUSE I
WANTED IT
TO BE!!!

WHAPF

IF THERE
WAS
ANOTHER
WAY, LET'S
HEAR IT!!

OW!

WHAPF

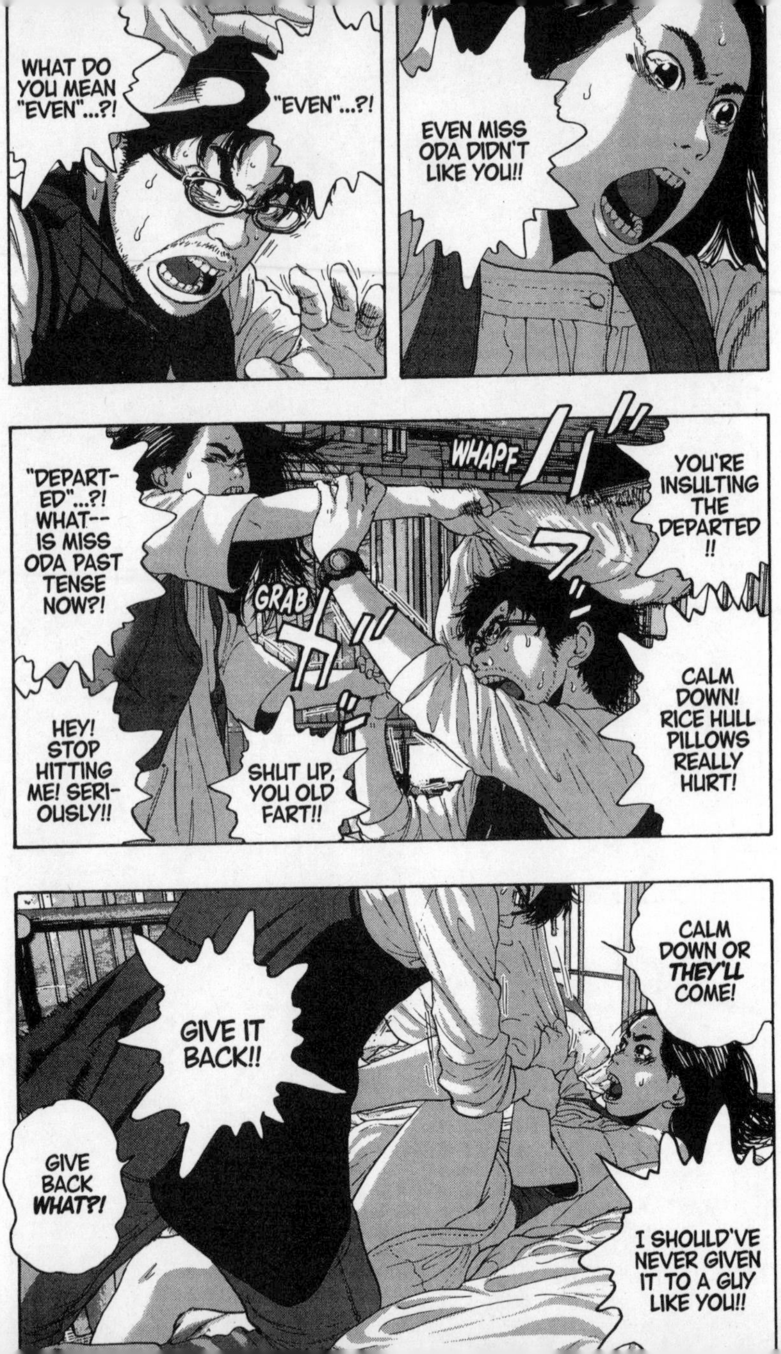
EVEN MISS ODA DIDN'T LIKE YOU!!
"EVEN"...?!
WHAT DO YOU MEAN "EVEN"...?!
YOU'RE INSULTING THE DEPARTED!!
WHAPF
"DEPARTED"...?! WHAT-- IS MISS ODA PAST TENSE NOW?!
GRAB
CALM DOWN! RICE HULL PILLOWS REALLY HURT!
SHUT UP, YOU OLD FART!!
HEY! STOP HITTING ME! SERIOUSLY!!
CALM DOWN OR *THEY'LL* COME!
GIVE IT BACK!!
GIVE BACK *WHAT?!*
I SHOULD'VE NEVER GIVEN IT TO A GUY LIKE YOU!!

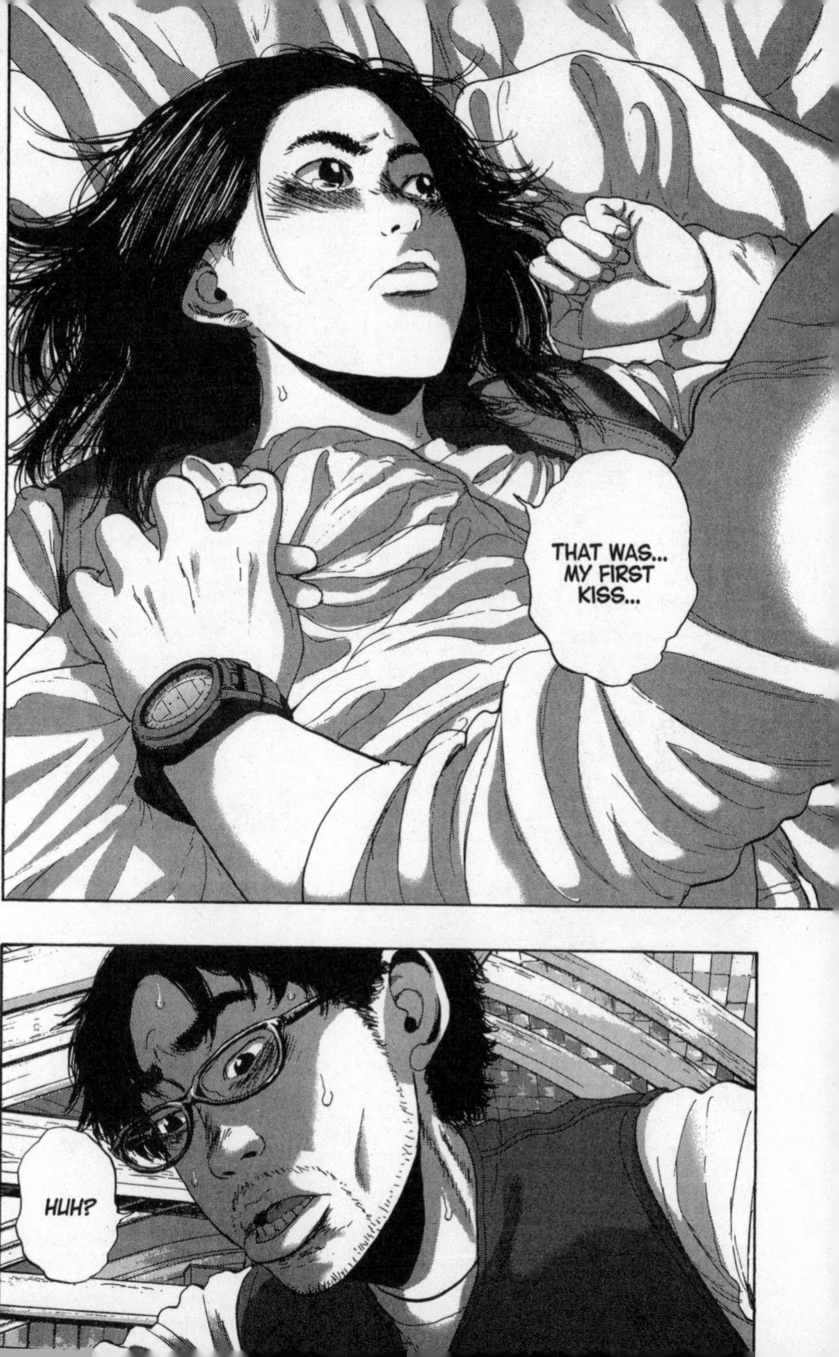
THAT WAS... MY FIRST KISS...
HUH?

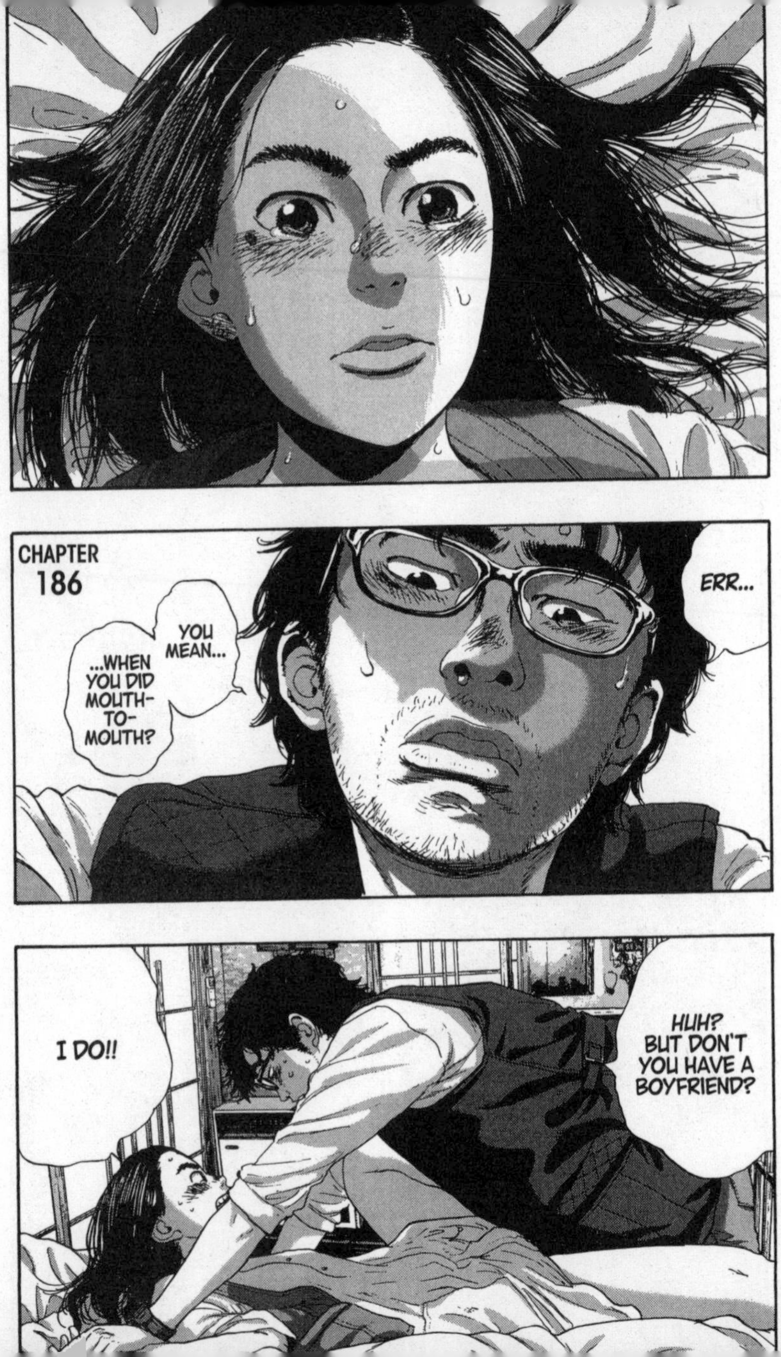
CHAPTER 186
ERR...
YOU MEAN...
...WHEN YOU DID MOUTH-TO-MOUTH?
HUH? BUT DON'T YOU HAVE A BOYFRIEND?
I DO!!

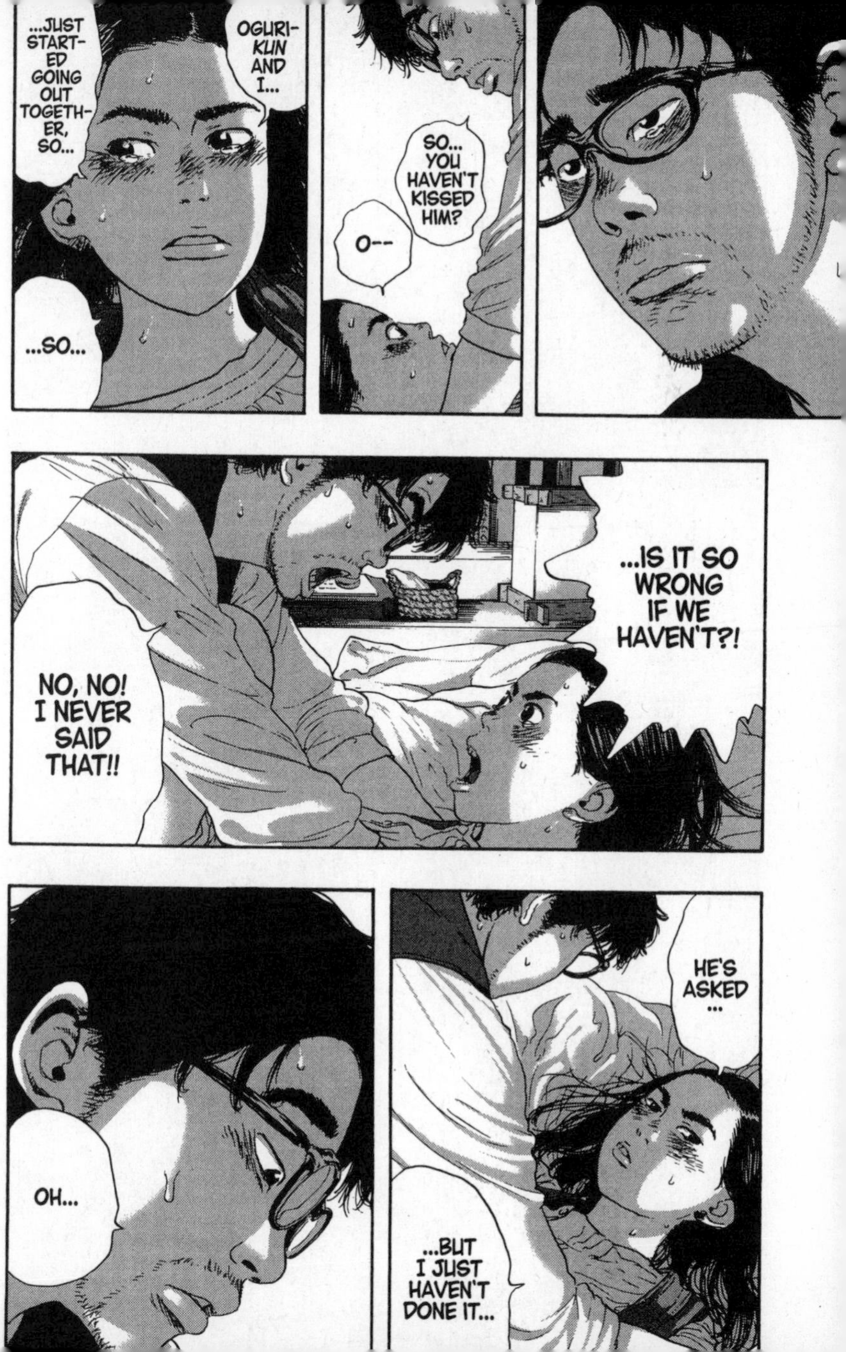
SO... YOU HAVEN'T KISSED HIM?
O--
OGURI-KUN AND I...
...JUST START-ED GOING OUT TOGETH-ER, SO...
...SO...
...IS IT SO WRONG IF WE HAVEN'T?!
NO, NO! I NEVER SAID THAT!!
HE'S ASKED ...
...BUT I JUST HAVEN'T DONE IT...
OH...

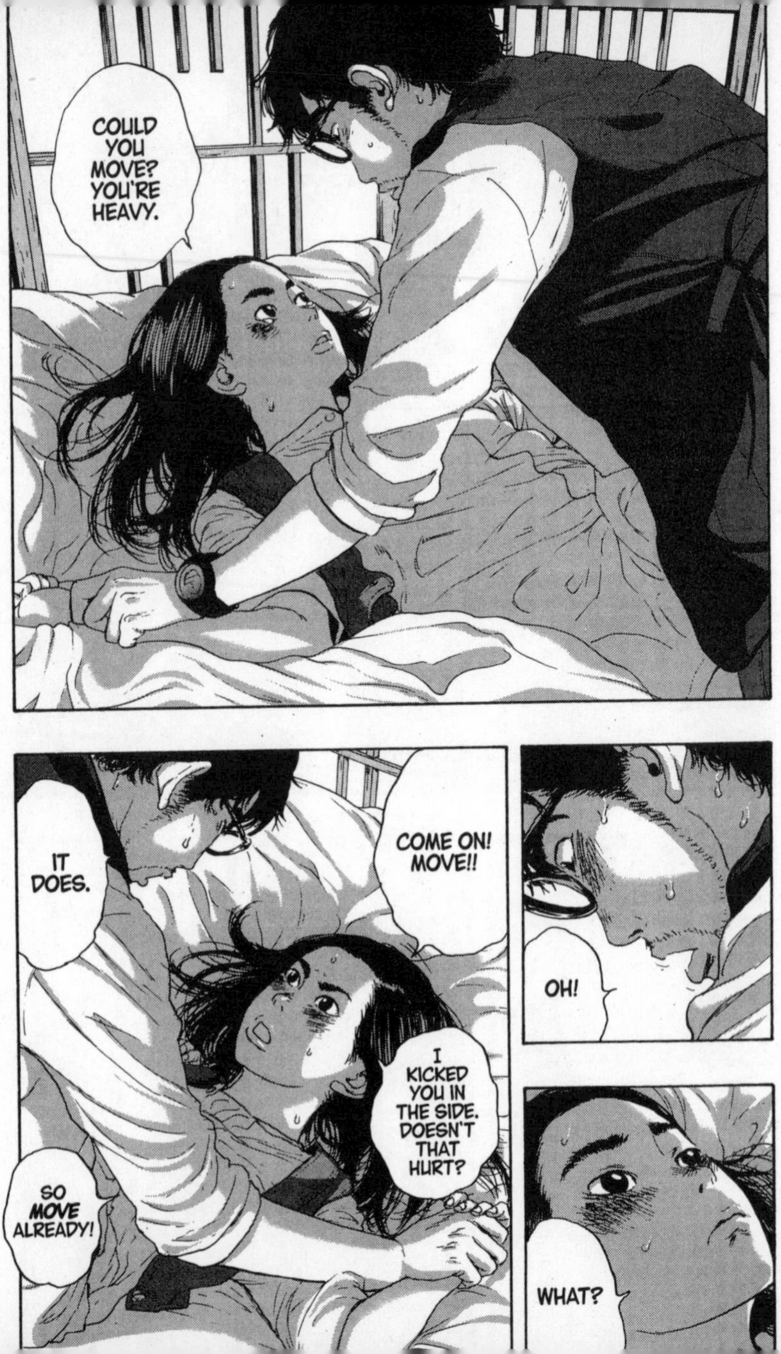
COULD YOU MOVE? YOU'RE HEAVY.
OH!
WHAT?
COME ON! MOVE!!
IT DOES.
I KICKED YOU IN THE SIDE. DOESN'T THAT HURT?
SO MOVE ALREADY!

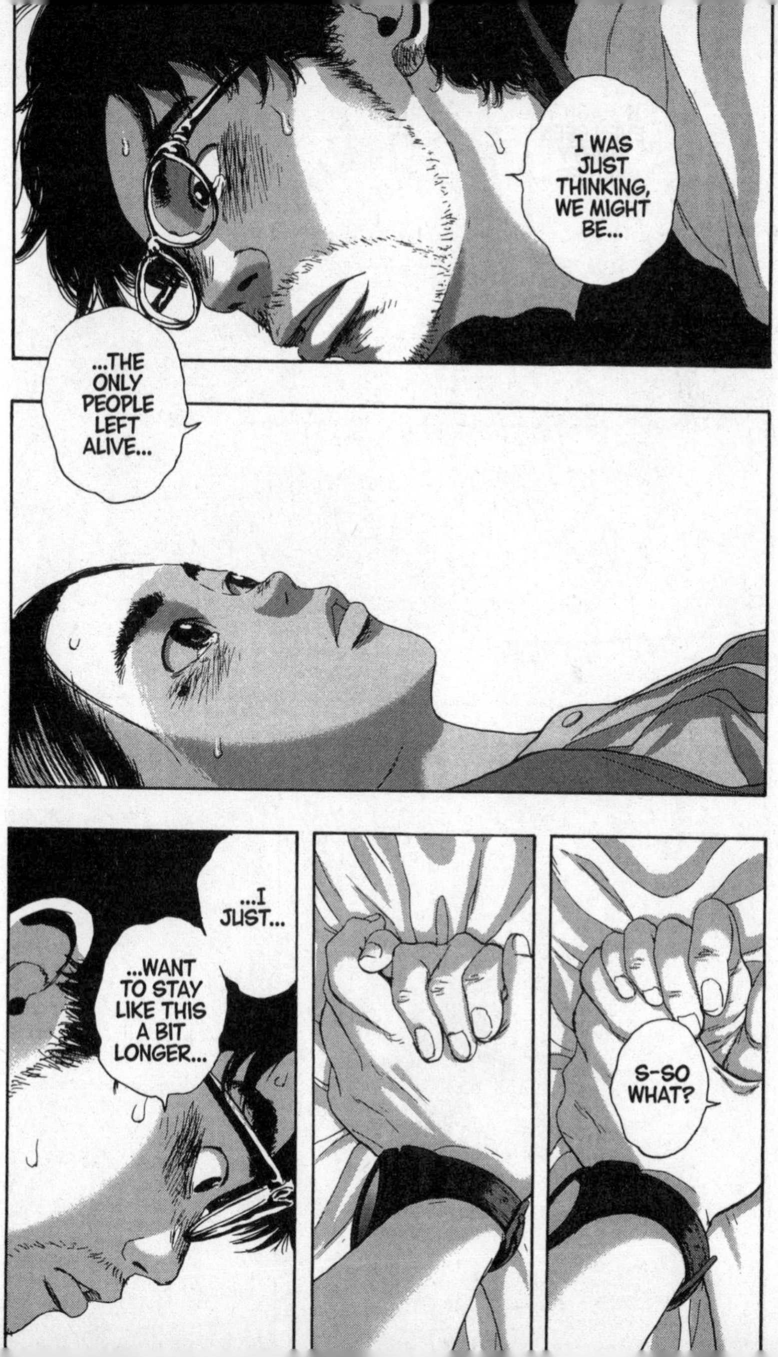
I WAS JUST THINKING, WE MIGHT BE...
...THE ONLY PEOPLE LEFT ALIVE...
S-SO WHAT?
...I JUST...
...WANT TO STAY LIKE THIS A BIT LONGER...

IT HASN'T EVEN BEEN THIRTY MINUTES...

...SINCE MISS ODA DIED.

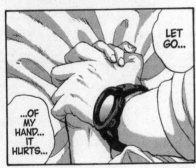

LET GO...

...OF MY HAND... IT HURTS...

NO! THAT'S--

OH!

SORRY.

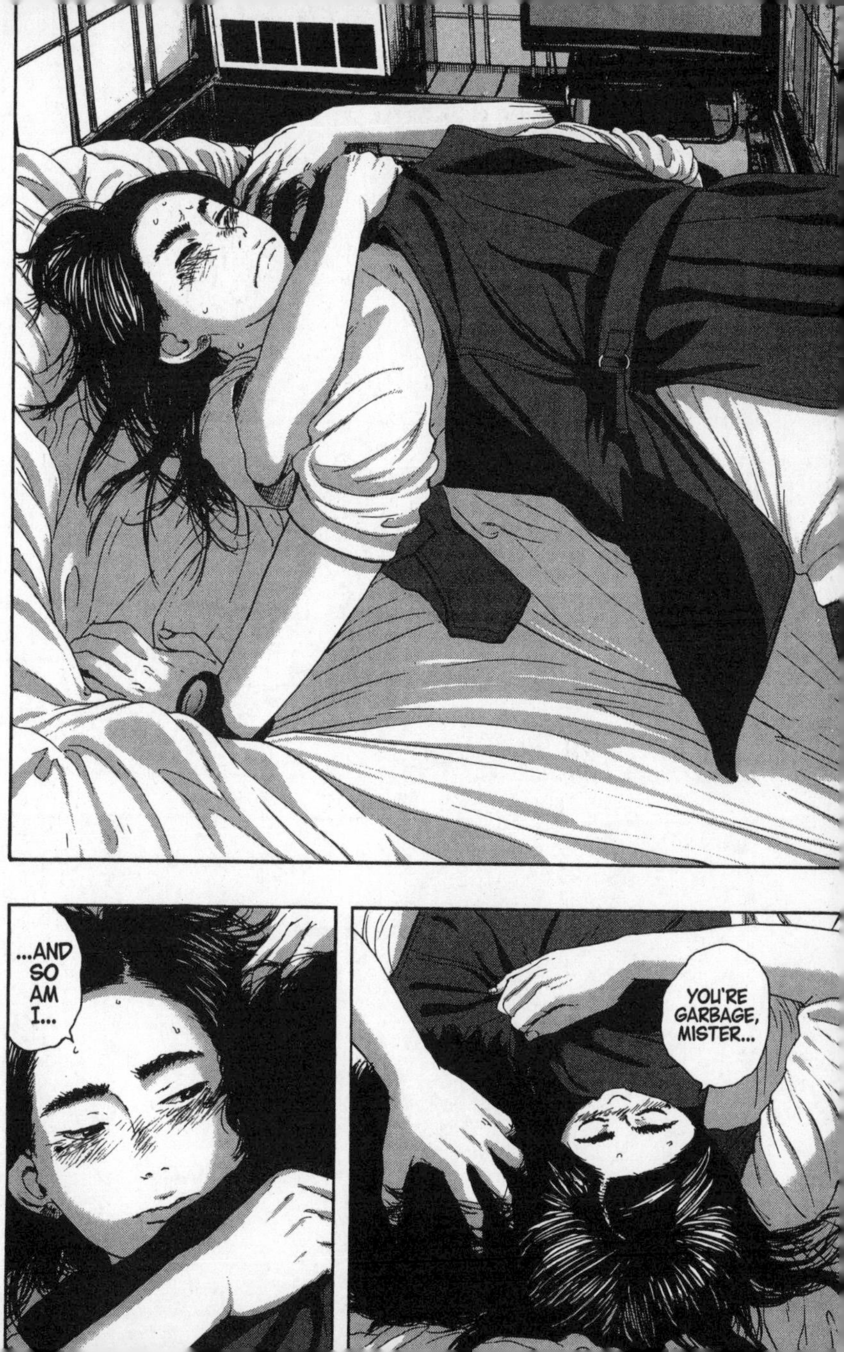
YOU'RE GARBAGE, MISTER...
...AND SO AM I...

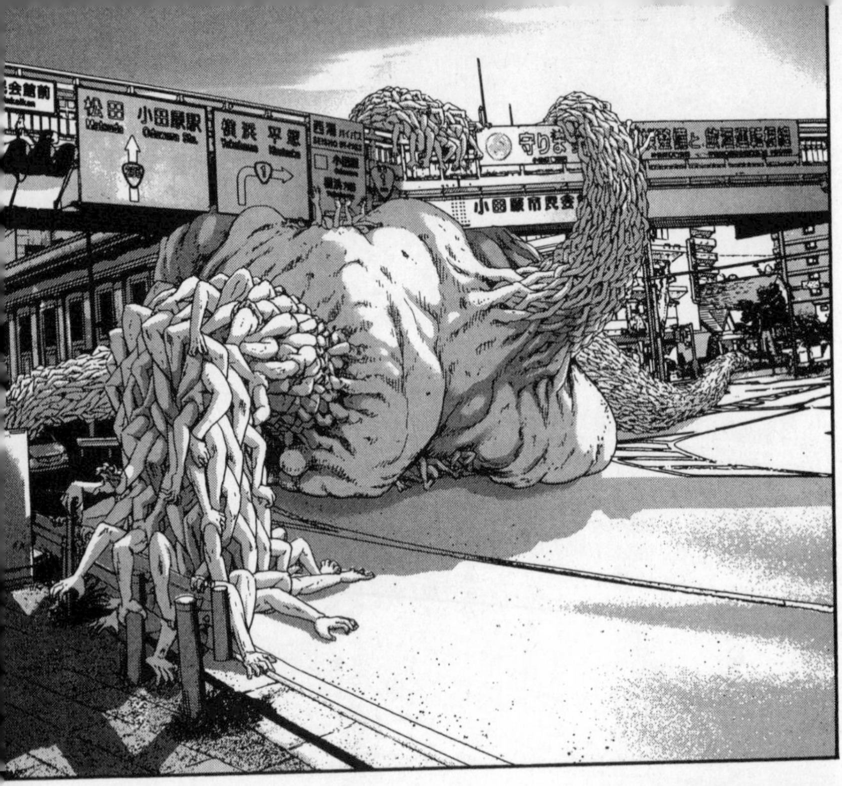
松田
小田原駅
横浜 平塚
西湘 バイパス
小田原市民会
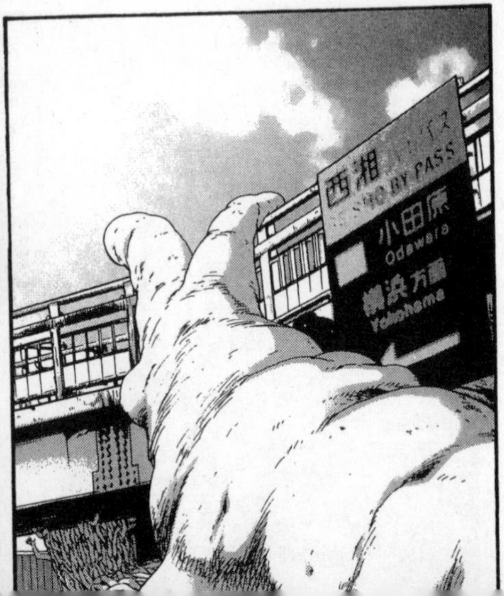
西湘 バイパス
BY PASS
小田原
Odawara
横浜方面
Yokohama
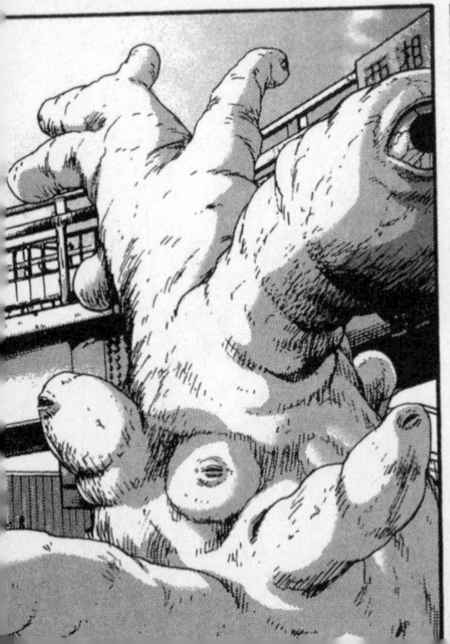
西湘

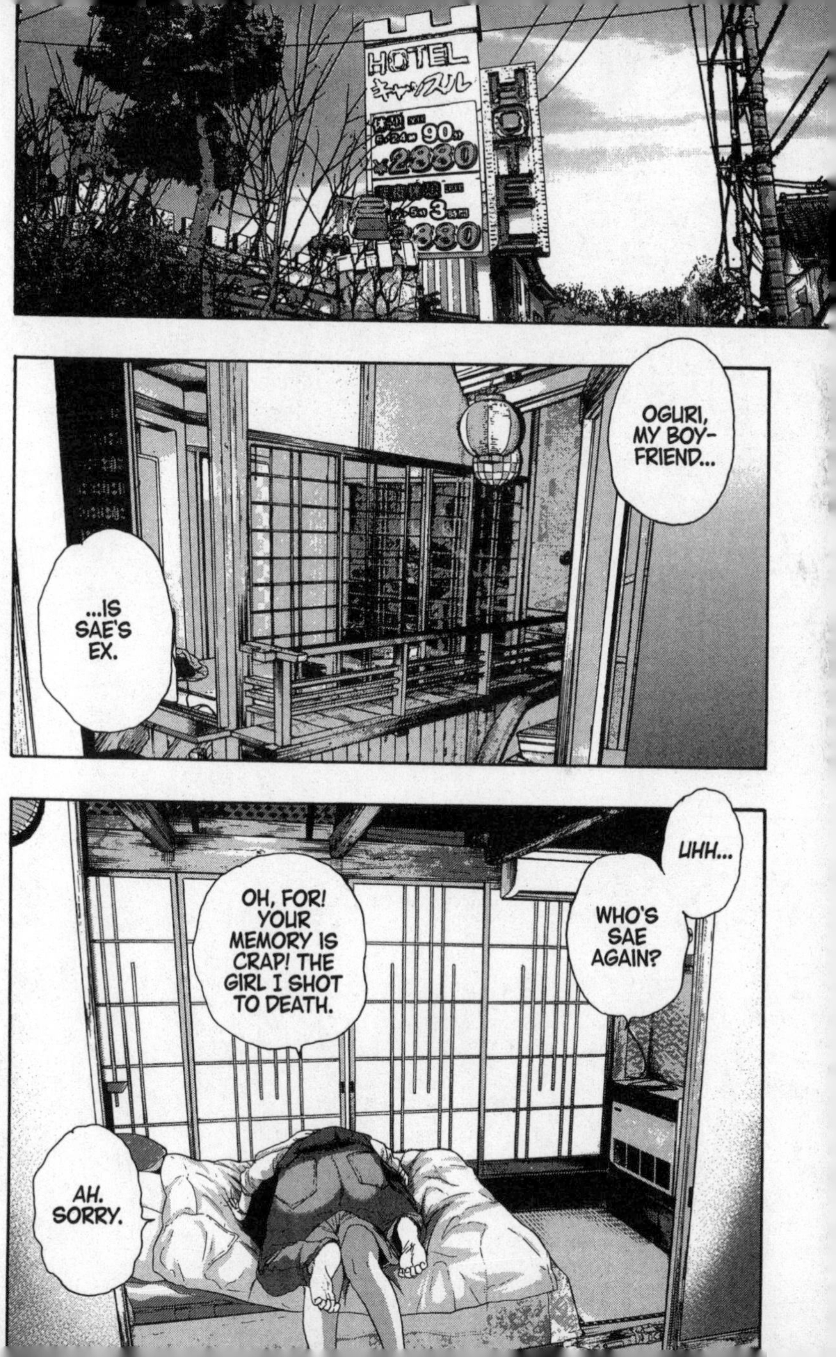
HOTEL
キャッスル
¥2380
HOTEL
OGURI, MY BOY-FRIEND...
...IS SAE'S EX.
UHH...
WHO'S SAE AGAIN?
OH, FOR! YOUR MEMORY IS CRAP! THE GIRL I SHOT TO DEATH.
AH. SORRY.

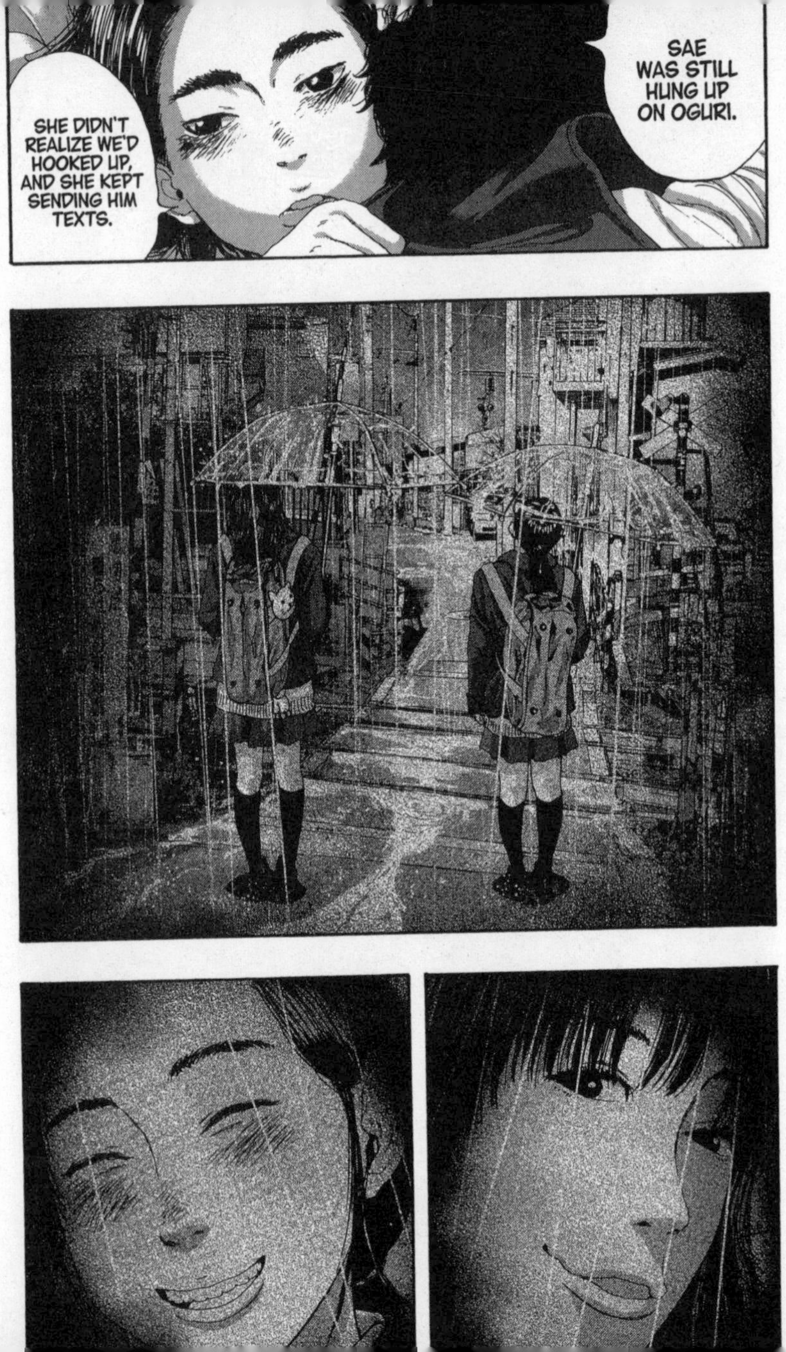
SAE WAS STILL HUNG UP ON OGURI.
SHE DIDN'T REALIZE WE'D HOOKED UP, AND SHE KEPT SENDING HIM TEXTS.

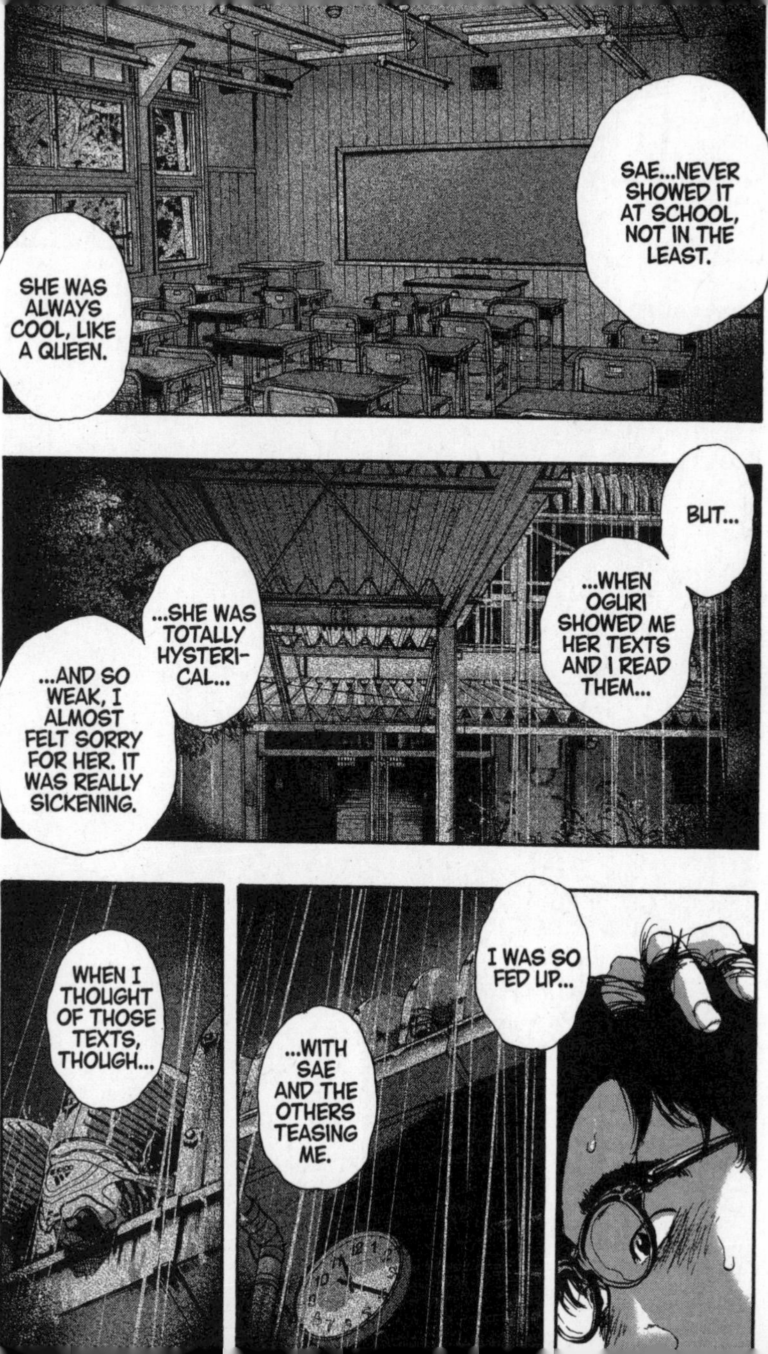
SAE...NEVER SHOWED IT AT SCHOOL, NOT IN THE LEAST.
SHE WAS ALWAYS COOL, LIKE A QUEEN.
BUT...
...WHEN OGURI SHOWED ME HER TEXTS AND I READ THEM...
...SHE WAS TOTALLY HYSTERI-CAL...
...AND SO WEAK, I ALMOST FELT SORRY FOR HER. IT WAS REALLY SICKENING.
I WAS SO FED UP...
...WITH SAE AND THE OTHERS TEASING ME.
WHEN I THOUGHT OF THOSE TEXTS, THOUGH...

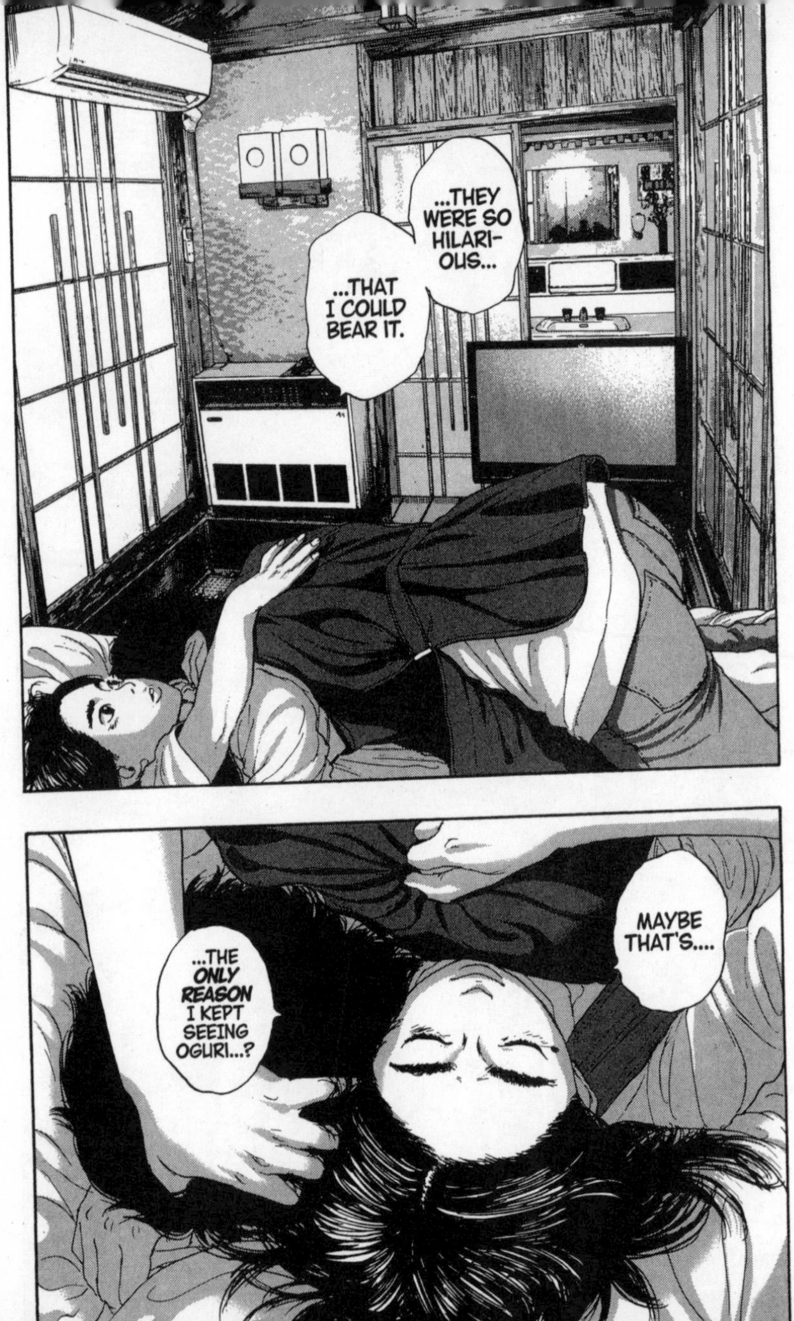
...THEY WERE SO HILARIOUS...
...THAT I COULD BEAR IT.
MAYBE THAT'S....
...THE ONLY REASON I KEPT SEEING OGURI...?

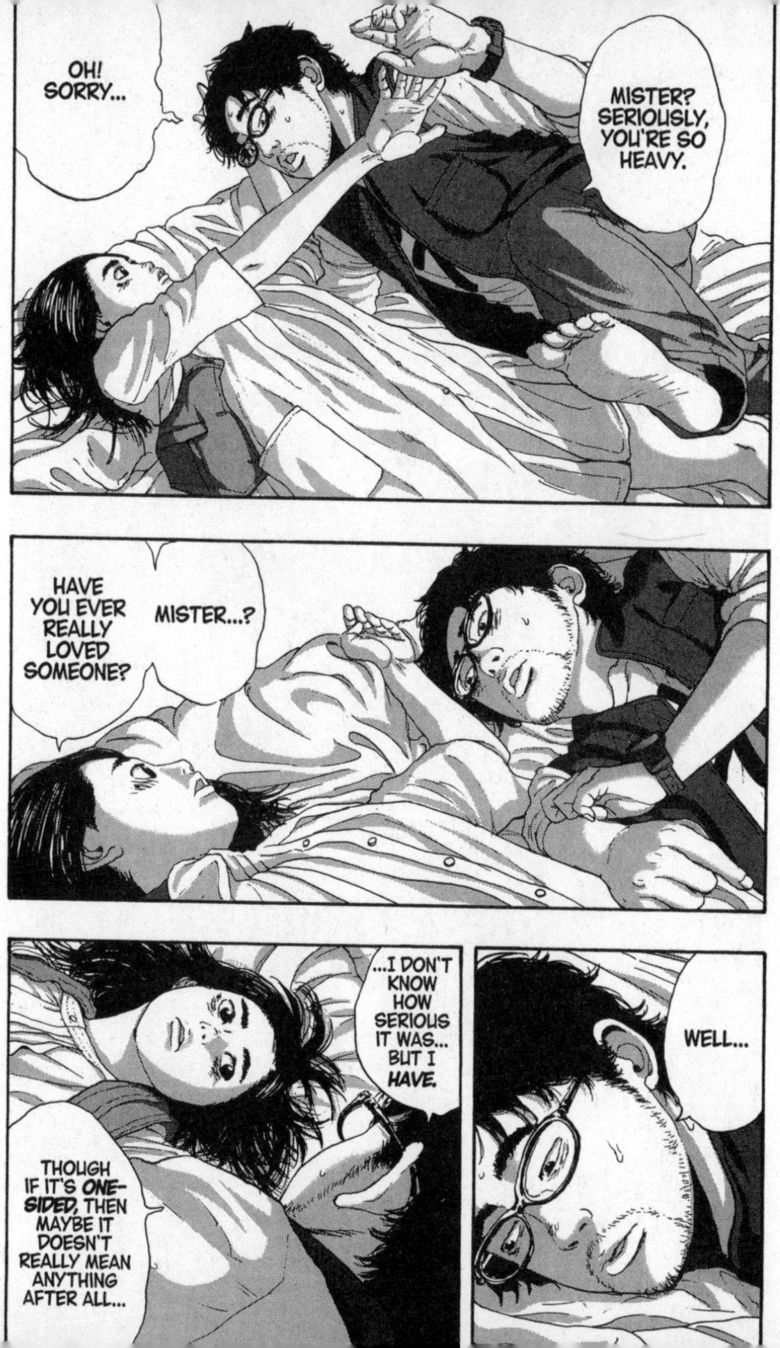
MISTER? SERIOUSLY, YOU'RE SO HEAVY.
OH! SORRY...
MISTER...?
HAVE YOU EVER REALLY LOVED SOMEONE?
WELL...
...I DON'T KNOW HOW SERIOUS IT WAS... BUT I HAVE.
THOUGH IF IT'S ONE-SIDED, THEN MAYBE IT DOESN'T REALLY MEAN ANYTHING AFTER ALL...

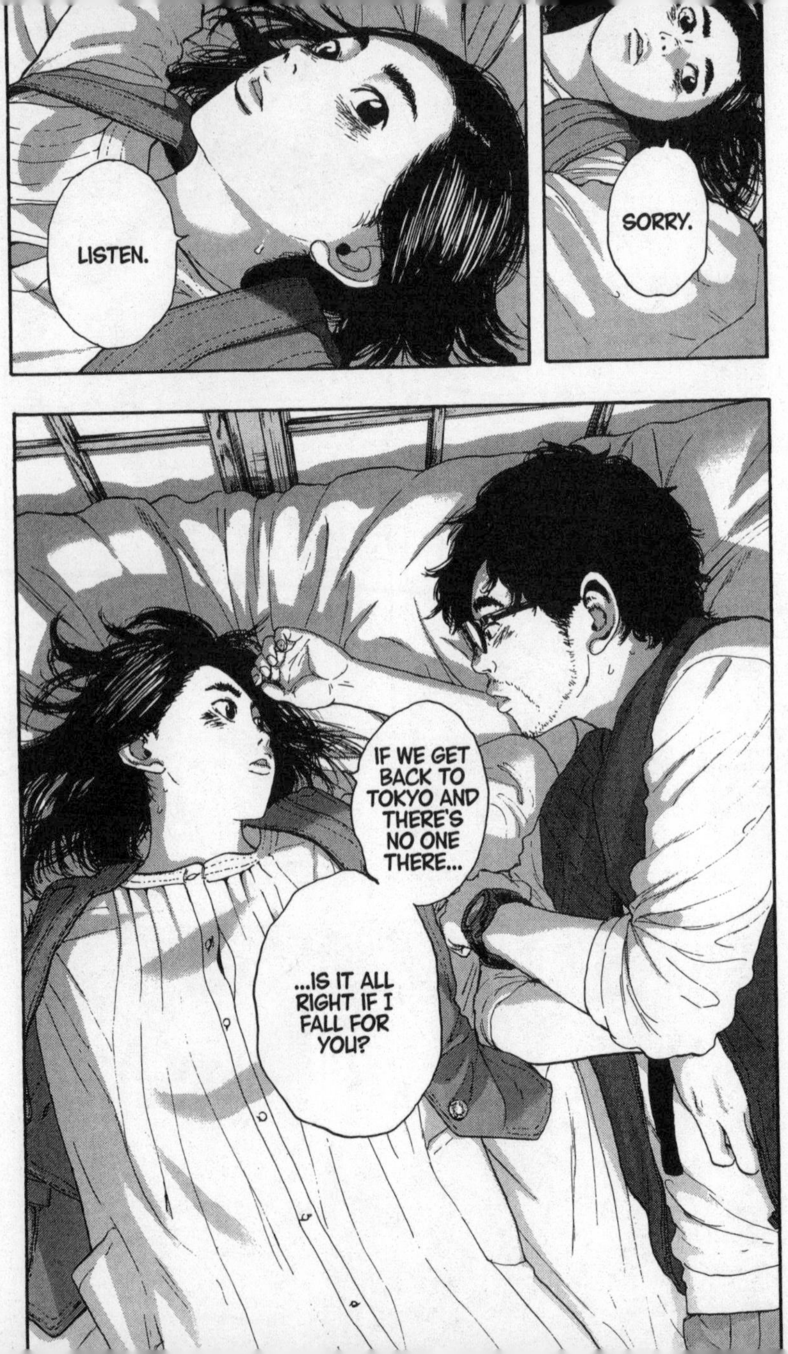
SORRY.
LISTEN.
IF WE GET BACK TO TOKYO AND THERE'S NO ONE THERE...
...IS IT ALL RIGHT IF I FALL FOR YOU?

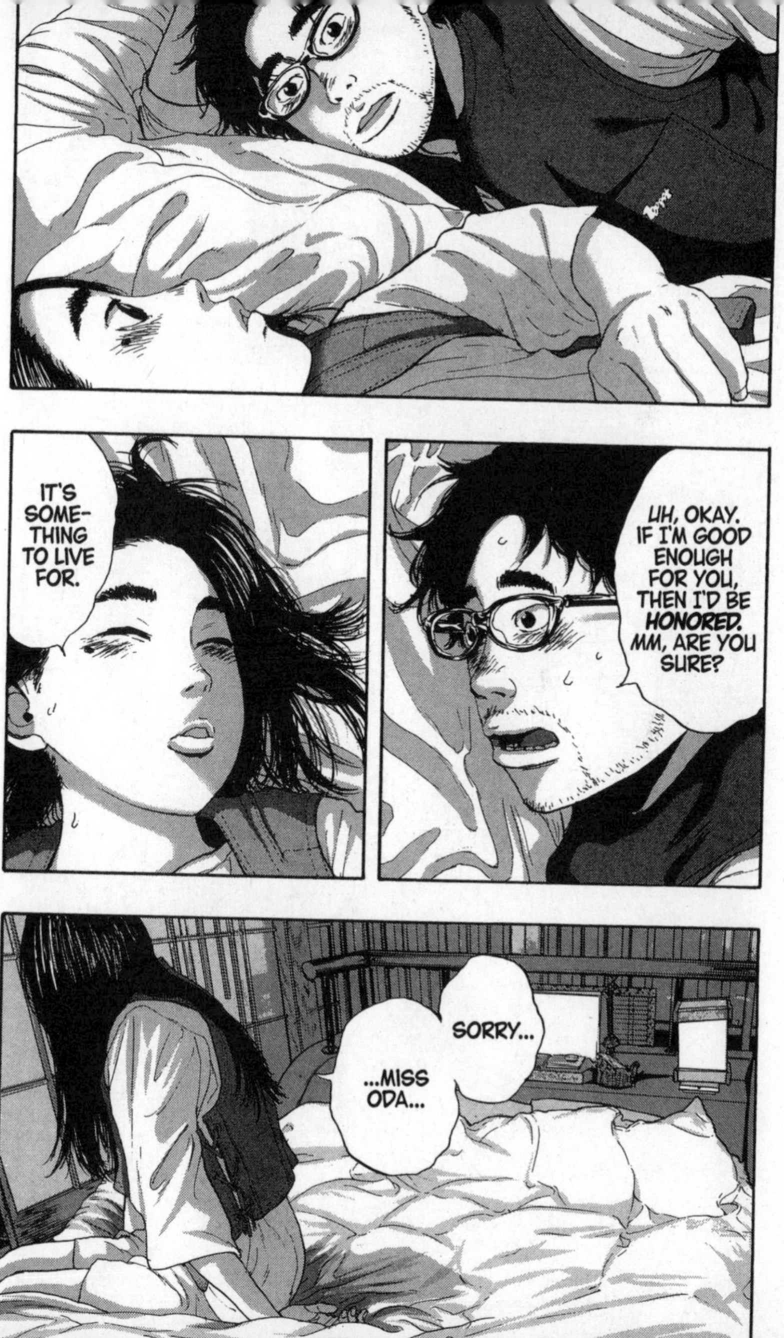
UH, OKAY. IF I'M GOOD ENOUGH FOR YOU, THEN I'D BE **HONORED.** MM, ARE YOU SURE?
IT'S SOME-THING TO LIVE FOR.
SORRY...
...MISS ODA...

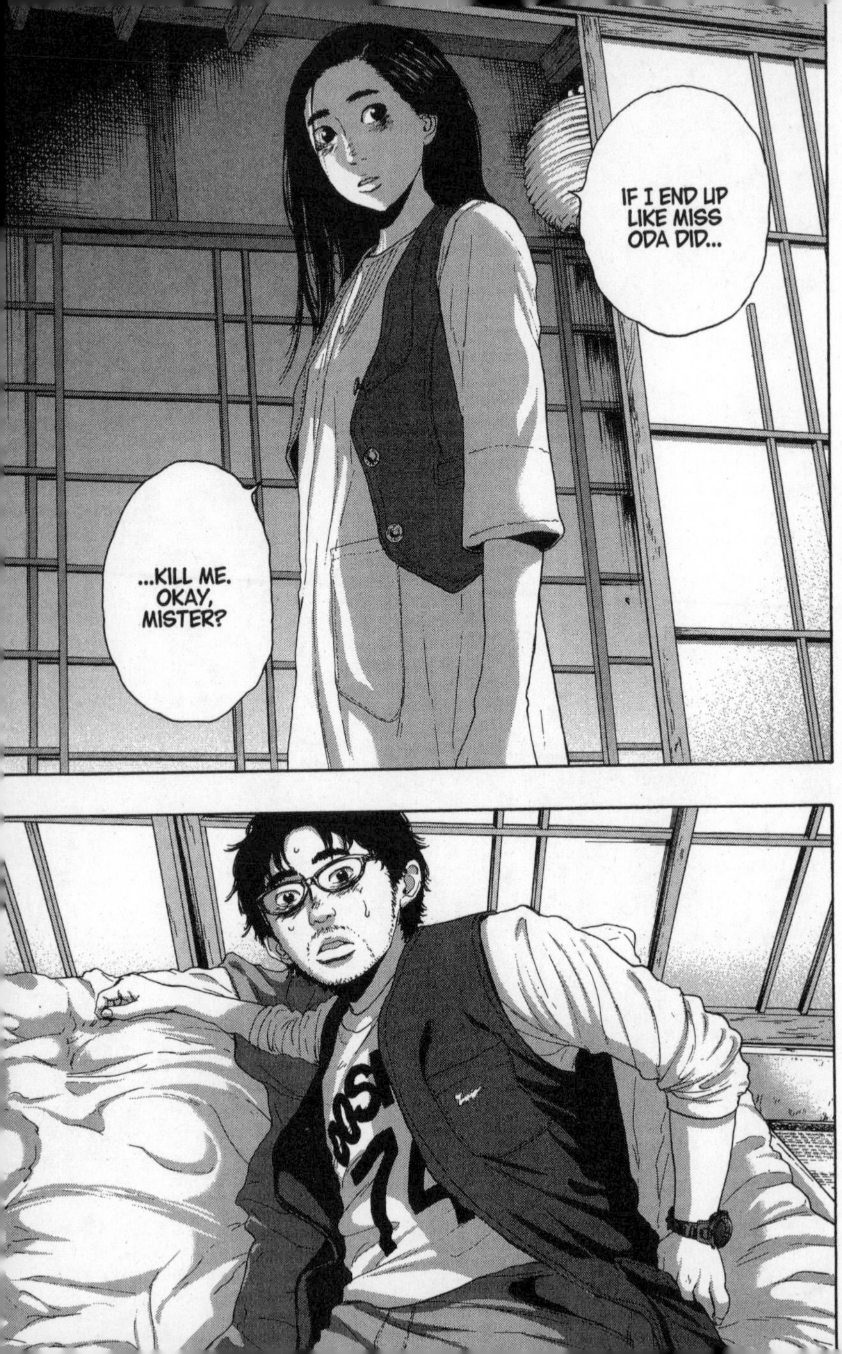
IF I END UP LIKE MISS ODA DID...
...KILL ME. OKAY, MISTER?

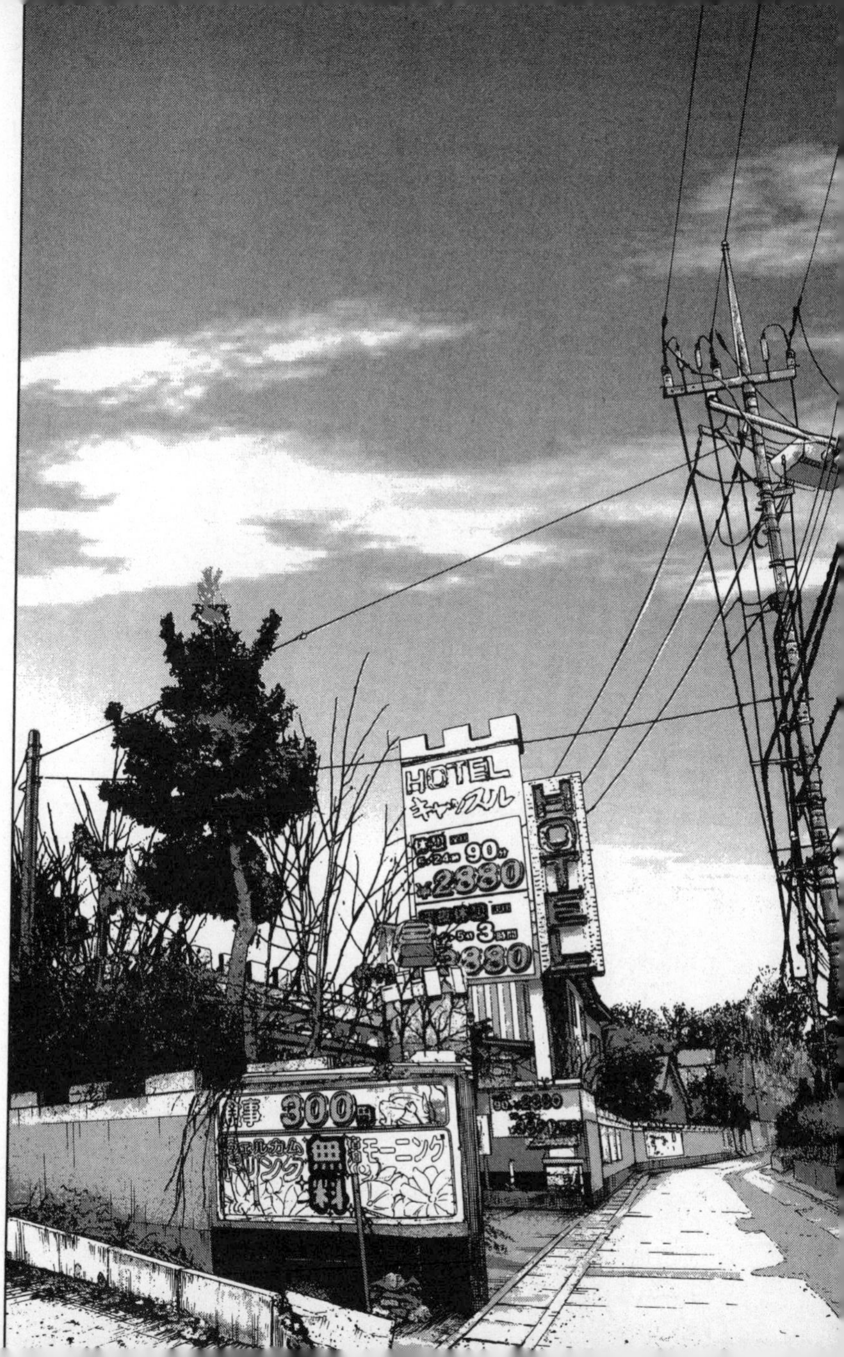
HOTEL
キャッスル
90分
¥2880
3時間
HOTEL
300円
モーニング
無料

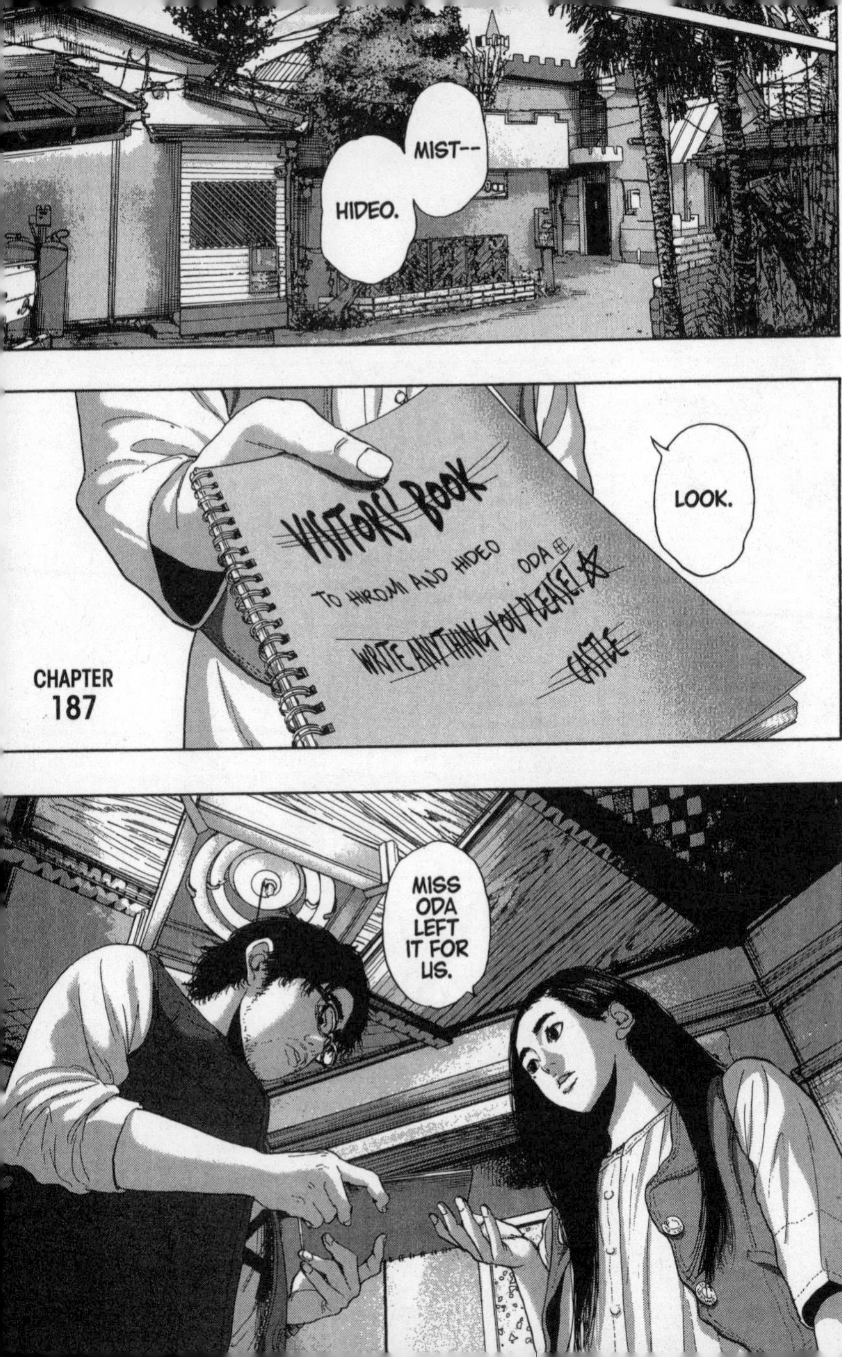
MIST--
HIDEO.
LOOK.
VISITORS' BOOK
TO HIROMI AND HIDEO ODA
WRITE ANYTHING YOU PLEASE!
CASTLE
CHAPTER 187
MISS ODA LEFT IT FOR US.

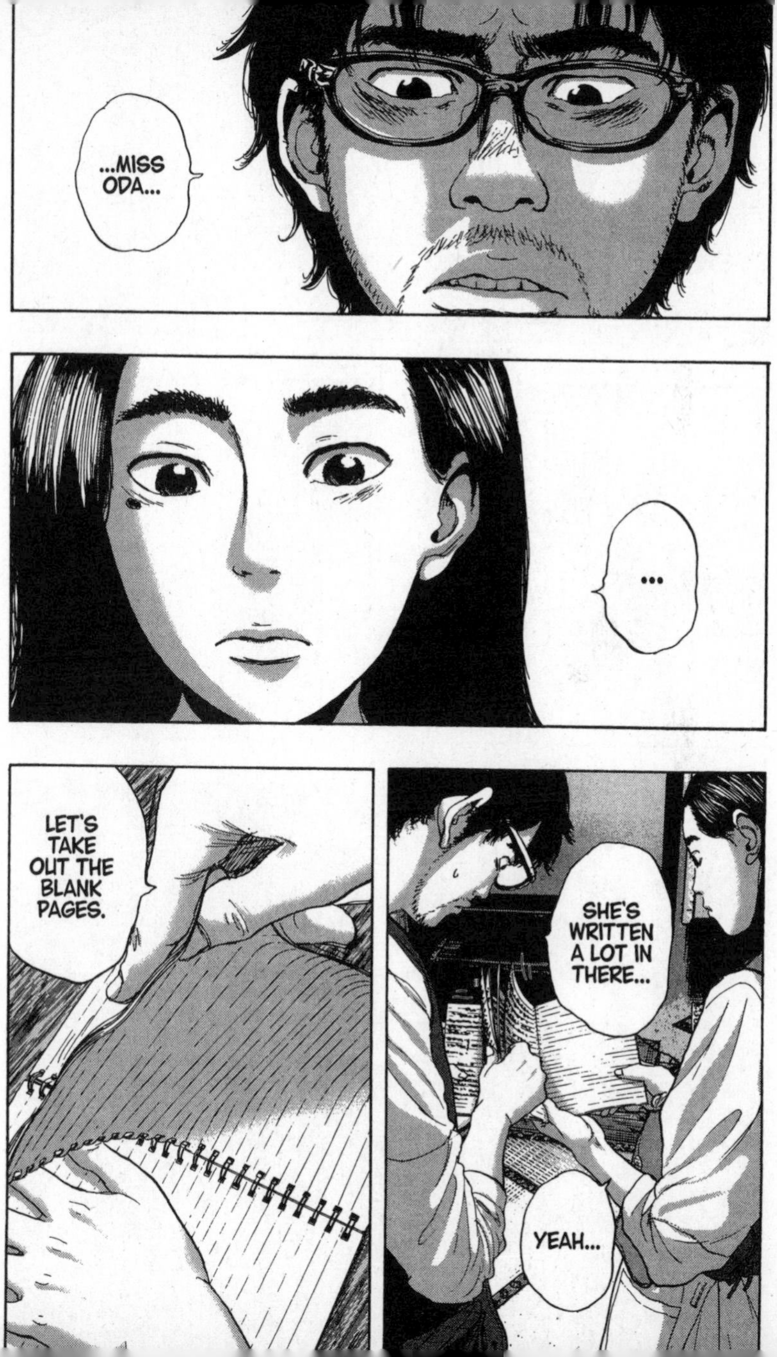
...MISS ODA...
...
SHE'S WRITTEN A LOT IN THERE...
YEAH...
LET'S TAKE OUT THE BLANK PAGES.

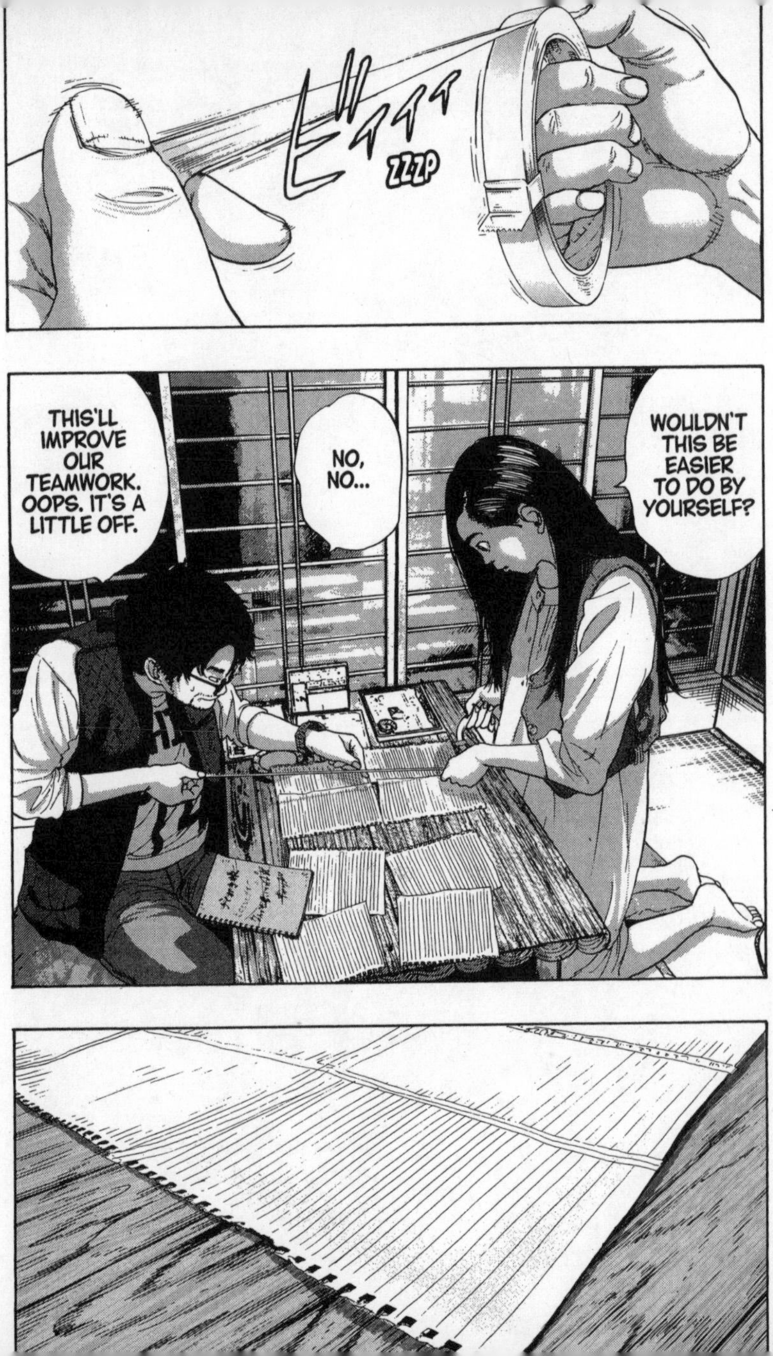
ZZZP
WOULDN'T THIS BE EASIER TO DO BY YOURSELF?
NO, NO...
THIS'LL IMPROVE OUR TEAMWORK. OOPS. IT'S A LITTLE OFF.

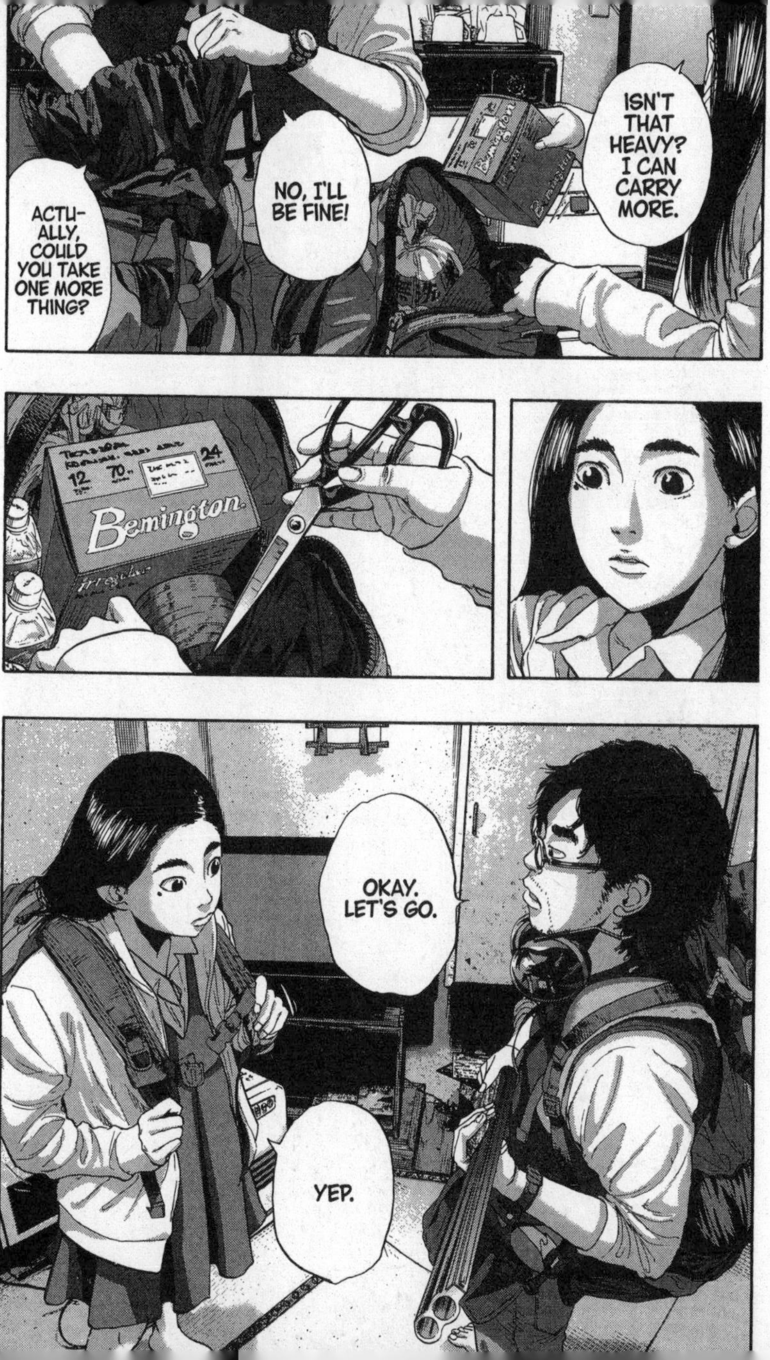
ISN'T THAT HEAVY? I CAN CARRY MORE.
NO, I'LL BE FINE!
ACTU-ALLY, COULD YOU TAKE ONE MORE THING?
Bemington
OKAY. LET'S GO.
YEP.

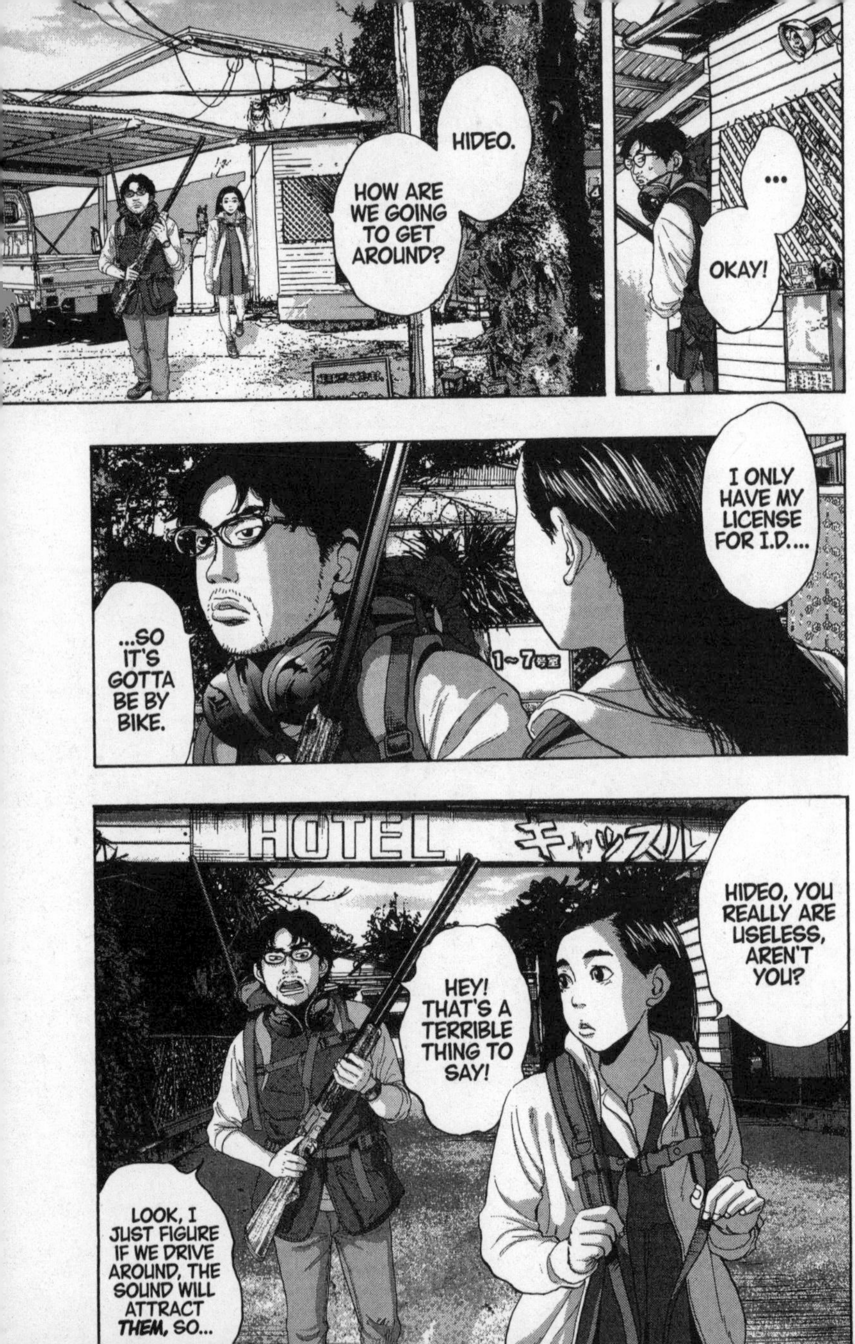
...
OKAY!
HIDEO.
HOW ARE WE GOING TO GET AROUND?
I ONLY HAVE MY LICENSE FOR I.D....
1~7号室
...SO IT'S GOTTA BE BY BIKE.
HOTEL キャッスル
HIDEO, YOU REALLY ARE USELESS, AREN'T YOU?
HEY! THAT'S A TERRIBLE THING TO SAY!
LOOK, I JUST FIGURE IF WE DRIVE AROUND, THE SOUND WILL ATTRACT *THEM*, SO...

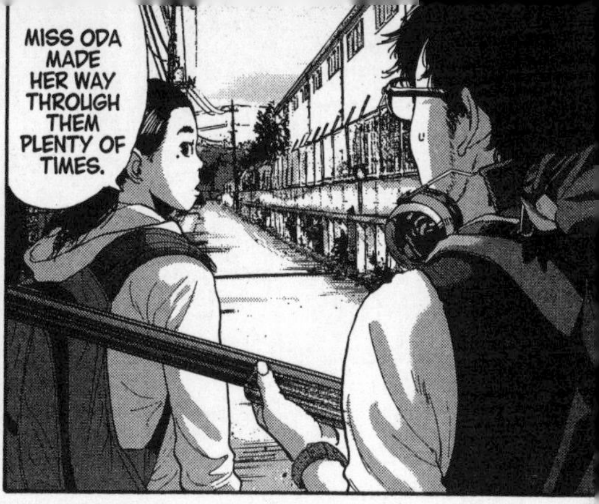
MISS ODA MADE HER WAY THROUGH THEM PLENTY OF TIMES.
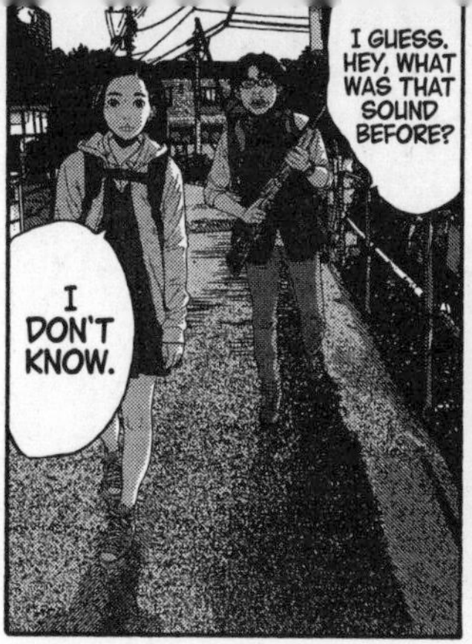
I GUESS. HEY, WHAT WAS THAT SOUND BEFORE?
I DON'T KNOW.
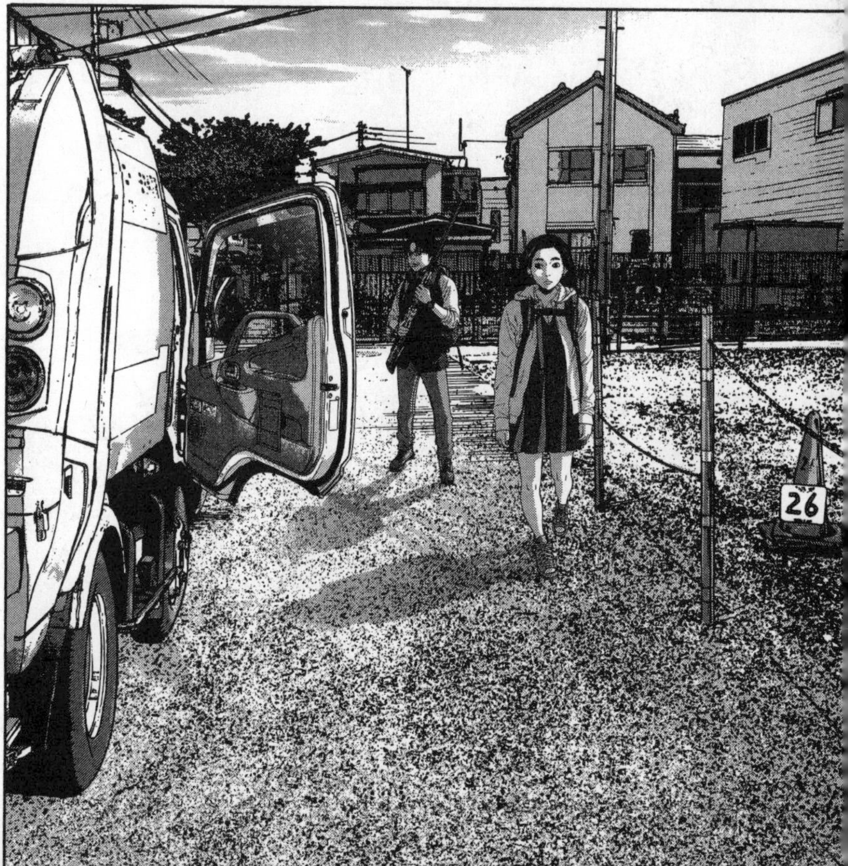
26

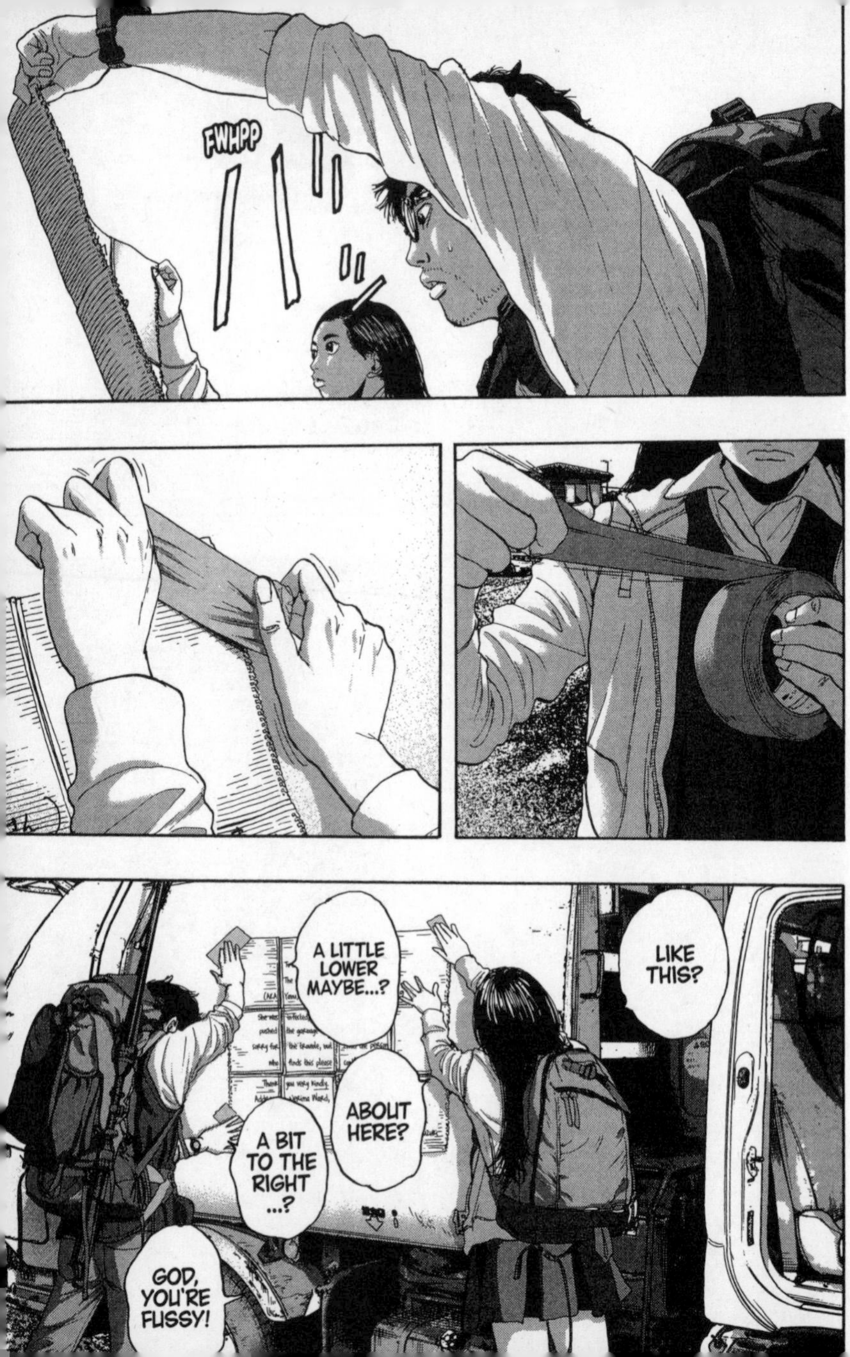
FWHPP
LIKE THIS?
A LITTLE LOWER MAYBE...?
ABOUT HERE?
A BIT TO THE RIGHT ...?
GOD, YOU'RE FUSSY!

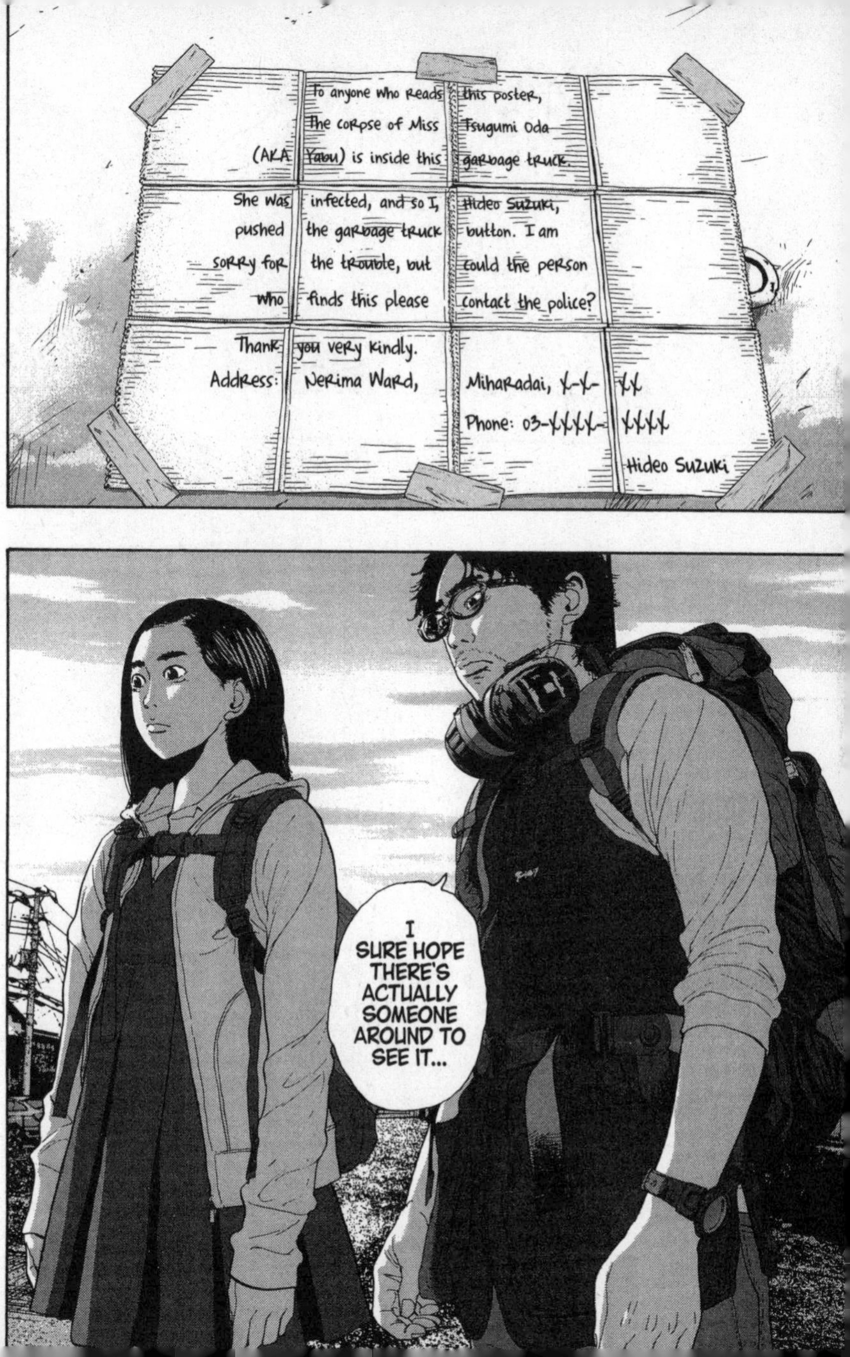
To anyone who reads this poster,
The corpse of Miss Tsugumi Oda
(AKA Yabu) is inside this garbage truck.
She was infected, and so I, Hideo Suzuki,
pushed the garbage truck button. I am
sorry for the trouble, but could the person
who finds this please contact the police?
Thank you very kindly.
Address: Nerima Ward, Miharadai, X-X-XX
Phone: 03-XXXX-XXXX
Hideo Suzuki
I SURE HOPE THERE'S ACTUALLY SOMEONE AROUND TO SEE IT...

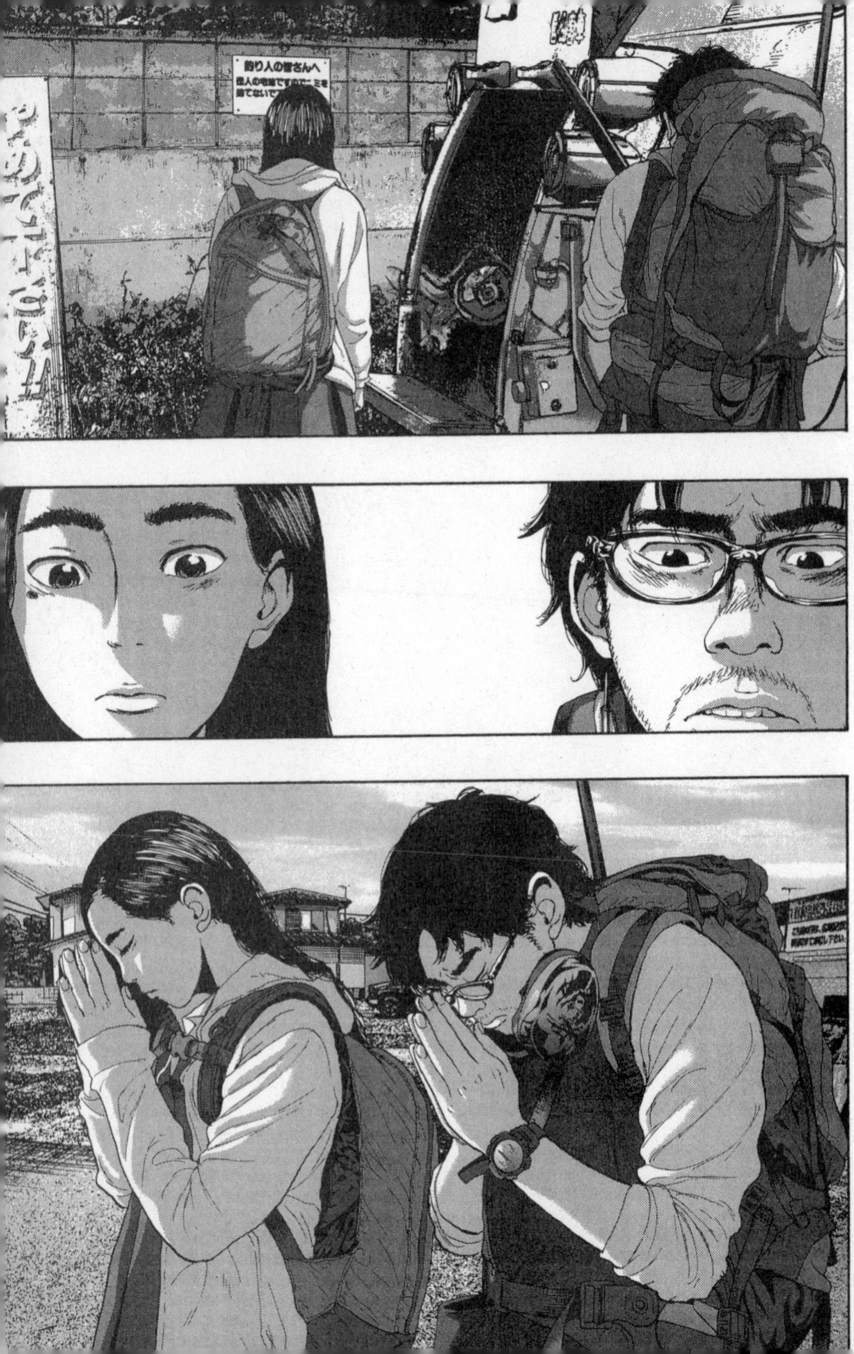
釣り人の皆さんへ

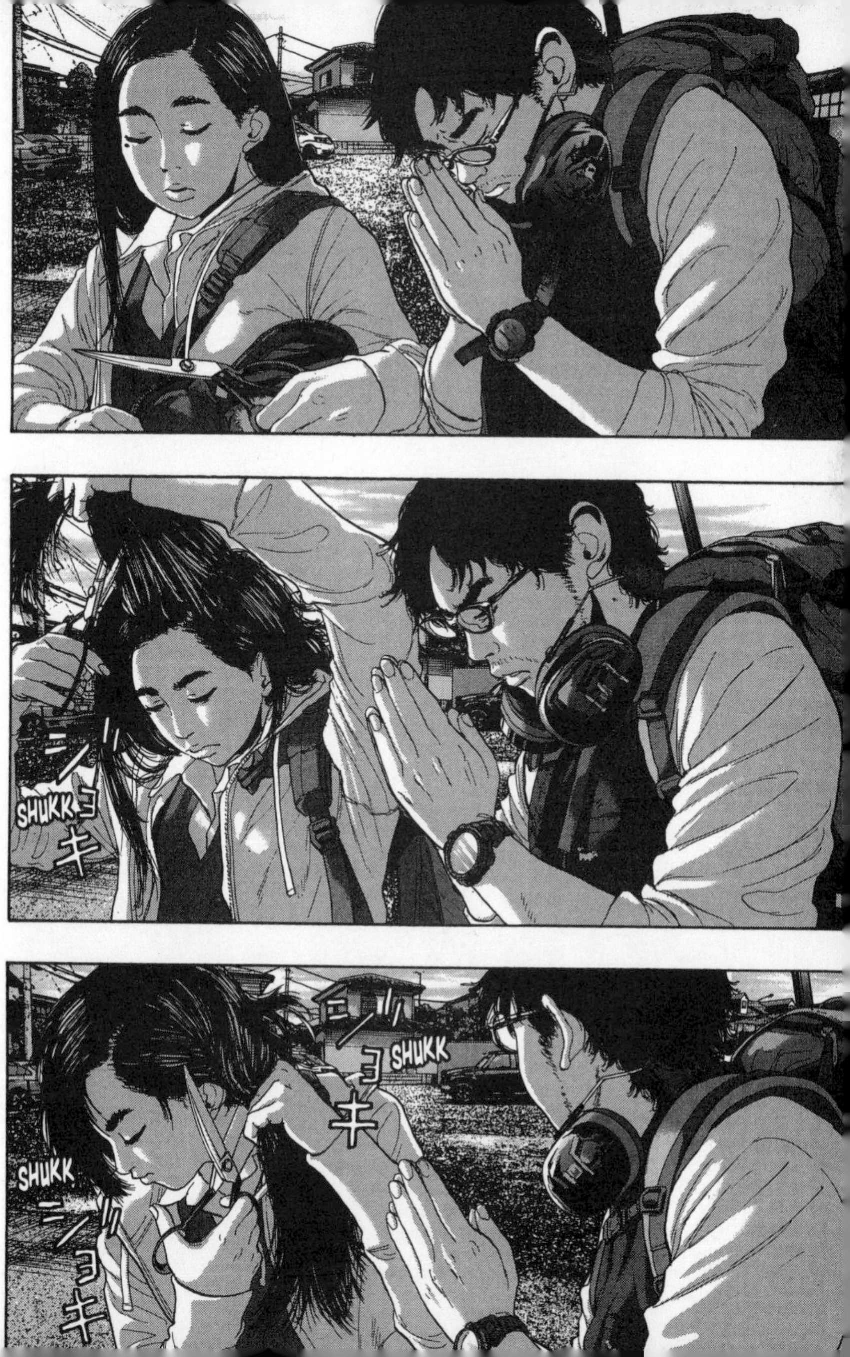
ジョキ
SHUKK
ジョキ
SHUKK
SHUKK
ジョキ

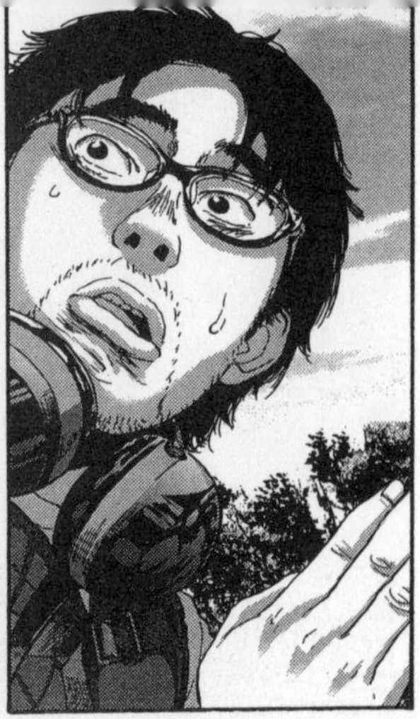

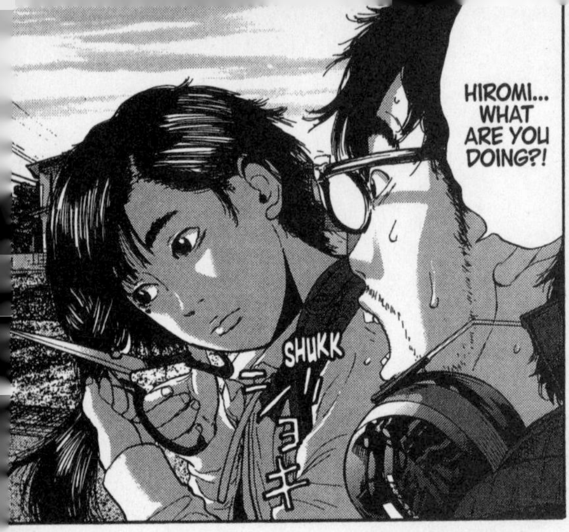
HIROMI... WHAT ARE YOU DOING?!
SHUKK

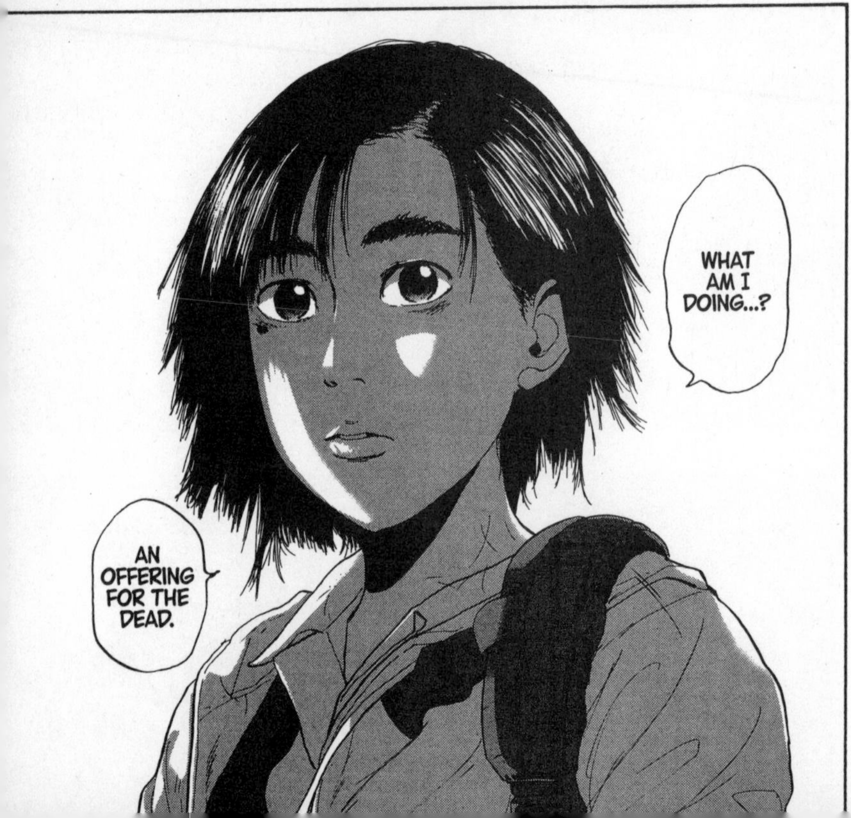
WHAT AM I DOING...?
AN OFFERING FOR THE DEAD.

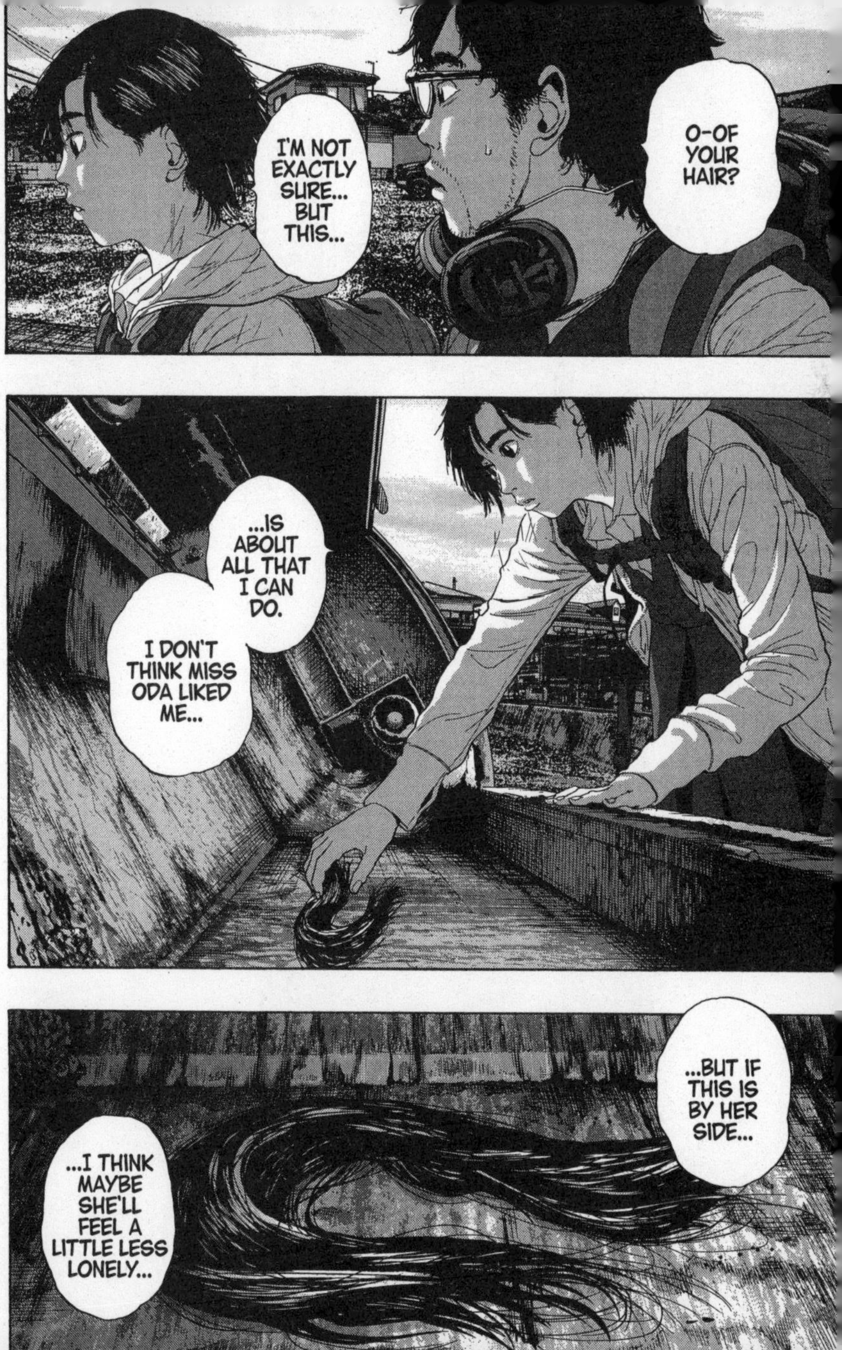
O-OF YOUR HAIR?
I'M NOT EXACTLY SURE... BUT THIS...
...IS ABOUT ALL THAT I CAN DO.
I DON'T THINK MISS ODA LIKED ME...
...BUT IF THIS IS BY HER SIDE...
...I THINK MAYBE SHE'LL FEEL A LITTLE LESS LONELY...

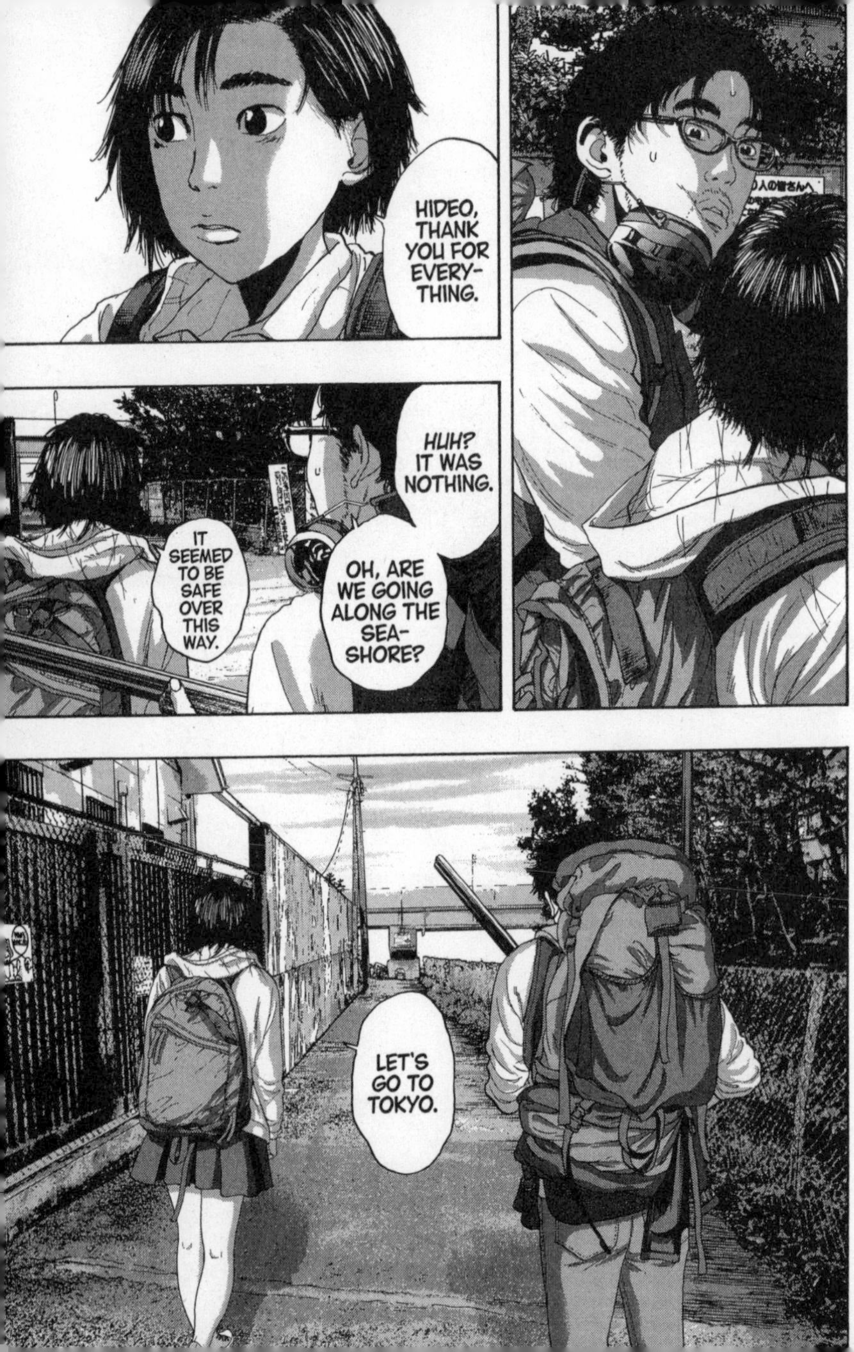
HIDEO, THANK YOU FOR EVERY-THING.
HUH? IT WAS NOTHING.
OH, ARE WE GOING ALONG THE SEA-SHORE?
IT SEEMED TO BE SAFE OVER THIS WAY.
LET'S GO TO TOKYO.

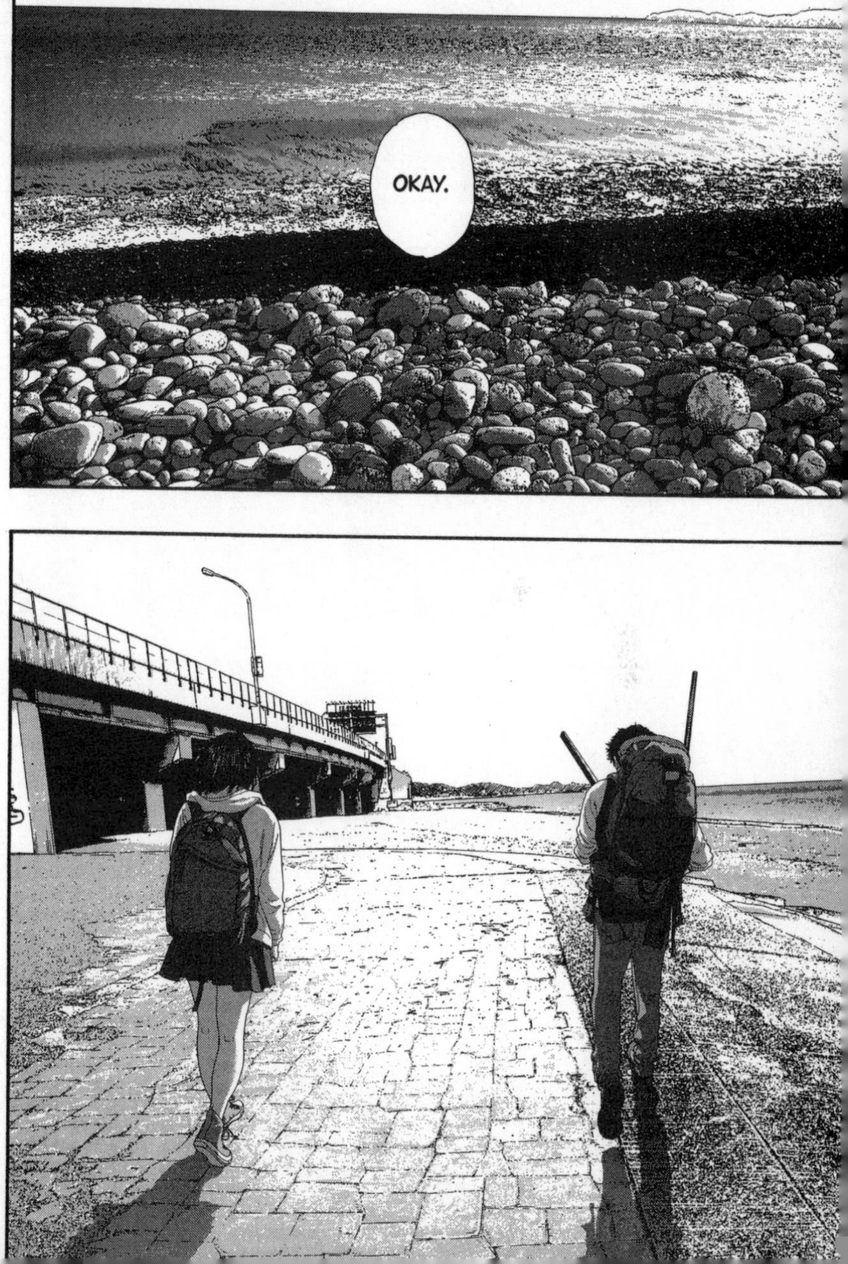
OKAY.

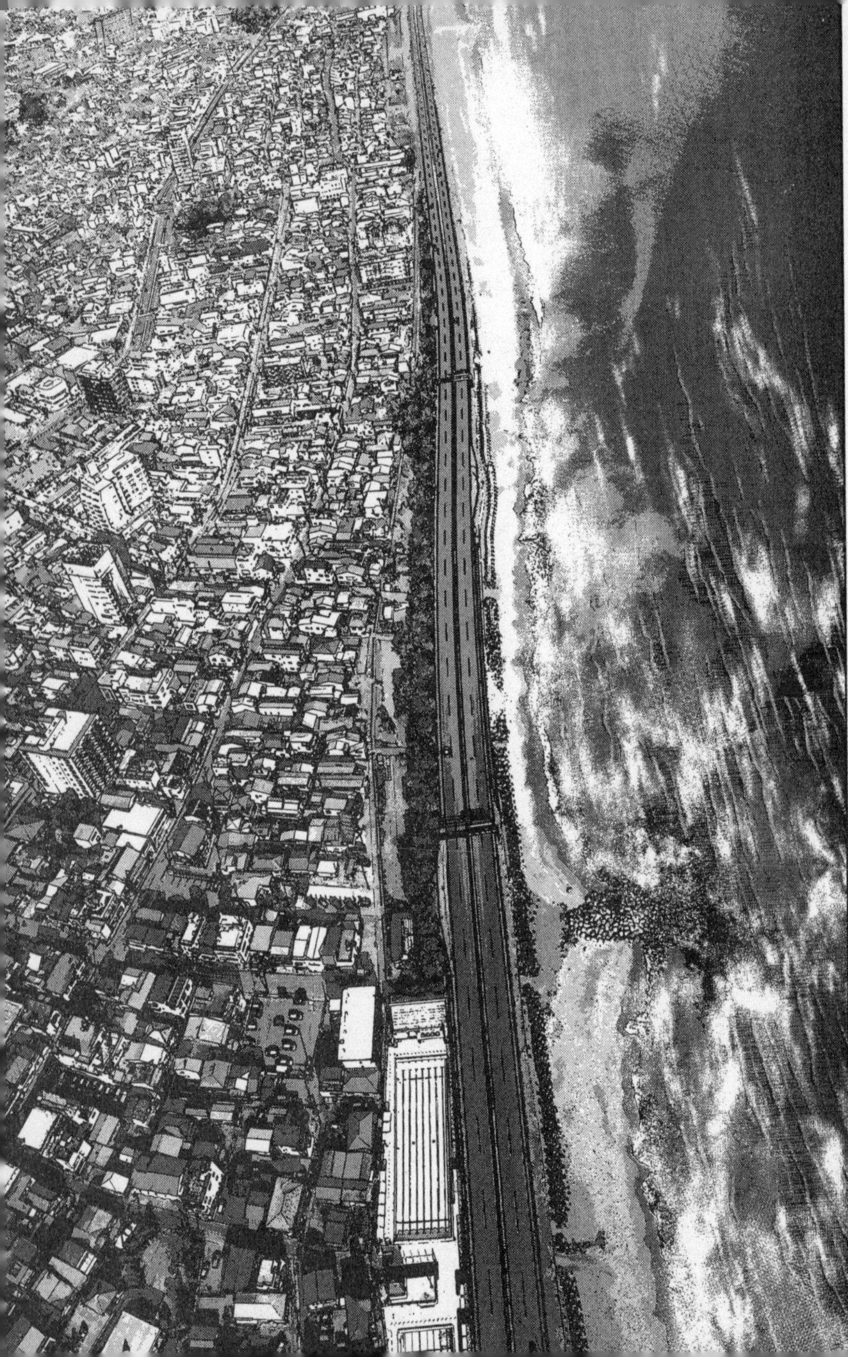

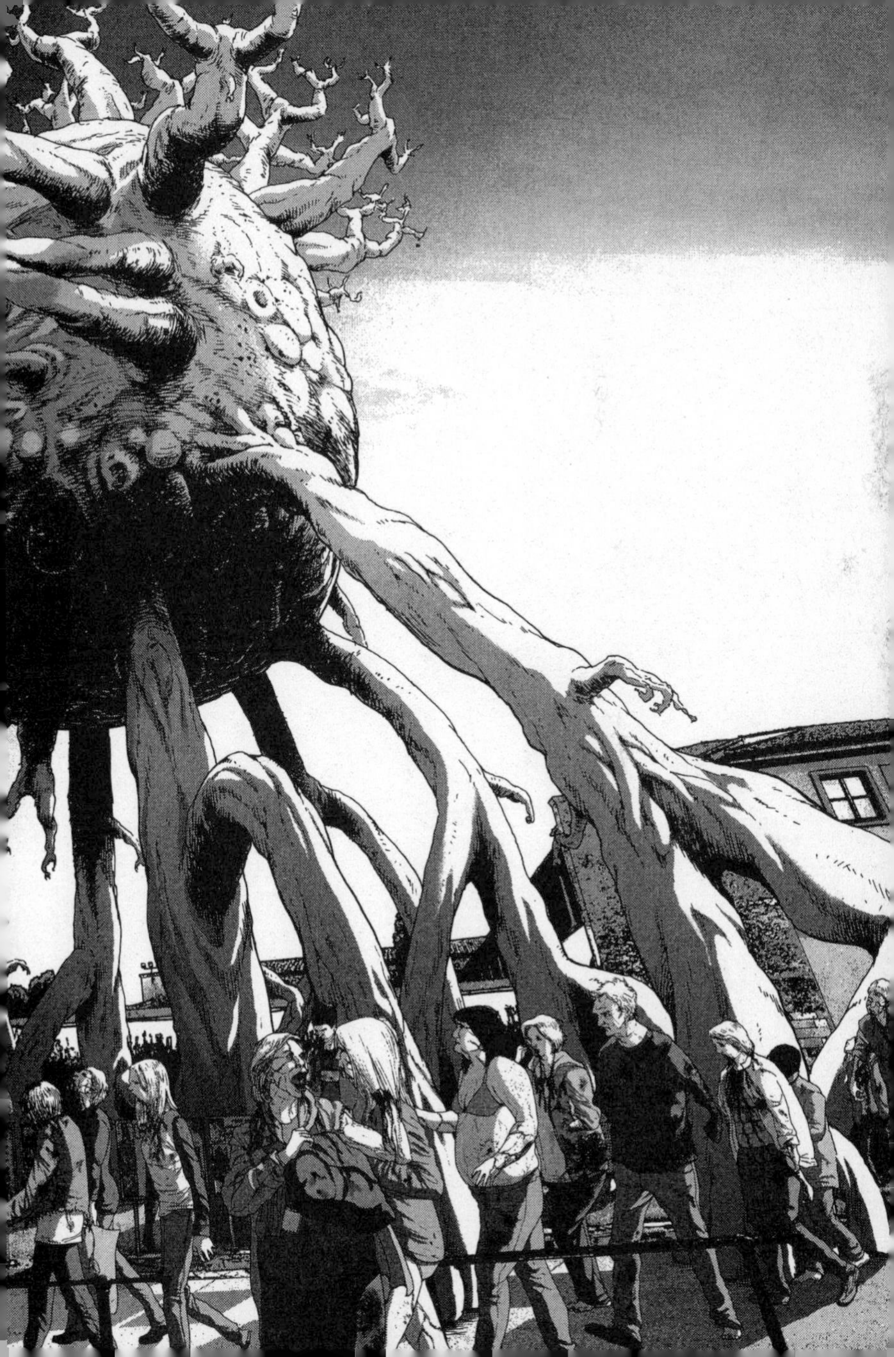

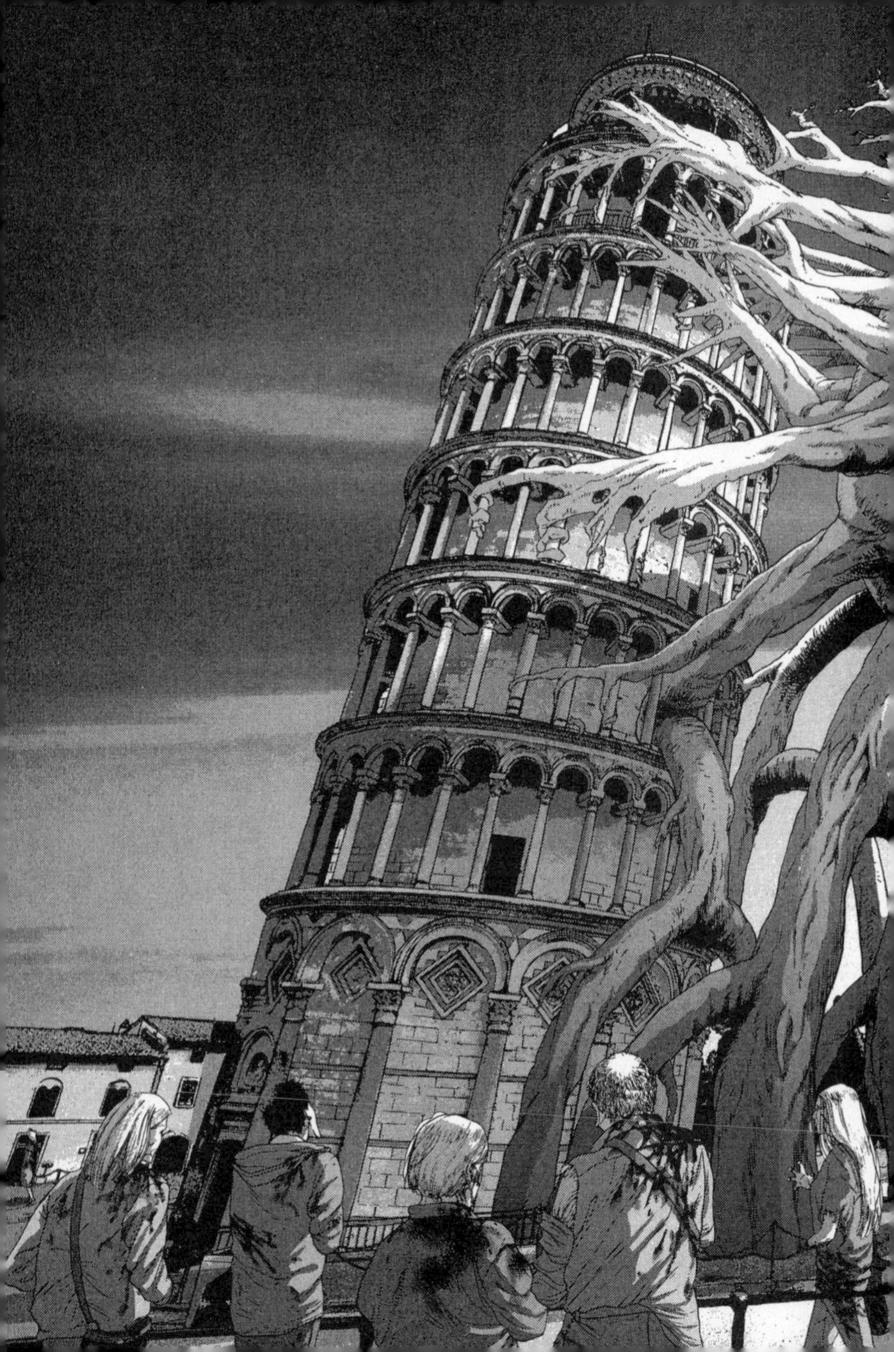

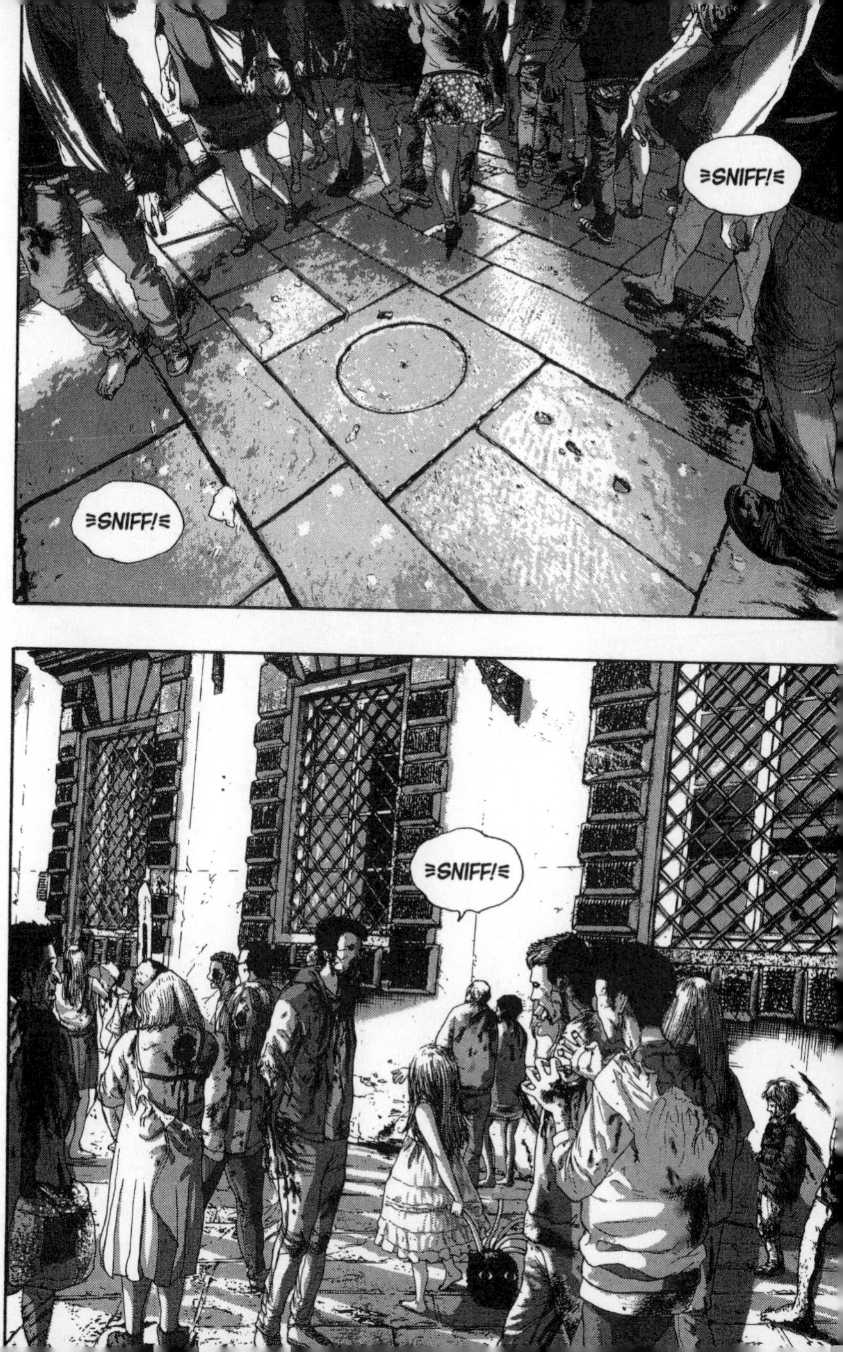
SNIFF!
SNIFF!
SNIFF!

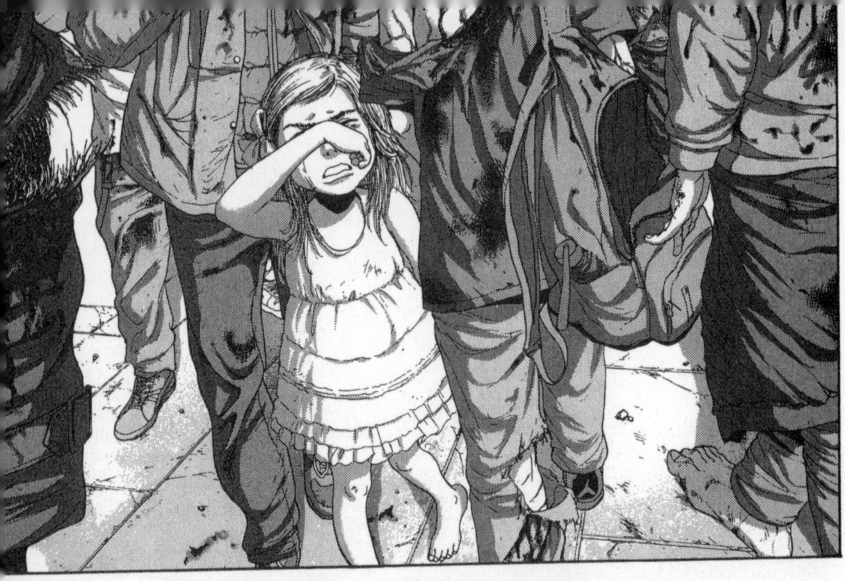

NOTE: SPOKEN ITALIAN WILL FALL WITHIN POINTED BRACKETS, <LIKE THIS>.

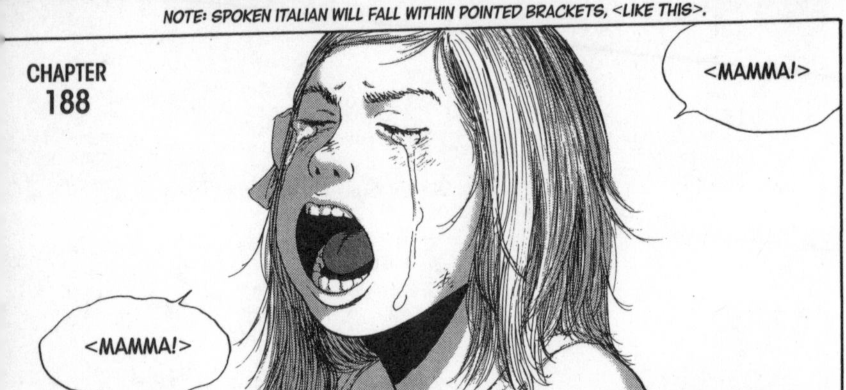
<MAMMA!>
CHAPTER 188
<MAMMA!>

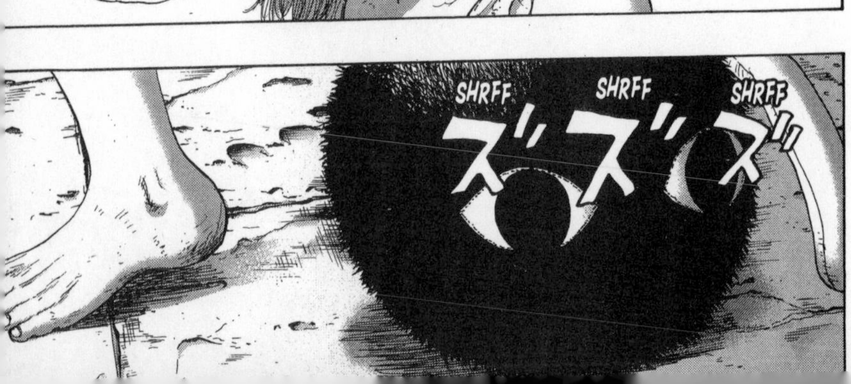
SHRFF
SHRFF
SHRFF
ズズズ

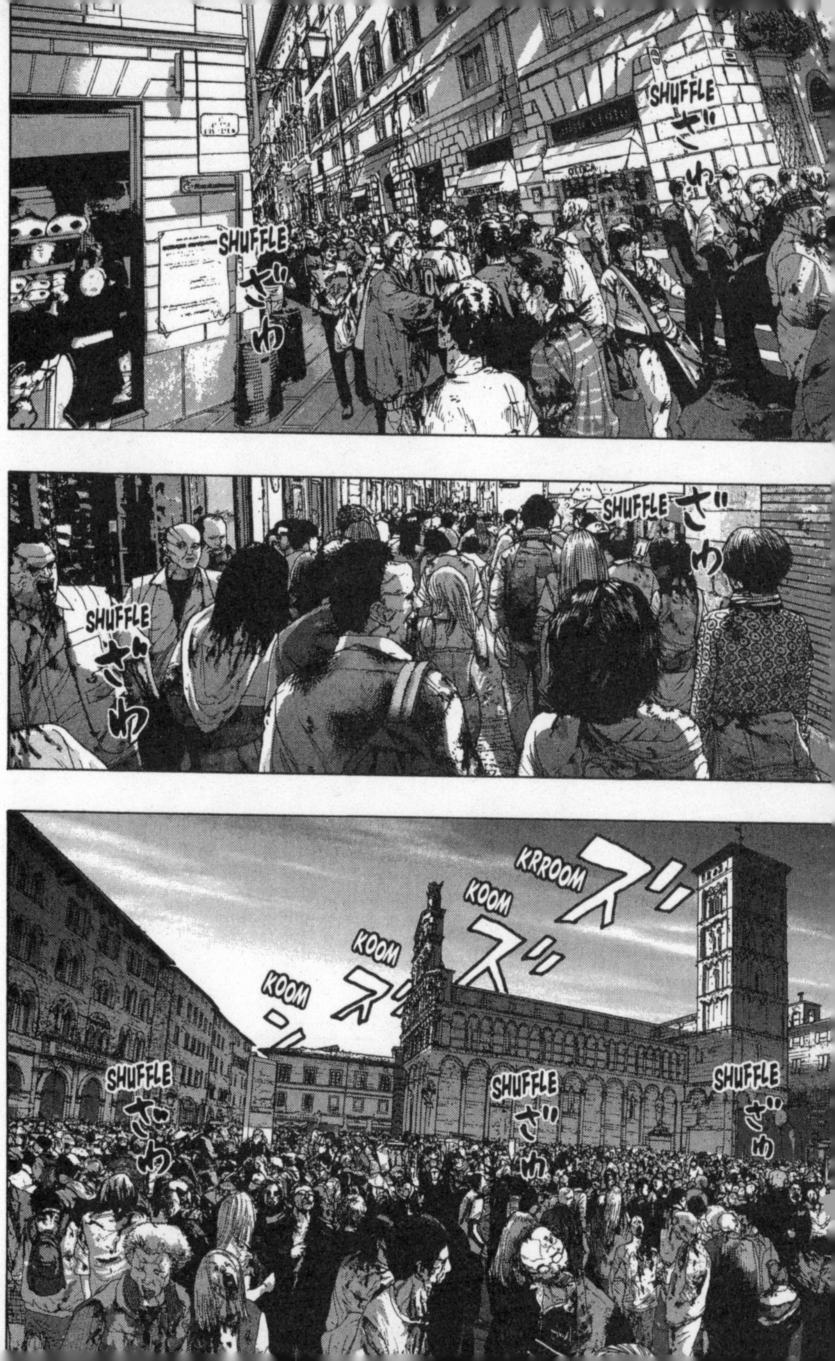
SHUFFLE
ざわ
SHUFFLE
ざわ
SHUFFLE
ざわ
SHUFFLE
ざわ
KRROOM
ズッ
KOOM
ズッ
KOOM
ズッ
KOOM
SHUFFLE
ざわ
SHUFFLE
ざわ
SHUFFLE
ざわ

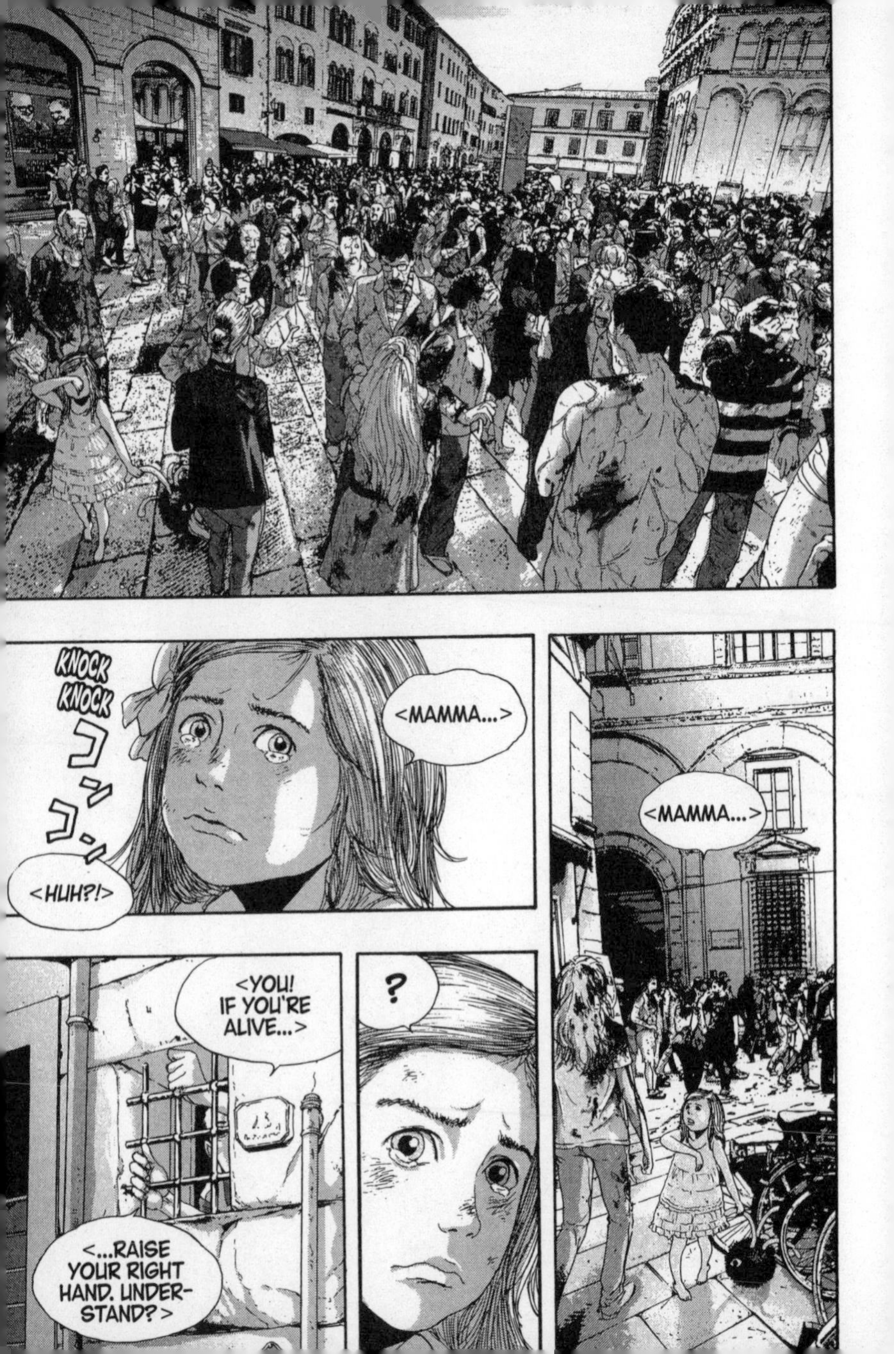

<MAMMA...>
<MAMMA...>
KNOCK KNOCK
<HUH?!>
?
<YOU! IF YOU'RE ALIVE...>
<...RAISE YOUR RIGHT HAND. UNDER-STAND?>

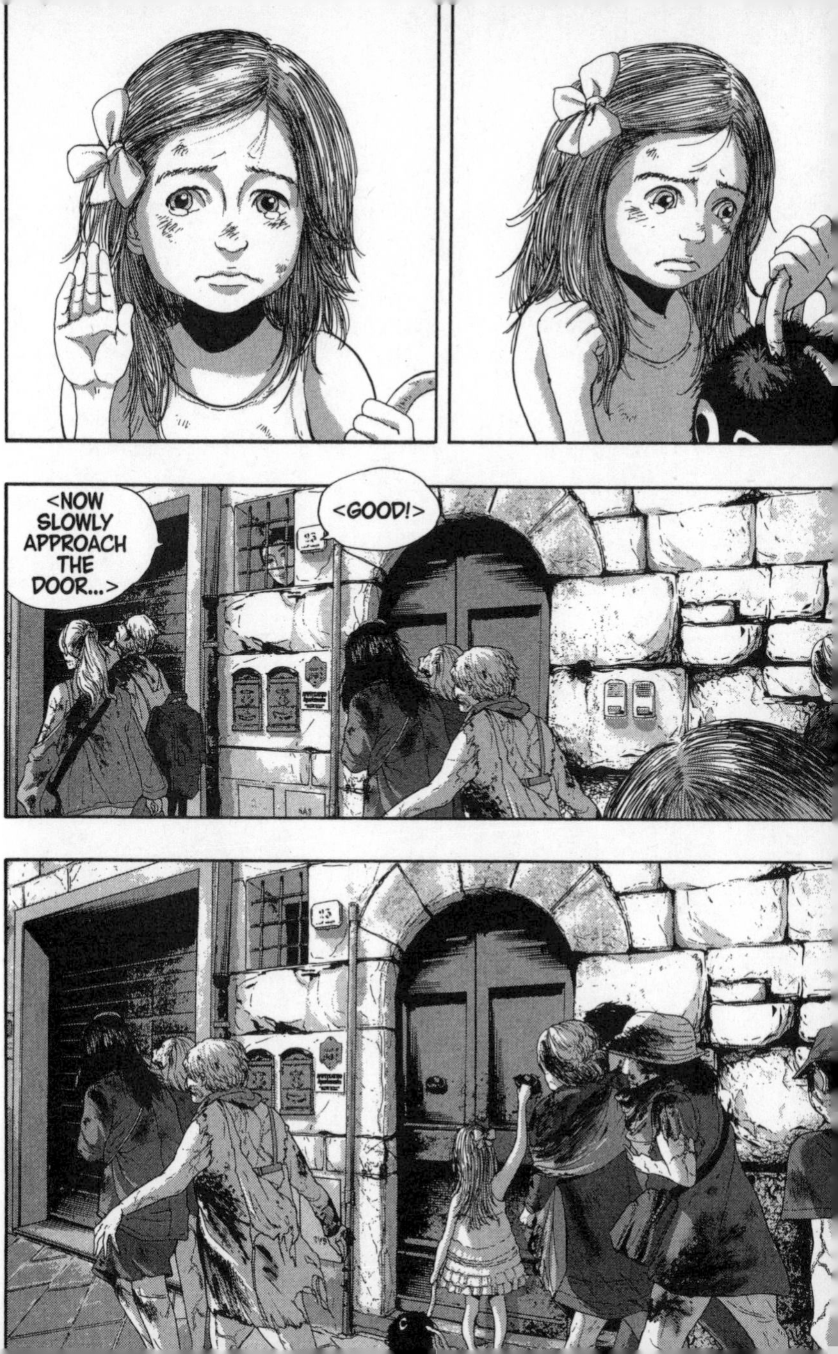
<GOOD!>
<NOW SLOWLY APPROACH THE DOOR...>

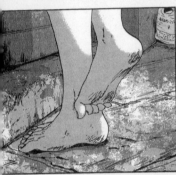

CREAK

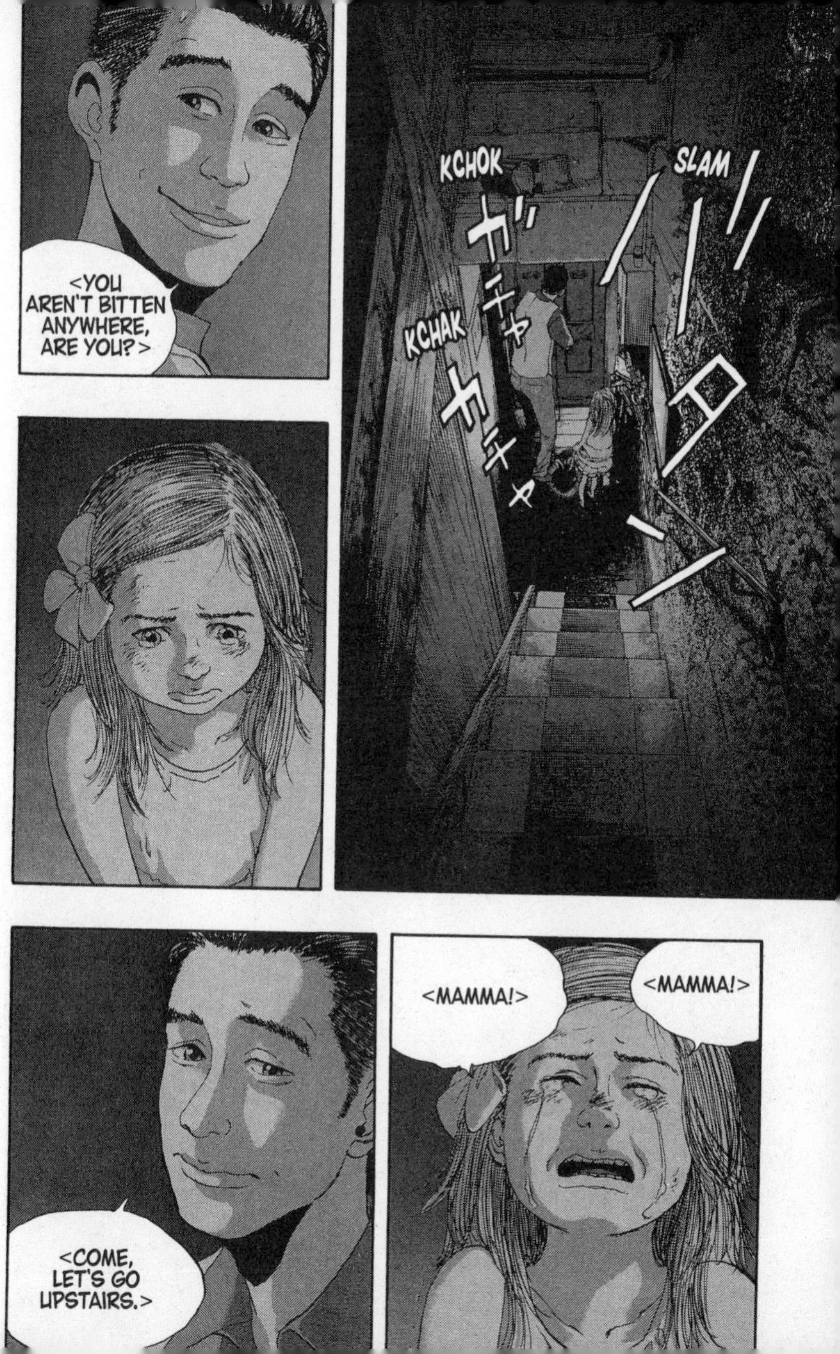
SLAM
KCHOK
KCHAK
<YOU AREN'T BITTEN ANYWHERE, ARE YOU?>
<MAMMA!>
<MAMMA!>
<COME, LET'S GO UPSTAIRS.>

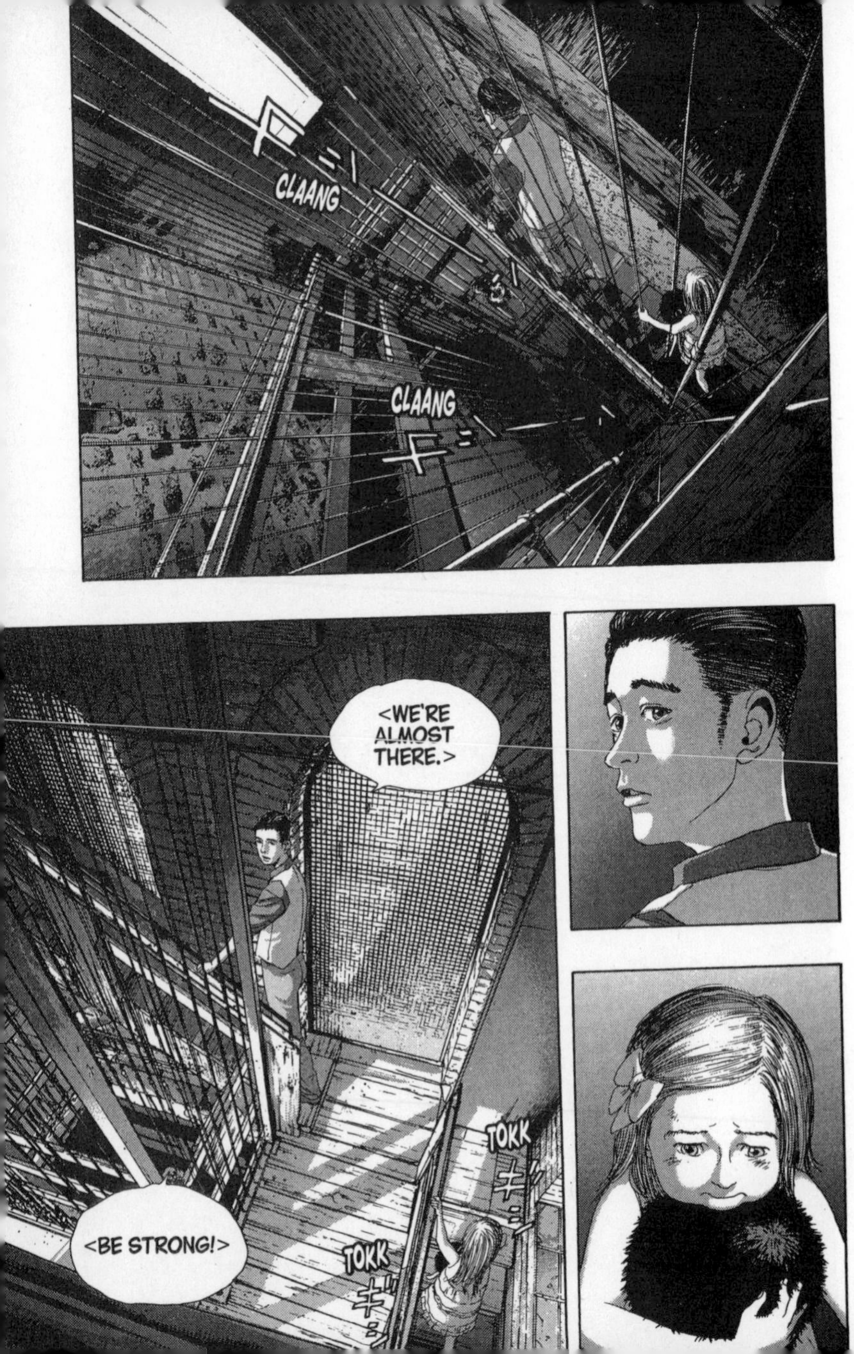
CLAANG
CLAANG
<WE'RE ALMOST THERE.>
TOKK
<BE STRONG!>
TOKK

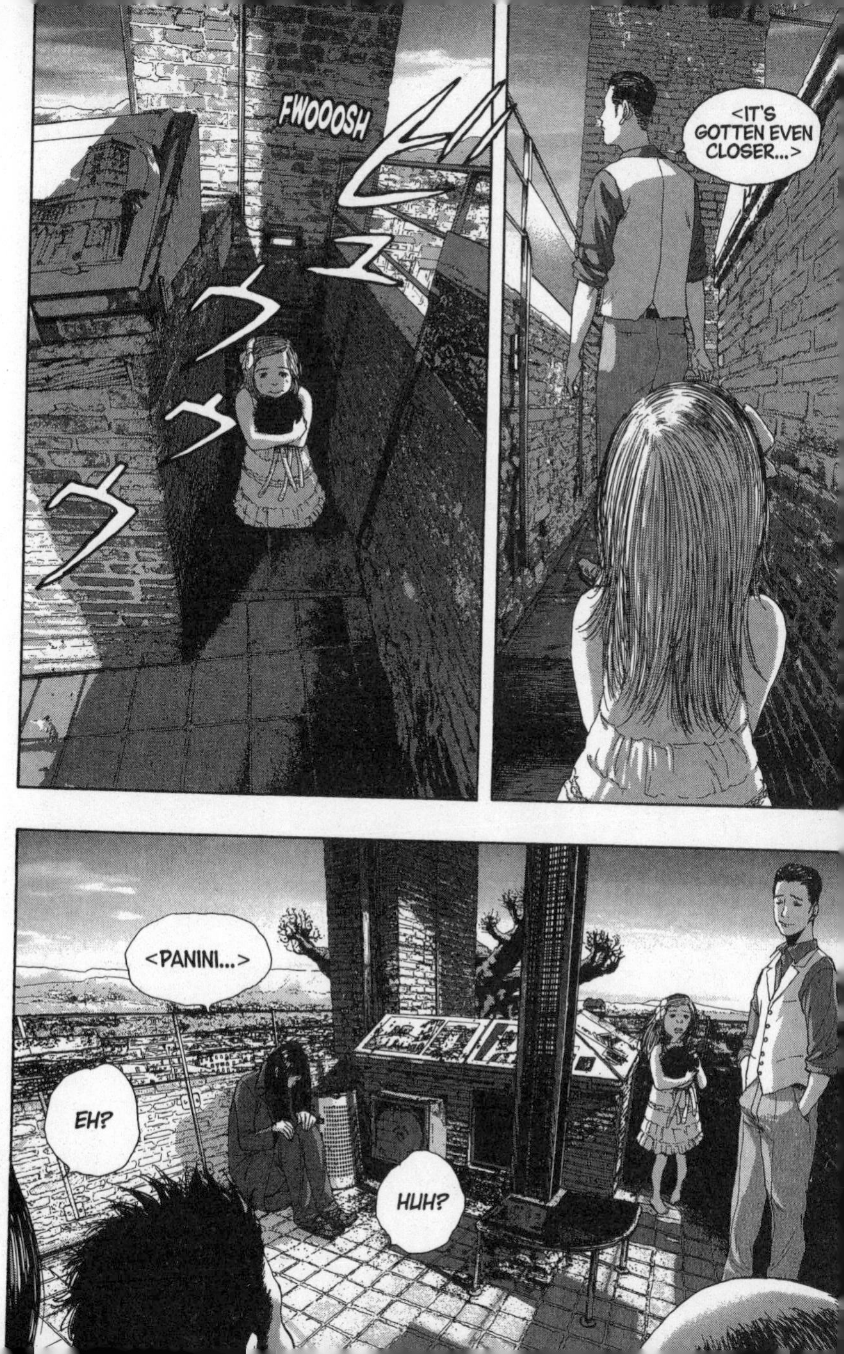
<IT'S GOTTEN EVEN CLOSER...>
FWOOOSH
ヒュウウウ
<PANINI...>
EH?
HUH?

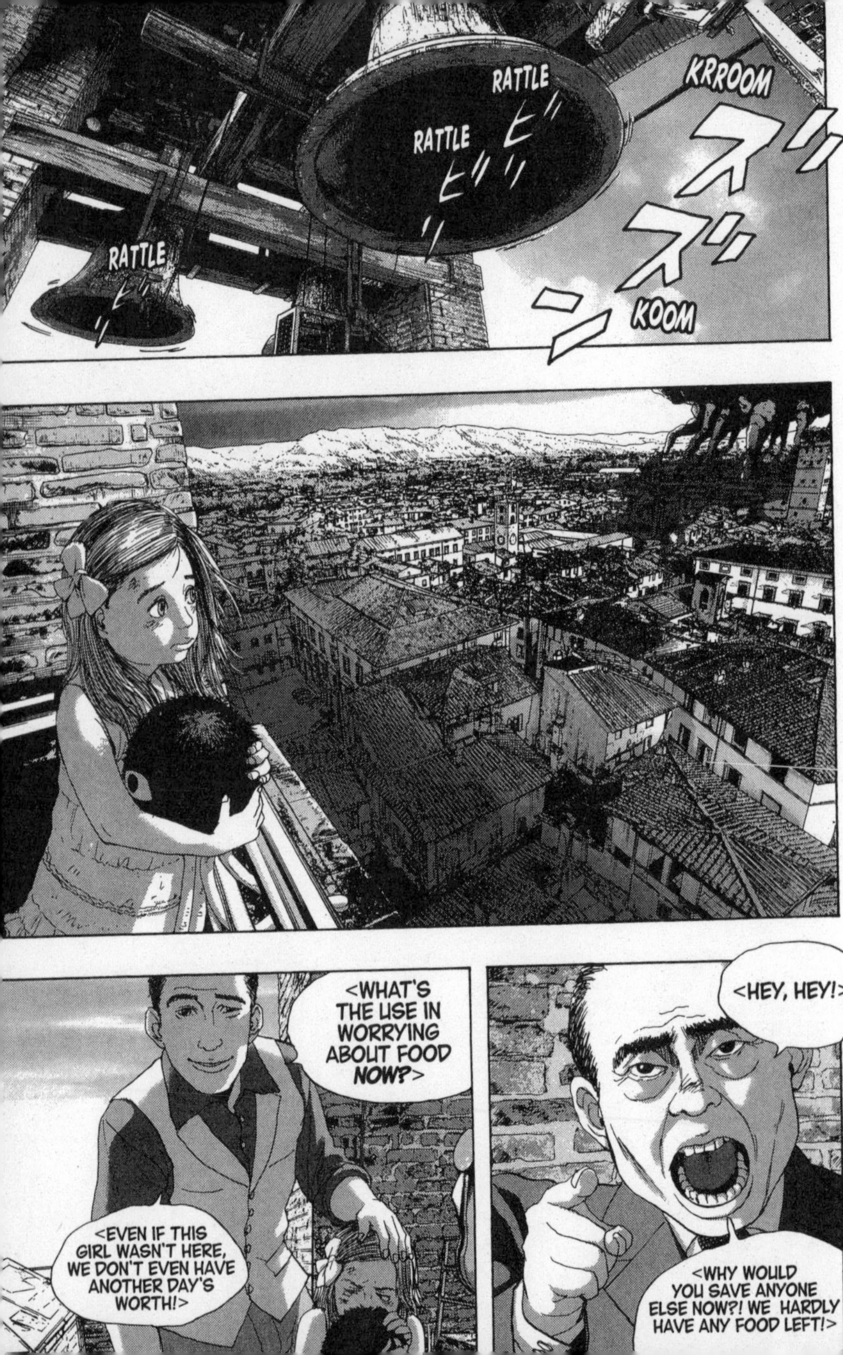
KRROOM
KOOM
RATTLE
RATTLE
RATTLE
<HEY, HEY!>
<WHY WOULD YOU SAVE ANYONE ELSE NOW?! WE HARDLY HAVE ANY FOOD LEFT!>
<WHAT'S THE USE IN WORRYING ABOUT FOOD *NOW?*>
<EVEN IF THIS GIRL WASN'T HERE, WE DON'T EVEN HAVE ANOTHER DAY'S WORTH!>

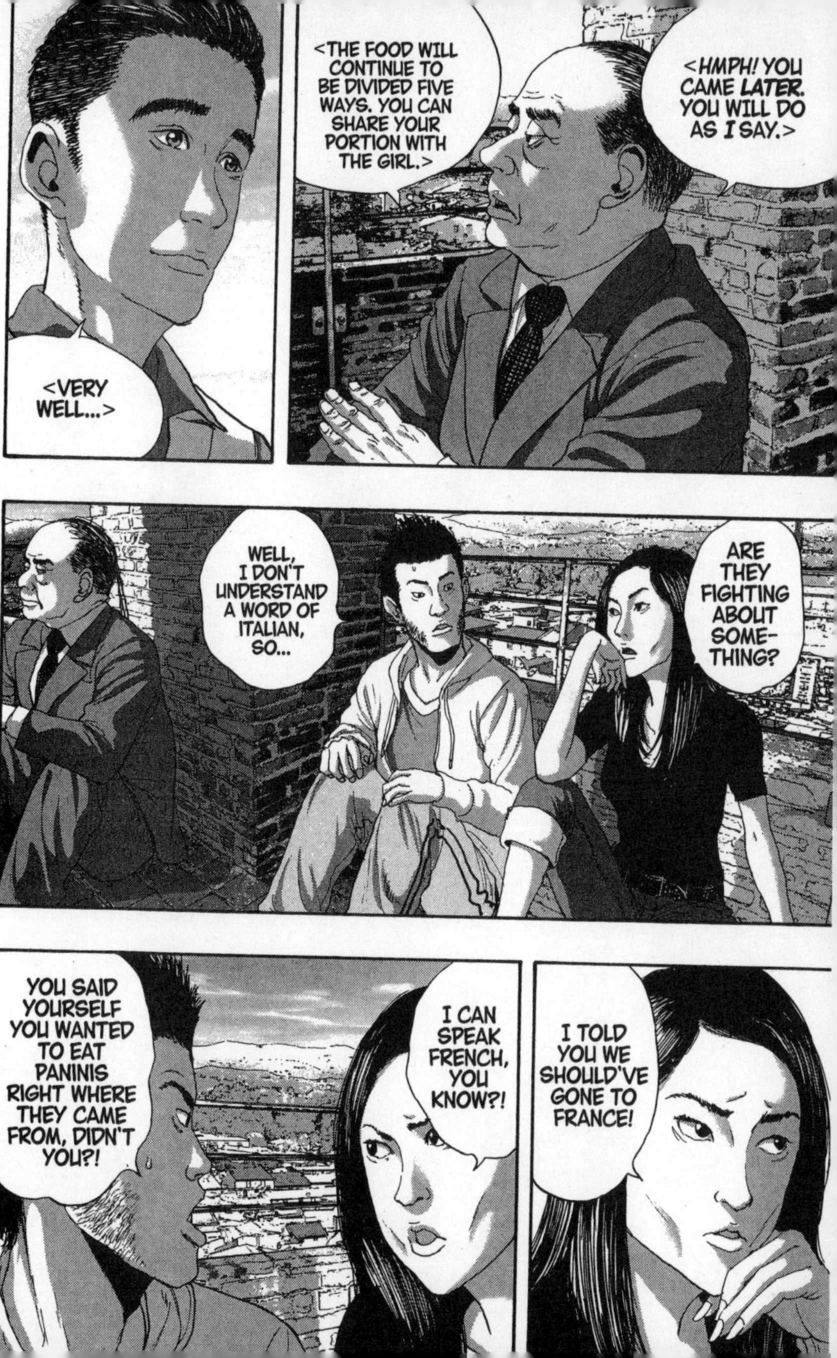
<HMPH! YOU CAME LATER. YOU WILL DO AS I SAY.>
<THE FOOD WILL CONTINUE TO BE DIVIDED FIVE WAYS. YOU CAN SHARE YOUR PORTION WITH THE GIRL.>
<VERY WELL...>
ARE THEY FIGHTING ABOUT SOME-THING?
WELL, I DON'T UNDERSTAND A WORD OF ITALIAN, SO...
I TOLD YOU WE SHOULD'VE GONE TO FRANCE!
I CAN SPEAK FRENCH, YOU KNOW?!
YOU SAID YOURSELF YOU WANTED TO EAT PANINIS RIGHT WHERE THEY CAME FROM, DIDN'T YOU?!

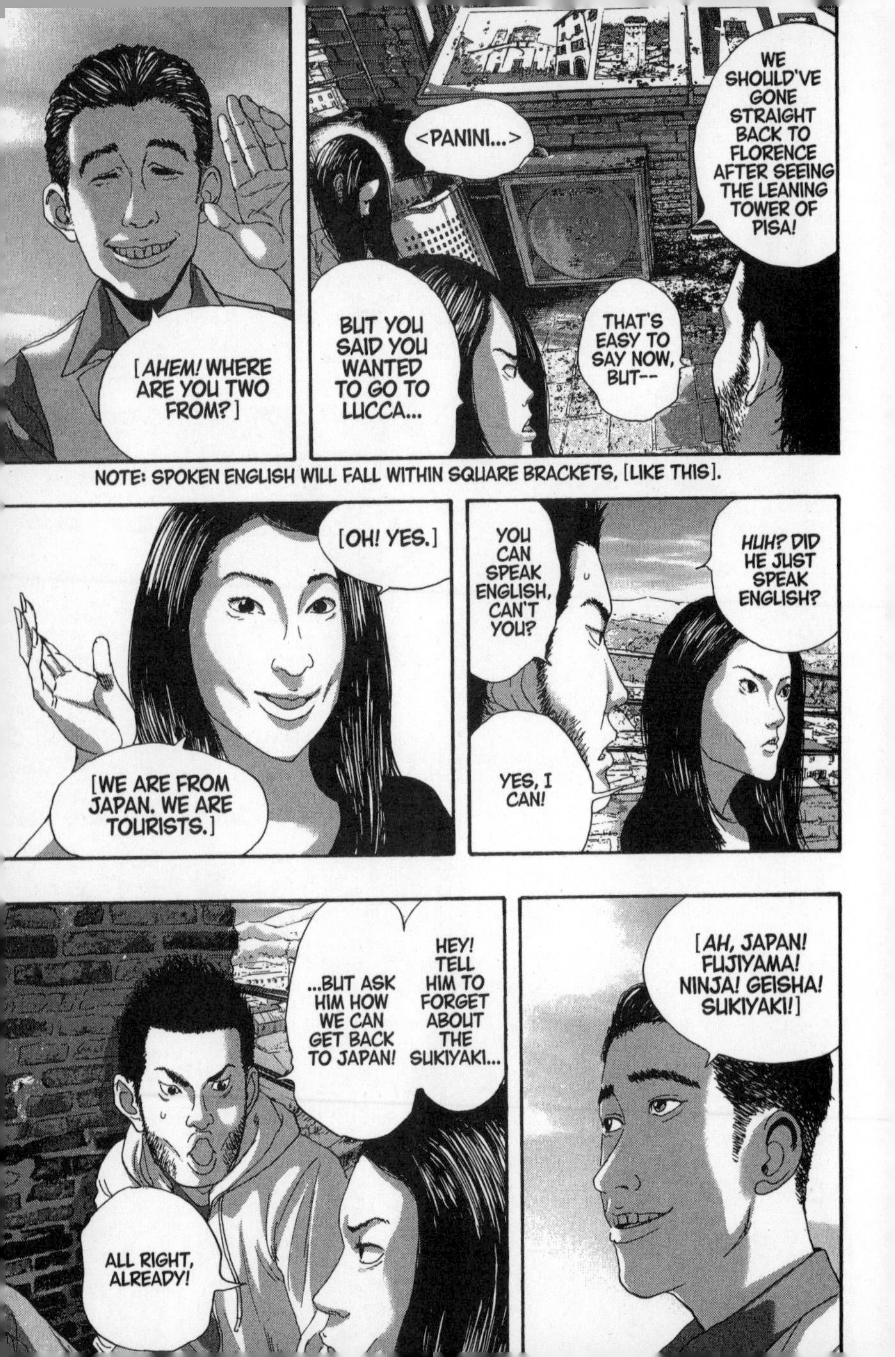
WE SHOULD'VE GONE STRAIGHT BACK TO FLORENCE AFTER SEEING THE LEANING TOWER OF PISA!
<PANINI...>
THAT'S EASY TO SAY NOW, BUT--
BUT YOU SAID YOU WANTED TO GO TO LUCCA...
[AHEM! WHERE ARE YOU TWO FROM?]
NOTE: SPOKEN ENGLISH WILL FALL WITHIN SQUARE BRACKETS, [LIKE THIS].
HUH? DID HE JUST SPEAK ENGLISH?
YOU CAN SPEAK ENGLISH, CAN'T YOU?
YES, I CAN!
[OH! YES.]
[WE ARE FROM JAPAN. WE ARE TOURISTS.]
[AH, JAPAN! FUJIYAMA! NINJA! GEISHA! SUKIYAKI!]
HEY! TELL HIM TO FORGET ABOUT THE SUKIYAKI...
...BUT ASK HIM HOW WE CAN GET BACK TO JAPAN!
ALL RIGHT, ALREADY!

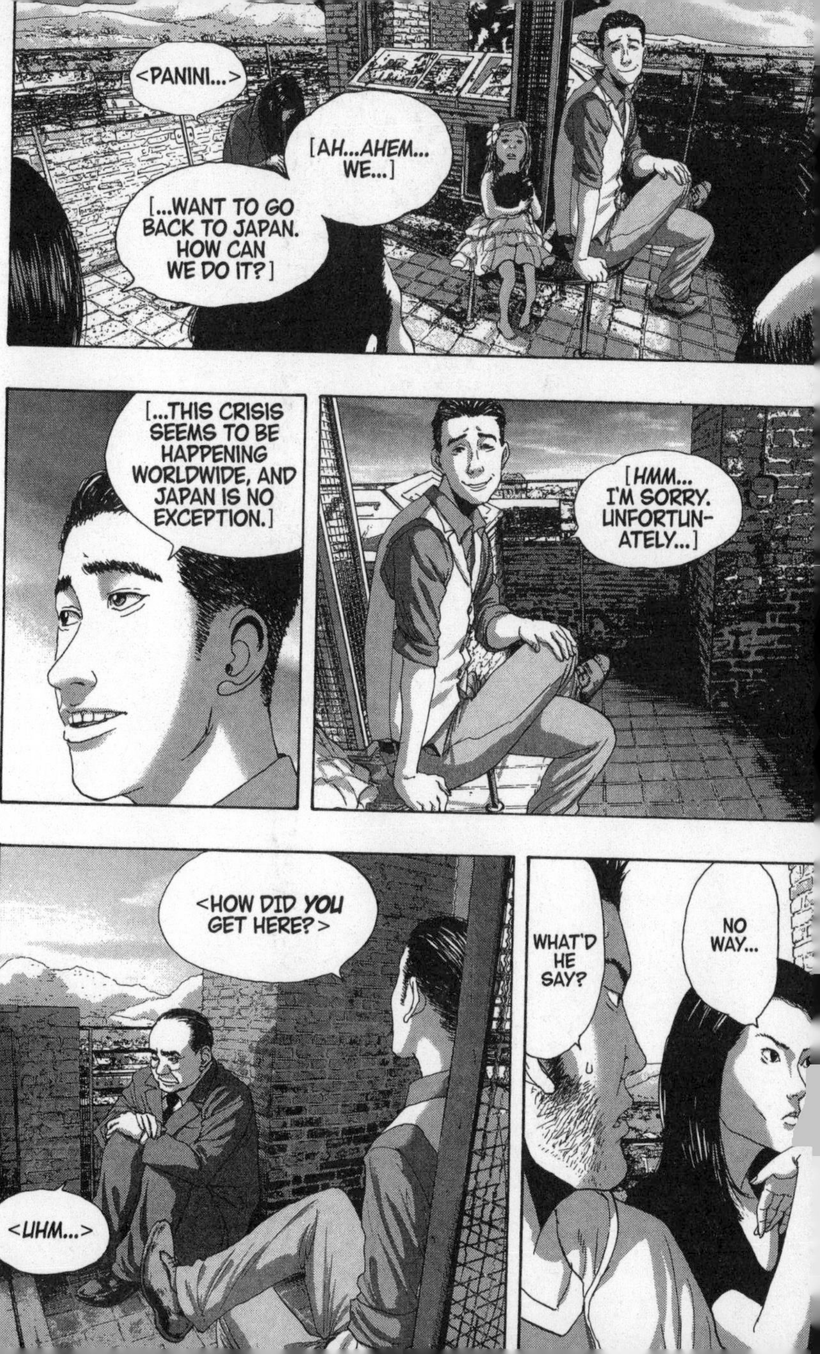
<PANINI...>
[AH...AHEM... WE...]
[...WANT TO GO BACK TO JAPAN. HOW CAN WE DO IT?]
[HMM... I'M SORRY. UNFORTUNATELY...]
[...THIS CRISIS SEEMS TO BE HAPPENING WORLDWIDE, AND JAPAN IS NO EXCEPTION.]
NO WAY...
WHAT'D HE SAY?
<HOW DID *YOU* GET HERE?>
<UHM...>

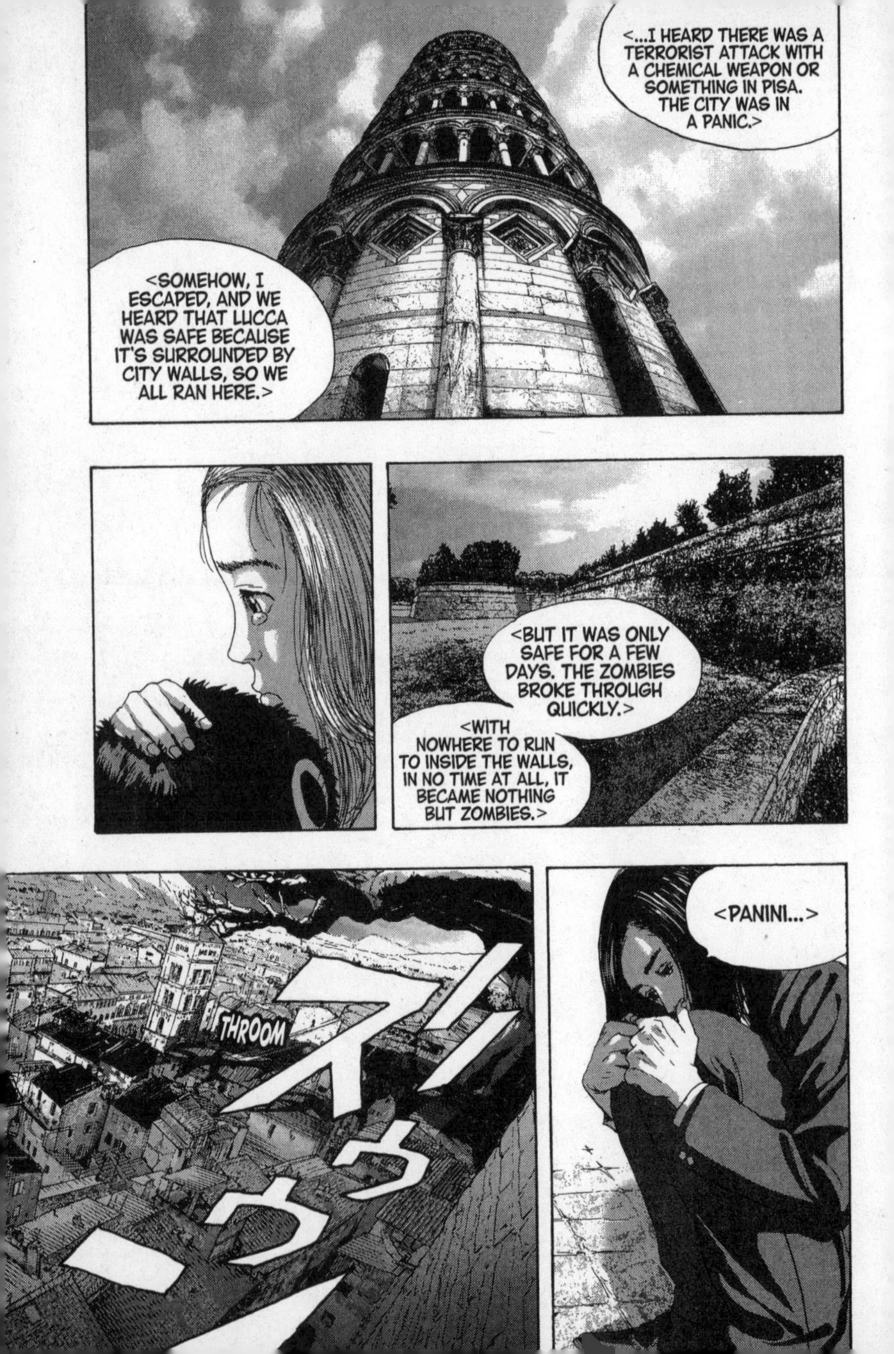
<...I HEARD THERE WAS A TERRORIST ATTACK WITH A CHEMICAL WEAPON OR SOMETHING IN PISA. THE CITY WAS IN A PANIC.>
<SOMEHOW, I ESCAPED, AND WE HEARD THAT LUCCA WAS SAFE BECAUSE IT'S SURROUNDED BY CITY WALLS, SO WE ALL RAN HERE.>
<BUT IT WAS ONLY SAFE FOR A FEW DAYS. THE ZOMBIES BROKE THROUGH QUICKLY.>
<WITH NOWHERE TO RUN TO INSIDE THE WALLS, IN NO TIME AT ALL, IT BECAME NOTHING BUT ZOMBIES.>
<PANINI...>
THROOM

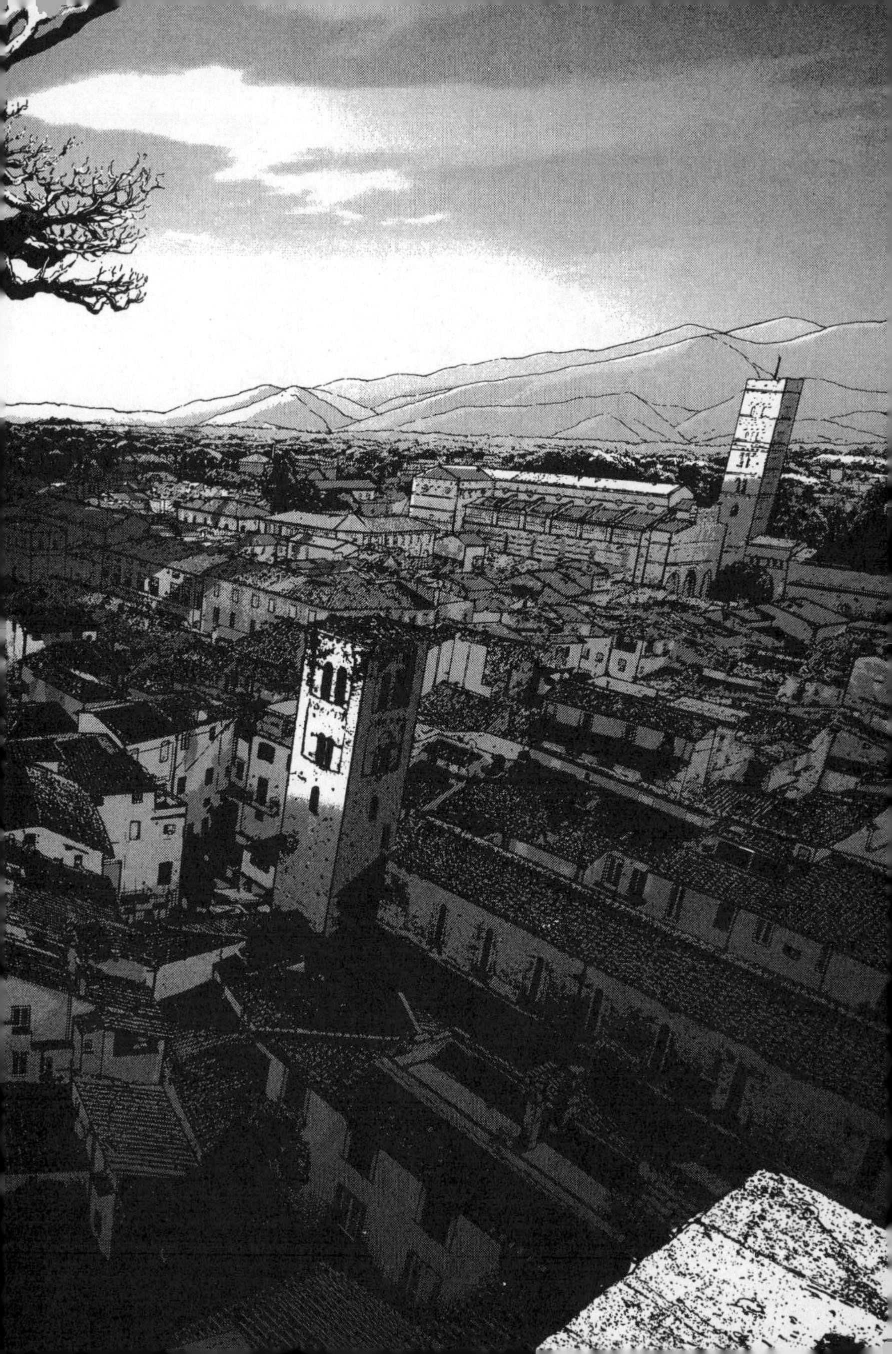

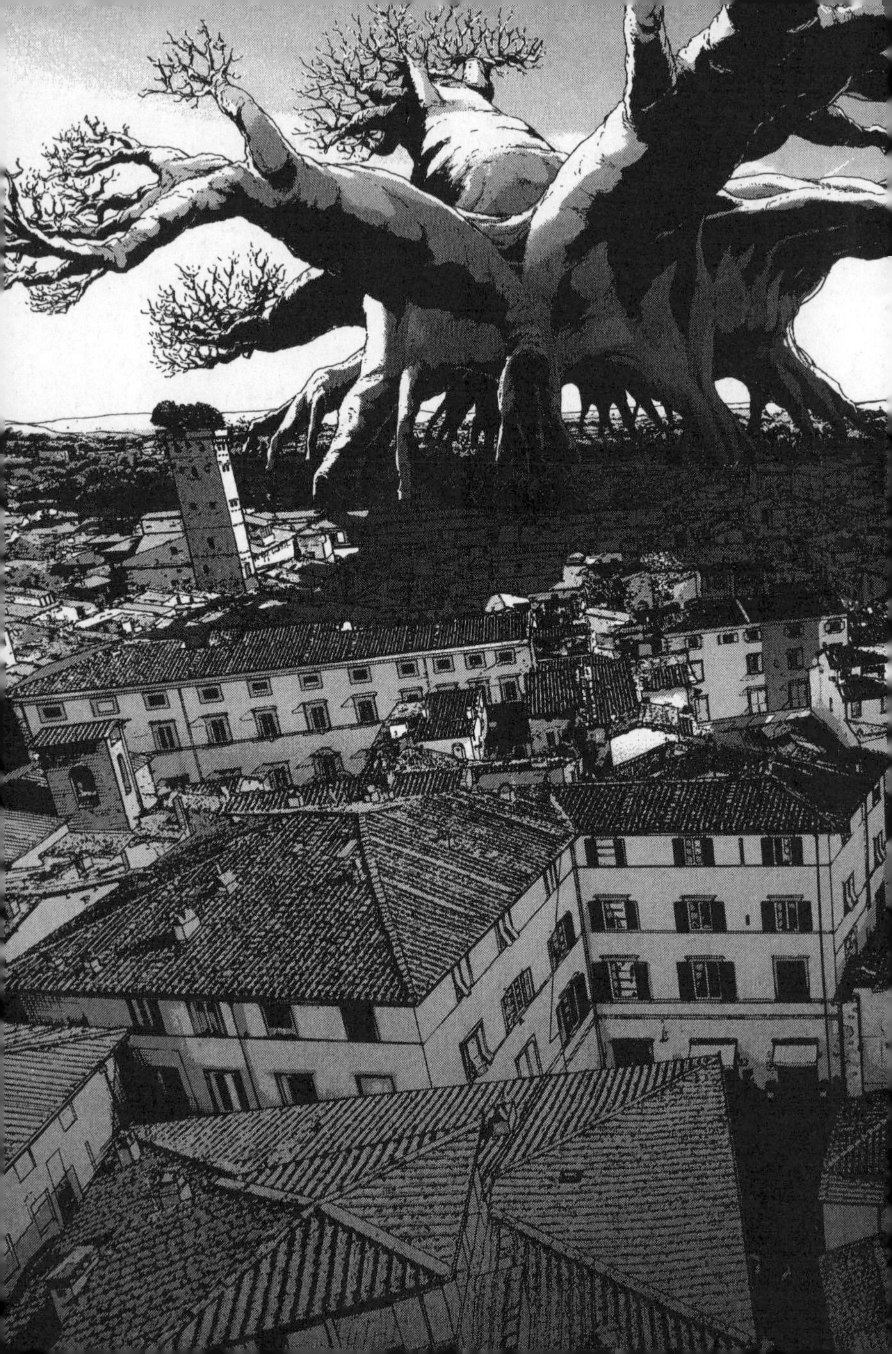

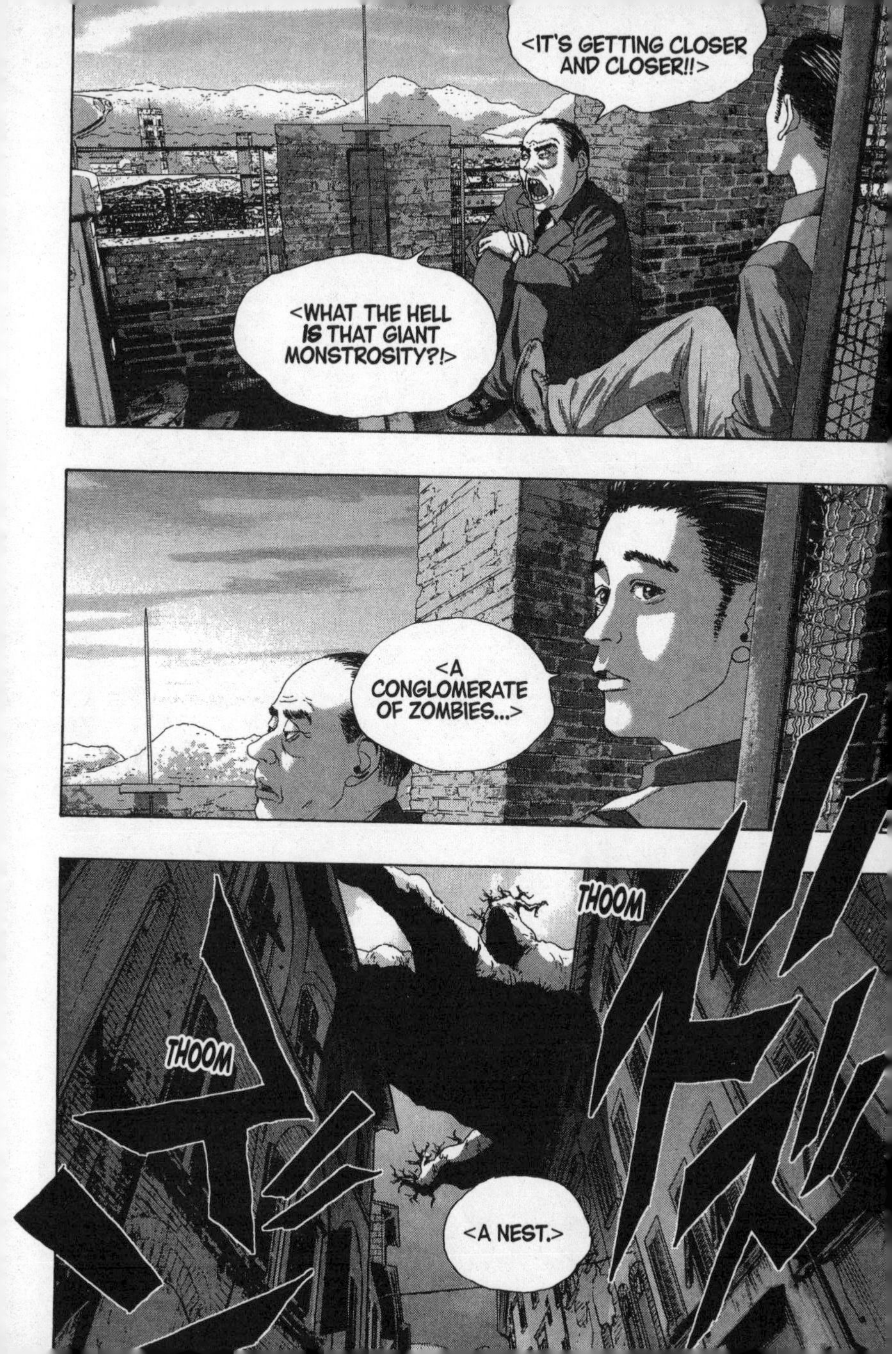
<IT'S GETTING CLOSER AND CLOSER!!>
<WHAT THE HELL *IS* THAT GIANT MONSTROSITY?!>
<A CONGLOMERATE OF ZOMBIES...>
THOOM
THOOM
<A NEST.>

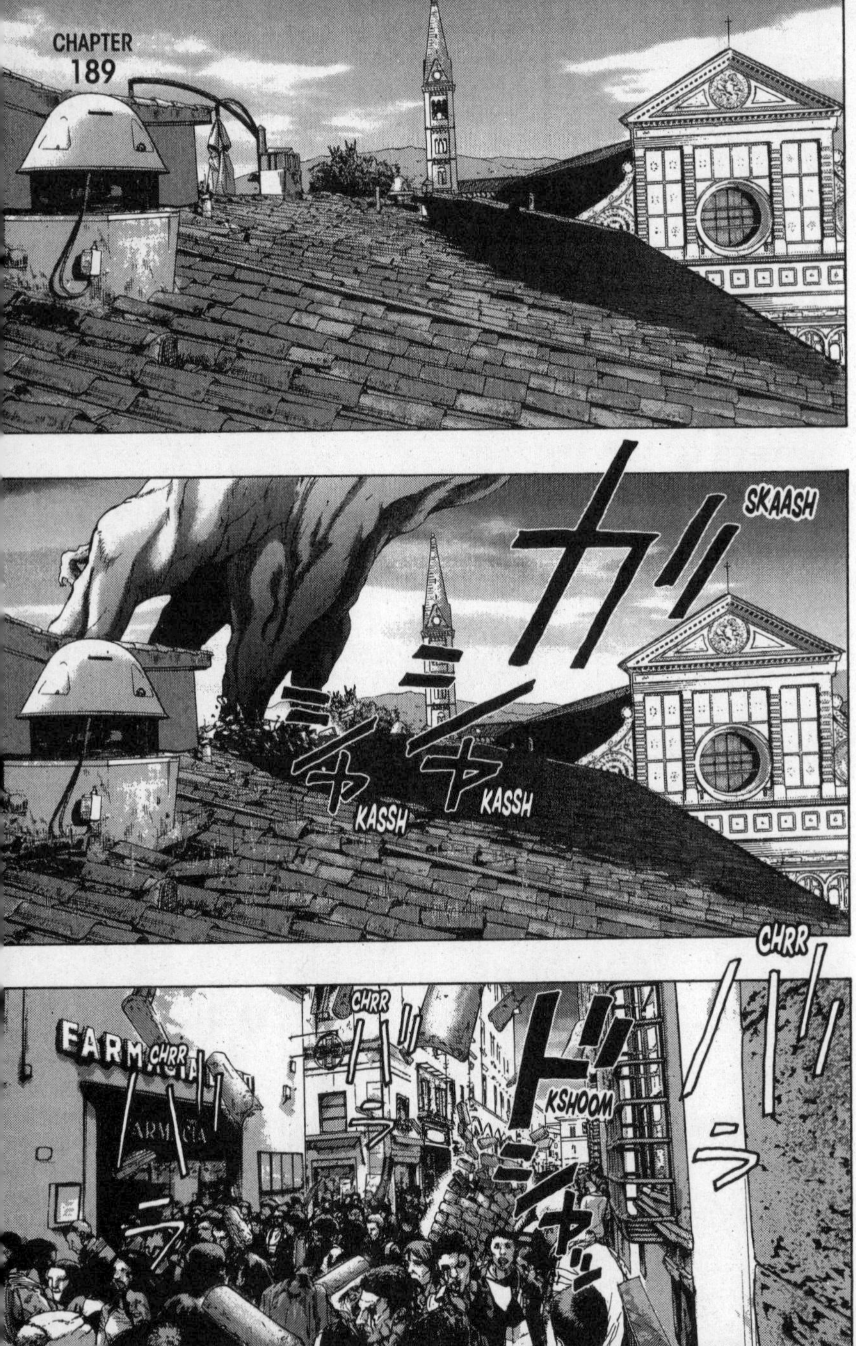
CHAPTER
189
SKAASH
KASSH
KASSH
CHRR
KSHOOM
CHRR
CHRR

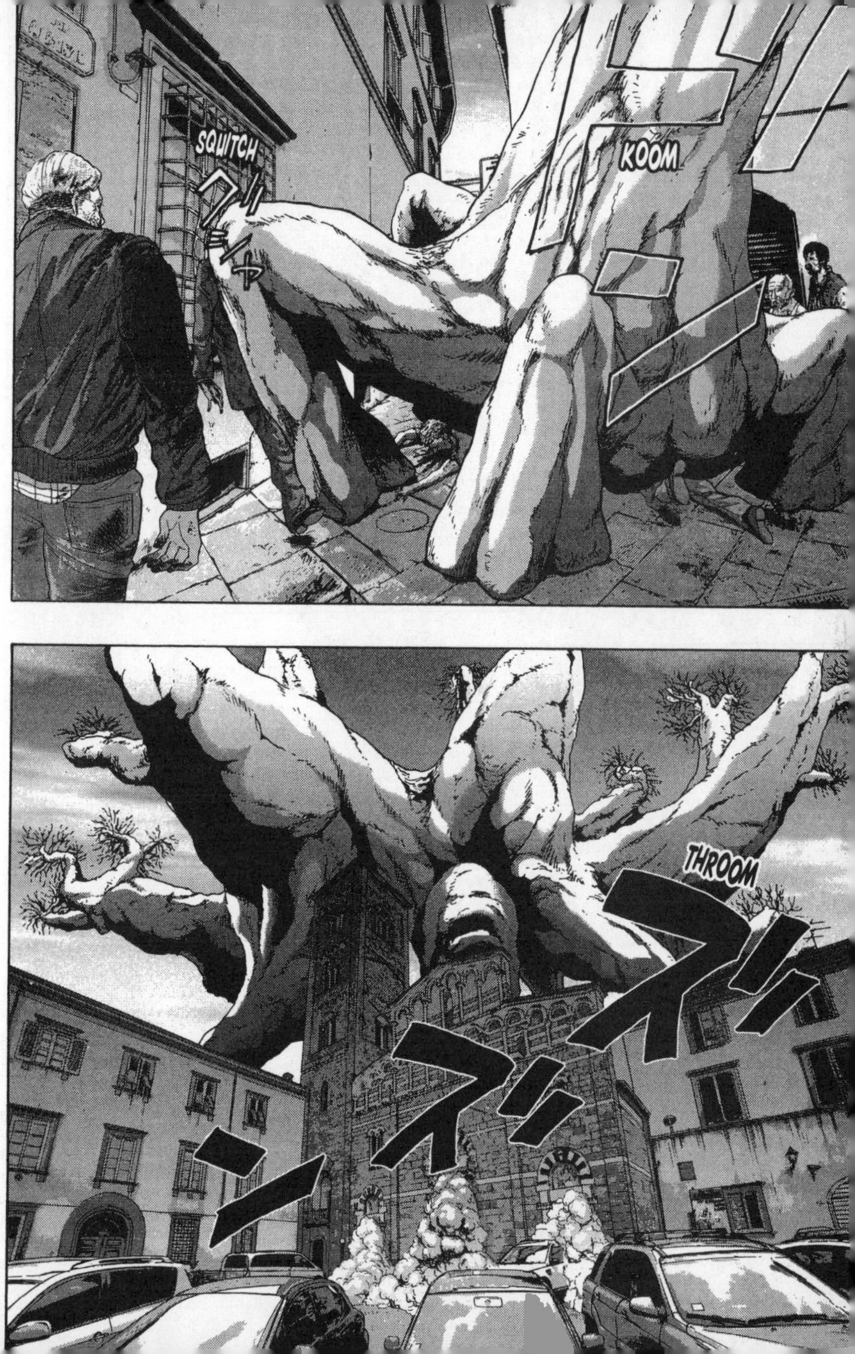
KOOM
SQUITCH
THROOM

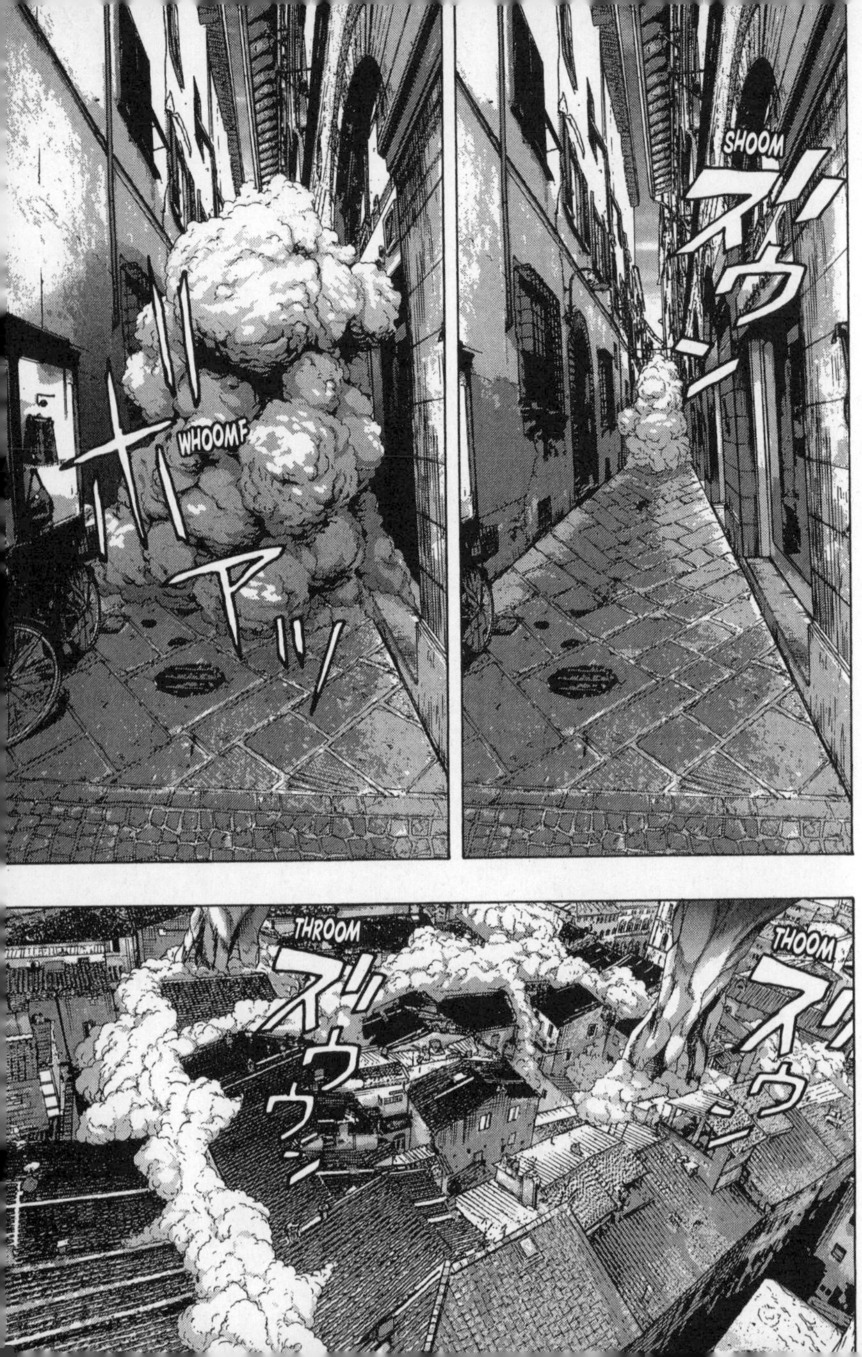
SHOOM
WHOOMF
THOOM
THROOM

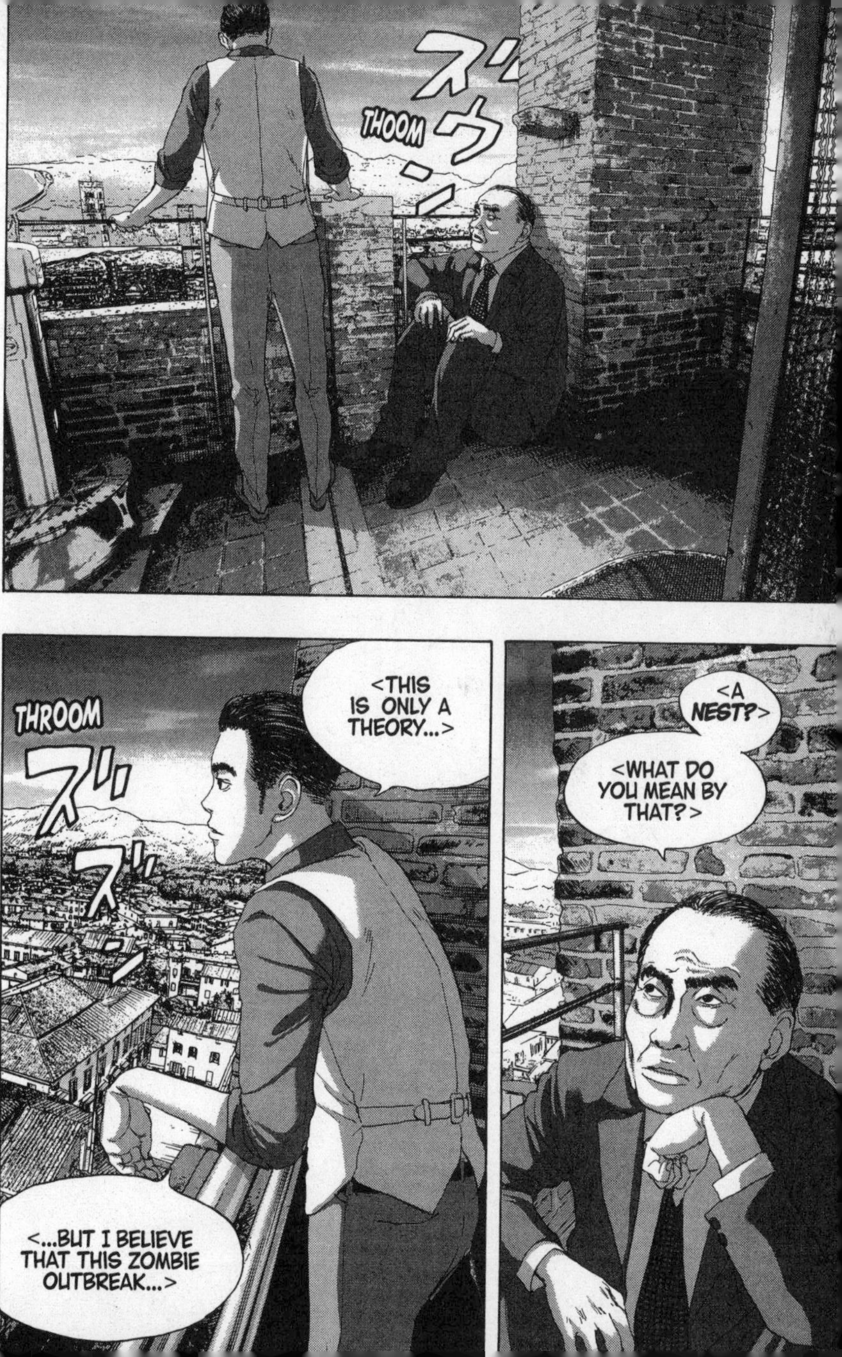
THOOM
<A NEST?>
<WHAT DO YOU MEAN BY THAT?>
THROOM
<THIS IS ONLY A THEORY...>
<...BUT I BELIEVE THAT THIS ZOMBIE OUTBREAK...>

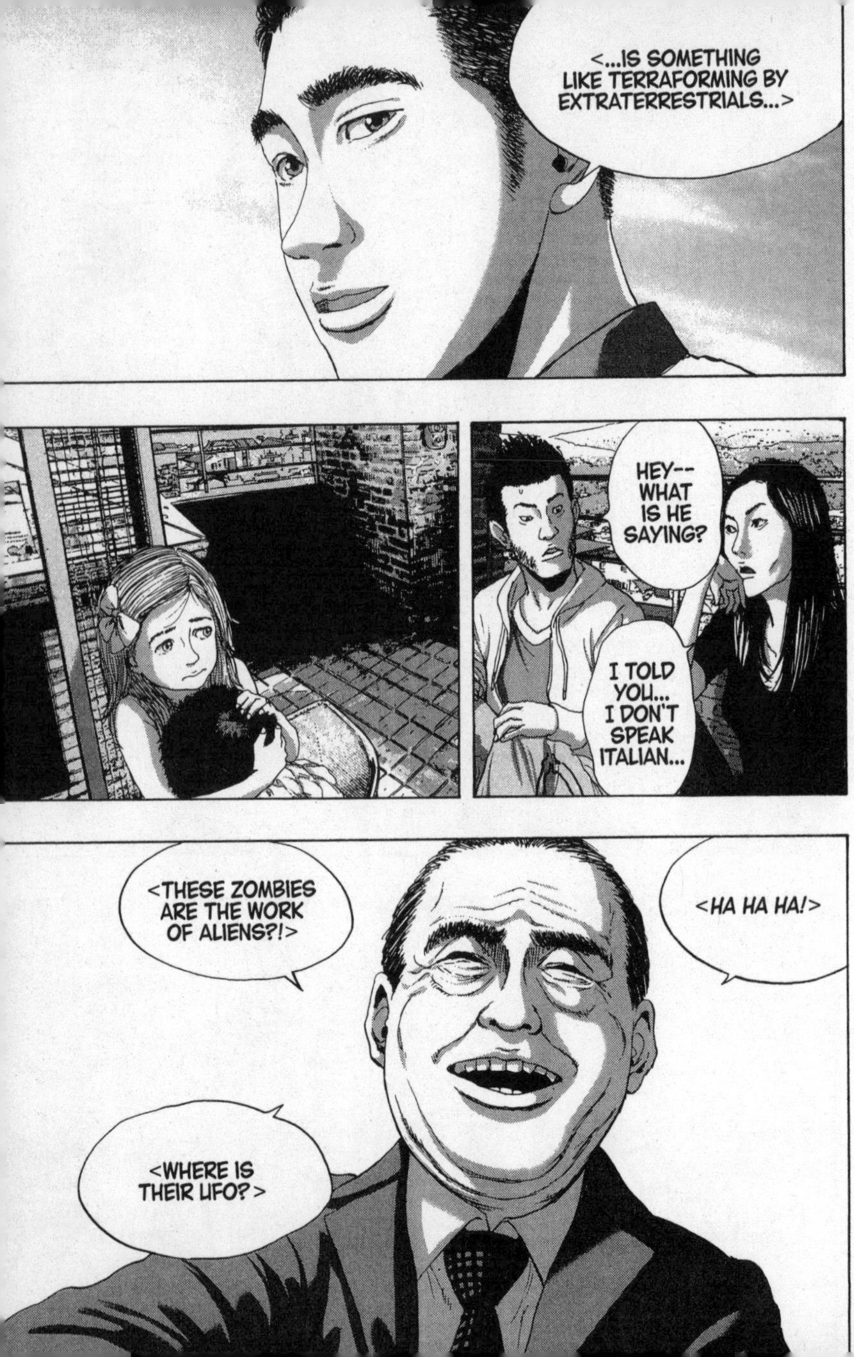
<...IS SOMETHING LIKE TERRAFORMING BY EXTRATERRESTRIALS...>
HEY-- WHAT IS HE SAYING?
I TOLD YOU... I DON'T SPEAK ITALIAN...
<HA HA HA!>
<THESE ZOMBIES ARE THE WORK OF ALIENS?!>
<WHERE IS THEIR UFO?>

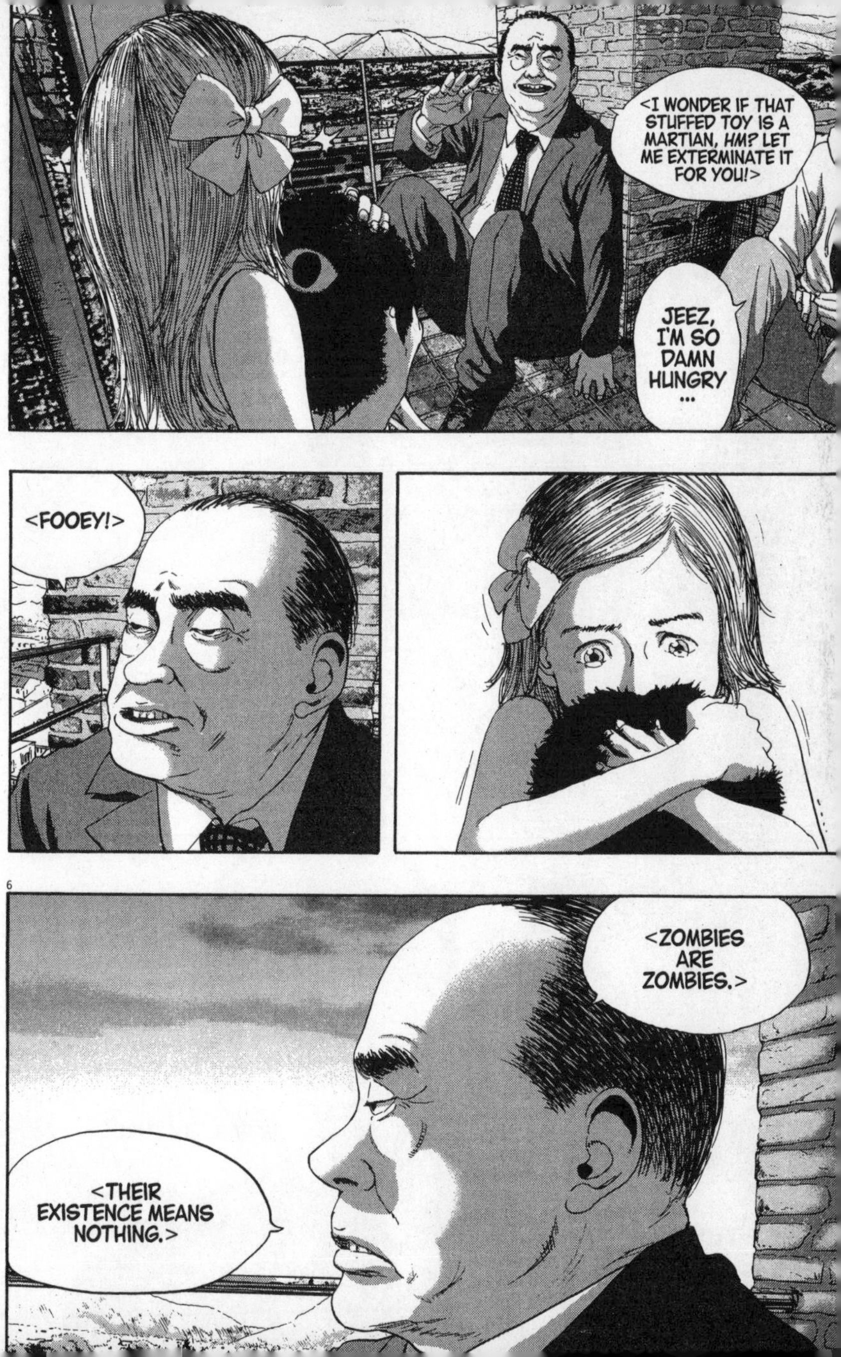

<I WONDER IF THAT STUFFED TOY IS A MARTIAN, *HM?* LET ME EXTERMINATE IT FOR YOU!>
JEEZ, I'M SO DAMN HUNGRY ...
<FOOEY!>
<ZOMBIES ARE ZOMBIES.>
<THEIR EXISTENCE MEANS NOTHING.>

6

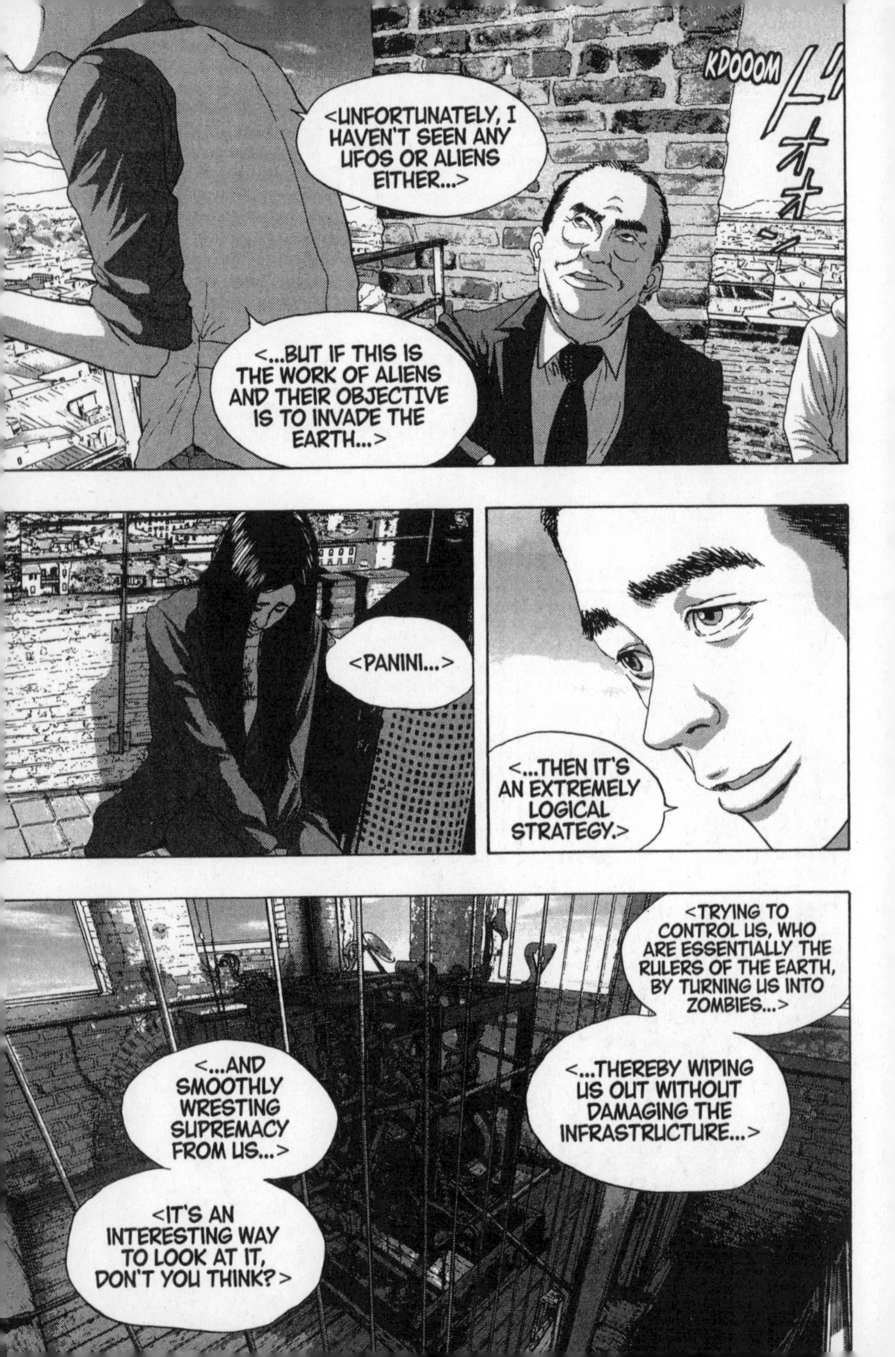
KDOOOM
<UNFORTUNATELY, I HAVEN'T SEEN ANY UFOS OR ALIENS EITHER...>
<...BUT IF THIS IS THE WORK OF ALIENS AND THEIR OBJECTIVE IS TO INVADE THE EARTH...>
<...THEN IT'S AN EXTREMELY LOGICAL STRATEGY.>
<PANINI...>
<TRYING TO CONTROL US, WHO ARE ESSENTIALLY THE RULERS OF THE EARTH, BY TURNING US INTO ZOMBIES...>
<...THEREBY WIPING US OUT WITHOUT DAMAGING THE INFRASTRUCTURE...>
<...AND SMOOTHLY WRESTING SUPREMACY FROM US...>
<IT'S AN INTERESTING WAY TO LOOK AT IT, DON'T YOU THINK?>

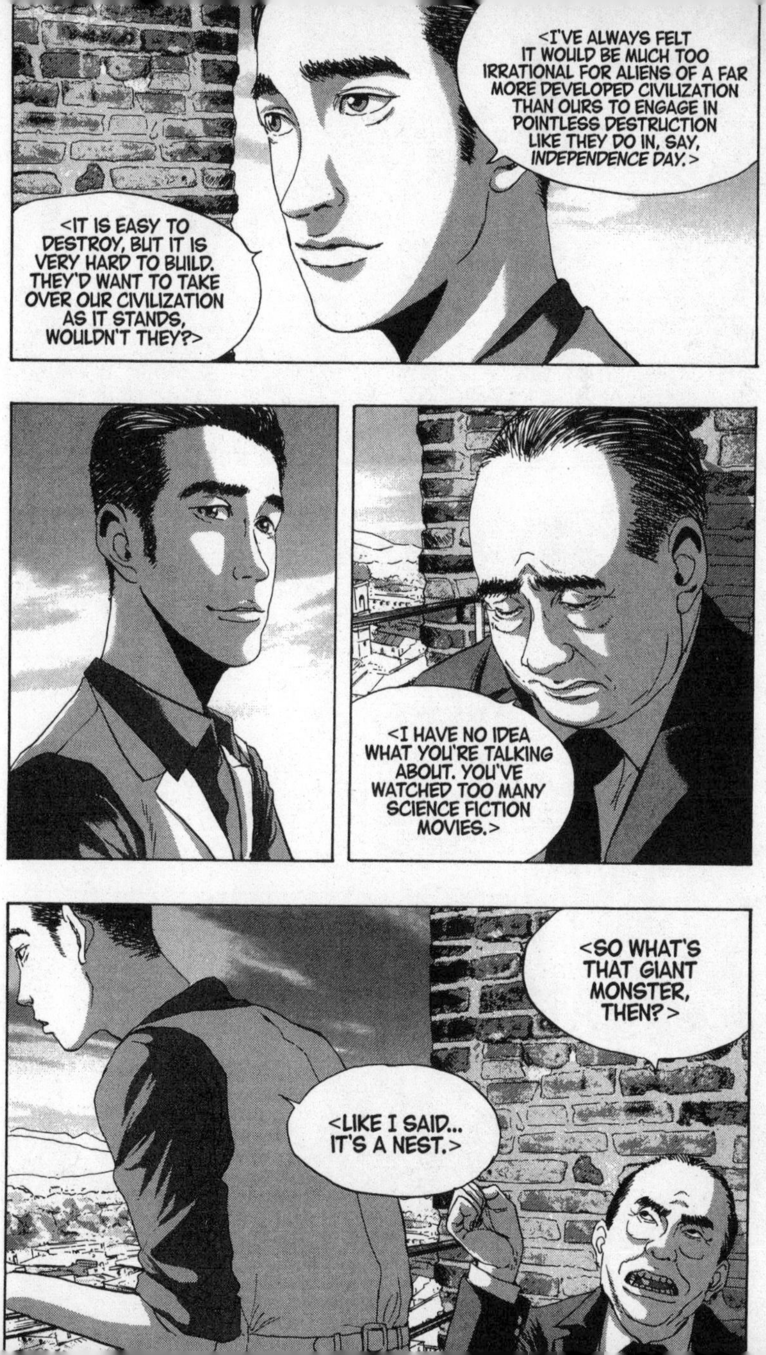
<I'VE ALWAYS FELT IT WOULD BE MUCH TOO IRRATIONAL FOR ALIENS OF A FAR MORE DEVELOPED CIVILIZATION THAN OURS TO ENGAGE IN POINTLESS DESTRUCTION LIKE THEY DO IN, SAY, INDEPENDENCE DAY.>
<IT IS EASY TO DESTROY, BUT IT IS VERY HARD TO BUILD. THEY'D WANT TO TAKE OVER OUR CIVILIZATION AS IT STANDS, WOULDN'T THEY?>
<I HAVE NO IDEA WHAT YOU'RE TALKING ABOUT. YOU'VE WATCHED TOO MANY SCIENCE FICTION MOVIES.>
<SO WHAT'S THAT GIANT MONSTER, THEN?>
<LIKE I SAID... IT'S A NEST.>

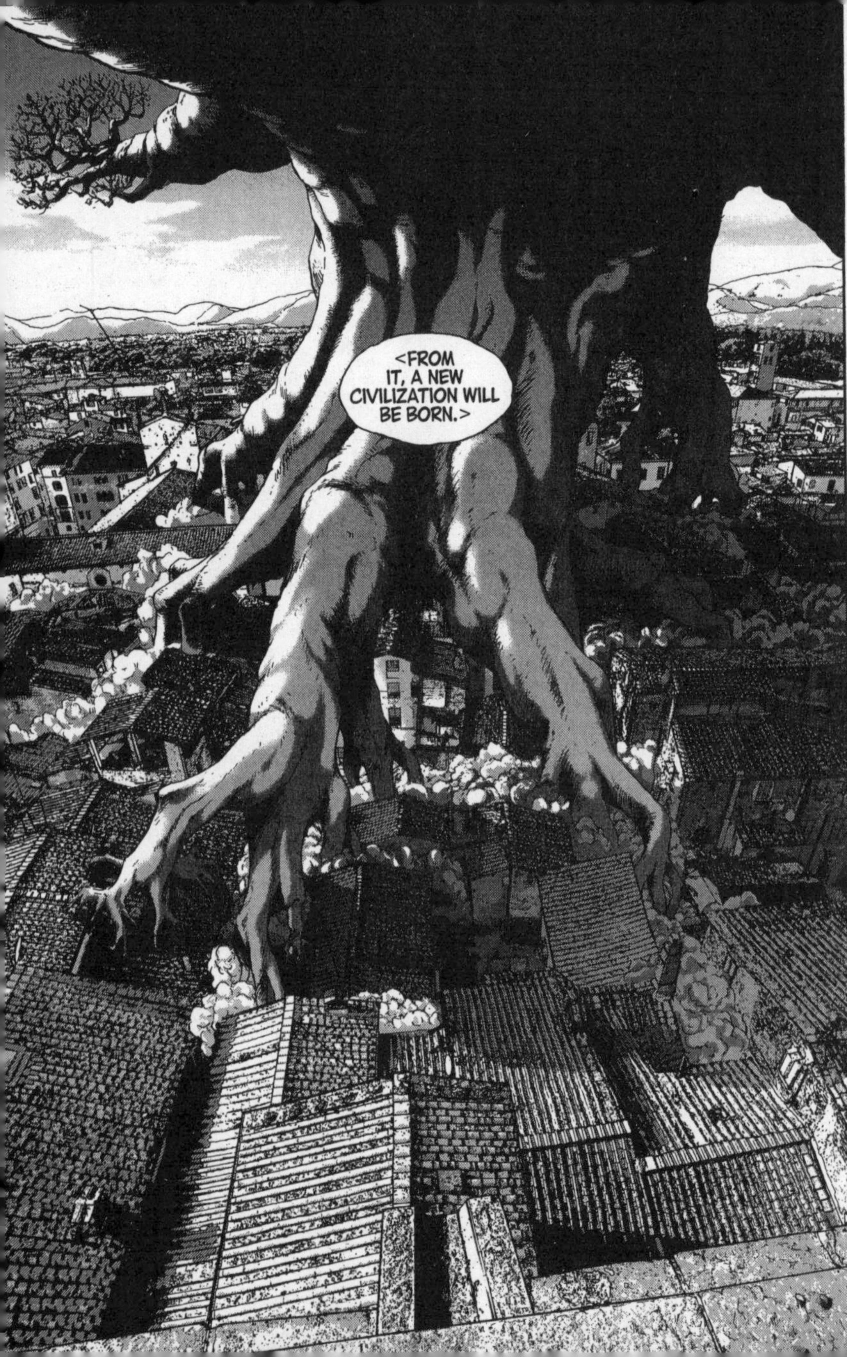
<FROM IT, A NEW CIVILIZATION WILL BE BORN.>

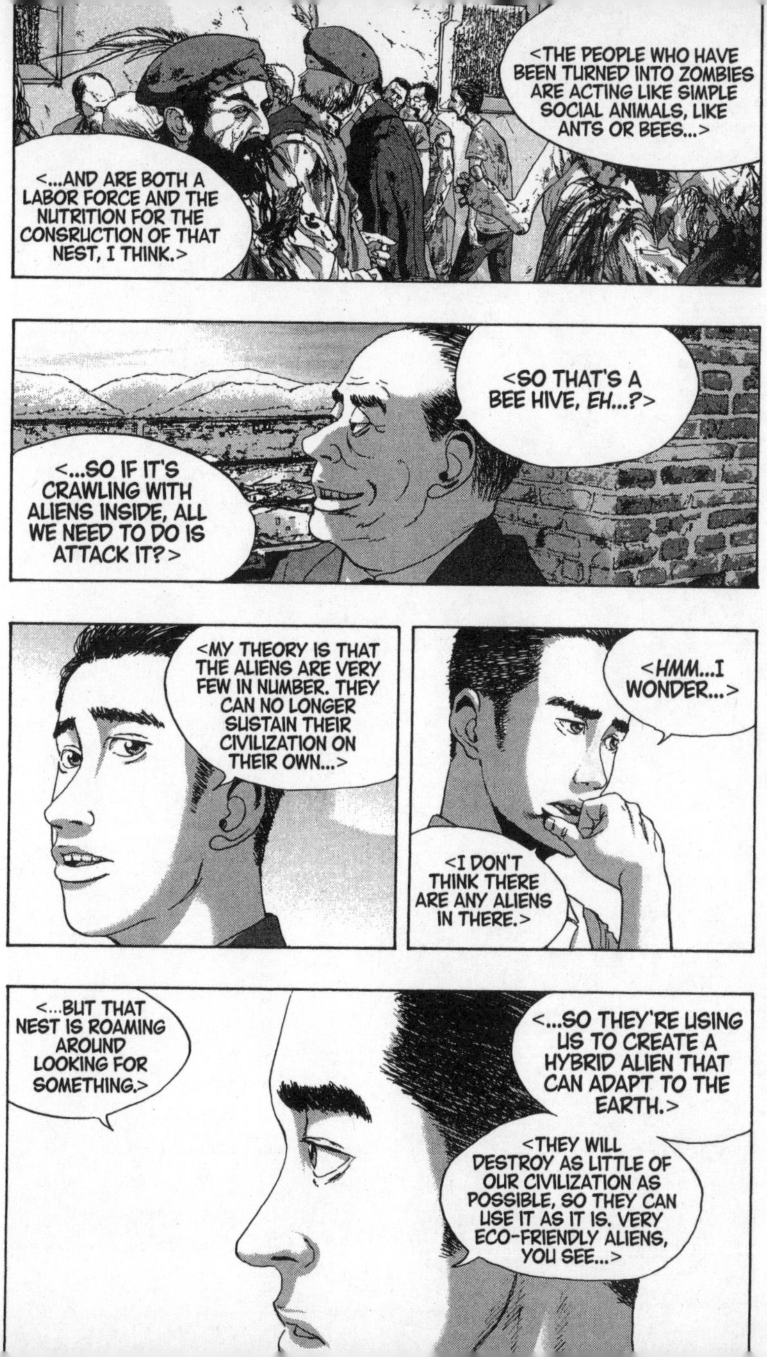
<THE PEOPLE WHO HAVE BEEN TURNED INTO ZOMBIES ARE ACTING LIKE SIMPLE SOCIAL ANIMALS, LIKE ANTS OR BEES...>
<...AND ARE BOTH A LABOR FORCE AND THE NUTRITION FOR THE CONSRUCTION OF THAT NEST, I THINK.>
<SO THAT'S A BEE HIVE, EH...?>
<...SO IF IT'S CRAWLING WITH ALIENS INSIDE, ALL WE NEED TO DO IS ATTACK IT?>
<HMM...I WONDER...>
<I DON'T THINK THERE ARE ANY ALIENS IN THERE.>
<MY THEORY IS THAT THE ALIENS ARE VERY FEW IN NUMBER. THEY CAN NO LONGER SUSTAIN THEIR CIVILIZATION ON THEIR OWN...>
<...SO THEY'RE USING US TO CREATE A HYBRID ALIEN THAT CAN ADAPT TO THE EARTH.>
<THEY WILL DESTROY AS LITTLE OF OUR CIVILIZATION AS POSSIBLE, SO THEY CAN USE IT AS IT IS. VERY ECO-FRIENDLY ALIENS, YOU SEE...>
<...BUT THAT NEST IS ROAMING AROUND LOOKING FOR SOMETHING.>

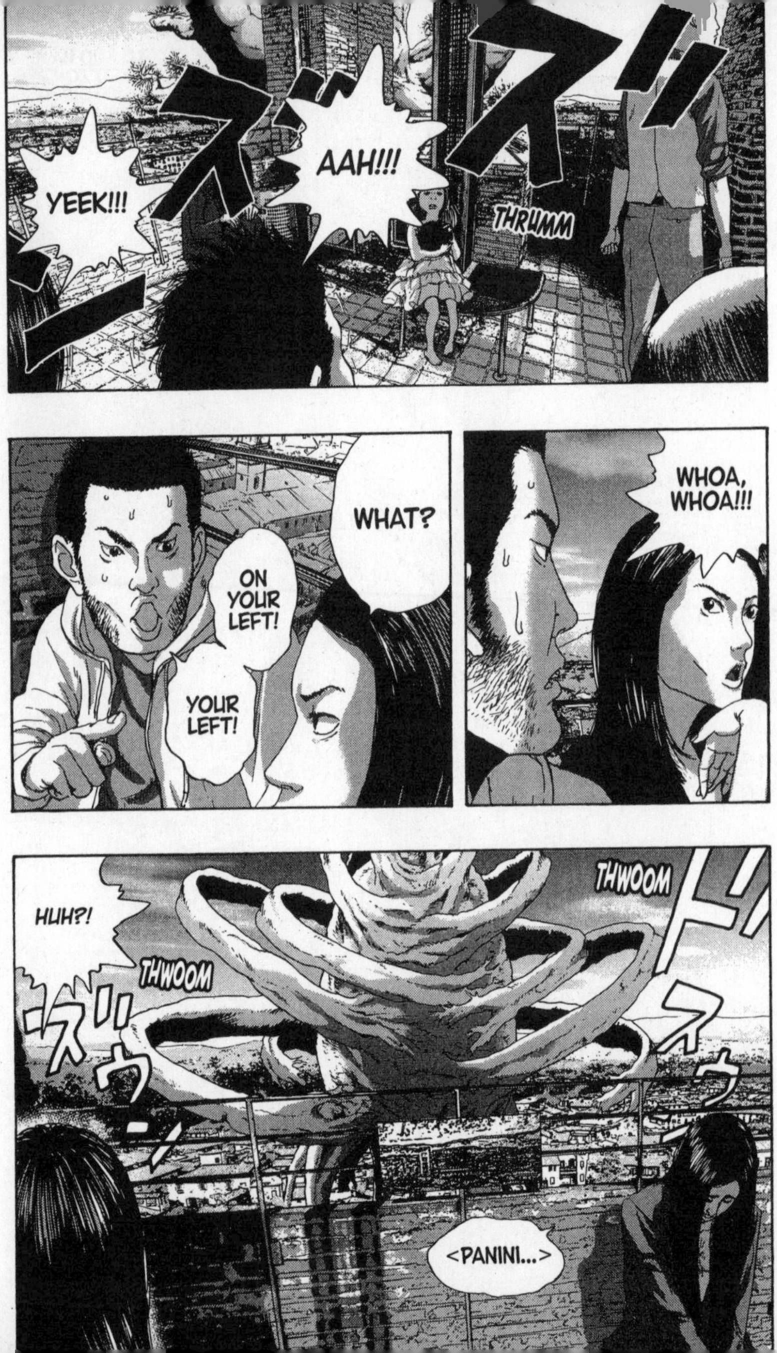
THRUMM
AAH!!!
YEEK!!!
WHOA, WHOA!!!
WHAT?
ON YOUR LEFT!
YOUR LEFT!
THWOOM
HUH?!
THWOOM
<PANINI...>

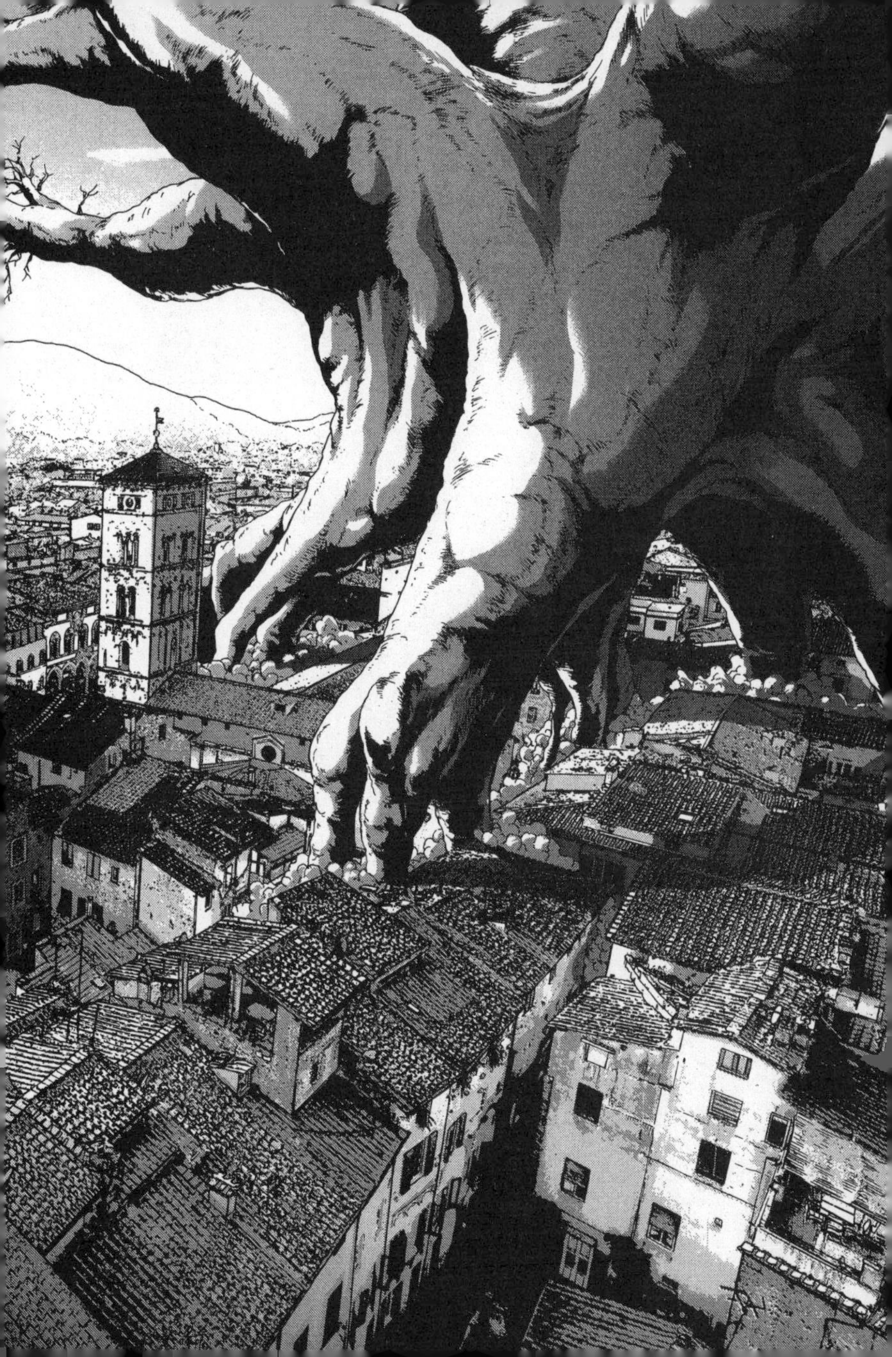

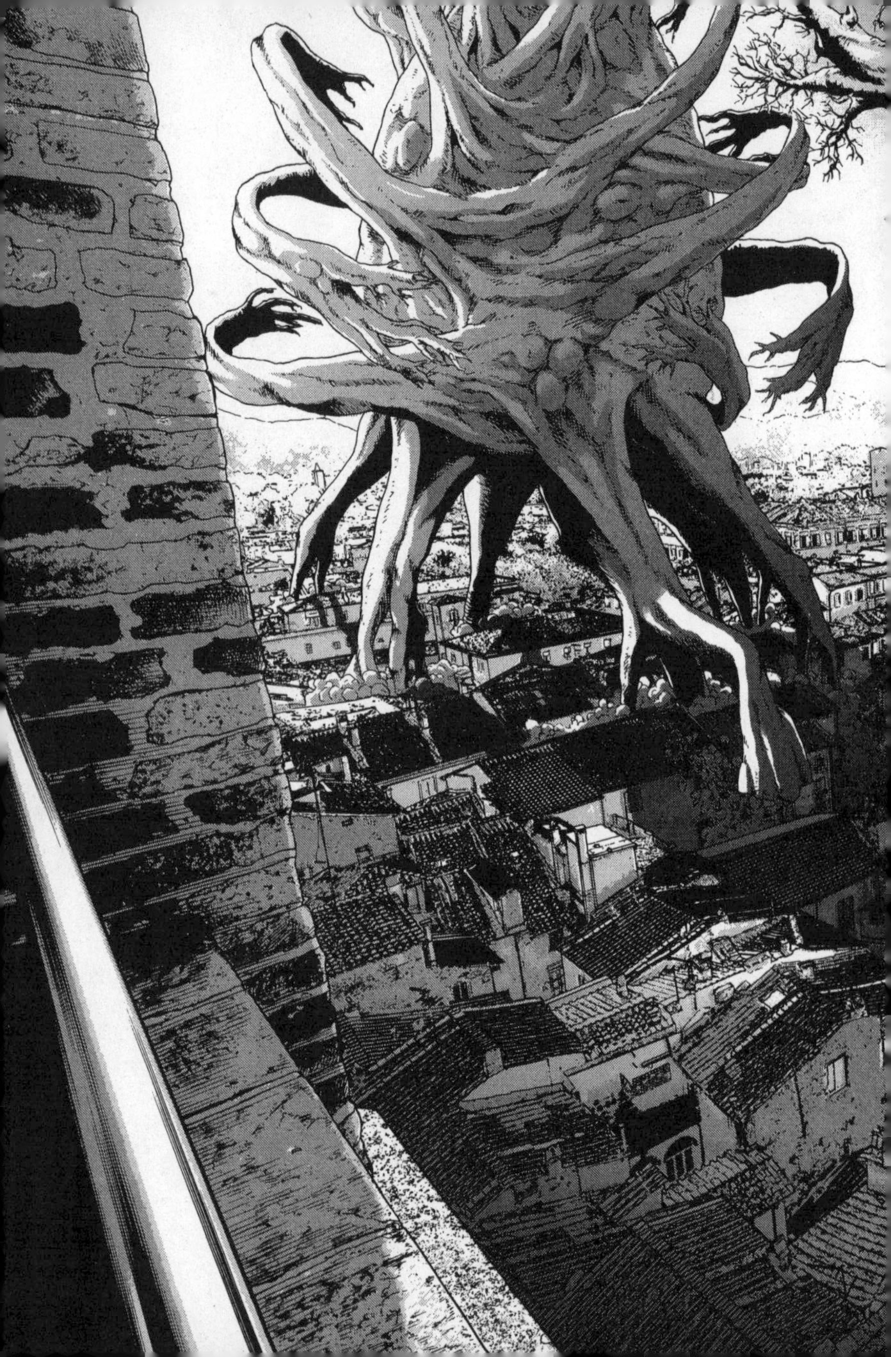

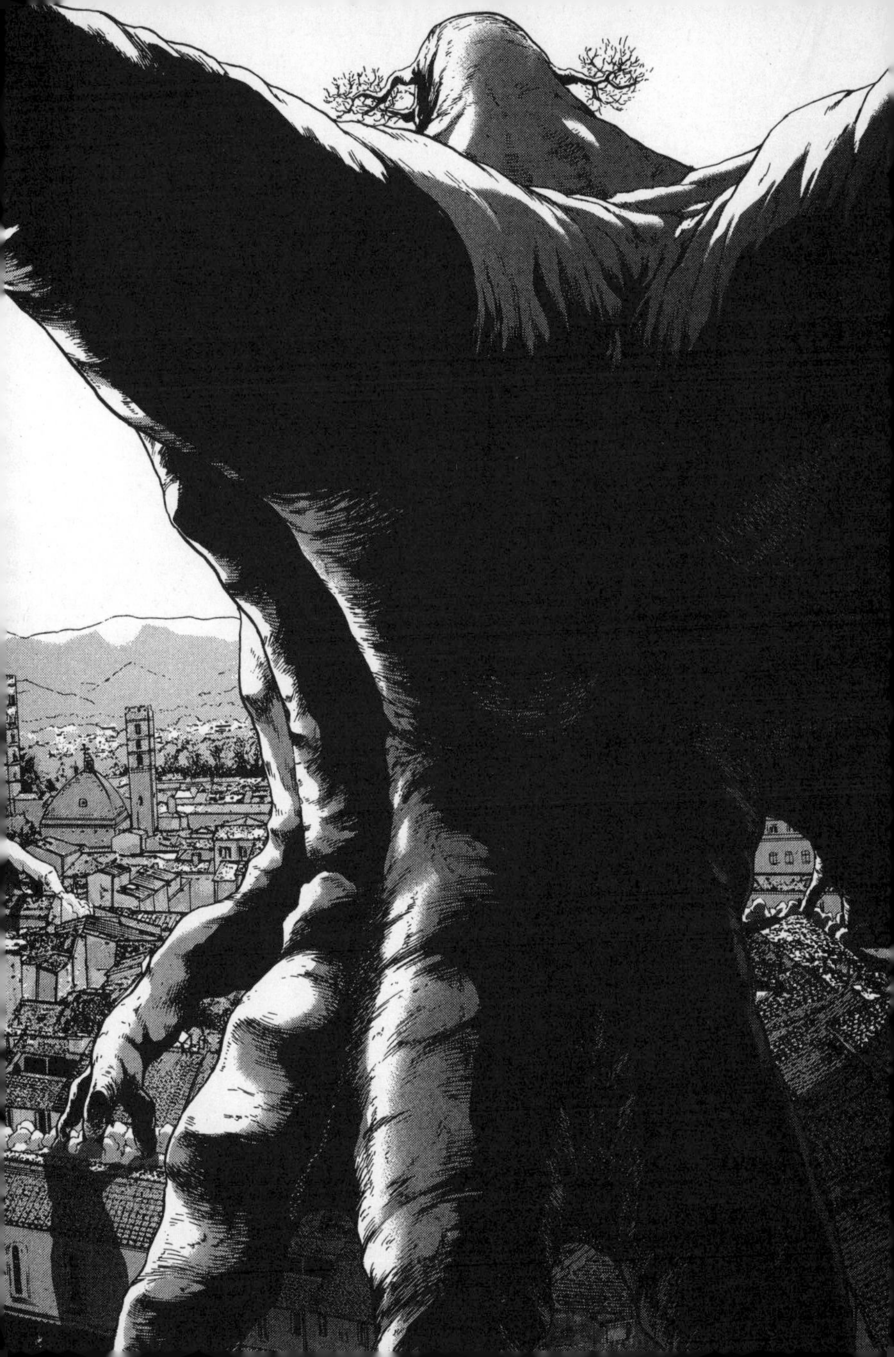

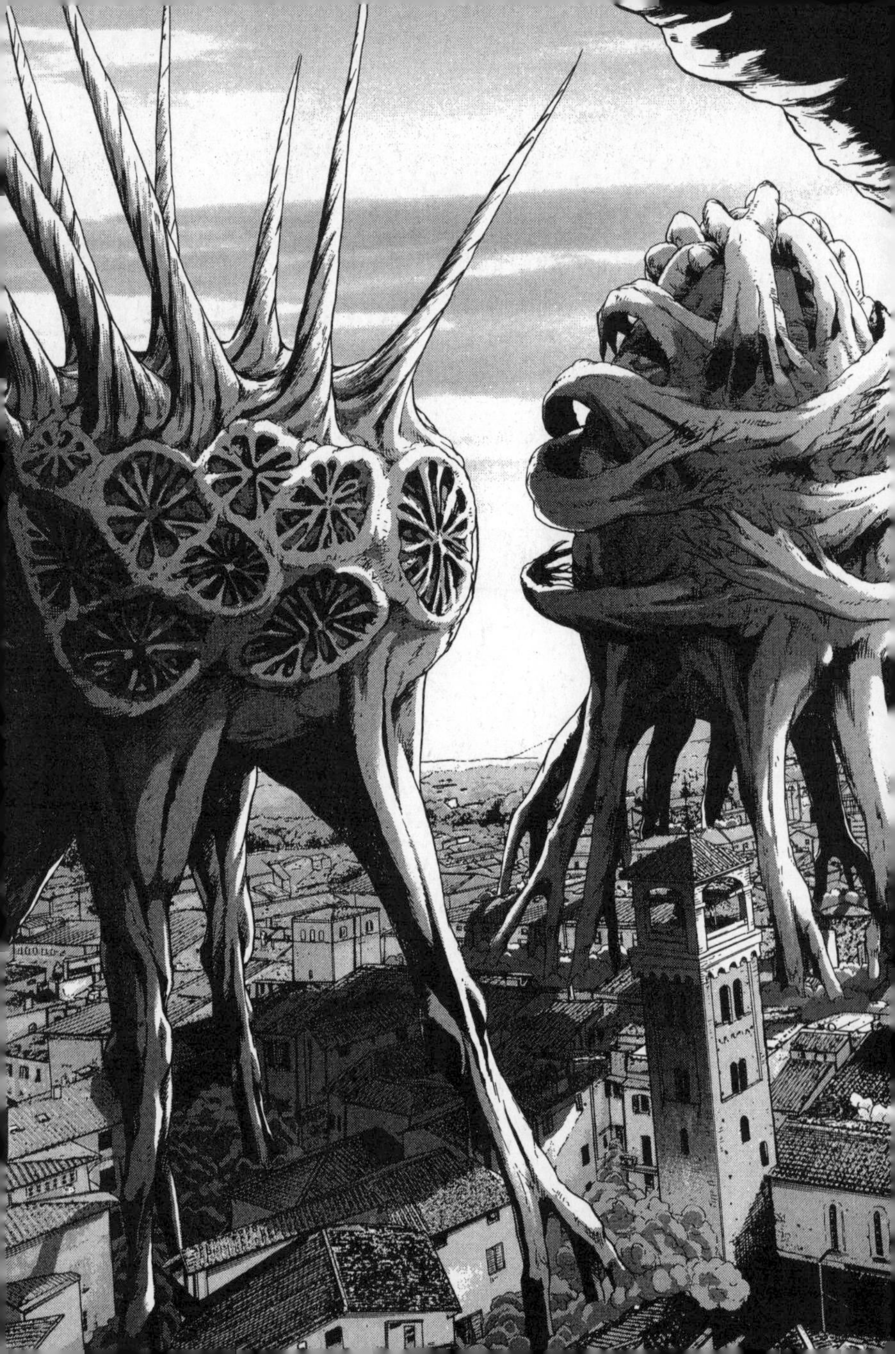

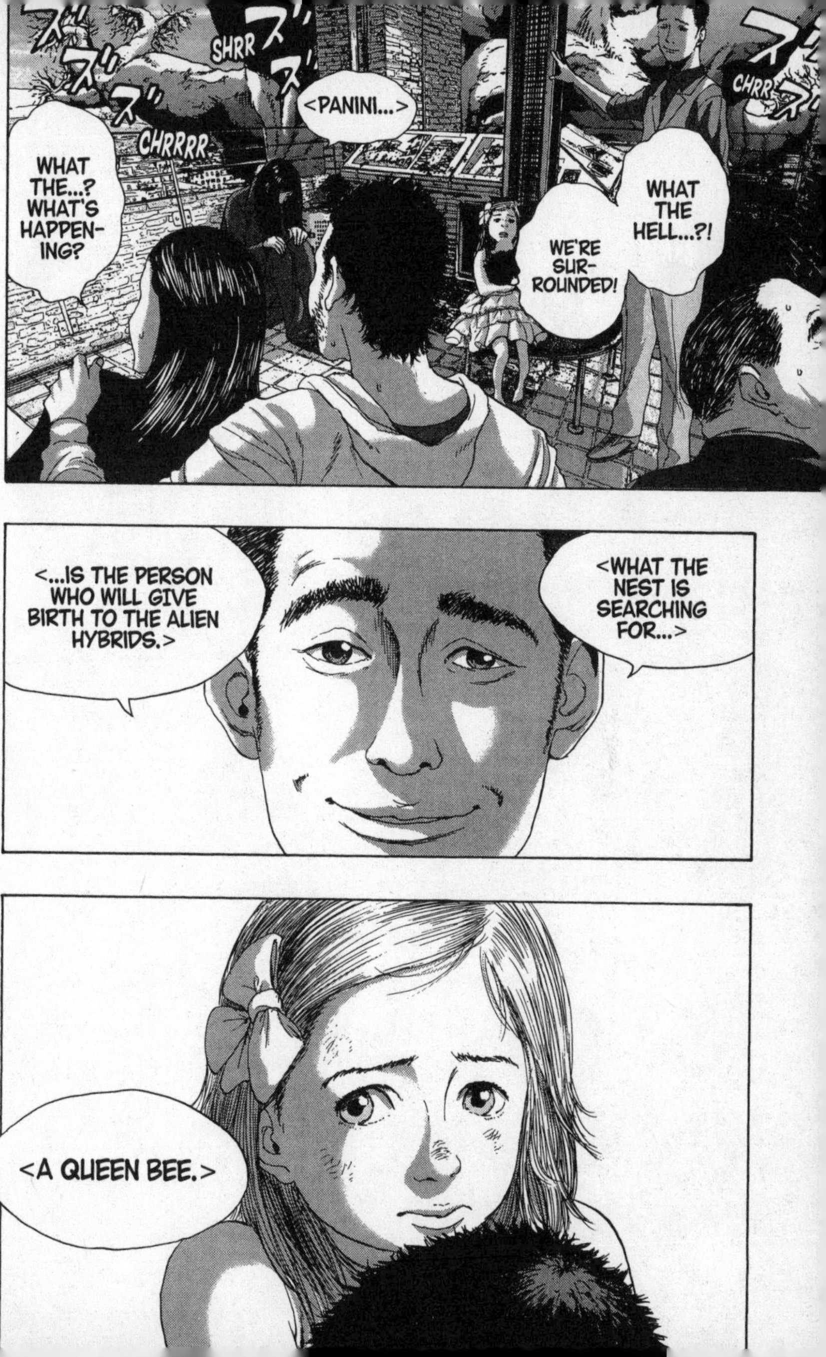
CHRR
WHAT THE HELL...?!
WE'RE SUR- ROUNDED!
<PANINI...>
SHRR
CHRRRR
WHAT THE...? WHAT'S HAPPEN- ING?
<WHAT THE NEST IS SEARCHING FOR...>
<...IS THE PERSON WHO WILL GIVE BIRTH TO THE ALIEN HYBRIDS.>
<A QUEEN BEE.>

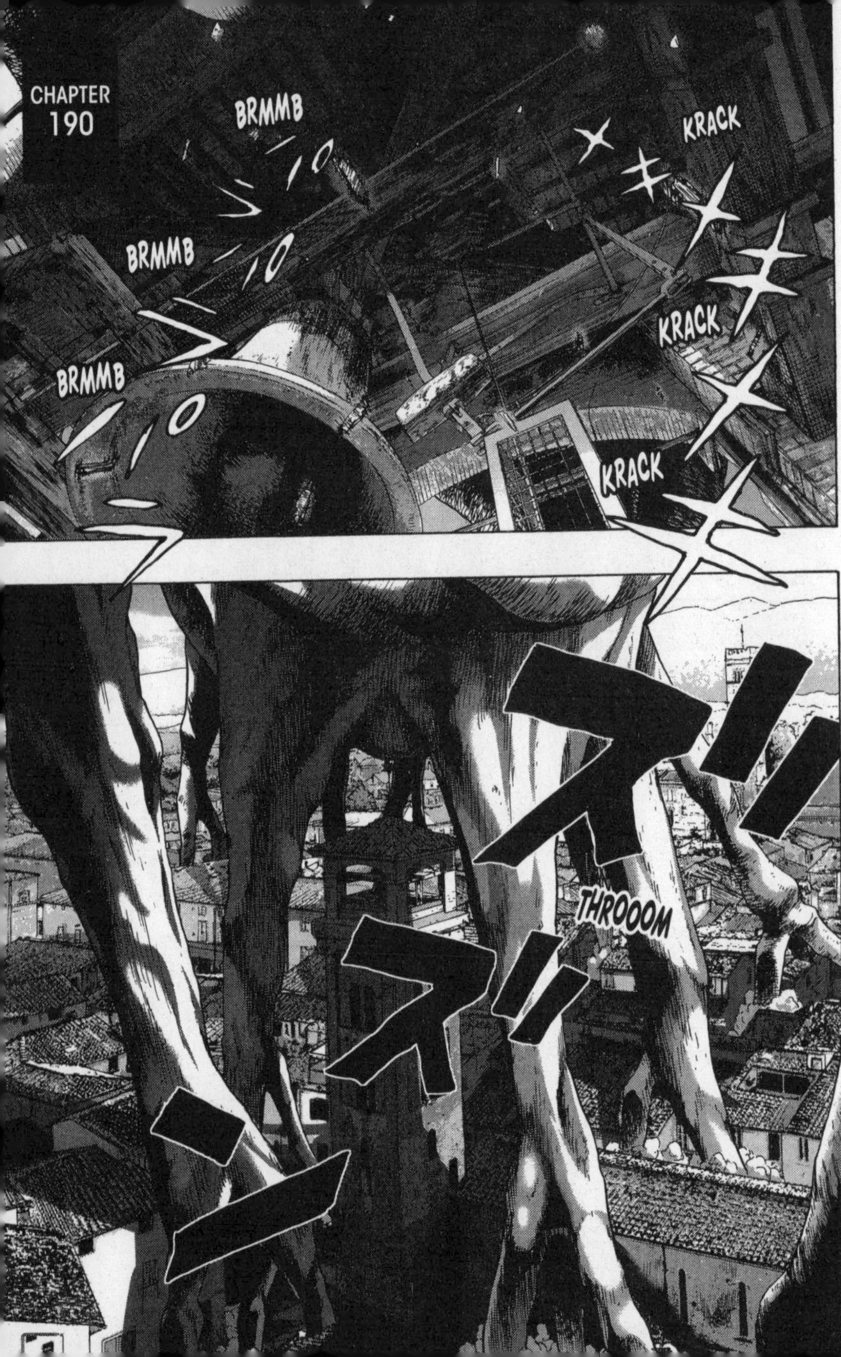
CHAPTER 190
KRACK
BRMMB
KRACK
BRMMB
KRACK
BRMMB
THROOOM

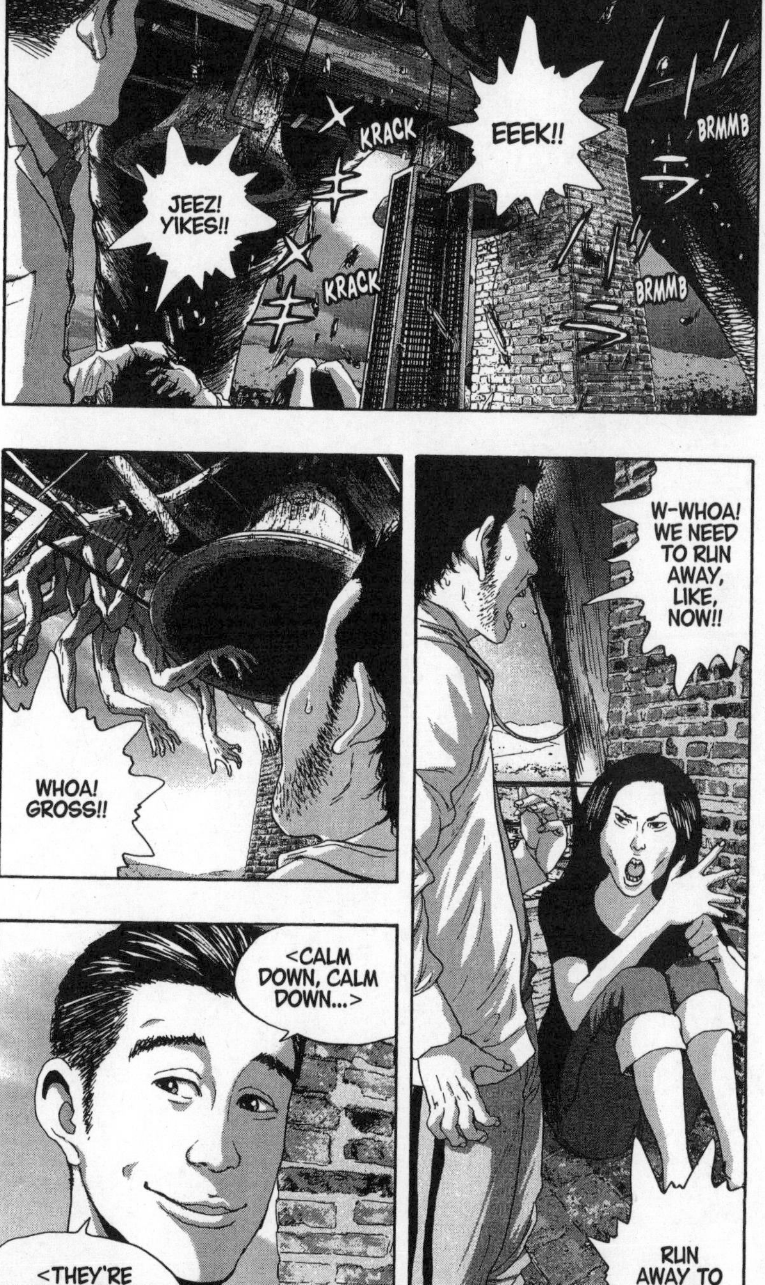
BRMMB
EEEK!!
KRACK
JEEZ! YIKES!!
BRMMB
KRACK
W-WHOA! WE NEED TO RUN AWAY, LIKE, NOW!!
RUN AWAY TO WHERE?
WHOA! GROSS!!
<CALM DOWN, CALM DOWN...>
<THEY'RE NOT GOING TO ATTACK US.>

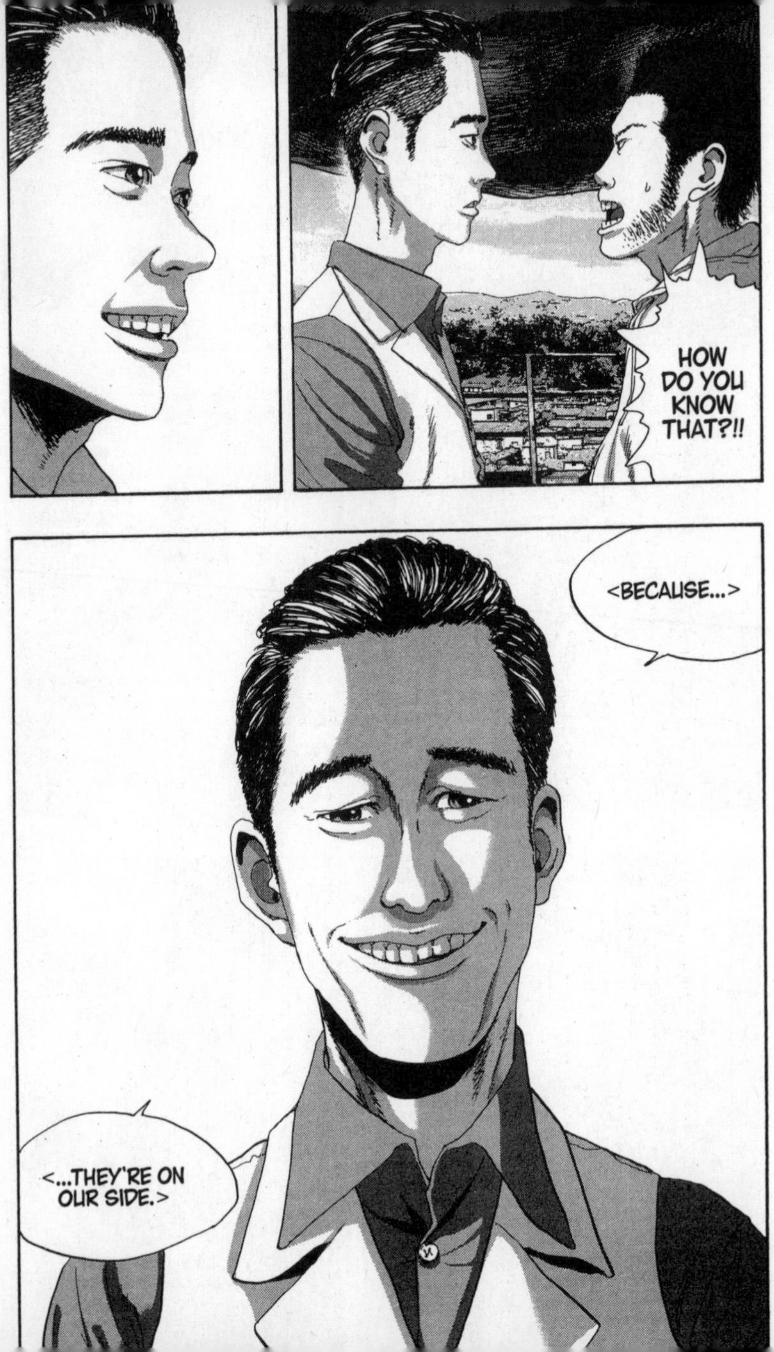
HOW DO YOU KNOW THAT?!!
<BECAUSE...>
<...THEY'RE ON OUR SIDE.>

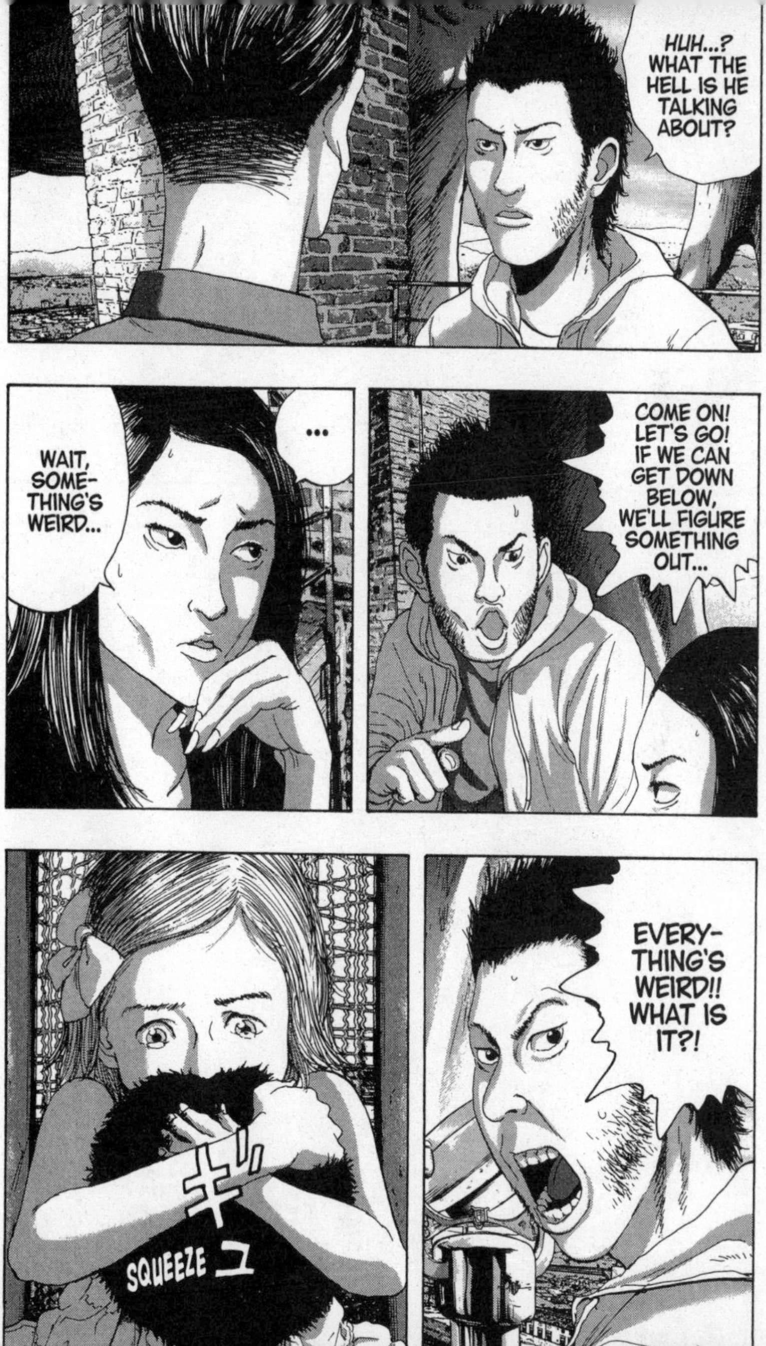
HUH...? WHAT THE HELL IS HE TALKING ABOUT?
COME ON! LET'S GO! IF WE CAN GET DOWN BELOW, WE'LL FIGURE SOMETHING OUT...
...
WAIT, SOME-THING'S WEIRD...
EVERY-THING'S WEIRD!! WHAT IS IT?!
SQUEEZE

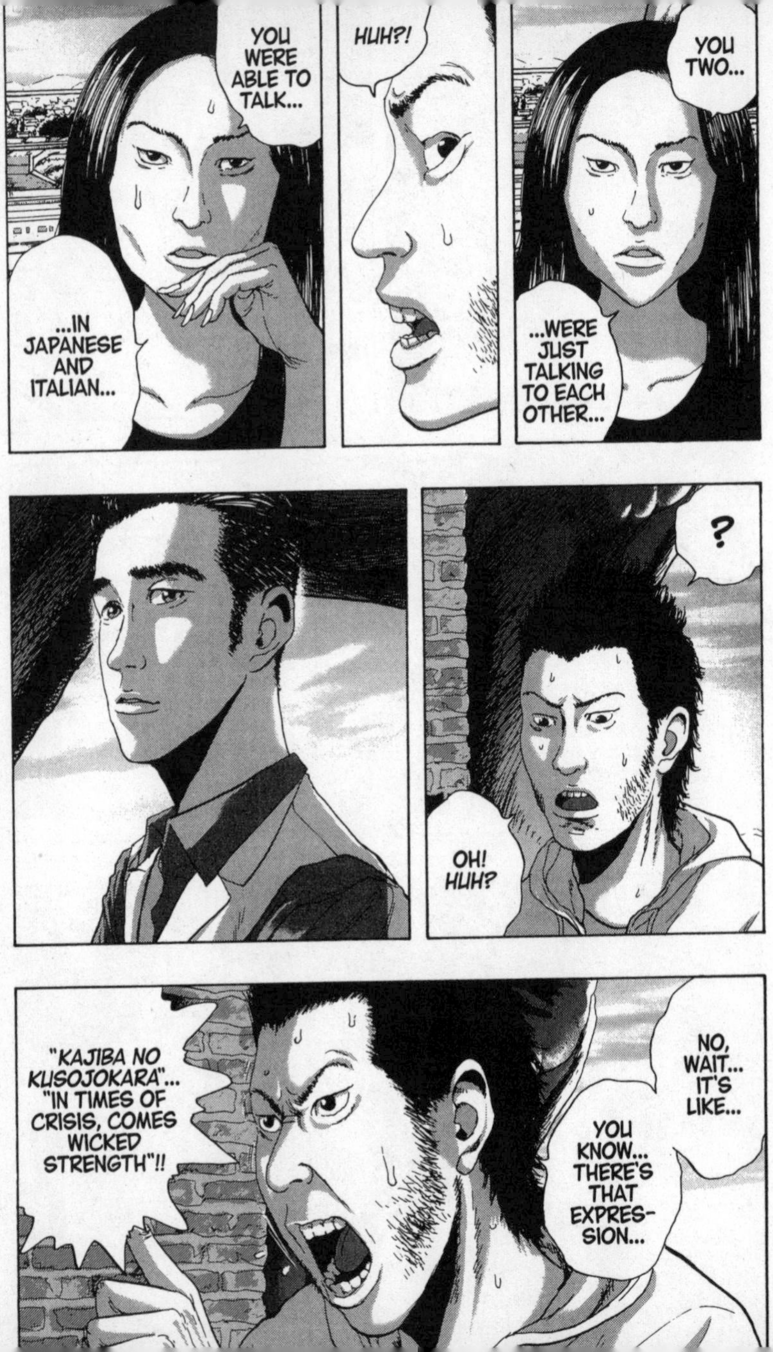
YOU TWO...
...WERE JUST TALKING TO EACH OTHER...
HUH?!
YOU WERE ABLE TO TALK...
...IN JAPANESE AND ITALIAN...
?
OH! HUH?
NO, WAIT... IT'S LIKE...
YOU KNOW... THERE'S THAT EXPRES-SION...
"KAJIBA NO KUSOJOKARA"... "IN TIMES OF CRISIS, COMES WICKED STRENGTH"!!

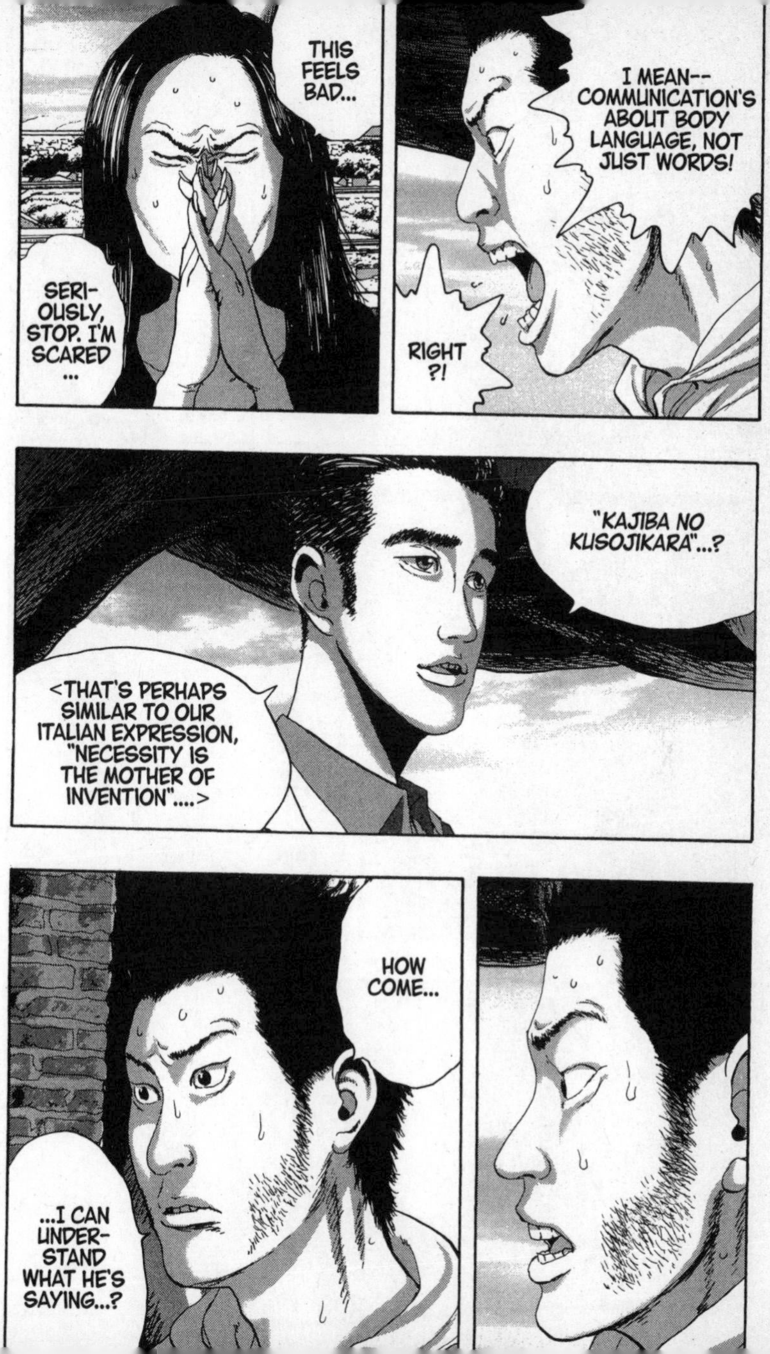
I MEAN-- COMMUNICATION'S ABOUT BODY LANGUAGE, NOT JUST WORDS!
RIGHT ?!
THIS FEELS BAD...
SERI- OUSLY, STOP. I'M SCARED ...
"KAJIBA NO KUSOJIKARA"...?
<THAT'S PERHAPS SIMILAR TO OUR ITALIAN EXPRESSION, "NECESSITY IS THE MOTHER OF INVENTION"....>
HOW COME...
...I CAN UNDER- STAND WHAT HE'S SAYING...?

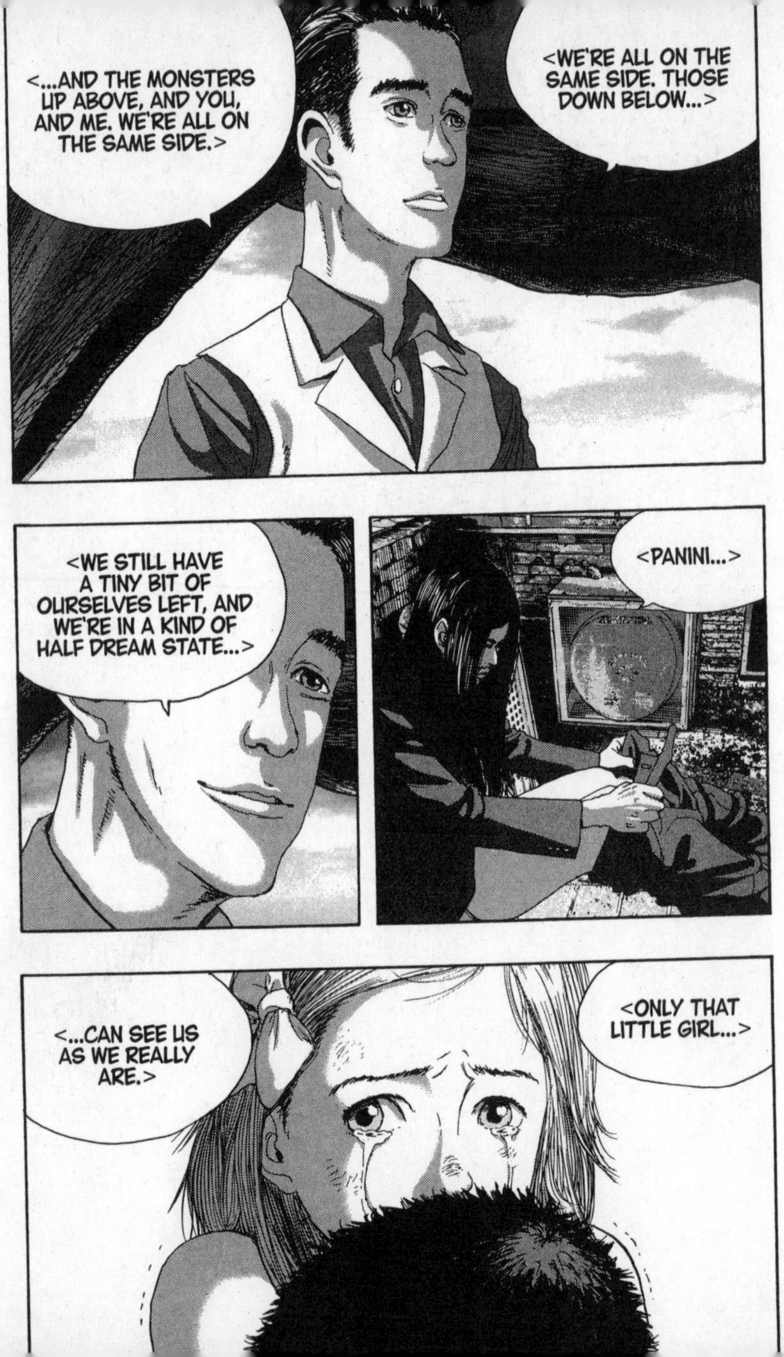
<WE'RE ALL ON THE SAME SIDE. THOSE DOWN BELOW...>
<...AND THE MONSTERS UP ABOVE, AND YOU, AND ME. WE'RE ALL ON THE SAME SIDE.>
<PANINI...>
<WE STILL HAVE A TINY BIT OF OURSELVES LEFT, AND WE'RE IN A KIND OF HALF DREAM STATE...>
<ONLY THAT LITTLE GIRL...>
<...CAN SEE US AS WE REALLY ARE.>

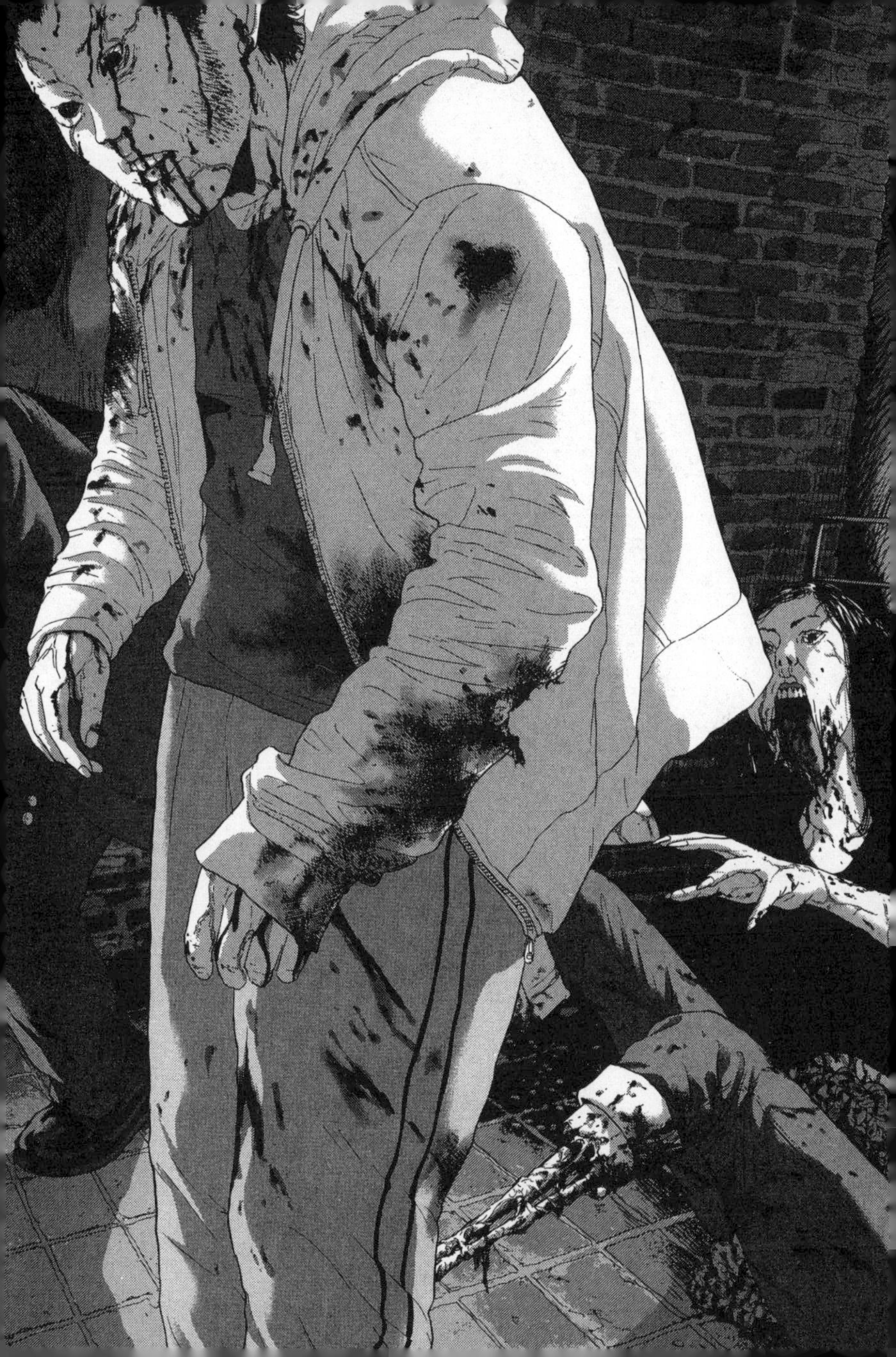

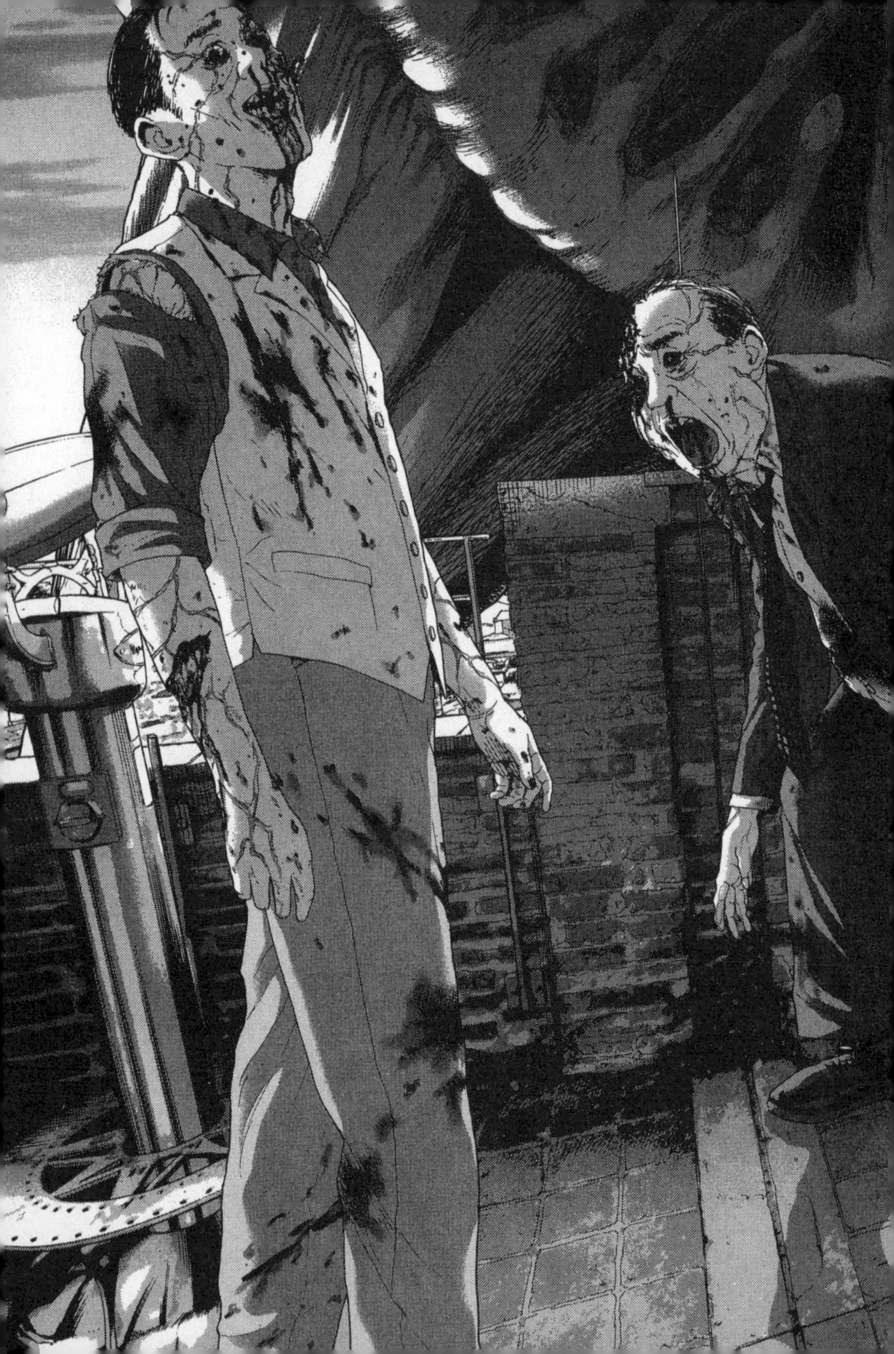

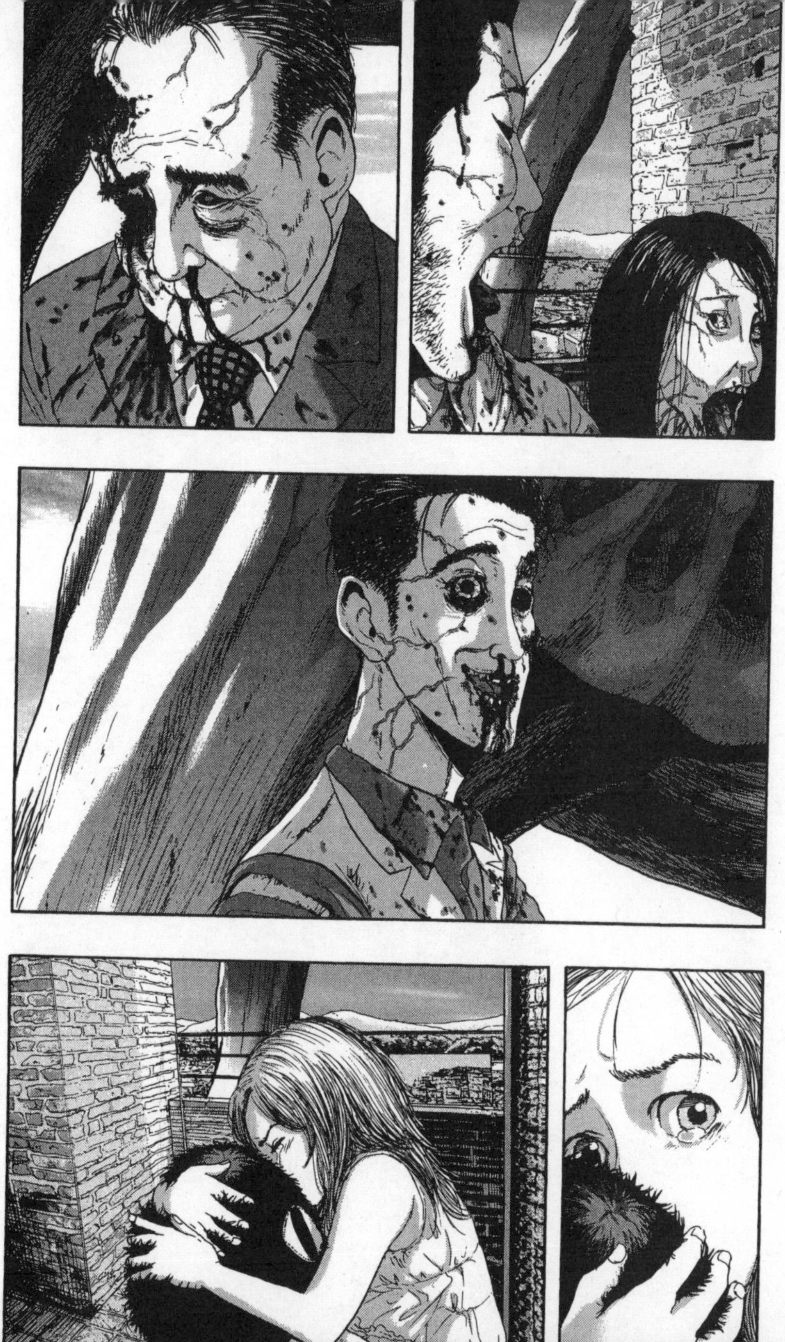

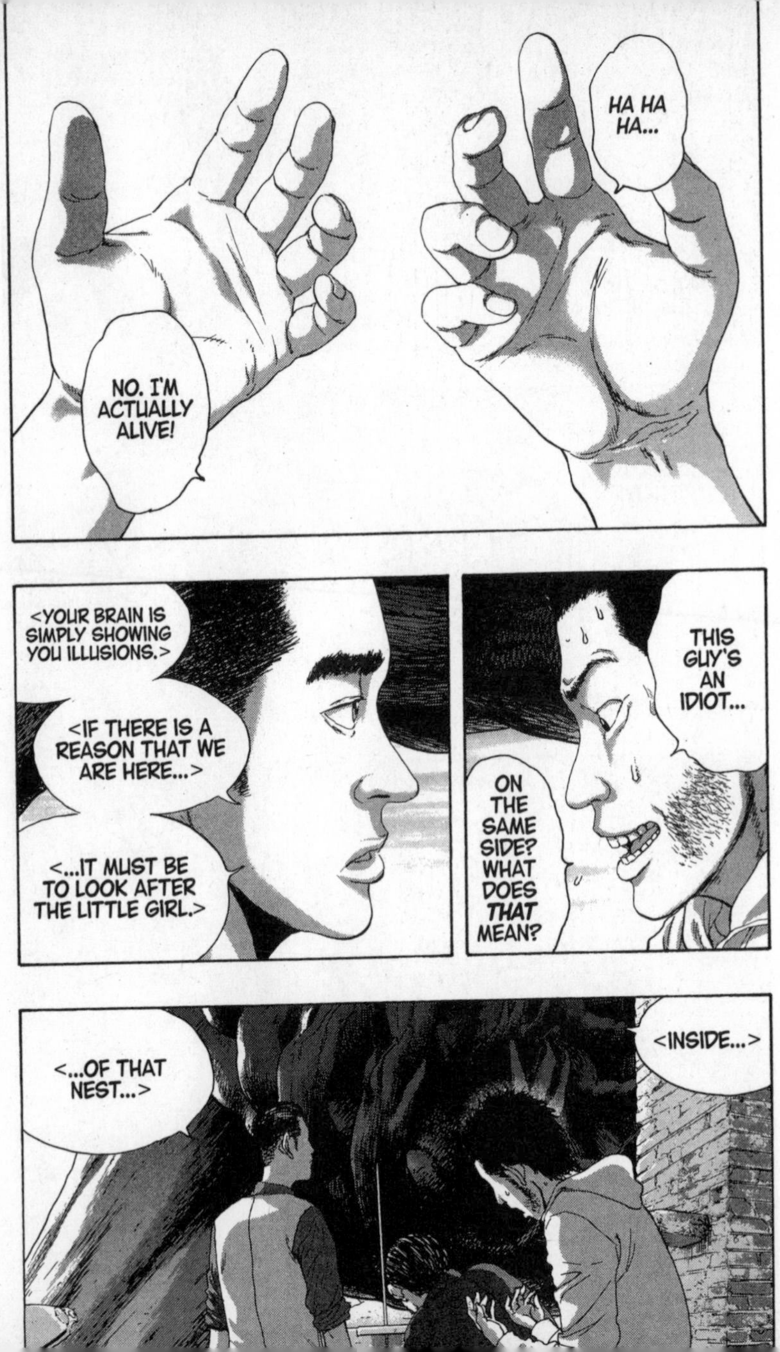
HA HA HA...
NO. I'M ACTUALLY ALIVE!
THIS GUY'S AN IDIOT...
ON THE SAME SIDE? WHAT DOES *THAT* MEAN?
<YOUR BRAIN IS SIMPLY SHOWING YOU ILLUSIONS.>
<IF THERE IS A REASON THAT WE ARE HERE...>
<...IT MUST BE TO LOOK AFTER THE LITTLE GIRL.>
<INSIDE...>
<...OF THAT NEST...>

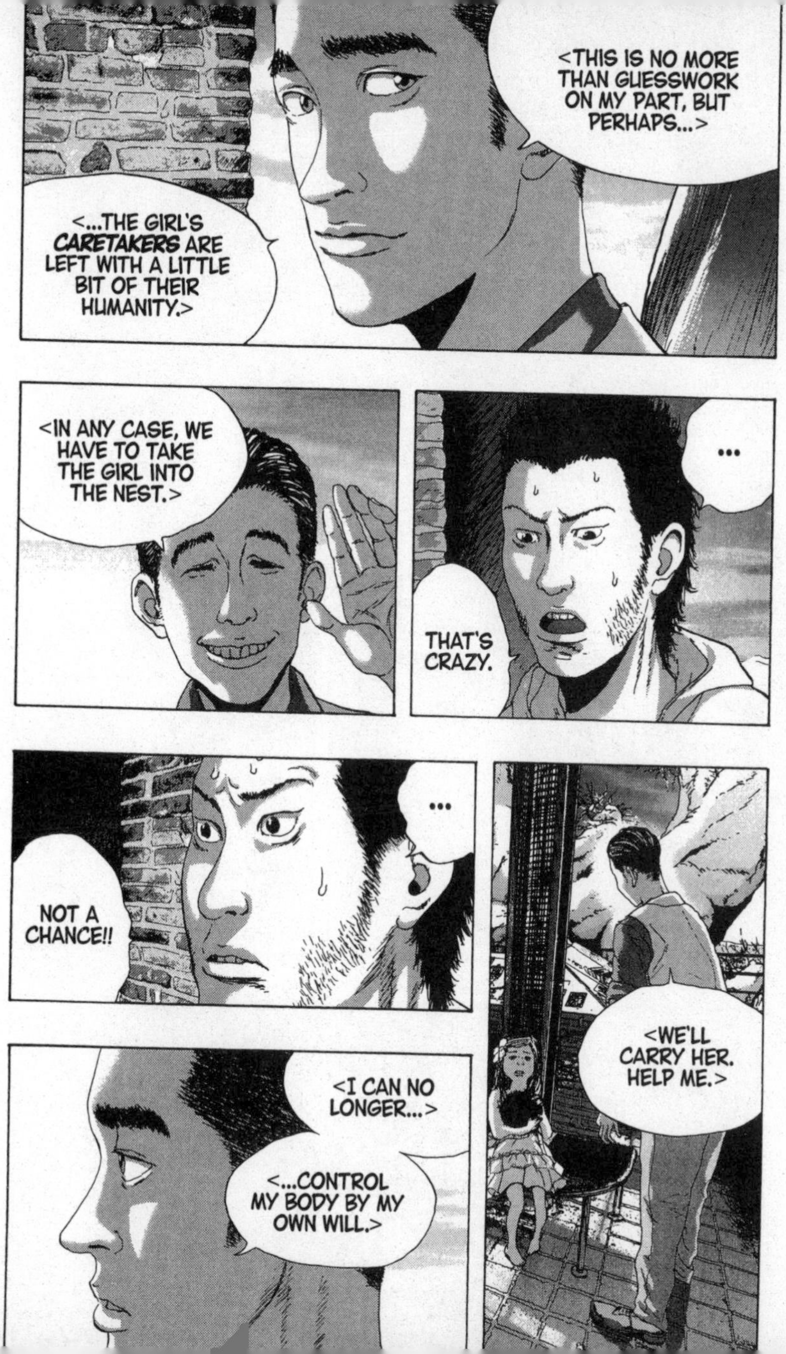
<THIS IS NO MORE THAN GUESSWORK ON MY PART, BUT PERHAPS...>
<...THE GIRL'S *CARETAKERS* ARE LEFT WITH A LITTLE BIT OF THEIR HUMANITY.>
...
THAT'S CRAZY.
<IN ANY CASE, WE HAVE TO TAKE THE GIRL INTO THE NEST.>
<WE'LL CARRY HER. HELP ME.>
...
NOT A CHANCE!!
<I CAN NO LONGER...>
<...CONTROL MY BODY BY MY OWN WILL.>

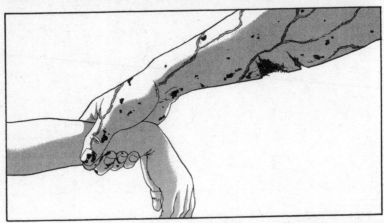

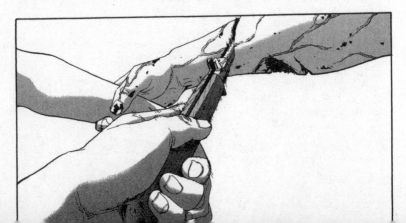

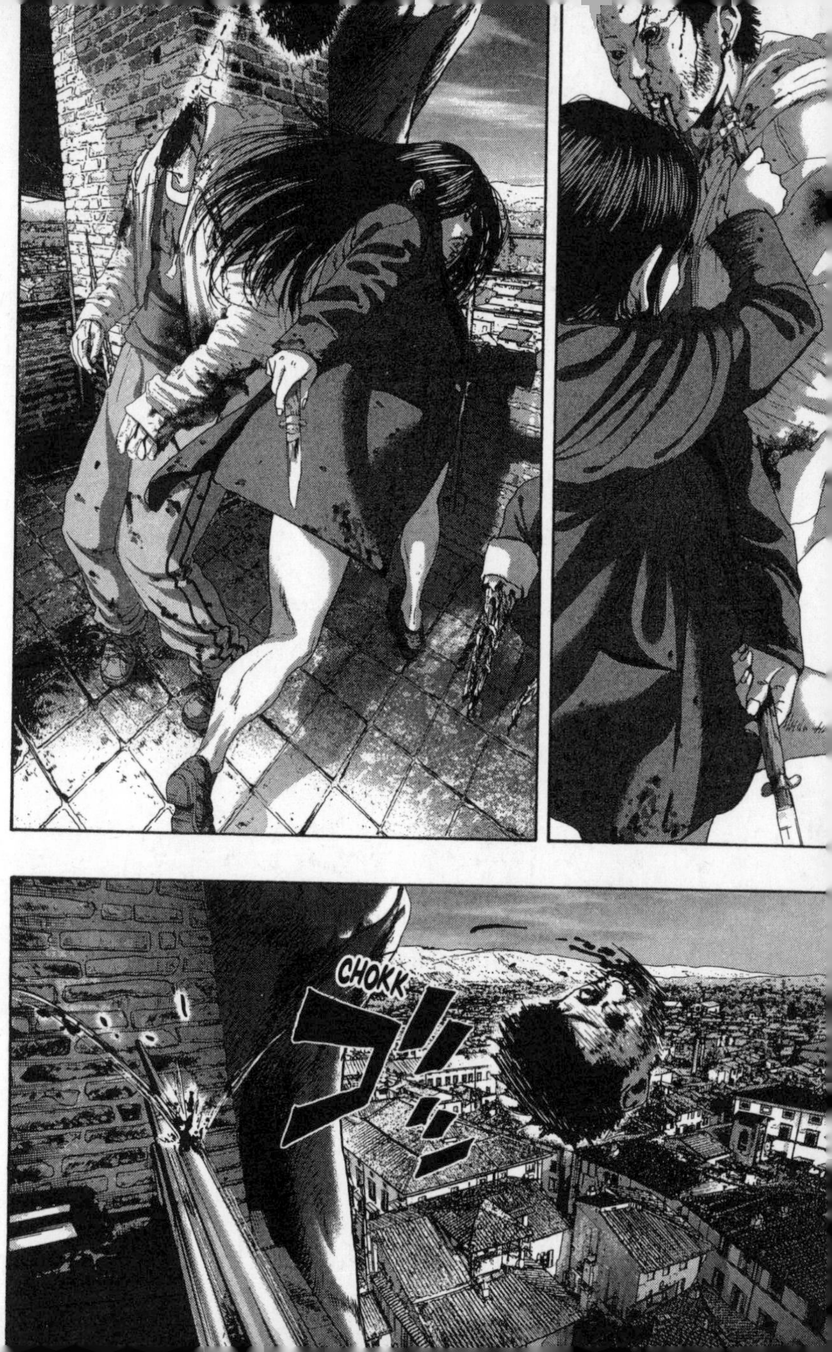
CHOKK

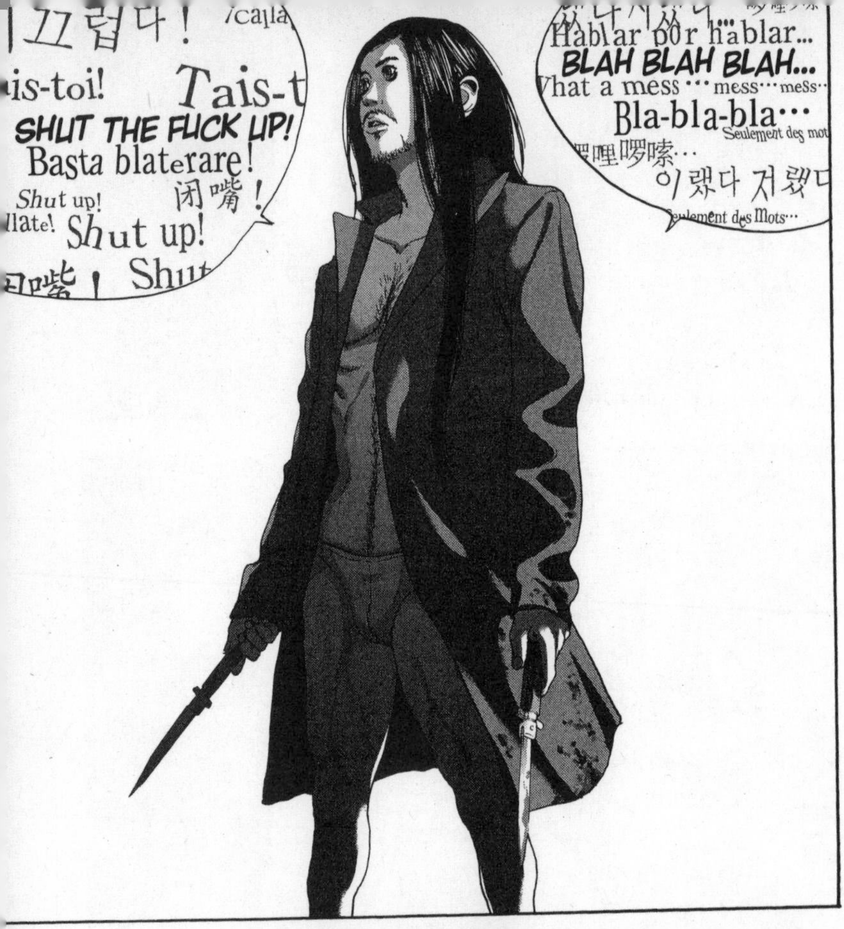
Hablar por hablar...
BLAH BLAH BLAH...
mess… mess…
Bla-bla-bla…
Seulement des Mots…
SHUT THE FUCK UP!
Basta blaterare!
闭嘴！
Shut up!
Shut up!

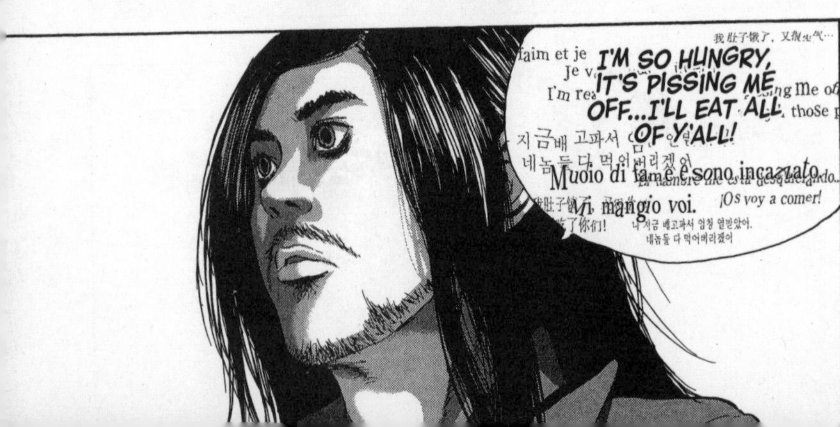
我肚子饿了，又很生气…
I'M SO HUNGRY, IT'S PISSING ME OFF...I'LL EAT ALL OF Y'ALL!
Muoio di fame e sono incazzato.
Mi mangio voi.
¡Os voy a comer!
나 지금 배고파서 엄청 열받았어.
네놈들 다 먹어버리겠어

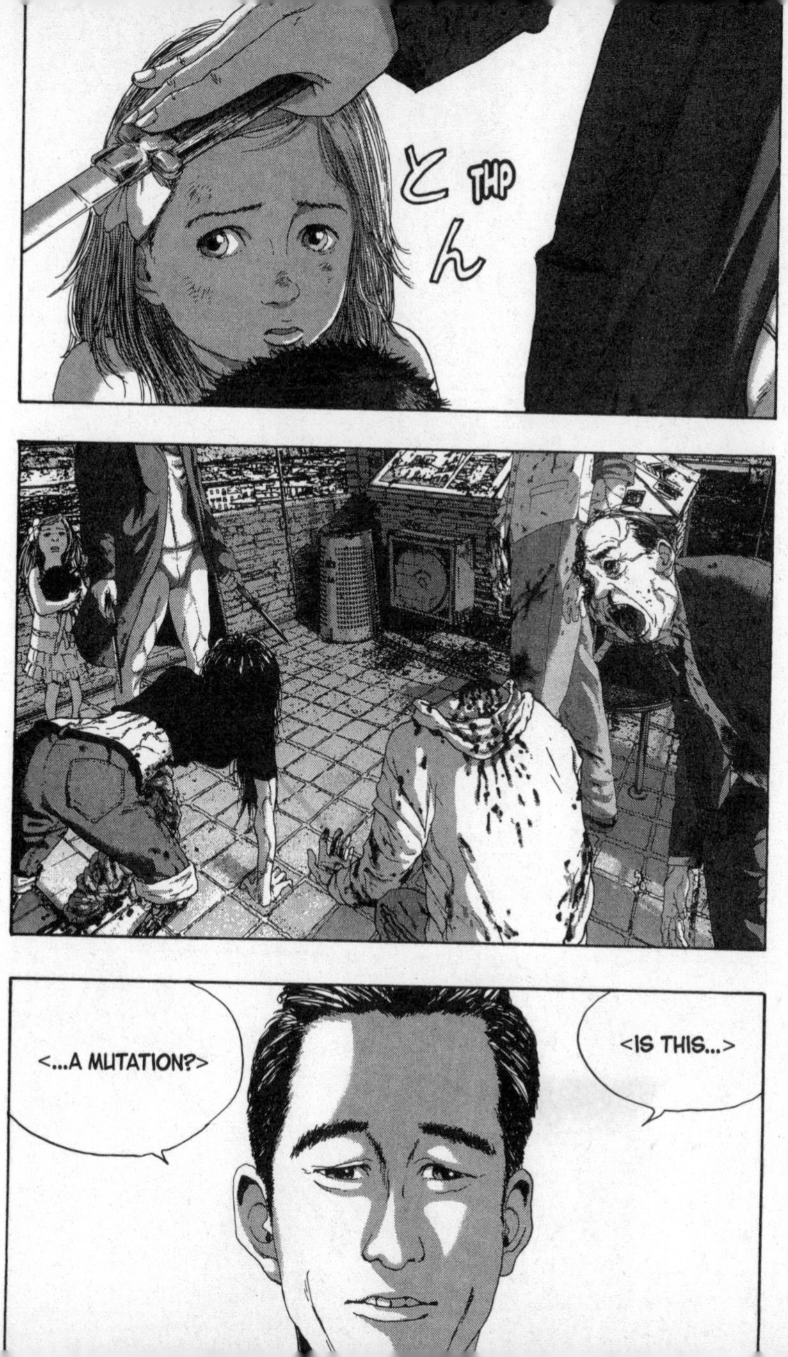
とん
THP
<IS THIS...>
<...A MUTATION?>

CHAPTER 191

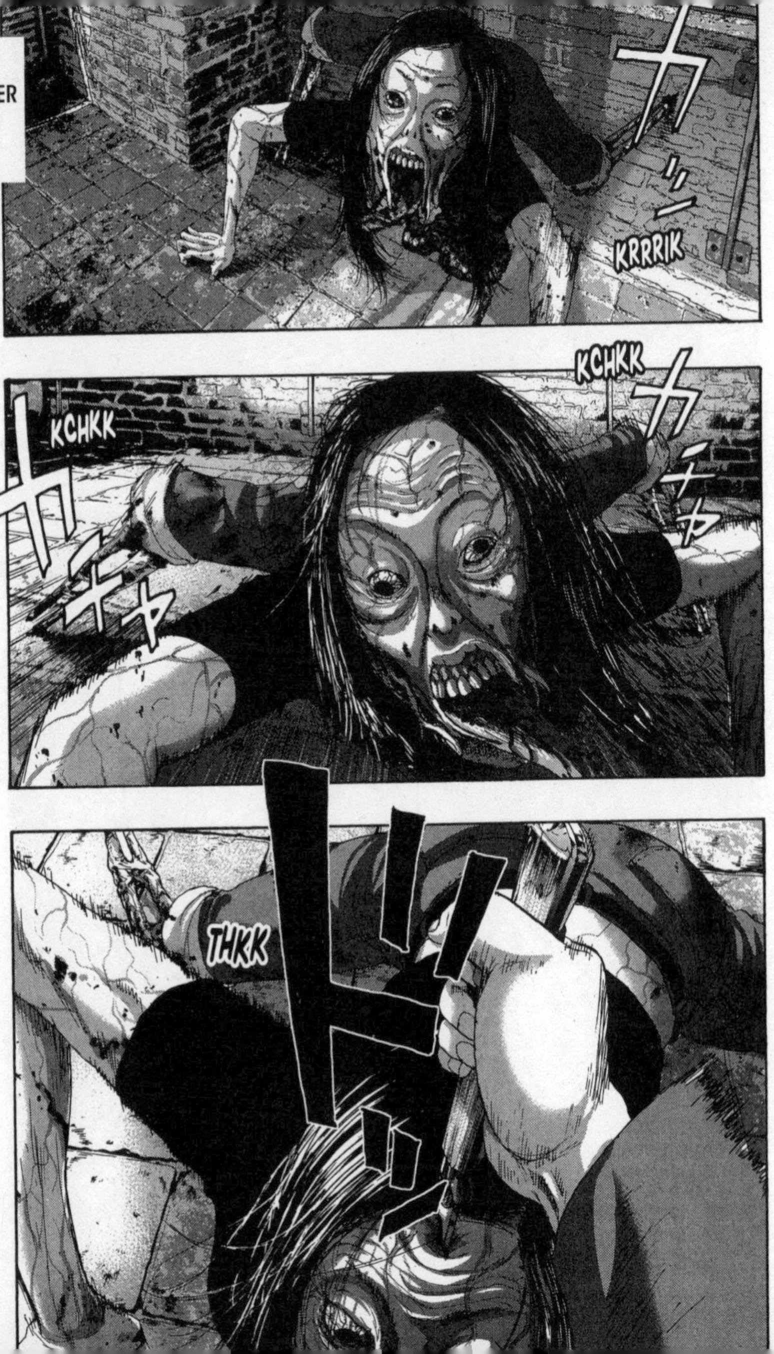
KRRRIK
KCHKK
KCHKK
THKK

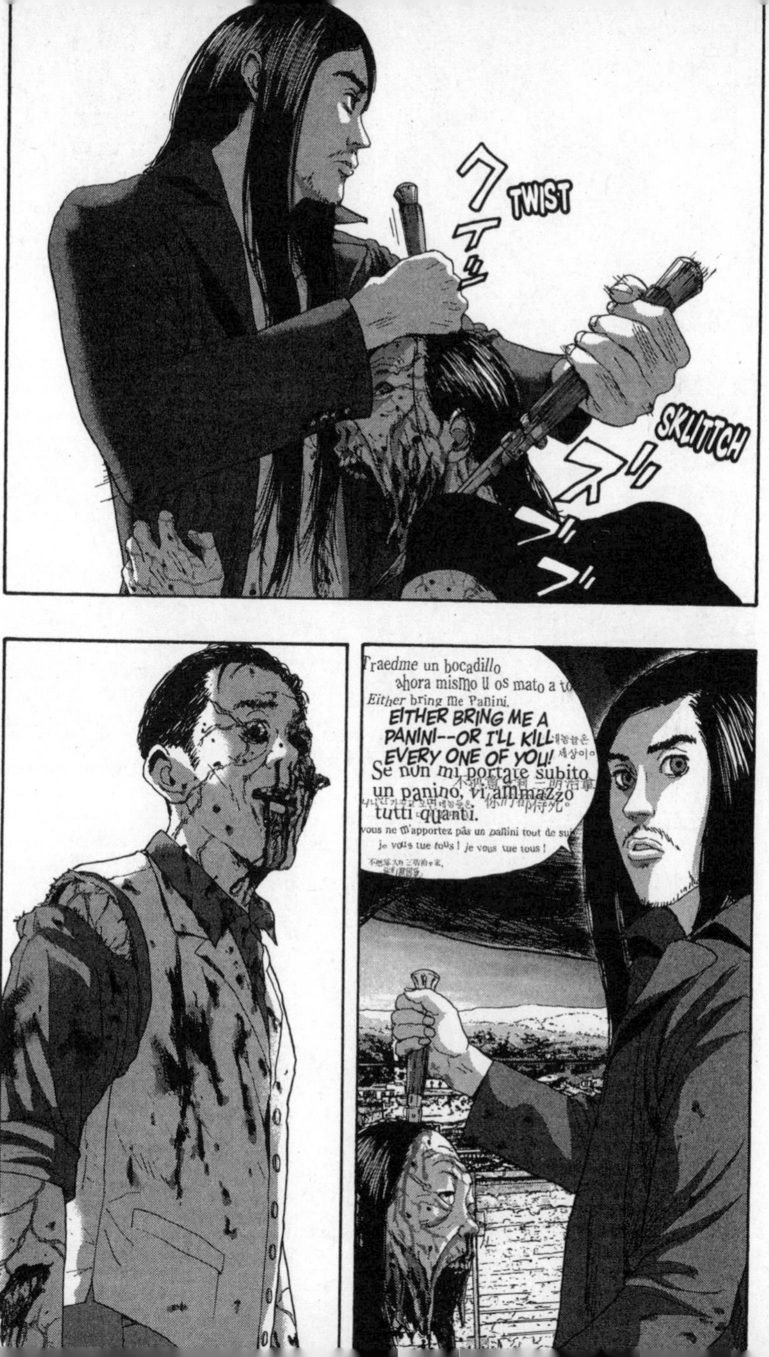
クイッ
TWIST
SKLITCH
ズブブ
Traedme un bocadillo
ahora mismo u os mato a to
Either bring me Panini.
EITHER BRING ME A PANINI--OR I'LL KILL EVERY ONE OF YOU!
Se non mi portate subito un panino, vi ammazzo tutti quanti.
vous ne m'apportez pas un panini tout de su
je vous tue tous ! je vous tue tous !

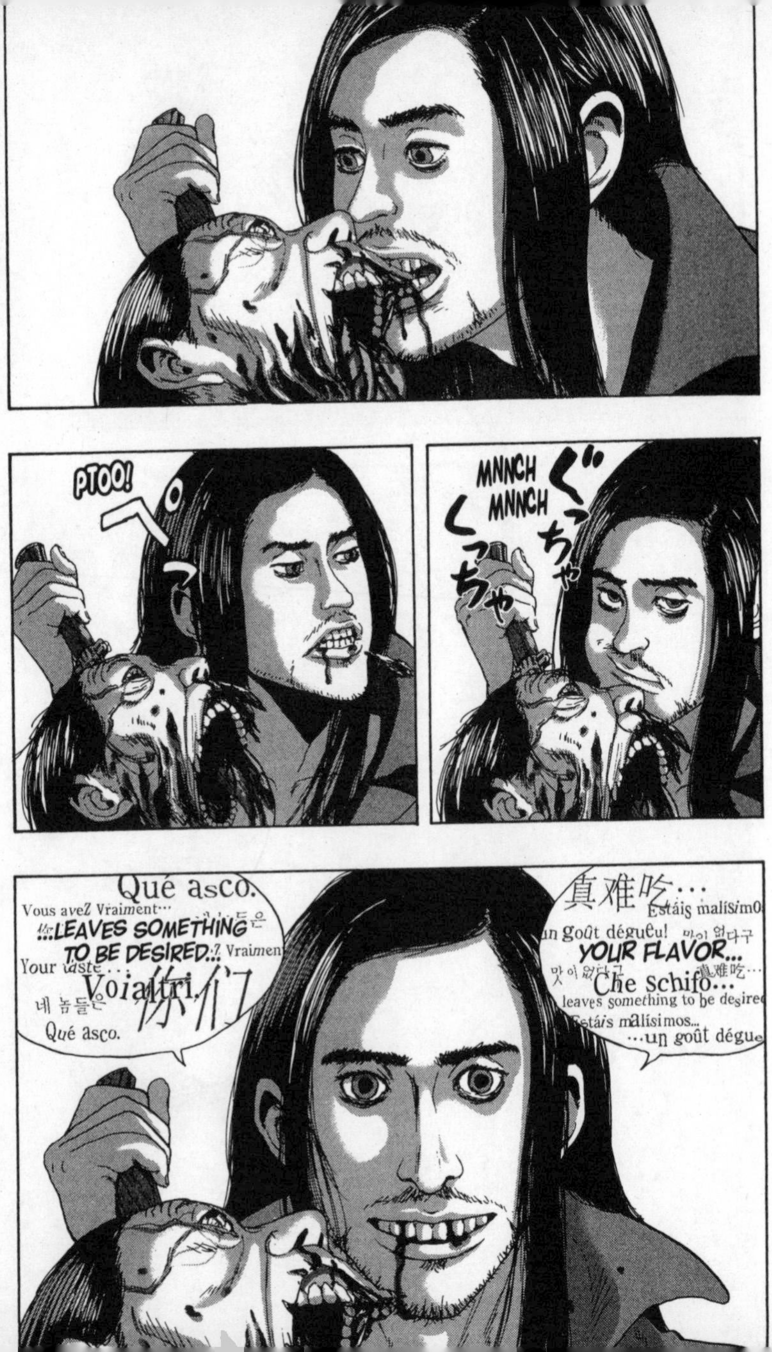
MNNCH MNNCH
ぐっちゃ
くっちゃ
PTOO!
ぺっ
真难吃… Estáis malísimo un goût dégueu! 맛이 없다구
YOUR FLAVOR...
맛이 없다구 真难吃… Che schifo… leaves something to be desired Estáis malísimos... …un goût dégue
Qué asco. Vous avez Vraiment…
...LEAVES SOMETHING TO BE DESIRED...
Your taste… Voialtri 你们 네 놈들은 Qué asco.

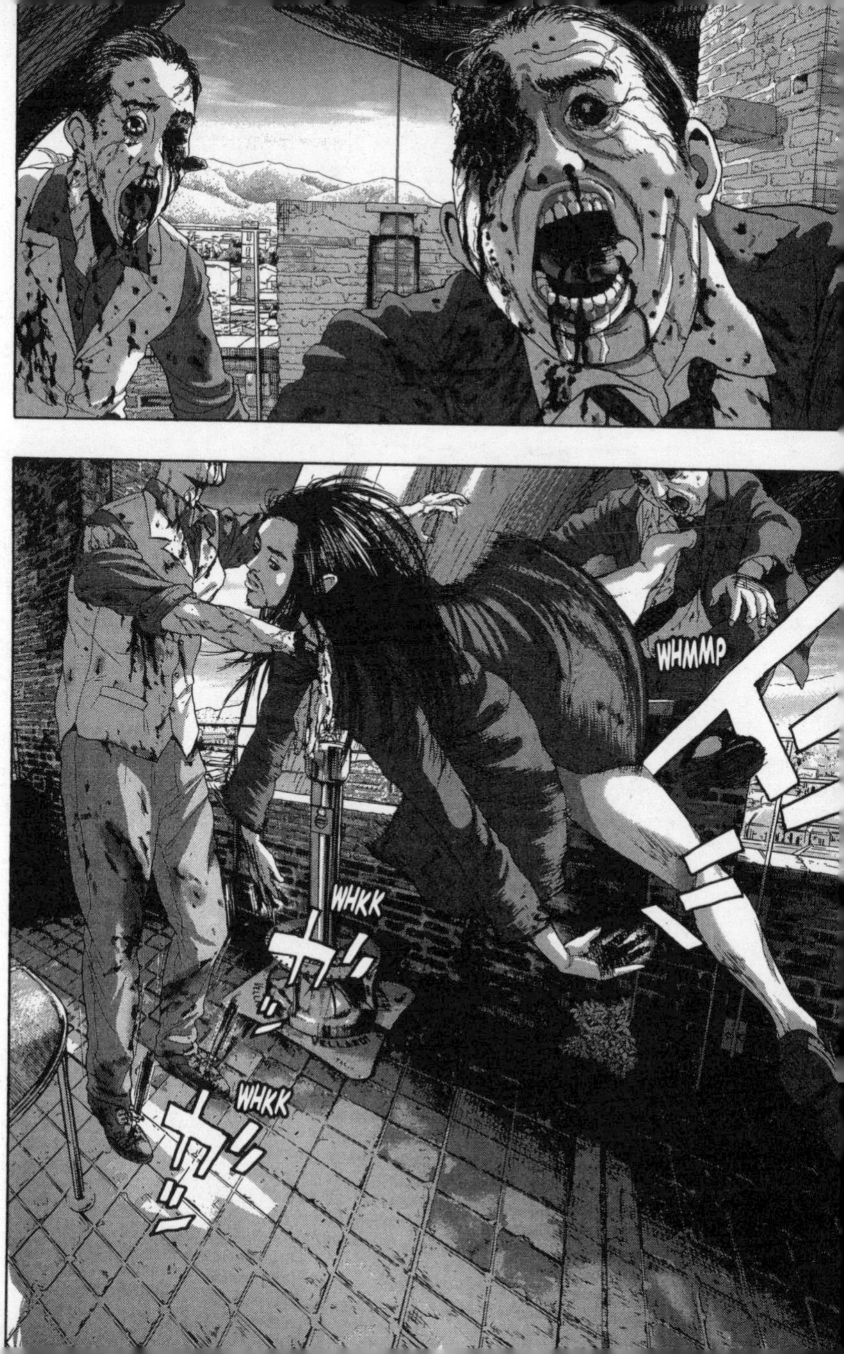
WHMMP
WHKK
WHKK

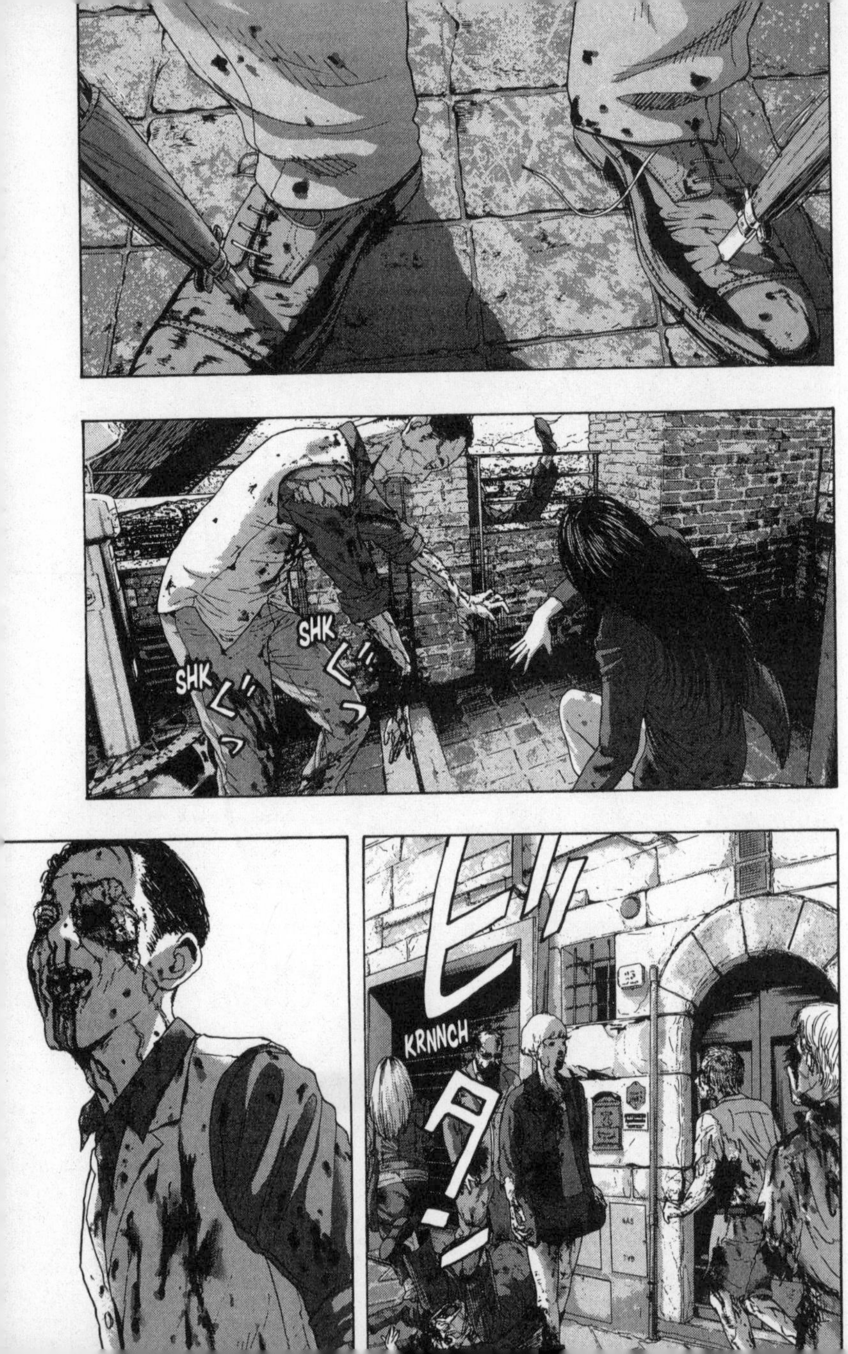
SHK
SHK
KRNNCH

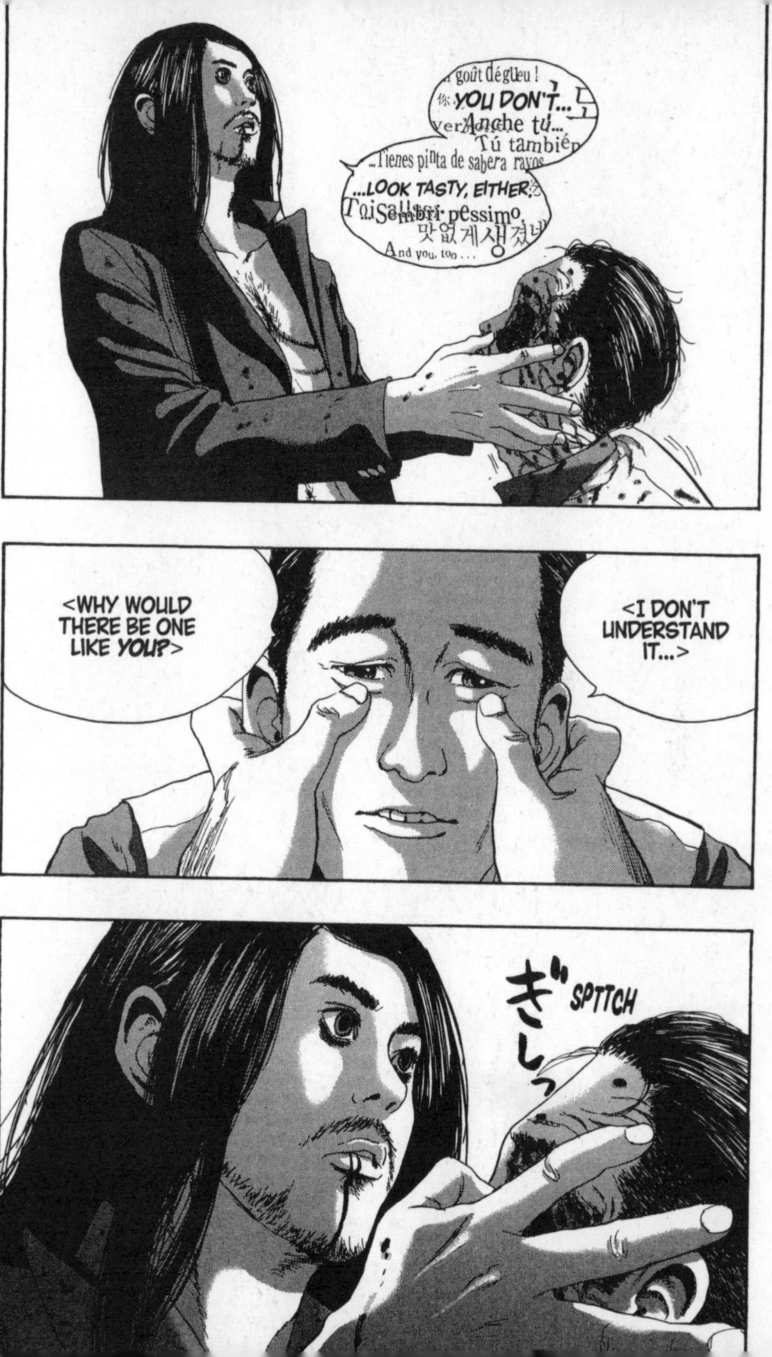
goût dégueu !
YOU DON'T...
Anche tu...
Tú también
...Tienes pinta de sabera rayos
...LOOK TASTY, EITHER.
...Sembri pessimo
맛없게생겼네
And you, too . . .
<I DON'T UNDERSTAND IT...>
<WHY WOULD THERE BE ONE LIKE YOU?>
ぎしっ
SPTTCH

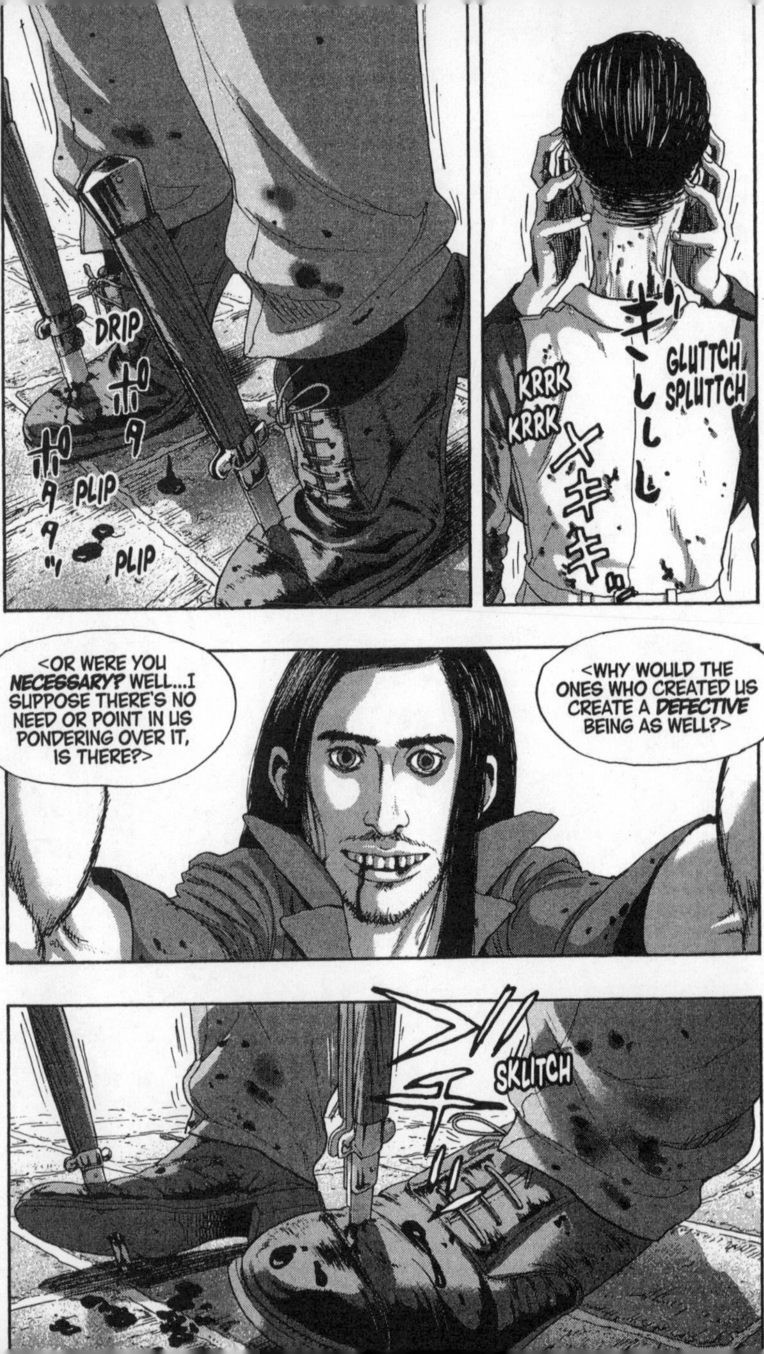
GLUTTCH SPLUTTCH
KRRK KRRK
DRIP
PLIP
PLIP
<WHY WOULD THE ONES WHO CREATED US CREATE A DEFECTIVE BEING AS WELL?>
<OR WERE YOU NECESSARY? WELL...I SUPPOSE THERE'S NO NEED OR POINT IN US PONDERING OVER IT, IS THERE?>
SKLITCH

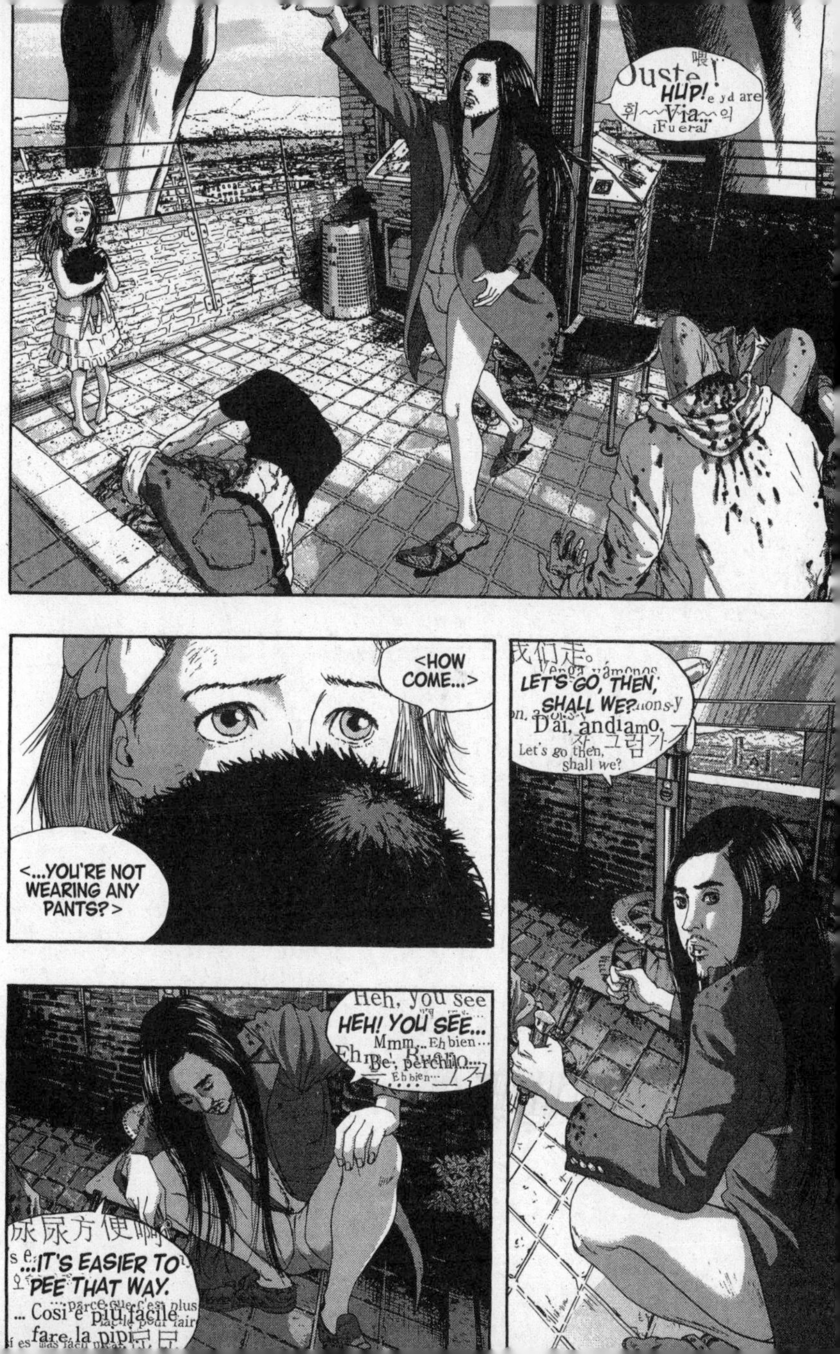

喂！
Ouste!
HUP!
Via...
¡Fuera!
LET'S GO, THEN, SHALL WE?
Dai, andiamo.
Let's go then, shall we?
<HOW COME...>
<...YOU'RE NOT WEARING ANY PANTS?>
Heh, you see
HEH! YOU SEE...
Mmm... Eh bien...
Be', perchè...
...IT'S EASIER TO PEE THAT WAY.
... Così è più facile fare la pipì

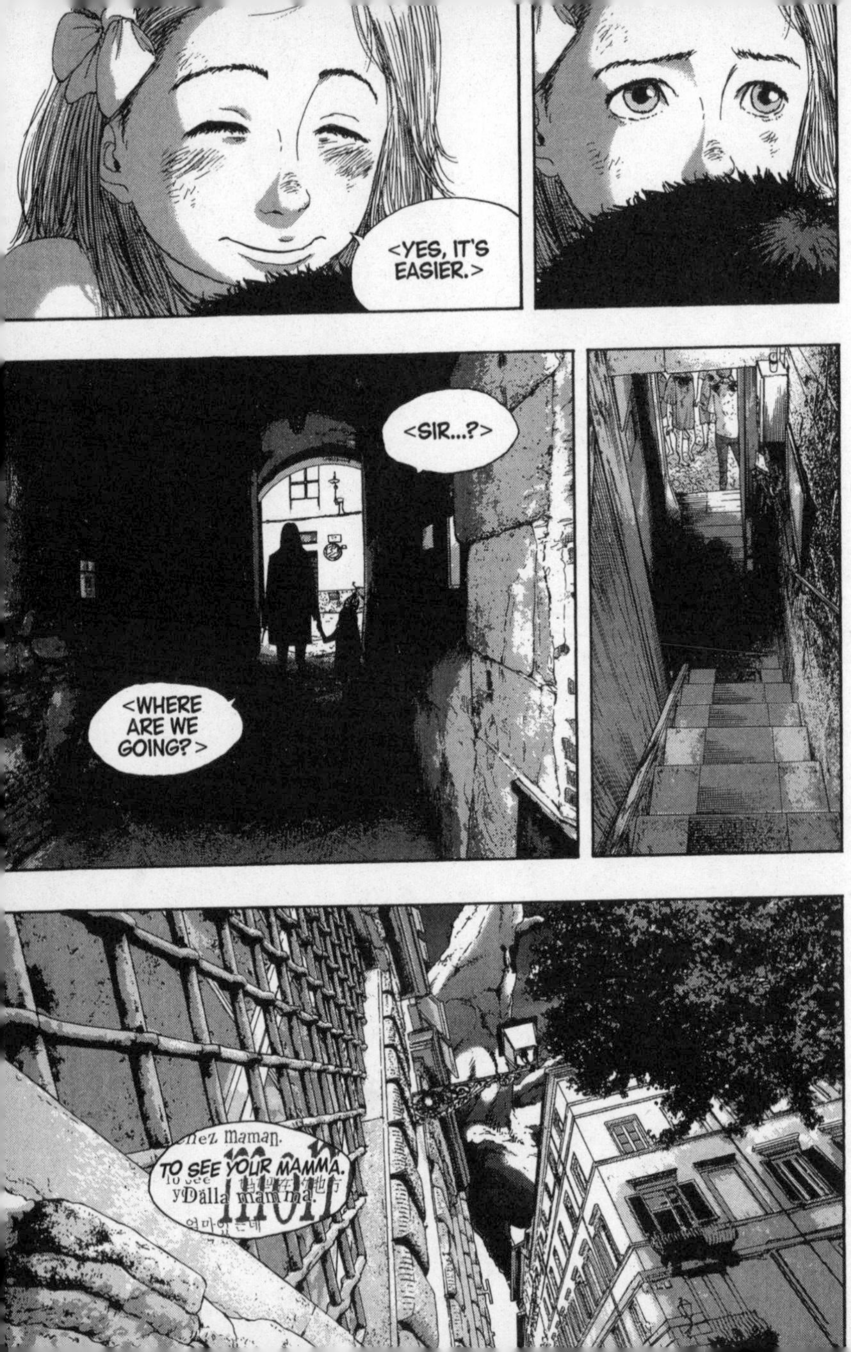
<YES, IT'S EASIER.>
<SIR...?>
<WHERE ARE WE GOING?>
...hez Maman.
TO SEE YOUR MAMMA.
Dalla mamma.

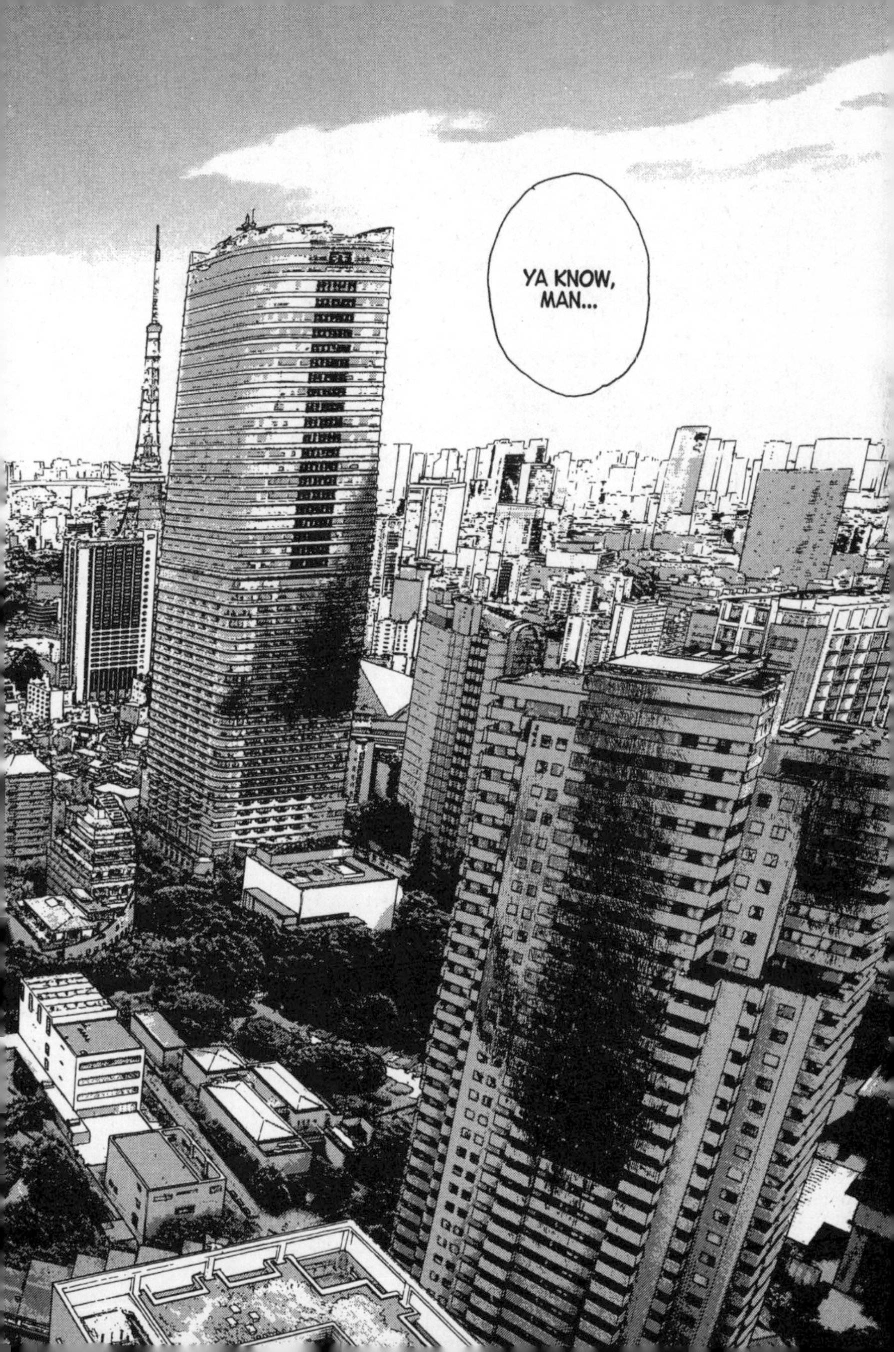
YA KNOW, MAN...

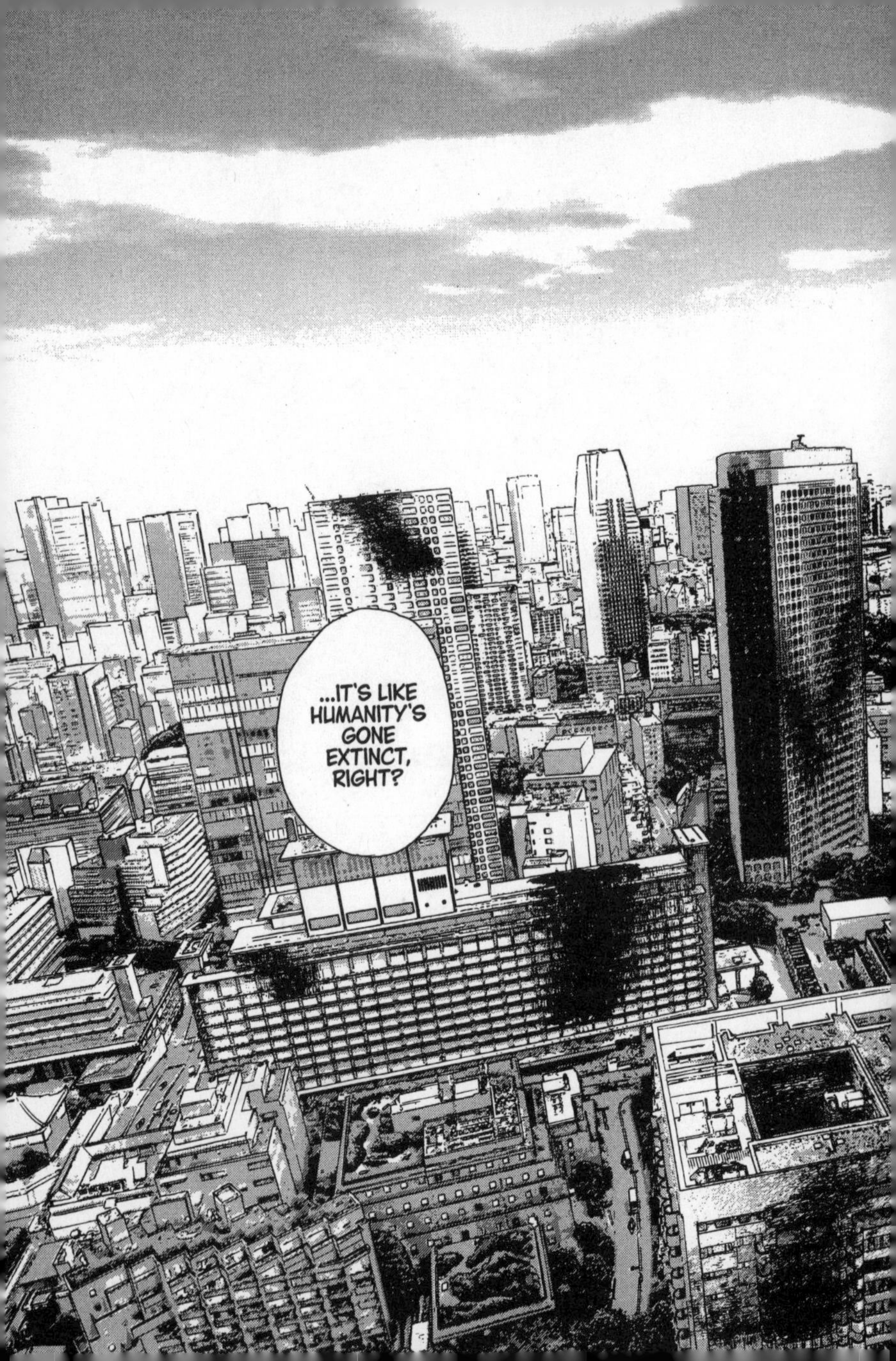
...IT'S LIKE HUMANITY'S GONE EXTINCT, RIGHT?

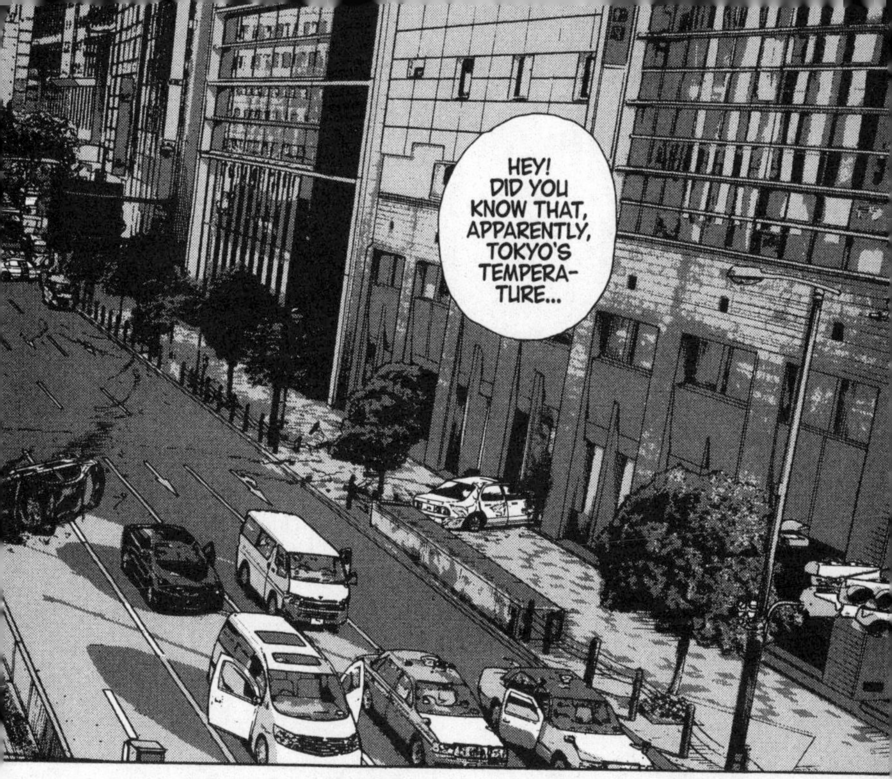
HEY! DID YOU KNOW THAT, APPARENTLY, TOKYO'S TEMPERA-TURE...

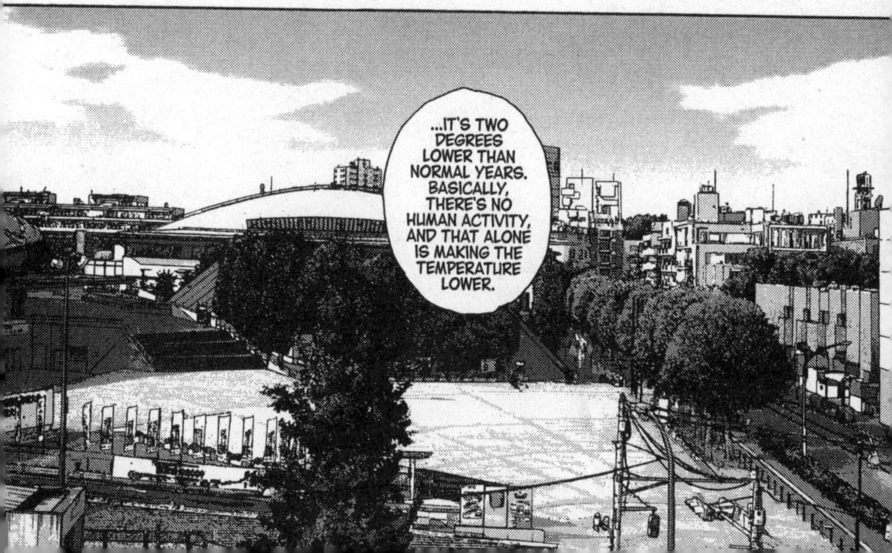
...IT'S TWO DEGREES LOWER THAN NORMAL YEARS. BASICALLY, THERE'S NO HUMAN ACTIVITY, AND THAT ALONE IS MAKING THE TEMPERATURE LOWER.

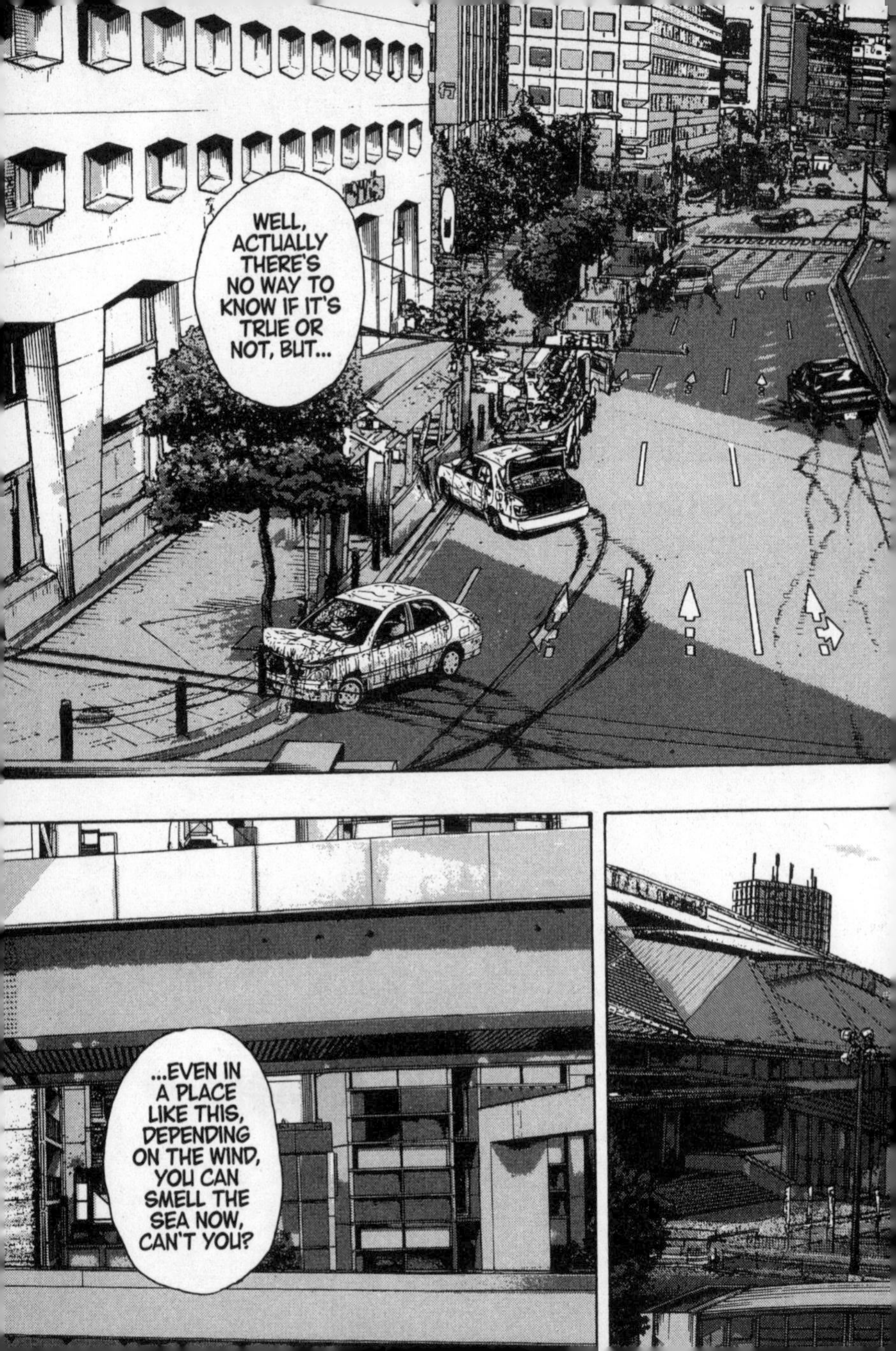
WELL, ACTUALLY THERE'S NO WAY TO KNOW IF IT'S TRUE OR NOT, BUT...
...EVEN IN A PLACE LIKE THIS, DEPENDING ON THE WIND, YOU CAN SMELL THE SEA NOW, CAN'T YOU?

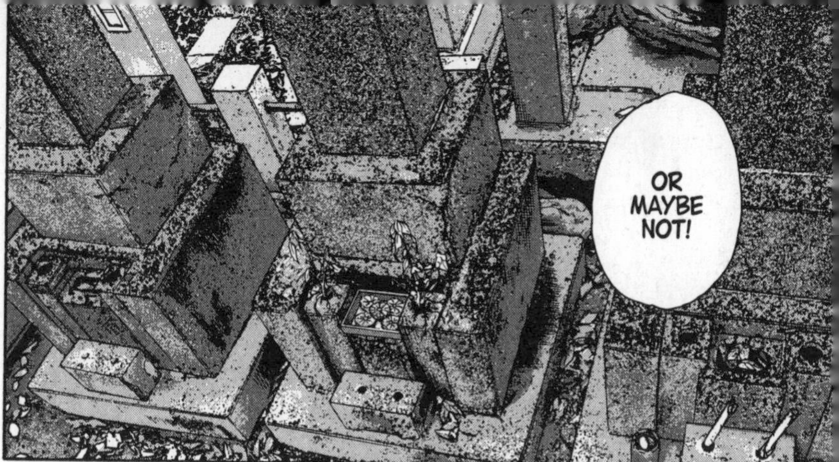
OR MAYBE NOT!
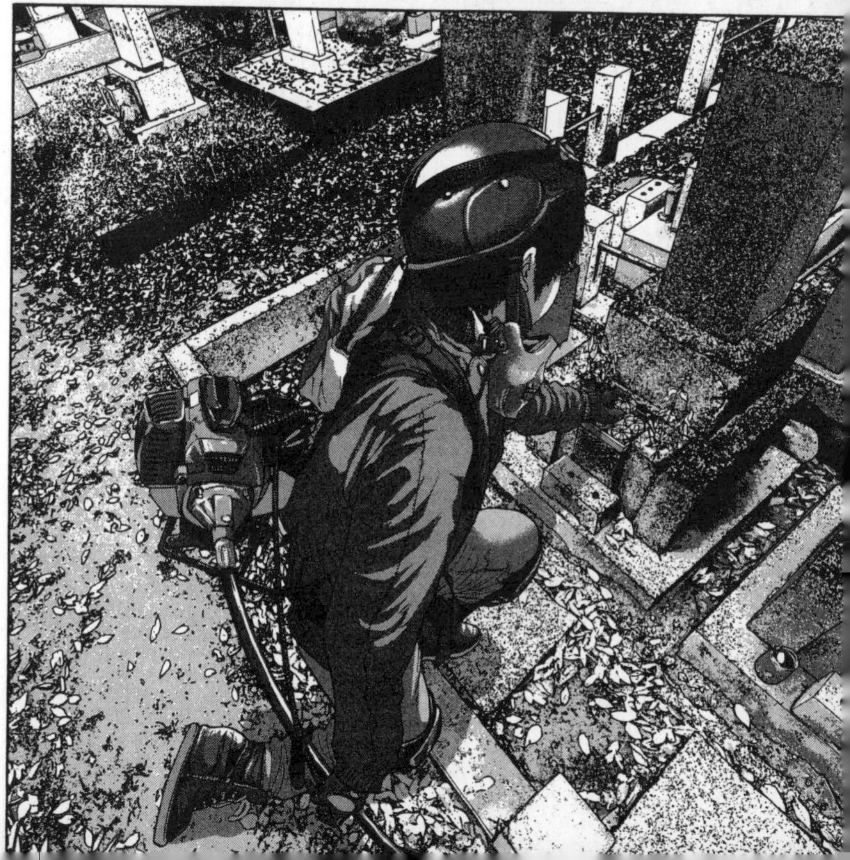

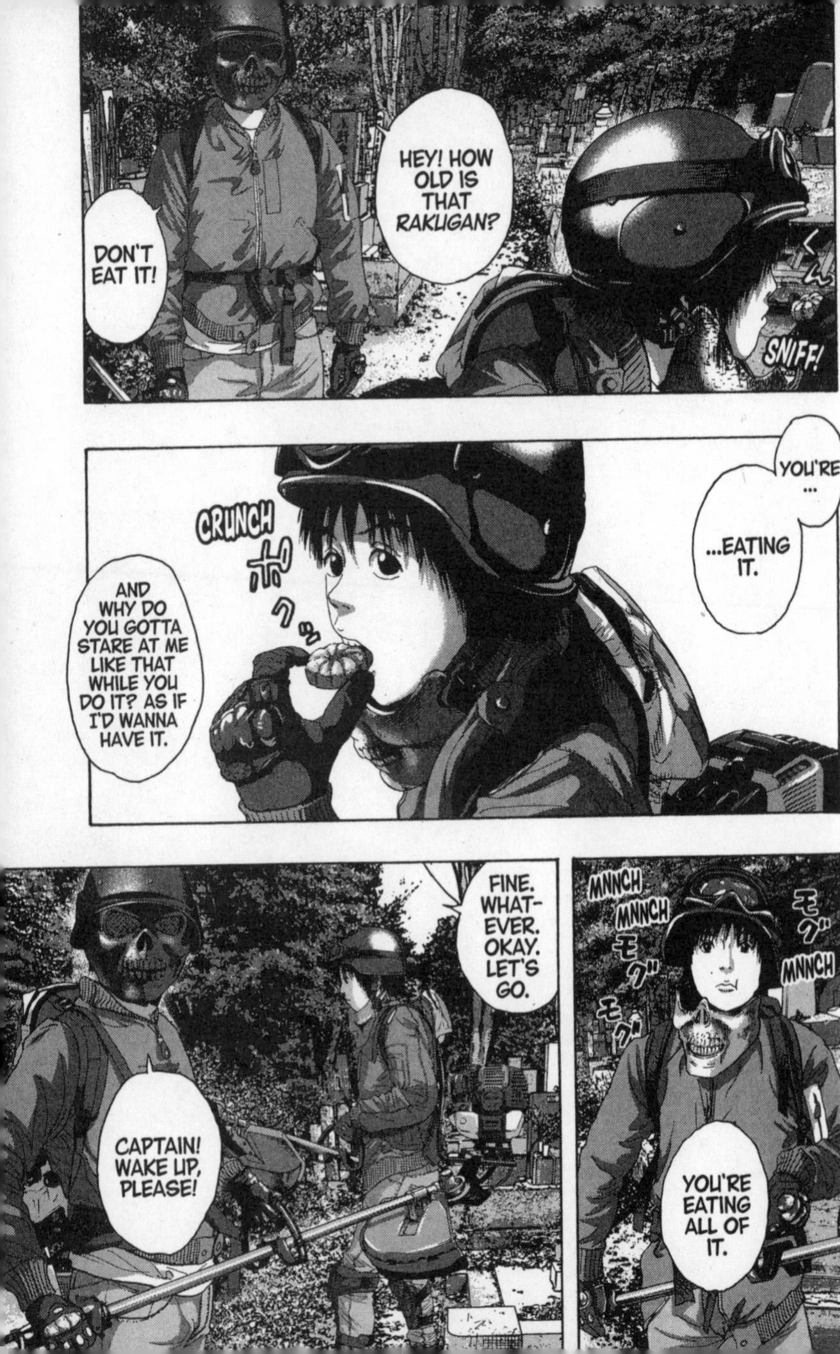
HEY! HOW OLD IS THAT RAKUGAN?
SNIFF!
DON'T EAT IT!
YOU'RE ...
...EATING IT.
CRUNCH
AND WHY DO YOU GOTTA STARE AT ME LIKE THAT WHILE YOU DO IT? AS IF I'D WANNA HAVE IT.
MNNCH
MNNCH
MNNCH
YOU'RE EATING ALL OF IT.
FINE. WHAT-EVER. OKAY. LET'S GO.
CAPTAIN! WAKE UP, PLEASE!

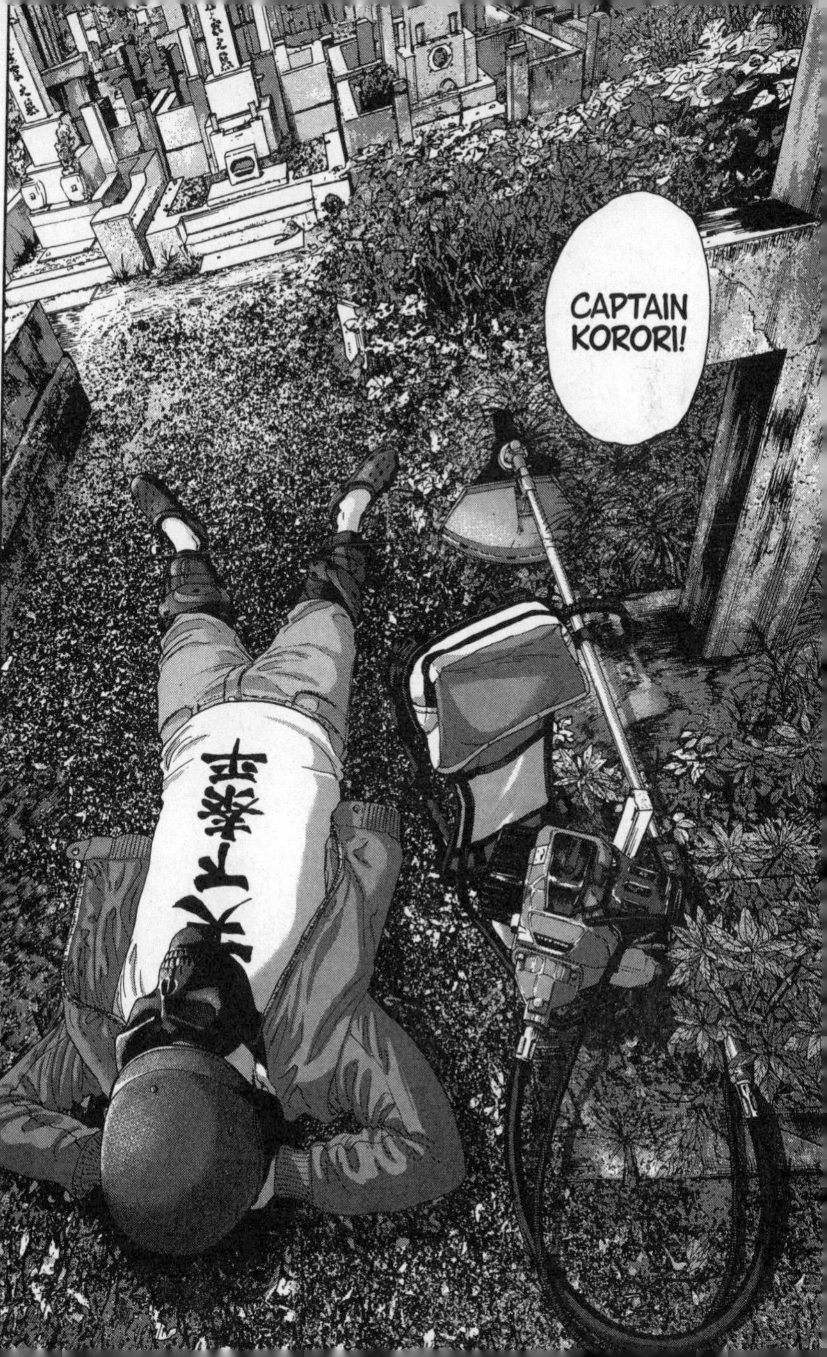
CAPTAIN KORORI!

SHIRT: WORLD PEACE

I AM
A HERO

I AM A HERO

TRANSLATION NOTES

CHAPTER 168

As seen in our previous volume, the creature who's carrying Hiromi and Miss Oda at the beginning of this chapter is capable of mentally commanding certain ZQNs to fight other ZQNs. In this chapter, before he's overwhelmed, the hybrid creature makes some ZQNs grab and punch other ZQNs in the hope that the human survivors can get away.

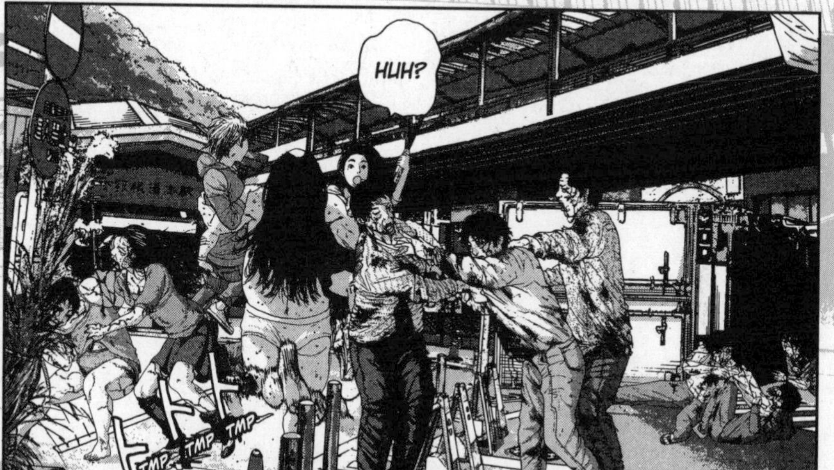
HUH?
TMP
TMP
TMP

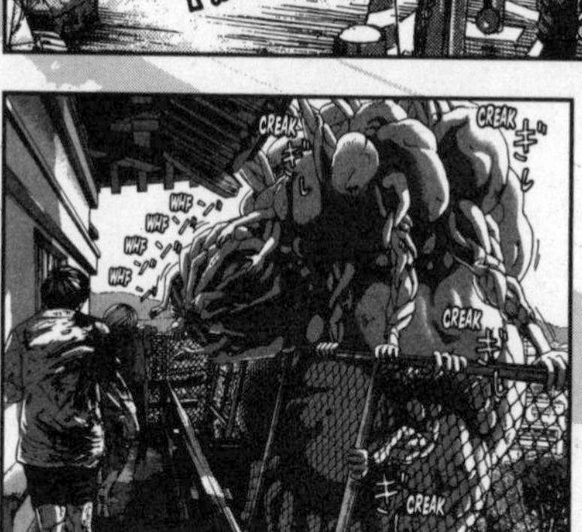
CREAK
CREAK
WHF
WHF
WHF
WHF
CREAK
CREAK

CHAPTER 172

In this chapter, we continue to see ZQNs coming together physically. It was revealed in an earlier volume that some ZQN beings can communicate telepathically. Some human-ZQN hybrids, like Hiromi, can gain strength while retaining memories and control over themselves. Now we're seeing a new type of mutation, as herds of ZQNs are linking up physically, merging and morphing into huge, moving masses.

CHAPTER 173

The "ya" has fallen off the Japanese sign "kyassuru," which means "castle," causing Hiromi to think that it says "kissuru."

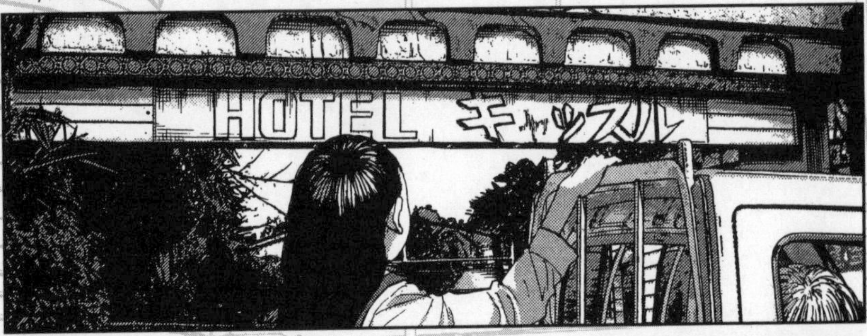
HOTEL

CHAPTER 174

Nikujaga is a boiled meat and potato stew with soy sauce and sugar. *Ochazuke* is boiled rice soaked with tea.

CHAPTER 176

Natto is a food made from fermented soybeans. It has a strong smell and a slimy texture.

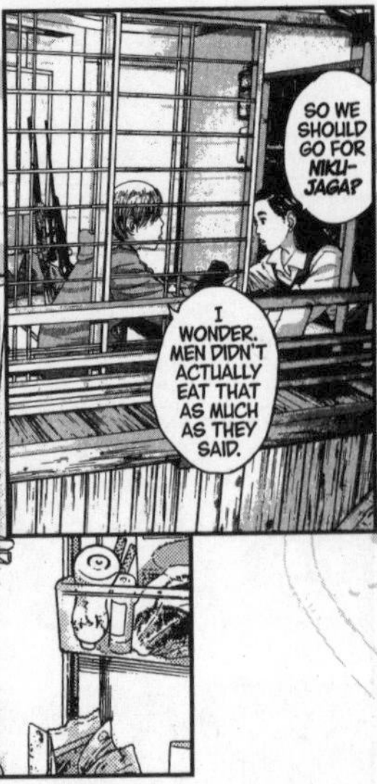
SO WE SHOULD GO FOR NIKU-JAGA?
I WONDER. MEN DIDN'T ACTUALLY EAT THAT AS MUCH AS THEY SAID.

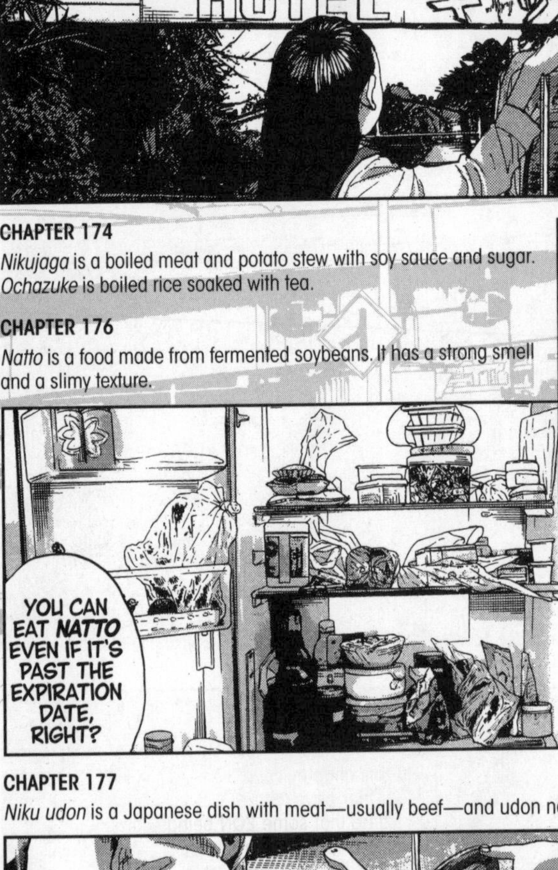
YOU CAN EAT NATTO EVEN IF IT'S PAST THE EXPIRATION DATE, RIGHT?

CHAPTER 177

Niku udon is a Japanese dish with meat—usually beef—and udon noodles.

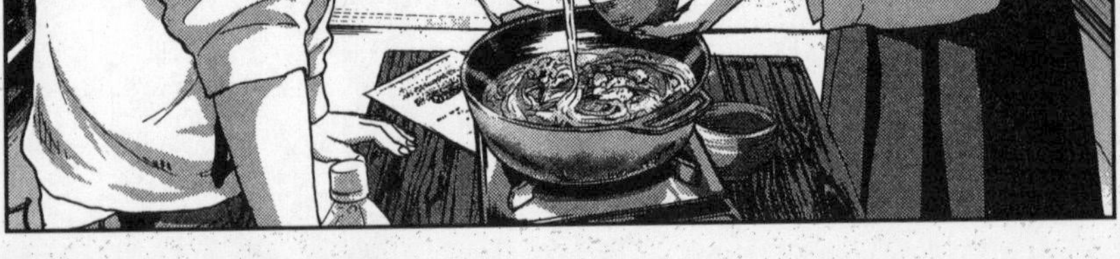

CHAPTER 178

When washing up for the night, the reason Hiromi thinks that the washroom is "kinda erotic looking" is because it's made to look like a hot springs bath and seems big enough to fit two people.

CHAPTER 179

Once again, the home pregnancy test that Miss Oda takes tells her that she is indeed pregnant. Looking through the "Visitors' Book" notebook, the hard-to-read first pages that Miss Oda flips through seem to read: "Let's be full of lovely-dovey feelings right now. –Saori" "So happy to be here with Mii-*kun*. I love you." And "I love you so much, I just can't help it."

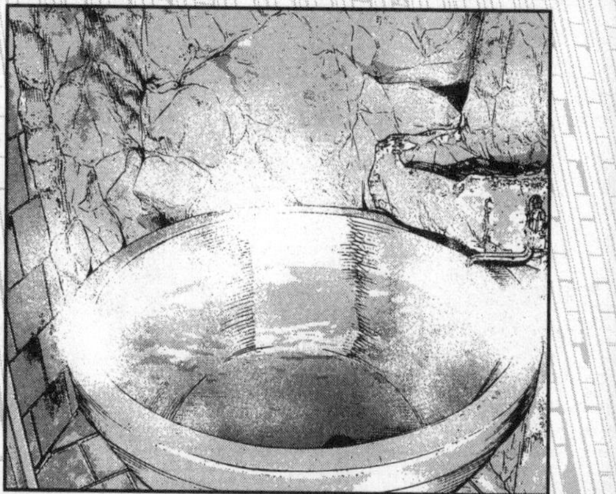

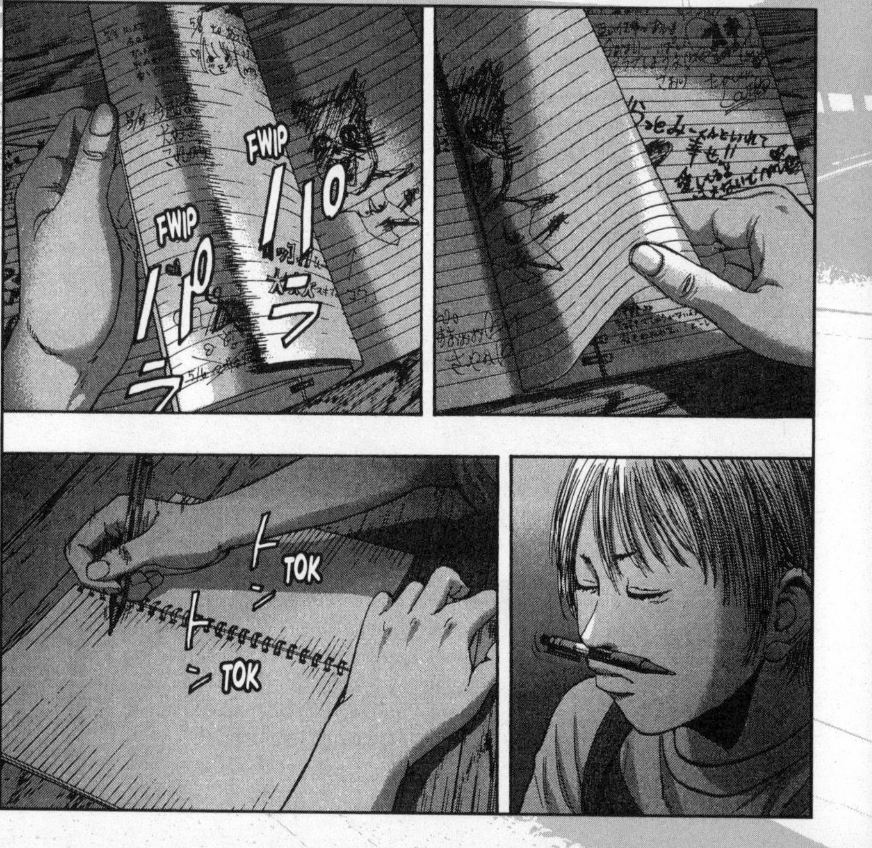

FWIP
パラ
FWIP
パラ
トン
TOK
トン
TOK

CHAPTER 180

The garbage truck that Miss Oda puts in reverse beeps a few times and has an electronic voice that says, "Backing Up."

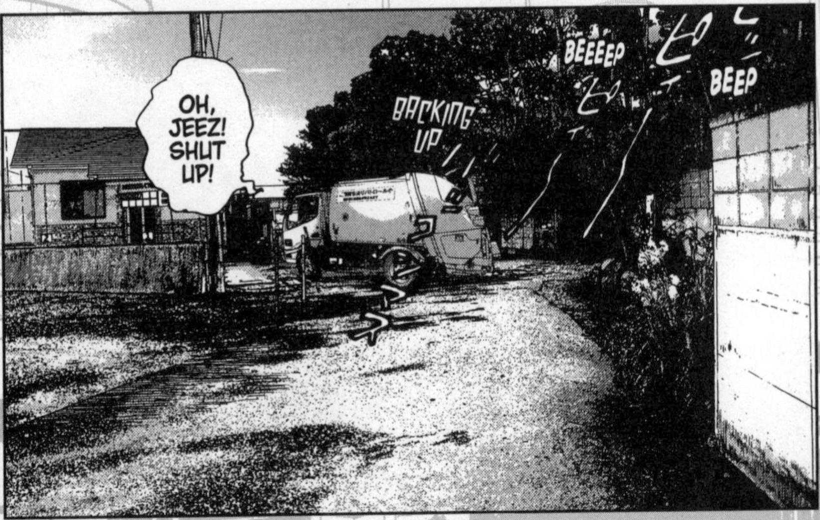
BEEEEP
BEEP
BACKING UP
OH, JEEZ! SHUT UP!

CHAPTER 191

Rakugan is a pressed mixture of soy flour and sugar that makes a hard, dry candy. In this case, it may have been left at the gravesite because it's something the deceased liked to eat when they were alive.

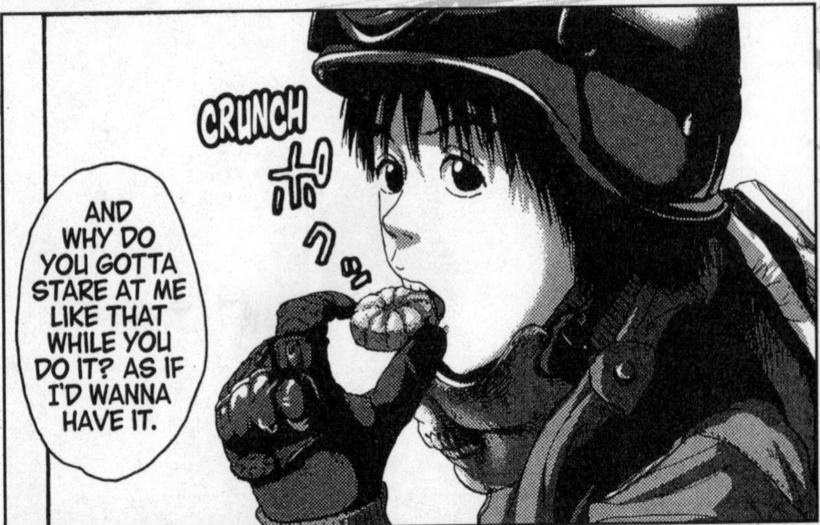
CRUNCH
AND WHY DO YOU GOTTA STARE AT ME LIKE THAT WHILE YOU DO IT? AS IF I'D WANNA HAVE IT.

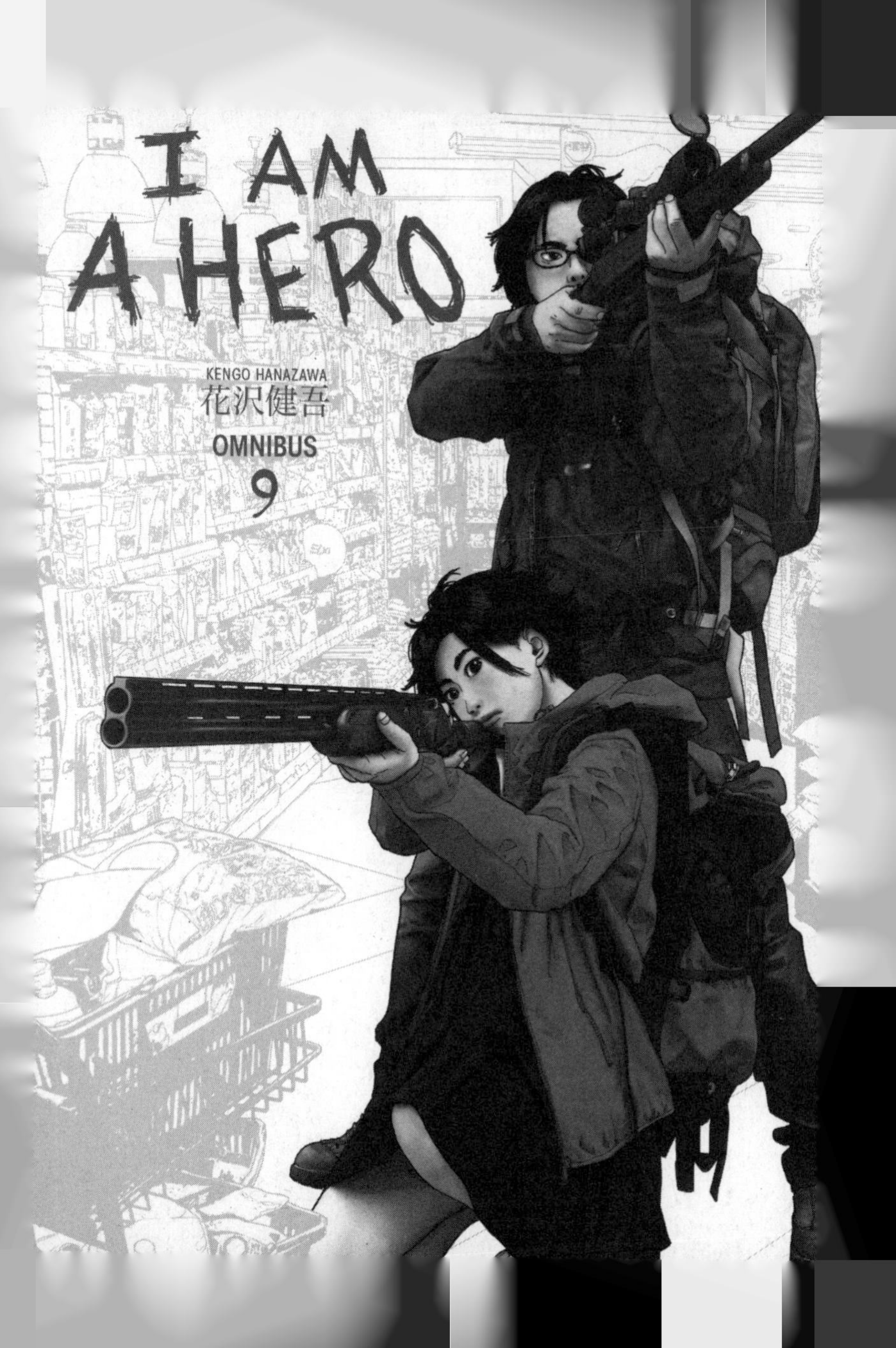
I AM A HERO
KENGO HANAZAWA
花沢健吾
OMNIBUS
9

I AM A HERO

OMNIBUS 9—COMING SOON!

THE WORLD'S STRANGEST ZOMBIE APOCALYPSE!

A small group of survivors, led by former manga creator Korori Nakata, considers breaking from a large, organized group of humans who follow cult leader "Asada" and have taken control of a high-rise apartment building. On a collision course with our heroes Hideo and Hiromi, the "high-rise survivors" face extremely powerful ZQNs and strange ZQN-human hybrids that may hold the key to unlocking the global zombie epidemic! Hideo and Hiromi continue to bond, while the rest of Japan falls apart. This omnibus collects two thrilling original Japanese volumes into one huge Dark Horse Manga edition!

Hiroaki Samura's Eisner Award–winning manga epic

BLADE OF THE IMMORTAL OMNIBUS

HIROAKI SAMURA
無限の住人
BLADE.
OF THE IMMORTAL
OMNIBUS I

Volume 1
ISBN 978-1-50670-124-0
$21.99

HIROAKI SAMURA
無限の住人
BLADE.
OF THE IMMORTAL

Volume 2
ISBN 978-1-50670-132-5
$21.99

HIROAKI SAMURA
無限の住人
BLADE.
OF THE IMMORTAL
OMNIBUS III

Volume 3
ISBN 978-1-50670-172-1
$21.99

HIROAKI SAMURA
無限の住人
BLADE.
OF THE IMMORTAL
OMNIBUS IV

Volume 4
ISBN 978-1-50670-569-9
$21.99

無限の住人
HIROAKI SAMURA
BLADE.
OF THE IMMORTAL
OMNIBUS V

Volume 5
ISBN 978-1-50670-567-5
$21.99

HIROAKI SAMURA
無限の住人
BLADE.
OF THE IMMORTAL

Volume 6
ISBN 978-1-50670-568-2
$21.99

無限の住人
HIROAKI SAMURA
BLADE.
OF THE IMMORTAL
OMNIBUS VII

Volume 7
ISBN 978-1-50670-655-9
$21.99

Also by Hiroaki Samura:

Hiroaki Samura's Emerald and Other Stories
ISBN 978-1-61655-065-3
$12.99

Ohikkoshi
ISBN 978-1-59307-622-1
$12.99

The Art of Blade of the Immortal
ISBN 978-1-59582-512-4
$29.99

DARK HORSE MANGA
DarkHorse.com

AVAILABLE AT YOUR LOCAL COMICS SHOP OR BOOKSTORE • To find a comics shop in your area visit comicshoplocator.com
For more information or to order direct visit DarkHorse.com or call 1-800-862-0052 Mon.–Fri. 9 AM to 5 PM Pacific Time.
*Prices and availability subject to change without notice

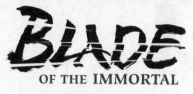

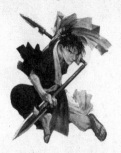

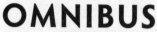

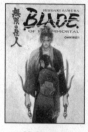

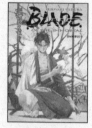

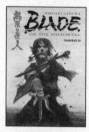

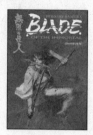

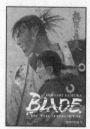

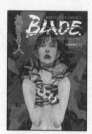

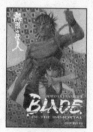

publisher
MIKE RICHARDSON

senior editor
PHILIP R. SIMON

associate editor
MEGAN WALKER

collection designer
LIN HUANG

digital production
SAMANTHA HUMMER

Special thanks to Michael Gombos and Carl Gustav Horn for editorial assistance and advice. Special thanks to Chitoku Teshima and Velan Sivasubramanian for translation assistance.

Art staff, original volumes 15 and 16: Jurii Okamoto, Yukihiro Kamiya, Hiroki Tomizawa, Kurao Nabe, Miki Imai, Yoshitaka Mizutani, Satomi Hayashi.

Original Cover Design: Norito INOUE Design Office

This omnibus volume collects the original *I Am a Hero* volumes 15 and 16, published in Japan.

I AM A HERO OMNIBUS 8 by Kengo HANAZAWA / TOCHKA

Dark Horse Manga | A division of Dark Horse Comics, Inc.
10956 SE Main Street, Milwaukie, OR 97222

DarkHorse.com

To find a comics shop in your area, visit the Comic Shop Locator Service at comicshoplocator.com

First edition: November 2018
ISBN 978-1-50670-750-1

10 9 8 7 6 5 4 3 2 1

Printed in the United States of America

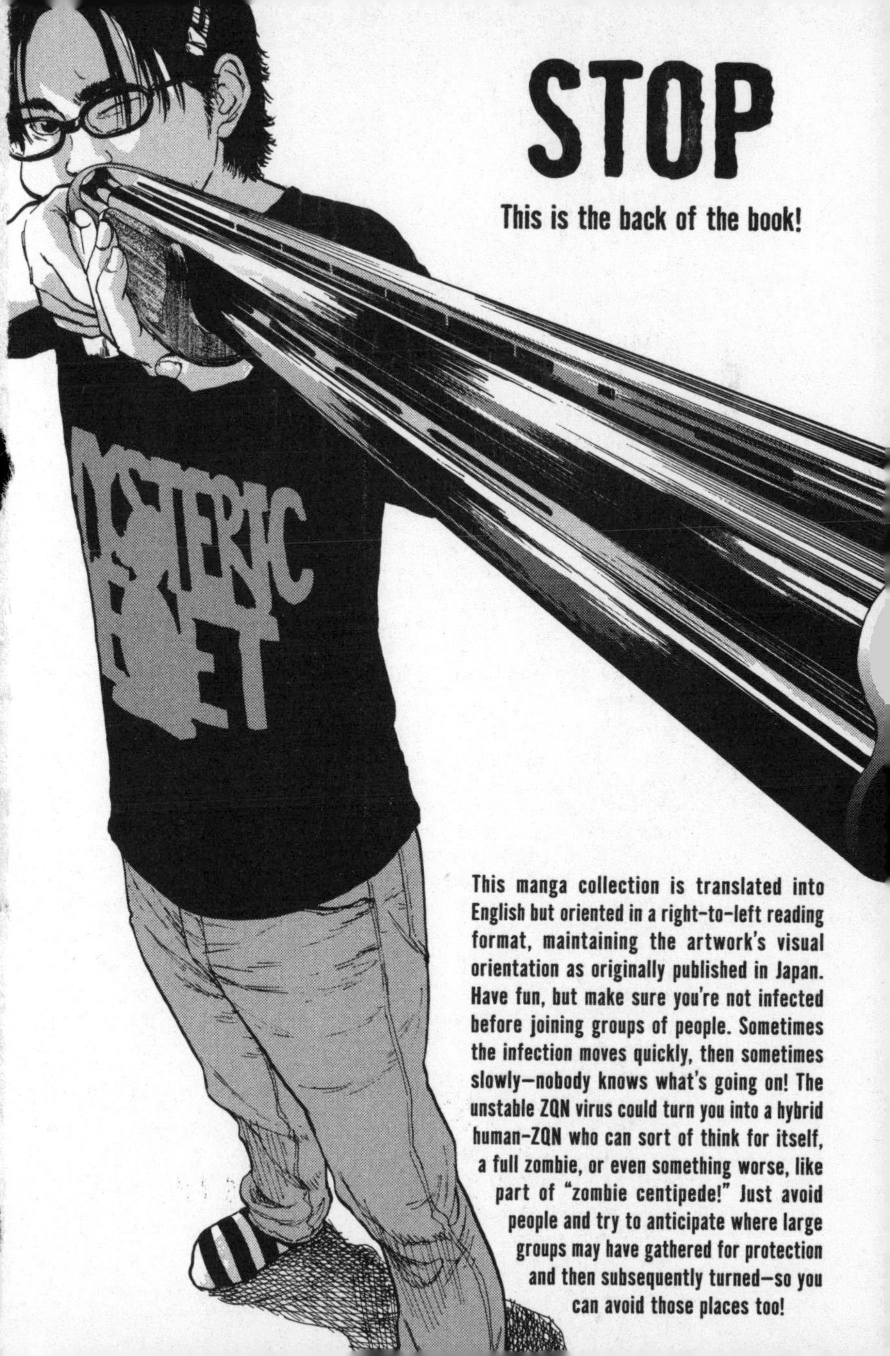

STOP

This is the back of the book!

This manga collection is translated into English but oriented in a right-to-left reading format, maintaining the artwork's visual orientation as originally published in Japan. Have fun, but make sure you're not infected before joining groups of people. Sometimes the infection moves quickly, then sometimes slowly—nobody knows what's going on! The unstable ZQN virus could turn you into a hybrid human-ZQN who can sort of think for itself, a full zombie, or even something worse, like part of "zombie centipede!" Just avoid people and try to anticipate where large groups may have gathered for protection and then subsequently turned—so you can avoid those places too!

Art and story
KENGO HANAZAWA
花沢健吾

This Dark Horse Manga omnibus
collects *I Am a Hero* chapters 168
to 191, first appearing in Japan as
I Am a Hero Volumes 15 and 16.

Translation
KUMAR SIVASUBRAMANIAN

English Adaptation
PHILIP R. SIMON

Lettering
STEVE DUTRO

OMNIBUS 8

I AM
A HERO